Asian Cinemas

ASIAN CINEMAS

A READER AND GUIDE

Edited by Dimitris Eleftheriotis
and Gary Needham

EDINBURGH UNIVERSITY PRESS

Edinburgh University Press Ltd
22 George Square, Edinburgh

Typeset in 10/12.5 Sabon
by Servis Filmsetting Ltd, Manchester and
printed and bound in Great Britain by
Antony Rowe Ltd, Chippenham, Wilts

A CIP record for this book is available from the British Library

ISBN 0 7486 1776 0 (hardback)
ISBN 0 7486 1777 9 (paperback)

CONTENTS

ACKNOWLEDGEMENTS

Dimitris Eleftheriotis wants to thank his colleagues Karen Boyle, Ian Craven, Ian Garwood, Christine Geraghty, Ian Goode and Karen Lury at the University of Glasgow for help and support throughout the project; Gary Needham for sharing his knowledge and his hard work on the book; Sarah Edwards for her encouragement; Lindsay Pratt for all her support.

Gary Needham would like to thank the friends and colleagues who have supported this project from its inception and provided the space to both discuss and teach Asian Cinemas. They are Karen Boyle, Phil Drake, Belen Vidal, Jules Pidduck, Lydia Papadimtriou, Patrick Williams, Roger Bromley and I-Fen Wu. I would like to extend a very special thanks to two people. They are: Yannis Tzioumakis, an invaluable friend and one-time colleague to whom I am always indebted, and my co-editor Dimitris Eleftheriotis who has seen me through many personal and scholarly transitions over the years and continues to keep me motivated and excited through his friendship and advice. Finally, I would like to thank my partner David for his support in what I do, for always being there, for having not complained when I made him sit through hundreds of films that he probably wished he'd never seen.

The extracts in this book are reprinted by permission, as follows:

David Desser, 'Introduction', 'A filmmaker for all seasons', in David Desser (ed.), *Ozu's Tokyo Story*, pp. 1–24. © 1997, Cambridge University Press. All rights reserved. Used by permission of the publisher.

Mitsuhiro Yoshimoto, 'The difficulty of being radical: the discipline of film studies and the postcolonial world order', in Masao Miyoshi and

H. D. Harootunian (eds), *Japan in the World*, pp. 338–53. © 1993, Duke University Press. All rights reserved. Used by permission of the publisher.

Chon Noriega, 'Godzilla and the Japanese nightmare: when *Them!* is U.S.', from *Cinema Journal*, 27: 1, pp. 63–77. © 1987 by the University of Texas Press. All rights reserved.

Philip Brophy, 'Monster island: Godzilla and Japanese sci-fi/horror/fantasy', from *Postcolonial Studies* (2002), vol. 3, pp. 39–42. © Taylor & Francis Ltd, http://www.tandf.co.uk/journals.

Ackbar Abbas, 'The new Hong Kong cinema and the *déjà disparu*', from Ackbar Abbas, *Hong Kong: Culture and the Politics of Disappearance*, University of Minnesota Press, 1997, pp. 16–47.

Siu Leung Li, 'Kung Fu: negotiating nationalism and modernity', from *Cultural Studies* (2001), vol. 15, pp. 515–42. © Taylor & Francis Ltd, http://www.tandf.co.uk/journals.

Tony Williams, 'Under "Western eyes": the personal odyssey of Huang Fei-Hong in *Once upon a Time in China*,' from *Cinema Journal*, 40: 1, pp. 3–24. © 2000 by the University of Texas Press. All rights reserved.

E. Ann Kaplan, 'Problematizing cross-cultural analysis: the case of women in the recent Chinese cinema,' from *Wide Angle* 11: 2, pp. 40–50. © 1989 Ohio University School of Film. Reprinted with permission of The Johns Hopkins University Press.

Rey Chow, 'Seeing modern China: toward a theory of ethnic spectatorship', from Rey Chow (1991), *Women and Chinese Modernity: The Politics of Reading Between West and East*, University of Minnesota Press, pp. 3–33.

Esther Yau, '*Yellow Earth*: Western analysis and a non-Western text', from *Film Quarterly*, 41: 2 Winter 1987–8, pp. 22–33. © 1988 The Regents of the University of California.

Nezih Erdoğan, 'Narratives of resistance: national identity and ambivalence in the Turkish melodrama between 1965 and 1975', from *Screen*, 39: 3, pp. 257–71. © 1998, Oxford University Press.

Nezih Erdoğan, 'Mute bodies, disembodied voices: notes on sound in Turkish popular cinema', from *Screen*, 43: 3, pp. 233–49. © 2002, Oxford University Press.

Rosie Thomas, 'Indian cinema: pleasures and popularity', from *Screen*, 26: 3–4, pp. 116–32. © 1985, *Screen*.

Ravi S. Vasudevan, 'Addressing the spectator of a "third world" national cinema: the Bombay "social" film of the 1940s and 1950s', from *Screen*, 36: 4, pp. 305–24. © 1995, Oxford University Press.

Lalitha Gopalan, '"Hum Aapke Hain Koun?" – cinephilia and Indian films', from Lalitha Gopalan, *Cinema of Interruptions*, pp. 1–33. © 2002, BFI.

Stephen Teo, 'Bruce Lee: narcissus and the little dragon', from Stephen Teo, *Hong Kong Cinema*, pp. 110–21. © 1997, BFI.

Leon Hunt, 'Han's island revisited: *Enter the Dragon* as transnational cult film', previously printed in Xavier Menolik and Graeme Harper (eds), *Unruly Pleasures,* ISBN 1 903254 00 0, FAB Press, 2000, www.fabpress.com

Yvonne Tasker, 'Fists of fury: discourses of race and masculinity in the martial arts cinema', from Harry Stecopoulos and Michael Uebel (eds), *Race and the Subject of Masculinities*, pp. 315–35. © 1977, Duke University Press. All rights reserved. Used by permission of the publisher.

The following have contributed commissioned work to this volume:

Dimitris Eleftheriotis is Senior Lecturer in Film Studies at Glasgow University. He is the author of *Popular Cinemas of Europe: Studies of Texts, Contexts and Frameworks* (2001).

Ian Garwood is Lecturer in Film and Television Studies at Glasgow University. He has published extensively on film music.

Ahmet Gürata is Lecturer at Gazi University, Ankara. He has recently completed a doctoral thesis on remakes in Turkish cinema.

Gary Needham teaches film in the Department of Media and Cultural Studies, Nottingham Trent University.

Julianne Pidduck is Lecturer at the Institute for Cultural Research at the University of Lancaster. She has written on queer cinemas and is the author of *Contemporary Costume Cinema: Spaces of the Self* (2005) and *La Reine Margot* (2005).

I-Fen Wu teaches in the English Department of Tamkang University, Taipei. She has written articles on Taiwanese cinema for the journal *CineAction.*

INTRODUCTION

Dimitris Eleftheriotis

The successful challenge of the hegemonic position of Hollywood and European art cinema within Anglo-US film studies has led to a rapidly increasing body of critical and theoretical work addressing what were traditionally perceived as 'other' cinemas. An intense interest in the films produced in Asia in particular has spearheaded the expansion of the scope of the discipline. In many academic institutions such interest is strongly reflected by a proliferation of undergraduate and postgraduate courses which are, at least partly, structured around the study of Asian films.

While we recognise the fact that organising the present *Reader and Guide* around a rather imaginary geographical entity (Asia) is in many ways problematic, we do believe that there are pedagogical and methodological merits in our decision. First, some of the problems surrounding the designation 'Asian' are explicitly addressed in Section 4, where the case study of a liminal country *par excellence*, Turkey, is closely considered. Secondly, what emerges from that particular section, and is reiterated in several other sections in this book, is that national Asian cinematic forms are approached, in strikingly similar ways by the contributors, as specific negotiations between local/national/regional traditions and 'Western' film conventions and aesthetics. Thirdly, it is important to realise that a similar but inverted process takes place when Western students and academics approach, for the purpose of study or research, various cinemas of Asia: their position, heavily informed by culturally familiar cinematic forms, is structured by a relationship, a negotiation between 'familiar' and 'unfamiliar', Euro-American and Asian.

This *Guide and Reader*, therefore, takes as its starting point the problematic relationship between Western scholar/student and Asian text. The experience of teaching courses on Asian cinemas suggests that the expectations of students from such courses (and consequently from any textbook servicing them) are very much based on problematic assumptions about the object of study. Such assumptions are usually informed by critical (mis)judgements and (mis)conceptions: these vary from complete and unqualified admiration of the masterpieces of directors such as Kurosawa and Ozu, to an equally unqualified adoration of Asian films as 'cult' objects, to an outright rejection, in extreme but not unusual cases, of the texts as culturally and aesthetically inferior products whose only value lies in their 'exoticism'.

It is essential, then, that we first challenge and then re-construct such positions. Part I of *Asian Cinemas: A Reader and Guide* directly addresses three different ways in which Euro-American critics and academics have historically approached Asian culture and cinema: the discourse of orientalism, the critical/historical context of post-coloniality, and the debate around the problems and possibilities of cross-cultural criticism. Such approaches are 'grounded' on specific case studies: that of the widely celebrated cinema of Ozu and the cult *Godzilla* films, recent Hong Kong cinema, and 1980s Chinese cinema, respectively.

Informed by the experience of teaching Asian cinemas, we have decided to adopt a 'debate-driven' approach, rather than one driven by texts or case studies. Thus, following on from the explicit addressing of the problems around approaching Asian cinemas, Part II focuses on specific case studies within the context of some of the most influential theoretical frameworks for the study of national/regional cinemas: the category of national cinema itself, genre criticism, auteurism and stardom. Engaging the readers/students initially with familiar areas of critical discourse, *Asian Cinemas: A Reader and Guide* introduces within such a context the 'unfamiliar' case studies which are then explored in depth and in detail. The advantage of such an approach is that it works with the familiarity/unfamiliarity dynamic inherent in the object of study, and it avoids constructing Asian cinemas as a gallery of exotic objects that might be particularly fascinating but remain deeply distant and foreign.

While individual sections are necessarily selective and limited, they do offer – we hope – intensity of engagement with key debates and historical moments. The choice of material is eclectic but not arbitrary. The collected reprinted essays represent important and formative contributions to the study of Asian cinemas by some of the most influential and incisive scholars in the field. The specially commissioned essays cover more recent histories and provide insights into contemporary scholarly developments in the field. The main objective of the opening essays of each chapter, written by the editors of this *Reader and Guide*, is to map out the discursive and historical context within which the other contributions operate. The topics of the individual sections collectively offer a kaleidoscopic view of crucial aspects of Asian cinemas: the 'othering' of the films of Ozu and the *Godzilla* movies; Hong Kong cinema as the privileged referent of post-colonial discourse; the mid-1980s as a key moment of 'change' in Chinese society and cinema, as well as film criticism; Turkish cinema in the context of the current debate around the country's European or Asiatic nature; Indian cinema at the peak of its global appeal; the exciting films of contemporary Taiwanese directors; and the 'legend' of Bruce Lee as the most popular star ever to emerge from the Asian film industries.

More specifically, Section 1 builds on the critical analysis of orientalism and explores the historical relationship between West and East in its investigation of critical approaches to the Japanese cinema of the 1950s and 1960s. The case study brings to the attention the process of 'othering' involved in both the positive evaluation of the work of Ozu and the dismissive criticism of the popular cycle of *Godzilla* films.

As the first section suggests, the encounter between West and East is inescapably informed by processes of colonialism. Post-colonial criticism conceptualises contemporary national identities as informed by, and at the same time transgressing, the colonial legacy. The case of the cinema of Hong Kong (especially in the past two decades) is particularly interesting both in terms of the critical attention it has attracted (for the ways in which it articulates post-colonial experiences, anxieties and formulations of identity), and in terms of its internationally significant commercial and critical success.

Theorists and critics have addressed the theoretical, methodological and political challenges involved in (Western) critical engagement with texts originating within cultural contexts marked by difference. The case study in Section 3 focuses on what has become a privileged point of reference in the debate: Chinese films of the 1980s.

The category of national cinema has been surrounded by (increasing) theoretical ambivalence as it remains recognised as a valuable context for the study of film but is also criticised for the limitations and restrictions that it imposes on the object of study. The category is interrogated in Section 4, which addresses the specific case of Turkish cinema.

Anglo-American genre criticism and theory becomes profoundly problematic when exercised in the context of Asian films and genres. The detailed study of Indian popular cinema in Section 5 foregrounds the inadequacies of a theoretical/critical/generic framework that are insensitive to difference, and examines closely the textual and contextual specificities of such cinema.

Authorship in the context of Asian cinemas is a particularly thorny category. *Auteur* as a critical concept has clear European origins and, with the exception of a handful of individuals, the term has been used to define directors working within either the Hollywood or the European art cinema paradigms. The case study in Section 6 considers a trio of Taiwanese directors (Edward Yang, Hsiou Hsiao-Hsien and Ang Lee) with international appeal, whose work is produced beyond strictly defined national contexts and transgresses the art/popular dichotomy.

The final section focuses on Bruce Lee as the most popular star to emerge from Asia. It addresses issues of national identity, masculinity and performance, as well as issues of stardom such as marketing and promotion.

Asian Cinemas: A Reader and Guide must be seen as precisely what its title suggests: a collection of important (but limited) reading, and a guide to an initial exploration of key aspects of Asian cinema. We hope that it will stimulate the appetite of students of Asian cinemas for further reading and more thorough explorations.

PART I
APPROACHING ASIAN CINEMAS

SECTION 1
ORIENTALISM AND JAPANESE CINEMA

Gary Needham, 'Japanese cinema and orientalism'
David Desser, 'A filmmaker for all seasons'
Mitsuhiro Yoshimoto, 'The difficulty of being radical: the discipline of film studies and the post-colonial world order'
Chon Noriega, 'Godzilla and the Japanese nightmare: when *Them!* is U.S.'
Philip Brophy, 'Monster island: Godzilla and Japanese sci-fi/horror/fantasy'

JAPANESE CINEMA AND ORIENTALISM

Gary Needham

Introduction

Asian Cinemas: A Reader and Guide begins with a section on Japan because, more than any other Asian cinema, Japan has consistently occupied a discursive position of otherness. Japanese cinema has been the object of constant and consistent fascination in Europe and particularly in the United States. Furthermore, the relationship between Japanese cinema and its Western reception, criticism and place within film studies operates upon terms similar to those attributed to the discourse of orientalism by Edward Said.[1]

For Said, orientalism involves the exercise of power operating through a body of knowledge (everyday, common sense and academic) that results to the legitimacy of 'the West' to govern, speak for and to shape the meaning of the 'Orient'. The Orient refers both to a geographical entity, most often Asia, and an imaginary construction, which has historically enabled the justification of colonial conquest and imperial mentalities to foster imagined spaces, representations and identities of the other. Such imaginations, fantasies, gross misrepresentations and stereotypes serve not to define the other, but rather to enable the self to be more clearly defined by what it is not.

This explanation of orientalism is a mere gloss in relation to the scale of the debate and its ongoing definition in post-colonial studies. However, I hope that it begins to raise an awareness of how ideas, representations, criticisms and selections of Asian films in the West is not a neutral venture. It is important to realise that the pleasures derived from, and the academic approaches to, Asian films cannot be divorced from their connection to historical discourses that have indeterminately shaped and distorted East/West self/other relations.

FROM *RASHOMON* TO *RING*

Despite the continued fascination with Japanese cinema and Japanese-ness since *Rashomon* (Kurosawa Akira, 1950), its role as the other seems to be hardly waning, with the emergence of a new wave of genre films being imported to Europe and the United States. This new wave of Japanese films is being taken up by a new and younger audience, who are familiar with Kurosawa Kiyoshi rather than Kurosawa Akira, and seek pleasures not found in Hollywood. Aiding the popularity of this new Japanese cinema are discourses of excess, difference and transgression, connected as they are to notions of otherness, promoted through marketing practices which recontextualise the films as extreme entertainment.

The obvious example is the distributor Metro-Tartan which has gathered together numerous contemporary Japanese genre films, as well as South Korean, Thai and Hong Kong films, under the banner of 'Tartan Asia Extreme'. The language of its promotional material speaks for itself, announcing that 'If the weird, the wonderful and the dangerous is your thing, then you really don't want to miss this chance to take a walk on the wild side.' The promise of danger and of the unexpected is linked with the way in which these films are marketed according to their otherness from Hollywood, and subsequently feeds in to many of the typical fantasies of the 'Orient' characterised by exoticism, mystery and danger.

Interestingly, the films are shown in British multiplex cinemas and not in arthouse cinemas, which have historically been the typical context of 'foreign film' exhibition – their position alongside Hollywood informed firmly by Hollywood/East distinctions. Many of the films, such as *Ring/Ringu* (Nakata Hideo, 1998), or the Hong Kong film *Infernal Affairs/Wu jian dao* (Andrew Lau, 2002), could hardly be thought of as extreme in the terms that the distributors want us to imagine. The way in which these films are promoted for theatrical consumption and their continued popularity on DVD does demonstrate that there is a loving audience for popular Asian film. However, the discourses surrounding the packaging of these films continue a relationship to Japanese and Asian cinema, cemented in the early 1950s, in which otherness becomes a necessary element in their appreciation and contextualisation.

Early interest in Kurosawa Akira and Mizoguchi Kenji arose not only from their formal differences but also from their status as Japanese cultural products, as being culturally other. The new emphasis for audiences of contemporary Japanese films, like those of Takashi Miike for example, is their subversive and explicit treatment of sex and violence and the multiple ways in which they transgress the norms and expectations of Hollywood cinema. However, these ideas of transgression and subversion must be understood as being based on Western notions of the self as they are firmly contextualised in relation to Hollywood and therefore may not be shared by audiences, Japanese or otherwise, whose cultural limits and boundaries are altogether different.

In what follows, I would like to outline some further ideas around the persistence of otherness in relationship to Japanese cinema initiated with the success of *Rashomon*, and then the continued interest in Japanese cinema and its otherness that is specific to film studies. I have chosen to organise this section around two key figures of Japanese cinema, the film director Ozu Yasujiro and the monster Godzilla, to examine how concepts of otherness relate to each other within the categories of genre cinema and art cinema and across the West-Japan dichotomy.

The Persistence of Otherness

The high-profile presence of Japanese cultural products and goods outside Japan – in the form of animated series like *Pokemon* and *Dragonball Z*, video games such as *Resident Evil, Super Mario* and *Final Fantasy*, games consoles such as the Sony Playstation and the Nintendo Gamecube, the popularity of sushi – could possibly lead one to think that it is now possible to partially 'demystify' Japan, as it is now an integral part of the everyday cultural fabric of life. From American children's leisure time to their parents' high-end electronic goods and motor vehicles, Japan is associated with quality entertainment and state-of-the-art technologies. If Japanese culture and cultural products are part of many people's everyday life, then why does Japan still remain distant and unknowable in this era of mass media saturation and local and global formations?

This is partly answered by Iwabuchi Koichi whose ongoing work disentangles the Japan-West relationship, as well as Japan's relationship to globalisation and its Asian neighbours.[2] For Iwabuchi, Japan enacts a self-orientalising tendency through perpetuating an idea of the 'West' that it constructs for itself through a relationship organised around a set of perceived differences from the United States. Japan's own image of itself, according to Iwabuchi, is shaped by a complicit orientalism that allows Japan to define itself as unique and unknowable on the basis that it remains separate from the 'West' in an unbridgeable cultural gulf. This is achieved through a self-constructed notion of otherness culturally bound to the equally imagined 'West'. Furthermore, Iwabuchi suggests that part of Japan's success in exporting culture is based on a strategy to de-Japanise many of its products, particularly the way in which characters in animated series and video games appear to look un-Japanese. Iwabuchi refers to this erasure of race and ethnicity as *mukokuseki* or 'the something or someone lacking any nationality'.[3] For Iwabuchi, Japan's uniqueness is bound to an acceptance of its role as other, perpetrated by the external factors of orientalism, an internal complicit position that sustains it, and *mukokuseki* in its popular culture exports.

Japan's relationship to the United States is also central to Yoshimoto Mitsuhiro's book on Kurosawa Akira.[4] While the book is a valuable study of every film made by Kurosawa, the first section of Yoshimoto's book is the most definitive account to date of the nexus between Japan, America and film studies. Yoshimoto suggests that US military intelligence used Japanese cinema as a way of getting to know the other, and that it informed cultural policy on how to 'treat' the Japanese. He argues that this World War Two American formation of Japanese identity, which is based on studying its cinema, is also coterminous with the emergence of film authorship as the proto-disciplinary formation of film studies. The starting point of the latter can be pinpointed to a time and a place: *Rashomon* winning the Golden Lion at Venice in 1951.

It is difficult to assess the US military's use of Japanese cinema but the surrounding discourses of Japanese-ness in both camps points to an increased visibility of cinematic Japan as a way of both knowing and maintaining Japan as an essentialist cultural Other, particularly as it is imagined to be separate from the United States and 'the West'. The chapter by Yoshimoto on Ozu Yasujiro in this *Reader and Guide* outlines some of the key concerns that form the basis for his more extensive survey of film studies' relationship to Japanese cinema in the Kurosawa book. This will be specifically addressed below in relation to Ozu.

Yoshimoto's Kurosawa book proposes three instances in the historicising of film studies in relationship to Japanese cinema: the humanist traditions associated with Donald Richie in the 1960s; the formal analysis associated with Noel Burch, David Bordwell and Kristin Thompson in the 1970s; and the mono-cultural and cross-cultural analyses by Japanese scholars and E. Ann Kaplan in the 1980s respectively.[5] Yoshimoto explains how these paradigm shifts within film studies are inextricably linked to changing attitudes. Thus, Yoshimoto argues that intrinsic to the history of film studies is its relationship to Japanese cinema.

Furthermore, the relationship to Japanese cinema has to be subsequently framed within the larger context of historical and theoretical discursive exchanges between Japan and the 'West', Japan's complicit oriental self-fashioning, and to the range of more general strategies of othering enacted through colonial and, ultimately, orientalist modes of thinking about non-Western cinemas. The repackaging in the West of contemporary popular Japanese films such as *Ichi the Killer/Koroshiya 1* (Takashi Miike, 2002), *Battle Royale/Batoru Rowaiaru* (Fukasaku Kinji, 2000), and *Ring*, as exotic and dangerous cinematic thrills, has a lot in common with the way in which the 'yellow peril' figure of the Japanese military sadist of *Boy's Own*-style fantasies functioned as a dangerous Other of popular culture. In both cases, horror, sadism and cruelty are passed off as an essentially integral part of 'the Japanese nature' and inform the way in which Japan is perceived to be a dangerous Other.

Another more recent and less offensive example here would be the two different versions of the film *Kill Bill Vol. 1* (Quentin Tarantino, 2003). This is, of course, a clear indication of the way in which Japanese and Hong Kong cinemas are appropriated to 'spice up' Hollywood while simultaneously maintaining the position of popular Asian cinema as one inferior to Hollywood. The Japanese version of *Kill Bill Vol.1* has numerous extended scenes of violence and gore not found in any other version. This is made common knowledge when Tarantino, discussing the film, suggests that this decision to have two different versions is justified because Japanese audiences demand more 'blood and guts', suggesting, thus, a kind of innate desire for cruelty and extreme violence as a typical trait of Japanese film audiences. Of course, this 'extreme version', the source of great cult appreciation and wide underground dissemination in the West, inevitably will garner the film a re-release, revealing it as a covert marketing strategy as well as an example of 'extreme Asia'.

Ozu Yasujiro, Japanese Filmmaker

The critical and scholarly interest in Ozu Yasujiro is more recent than that of Kurosawa Akira, Mizoguchi Kenji and Oshima Nagisa. Oshima, who was a key figure in establishing Western interest in Japanese cinema, along with other directors of the Japanese New Wave in the 1960s, has not continued to generate a sustained level of inquiry in comparison to Kurosawa or Ozu.

What differentiates Ozu from Kurosawa is the way in which the former is maintained within a role that perpetually raises questions of the uniqueness of his films and makes Japanese-ness, otherness and modernism integral components of his identity as an *auteur*. Kurosawa seems to provoke a lesser response primarily because his more popular films are perceived to be largely more accessible through their generic status in easily, if complexly executed, conventions of action cinema and period drama, and through their ability to convey a humanistic message. Kurosawa is also well known for his engagement and adaptation across a range of both popular and high-culture texts from American westerns (*Yojimbo*) to Shakespeare (*Throne of Blood, Ran*) and Maxim Gorky (*The Lower Depths*).

Ozu, on the other hand, is primarily thought of in more essentialist terms of detailing the specificities of postwar Japan through modernity, domesticity and intergenerational relationships, mapped out through the formal aspects of his authorial style. However, it is through film form, rather than theme, that Ozu comes to be associated with otherness, particularly as he has been positioned in relationship to the formal regulations of the Classical paradigm. The three most influential texts here are Paul Schrader's *Transcendental Style in Film: Ozu, Bresson, Dreyer* (1972), David Bordwell and Kristin Thompson's 'Space and narrative in the films of Ozu' (1976), and Noel Burch's *To the Distant Observer* (1976/1979). Grouped together, these three texts have been central in establishing Ozu as an important figure within film studies in terms of his departures from the dominant conventions of film construction.

Thus, Ozu, also situated outside the European art cinema, is clearly positioned as the other to a Hollywood-defined filmmaking norm. The championing of Ozu does come from an overwhelming respect for his films as art but we must ask why Ozu's formal otherness is validated against a set of conventions operating as a normative paradigm chiefly associated with Hollywood cinema.

Ozu's cinema represents, like many other Japanese films, a form of transgression but of a different kind than that of the contemporary Japanese films discussed above. The key transgressions outlined by Schrader, Bordwell and

Thompson, and Burch are identified as ruptures in continuity. Continuity in cinema determines and regulates time and space for the purposes of narrative realism and spectator identification and works towards masking the constructed nature of the film text. In an often-laboured point, it is demonstrated that Ozu favours shooting in a 360-degree space as opposed to the standard 180-degree space favoured by most popular cinemas. In terms of the (dis)continuity of the 360-degree space, screen direction can be difficult to determine and backgrounds do not always remain constant or enable match-cuts. Ozu also favours a low camera height, often mistakenly referred to as low-angle, in order to convey the low seating position of his characters on *tatami* flooring.

The most debated formal device that Ozu employs is the apparently unmotivated or empty shots, shots of vases being the most cited, that appear to form various kinds of transitional purposes. It is these shots, labelled 'pillow shots' by Burch, that have caused the most concern to scholars like Yoshimoto since they are often determined through their supposed aesthetic embodiment of Zen (as Schrader does) or other cultural concepts such as *mono no aware* and modernism. As Yoshimoto has pointed out, it is unlikely that the average Japanese audience even understand the philosophical underpinnings of Zen to the degree that it would inform their enjoyment of the films of Ozu, let alone perceive Ozu's work to embody any principles of Zen, *mono no aware* or modernism in the first place.

The renowned Japanese film scholar Sato Tadao refers to these shots as 'curtain shots' for the way in which they function to divide scenes as a curtain would do in the theatre. Sato also tells us that when Ozu's films are shown on Japanese television, these shots are often removed by the television channel as an alternative to lexiconing and as a means to tighten scheduling for more advertising.[6] These different understandings of the seemingly unmotivated shots point to the biggest gap across the study of Asian cinema, the question of reception.

The two essays on Ozu that follow this chapter each set a different agenda but – I hope – complement each other in a way that facilitates the ongoing debates of Ozu's position within critical and scholarly writing on film. Certainly recent work on Ozu by Catherine Russell and Alastair Philips is setting contemporary agendas by opening up new possibilities in Ozu scholarship, on stardom, modernity and femininity.[7]

Yoshimoto Mitsuhiro's essay is closely related to his later work in the Kurosawa book by tracing the interrelationship between post-colonial politics, Japanese cinema and film studies. Yoshimoto takes to task not only the earlier approaches to Ozu mentioned above, but the critiques of those approaches by other scholars, such as Peter Lehman and Scott Nygren, more sensitive to the cultural politics of difference. Yoshimoto untangles the Anglo-American struggle over politics and identity revolving around the position of Ozu as a modernist filmmaker. He reveals that what at first glance appears to be a tension between Japan and the West is in fact a tension between history and theory, with Ozu at its centre. Yoshimoto's chapter also makes us aware of the difficulty in approaching any cinema that is remote from our own locality of everyday culture and experience even when such an approach involves the most careful of cross-cultural frameworks which, he suggests, may only serve to depoliticise 'the structure of domination found in West/non-West opposition'.

The essay by David Desser is more concerned with the specificities of Ozu's authorship through his most canonical film *Tokyo Story/Tokyo Monogatari* (1953). The chapter reprinted here comes from the edited collection on *Tokyo Story*.[8] In his essay Desser specifies the formal strategies of Ozu such as narrative ellipses and the 360-degree shooting space. Desser is also aware of the histories of reductive framing of Ozu as 'the most Japanese of filmmakers' and through his textual analysis points out with great accuracy both the identifiable formal tendencies of Ozu and the culturally specific parameters that engender his work.

GODZILLA, JAPANESE MONSTER

The films featuring the monster Godzilla and produced by Toho studios constitute one of the most popular Japanese film series. They begin with the first film, *Godzilla/Gojira* (Ishiro Honda, 1954), and continue up to the most recent, *Gojia tai Mosura tai Mekagojira: Tokyo S.O.S* (Tezuka Masaaki, 2003). Godzilla is part of a genre called *kaiju eiga* or monster film, increasingly identified as a children's genre, that also includes equally important characters such as the giant moth *Mothra/Mosura* and Daiei studio rival *Gamera*, a giant flying space-turtle. The genre is commonly associated with rubber-suited monsters, the pleasures involved in the spectacle of destruction of identifiable landscapes (such as Tokyo Bay, carefully crafted in miniature) and often easily understood messages such as the dangers of nuclear power, technological determinism or in the case of *Godzilla and the Smog Monster/Gojira tai Hedorah* (Banno Yoshimitsu, 1971), pollution.

Godzilla – both the films and the figure of the monster itself – engages with otherness on a different level from Ozu, a level that suggests multiple layers of otherness in relation to Japanese cinema. Godzilla, as a science-fiction/horror monster, is naturally understood to be Other through generic definition but, as Chon Noriega reveals in his essay, far from being the monstrous Other, Godzilla is actually a crucial point of identification for its local audience.

Noriega also compares the two versions of the original 1954 *Godzilla*, revealing the difference in meaning attached to Godzilla and the ways in which both Godzilla's otherness and the Japanese-ness of the original text are managed through the alternative American version. The American re-edited version is by far the most widely distributed version of the film. Noriega uses *Godzilla* as a way to explore the Cold War narrative between Japan and the United States in the 1950s and to investigate the way in which a self/other, Japan/United States tension operates within the text. The original Japanese version of the film contains numerous references to American nuclear testing in the Pacific islands that are edited out of the American version, which substitutes the material with scenes with American actors. This practice is not only a deliberate move to cover up the original version's anti-nuclear stance; it can also be seen in a number of other Japanese science-fiction films distributed in the United States that substitute scenes with the Japanese cast for an American cast, such as Honda Ishiro's 'monster on Mount Fuji' film *Ju jin yuki otoko* (1955) which becomes almost unrecognisable two years later as *Half Human*, and is credited to an American director. This also allows the narratives of horror, mutation and transformation to be altered in order to deflect any blame or reference to America's programme of nuclear testing in the 1950s; it also strategically increases their popularity with American audiences by managing their otherness as Japanese cultural products.

This 'remaking' of Japanese films also cuts across the construction of the monster as other. Noriega suggests that for Japanese audiences the concept of the other as something separate from the self is not conceivable: thus, Godzilla is always part of the self and creates a sympathetic point of identification for its audience. Godzilla's transition to loveable hero throughout most of the series was not far off. In the US version, Godzilla is maintained as completely other through his position as an unknowable monster, along with the countless other foreign nasties that grace the American science-fiction movies of the period.

Noriega lays out a framework for thinking through self/other distinctions in Japanese genre films such as *Godzilla*, which should also prove fertile ground for addressing the recent boom in Hollywood remakes of Japanese horror films initiated by *Ring*. Attention to how *Ring* has been remade in Hollywood might also reveal how the tragic figure and ghost called Sadako becomes a franchise-driven monster named Samara in Hollywood, much in the same way as Gojira the victim became Godzilla the perpetrator. However, this recent development does not account for the unexpected popularity of the Hollywood remakes in Japan, nor for the decision of Japanese directors to helm their own remakes in Hollywood, indicating that a more complex transcultural dynamic is at play than simple and often reductive self/other dichotomies will allow.

The final essay of this section by Philip Brophy, on Godzilla and other monsters, is concerned with the symbolic elements and meanings at play in Japanese science-fiction and horror film genres. He identifies how the landmark of Tokyo Bay becomes a central and symbolic motif in the movies. Brophy also teases out similar theoretical concepts employed in Noriega's chapter around the interpretation of genre by suggesting that the difference between Western horror and Japanese horror exists at the level of repression and energy. Brophy argues that Godzilla deals in monstrous energy as opposed to the commonly-held assumption about horror's sexual energy, based on the universalising tenets of psychoanalysis.

Notes

1. Edward Said (1978), *Orientalism*, New York: Vintage.
2. Koichi Iwabuchi (1994), 'Complicit exoticism: Japan and its other', *Continuum*, vol. 8, no. 2, and Koichi Iwabuchi (2002), *Recentering Globalization: Popular Culture and Japanese Transnationalism*, Durham: Duke University Press.
3. Koichi Iwabuchi (2002), *Recentering Globalization: Popular Culture and Japanese Transnationalism*, Durham: Duke University Press, p. 28.
4. Mitsuhiro Yoshimoto (2000), *Kurosawa: Film Studies and Japanese Cinema*, Durham: Duke University Press.
5. Joseph L. Anderson and Donald Richie (1981), *Japanese Cinema: Film, Art and Industry*, Princeton: Princeton University Press [first published in 1959]; David Bordwell and Kristin Thompson (1976), 'Space and narrative in the films of Ozu', *Screen* vol. 17, no. 2; Noel Burch (1979), *To the Distant Observer: Form and Meaning in the Japanese Cinema*, Berkeley: University of California Press; E. Ann Kaplan (1989), 'Problematizing cross-cultural analysis: the case of women in recent Chinese cinema' *Wide Angle* vol. 11, no. 2.
6. Sato Tadao (1982), *Currents in Japanese Cinema*, Tokyo: Kodansha International, p. 190. Lexiconing is the practice in television of reducing the duration of a film by slightly and also imperceptibly speeding it up in order to lose several minutes from its proper running time, thus allowing more space to advertising.
7. Catherine Russell (2003), 'Three Japanese actresses of the 1950s: modernity, femininity and the performance of everyday life', *Cineaction* no. 62, and Alastair Phillips (2003), 'Pictures of the past in the present: modernity, femininity and stardom in the post-war films of Ozu Yasujiro' *Screen* vol. 44, no. 2.
8. David Desser (ed.), *Tokyo Story*, Cambridge: Cambridge University Press.

1

A FILMMAKER FOR ALL SEASONS

David Desser

An aging couple, Hirayama Shukichi and his wife, Tomi[1] living in retirement in the port city of Onomichi, prepare for a train trip to Tokyo to visit their children. A stopover to see a son in Osaka is to be followed by a stay with their eldest son, Koichi, a doctor. Their quiet preparations and gentle banter set a tone of contemplation and nostalgia. Once in Tokyo, however, they realize that Koichi, living in a poor suburb and with a small pediatric practice, is hardly the success they thought he was and seems barely to have time for them. Their daughter Shige, owner of a beauty salon, seems even less interested in their company; indeed, she appears to be outright resentful of their presence.

Koichi and Shige send their parents to Atami, a hot springs resort highly unsuitable for this elderly couple. When they return early to Tokyo, neither Koichi nor Shige is willing to take them in. Only their daughter-in-law, Noriko, a war widow, seems genuinely loving and kind to them; she invites Tomi to stay at her small apartment, while Shukichi must stay at an old friend's. When a drunken Shukichi and his friend are brought to Shige's home by the police, the anger and disappointment the parents feel toward their children and the children toward their parents send the old Hirayamas back home.

On the way home, Tomi is taken ill. A stopover in Osaka to recover for the moment finds the old couple reflecting on their life with a mixture of bitterness and resignation. When the Hirayamas return home, Tomi gets worse. Their youngest daughter, Kyoko, still living at home, sends for her brothers, sister,

From David Desser (ed.) (1997), *Ozu's Tokyo Story*, Cambridge: Cambridge University Press, pp. 1–24.

and sister-in-law. Shortly after their arrival in Onomichi, Tomi dies. Only Kyoko and Noriko seem genuinely saddened. As Noriko prepares to return to Tokyo, the widowed Shukichi extends his gratitude to her for her love and kindness and urges her to remarry. Noriko's contemplative journey home ends the film.

That is the simple plot of Ozu Yasujiro's *Tokyo Story* (*Tokyo monogatari*, 1953). Little of this description would indicate that the film is generally acknowledged to be one of the greatest ever made, as indicated, for example, by *Sight and Sound* magazine's respected surveys of film critics. It is probably the best-known film directed by Ozu Yasujiro, both in the West and in Japan. Ozu himself, at least since the middle of the 1970s, has been considered one of Japan's best known and most respected directors in the West; in Japan his status as a major filmmaker was established by 1932, and he remained preeminent among film directors until his death in 1963. His position in the pantheon of Japanese film directors in Japan and the West is unmatched.

Ozu's recognition in the West was a long time in coming compared with that of many Japanese directors working in the 1950s and 1960s. The success of *Rashomon* at the 1951 Venice Film Festival should not make us oblivious to the reality that Japanese producers and distributors created films almost specifically for export to the burgeoning film festival and 'art theater' circuit in the United States and around the world, or else sought in their massive output of the 1950s and early 1960s suitable films for export.[2] Such films for export were far more often than not period films, costume dramas, portrayals of the world of the samurai or the geisha. Though Ozu's first film, *The Sword of Penitence* (*Zange no yaiba*, 1927), was a period piece, he never made another one. So as films like *Ugetsu* (Mizoguchi Kenji, 1953), *Gate of Hell* (*Jigokumon*, Kinugasa Teinosuke, 1953), and the Samurai trilogy (1954–5) by Inagaki Hiroshi were winning accolades in the West for their lush visual style or exotic appeal, Ozu quietly went about the business of directing films, typically one and sometimes two per year starting in 1948.[3] For the Japanese exporters of films to the West, Ozu, it appeared, was just 'too Japanese.' That this was far from the truth, that the West responded to Ozu with as much enthusiasm as ever a Japanese audience did, became clear only after his death.

As the Japanese film industry declined in the 1960s, the export market paradoxically increased, at least in the United States because of a precipitous decline in Hollywood's output and the American film industry's growing inability to reach a target audience. A more demanding college and college-educated audience began turning its back on the perceived immaturity and escapism of Hollywood and found in foreign films, from France, Italy, and Sweden, among other countries, an intellectual content and maturity of themes absent from Hollywood's wheezing attempts to hold on to its former glory. Thus an audience for Japanese films was ready and waiting. The showing of a handful of Ozu's films in the mid-1960s at festivals, museums, and New York theaters gradually revealed a director seemingly at odds with the wandering swordsmen and magnificently costumed women that defined the Japanese cinema for some. Here was a director so steeped in contemporary Japanese culture as to be making films without concessions to an international mass audience. That Ozu was, in fact, very much in tune with the Japanese mass audience (though his films were not box-office giants in the year of their release) made U.S. intellectuals excited about coming to terms with a foreign culture that could produce a filmmaker of this originality and particularity. That his films were relatively plotless and steeped in everyday life made them seem if not part of, then related to, the French New Wave or the severe style and themes of Michelangelo Antonioni and Ingmar Bergman. Seemingly endless arguments over Ozu's 'Japaneseness,' his place in world cinema history, and the depths of his stories and themes testify to this filmmaker's international significance and universality.

The respect accorded both *Tokyo Story* and Ozu himself stems from a number of factors. The film is, paradoxically, both intensely insular and immensely universal. Rarely has a film been so immersed in specifics of setting and period, so thoroughly pervaded by the culture from which it was produced. Indeed, so completely does the film derive from particularities of Japanese culture – marriage, family, setting – that critics have argued over the film's basic themes. Is it about the breakup of the traditional Japanese family in the light of postwar changes (increased urbanization and industrialization, which have led to the decline of the extended family)? Or is it about the inevitabilities of life: children growing up, getting married, moving away from home, having children of their own, leaving their aging parents behind? Of course, though the film is set in a specific time and place, such questions concerning the breakdown of tradition and the changes that life inevitably brings are universal in their appeal. Like *Bicycle Thieves* (*Ladri di biciclette*) made just a few years earlier, *Tokyo Story* derives its power from both its unique setting and the universality of its characters and theme.

For film scholars and students, the pleasures and power of *Tokyo Story*, indeed of Ozu's oeuvre in its entirety, stem not just from the way in which the film's thematic range is steeped in Japanese culture, but also, and perhaps more interestingly, from its stylistic practices. Under the influence of critics and historians, ranging from film-critic-truned-director Paul Schrader to Donald Richie (the best-known and most prolific scholar-critic of the Japanese cinema), Noel Burch, and David Bordwell, the Western fascination with Ozu has revolved around his cinematic techniques, which, like his films' themes, have been endlessly debated and discussed. One debate has centered on his proclivity for the low camera position, said by some to reproduce the typical Japanese perspective of someone sitting on a tatami mat. A more intense debate has concerned his use of 'empty shots,' said by many to reproduce the worldview of Zen Buddhism or to reflect the modernist fascination with surface and materiality. In addition to issues of camera placement and *mise en scène*, critics have noted Ozu's narrative strategy whereby plot is completely deemphasized.

This is considered by some to deny the cause-effect chain that is a function of Western logocentrism, individualism, and bourgeois capitalism, or to draw viewer attention away from results and toward process. These are just some of the issues that situate Ozu as a filmmaker with a unique and uniquely important cinematic consciousness. Moreover, Ozu is prized by so many film scholars and critics because he offers an alternative to mainstream American cinema (the vaunted 'classical Hollywood cinema').

Thus *Tokyo Story* can be appreciated as a film with universal appeal in its story of aging parents and their disappointments with their children and their lives or as a paradigm of the unique cinema of Ozu. From either perspective, the film is rich in its implications.

Narrative and Space in *Tokyo Story*

One technique whereby a film viewer or 'reader' learns to appreciate the particularities of a film is to make comparisons, implicitly or explicitly, with other films. In other words, the viewer analyzes the film against a set of 'norms.' In film studies, those norms are based on the classical Hollywood cinema, and indicate not what is right or wrong, but what is usual, typical, or standard, but without value judgment. (For example, there is nothing good or bad about an 'inch' or a 'meter'; either is just a standard measurement.) Thus the characteristics of 'ordinary' American film may be used to grasp the uniqueness of Ozu's cinema in general and of *Tokyo Story* in particular.

What the typical viewer, Western or Japanese, ordinarily first realizes about Ozu's films is the apparent lack of plot – not of story, but of story-events. Plot in American cinema is usually tied to the dramatic, the action-packed, the revelatory; it relies on a rigid chain of cause and effect from which extraneous detail is eliminated in the interest of 'moving the plot along.' Not so in an Ozu film, where 'extraneous event' is an almost meaningless term because the film is made up of a series of moments, cumulative in their power and their emotional effect, but not causal, not story-driven. The clearest indication of how this works can be found, so to speak, precisely in the sorts of things Ozu leaves out.

An important narrative principle for Ozu is the ellipsis, the omission of plot material or even an event. In films like *Late Spring* (*Banshun*, 1949) and *An Autumn Afternoon* (*Samma no aji*, 1962) the plot point, the dramatic highlight, to which the film has been leading, is elided: these films about a daughter who ought to marry never show the husband-to-be when the daughter agrees to marry. In *Tokyo Story* we are aware of various sorts of ellipses. There is the 'minor ellipsis,' in which certain plot points are dropped. For instance, in one scene, the two oldest children discuss sending their parents on a trip to Atami. This is followed by a shot of people on a seawall then by a shot of the sea seen from an interior, then a shot down the length of a hallway, and, finally, a shot of the old couple in a hotel. Thus we see that the parents are already at the spa, and we understand that Ozu has eliminated scenes in which the parents are told about the trip, are put on a train to Atami, and arrive at the resort.

This sort of minor ellipsis is common in worldwide cinema, but nevertheless needs highlighting here. It involves the principle of retrospectivity, the active participation of viewers, who must constantly reintegrate themselves into the action, reorient themselves within filmic time and space. The greater the ellipsis the more active, the more involved we must be. In Ozu's films, the variety of ellipses requires that we pay attention. For instance, Ozu often uses what may be called a 'surprise ellipsis.' Here plot points prepared for by dialogue and action are, in fact, elided. At the start of *Tokyo Story* the parents discuss changing trains in Osaka and thus seeing their younger son, who lives and works there. The next scene begins in Tokyo at the home of the older son, and shortly thereafter the parents arrive. The Osaka visit discussed by the parents is thus never shown, although we learn that the rendezvous did, in fact, take place. Preparing us for a scene that never occurs onscreen is a daring strategy. Even more daring is the fact that the scene has occurred offscreen. Talked about, prepared for, clearly mentioned, it is then simply elided.

More daring yet is the 'dramatic ellipsis,' whereby something important has occurred, but offscreen. In *Tokyo Story* this is the parents' arrival in Osaka on the return trip and their overnight stay because the mother has become ill. We learn about their arrival secondhand, as it were, after the fact, from the second son, who mentions that they are now in Osaka because of the mother's illness. By the time we see the couple, they are already at the son's home and the mother is, for the moment, recovering (though, somewhat rare for Ozu, this prepares us for her eventual demise). The point is that the drama of her illness, the sudden change in plans, is not shown. As just mentioned, the first Osaka trip, which we expect to see, is not shown (something not atypical of Ozu). The second, unexpected stop in Osaka, is shown, however.

Now if the sorts of things Ozu eliminates are often the sorts of things most American films are specifically built around, moments of intense emotion surrounding events like reunions, marriages, illness, we may need to account for this difference. Ozu's strategies are rooted in elements of the Japanese aesthetic tradition – the deemphasis of drama and the elision of plot elements in theatrical works, the emphasis on mood and tone instead of story in literature. Some of the essays in this volume discuss Ozu's films in relation to other modes of Japanese art, history, and religion. For now, the important point is the manner in which the story, the drama, is told differently than in American cinema, if just a bit differently.

Ozu's spatial composition, specifically his 'screen direction' and 'mismatched action,' can similarly be linked to elements of the Japanese aesthetic tradition. We will look first, briefly, at the way Ozu handles transitional spaces.

Transitional spaces are linked to retrospectivity in general and often ellipsis in particular. Instead of a direct cut between scenes, Ozu often finds 'intermediate spaces.' These are sometimes intermediate in a literal sense, in that they fall between the action just completed and the action forthcoming. Many critics have seen in these intermediate spaces evidence of Japanese aesthetic practices – Zen Buddhism, say, for Paul Schrader and 'pillow shots' for Noel Burch. Such spaces are sometimes called 'still lifes' and, like the still lifes of classical painting, are often devoid of human figures. Ozu achieves a particular poignancy in many of his still lifes by highlighting the paradox of humanity's presence by its absence. Transitional spaces help viewers understand that a scene is changing and prepare them for the retrospective activity of reorienting themselves in the next scene. However, though transitional spaces help to indicate a change of scene or locale, it is not always clear where the new locale is until a later shot in the sequence (postponement of narrative information). And transitional spaces do little to help viewers understand how much time has passed. Here is an example of spatial change and temporal retrospectivity in *Tokyo Story*.

Between the first scene of the film, in which the older Hirayamas pack for their trip and discuss the stop in Osaka, and the second scene, which takes place in Koichi's house in Tokyo, there are three transitional spaces. The first is a shot of smokestacks, a recurring image of Tokyo in the film. It is not, however, an image unique to Tokyo and might as well be one of Osaka, Japan's commercial heartland. And since the film has prepared us for an Osaka outing, this may very well be our guess.[4] The next shot of power lines and a small railroad crossing might be taken as representative of Tokyo, with its high energy and prominence in the postwar era. The following shot, however, makes it clear that we are in Tokyo, with its sign outside of Dr Hirayama's office (though we do not know that Koichi, the oldest child, is a doctor; in Ozu's films it is typically difficult to follow familial relationships at first). Careful examination of the exterior shots in the rest of the film reveals that the smokestacks and train station are, in fact, spaces 'connected' to Dr Hirayama's, but nothing so indicates that at the start.

If we have, however, made the spatial transition from Onomichi to Tokyo, nothing in these intermediate spaces, these still lifes, has indicated any specific passage of time. For we find out shortly thereafter, though not before some small, seemingly irrelevant business about cleaning the house and asking a child to give up his room for his grandparents' visit, that not only has the film made the spatial transition from Onomichi to Tokyo, but so has the old couple. This is the ellipsis we discussed earlier, but we now understand that it occurred in the space and time of the intermediate shots.

This is not to say that Ozu handles all spatiotemporal changes in a deceptive or playful manner. For instance, when Ozu wants to introduce the sequence in which Shukichi and Tomi stay over in Osaka when the latter takes ill, his intermediate spaces are clear and straightforward. The Osaka setting is established beyond a doubt by a shot of Osaka Castle, a massive stone structure instantly recognizable to virtually every Japanese. This is reinforced by a second shot of the Osaka skyline, this time with Osaka Castle in the background, a typical Ozu maneuver whereby the space of a scene is thoroughly explored by reverse angles and camera shifts. And it is to such strategies to which we now turn.

Ozu's scenic construction and segmenting of screen space are among the most notable characteristics of his cinema, yet casual viewers often fail to notice them. One of these is the frequency with which Ozu crosses the so-called 180-degree line. This crossing of the line results in what would be called in American film 'mismatched' action within the same space. Characters who converse with each other seem to shift spatially in relation to each other and to the space in which they are filmed. Examples from *Tokyo Story* abound. For instance, the first time we see the Hirayamas in the film, they are seated next to each other, each facing right. Yet by the time the sequence ends we suddenly notice that now they are facing left! So bald a juxtaposition seems a bizarre mistake. One might explain it away in terms of the numerous angles and shots between the first time we see the couple and this last time at the end of the sequence. Numerous close-ups have been intercut, and cutaways to a neighbor lady have also occurred. Thus the precise moment of the shift from right to left may have passed us by.

More daring, yet more typical of Ozu, such apparent mismatches are not always disguised by cutaways but, in fact, represent a principle of cinematic spatial construction different from Hollywood's 'norms.' Critics have come to understand that Ozu uses a principle of 360-degree space instead of the 180-degree rule applied in Hollywood. For instance, in one of the most moving scenes of the film, in which the old mother tells her widowed daughter-in-law how much she enjoys her visit, the daughter-in-law is initially screen right! Noriko gently massages Tomi's shoulders as they talk. Noriko then stands to move across the room. In the midst of her standing, Ozu cuts. In a typical American film this would be a cut on action, the action in some sense 'disguising' the actual cut. Ozu cuts on her motion, too, but at the same time shifts the camera across the 180-degree line. Thus, when the cut on Noriko's motion is completed, she is now screen left.

In fact, the rest of this sequence, an important one in terms of its portrayal of loss, regret, and change, Ozu's camera traverses the entire space of the room, utilizing two-shots, close-ups, and reverse shots from every possible angle. Characters sitting side by side are typical in Ozu's cinema, reflective of the non-confrontational stance of the Japanese, a certain politeness.[5] Notice here that Tomi, the mother-in-law, is facing screen left. When Ozu cuts to a close-up of her, however, she is facing screen right. Without the benefit of a cutaway this again appears to be a 'mismatched action.' And when Ozu returns to a two-shot, the screen direction does not correspond to the preceding shot, nor to the one before that. Careful examination of the individual setups reveals that Ozu rarely shoots a scene in a master shot, the whole scene or dramatic sequence done in one angle to which an editor can return periodically after using close-ups, reverse shots, over-the-shoulder shots, or other shots.

Changes in screen direction or seemingly mismatched action also occur regularly when Ozu shows continuous action across contiguous spaces. That is, when a character leaves one room of a house and enters another, Ozu does not typically imply spatial contiguity in the conventional way. Simply put, in a Hollywood film, when a character exits the frame to enter a contiguous space, screen direction hides the cut. If a character exits screen right, the next shot shows the character entering screen left. A smoothing out of the cut is thus made by the apparent continuity of motion left to right. Hollywood style and other variations on this classical continuity mode strive to achieve the *appearance* of contiguity, whereas such sequences may have no basis in a real space and time. (The Soviet theoretician and filmmaker Lev Kuleshov convincingly proved this with regard to 'creative geography.') Hollywood filmmakers regard the cut as something to be elided, to be made 'invisible,' and so principles of matching screen direction and eyeline matches have been developed over the years. As we have demonstrated, Ozu often disregards such principles.

Attempting to account for these spatial anomalies can be difficult. Are they a cultural or an individual particularity? I am convinced that a 'cultural reading' of screen space in Ozu would be reductive and essentialist, if not basically incorrect. I do think, however, that Ozu has drawn inspiration for his spatialization from aspects of traditional Japanese culture, including, most prominently, architecture. The 'mismatched' screen direction in interior sequences (especially in houses) in which characters exit screen right and enter the next scene from the same direction may derive from the modularity of the Japanese home, in which space can be changed by the movement of sliding screens. Lower-level entryways that make a ring or border around the living area in a typical Japanese home provide a variety of entrances and exits into and out of rooms as well. Thus the space of the home itself can shift.[6] Combined with Ozu's proclivity for using individual setups for most shots, spatial configurations become important in individual scenes but much less so across the cut.

This is not to say that cutting, as such, is not important to Ozu, that the juxtaposition of shots to make meaning, to carry thematic weight, does not occur. There is a very shocking use of such a cut, in fact, in *Tokyo Story*. Tomi, playing with her youngest grandson, Isamu, muses over her fate and his. This, of course, is typical foreshadowing in which a character thinks about the future, cueing the audience to the possibility of the future being cut short. Though rare for Ozu (unlike other filmmakers), this is indeed what happens. But when Tomi muses about Isamu's future, wondering what will become of him, Ozu cuts to a shot of Shukichi, the grandfather, sitting alone. Is this a kind of 'melodramatic' cut, Ozu implying that the same fate, of old age, loneliness, and disappointment, awaits Isamu? Yes and no.

Ozu has said that *Tokyo Story* was his 'most melodramatic' film. Indeed, for critic Tony Rayns, Ozu may be taken at his word. The cut just described seems clearly to indicate that Isamu is doomed to a life like Shukichi's. But Ozu is too subtle a filmmaker, after all. Yes, Isamu may very well be doomed to such a life, but is such a life so bad? Or is there any alternative to such a life? Aging is inevitable, children grow up and grow apart from parents; that is to say, time brings changes. Yet there is also a cycle to life: birth, growth, death, the birth of a new generation and the pattern begins again. So if *Tokyo Story* is melodramatic in terms of its didacticism, teaching us to respect our elders, for instance, it is also realistic: life goes on no matter what one does. And in being so Japanese in terms of its historical setting and its familial characteristics, the film is also universal.

A Routine Production

Tokyo Story is only one of fourteen films Ozu made between 1948 and 1962. Oddly, this averages out to one film a year, a reminder of the vibrancy of the Japanese cinema in the 1950s, when directors routinely made a film each year, with many making as many as two or three. *Tokyo Story* was little different in its script preparation from most of Ozu's films. As was their habit, Ozu and co-writer Noda Kogo, with whom Ozu had worked for virtually his entire film career, went to an inn and hashed out the ideas over food, drink, and conversation. In this case, the inn was in Chigasaki and the script took 103 days to complete along with forty-three bottles of sake.[7] Location scouting with Noda and cinematographer Atsuta Yuharu, script in hand, took a little less than one month, first in Tokyo, then in Onomichi. The film itself was shot and edited from July to October 1953. This four-month schedule is typical of Ozu: virtually all of his postwar films took four to five months to shoot and edit. There was no hint that *Tokyo Story* would surpass his other films in worldwide popularity and esteem.[8] In fact, it is arguable to say that *Tokyo Story* is his finest film, whatever one might mean by that. The point is, rather, that this film, made with the same crew Ozu had been using for years and featuring many of the same actors with whom he had worked so often before (Ryu Chishu had been in virtually every Ozu film since *Dragnet Girl* (*Hijosen no onna*) in 1933, was part of a routine, yet unique 'project.' With films spanning his career devoted to similar themes and with similar titles (the Japanese titles no less confusing than the English ones; 'Tokyo' cropped up in four other films, for instance), Ozu played with variations on a theme. *Tokyo Story*, while it stands by itself as a masterpiece of world cinema, may also be taken as paradigmatic of Ozu's films, certainly his postwar films geared to the seemingly insular world of the Japanese middle-class family, yet speaking volumes about Japan as a whole and the world around.

Notes

1. The name order is given in Japanese style, last name first, given name second.
2. The Japanese economic miracle, a theme that underlies *Tokyo Story* to some extent, was responsible, too, for making Japan the world's largest film producer: for instance, between 1957 and 1961 the Japanese averaged 500 feature films per year. Though a decline began in 1962, throughout the rest of the 1960s the Japanese averaged more than 350 films per year.
3. With an output of just over forty films, Ozu is far from being Japan's most prolific director. With directors like Inagaki and Misumi Kenji, who directed more than 100 films, and Makino Masahiro, who directed well over 200 films, Ozu's relatively scant output suggests that he was able to invest great care and effort into each film.

4. As if to illustrate the difference between Ozu's style and that of Hollywood, a 16-mm subtitled version of *Tokyo Story* available in the United States uses subtitles to identify the new location where no such indications are present!
5. Of course, one should be leery of such a sweeping cultural generalization. To converse, the Japanese naturally sit opposite each other, or at right angles, or obliquely, or many possible ways. Yet this 'norizontality' not only is characteristic of Ozu but may be seen throughout the Japanese cinema. For instance, recall the many dinner scenes in *Family Game* (*Kazoku geemu*, Morita Yoshimitsu, 1984) in which the family members are eating side by side, to great comic effect.
6. For a further discussion of this issue, consult my essay on Ozu's *Ohayo*, in 'Childhood and Education in Japan,' Teaching Module 3 (New York: The Japan Society, n.d.).
7. See Donald Richie, *Ozu* (Berkeley: University of California Press, 1974), 26.
8. Ozu's films received more *Kinema Jumpo* Best One awards than any other director (six), yet *Tokyo Story* did not win the Best One in 1953 (it was second).

2

THE DIFFICULTY OF BEING RADICAL: THE DISCIPLINE OF FILM STUDIES AND THE POST-COLONIAL WORLD ORDER

Mitsuhiro Yoshimoto

Discourse on the Other

Dilemmas of Western Film Scholars?

Writing about national cinemas used to be an easy task: Film critics believed all they had to do was to construct a linear historical narrative describing a development of a cinema within a particular national boundary whose unity and coherence seemed to be beyond all doubt. Yet, this apparent obviousness of national cinema scholarship is now in great danger, since, on the one hand, we are no longer so sure about the coherence of the nation-state and, on the other hand, the idea of history has also become far from self-evident. As the question of authorship in the cinema was reproblematized by poststructuralist film theory, the notion of national cinema has been similarly put to an intense, critical scrutiny.

The problematic of national cinema scholarship becomes further complicated when we deal with non-Western national cinemas; these pose an additional problem with regard to the production of knowledge. It is often argued that any attempt to write about non-Western national cinemas should be accountable for all the complicated questions concerning the discourse on the Other. Writing about non-Western national cinemas has been situated in such a way that it is inescapable from the question, 'Can we ever know the Other as the truly Other?'[1] What is required by the hermeneutics of the Other

From Masao Miyoshi and H.D. Harootunian (eds) (1993), *Japan in the World*, Durham: Duke University Press, pp. 338–53.

sought out in non-Western national cinema scholarship is neither a simple identification with the Other nor an easy assimilation of the Other into the self. Instead, it is a construction of a new position of knowledge through a careful negotiation between the self and the Other.

To further explore this problematic of non-Western film scholarship, let us focus on the study of Japanese cinema. Not surprisingly, the axiomatics of the discursive mode of Japanese film scholarship has also been constructed on the opposition between the self and the Other or between Western theory and Japanese culture. This opposition in Japanese film studies creates a certain epistemological difficulty, which Peter Lehman summarizes as follows:

> Japan raises unique problems for Western film scholars. The situation can be summarized, perhaps a little too cynically, as follows: Western film scholars are accusing each other of being Western film scholars. Or to put it a bit more accurately, Western film scholars are accusing each other of being Western in their approach to Japanese film. Is this a genuine dilemma with possible solutions or is it a pseudo-issue which obscures the real issues? Is it productive for us as modern Western film scholars to pursue this quest for the proper Japanese response?[2]

As this passage suggests, there are many writings or meta-discourses on how to study the Japanese cinema properly, and by problematizing dilemmas of Western scholars of Japanese film, Lehman himself contributes to this thriving meta-discourse industry. More specifically, Lehman intervenes in critical exchanges between David Bordwell/Kristin Thompson and Joseph Anderson/Paul Willemen.

One of the points of dispute in this controversy is whether we should call Ozu Yasujiro a modernist filmmaker. It starts with Bordwell and Thompson's claim that since the narrative mode of Ozu's films systematically defies the rules established by the classical Hollywood cinema, Ozu should be regarded as a modernist director. Paul Willemen criticizes Bordwell and Thompson by saying that to call Ozu a modernist is not so much different from European modernist artists questionable appropriation of African tribal sculpture in the early twentieth century. Bordwell responds that Willemen's critique does not hold, since African sculptors never saw modernists' art work, but Ozu was thoroughly familiar with the Hollywood cinema. Lehman intervenes in this skirmish and takes side with Willemen. According to Lehman, Bordwell dismisses too easily the similarities between traditional Japanese art and Ozu's films, both of which, as Joseph Anderson points out, construct discontinuous, non-narrative space. Furthermore, Lehman quotes Willemen to claim that Bordwell has completely misunderstood the meaning of modernism:

> Ozu's films cannot be claimed as modernist, since the point about modernism is precisely that it is a *critique* of, not a neutral alternative to, dominant aesthetic practices.[3]

Lehman's critique of Bordwell and Thompson is well taken. We should all join Lehman and be 'baffled as to why Bordwell and Thompson ever characterized Ozu as a modernist in the first place.'[4] At the same time, we should also be appalled by Willemen's and Lehman's Eurocentric view of modernism, which does not consider what modernism possibly means for the non-West. A seemingly innocent question of Ozu's modernity, in fact, cannot be answered unless we carefully take into account the specificities of Japanese cinema, social formations, and history. Such a problematic in Japanese or non-Western cinema scholarship will finally lead to many more fundamental questions concerning the definitions of a nation and of a cinema.

The Subject of Cross-Cultural Analysis

The possibility of studying a non-Western national cinema without erasing its own specificities has been recently attempted in the emerging field of Chinese film studies. E. Ann Kaplan's essay on the Chinese cinema shows great sensitivity toward the issue of cultural specificities and the difficulty of what she calls 'cross-cultural analysis.'[5] As Kaplan points out, 'Cross-cultural analysis . . . is difficult – fraught with danger,' since '[w]e are forced to read works produced by the Other through the constraints of our own frameworks/theories/ideologies' (CCA, 42). Yet, despite its inherent danger, according to Kaplan, it is still worth attempting cross-cultural analysis, because 'theorists outside the producing culture might uncover different strands of the multiple meanings than critics of the originating culture just because they bring different frameworks/theories/ideologies to the texts' (CCA, 42). The question is whether cross-cultural analysis can really contribute to a cultural exchange between two different cultures on an equal basis, to the understanding of the Other without making it fit to the underlying assumptions of the analyst's own culture, or simply, to a non-dominating way of knowing and understanding the Other.

The major feature of Kaplan's essay is its nonlinearity. It contains so many questions, self-reflexive remarks, and qualifications; that is, the tone of the essay is, as Kaplan says, 'tentative':

> So, on the one hand, we have Chinese film scholars turning to American and European film theories to see what might be useful for them, in their writing on both American film and their own cinema; on the other hand, we have some American scholars writing tentative essays on Chinese films. (Those scholars, like Chris Berry, who have lived in China and know the culture and the language are obviously no longer 'tentative.') We have, then, a sort of informal film-culture exchange of a rather unusual kind, precisely because of its relative informality. (CCA, 40).

Kaplan's essay on the Chinese cinema is tentative because she has not lived in China and does not know the Chinese language and culture. Yet, according to Kaplan, this tentativeness of informal discourse can become formal knowledge if one goes to and lives in China and becomes an expert in things

Chinese. Thus, there is nothing *unusual* about this 'informal film-culture exchange'. On the contrary, the model of cross-cultural exchange presented here is a classic example of what Gayatri Spivak calls the 'arrogance of the radical European humanist conscience, which will consolidate itself by imagining the other, or, as Sartre puts it, "redo in himself the other's project," through the collection of information.'[6]

As we will see in a moment, the mapping of critical discourses on the Chinese cinema by Kaplan is remarkably similar to the polarized scholarship on the Japanese cinema. While either the Western or native expert on a national cinema provides specific information about the cultural background of that cinema, the Western theorist constructs a theoretical framework that gives rise to new insight on the aspects of the national cinema never noticed by area studies experts before. The only difference is that the position of the theorist has become less certain vis-à-vis the non-Western culture, so that any theoretical analysis of the Other can no longer escape a certain sense of hesitation that is hard to find in actual writings on the Japanese cinema.

This sense of hesitation about Western intellectuals' own critical position on and distance from the non-Western culture is widespread in the postmodern West, and compared to the extreme logical consequences reached by postmodern critical ethnography, Kaplan's self-reflexive essay does not go far enough. By pushing to the limit the self-examination of knowledge production in relation to the Other, postmodern critical ethnography has radically put into question not only the position of the analyzing subject, equipped with the latest knowledge of theory and critical methodologies, but also those of the expert subject and the 'radical European [or American] humanist conscience' that claim to know the Other based on the authenticity of experience and self-claimed deep understanding of the Other's culture.

In his essay on the Japanese cinema, Scott Nygren attempts to re-articulate the terms of cross-cultural exchange between Japan and the West from a 'postmodern perspective.' Nygren argues that postmodernism puts into question a linear, evolutionary model of history constructed by a paradigm of modernism, so that 'a discontinuous and reversible model of history now seems more productive in conceptualizing cross-cultural relationships.'[7] Instead of accepting the traditional view that modern Japanese history is a history of mere imitation and assimilation of the West, Nygren proposes an alternative relation between the West and Japan, characterized by a mutual cross-cultural exchange: Traditional Japanese culture gave inspiration to Western modernists as much as Western humanism had a deconstructive impact on feudal aspects of Japanese society. Nygren thus posits a chiasmatic correspondence between Japan and the West on the one hand and between tradition and modernism on the other:

> This paper will argue that classical Hollywood conventions often valorized (although misleadingly) under the name 'realism' served to

> reinforce dominant cultural ideology in the West, while functioning to deconstruct dominant values in Japan . . . Although the influence of Japanese traditional culture on the formation of Western modernism is well known, in many respects the situation in Japan was the reverse: it was Western tradition, not Western modernism, that played a key role in the formation of what we call 'Japanese modernism.'[8]

What Nygren attempts to find in this reversed specularity is an 'alternative access to a postmodern situation':

> If postmodernism is conceived in the West as a non-progressivist freeplay of traditionalist and modernist signification without progressivist determinism, is it possible to discuss a postmodernist reconfiguration of Japanese culture where Western values of humanism and anti-humanism seem reversed in their relation to tradition and the modern? Can Asian societies in general be theorized in terms of an alternative access to a postmodernist situation?[9]

Yet, this particular model of cross-cultural exchange between the West and Japan, in light of the postmodernism articulated in the passages above, begs the basic facts of West/non-West relations.

There is no need for us to remind ourselves that the West and the non-West do not voluntarily engage in cross-cultural exchange. The relation between the two has always taken the form of political, economic, and cultural domination of the non-West by the West. Not surprisingly, the emergence of modern Japanese literature and film more or less coincides with the age of high imperialism and nationalism. Yet, nowhere in the text do we find questions concerning the ineluctable relations existing among modernism, imperialism, and nationalism (or nativism). Is it the case that by providing Japan with Western tradition, which is said 'to deconstruct dominant values in Japan,' Western imperialism had some empowering effect on Japan? I don't think this is what is argued in the essay; yet at the same time, it is hard not to deduce this disturbing conclusion from the essay's logic, either.[10]

The notions of cross-cultural analysis and cross-cultural exchange are ideologically dubious for the following reasons. First, as we will see in a moment, it contributes to the concealment of the questionable, complicit division of national cinema scholarship between history and theory. Second, it also contributes to the myth of a specular relation between Western theory and non-Western practice. In film studies, there are many examples of arguments perpetuating this myth. We have just discussed two examples above. Another powerful instance can also be found in the field of Japanese film studies. In *To the Distant Observer: Form and Meaning in the Japanese Cinema*, which still remains the most provocative study on the Japanese cinema in any language. Noel Burch calls for the 'possibility of an immense productive relationship which could and should be developed between contemporary European theory and Japanese practice.' 'And,' continues Burch, 'Marxism had always regarded such mutually informative relationships between theory and practice as essential to its growth.'[11] Inspired by Roland Barthes's 'study' of 'Japan,' *Empire of Signs*, Burch constructs a utopia called 'Japan,' in which Western critical theory materializes its critical insight in concrete artistic practices. Japan as the Other is then conceived as mere supplement, safely contained within the epistemological limit of the West.

Examples of this discursive mode are not confined within Japanese film scholarship. Julianne Burton presents a similar view in her article on Third World cinema and First World theory, 'Marginal Cinemas and Mainstream Critical Theory.'[12] While Burch tries to establish a complimentary relation between Western theory and Japanese practice. Burton attempts to appropriate Third World cinema within the sphere of Western critical discourse by designating the former 'marginal' and the latter 'mainstream.' In Burton's scheme, critics of Third World cinema should be enlightened by the insights of Western critical theory, particularly by the 'theory of mediation,' and Western critical theory in turn should be modified so that it can accommodate and appropriate Third World films and the specific contexts surrounding them. This sounds good as far as it goes. But who in the end benefits by this cross-cultural exchange? Who dictates the terms of this transaction between the West and the Third World?[13] Burton's critique of Third World filmmakers and critics is dependent on her misuse of the concept of mediation. She does not use this crucial concept to articulate the relation between Third World film practices and various subtexts of film production and consumption. Rather, Burton has recourse to the concept of mediation to insert Western theorists into the position of subject, which, by criticizing the naïveté of Third World practitioners who believe in 'un-mediated' transparency of meaning, plays the role of 'mediator' between Western high theory and Third World practice not only for the First World audience of Third World film but also for Third World people as the uninitiated.

In his essay on the Third Cinema debate, Homi Bhabha argues that critical theory's appropriation of the Other as a good object of knowledge is an epistemological colonization of the non-West:

> Montesquieu's Turkish Despot, Barthes' Japan, Kristeva's China, Derrida's Nambikwara Indians, Lyotard's Cashinahua 'pagans' are part of this strategy of containment where the Other text is forever the exegetical horizon of difference, never the active agent of articulation. The Other is cited, quoted, framed, illuminated, encased in the shot/reverse-shot strategy of a serial enlightenment. Narrative and the *cultural* politics of difference become the closed circle of interpretation. The Other loses its power to signify, to negate, to initiate its 'desire,' to split its 'sign' of identity, to establish its own institutional and oppositional discourse. However impeccably the content of an 'other' culture

> may be known, however anti-ethnocentrically it is represented, it is its *location* as the 'closure' of grand theories, the demand that, in analytic terms, it be always the 'good' object of knowledge, the docile body of difference, that reproduces a relation of domination and is the most serious indictment of the institutional powers of critical theory.[14]

Interestingly, the title of Bhabha's essay is 'The Commitment to Theory,' not 'The Indictment of Theory,' although what Bhabha argues is diametrically opposite to Burton's project. This false resemblance between the two, or the double nature of theory in relation to the Other, is precisely a sign of the complexity of the problem we must deal with. What is to be done is neither a simple celebration nor condemnation of critical theory; instead, what is at stake is the precise location of theory in critical discourse on/of/by the non-West. This problematic of theory will be discussed more fully in the following sections, but for a moment. I would like to come back to my third point about the notion of cross-cultural exchange (or analysis). By designating only one direction of subject-object relation, this popular notion elides the issue of power/knowledge. While Western critics as subject can analyze a non-Western text as object. non-Western critics are not allowed to occupy the position of subject to analyze a Western text as object. When non-Western critics study English literature or French cinema, it is not called cross-cultural analysis. Whatever they say is interpreted and judged only within the context of Western discourses. The cross-cultural analysis, which is predicated on the masking of power relations in the production of knowledge, is a newer version of legitimating cultural colonization of the non-West by the West.

A binarism of self/Other, which underlies the project of cross-cultural analysis, is a trap. It abstracts the role of power in the production of knowledge, and depoliticizes the structure of domination found in West/non-West opposition. The studies of non-Western national cinemas based on the axiomatics of self/Other opposition cannot but reproduce the hegemonic ideology of Western neo-colonialism. It can produce knowledge on non-Western national cinemas only for those who can put themselves into the position of the subject (i.e., Western theorists. Discourse on the Other and its corollary, cross-cultural analysis, not only fix the non-West as the object to be appropriated but also transform serious political issues into bad philosophical questions. For instance, as we have already observed, Peter Lehman's critique of Bordwell, Thompson, Heath, and so forth is right on target; however, the dilemmas of Western scholars of Japanese film on which he speculates are also false dilemmas created by the mistaken assumptions and premises of meta-discourses on Japanese film criticism. Being dependent on the framework of self/Other dichotomy, Lehman misses what is fundamentally at stake: The structural dilemma created by discourse on the Other is in fact only a disguise for a legitimation of Western subjectivity supported by another fundamental opposition underlying Japanese film scholarship.

History and Theory

Two Types of Japanese Film Scholarship

In *Cinema: A Critical Dictionary*, edited by Richard Roud, there are seven entries on Japanese directors; of these seven, three essays (on Mizoguchi, Naruse, and Ozu) are written by Donald Richie, while Noel Burch contributes two essays (on Kurosawa and Oshima).[15] This division of labor in Roud's volume mirrors the two different types of Japanese film scholarship: On the one hand, the Japanese film and area studies specialists tend to take up the historical study of Japanese cinema, since they possess a good command of the Japanese language and are familiar with Japanese culture but not with the theoretical advancement made in film studies; on the other hand, film critics well versed in theory but not in the Japanese language write on Japanese cinema from 'theoretical perspectives.'

The critic who represents area studies specialists is Donald Richie, whose *Japanese Film: Art and Industry*,[16] cowritten with Joseph Anderson, is a combination of conventional, linear narrative sketching the development of the Japanese film industry and a compilation of chronologically arranged, short commentaries on hundreds of films. If, as the blurb by David Bordwell on the back cover of the book says, *The Japanese Film* is really 'the definitive study in any Western language of the Japanese cinema,' it is presumably because Richie and Anderson know the language and culture, or simply Japan. The fact that Richie freely draws on his firsthand knowledge of directors like Ozu and Kurosawa also seemingly gives a sense of authenticity to his other important books on those directors and secures his position as the authority of the Japanese cinema. What Richie embodies in Japanese film scholarship is the figure of cultural expert. What is appreciated and valued is the authenticity of the personal experience of the (anthropologist) expert 'who was actually there.'

In contrast to the empiricism of Donald Richie, the strength of a theoretical study is said to lie in the analyst's mediated detachment from the object of study. The importance of Noel Burch's work on the Japanese cinema is derived precisely from this sense of detachment as a result of his unfamiliarity with the mass of native Japanese discourses. By radically de-contextualizing the Japanese cinema, Burch has succeeded in displacing the Japanese cinema from the margin to the forefront of contemporary film scholarship and, however indirectly, has contributed to the critique of ethnocentrism in the institution of film studies.

Thus, the real division in Japanese film scholarship is created not by the West/Japan dichotomy but by the opposition between theory and history. What is at stake is not simply the shortcomings of either theoretical work (Burch) or historical study (Richie) but the unproblematic division between history and theory itself. Generally speaking, both sides are quite respectful of each other and do not meddle in the affairs of the other group. Far from creating antagonism, the split within Japanese film studies has reached a curious equilibrium, a peaceful coexistence of theorists with area studies specialists. It is this mutually complicit relation between theory and history that should be questioned and re-articulated. Put another way, we need to reexamine how the differentiation of empirical history from abstract theory creates an illusion that different critical approaches could democratically coexist side by side without any interference. What is at stake in the end is not a specific problem debated in the field of Japanese film studies but the question of how Japanese film studies is constructed as an academic sub-discipline.[17]

The Classical Hollywood Cinema and a New Tribal Art

The theoretical mode of Japanese film studies derives its impetus from the rigorous theorization of the narrational mode of Hollywood cinema and a renewed interest in possible radical alternatives. One of the major accomplishments of film studies is the deconstruction of the sense of continuity and the impression of reality created by the Hollywood cinema. It has been shown that that sense of continuity becomes possible precisely because of, for instance, numerous discontinuities whose existence is concealed by a series of alternations and repetitions constructing symmetrical structures. In theoretical studies of the Japanese cinema, the indigenous mode of Japanese film practice, based on structural principles of traditional art – privileging of surface over depth, presentation instead of representation, organization of nonlinear, non-narrative signifiers, and so on – is said to be inherently radical and thus puts into question the representational mode of the classical Hollywood cinema. From this particular theoretical perspective, Burch rewrites the history of the Japanese cinema in order to present the Japanese cinema as a prime example of an alternative to the institutional mode of representation.

Understandably, this theoretical tyranny of Burch's argument is not unchallenged. David Desser is one of those who question Burch's formalist position; however, by accepting formalist reification of a form/content division, he presents a confused counterproposal. According to Desser, 'since traditional Japanese art is already formally subversive, a genuinely radical, political Japanese art must move beyond the merely formally subversive; it must also move beyond the kind of radical content apparent in the prewar tendency films or the postwar humanistic, left-wing cinema of the 1950s.'[18] To the extent that he asserts the formal subversiveness of traditional Japanese art, Desser writes within the framework constructed by Noel Burch, and his criticism is not really a criticism but a revision within a formalist framework. The questions I would like to ask are much more simple and fundamental: What does traditional Japanese art subvert? Is it, as Burch argues, the representational mode of the classical Hollywood cinema? What does traditional Japanese art have to do with the Hollywood cinema?

The classical Hollywood cinema has certainly played a crucial role in the formation of any national cinema that had access to it, yet it can never have complete control over how a particular national cinema is constructed. A national cinema as the culture industry exists in a complex web of economic, ideological, and social relations, and the classical Hollywood cinema constitutes only one element of those relations. As Judith Mayne correctly points out, the excessive emphasis on the classical Hollywood cinema as the norm has a constrictive effect on the attempt to study and/or search for an 'alternative' cinema:

> The classical Hollywood cinema has become the norm against which all other alternative practices are measured. Films which do not engage the classical Hollywood cinema are by and large relegated to irrelevance. Frequently, the very notion of an 'alternative' is posed in the narrow terms of an either-or: either one is within classical discourse and therefore complicit, or one is critical of and/or resistant to it and therefore outside of it.[19]

Nobody can question the dominance of the Hollywood cinema in the world film market. However, this does not automatically mean that the Hollywood cinema has been dominant trans-historically or trans-culturally. We need to put the Hollywood cinema in specific historical contexts; instead of talking about the Hollywood cinema as the norm, we must examine the specific and historically changing relations between the Hollywood cinema and other national cinemas.[20]

Other questions concern a special position accorded to the Japanese cinema in non-Western national cinema scholarship. Why has the Japanese cinema become so important in the battle against the institutional mode of representation? Why can the Japanese cinema be so easily incorporated into theoretical discourses of Anglo-American film studies, while theory seems to become problematic in the analysis of, say, the Chinese cinema? Why suddenly has the possibility of cross-cultural analysis become an issue in the analysis of the Chinese cinema, while it has never been an issue in studies of the Japanese cinema, except in various meta-discourses that appeared mostly in the form of review essays?

One way of approaching these questions is to go back to the issues of modernism, the avant-garde, and the Japanese cinema to which I briefly refer in the beginning of this essay. For Bordwell and Thompson. Ozu is a modernist filmmaker in a class with Dreyer, Bresson, Godard, and the like. For Burch, the prewar Japanese cinema as a unified whole is comparable to European avant-garde cinemas. Despite the difference in their claim and the register of concepts used in their argument, Burch and Bordwell/Thompson participate in the same critical project. In both cases, the logic used to legitimate their claims is dependent on the observable formal features commonly found in two groups of objects that are drastically different in other aspects. To this extent, Burch, Bordwell, and Thompson's argument seems to be a variation of the discourse of art history claiming the existence of affinity between modern and tribal artifacts. This formalist logic is criticized by James Clifford as wishful thinking by Western critics.

> Actually the tribal and modern artifacts are similar only in that they do not feature the pictorial illusionism or sculptural naturalism that came to dominate Western European art after the Renaissance Abstraction and conceptualism are, of course, pervasive in the arts of the non-Western World. To say that they share with modernism a rejection of certain naturalist projects is not to show anything like an affinity . . .
>
> The affinity of the tribal and the modern is, in this logic, an important optical illusion – the measure of a *common differentness* from artistic modes that dominated in the West from the Renaissance to the late nineteenth century.[21]

But what Burch and Bordwell/Thompson argue is more 'radical' than a kind of colonial discourse questioned by Clifford. For what they find is not just affinity but identity between the Western avant-garde and the Japanese cinema or Ozu and Western modernist filmmakers. For their projects a mere affinity or optical illusion is not enough, so that, for instance, according to Burch, instead of merely resembling avant-garde practices, the Japanese cinema should be an avant-garde art. Burch's purpose is to find an autonomous group of film practices that is not analogous to but identical with what he calls avant-garde.

By the recent Japanese film scholarship, the Japanese cinema is construed as a new tribal art. At the same time, the emphasis on identity instead of affinity also makes it the avant-garde in the guise of a tribal art. For this reason, Burch and others choose to study Japanese but not Chinese, Indian, or any other non-Western national cinemas. The double identity of the cinema – tribal *and* avant-garde – requires them to choose the cinema of a nation that is perceived to be sufficiently different from, but have some common elements with, Western capitalist nations. Japan fulfills their utopian dream. On the one hand, Japan is exotic; according to Burch, 'Japan offer[s] traits which seem even more remote from our own, Western ways of thinking and doing, more remote than comparable traits of other Far-Eastern societies' (*JC*, 89). On the other hand, an exotic Japan is similar enough to the West, since 'these traits also lend themselves to *a Marxist critique of modern Western history in many of its aspects*' (*JC*, 89). Burch sublates the contradiction of Japan and the Japanese cinema by situating them 'with regard both to the dominant ideological profile of Western Europe and the Americas, and to those practices, scientific, literary and artistic, which instantiate the Marxist critique of that dominance' (*JC*, 89). What makes Burch's sublation possible is Japan's ambivalent geopolitical position: economically part of the First World but culturally part of the Third World. The dialectic of the traditional art form and Western influences that Burch finds in the history of the Japanese cinema is homologous with the schizophrenic division of Japan's relations to other nations.

CONCLUSION

The genealogy of film studies shows that it started as a contestation against the academicism in the 1960s and remained in the forefront of the changing humanities and a redrawing of disciplinary boundaries. In the name of the avant-garde and subversion, however, film studies has consolidated itself as a respectable academic discipline whose discursive organization is not very different from such a traditional discipline as literary studies. One of the concrete examples of this irony can be observed in the division of labor in national cinema studies, which uncannily mirrors the geopolitical configuration and division of a contemporary post-colonial world order. The opposition between the classical Hollywood cinema and the alternative modes of film practices is created with a good intention of avant-garde radicalism; however, the kind of politics articulated in this binarism is a different matter entirely. In the peculiar division of national cinema studies, American, European, Japanese, and other non-Western cinemas are studied to promote distinctively different critical and political agendas. Therefore, we need to carefully reexamine whether, by engaging ourselves in national cinema studies, we are mechanically reproducing, instead of analyzing, the ideological picture of a post-colonial world situation constructed by Western postindustrial nations. More precisely, we must question whether, in the name of critical opposition to Hollywood, we are, on the contrary, contributing to the hegemony of and the accumulation of cultural capital by the United States.

How can we stop fashioning the discipline of film studies into a mirror of post-colonial world geopolitics? Can the neo-colonial logic of film studies be corrected by going back to that perennial epistemological question, 'Can we ever know the Other as the truly Other?' The problem here is not that this question is too complicated to be sufficiently answered by any response; that is, the problem is not the impossibility of the answer but the formulation of this particular question itself. By construing the Other as the sole bearer of difference, this seemingly sincere question does nothing but conceal the fundamentally problematic nature of the identity of the self.

The so-called imperialist misrepresentation or appropriation of the Other is an oxymoron. The Other cannot be misrepresented, since it is always already a misrepresentation. Imperialism starts to show its effect not when it domesticates the Other but the moment it posits the difference of the Other against the identity of the self. This fundamental imperialism of the self/Other dichotomy can never be corrected by the hermeneutics of the Other or cross-cultural exchange; on the contrary, the latter reinforces the imperialist logic under the guise of liberal humanism, or what Spivak calls 'neo-colonial anti-colonialism.'

Let us debunk once and for all the imperialist logic of questions based on the self/Other dichotomy. Let us go back to that spirit of true radicalism that once made film studies such an exciting space for critical thinking.

Notes

1. Zhang Longxi, 'The Myth of the Other: China in the Eyes of the West,' *Critical Inquiry* 15, no. 1 (Autumn 1988): 127.
2. Peter Lehman, 'The Mysterious Orient, the Crystal Clear Orient, the Non-Existent Orient: Dilemmas of Western Scholars of Japanese Film,' *Journal of Film and Video* 39, no. 1 (Winter 1987): 5.
3. Lehman, 'The Mysterious Orient,' 8. Lehman quotes this passage from Paul Willemen, 'Notes on Subjectivity: On Reading Edward Braingan's "Subjectivity under Siege," ' *Screen* 18, no. 1 (1978): 56.
4. Lehman, 'The Mysterious Orient,' 8.
5. E. Ann Kaplan, 'Problematizing Cross-Cultural Analysis: The Case of Women in the Recent Chinese Cinema,' *Wide Angle* 11, no. 2 (1989): 40–50; hereafter cited in my text as CCA.
6. Gayatri Chakravorty Spivak, 'Theory in the Margin: Coetzee's *Foe* Reading Defoe's *Crusoe Roxana*,' in *Consequences of Theory*, ed. Jonathan Arac and Barbara Johnson (Baltimore: Johns Hopkins University Press, 1991), 155. The passage quoted continues as follows: 'Much of our literary critical globalism or Third Worldism cannot even qualify to the conscientiousness of this arrogance.'
7. Scott Nygren, 'Reconsidering Modernism: Japanese Film and the Postmodernist Context,' *Wide Angle* 11, no. 3 (1989): 7.
8. Nygren, 'Reconsidering Modernism,' 8.
9. Nygren, 'Reconsidering Modernism,' 7.
10. In her essay on the writing of history, Janet Abu-Lughod cautions us that 'with each higher level of generality, there are reduced options for reconceptualization. That is why I believe it is absolutely essential, if we are to get away from Eurocentric views of the universe, to pick our respondents carefully and broadly,' See 'On the Remaking of History: How to Reinvent the Past,' in *Remaking History*, ed. Barbara Kruger and Phil Mariani (Seattle: Bay Press, 1989), 118. Those who write on Japan as non-specialists necessarily have to depend on the works by specialists, which are already interpretations of the primary materials. There is nothing wrong with this dependency itself; the problem is that they often choose wrong authorities to support their argument.
11. Noel Burch, *To the Distant Observer: Form and Meaning in the Japanese Cinema* (Berkeley: University of California Press, 1979). 13; hereafter cited in my text as *JC*.
12. Julianne Burton, 'Marginal Cinemas and Mainstream Critical Theory,' *Screen* 26, nos. 3–4 (May–August 1985): 2–21.
13. For an extensive critique of Julianne Burton's argument, see Teshome H. Gabriel, 'Colonialism and "Law and Order" Criticism,' *Screen* 27, nos. 3–4 (May–August 1986): 140–7. See also Scott Cooper, 'The Study of Third Cinema in the United States: A Reaffirmation,' in *Questions of Third Cinema*, ed. Jim Pines and Paul Willemen (London: BFI, 1989): 218–22.
14. Homi K. Bhabha, 'The Commitment to Theory,' in *Questions of Third Cinema*, 124.
15. Richard Roud (ed.), *Cinema: A Critical Dictionary*, 2 vols. (London: Martin Secker and Warburg, 1980).
16. Joseph L. Anderson and Donald Richie, *The Japanese Film: Art and Industry*, expanded edn (Princeton: Princeton University Press, 1982).
17. For instance, see David Desser, *Eros Plus Massacre: An Introduction to the Japanese New Wave Cinema* (Bloomington: Indiana University Press. 1988), 2–3. Desser argues that his purpose is to 'situate the New Wave within a particular historical, political, and cultural context' without challenging the already existing other modes of critical discourse. Yet contextualization should not be mere supplement to theoretical abstraction or formalism. If it is merely supplemental, then, that mode of contextualization is nothing more than vulgar historicism.

When it takes the form of a radical questioning, contextualization becomes a critical practice of *mediation*, which demolishes the edifice of democratic pluralism.

18. Desser, *Eros Plus Massacre*, 24.
19. Judith Mayne, *Kino and the Woman Question* (Columbus: Ohio State University Press, 1989), 3.
20. For the specific place of Hollywood in the postwar Japanese cultural system, see my forthcoming 'The Aporia of Modernity: The Japanese Cinema and the 1960s,' (Ph.D. dissertation, University of California, San Diego).
21. James Clifford, *The Predicament of Culture: Twentieth-Century Ethnography, Literature, and Art* (Cambridge: Harvard University Press, 1988), 192.

3

GODZILLA AND THE JAPANESE NIGHTMARE: WHEN *THEM!* IS U.S.

Chon Noriega

History shows again and again how nature points out the folly of man;
Go, Go, Godzilla.

Blue Oyster Cult

In 1954, Japan's Toho Studios – in what appeared to be merely an imitation of the 1953 American film *Beast from 20,000 Fathoms* – unleashed *Godzilla*. The film was Japan's first international hit, inspiring sixteen sequels and a dozen other radioactive dinosaurs. Today, Godzilla has achieved icon status in Japan and America, making plausible James Twitchell's jibe in *Dreadful Pleasures* that 'it is one of the first images Westerners think of when they hear the word "Japan."' If the word *Japan* evokes Godzilla – and not Hiroshima, 1985's \$62 billion trade surplus, and compact cars – one wonders why these films are so easily dismissed by Twitchell and ignored by others.[1] That this genre – Japan's most popular filmic export – has been neglected seems in itself to indicate a mechanics of repression at work. These movies are ascribed the same attributes as those 'made in Japan' products that in the fifties connoted shoddiness. When examined, however, they reveal a self-conscious attempt to deal with nuclear history and its effects on Japanese society.

There are two related impediments to a sociohistorical reading of Godzilla films: critical approach and the concept of Otherness. Noel Carroll sums up the prevailing approach to the horror film when he states that 'as a matter of social tradition, psychoanalysis is more or less *lingua franca* of the horror film and

From *Cinema Journal* 27: 1, pp. 63–77.

thus the privileged critical tool for discussing the genre.'[2] He also notes that 'the horror and science fiction film poignantly expresses the sense of powerlessness and anxiety that correlates with times of depression, recession, Cold War strife, galloping inflation, and national confusion.'[3] Ironically, Carroll does not attempt to historicize the psychoanalytic archetypes he goes on to posit.

Unlike Carroll, Robin Wood makes a direct link between psychoanalysis and history in examining the horror film. In 'An Introduction to the American Horror Film,' Wood applies the psychoanalytic concepts of repression and projection to the horror film: 'It is repression . . . that makes impossible the healthy alternative: the full recognition and acceptance of the other's autonomy and right to exist.'[4] While Wood argues that such repression is ultimately sexual, he outlines a process very similar to Fredric Jameson's doctrine of the political unconscious. In both cases, repressed social contradictions that threaten the hegemonic 'self' are projected onto a text where they struggle for recognition, but are ultimately 'resolved.'[5] Central to Wood's sexual repression and Jameson's 'absent cause' is the concept of Otherness.

The concept of Otherness defines a dynamic in Western culture that extends to the psychoanalytical, anthropological, and historical. According to this dynamic, the individual and/or society project 'what is repressed (but never destroyed) in the self' onto an Other in order to define or delimit a self.[6] Interpolating an Other then becomes an externalized way of dealing with oneself, a point made again and again by historians of American foreign policy: 'For most Americans, the external world has been a remote, ill-defined sphere which can be molded into almost anything they wish. More often than we might care to think, this attitude has translated into foreign policies which have relieved and encouraged a nation struggling with tormenting domestic concerns.'[7]

That American foreign policy so closely follows the self/Other model outlined above implicates the model in the problem it describes, becoming the mechanism whereby the Soviet and nuclear threats are variously appropriated, and the cold war perpetuated. Because the political environment encourages literal adherence to the self/Other model, while at the same time political realities have become increasingly multilateral and fragmented since the 'two camp' days of the late forties and early fifties, a sociohistorical reading requires an examination of the gaps and fissures in both the concept and implementation of the self/Other model.

A good place to begin would be Japan, given its unique position in the cold war, where, curiously enough, Godzilla films provide an opportunity to challenge our constructions of the self and the Other. These films were popular in the United States during the fifties and early sixties, while Godzilla remains a cultural icon used in numerous commercials and parodied in television's *Saturday Night Live* and the 1986 film *Pee Wee's Big Adventure*. But in many ways Japanese culture, foreign policy, and language complicate the cold war paradigm. Any sociohistorical interpretation must remain sensitive to differences in culture and language in order to register the difference between

American and Japanese reception. Psychoanalysis – if it is to be 'the privileged critical tool' – must account for these differences. In Godzilla films, it is the United States that exists as Other – a fact that Hollywood and American culture at large has masked. To see how we are seen by another culture is central to understanding that culture as other than a projection of our own internal social anxieties. We are then on the way to answering some seemingly simple questions. Why does Japan produce radioactive-dinosaur films while the United States imports them? And if Godzilla is so destructive, why do the Japanese sympathize with him as a tragic hero, while Americans see him as little more than a comic icon?

The original *Godzilla* (1954) had no national filmic tradition per se, because it was the first Japanese monster *cum* science fiction film. Bill Warren argues that the 1952 rerelease of *King Kong* strongly influenced Eiji Tsuburaya, the special effects artist for *Godzilla*.[8] American newspaper reviews at the time label *Godzilla* a remake of *King Kong*.[9] It should be noted, however, that Embassy Pictures encouraged such comparisons, emphasizing them heavily in their advertising campaign.[10] In any case, the emphasis on special effects ignores the re-inscription of *King Kong* (1933) into the emerging cold war, reducing the text to its special effects rather than acknowledging how those effects – central to the film's impact during the depression[11] – were received in the fifties. To understand why *Godzilla* developed its own genre, it is necessary to look at its historical environment, and not just apparent American precursors. Edwin Reischauer gives a cultural impetus to such an approach: 'Unlike the Americans . . . the Japanese have a strong consciousness of history. They see themselves in historical perspective. They will delve a thousand years and more into their past in analyzing their contemporary traits.'[12]

For the moment we need only go back to the ten years between Hiroshima and *Godzilla*. After the United States dropped two atomic bombs on Japan in 1945, an essentially American military occupation force dismantled and rebuilt the Japanese family and society in such a way as to ensure that Japan could never again become a *military* threat to the Allies. Reform gave women full *legal* equality and ended the authority of the clan over the family and the father over adult children. Compulsory education was extended to nine years, further reducing parental influence. So-called reform exceeded what American society would have accepted for itself at the time, indicating that the purpose was more to undermine the patriarchal base of Japanese society than to reform it. (In America, women were being forced out of the workplace in order to make room for returning soldiers *cum* patriarchs.) For the most part, however, the Japanese cooperated with the Americans, bringing about enormous socioeconomic and political change during the relatively short occupation (1945–52). Such change, however much desired by both Japanese and Americans, required repression in order to succeed; and as Wood aptly puts it, 'what is repressed must always strive to return.'[13]

Occupation ended in 1952, but the United States nuclear presence did not. On November 6, the United States exploded its first H-bomb, a ten-megaton weapon 1,000 times more powerful than the one dropped on Hiroshima, on a Pacific Island near Japan. The island evaporated. In 1953, on the other side of Japan, the Soviet Union exploded its first H-bomb. Then in March 1954, the United States exploded a fifteen-megaton H-bomb that unexpectedly sent substantial fallout across a 7,000-square-mile area. Twenty-eight military personnel and 239 Marshall Islanders at a presumably 'safe' distance were exposed to high radiation. The United States attempted to downplay the incident until it was discovered that a Japanese tuna boat, the Fukuryû Maru or 'Lucky Dragon,' had also been hit by fallout. The entire crew developed radiation sickness, and one member soon died. Japanese protest against the tests escalated, especially when the United States, accepting blame for the fisherman's death, paid his widow less than $4,000: 'Almost overnight, the Japanese revived a buried interest in their own nuclear victims. For the first time in nearly a decade, the condition of the survivors of Hiroshima became a national preoccupation. The protests quickly became international . . .'[14] Amid these events, Toho Studios began shooting Japan's first monster film, *Godzilla*.[15] *The repressed had returned.*

Go, Go, Godzilla

> How do American actions since V-J day appear to other nations? I mean by action concrete things like $13,000,000,000 for the War and Navy Departments, the Bikini tests of the atomic bomb and continued production of bombs . . . I cannot but feel that these actions must make us look to the rest of the world as if we were only paying lip service to peace at the conference table.
>
> How would it look to us if Russia had the atomic bomb and we did not, if Russia had 10,000 mile bombers and air bases within 1,000 miles of our coastline and we did not. (Secretary of Commerce Henry Wallace, letter to President Truman, 23 July 1946)[16]

On 18 September 1946, *The New York Times* reprinted Wallace's letter to President Truman. Two days later Truman fired Wallace: such questions were not open to public debate. Wallace validated the Other's perspective and threw into question the motives behind United States actions. To accept Wallace's criticism would threaten the perceived (perhaps willfully misread) Manichaean opposition against the Soviet Union. As the cold war developed. American monster films reflected this inability to identify with the Other. In concurrent Japanese monster films, however, the relationship between monster and society became integral. A comparison of American and Japanese horror films in the fifties reveals fundamentally different cultural and political attitudes toward nuclear history and the Other. The Japanese monster film also provides a look at the cold war from somewhere between the United States–Soviet Union dichotomy. Perhaps it is at this point that a nuclear dialectic can begin.

The Fifties

The American monster films of the fifties are notable for their support of the bomb and cold war attitudes. *The Beast from 20,000 Fathoms* (1953) was the first Hollywood movie that dealt with the problem of nuclear testing, and it was a box office success. In the film, a nuclear explosion in the Arctic melts an iceberg, awakening the 'rhedosaurus' frozen within. The rhedosaurus heads for New York, where it destroys Coney Island and Manhattan. Eventually, the military kills the monster by shooting a nuclear missile into its mouth. The message is clear: nuclear weapons can solve the problems and anxieties they create. But in order to provide such a resolution, the real site of United States nuclear testing is displaced onto the more politically distant and isolated Arctic – locus or final destination of other American monsters like the Thing and the Blob that threaten to subsume 'civilization' or 'us.'

While *Beast* is the only American radioactive-dinosaur film, other radioactive-monster films from the fifties use the same plot: *Them!* (1954), *Tarantula* (1955), and *The Beginning of the End* (1957). The complete Otherness of these monsters is emphasized by their impersonal names: 'Them' and 'It.' The monsters are hated, feared, and eventually destroyed through force, often a variation of the technology that created them. The films' apparent self-examination – 'look at what we've accidentally created' – lasts until the monster's autonomy and threat shifts responsibility from American science onto the monster itself. The films effectively destroy any causal relationship, thereby constructing the monster as complete Other. The Americans in the film, freed from implication in the monster's threat, can now use nuclear or other force to destroy it.

Derek Hill and Susan Sontag, writing at the time these films were still in vogue in the United States, equate the monster as Other with the bomb. But perhaps an attempt to avoid the pitfalls of McCarthyism and cold war consensus prevents either from acknowledging or analyzing the political context within which the monster as bomb existed. Twenty years later, Peter Biskind writes that 'like the Bomb, the Red Menace theory stands in the way of thinking through the idea of the Other . . . [these theories being] no more than a smoke screen for a domestic power struggle.'[17] Here, however, the problem with the concept of the Other is that it allows only a reading of the self. True, the bomb and the Red Menace are powerful smoke screens for internal struggles and problems. But what also hides behind these smoke screens is a very real cold war relation between the Soviet Union and the United States. These films both perpetuate cold war attitudes and resolve anxieties about possessing annihilatory weapons in a warlike environment. Describing fifties foreign policy – although it could also have been American monster films of the period – Eisenhower once said, 'Our armaments did not reflect the way we wanted to live; they merely reflected the way we had to live.' The monster created by the bomb requires the bomb to kill the monster. This is the circuitous logic of the arms race.

Japanese monster films of the same period likewise have origins in American and cold war history. And yet within the films – contrary to Wood's claim – the Japanese sympathize with the 'totally non-human' monsters.[18] Unlike American monsters, Japanese monsters have personalities, legends, and *names*: Godzilla, Rodan, Mothra.[19] Clearly Western conceptions of the Other or monster as repressed sexual energy (Wood), class struggle (Jameson), or 'archaic, conflicting impulses' (Carroll) do not fully explain the Japanese monster. Takao Suzuki's sociolinguistic examination of the Other as it operates in Japanese – as opposed to Western – culture helps explain how the Other operates in Japanese monster films.[20] Suzuki notes that the Japanese language, unlike Indo-European languages, does not have a long or consistent history of personal pronouns to distinguish between 'I' and 'You,' 'We' and 'Them' that make it easy for the repressed in Western culture to be, in Wood's words, 'projected outward in order to be hated and disowned':[21] 'It is frequently pointed out that whereas Western culture is based on the distinction between the observer and the observed, on the opposition of the self versus the other, Japanese culture and sentiment show a strong tendency to overcome this distinction by having the self immerse itself in the other.'[22]

In Japan, Suzuki argues, the above-described 'other-oriented self-designation' operates *as long as the other belongs to the culture*.[23] While cultural criticism in the West generally acknowledges that construction of an Other primarily defines a self, the Japanese language carries within it the added stipulation that both self and Other remain within the culture. The monster's name and legend necessarily insert the monster into the culture as always-already-extant. Because the monster has always-already-been Japanese, its continuance is assured: the legend will continue to return as an archetype of Japanese horror that explicates the present. Consequently, the monster's American and cold war historical origins, now rooted in Japanese mythology,[24] allow it to serve as an intermediary in the Japanese designating themselves vis-à-vis the United States and, later, the Soviet Union. The plot must then uncover why the *distant* past (embodied in the dinosaur) again confronts the present.[25]

While the Japanese monster does not constitute a projected Other, it can be seen to operate according to the defense mechanism that is central to therapeutic psychoanalysis: transference. The shift from theoretical to therapeutic psychoanalysis provides a critical analogue to cultural and historical processes that struggle against a cold war ideology based on repression and projection. In Freud's paradigm, the analysand transfers onto the analyst a central role in a symbolic reenactment of a problem that would cause 'unpleasure' to remember outright. Godzilla films exhibit this compulsion to repeat a traumatic event in symbolic narrative. The necessity for a quick solution is inherent in each film, because the monster must be destroyed or pacified in order to save Japan and the world. Because brute force cannot affect the monster, the search for a solution ('What does Godzilla want?') becomes equally as fascinating as the spectacle of mass destruction. In later films, the search becomes the central plot element, a sign that these films are serious attempts at dealing with trauma therapeutically. For the first step toward psychic health is exactly at that point where the search for answers (the psychoanalytic process) is seen as more attractive than the drive toward destruction.

The films transfer onto Godzilla the role of the United States in order to symbolically re-enact a problematic United States – Japan relationship that includes atomic war, occupation, and thermonuclear tests. The films, however, in their search for a solution do more than blame and destroy the transferred object, and thereby 'resolve' the 'problem' 'Other-oriented self-designation' mitigates the sharp division between self and Other implicit in the transference process, so that Godzilla comes to symbolize Japan (self) as well as the United States (Other). Like Godzilla, identified as a four-hundred-foot tall dinosaur marking a transition between sea and land creatures and aroused 'after all these centuries' by Strontium-90 (a radioactive product of H-bomb explosions), Japan in 1954 is a transitional monster caught between the imperial past and the postwar industrial future, aroused by United States H-bomb tests. Thus the monster expresses more than impotent rage made powerful in fantasy, because the anxieties Godzilla reflects are as much about Japan as the United States. The films must balance these two anxieties, but cannot resolve them since they reside in one figure: they must be simultaneously repressed in order to rebuild the 'beloved land' (to make the transition) and yet be actively directed at United States H-bomb testing in order to address a pressing concern at the mass cultural level.

In the films, the news media function as psychoanalyst at the mass cultural level, mediating between society and the monster. The psychoanalyst plays two roles in the transference relationship: a symbolic one and an investigative one. The Japanese monster film divides these roles between the monster (symbolic) and the reporter (investigative). The reporter represents an institutionalized attempt to discover and expose social anxieties (the monster) and their causes, while working 'behind the scenes' to discover and implement a solution. The investigative role, both within psychoanalysis and the news media, is not without inherent contradictions. The reporter in *Godzilla vs. Mothra* (1964) realizes 'that newspapers have a limited capacity to influence people . . . the more I write, the more Happy Enterprises [which works against the interest of the investigation] benefits from the publicity.' The statement reveals more about the news media – and its reliance on larger structures of authority for information and advertising – than it does about those who actually read newspapers. Similarly, implicit in the transference relationship is the underlying problem of authority in psychoanalysis, especially given the complicity assumed by the analyst when in the transference role. The Japanese monster films acknowledge these problems and attempt to work around them.

The United States release of *Godzilla* shows the two approaches to the radioactive monster (projection and transference) in high-relief. Embassy

Pictures reedited the film, cutting more than thirty minutes and adding new scenes with Anglo-American Raymond Burr as reporter Steve Martin. Included in the cuts were direct references to Hiroshima ('First the radioactive rain. Then the evacuation. What's next?') and songs about peace. The film was renamed *Godzilla, King of the Monsters* in an effort to link the film with *King Kong*. Additional dialogue about young women sacrificed to Godzilla by Micronesian Islanders backs up the advertising and the title's reference to *King Kong*. Thus the film tells a different story to its new audience.

Although the scenes with Martin largely replace similar scenes with a Japanese reporter, the shift in narrative perspective is crucial to the subsequent appropriation of the film's message. The film begins with a voiceover by Martin of inserted scenes showing 'scorched flesh' and the destruction of Tokyo. He describes himself as a reporter cast into 'the living Hell of another world that lives in the paralyzing fear that *it* could happen again today or tomorrow.' But 'it' is never named, merely encoded as 'an incident that has shaken the foundations of the civilized world.' The film then switches to the chronological beginning in which the first Japanese ship is engulfed by white light mushrooming up from beneath the water. The sustained ambiguity implies the initial cause ('it') to be the atomic bombs dropped on Japan in 1945, and not the Godzilla mentioned in the title. The second scene alludes to the 'Lucky Dragon' (at this point still a sensitive issue in the United States), confirming 'the paralyzing fear that *it* could happen again.'

The Hollywood re-edited film plays on an American sense of guilt toward the Japanese in the early fifties, saying in effect, 'look at what we've done/are doing to Japan.' As with other American radioactive-monster films, this guilt is then projected onto the monster, who is revealed to be the true cause within the movie. Godzilla's death represses American guilt and anxieties about nuclear weapons: both history and Japan's own filmic rendition are retextualized to erase the bomb and thereby relieve anxieties about the American occupation and H-bomb tests.

Détente

In 1961, Mothra became the first Japanese monster to be recognized as a moral force and consequently to be alive at the fade-out. *Mothra* (U.S. release, 1962) pits a giant Micronesian caterpillar/moth against an entrepreneur who steals a pair of twelve-inch-tall female twins who protect the islanders from the effects of nuclear testing. Mothra proves indestructible, even against the United States Army's new atomic heat gun. Because force cannot stop the monster, the Japanese must discover what it is Mothra wants. To appease the creature, they catch the entrepreneur and return the twins, using church bells to attract Mothra because they sound like the twins singing, in addition to a large cross which resembles the cross found on Mothra Island.

The connection between Mothra and the Christian church suggests a facile 'resolution' to the monster's existence. The connection, however, works at a deeper level to explicate Japan's Westernization. Mothra, like Godzilla, represents repressed consequences of Western actions. Initially, it is the Other (the West) who causes Japan's social contradictions, but it is also that same Other who offers new spiritual ideals along with the socioeconomic realities. Unlike Godzilla, who is a transitional monster, Mothra is a monster in transition. Both monsters, like postwar Japan, are awakened by H-bomb tests. Mothra, however, changes from a larva into a moth. This represents a shift in the nature of the repressed-returned-as-monster and points to the positive and moral forces within history that can arise out of the negative. The film uses the Judeo-Christian tradition to construct a nuclear dialectic within the West that speaks to Japanese concerns (for example, industrial pollution) as well.

Godzilla vs. Mothra (1964) brings the nuclear dialectic into open conflict: Godzilla (the bomb) versus Mothra (Christianity). The following dialogue on Mothra's island appears to make nuclearism a central concern:

Photographer: This is the result of atomic tests.

Reporter: At one time this was a beautiful green island.

Scientist: As a scientist I feel partly responsible for this.

Photographer: All of mankind is responsible.

Reporter: Like the end of the world here.

Scientist: This alone is a good reason to end nuclear testing.

Reporter: Those who dream of war should come see this.

Photographer: Can anyone really live here? . . . I'm sure they hate us for what happened here . . . the nuclear tests.

Here, however, the emphasis is on Japan as cause: United States nuclear testing becomes something for which the Japanese feel guilt. The reporters and scientist act out the investigative role in a transference relation with Japanese society, becoming both the focus of guilt and the source of therapy. Godzilla's emergence out of the ground of an industrial development reinforces the idea that Japan itself is at issue. Godzilla does not return from some distant island, but exists beneath the soil upon which Japan rebuilds itself.

Mothra fights Godzilla and dies. Her[26] egg – stolen by a self-proclaimed 'great entrepreneur' – hatches and two caterpillars emerge to wrap Godzilla in silk, causing him to fall into the sea. It is conceivable, however, that the sea beast breaks its silk bonds. In any case, Godzilla's repression, in light of its sudden eruption from the ground, is by no means final. Rather than resolve the anxieties and social problems Godzilla embodies, the film instead exposes these problems for recognition and at the same time points to Mothra, whose previous embodiment of Christian morality is doubled in this film. The reporter calls Mothra 'one of us' in convincing her to fight Godzilla. It is the moral relationship between the Japanese and Mothra that succeeds in dealing with (though not destroying) Godzilla and the problems of capitalism and industrialism. Thus we have one return of the repressed dealing with another, a standard process in later Japanese monster films.[27]

The Limited Test Ban Treaty in 1963, which prohibited atmospheric nuclear tests, resolved the problem behind Godzilla and the other radioactive monsters. By 1965, Toho Studios' president had decided to tailor Godzilla to its primary audience: children. Thus in *Ghidrah, the Three-Headed Monster* (1965) Mothra convinces Godzilla and Rodan to stop fighting each other and to join together to save the earth from the three-headed monster from outer space. The film transformed Godzilla into a hero, especially among Japanese children, his image soon adorning their clothing, lunch boxes, toys, and candy. But Godzilla did not become a monster without a cause; he would continue to rely on his nuclear origins to explicate new social problems to a younger audience.

The genre now focused on the role of a child guiding the monster to save Japan from another monster, reflecting changes in postwar Japan. The family, atomized by occupation reform, began to restabilize in the mid-sixties when Japan's economic success began to alleviate social anxieties. Children born in the sixties were also a generation removed from World War Two. The realities Godzilla reflects became 'history' rather than lived experience.

The introduction of children in the films of the sixties and seventies is central to reconstructing society. (It is interesting to note that both the original *Godzilla* and *Godzilla 1985*, occurring amid times of increased cold war tensions, have no children in the plot.) The male reporter and female photographer in both Mothra films represent an intramedia 'marriage' bound by an urgent need to return history to the conscious. The central child in these films aligns himself with the reporter and photographer, suggesting a nuclear family constructed in relation to the monster. Each film recreates the entire society around the problem(s). We see where women, men, and children fit in, what types of marriages and families are constructed and under what conditions. As the political dimension changes with time so does the sociofamilial, here seen as the 'unconscious' within the Japanese films. Thus history (in addition to cultural difference) must temper purely psychoanalytic interpretations.[28]

The Eighties

Godzilla 1985, the first Godzilla film since 1976, ostensibly celebrates Godzilla's thirtieth birthday. The film was released in the United States in September 1985. Because the narrative takes place in August 1985, the film provides a retrospect on the bombings of Hiroshima and Nagasaki in early August 1985 and the fortieth-year commemorations in early August 1985.[29] In early 1985, NATO decided that Japan should have a nuclear arsenal in order to 'pay for peace' like the other (less economically stable) NATO members. But Japan's three non-nuclear principles – no manufacture, no introduction, and no possession of nuclear weapons – formally codified in 1967, have been a centerpiece of Japanese policy since it became the only country ever to suffer atomic attacks.

In *Godzilla 1985*, Godzilla – as yet the absent cause – attacks a Japanese fishing boat and then a Soviet submarine. The Soviets mobilize, while the Americans – portrayed as LBJ/Reagan-style cowboys – are unable to clear themselves because the hotline is 'down for repairs.' The Japanese news reports: 'tension increases as Soviet and U.S. forces step up mobilization for an all out confrontation. Concerns are mounting throughout Europe, the most likely battleground for a limited nuclear exchange.' It is at this point that the Japanese prime minister reveals Godzilla to be the cause.

American and Soviet delegations meet with the prime minister to demand that he allow them to use nuclear weapons to destroy Godzilla. The prime minister refuses: 'Japan has a firm nuclear policy: we will not make, possess, or allow nuclear weapons. We cannot make an exception, not even in a situation as grave as this.' The Japanese use their self-defense forces to 'kill' Godzilla, but in all the confusion the Soviets accidentally launch a space-based nuclear missile at Tokyo. The United States successfully intercepts the Soviet missile. The blast and fallout, however, revive Godzilla, who proceeds to rampage until the Japanese use a birdcall to lure Godzilla away to a volcano lined with explosives. The volcano is activated, and Godzilla is consumed by the lava. Where weapons fail, nature succeeds. And the Japanese prove that they can deal with Godzilla outside an East-West framework.

In *Godzilla 1985*, it is the Japanese who can defuse the nuclear crisis. To do so, they must name (textualize) the absent cause: Godzilla. The immediate crisis is resolved, but the United States and Soviet Union now join together and threaten to use nuclear weapons to stop Godzilla. Japan, therefore, becomes a nuclear target upon which, forty years later, the Soviets drop the bomb, Japan – as the NATO member purposefully without nuclear weapons – takes on a pivotal role in critiquing the United States – Soviet Union dichotomy. Both countries are represented not as enemies dividing the world between them but as a single interactive force that has brought the world together under the threat of global annihilation. Japan and Europe (the first 'nuclear theater') become Other to what is now seen as a schizophrenic self.

Just as the politics of using nuclear weapons conflates the United States and Soviet Union, the specter of nuclear annihilation effectively conflates civilization and nature (often symbolized respectively as the United States and the Soviet Union in American cold war politics and films), so that Godzilla becomes at once a sign from nature and a product of human civilization. Godzilla is almost never referred to as a monster, but is described instead through simile and metaphor. The sole survivor of Godzilla's first attack describes it as 'like a monster.' To Professor Hayashida, 'Godzilla is more like a nuclear weapon. A living nuclear weapon destined to walk the earth forever – indestructible – a victim of the modern nuclear age.' To Steve Martin, 'Godzilla is like a hurricane or tidal wave. We must approach him as we would a force of nature: we must understand him, deal with him, perhaps even try to communicate with him.' Hayashida, responding to the Japanese plan to shoot cadmium bombs into Godzilla's mouth, explains that it will not work because 'Godzilla is not a reactor.' Shortly before Godzilla attacks Tokyo, Hayashida states, 'Godzilla is a warning – a warning to every one of us. When mankind falls into conflict with nature, monsters are born.' These descriptions obscure the nature/civilization distinction, especially Martin's admonition to deal with Godzilla as 'a force of nature' and '*communicate* with him' (emphasis added).

This done, the film can be more directly historical. The film contains numerous historical allusions: the fishing boat evokes the 'Lucky Dragon,'[30] while the hotline being 'down for repairs' evokes Reagan's stance toward the Soviets and arms control in which, ironically, technology will solve political problems. While, ultimately, it is Japan's non-nuclear efforts that 'kill' Godzilla, the film enacts a 'Star Wars' or Strategic Defense Initiative scenario between the Soviets and the United States, played out over Japan. A variation on the *Star Wars* (1977) musical theme underscores these scenes. Steve Martin historicizes the event after an elated major explains, 'Mr. Martin, this is the natural aftermath of stratospheric nuclear blast: absolutely harmless.' Martin replies, 'Major, in 1962, for forty whole minutes, a high atmospheric test shut down transmissions across a 7,000-mile perimeter – all the way from Australia to California.' The stunned major walks away. Martin invokes the apex of the cold war to show that no nuclear blast is politically harmless in citing the test that 'first' made electromagnetic pulse (EMP) known. 'The 7,000-mile perimeter' recalls the 1954 test that spread fallout across 7,000 square miles.

Godzilla 1985, more than anything else, is a nuclear parable. As in the fifties original, Godzilla represents nuclear fears 'too terrible for humans to see.' Rather than 'resolve' the unthinkable, the film uses Godzilla as a focal point, which allows a marginal examination of current nuclear instabilities and fears: the clash between Japan's non-nuclear principles and the new cold war centered around Reagan's 'Star Wars.' The film addresses an internal dllemma as well as one of global politics, because the non-nuclear principles are not universally accepted among Japanese voters. When Godzilla 'dies,' these problems remain. The final voiceover by Martin emphasizes the film's moral/warning: 'The reckless ambitions of man are often dwarfed by their dangerous consequences. For now, Godzilla, that strangely innocent and tragic monster, has gone to earth. Whether he returns or not, or is ever seen again by human eyes, the things he has taught us remain.'

Surprisingly, American film reviewers did not comment on the nuclear issues raised by the film. One scene may explain why the film – so popular in Japan that a sequel is underway – showed less than a week in the United States. In the scene following Godzilla's attack on a Japanese nuclear reactor, a small American boy plays with a toy Godzilla robot. Shiny black shoes appear at his feet. The camera, using the boy's perspective, tilts up to the body's full height to reveal a towering MacArthur-like officer in sunglasses. The man asks for Steve Martin, the boy's grandfather. The same tilt and perspective had been used in the previous scene to reveal (for the first time in the film) Godzilla to an unsuspecting worker at the nuclear reactor. The contrast inverts General Douglas MacArthur's description of Japan as a twelve-year-old boy (above which he towered), and implicates the American audience in the current nuclear crisis: the boy returns to play, smashing Godzilla into other plastic weapons, himself mimicking the American and Soviet military actions within the film and in real life. The scene implies that American popular culture – in its 'escapism' – underscores the military-industrial complex, creating a plastic/video replica in which nuclear war is quite thinkable.

Unfortunately, Godzilla (horror) films are not perceived historically, but aesthetically according to Hollywood technical standards. These films received critical and popular attention in the United States in the fifties and early sixties, when they contained state-of-the-art special effects.[31] But by the eighties, these films were considered to have fallen behind in a special effects race similar to the nuclear arms race. *Magill's Cinema Annual 1986* provides the most concise example of this view in its review of *Godzilla 1985:* 'This upgrading of the Godzilla saga does not improve on the original 1956 film, despite thirty years of progress in special-effects technology.'[32] This in itself seems to be a mechanism of repression that assures we will miss the point when *Them!* is U.S. The evaluation according to Hollywood standards de-historicizes the text, assuring an ethnocentric reading. Likewise, in film criticism the concept of the repressed-returned-as-Other allows us to examine the projection of ourselves onto another's existence. In doing so, we avoid the other culture. Finally, because we are unable to acknowledge ourselves as the Other in another culture's text, we can only colonize the other's text.

Most Godzilla films end with the monster(s) swimming out to sea. The scenes are almost always melancholic, filled with restrained music and close-ups of pensive faces. Rather than celebrate the monster's retreat, the films reveal the narrative 'resolution' to be incomplete. They acknowledge that necessary confrontation has been avoided within the narrative and that pensiveness outside the narrative is needed to understand what the monster's return means. The end also indicates a prescience of the monster's (re)return, or worse. After all, the nuclear threat the monster signifies never leaves; it is always here. What returns then is narrativity itself, the act of resolving contradictions by retextualizing them into one polysemous figure and 'killing' it. The films, however, deconstruct themselves in an attempt to link the 'thinkable' monster to the 'unthinkable' nuclear environment. In this sense, the films are aimed not at resolving an absent cause, but providing a reinterpretation (or retextualization) of the past that allows Japan to examine repressed anxieties within a historical context. The monster surfaces only when – as in the case of rapid postwar industrialization and the new cold war – the lessons of the past are overlooked in writing the future.

NOTES

1. James B. Twitchell, *Dreadful Pleasures: An Anatomy of Modern Horror* (New York: Oxford University Press, 1985), 259, 320. Most monster anthologies either ignore the Godzilla films or use them as a half-page foil to other, 'better' films. Donald Richie does much the same in his books on Japanese film. For critical works that consider Godzilla films, see Charles Derry, *Dark Dreams: A Psychological History of the Modern Horror Film* (New York: A. S. Barnes, 1977), 68–74; and Susan Sontag, 'The Imagination of Disaster,' *Against Interpretation* (New York: Farrar, Straus and Giroux, 1978): 209–25. For perhaps the only monster anthology with an extended treatment of Godzilla films, see Donald Glut, 'Godzilla, the New King,' *Classic Movie Monsters* (Metuchen, N.J.: Scarecrow Press, 1978), 374–412.
2. Noel Carroll, 'Nightmare and the Horror Film: The Symbolic Biology of Fantastic Beings,' *Film Quarterly* 34 (Spring 1981): 17.
3. Carroll, 'Nightmare and the Horror Film,' 16; Derek Hill noted the correlation between the horror film and 'hard times' as early as 1958: 'Every horror film cycle has coincided with economic depression or war.' Hill concluded: 'Now we have the biggest, ugliest threat of them all, and a bigger, uglier horror boom than ever before.' He referred of course to the newly arrived at situation of Mutually Assured Destruction (MAD) and the coinciding popularity of the numerous American, Japanese, and British movies about radioactive insects, dinosaurs, and humans. (Derek Hill, 'The Face of Horror,' *Sight and Sound* 28 [Winter 1958–9]: 6–11.)
4. Robin Wood, 'An Introduction to the American Horror Film,' *Movies and Methods*, vol 2, ed. Bill Nichols (Berkeley: University of California Press, 1985), 199.
5. Wood, 'American Horror Film,' 201, and Fredric Jameson, *The Political Unconscious: Narrative as Socially Symbolic Act* (Ithaca, N.Y.: Cornell University Press, 1981), 79–83. Wood and Jameson argue that the text can nonetheless contain 'progressive' or 'utopian' elements.
6. Wood, 'American Horror Film,' 199; and James Clifford, 'Introduction: Partial Truths,' in *Writing Culture: The Poetics and Politics of Ethnography*, ed. James Clifford and George Marcus (Berkeley: University of California Press, 1986), 23–4.
7. Robert Dallek, *The American Style of Foreign Policy: Cultural Politics and Foreign Affairs* (New York: New American Library, 1983), xii–xiii.
8. Bill Warren, *Keep Watching the Skies! American Science. Fiction Movies of the Fifties: 1950–1957* (London: McFarland, 1982), i, 276.
9. For representative reviews, see Bosley Crowther, 'Film Reviews,' *New York Times*, 28 April 1956, sec. C, 11; 'Movies,' *Newsweek*, 14 May 1956, 126; and Gilb., 'Film Reviews,' *Variety*, 25 April 1956, 6.
10. Warren, *Keep Watching*, 276. The film's poster stated something to the effect that Godzilla 'makes King Kong look like a chimpanzee.'
11. Claude Ollier, 'A King in New York,' in *Focus on the Horror Film*, ed. Roy G. Huss and T. J. Ross (Englewood Cliffs, N.J.: Prentice-Hall, 1972), 110–20.
12. Edwin O. Reischauer, *The Japanese* (Cambridge: Harvard University Press, 1980), 41.
13. Wood, 'American Horror Film,' 205.
14. Peter Pringle and James Spigelman, *The Nuclear Barons* (New York: Holt, Rinehart and Winston, 1981), 245.
15. Denmark, Great Britain, and America also produced radioactive-dinosaur films between 1953 and 1962 – that is, between the first H-bomb tests and the Limited Test Ban Treaty. Inoshira Honda directed *Godzilla* and almost all sequels. In a recent interview he stated the importance of *Godzilla* as a political statement. (*Our World*, ABC News, 6 Nov. 1986)
16. Edgar M. Bottome, *The Balance of Terror* (Boston: Beacon Press, 1971), 5–6.
17. Peter Biskind, *Seeing Is Believing: How Hollywood Taught Us to Stop Worrying*

and Love the Fifties (New York: Pantheon Books, 1983), 111.

18. Wood, 'American Horror Film,' 216.
19. Mothra is sometimes refered to as 'the Thing' in American releases. This impersonal name, however, is the result of Hollywood reediting obviously aimed at making Mothra 'Other' enough to appeal to American audiences. Thus, Mothra might have been renamed 'the Thing' in order to capitalize on *The Thing (from Another World)* (1951). Mothra did not appear in the film's American advertising, which instead asked 'What is *it* . . . how much terror can you stand?' (Glut, *Classic Movie Monsters* 386; emphasis added)
20. Takao Suzuki, *Words in Context: A Japanese Perspective on Language and Culture* (Tokyo: Kodansha International, 1984).
21. Suzuki, *Words in Context*, 116–24; Wood, 'American Horror Film,' 199.
22. Suzuki, *Words in Context*, 167.
23. Ibid. 169.
24. Charles Derry argues that these films create a Japanese popular culture mythology that 'redefines the atomic bombs in terms of overt animalistic, natural instincts rather than in terms of some intellectual "humanity" ' (Derry, *Dark Dreams*, 69–70). As I will discuss, however, the films actually conflate civilization and nature in order to foreground a more immediate nuclear history. Thus the mythology serves primarily to enculturate the bomb.
25. The dinosaur symbolizes nuclear annihilation (extinction) and the uncontrollable power in a nuclear explosion. The dinosaur's small bram and huge size implies that neither reason nor force can 'resolve' its return. On the other hand, the dinosaur as merchandise has become increasingly popular, especially among women and children, those denied power.
26. I do not go into the full implications of the monsters' sex because it is not known whether Godzilla is actually male or female. See Glut, *Classic Movie Monsters*, 391. I refer to Godzilla as 'he' only because most films do so. That Mothra and Godzilla reproduce does not pose the problems seen in American cold war films in which 'promiscuous, undifferentiated, vegetable reproduction threatens family bonds' with female-engendered mass society. (Michael Rogin, 'Kiss Me Deadly: Communism, Motherhood, and Cold War Movies,' *Representations* 6 [Spring 1984]: 26–7.) But I cannot say what the monsters' sex does say about Japanese society.
27. For example, *Godzilla vs. the Smog Monster* (1971).
28. The films – now dealing more and more with Japanese children – were, as a consequence, marketed in the United States as 'kiddie flicks.' Since the early seventies, these movies have been shown primarily on UHF channels on weekend mornings and afternoons. The basic framework the films establish may explain why these films have been popular among younger viewers. The monster can be seen to symbolize the viewer-child's conscious and unconscious antisocial impulses, which are simultaneously acted out in grand spectacle while being redirected toward the good of society by the filmic-child with whom the viewer identifies. The films resolve or alleviate the contradictions inherent in childhood and puberty. Thus Godzilla joins the ranks of the Teenage Werewolf and other archetypal monsters in expressing anxieties about the uncontrollable changes of puberty. As such, its political message seems to be lost in America.
29. August is a pivotal month in nuclear history: in August 1949, the Soviets exploded their first nuclear bomb, prompting the United States and Western Europe to form NATO.
30. The boat's name, Yahada Maru, sounds similar to Fukuryû Maru (or Lucky Dragon).
31. James Morgan, 'In Brief,' *Sight and Sound* 26 (Winter 1956–7): 154; Gilb., 'Film Reviews'; and Sontag, 'The Imagination of Disaster,' 213.
32. Frank N. Magill, ed. *Magill's Cinema Annual 1986: A Survey of the Films of 1985* (Pasadena: Salem Press, 1986), 444.

4

MONSTER ISLAND: GODZILLA AND JAPANESE SCI-FI/HORROR/FANTASY

Philip Brophy

To stand in front of the large shallow pool that served as Tokyo Bay for over a dozen Toho Godzilla movies evokes a strange sensation. Two sides of the pool are accessible; the other sides touch walls across which curves a cyclorama of painted sky and clouds. A carney fakeness is exuded typically enough, but the strangeness arises from the potency with which this theatrical seaside recalls the precise plasticity of the movies themselves. When one sees the Bates residence from *Psycho* (1960) for the first time on the Universal lot, one is struck by how small it appears, and wonders at how such slight architecture could have induced dread on the silver screen. When one sees the Toho pool, the inverse occurs: one feels incongruously transported into the world of the Godzilla movies' blatant simulacra. This sensation of being disoriented by overt fakery rather than overcome by verisimilitude is worth investigating further, for those shallow waters belie greater depths of meaning.

In nearly all the Godzilla films,[1] Tokyo Bay is sited as the epidermis of Japan's postnuclear urb. Its still waters lap at docks whose perimeters are lined with giant gas tanks and towering electrical stations, creating a halo of energy which hums at the peripheries of Tokyo's expanse. Time and time again, Godzilla and fellow monsters wade towards that fatal shore, attracted to its glowing ring of tensile danger – then blithely careen through it, detonating all in their path. In much Japanese sci-fi/horror/fantasy (*kaiju eiga, anime* and *manga*),[2] the insecurity of Japan's island status is founded equally on an isolationist perspective and a technologically compensated concept of fortification: no moats with bridges, no walls

From *Postcolonial Studies* (2002), vol. 3, pp. 39–42.

with turrets, no mountains with crags. Tokyo is figured as a floating berg of energy: impenetrable and omnipotent. Arguably, this marriage of psyche and technology resides so deeply in the Japanese consciousness that the ways in which images and narratives of the city are generated constitutes a kind of 'psycho-islanding', with the designs of Tokyo's futuristic metropoli serving to fortify a sense of Japanese self-security as much as to project how Japan might socially and industrially navigate the globe as an island. Not surprisingly, the invasion of Japan in general and the destruction of Tokyo in particular remain traumatic fixtures in those images and narratives, especially as they fuse Japan's latent imperialist itches with its own graven misfortune at the hands of America's atomic and pyrotechnic tactics during World War Two. Every time Neo-Tokyo is razed to the ground, silent footage of Hiroshima seems to be subliminally superimposed in a way that collapses Us – Them binaries into a common ground of regret peculiar to Japanese sci-fi/fantasy.

If the docks of Tokyo Bay symbolically function as a haunting epidermis of the Japanese embodiment of such regret, Godzilla and company ritually rupture that outer skin of the metropolis like fallout on flesh. Within minutes, the horizon of Tokyo Bay will resemble any fiery catastrophe the mind can recall, from engraved etchings of the Great Fire of London to helicopter videos of the blazing oil wells of Iraq. The pool at Toho Studios which served as the setting for Godzilla's diabolical dioramas is thus a strangely calm lake of discontent. It has been the psychological stage for playing out both Japan's self-critical past (how Japan persisted in nuclear testing after the Hiroshima and Nagasaki bombings to create accidentally the ray of destruction genetically fused into Godzilla's spinal column) and its problematised future (how Japan might control a frantic increase in energy production and consumption which is forever on the verge of growing beyond the available land of Japan). The Toho monster movies document this moral drama of postnuclearity, and imply an inevitability on a multitude of narrative planes: nuclear testing will produce mutations; Japan's postwar industrial boom will explode; Godzilla will destroy Tokyo. Fission aptly works as a deadly metaphor for two trajectories hurtling towards a head-on collision.

Yet this eerie feeling of cultural scarring is not simply borne by mournful poetics. Phenomenological aspects of direct physicality also come into play. Standing in front of the Toho pool, one feels like Godzilla himself, for this stage is set to amplify human scale while retaining a sense of human presence. This feeling is not uncommon when one is placed in front of or within any miniature diorama. From young girls playing with doll houses to grown men playing with train sets, one engages in play with an enlarged sense of self. While this tends to suggest notions of Olympian godliness under a Judeo-Christian light, such notions are not pertinent to Oriental shades of mortal existence. This crucial difference becomes clear when identifying modes of practice in American and Japanese cinema. The predigital mechanics of fantasy in American cinema lean toward the human-as-engineer, with Willis O'Brien (*King Kong*, 1933) and Ray

Harryhausen (*Jason and the Argonauts*, 1963) exemplifying and perfecting the stop-motion animation technique of articulated figurines. The engineer in this process is the unseen God, operating beyond the frame and between the edit; invisible in the act of animation yet perceivable through the product of motion. By contrast, concurrent Japanese fantasy privileges the human-as-agent, building upon the parallel crafts of *Bunraku* and *Kabuki*. These theatrical traditions invoke the phantasmagorical, but always through the presence of the human within the proscenium arch (as black-clothed puppeteer in the former and ornately costumed actor in the latter). It logically follows that Japanese sci-fi/fantasy cinema embraces the human figure within the cinematic frame rather than denies its status just because of the photographic medium's propensity to be seemingly more 'realistic' (which itself is less relevant to Japanese visuality and its calligraphic base).

While America (and Britain) employed rubber suits for human-scaled monsters, Japan employed rubber suits to depict gigantic monsters. But what seems like a simple distinction between the role of costumery is a fundamental schism in human characterisation and performance which illuminates the specificity of Japanese sci-fi/horror/fantasy. Virtually all American rubber-suit movies redirect initial fears of the monstrous Other into a paraphiliac exploration of the expanded tactile self. Movies like *The Creature from the Black Lagoon* (1954), *The Monster that Challenged the World* (1957), *The She-Creature* (1957), *Curse of the Demon* (1958) and many other 1950s horror/sci-fi movies foreground their plasticity in the form of sexual grotesqueries. The Creature's gelatine lips, the Demon's hairy nostrils, the Monster's cellulite bulk, the She-Creature's crustaceous breasts – all stir up a gorgeous heady confusion between the penile, the vaginal, the mammarian, the anal. In key dramatic scenes, the costumed form of these monsters comes into heaving and salivating proximity of the normalised human body, suggesting acts of sex more than death. The man in the Godzilla suit has no such contact with humans. Instead he chews trains, crushes buildings, destroys power lines and melts army tanks. For Godzilla is not there to titillate with the prospect of aberrant sex (which is the key charm of the Western monster movie); he is there to embody energy *per se*, and to perform the action of wilfully unleashing that energy without control. In short, the Japanese monster movie is more about monstrous energy than it is about the 'monstrous-ising' of sexuality. This is the subtextual drive of the Toho monster movies: to plainly destroy. The use of a human-in-a-suit is crucial to one's identification with this act, so that one might imagine the power in being that person who is the agent of destruction. As juvenile as it sounds, destroying things can be highly gratifying. Destroying whole cities has to be exhilarating.

Accepting this subtextual drive as a pleasure push within the Toho monster movie cycles, one is confronted by a chaotic swirl of contradictions which the movies themselves eventually affirmed. This is most noticeable in the change from Godzilla as innocent victim of nuclear testing (*Godzilla*, 1959) to Godzilla as evil monster (*Godzilla vs. Mothra*, 1964) to Godzilla as tamed being (*Ghidrah – The Three-Headed Monster*, 1965) to Godzilla as heroic champion (*Godzilla vs. The Smog Monster*, 1972). His might and energy shifted from one of critical neutrality to modified humanism, and in doing so struck unsettling angles in relation to his original embodiment of Japan's doubts in advocating nuclear energy. Once the American occupation of Japan ceased in 1958, Japanese popular cinema certainly shifted its axis away from regret and atonement to rebuilding and rejuvenation. Godzilla accordingly wavered between being a threat to super-industrialization and a symbol of Japan's super-industrial strength, and in doing so was aligned more to the ambivalent amorality of tag-team wrestling (where good and evil change between bouts and managers) and less to the social critique instigated in the original *Godzilla*. The wildest and most fantastic attempt to create a coherent fictional realm for the cohabitation of Godzilla and Japan has to be in *Destroy All Monsters* (1968). No fewer than eleven monsters (including Godzilla, Mothra, Rodan and Ghidrah) are interred on Monster Island and controlled by a sonic perimeter which keeps the monsters at peace with one another. Presented as a holiday resort while operating as a high-tech penal colony, the songs of praise for Japan's futuristic control of unstable energy drown out issues of colonisation (where exactly in the Pacific is this 'uninhabited island'?) and individualism (who has the right to reprogramme monsters into not being themselves?). As hidden cameras monitor the monsters on the island for the scientists and technicians housed deep below the ground, the desperate dream of human and monster control in *Destroy All Monsters* uncannily recalls Disneyland's 'It's A Small World' ride. Both miniaturise life in diorama form to be viewed from a safe distance; both induce dread through their aim to create utopia.

However, this is not to say that the character or figure of Godzilla was rendered impotent or vague, or that somehow the first cycle of Toho monster movies (between 1954 and 1976) was corrupted by these contradictions. The figure of Godzilla – as famous as a suit as he is a character – is less a vessel for consistent authorial and thematic meaning as he is a shell to be used for the generation of potential and variable meanings. As puppet, doll and prop on a stage of special effects, his theatricalised unreality is never hidden. To this day, most Westerners cannot comprehend the sensibility that unflinchingly photographs a man in a rubber suit squashing toy cars and crumbling cardboard buildings and presents it as cinema. Yet that sensibility explains how the non-human (from a rubber suit to plastic doll) can be invested with such a flux of dramatic sway and cultural signification. The meta-issues and socioeconomic fissures that irrationally sprout forth from the 'psycho-islanding' of the first Godzilla movie cycle are perfectly captured in all their opposing aspirations, and constitute the basis for many postnuclear, post-human and post-robotic figures and themes which define the uniqueness of Japanese sci-fi/horror/fantasy from the late 1970s through to the present day.

Notes

1. The first cycle of Godzilla movies starts with *Godzilla King of Monsters* (1959) and concludes in 1976 with *Godzilla vs. Mecha Godzilla*. The second cycle starts with Toho's intent to re-market Godzilla in 1985 with *Godzilla 85*. This second cycle – a set of remakes that are glossy, hi-tech, but still replete with rubber suits and dioramas – continues to this day. The American release of their own version of Godzilla (*Godzilla*, 1998) will possibly ensure that this second cycle of Toho-produced films will continue for some time.
2. This brief article does not wish to define the specifics of 'sci-fi', 'horror' and 'fantasy'. The term *kaiju eiga* refers simply to 'monster movies', which in Japan combine elements of both horror and science fiction. *Anime* is the romanised contraction of the phonetic pronunciation of 'animation'. *Manga* is the field of comics. While *anime* and *manga* are entirely different from their counterparts in English-speaking cultures, the birth and various rejuvenations of both media forms in Japan are largely built upon innovative work produced in the genres of science fiction (or what in the 1980s was dubbed 'hard sf').

SECTION 2
COLONIAL ENCOUNTERS, POST-COLONIAL CRITICISM AND HONG KONG CINEMA

THE POST-COLONIAL HONG KONG CINEMA

Gary Needham

Introduction

This section is concerned with the construction of Hong Kong cinema of the past fifteen years as a post-colonial cinema that has been brought about through both sociohistorical change and academic and critical discourse. This introductory essay critically examines the relationship between post-colonial interpretation and Hong Kong cinema as both a blessing and a curse. The post-colonial meta-discourse that frames contemporary Hong Kong cinema is rightly concerned with the historical moment before the 1997 handover. As productive as this might be, however, it can also overshadow and limit the definitions of Hong Kong cinema, certainly those that go beyond the scope of Hong Kong's historical significance at the end of the twentieth century.

All three of the essays included in this section are concerned with the cultural transformation in Hong Kong culture and identity, with specific reference to recent films. Present in all three is a focus on genre as an essential component responsive to social, cultural and historical change. Genre is perhaps one of the most conducive of cultural forms to respond to change, particularly in the regularising of meaning and the positioning of identity. The dominant genre explored in the following chapters, and in the case study on Bruce Lee later in this *Reader and Guide*, is the martial arts film. It is the genre synonymous in the West with Hong Kong cinema, but, as the authors of the three essays reveal here, it is also the genre through which many of Hong Kong's post-colonial concerns can be articulated. The film that is most commonly discussed, and forms the sole focus of Williams' chapter, is *Once Upon a Time in China/Wong Fei-Hung* (1991) and its sequels. The significance of *Once Upon a Time in*

China, and its director Tsui Hark, is woven through both Abbas and Li's essays and further reference will be made to this important film in this Introduction. *Once Upon a Time in China* stands as the clearest example of the synthesis between popular film and post-colonial identity, as well as being a testament to the imagination, energy and craft of Hong Kong cinema.

Post-ing Hong Kong Cinema: Colonial and Post-colonial Definitions

One of the problems with the post-colonial is the relationship between the 'post' and the 'colonial' through the various uses and meanings of the term. Do we use it with or without the hyphen? Does the term indicate a clear-cut historical shift from colonial governance to decolonisation? Is it quite simply after colonialism? Is it the same kind of 'post' as in postmodernism and post-structuralism? The many uses and abuses of the term 'post-colonial' have been debated and contested for the multiple meanings and positions that the term suggests and designates.[1]

As many others have indicated, the term neo-colonial is perhaps more accurate since new regimes of control are enacted through the powers of multi-national corporations, media empires and most of the inequalities brought about through globalisation. The term 'post-colonial' is fraught with problems of usage, at worst careless and insensitive, at best rendered meaningless; it seems, therefore, better to acknowledge that it comes into being from multiple speaking positions, and to identify from where such speaking and positioning is taking place. What we would like to indicate is that it is perhaps a case of one's position as a native Hong Kong film director, a diasporic British-Chinese audience, a Jackie Chan aficionado or an American film studies scholar that potentially comes to shape one's understanding of the term and one's experience and understanding of post-coloniality as a legitimating and appropriate discourse of theoretical practice, cultural production and lived experience.

What I also want to suggest in this section is that the use of the term post-colonial in relation to Hong Kong cinema appears to have been employed rather unproblematically to cover all post-1980s Hong Kong cinema, right after the earliest stages of the British-Chinese negotiations. Like the authors of the influential text *The Empire Writes Back*, who suggest that they 'use the term "post-colonial" to cover all the culture affected by the imperial process from the moment of colonisation to the present day', the framing and interpretation of a post-colonial Hong Kong cinema seems to operate by similar definition. However, this has the potential to erase many of the differences, nuances and periodisations further implied by the terms colonial and neo-colonial.[2] Again, this is a matter of one's politics, position and experience, but the designation of everything as post-colonial with regard to Hong Kong evidently has an appeal that is able to define, unify and limit ones thinking about Hong Kong cinema, thus making it function as an almost essentialist category fundamentally and paradoxically based on a politics of anti-essentialism.

Hong Kong cinema has also been challenged on more than one occasion for its history of colonial-style domination over smaller and more fragile film industries across Asia. This is a detail also relevant to the section on authorship and Taiwanese cinema in this *Reader and Guide*. Ding-Tzann Li has called Hong Kong cinema a 'marginal imperialism' for the way it has conducted its film business in Asia in terms almost synonymous with Hollywood's global reach of power.[3] However, this notion of Li's of Hong Kong cinema as a 'marginal imperialism', a colonial film power, while evidently true if one takes box-office statistics at face value, seemingly overlooks many of the aspects that have shaped Hong Kong cinema. The Hong Kong film industry that Li refers to is not a monolithic entity; rather, it is transcultural, and was in part the product of local Cantonese film production and Malaysian business tycoons such as the Shaw Brothers and Cathay's Loke Wan Tho, as well as the large and widespread post-1949 Chinese diasporic audiences whose tastes and memories the films also catered for. This notion of 'marginal imperialism' does not account for the transnational and inter-Asian networks of culture and people connected through the multiple production and consumption sites of Hong Kong cinema since its inception, including complex histories of interaction with both Malaysia and Taiwan. Furthermore, when Hong Kong cinema is positioned against Taiwanese cinema around the 1980s, as Li does, one only needs to look at the opposition in this period between, say, Jackie Chan's *The Young Master/Shi di chu ma* (1980) and the Taiwanese New Wave *In Our Time/Kuangyin de kushih* (1982) to hazard a fairly accurate guess about popular film and what audiences tend to gravitate towards for an evening's entertainment. As much as we would champion a film like *In Our Time*, the fact that audience pleasure is fairly consistent and often aligned with the immediate pleasures of the most popular of forms is evidenced through the broad appeal of the action and martial arts film genres across Asia.

Framing the Meaning of Post-colonial Hong Kong Cinema

The energetic burst of scholarship on Hong Kong cinema since the mid 1980s, and its mapping within film studies, was, for the most part, framed in relation to the post-colonial context. Early dossiers in *Film Comment* and *Cahiers du Cinéma* and festival reports, such as the one in *Screen*, read Hong Kong films in a highly allegorical way as explicitly or implicitly symptomatic of a culture responding to the negotiations between Britain and China that resulted in the 1984 Sino-British agreement.[4] The formal experimentation, energy and speed of Hong Kong films from the New Wave onwards, through films like *A Chinese Ghost Story/Sinnui yauman* (1987), *A Better Tomorrow/Ying huang boonsik* (1986) and *Aces Go Places/Zuijia paidang* (1982), are understood as formally embodying a concern about acceleration towards a deadline and exhibiting some sense of postmodern crisis. North American and European scholarship is concerned with an investigation of the generic, formal, and aesthetic qualities of the contemporary Hong Kong film, as well as with addressing questions of history and identity. Often the films under discussion – those of John Woo, Stanley Kwan and Tsui Hark for example – are those of a post-1980 period, which fits neatly within the colonial context of the early British-Chinese negotiations and the Sino-British agreement of 1984.

Li's essay on the martial arts genre, reprinted here, highlights the post-colonial concerns around national identity, despite Hong Kong's own non-nation or quasi-nation status, through the contemporary kung fu genre's encounter with modernity and China from the early 1970s onwards. Li, therefore, takes us back to a cinema before the 1980s in order to render problematic questions of identity and to consider a national self-fashioning through a popular genre's obsession with Chinese-ness and the male body. The Hong Kong martial arts film has always flirted with heavy-handed allegory in articulating a relationship to both China and the colonial government. For example, the mid-1960s 'new era swordplay films' (*wuxia pan*), produced by the highly productive Shaw Brothers Studio and often directed by Chang Cheh/Zhang Che (such as *Have Sword Will Travel/Bao biao* (1969) and *The One Armed Swordsman/Dubei dao* (1967)), are celebratory in their vision of heroic Chinese masculinity and are set in a quasi-fictional world of a pre-communist mythical China. In contrast, the kung fu films set in the modern day, like Chang's *The Delinquent/Fen nu qing nian* (1973) and *Chinatown Kid/Tang ren jie xiao zi* (1977), set in Hong Kong and an invented American Chinatown respectively, reflect the social unease of the Hong Kong anti-colonial riots at the end of the 1960s, migration fears and the disaffection and generational conflict of Hong Kong youth. This tension between a fantasy of past China and a concern for contemporary Hong Kong, articulated through the martial arts genre's historical and contemporary variants, is what Sek Kei identifies as two dominant themes in pre-1980s Hong Kong cinema, 'the China Dream' and the 'Hong Kong sentiment'. Sek Kei's analysis, along with Li's essay, certainly should be noted for their re-centering of Hong Kong's post-colonial narrative to well before the 1980s.[5]

This section is not intended as a criticism of the excellent scholarship on Hong Kong cinema – it is without doubt some of the richest work on any non-Hollywood cinema – but rather as a suggestion that much of the scholarly interest in Hong Kong cinema is invoked and inspired, consciously or not, through a relationship to colonial history and the end of British-governed Hong Kong. Again, this is not to lay blame on the scholars themselves, as the films also respond to and solicit theoretical engagement with historical revisionism, experimentation and an anxiety around identity – what Ackbar Abbas has referred to as Hong Kong's desperate search for identity.[6] This particular historical moment by its very nature needs theorisation from different perspectives. The perceived end of Hong Kong is more significant from the local perspective of cultural production rather than global reception, and with good reason, for all senses of our identity hinge on the existence of locality, home and memory and the narrativising of that memory in multiple ways through culture.

Both Ackbar Abbas and Eric Kit-wai Ma illustrate that one of the dominant cultural trends attending to Hong Kong's then uncertain future was nostalgia.[7] The memorialising of the past in terms of nostalgia has become a key trope in contemporary Hong Kong films, especially those films of Stanley Kwan (*Rouge/Yin ji kau* (1987) and *Centre Stage/Yuen Ling-yuk* (1992)). Less obvious examples of the trend can be seen in Jackie Chan's Shanghai-set 1930s gangster film *Mr Canton and Lady Rose/Qiji* (1989). There is also an evident nostalgia for local folk heroes of the past, like Wong Fei-Hung and Fong Sai-Yuk, revived as they are through the genre revisionism of Tsui Hark and Yuen Wo-Ping.

Many of these nostalgia films focus on an over-investment in detail and period minutiae in the *mise en scène*, a tapping in to the memory of an older Hong Kong cinema, and the skilful use of music as an affective strategy, a 'sonic period landscape' used to evoke feelings of loss. Part of the construction of 1960s Hong Kong by Wong Kar-Wai in *In the Mood For Love/Hua yang nian hua* (2000) is through the music and *mise en scène* that both work hard towards fixing and sentimentalising the period in terms of nostalgia, which is a nostalgia for lost femininities and diasporic communities.

For Abbas, nostalgia is one of the defining characteristics of Hong Kong at the end of the twentieth century: the experience of loss for something already gone, what he calls the *Déjà Disparu*, forms his central thesis. Abbas's thesis is one of the most influential arguments for thinking about the cultural dimension of Hong Kong's post-colonial context in the 1980s and 1990s. We include here one of his two chapters on cinema from his book *Hong Kong: Culture and the Politics of Disappearance* where he fleshes out in detail the relationship between several film texts, including some of those mentioned above, and the concept of the *Déjà Disparu*.

What we want to reinforce, along with others such as Sheldon H. Lu and Poshek Fu, is that both a contemporary and a post-colonial Hong Kong cinema is a limiting definition of Hong Kong cinema.[8] While shifts towards a proper historical narrative of Hong Kong cinema are being championed in the work of Lu and Fu, as well as the ongoing publications and oral projects of the Hong Kong Film Archive, we must stress that Hong Kong cinema is, by definition, in danger of becoming singular and fixed by its anchoring around the context of 1997. When one actually looks at the range of Hong Kong postwar film culture, such as the popular Mandarin-language film production studios of Shaw Brothers and Cathay, modelled as they were on the classical Hollywood system of vertical integration, the left-wing studios of Great Wall, Feng Huang and Sun Luen Film Company, and the locally produced Cantonese-language genre films of the 1950s and 1960s, one cannot simply build a picture of a unified and coherent idea of Hong Kong cinema.

Hong Kong cinema has multiple histories of economic and cultural connections with Taiwan, China, Hollywood and Singapore. What the events of decolonisation do indeed lend themselves to is a neat way of unifying a concept of Hong Kong cinema – in theory and in practice – around dates and timelines concomitant with the end of British colonial governance and the subsequent Chinese rule as Special Administrative Region. However, conflicts of form, reception and ideology, always threaten to rupture such *laissez faire* conceptualisations when one tries to contain the diverse talents of recent filmmakers like Clara Law, Stephen Chow, Johnnie To and Fruit Chan within a singular framework. It might be more useful to approach Hong Kong cinema in the plural, through multiple discursive meanings, since its entire existence comes out of flux between China, Taiwan, Asia and Hollywood, and, historically, the struggle between Cantonese and Mandarin-language film production. As our concern in this section is with post-colonial definitions, we need also to acknowledge such a definition as only one of a number of possible framing discourses, and to remain aware of limitations as well as productivities of such definitions.

Another understanding of Hong Kong cinema, following on from Sheldon Lu, is in terms of being one of a number of Chinese-language cinemas but not singularly as the monolithic and essentialising category of 'Chinese cinema'. In contrast to Lu, Wimal Dissanayake and Kwok-Kan Tam, in their introductory text, see the Hong Kong director Stanley Kwan as belonging to a New Chinese cinema, along with mainland directors Chen Kaige and Zhang Yimou, and even more problematically, alongside Taiwanese directors Hou Hsiao-Hsien and Edward Yang. Yingchi Chu on the other hand, convincingly argues that Hong Kong cinema functions like a quasi-national cinema, caught between self-representation, a Chinese motherland and a Western coloniser, as the subtitle of her book *Hong Kong Cinema: Coloniser, Motherland, Self* indicates. Rey Chow, in her more general concerns, goes as far as to suggest that Hong Kong (and that includes its cinema) imagines itself as having an authentic native origin in China, which is a fundamental misrecognition of a culturally hybrid Hong Kong defined precisely by its 'lack of Chinese-ness'.

It is important, therefore, to stress that definitions of a cinema of this complexity are often struggles, even battlegrounds, for the control of meaning and to avoid the equation of Hong cinema as only and uniquely defined vis-à-vis the post-colonial.[9] A good example would be the 2002 film *Golden Chicken/Gam gai*, as it challenges the overarching history of Hong Kong in terms of colonial history and politics. While the film is about the history of Hong Kong through the experiences of a prostitute called Lum, the colonial is thoroughly de-emphasised through the way it comes to be understood in intertextual mediation. The official history of Hong Kong is revealed to be of little relevance to the lives of everyday Hong Kong folk, particularly the large numbers of people at the lower end of the social and economic spectrum.

In *Golden Chicken* the handover is shown as a very brief item on the news on a TV set discernable in the *mise en scène*. Often the characters in the film are not even paying attention to these supposedly grand social changes which are made even less significant when deliberately juxtaposed against other televised moments such as the appearances of (a pre-John Woo) Chow Yun-Fat as the romantic lead of early 1980s TVB soap operas. If the characters in the film are cueing the spectator in any way, then the significance afforded to Chow's TVB soap operas are signalled out as being of much greater historical significance and meaning to the individuals in the film and to the memory of its Hong Kong film audience. *Golden Chicken* therefore suggests that for ordinary folk like Lum, the appearance of Jackie Chan in *Drunken Master/Jui kuen* (1978) as Wong Fei-Hung (a performance Lum parodies) is more significant to her life than the death of Deng Xiaoping. *Golden Chicken* is also a perfect example of a trend where the history of Hong Kong collapses into the history of Hong Kong cinema, the line between reality and fiction is increasingly blurred, and popular culture takes precedence over politics. In this film, the transfer from one power to another is seen as having no bearing on the daily lives of the ordinary Hong Kong citizen; it is certainly not as important as Lum's encounter with film star Andy Lau. Far from being apolitical, *Golden Chicken* rewrites official history by working with the appeal and impact of popular culture, cinema and television as an alternative historical narrative for Hong Kong, one that privileges the personal and everyday experience of popular media and culture over the political arena.

Once Upon a Time in China

No set of films deal with post-colonial issues more concretely and explicitly than the *Once Upon a Time in China/Wong Fei-hung* series of films directed and/or produced by Tsui Hark between 1991 and 1997. As the post-colonial Hong Kong film *par excellence, Once Upon a Time in China* covers many of the bases that have come to define the appeal of contemporary Hong Kong cinema for both audiences and scholars. The series is an update of a long-running Cantonese film series from the 1950s and 1960s that was based on the real-life legendary figure Wong Fei-Hung. The real Wong was a Chinese medical practitioner and a revered martial arts expert, who has been fictionally represented on screen in more than 100 different films and by different actors including Kwan Tak-Hing, Jackie Chan and Jet Li. The re-emergence of this figure of Cantonese culture takes on a new cultural significance in *Once Upon a Time in China* as for the first time he is played by an actor from mainland China, Li Lian-jie or Jet Li.

The character is also placed within the historical juncture of the late nineteenth century, when China ceded many of its territories (including Hong Kong) to foreign rule. Explicit parallels can be drawn between the contemporary climate of change in Hong Kong and the turbulence depicted in the films' construction of history at the end of the Qing period. Tsui positions the character of Wong as an agent of social change in moments such as that in which he secures the safe departure of another real-life figure, Sun Yat-Sen, to China. Thus, a Cantonese folk hero is written into the history of China and given agency in the formation of twentieth-century China. A mainland Chinese actor portrays Wong, but the films tap into nostalgia for an older Cantonese culture, not just through the character revival but also in the use of the familiar signature tune of the character (a topic also raised in Li's chapter) that overwrites moments of history through generic pleasure. When we see the second film's nemesis, a Manchurian capitan, defeated by Wong, the music continues over to the next scene where we see the safe departure from Canton of 'father of the people' Sun Yat-Sen. The film mobilises the generic pleasures of the final duel, and carries that pleasure over to a fictionalised key moment of historical significance, one that ultimately ends in the formation of modern China, thus resolving both the narrative and the historical separation between Hong Kong and China.[10]

The *Once Upon a Time in China* films, therefore, attempt to soothe the differences between China and Hong Kong, tradition and modernity, while demonising the 'foreign devils' of Britain, Russia, France and the United States. However, the films punish just as readily the corrupt Chinese officials and xenophobic nationalist cults, as well as portraying the benevolence of British priests and westernised Chinese characters like Aunt Yee. Like many other responses to post-coloniality, there is in the series a resistance to the logic of clear-cut binary opposition and reductive thinking that would otherwise define good and bad in simple terms. More of these issues are explored at length in the following chapters.

A Slip Towards Insignificance?

Early in 2005, Wong Kar-wai's film *2046* (2004), was released throughout Europe to mixed response. While critical and journalistic opinions are irrelevant for the purposes of this section, there seemed to be a notable omission from the majority of them. That omission was the question of the post-colonial which was overlooked by attempts to cement the stylistic idiosyncrasies of Wong as the new boy of world cinema. Earlier films that brought Wong his international reputation, such as *Fallen Angels/Duoluo tianshi* (1995), *Chungking Express/Chongqing senlin* (1994) and *Happy Together/Cheungwong tsasit* (1997), were framed precisely against a context through which Wong's authorship has always been measured, namely his relevance to post-colonial Hong Kong, often attended through reference to both his organisation of time and space and his deconstruction of genre.

Thus, taking Wong as a prime example, we have seen within a short period the relevance of the post-colonial slip away as if it is not important – not just as a relevant context for Wong as a Hong Kong filmmaker, but for all manner of ideas that have informed discussion, debate, and definition for both the cultural and lived contemporary Hong Kong. *2046*, like 1997, is an imaginary telos of history. 2046 will be fifty years on from 1997 and the period in which Hong Kong's projected realignment with China will be complete after fifty years of grace as a Special Administrative Region (SAR). It will, it is hoped, come to a peaceful, harmonious and democratic conclusion. The question that needs to be asked is that when Hong Kong was returned, passed on or handed over to China – a politically loaded and controversial process – was it the end of the (post) colonial Hong Kong period or, as some have suggested, the start of a new phase and a new master? From a British perspective it would obviously mark a logical closure to that part of British colonial history. It is also worth remarking how late the decolonisation process took place in Hong Kong in comparison with other previously colonised territories and nations within Asia.

What is striking is the irrelevance of the post-colonial in general that now marks not just the lay approach to contemporary Hong Kong cinema, but also the distance of concern for Hong Kong in light of its ongoing tensions with China over governance and democracy, not to mention the financial crisis at the end of the 1990s in which China came to the rescue. Somehow seen as beyond the post-colonial, returned to China, and now entering the transnational context of globalisation, the terms of Hong Kong's cultural significance have shifted. A certain tendency can be observed in this shift towards colonial insignificance which is possibly the result of a new vogue of situating Asia in the frame of transnationalism, or possibly a complacent silence bound by a desire to avoid offending China, the new resource of global capital.

There are many questions still to be answered as Hong Kong's position vis-à-vis China and the rest of the world is still, according to John Nguyet-Erni, a process of becoming rather than being and still relatively uncertain.[11] Any close examination of Hong Kong, it seems, produces many more questions than it does answers, a trend that seems unavoidable even in this Introduction. One thing is for sure: that if the previous two decades are anything to go by, we should certainly keep an eye on the cinema of Hong Kong. The other side of this, however, is the recent trends in high-concept filmmaking and transnational funding which have resulted in a recent spate of pop-star driven vehicles, for example, *Twins Effect* (2003), bogged down by the wholesale economic determination of media synergies as well as a rash of uninspired digital effects. Pan-Asian appeal seems to lead to the complete erasure of any commitment to identity politics that would reflect Hong Kong's cultural specificity and processes of becoming.

What we hope the following three essays achieve is a way of understanding Hong Kong films at the post-colonial moment. By revealing the way in which aesthetics and genre are closely bound to the political, social and cultural system of identity formation and meaning, the authors reveal a cultural milieu under the shadow of transformation and uncertainty as seen through a number of immensely popular yet complex texts that have come to define the contemporary Hong Kong cinema as post-colonial.

Notes

1. Ella Shohat (1992), 'Notes on the "Post-Colonial" ', *Social Text*, 31/32; Ann McClintock (1992), 'The angel of progress: pitfalls of the term "Postcolonialism" ', *Social Text*, 31/32; Anthony Appiah (1991), 'Is the post- in postmodernism the post-in postcolonial', *Critical Inquiry*, 17, Winter.

2. Bill Ashcroft, Gareth Griffiths and Helen Tiffin (eds) (1989), *The Empire Writes Back: Theory and Practice in Post-Colonial Literatures*, London: Routledge, p. 2.
3. Ding-Tzann Lii (1998), 'A colonized empire: reflections on the expansion of Hong Kong films in Asian countries', in Kuan-Hsing Chen (ed.), *Trajectories: Inter-Asia Cultural Studies*, New York and London: Routledge, p. 125.
4. Rosalind Coward and John Ellis (1981), 'Hong Kong – China 1981', *Screen*, vol. 22, no. 4; 'Made in Hong Kong' (1984), *Cahiers du cinéma* no. 362/363, April; David Chute (ed.) (1988), 'Made in Hong Kong', *Film Comment*, vol. 24, no. 3.
5. Sek Kei (2003), 'Shaw Movie Town's "China Dream" and "Hong Kong Sentiments" ', in Wong AiLing (ed.), *The Shaw Screen: A Preliminary Study*, Hong Kong: Hong Kong Film Archive.
6. Ackbar Abbas (1997), *Hong Kong: Culture and the Politics of Disappearance*, Minneapolis: University of Minnesota Press.
7. Eric Kit-wai Ma (2005), 'Re-advertising Hong Kong: nostalgia industry and popular history', in John Nguyet Erni and Siew Keng Chua (eds), *Asian Media Studies*, Oxford: Blackwell Publishing.
8. Sheldon H. Lu and Emilie Yueh-yu Yeh (eds) (2005), *Chinese Language Film: Historiography – Poetics – Politics*, Honolulu: University of Hawaii Press; Poshek Fu (2003), *Between Shanghai and Hong Kong: The Politics of Chinese Cinemas*, Stanford: Stanford University Press.
9. Wimal Dissanayake and Kwok-kan Tam (1998), *New Chinese Cinemas*, Hong Kong: Oxford University Press; Yingchi Chu (2003), *Hong Kong Cinema: Coloniser, Motherland, Self*, New York: Routledge; Rey Chow (1998), 'Between colonizers: Hong Kong's postcolonial self-writing in the 1990s', in Rey Chow (ed.), *Ethics After Idealism: Theory-Culture-Ethnicity-Reading*, Bloomington and Indianapolis: Indiana University Press.
10. Gary Needham (2004), 'Once upon a time in Hong Kong: film music and identity in contemporary Hong Kong cinema', *Media Education Journal*.
11. John Nguyet-Erni (2001), 'Introduction – like a postcolonial culture: Hong Kong re-imagined', *Cultural Studies*, vol. 15, no. 3/4.

5

THE NEW HONG KONG CINEMA AND THE *DÉJÀ DISPARU*

Ackbar Abbas

The Déjà Disparu

According to Gilles Deleuze, the various European cinemas became 'modern' at different times, but always at the moment when they had to come up with new cinematic images in response to new historical situations: 'The timing is something like: around 1948, Italy, about 1958, France, about 1968, Germany.'[1] We might now arguably add, going beyond Europe, about 1982, Hong Kong, which was the year of Margaret Thatcher's visit to China. Since that date, it has become increasingly apparent that a new Hong Kong cinema has been emerging. It is both a popular cinema and a cinema of auteurs, with names like Ann Hui, Tsui Hark, Allen Fong, John Woo, Stanley Kwan, and Wong Kar-wai gaining not only local acclaim but also a certain measure of international recognition. Contrary to a widespread impression, however, this new cinema is not essentially a cinema of action or a 'cinema of blazing passions,' which was how one popular festival of Hong Kong films was billed in the United States. What is interesting is that it is a cinema that responds to a specific and unprecedented historical situation, what I have called a space of disappearance where 'imperialism' and 'globalism' are imbricated with each other. History now goes through strange loops and becomes difficult to represent in terms of traditional realism. If real history is becoming more incredible by the day, we will have to resort to the incredible to keep up with it.

From Ackbar Abbas (1997), *Hong Kong: Culture and the Politics of Disappearance*, Minneapolis: University of Minnesota Press, pp. 16–47.

Hence the frequent excesses and exaggerations of the new Hong Kong cinema: they register a sense of the incredible as real, somewhat as in Jorge Luis Borges's story *Emma Zunz*. Certain of the justice of her vengeance, Emma Zunz commits a murder and presents it as self-defense by telling an incredible story: 'Actually, the story *was* incredible, but it impressed everyone because substantially it was true. True was Emma Zunz's tone, true was her shame, true was her hate. True also was the outrage she had suffered: only the circumstances were false, the time and one or two proper names.'[2] In Borges's story, it is not so much that the end justifies the means, but, rather, that ends and means have become disconnected, in a time that is out of joint. Hence other kinds of connections have to be made. Such dislocations and novel connections also typify the new Hong Kong cinema and the images we find in them.

This allows us to see why cinema has such a privileged position in Hong Kong's culture of disappearance, quite apart from the fact that it is the most developed and popular of Hong Kong's cultural forms. It is in the images of the new cinema that the history of contemporary Hong Kong with all its anxieties and contradictions can be read. However, the response to this new cinema, even by well-informed local and foreign critics, is largely misleading, suggesting that the question of its evaluation is far from simple. In fact, on the evidence of what has been written about it, the more interesting examples of recent Hong Kong cinema must be among the most elusive films being made today.

Most critical opinion on Hong Kong films seems divided between criticizing it for its relentless commercialism or applauding it for (what is perceived as) its high camp qualities: neither view is very instructive. For example, Paul Fonoroff, a Hong Kong-based student of local film history, can ask about films currently being made, 'What makes Hong Kong films so mediocre?'[3] and suggest commercialism, low audience expectations, the lack of imaginative producers as answers. The respected local film critic Li Cheuk-to, in a review of films made in 1988–9, also points to the relentless commercial pressures exerted by film producers and distributors that leave Hong Kong directors little room for artistic maneuvering. He concludes his review by noting that 'the defects of the system and the lack of creative talent form the greatest obstacles and sources of worry that hamper the emergence of an artistically excellent Hong Kong cinema.'[4] Other critics go on to link commercialism to a certain filmic 'style' that is associated with the Hong Kong cinema. 'Welcome to the new wave of Hong Kong cinema,' writes Jeffrey Ressner in the *New York Times* – 'films characterized by comic-book images, hyperkinetic quick cuts and mind-boggling story lines . . . Unlike American films, Hong Kong movies are produced in assembly-line fashion.'[5] And even in many ways an astute and thoughtful essay by Geoffrey O'Brien (in the *New York Review of Books*) cannot finally resist taking up the refrain about commercialism: 'It is one of the ironies of the situation that the dangers of 1997 can make a frankly commercial, assembly-line cinema – dedicated to nothing more uplifting than the fleeting pleasures of spectacle and narration – look somewhat like an endangered ecosystem.'[6]

On the other hand, when the Hong Kong cinema is praised (interestingly enough, more often by foreign than by local critics), it is for its action sequences, its slick editing, its mastery of special effects that would 'make even George Lucas envious' (Ressner), as if the mere downplaying of dialogue, narrative structure, or even intelligence somehow made Hong Kong cinema more immediate, more like 'pure cinema,' more akin to the work of Buster Keaton or the Keystone Cops. It is thus that the Hong Kong cinema is elevated from commercial trash status to cult art status by way of the axiological reversals of camp. O'Brien writes, with more than a hint of lyricism, about the kung fu movie:

> In the best examples of the genre . . . the grace and flexibility of the performers – augmented by razor-fast editing, slow-motion trampoline leaps, and the guttural and percussive punctuations of the soundtrack – created unmediated cinematic pleasure. The movie did not represent anything at all; it presented . . . the Hong Kong cinema retains an athleticism which Hollywood, with a few fleeting exceptions, lost after the era of Douglas Fairbanks and Buster Keaton.

In other words, a film should not mean but be, and in a backhanded kind of way, Hong Kong films are seen to satisfy this requirement very well. To praise the Hong Kong cinema in these terms is not only to prize it loose of its very specific cultural space, it is also to place the kung fu films of Bruce Lee and Jackie Chan, and more recently the gangster epics of John Woo and his imitators, at the center of Hong Kong's film history, and to present them as the examples par excellence of an emergent international Hong Kong cinema. The question is whether such an evaluation is either justified or perceptive enough.

The problem with putting the whole emphasis on commercialism and the campiness of the action movie is that Hong Kong cinema tends to be *too easily homogenized* as a result. It is true that the films of Bruce Lee, Jackie Chan, and John Woo have had the most international exposure and are therefore the best-known Hong Kong films abroad. Of the trio, it is John Woo who has succeeded in exporting his idea of the action film to Hollywood, his latest films (*Hard Boiled*, 1992, *Hard Target*, 1993) were produced there. But all these action films – which are undeniably important for the Hong Kong film industry and which, it must be said, have their own interest – represent only one side of the new Hong Kong cinema. Even if we agree with O'Brien that 'Hong Kong at present makes the most raucous and least contemplative films on the planet,' it also makes other kinds of films as well. There is, in other words, no easy homogeneity to Hong Kong cinema, in spite of appearances. It is a gross simplification to say, as O'Brien does, that 'taken together, Hong Kong movies . . . constitute a single metanarrative, incorporating every available variant of sentimental, melodramatic and horrific plotting, set to the beat of non-stop synthesized pop music.' How, we might ask, could such a cinema of mindless pleasures command any but the most superficial kind of international attention or merit anything more than a casual sociological study? What makes the Hong Kong cinema an international cinema will have to be sought elsewhere, especially if we realize that it is a cinema that can now accommodate the stylish baroque obsessions of a Stanley Kwan, the visual and cognitive ambivalences of a Wong Kar-wai, the dismantlings of nostalgia of an Ann Hui, the reworkings of traditional storytelling of a Tsui Hark. The films that are made cannot be reduced to 'a single metanarrative' but represent so many disparate attempts to evoke a problematic cultural space. And it is ultimately by attending to the relationship of Hong Kong cinema to this cultural space that we will arrive at a different account of Hong Kong cinema and its history.

To address the nature of Hong Kong's cultural space as it relates to cinema, we must again raise the question of commercialism, but in a different way. We need to reexamine the assumption that strong commercial pressures can result only in poorly made films, by questioning the old paradigm that constructs an absolute opposition between 'commercialism' and 'art.' The terms of this opposition are extremely unstable in any case, as indeed the history of cinema itself can testify. Cinema was never art in any docile sense, on the contrary, it has always challenged accepted notions of art. But this lesson is always one that has to be learned anew because the old paradigm can resurface in a different guise, as in the distinction between a mainstream commercial cinema and an alternative art cinema.

As far as the Hong Kong cinema is concerned, the notion of the art film is more a liability than an asset. It would be much better, therefore, to begin by saying that the innovative Hong Kong cinema is not primarily directed at establishing itself as an alternative or art cinema, and to draw out the implications of this statement. With few exceptions, films made in Hong Kong are all part of the mainstream; all make use, to the full extent that their budgets allow, of established stars, established genres, and spectacle. To speak of 'new wave' directors or 'alternative' cinema in this situation is misleading, especially if one's idea of the new wave is Jean-Luc Godard or Alain Resnais. However – and this is the crucial point – such a state of affairs is not as limiting as it sounds because there are different ways of being part of the mainstream. If commercialism is indeed a necessary given that turns films into commodities, it is still possible, as Walter Benjamin said of Charles Baudelaire, to elicit the aura proper to the commodity – that is to say, to explore the cultural possibilities of what looks like a negative situation.[7] Such an enterprise may require the invention of new kinds of filmmaking strategies other than, say, the direct subversions of mainstream film practices that we see in Godard and Resnais. These new strategies should be the focus of our critical attention, and I shall be turning to them later when I discuss individual films. The point at the moment is that the use of mainstream forms in Hong Kong cinema is not *necessarily* a sign of intellectual inertia or of pandering to the masses. It is more a sign of the slippery nature of Hong Kong's cultural space.

The ambiguity of the commercial in Hong Kong cinema can be clarified to some extent by a comparison with the new Chinese cinema on the mainland. The early films of Chen Kaige, Zhang Yimou, Tian Zhuang-zhuang, Huang Jianxiu, and so on – the so-called Fifth Generation – are quite militantly non-commercial compared to their Hong Kong counterparts, with few compromises made to please an audience. There are many reasons for this, but one major reason is that while economics has always been a factor in film production, it was less decisive in the case of the Fifth Generation insofar as the Chinese system of film production and distribution in the early- and mid-eighties amounted almost to a form of state subsidy. This meant that the Fifth Generation could reinvent modernism, explore the possibilities of the spare image, experiment with nonlinear narration, and so on, without having to worry too much about any but an ideal audience. Their 'sharply defined pictures devoid of any didactic purpose, surrounded by silence and open to multiple interpretations' that so impressed O'Brien and that he contrasts to the noisiness of the Hong Kong cinema were made possible at least partly by state support.

The new Chinese cinema, however, presents a paradox of its own, one that George S. Semsel captures well when he notes with some surprise that 'what my American colleagues and I failed to acknowledge was that the films we celebrated as signs of a Chinese "new wave" had been produced within the dominant studio system of China, that those who made them did not represent an alternative, independent cinema.'[8] He goes on to speak of other filmmakers who tried to work independently of the state and hence had to fall back on market support. Although Semsel puts his point a little too baldly, he does make the valid suggestion that independence could mean different things: freedom from the market or freedom from state support, that is, that independence, too, could be as ambiguous as commercialism. Significantly, when the situation changed dramatically after the 1989 Tiananmen Massacre when state funding for films dried up and Chinese directors had to look to Hong Kong and Taiwan for financial backing, so, too, did the film aesthetics of the Fifth Generation change to some extent. *Yellow Earth* (1984) and *Red Sorghum* (1987) are very different from *Raise the Red Lantern* (1991) and *Farewell My Concubine* (1994). The second pair of films, in their use of spectacle, big-name stars, and familiar forms of narrative appropriate the devices of the commercial film, but not entirely to their own detriment. It was ironically *Farewell My Concubine*, Chen Kaige's 'commercial' film, that finally won him the major international film award that had eluded him for so long.

Unlike the Chinese cinema, the Hong Kong cinema cannot rely on any form of subsidy. It cannot therefore reject commercialism, which is the sine qua non of its existence. The Hong Kong cinema has to be popular in order to be at all. The effective strategy consists not of finding alternatives to the system, but alternatives within the system. The commercial is not necessarily the junkyard of cinema, just as the noncommercial is not necessarily the guarantee of quality or even of integrity. In any case, a certain impurity in the form of an ambiguity toward commercialism is the rule in Hong Kong cinema. But it is an impurity that can yield positive results, as a number of outstanding Hong Kong films made recently show, insofar as it goes together with an awareness that good films are not made according to one immutable set of rules.

In relation to commercialism, the isolated case of Allen Fong, who is very much the exception that proves the rule, becomes highly interesting. His non-commercial work seems to me to be a failure of a particularly valuable and significant kind. Take his best-known film *Father and Son* (1981), which is a semiautobiographical story about growing up in Hong Kong's crowded housing estates. It is a film shot in a kind of neorealist documentary style, which eschews the use of big-name stars and spectacular effects.

The film shows us another side of Hong Kong, not the sensational world of rapacious consumption and high-tech information but the everyday world of common people. *Father and Son* has all the uncompromising integrity of the early work of the Fifth Generation, even without the benefit of state subsidy. Fong does not make use of currently popular film genres and is relatively unconcerned about packaging, publicity, and distribution. Not surprisingly, he finds it particularly difficult to get funding for his projects. He wryly describes himself and like-minded filmmakers as 'magicians on how to survive.'[9] Fong has introduced a note of honesty and sincerity to Hong Kong cinema. For reasons that will be obvious in a moment, however, his straightforward neorealist style of filmmaking seems incapable of addressing the historical paradoxes of contemporary Hong Kong and the problematics of disappearance. *Father and Son* is set almost exclusively in the past, showing in one long flashback a Hong Kong that has almost completely vanished with the advent of air travel. The film is bracketed significantly by shots of an airplane landing and taking off. When Ann Hui uses flashback, it will not be to suggest the stability of the past, and when Stanley Kwan uses the documentary style, it will not imply a faith in the ability of 'the real' to speak and be heard. For better or for worse, it has been left to other directors less wary of the dangers of working within the system to make the decisively important films of the new Hong Kong cinema.

We turn now to the question of disappearance. It is not enough to think about Hong Kong cinema simply in terms of a tight commercial space occasionally opened up by individual talent, on the model of auteurs in Hollywood. The situation is both more interesting and more complicated, brought about by the social and political transformations that took place in the early eighties when it became clear that Hong Kong would revert to Chinese rule in July 1997. These transformations have produced an open-ended situation that is still in the process of definition – who knows what will happen to Hong Kong after 1997? Nevertheless, in relation to cinema, a number of changes are already discernible, like a new kind of filmmaker, an urgent new subject matter, and changes both in the nature of the audience and in the conditions of viewing. July 1997 is not just a terminal date that falls sometime in the future. It is, all at once, an ever-present irritant, a provocation, and a catalyst for change. It turns Hong Kong into what Paul Virilio calls a 'hyper-anticipatory and predictive' society, where time is experienced very much in the future perfect tense.[10]

The emergence of the new Hong Kong cinema could be dated to the early eighties because, while on one level the Hong Kong film industry just went on doing what it had been doing with relative financial success, on another level the eighties saw decisive changes that would turn Hong Kong cinema into something qualitatively different from what went before. This is not to dismiss the earlier cinema, but simply to affirm that the new cinema has to be judged by different rules. In the first place, the early eighties was the moment when a new generation of Hong Kong-born filmmakers, educated in film schools abroad and with no direct ties to either China or Taiwan, turned to filmmaking after a period of apprenticeship in local television. The result was a cinema that in terms of technical competence and thematic richness represented a qualitative leap forward. Three films released in 1982 can be taken to exemplify this moment: Tsui Hark's *Zu: Warriors from the Magic Mountain*, a kung fu film distinguished by its brilliant mastery of special effects; Ann Hui's *Boat People*, about Vietnamese refugees, where cinema is used to deal with pressing social and political issues; and Patrick Tam's *Nomad*, about disaffected youths in urban Hong Kong. But 1982 was also the year of Margaret Thatcher's visit to China, which began a process of negotiation that culminated in the Joint Declaration of 1984 returning Hong Kong to China in 1997. The Joint Declaration caused a certain amount of anxiety, even though one of its terms is that the sociopolitical structure of Hong Kong will remain unchanged for fifty years (according to the slogan 'One country, two systems'). But it also had another effect: it made Hong Kong people look at the place with new eyes. It is as if the possibility of such a social and cultural space disappearing, in the form we know it today, has led to our seeing it in all its complexity and contradiction for the first time, an instance, as Benjamin would have said, of love at last sight. The consequences for cinema are considerable. The Hong Kong cinema, even while it remains a popular commercial cinema, now addresses a public in the process of changing – a public suddenly anxious about its cultural identity because so many issues of social and political liberties hinge on that question. It would be that much harder for Hong Kong citizens to argue the case for political autonomy after 1997 if it could not make the case for cultural identity now. This might allow us to try out the following initial formulation: the new Hong Kong cinema deserves attention because it has finally found a worthy subject – it has found Hong Kong itself as a subject. Is it possible, then, to say about the new Hong Kong cinema that its real emergence could be dated not to the moment when Bruce Lee punched and kicked his way to international stardom, or to the moment when it caught up in terms of technical competence and sophistication with the rest of the world, but to the moment when it could take Hong Kong itself as its privileged subject of interest and inquiry?

Such a generalization would be tempting to make, but it could not be made without some very careful qualifications. It is not the *appearance* of new themes or new subject matter that is significant, for example, like reiterations of the question of Hong Kong's cultural identity or anxiety over 1997. Once these themes begin to appear, they tend to get repeated ad nauseum, very much like gossip. Almost every film made since the mid-eighties, regardless of quality or seriousness of intention, seems constrained to make some mandatory reference to 1997. For example, it is an issue that dominates Evans Chan's *To Liv(e)* (1990), a film that takes itself very seriously indeed, about the international response to Hong Kong's treatment of the Vietnamese boat people. The pun in the title alludes to Liv Ullmann, the celebrated star of Ingmar Bergman films turned human-rights campaigner, to whom the protagonist writes agonized letters. But 1997 is just as important a reference in Tsui Hark's shameless potboiler *Wicked City* (1992), a *Bladerunner* rip-off about reptilian humanoids plotting to take over the city on that fatal date. Similarly, many gangster films from A *Better Tomorrow* to Johnny Mak's *Long Arm of the Law* can be read as allegories of 1997. It is not the appearance of 'Hong Kong themes,' then, that is significant in the new Hong Kong cinema, but, rather, what I call a problematic of disappearance: that is to say, a sense of the elusiveness, the slipperiness, the ambivalences of Hong Kong's cultural space that some Hong Kong filmmakers have caught in their use of the film medium, in their explorations of history and memory, in their excavation of the evocative detail – *regardless of subject matter*. More often than not, these films do not even make any direct reference to Hong Kong's political situation today, and they cover a wide spectrum of popular genres. Nevertheless, as films they are both products and analyses of a cultural space of disappearance, as well as responses to it. A short list would include Wong Kar-wai's first four films; Ann Hui's *Song of the Exile*; Stanley Kwan's *Rouge* and *Center Stage*; and Tsui Hark's *Once upon a Time in China* series. It is the representation of disappearances in new cinematic images that is crucial for the Hong Kong cinema.

One way of explaining the problematic of disappearance is by considering the current interest in Hong Kong by Hong Kong people themselves. This is in some strange way a new phenomenon that requires some comment. There has of course always been widespread interest in Hong Kong on the part of locals and foreigners alike, especially since 1949 when the city embarked in earnest on its spectacular international career. The economist Milton Friedman, we remember, once put Hong Kong forward as the model of a capitalist utopia. But until recently this interest was focused primarily on economics and politics, and to a lesser extent (attributable perhaps to colonialist embarrassment) on history. From these kinds of perspectives, many studies of Hong Kong are available. However, when it came to the much more elusive question of Hong Kong culture, all we found was largely mystification and disavowal. To avoid the issue of Hong Kong culture, locals and expatriates alike used to take refuge behind the ideological image of Hong Kong as a 'cultural desert,' as if culture meant only Shakespeare, Beethoven, and the like, or even Peking Opera for that matter, the scarcity of all of which was loudly bemoaned. On the question of culture, it was as if the Hong Kong person lived through a version of what Sigmund Freud called the 'family romance': the fantasy that some children have that their real parents are not their actual parents. The result is that stories about Hong Kong always turned into stories about somewhere else, as if Hong Kong culture were somehow not a subject. This is a case of what Freud calls 'negative hallucination': to reiterate a point I made in chapter 1, if hallucination is seeing what is not there, then reverse hallucination is not seeing what is there.

This reverse hallucination requires us to qualify a little our initial formulation about Hong Kong cinema: it may have found a subject, Hong Kong itself, but Hong Kong as a subject is one that threatens to get easily lost again. This time around the threat will not be that there is no interest in Hong Kong – Hong Kong is today very much on the agenda. The threat will be that Hong Kong as a subject will be presented and represented in terms of some or the old *binarisms* whose function it is to restabilize differences and domesticate change, for example, binarisms like East and West, or tradition and modernity. In other words, the danger now is that Hong Kong will disappear as a subject, *not by being ignored but by being represented in the good old ways*. Precisely because Hong Kong is such an elusive subject, there is a temptation to use, and to believe in, the available forms of representation and misrepresentation. This is *dis-appearance* in a very specific sense (imagine the term as hyphenated), in that it gives us a reality that is not so much hidden as purloined, a reality that is overlooked because it is looked at in the old familiar ways. Furthermore, the binarisms used to represent Hong Kong as a subject give us not so much a sense of déjà vu, as the even more uncanny feeling of what we might call the *déjà disparu*: the feeling that what is new and unique about the situation is always already gone, and we are left holding a handful of clichés, or a cluster of memories of what has never been. It is as if the speed of current events is producing a radical desynchronization: the generation of more and more images to the point of visual saturation going together with a general regression of viewing, an inability to read what is given to view – in other words, the state of reverse hallucination.

There is an important relation, then, between the new Hong Kong cinema and the *déjà disparu*: its main task is to find means of outflanking, or simply keeping pace with, a subject always on the point of disappearing – in other words, its task is to construct images out of clichés. Some examples might be Stanley Kwan's drawing on the uncanniness of the ghost story in *Rouge*, or Wong Kar-wai's representations of violent actions that do not quite resolve themselves into clear images in *As Tears Go By*, or Ann Hui's *mise-en-abîme* of memory in *Song of the Exile*. These are some of the films of the new Hong Kong cinema that define for us the spatial conditions of viewing and of filmmaking, where the act of looking itself has become problematic: the more you try to make the world hold still in a reflective gaze, the more it moves under you.

These films do not so much thematize Hong Kong culture as they give us a critical experience of Hong Kong's cultural space by problematizing the viewing process. This may also explain why so many of the innovative films are situated in a space between 'fact' and 'fiction,' allowing the specular, the given-to-be-seen, to retain a certain critical speculative edge.

The ambiguity of commercialism and the paradoxes of disappearance can now be related to five features of the new Hong Kong cinema, the first of which involves the question of history and its spatialization. As a city, Hong Kong has been very much the plaything and ambiguous beneficiary of history. Colonized by the British in the nineteenth century; occupied by the Japanese in the Second World War, swelled by the influx of refugees from communist China after 1949, which gave it so many of its cooks and tailors and entrepreneurs; taken in hand by the multinationals as it developed into an international city; and now to be returned to China – Hong Kong's history is one of shock and radical changes. As if to protect themselves against this series of traumas, Hong Kong people have little memory and no sentiment for the past. The general attitude to everything, sometimes indistinguishable from the spirit of enterprise, is cancel out and pass on. But history exists, if not in surviving monuments or written records, then in the jostling anachronisms and spatial juxtapositions that are seen on every street; that is, history is inscribed in spatial relations. When the Hong Kong Shanghai Bank building designed by Norman Foster was being built, for example, this ultra-high-tech multinational building was surrounded by traditional Chinese bamboo scaffolding: an image of history as palimpsest. One of the features of new Hong Kong cinema is its sensitivity to spatial issues, in other words, to dislocations and discontinuities, and its adoption of spatial narratives both to underline and to come to terms with these historical anachronisms and achronisms: space as a means of reading the elusiveness of history. We get a better sense of the history of Hong Kong through its new cinema (and architecture) than is currently available in any history book.

Related to the question of space is that of affectivity. In a dislocated space, affectivity in turn becomes problematic. It is as if all the ways of relating have somehow shifted, the bonds that join us to others as friends and lovers, as daughters and sons blurring like the lines on a television screen that is not tracking properly. It is not just a question of traditional emotional responses versus modern indifference: the opposition between tradition and modernity is already too stable and predictable. Rather, what we find represented now are emotions that do not belong to anybody or to any situation – affective intensities with no name. Thus in Stanley Kwan's *Love unto Waste* (1986), a kind of Felliniesque study of decadence, love is a bad habit or a whim or a weakness, an expense of spirit in a waste of shame, a theme he explores again in the more recent *Red Rose, White Rose* (1994). In *Rouge* the most intense emotion belongs to a ghost. In Wong Kar-wai's *Days of Being Wild* (1991), with its structure of interlapping stories, human relations may still be painful, but they have lost all their *serious* aspects and take on instead a *serial* quality of transferences, exchanges, and repetitions – all to the background music of old dance-hall songs with their suggestions of faded passions.

From what vantage point can the filmmaker describe this cultural space and sick eros? Certainly not from the outside, from a privileged critical distance. So while there are a number of successful comedies, there are no parodies or ironic presentations of Hong Kong society in the new Hong Kong cinema comparable to, say, Robert Altman's ironic portraits of America in *Nashville* (1975) or *A Wedding* (1978). The position of the Hong Kong filmmaker, then, is what we might call a position of critical proximity, where one is always a part of what one is criticizing. This brings me to a third observation about the new Hong Kong cinema, which concerns the use of genres. Given commercial pressures, it is understandable that even the most independent of filmmakers find themselves working with popular genres like the gangster (or 'hero') film, the ghost story, and the kung fu movie. What is remarkable, however, is that these filmmakers produce some of their best work within these genres (this is an example of what I mean by critical proximity). Although many Hong Kong films are meretricious and formulaic, we also find Wong Kar-wai's *As Tears Go By* (a gangster film), Stanley Kwan's *Rouge* (a ghost film), and Tsui Hark's *Once upon a Time in China: Part I* (a kung fu movie). By no means parodies of their respective genres, these films use the limits of genre as a discipline and a challenge.

Fourth, the language of the new Hong Kong cinema is Cantonese (or more precisely, that version of Cantonese practiced in Hong Kong). This was not always the case. In the late seventies the sociologist I. C. Jarvie divided Hong Kong film into Cantonese and Mandarin, arguing that Cantonese movies were un-Westernized and designed entirely for local consumption, while Mandarin movies were cosmopolitan, technically accomplished, and in touch with the contemporary world.[11] If these observations had some cogency for the early seventies, they have proved to be irrelevant for Hong Kong cinema in the eighties and nineties. The new Hong Kong cinema has indeed gone over to Cantonese, as has pop music (what is called Canto-rock). But in doing so, it has not simply asserted the importance of the local; it has also changed the way in which the local is regarded. In the older Cantonese movies, the local was an ethos of exclusion: it defined a narrow homogeneous social space where foreigners and foreign elements had no place, which is what gives these old movies, when we watch them now, a certain campy quality. The new localism, on the other hand, investigates the dislocations of the local, where the local is something unstable that mutates right in front of our eyes, like the language itself. Hong Kong Cantonese now is sprinkled with snatches of Mandarin, English, and barbarous sounding words and phrases – a hybrid language coming out of a hybrid space. It is by being local in this way that the new Hong Kong cinema is most international. Conversely, some of the attempts to be international – by using a foreign city as background, for example, as in Clara

Law's well-regarded *Autumn Story*, a film about Hong Kong Chinese in New York made in the late eighties – may strike us as awkward and provincial.

Finally, the new localism does not just present Hong Kong as a subject worthy of attention; it develops what we might call a new Hong Kong subjectivity as it moves toward a difficult and idiosyncratic form of post-coloniality. The fifth feature of the new Hong Kong cinema is the presence of a politics of identity, but it is a politics that expresses itself best when expressed indirectly, for example, in the introduction of new kinds of cinematic images or in the rewriting of film genres. We will come back to the question of images and other features of the Hong Kong cinema when we look at individual films, but this may be the place to say a word about the politics of the kung fu genre, about kung fu as an indirect representation of the changing nature of coloniality in Hong Kong.

The kung fu/martial arts genre, from Bruce Lee's *The Big Boss* (1971) through the offerings of Jackie Chan and Tsui Hark, to Wong Kar-wai's recent *Ashes of Time* (1994), has gone through a number of distinct transformations, each one a rewriting of the genre. Such films are not expected to do much more than provide entertainment through visual spectacle (which is one reason why the brilliant and long-awaited *Ashes of Time* was such a disappointment to local audiences); but perhaps exactly because of that, we see all the more clearly the unstable shape of coloniality inscribed in these films over a period of roughly twenty-five years, undoubtedly the most important years in Hong Kong's short history. It is not that the kung fu film is ever a direct critique of colonialism, rather, that the ethos of (mainly) male heroism and personal prowess so central to the genre has to define itself in relation to *what is felt to be possible* in a changing colonial situation. In defining heroism, it defines by implication the colonial situation itself.

Bruce Lee was a child star in the local Cantonese cinema, and he learned his kung fu in Hong Kong. In the United States, he became a martial arts instructor who taught kung fu to Hollywood stars and got a minor and ethnically stereotyped part in the television series *The Green Hornet*. He was passed over for the role of Kane in the successful series *Kung Fu* that went to David Carradine. However, when he returned to Hong Kong in the early seventies at the beginning of the local craze for better-quality martial arts films, which came in the wake of the international success of Akira Kurosawa's sword-play epics *Sanjuro* and *Yojimbo*, things were very different. He returned with the cachet of foreignness: the repatriate was an expatriate. And he returned with impeccable martial arts credentials, having won a number of international martial arts competitions. His first film, *The Big Boss*, set the pattern. Here was an actor who could really kick and punch, and it introduced a new level of authenticity and a new type of hero to the Hong Kong cinema, what Geoffrey O'Brien calls the stuntman as hero. But there was another equally important element in Lee's series of films, whether directed by him or others. The physical authenticity was keyed to something else, something much more elusive, namely, the reassertion of an authentic and heroic Chinese identity. The repatriate/expatriate was also a patriot, the patriotism expressing itself as a form of anticolonialism. There was a strong xenophobic tone in the Lee films, which took the form of the Chinese hero beating up Japanese or Caucasians in beautifully choreographed action sequences. The anticolonialism was slightly forced, however, and cannot be taken too literally. It came at the moment when both Bruce Lee and Hong Kong began to embark on very successful international careers. Hence two features can be noted. First, the anticolonial anger did not refer to very much in the present, but only to *memories* of slights and insults suffered in the past: memories belonging to another place and to an older generation. It was as if Bruce Lee were fighting again in a new Boxer Rebellion through the medium of cinema, in much the same way that Hollywood refought the Vietnam War. The second feature was the vaguely directed animus and the stereotyped opponents, as if there were no idea who the 'enemy' really was. Every time Lee fights, he seems to fall into a trance and acts like someone shadow-boxing. As a result the films kick and punch themselves into a corner. *Fist of Fury* (1972) ends emblematically with Lee caught in a freeze-frame executing a high kick, leaving both its star and all the plot strands up in the air.

Jackie Chan marks a second moment in the development of the martial arts genre, and a different moment in colonial history. With Lee's death, a successor had to be found. Like Lee, Chan is a martial arts expert, and he makes it a point of honor to perform all the action stunts himself. One of Jackie Chan's first films is called in fact *New Fist of Fury* (1976) to underline the succession. But while villainous colonizers are still around, everything now has a touch of slapstick. The result is essentially a transformation of the genre into kung fu comedy. The Jackie Chan character created in *Drunken Master* (1978) is neither a patriot nor an expatriate; he is just a regular local boy with good but not invincible skills. The heroism is not to be taken too seriously. Jackie Chan has the good humor of the professional rather than the dark taciturnity of Bruce Lee's avenging angel. The good humor is significant because it could be related very closely to the relaxation of colonial tensions in Hong Kong so noticeable in the late seventies, a mood that lasted until Thatcher's visit to China in 1982. This was a moment when signs for optimism, like the end of the Chinese Cultural Revolution, were everywhere, and colonialism seemed almost an irrelevance, no more than a formal administrative presence that did not interfere with the real life of the colony. A new sense of how it was local ingenuity and professionalism more than imported talent that had brought about the city's great success came with the force of a revelation. In other words, it was a growing confidence in Hong Kong's international viability that led to a rediscovery of the local, just as it was Bruce Lee who prepared the way for Jackie Chan. Nor is it accidental that Jackie Chan's kung fu comedy coincided with the new brand of comedy introduced by the Hui brothers, Michael and Sam, who used current Cantonese slang to explore the peculiarities of the local situation, often to brilliant effect. It was also during this period that Sam Hui introduced what has since been known as Canto-pop, where the lyrics are in the local idiom rather than in English or Mandarin. The new 'local' culture was nonprovincial and exciting, and it appealed to a wide audience, unlike the earlier localism that appealed mainly to the non-Anglophone sectors of the community. All these developments changed the way Hong Kong people looked at local culture and, for a while, at colonialism – that is to say, until the eighties, which experienced the double trauma of the Sino-British Joint Declaration and the Tiananmen Massacre. Significantly, in the eighties the kung fu genre, too, fell into decline, only to reemerge in the nineties in two different forms in films by Tsui Hark and Wong Kar-wai. It is in the style of these new kung fu films that we sense that some radical changes in the nature of coloniality in Hong Kong have indeed taken place.

In these kung fu films of the nineties, two realizations have sunk in. First, it is no longer possible to appeal with any conviction to some vague notion of Chineseness, as China itself may turn out to be the future colonizer, in fact if not in name, once the present one has departed. Second, it is no longer possible to see local developments as separable or proceeding in isolation from global developments. It is from this perspective that we can interestingly consider the kung fu films of Tsui Hark, which obliquely convey the message that colonialism is on the point of becoming obsolete. This is particularly clear in the series *Once upon a Time in China*, the first of which appeared in 1991. The series deals with stories about the legendary Chinese master, Wong Fei Hung, and there are many action sequences and references to history and colonial history. At one point, Sun Yat-sen makes an appearance, reminiscent of the way historical figures keep appearing in *Forrest Gump*. This comparison with *Gump* suggests that what sets the series apart are not the authenticities of action or history but its mastery of *special effects*. In Tsui Hark's films, it is no longer stuntmen but special effects that are the real heroes. Tsui Hark's star Jet Li (who interestingly enough is mainland Chinese) knows his kung fu, but there are no more authentic stars/heroes of the order of Bruce Lee, as the real is more and more being 'coproduced' through special effects. For example, in the marvelous fight between Wong Fei Hung and another kung fu master that climaxes the first *Once upon a Time in China*, Tsui Hark makes the two characters do wonderful gravity-defying things with ladders, but our main interest is focused on how Tsui Hark *films* these sequences rather than on the athleticism of the actors. This interest in special effects implies not only that the Hong Kong cinema has caught up with the new technologies; more important, it now places the filmic action in a new technological and, by implication, transnational space where (we might be tempted to believe in an optimistic moment) the problem of colonialism will have been a thing of the past. Tsui Hark's kung fu series may be set in the past, but it is a past reproduced by laser.

Another view of technology and colonialism can be read in Wong Kar-wai's *Ashes of Time* (1994), one of the most remarkable films to have come out of the new Hong Kong cinema. It is Wong's version of the martial arts epic, made almost contemporaneously with Tsui Hark's kung fu films, but the style and emphases are very different. The beautiful cinematography of Chris Doyle merely serves to emphasize the film's somber tone, its focus on a landscape of ruins. As we watch the characters in their Issey Miyake-like costumes parade across desert and swamp in a series of fascinating tableaux, it is like watching a pavane. There is not one but four heroes, and the film uses a number of spectacular special effects; but it soon becomes clear that both heroism and special effects, as well as visuality itself, are being reexamined and found wanting. Consider the fight sequence that opens the film, involving the story's main figure Ouyang Feng. It is no longer a choreography of human bodies in motion that we see. In fact, we do not know what it is we are seeing. Things have now been speeded up to such an extent that what we find is only a composition of light and color in which all action has dissolved – a kind of abstract expressionism or action painting. It is not possible, therefore, to discern who is doing what to whom. The heroic space of Bruce Lee is now a *blind space* (one of the four heroes in fact is going blind); moreover, it is a blind space that comes from an *excess* of light and movement, that is to say, an excess of Tsui Hark-style special effects. *Ashes of Time* gives us a kind of double dystopia, where heroism loses its raison d'être and special effects lose their air of optimism and exhilaration. Wong's film marks a point of *degeneration* of the genre, the moment when the genre self-destructs. The idea of presence and authenticity implied in the ethos of heroism is subverted, and the hope of happy inscription in a technology-based global utopia implied in the optimistic use of special effects is imploded. In this indirect way the film speaks to some of the problems and anxieties of *technocolonialism*, which *shows* itself only abstractly and negatively as something that cannot be directly represented, particularly not by means of sophisticated technological equipment. As for the Hong Kong kung fu film as a whole, it suggests that colonialism itself is made up of a series of slippery dislocations: a kind of *morphing*.

Some Representative Films of the New Hong Kong Cinema

The four films I have chosen as representative of the new Hong Kong cinema are Wong Kar-wai's debut film *As Tears Go By* (1988); Ann Hui's domestic melodrama *Song of the Exile* (1990); Stanley Kwan's ghost film *Rouge* (1988); and his 'bio-pic' *Center Stage* (1991). While these four films are very different from each other, what they do have in common is that each is formally innovative. Each begins by working within the conventions of a specific genre, only to depart quite radically from them. Even more important is the fact that the formal innovation points to a historical situation that can only be felt and understood in some new and original way. We can use these films to exemplify and extend the general observations that have been made about Hong Kong cinema – its adoption of spatial narratives to suggest dislocations, a new complexity in the treatment of affects and emotions, a creative use of popular genres, a new localism, and a politics that can only be indirect.

The genre that Wong uses in *As Tears Go By* is what is known in Hong Kong as the hero movie, after the Chinese title of the series of very popular films made by John Woo. (The English title of the series is *A Better Tomorrow*.) In the Hong Kong cinema, Woo can be considered to be the polar opposite of Allen Fong, and not only in commercial terms. We must not hold John Woo's success in Hollywood against him, as his contribution to Hong Kong filmmaking is considerable. While Fong goes for a relatively pure 'realist' image, Woo introduces a 'mixed image.' In Woo's films, two qualities stand out: a fascination with extreme violence, often filmed in slow motion for emphasis, on the one hand; and on the other, a plot that underlines the need for personal loyalties, usually between male friends, in a crumbling world. Action and affection are two distinct series, but they are two series that nevertheless interrupt each other, resulting in a mixed image. For example, in *A Better Tomorrow: Part I* (1986), Ho, one of the three main characters, intends to give up his lucrative career in crime for the sake of his younger policeman brother Kit. Ho is betrayed on his last job. Mark, Ho's friend and partner, avenges the betrayal in one of the classic shoot-out scenes of the Hong Kong cinema that so impressed Hollywood, and he gets crippled in the process. In both cases, it is the affection series that pushes the action series forward and eventually off course. Action therefore takes on a certain reflexivity and affection, an incipient note of violence. The limitation of the film, however, is that ultimately these two series interact without transforming each other. The moral and affective issues remain relatively simple. We do not find the moral ambiguities of film noir, much less those of disappearance. It has been said that Woo's hero films are allegories of the Hong Kong situation, the romanticization of the outlaw a displaced sign of resistance to Chinese rule. If so, they are allegories based on a *simplification* of the Hong Kong situation. Nevertheless, the twist in the genre that Woo introduced opened up new possibilities for other directors like Wong Kar-wai.

Up to a point, *As Tears Go By* follows quite closely the hero genre established by John Woo. One main part of the story deals with the friendship between two local hoods, the hero and his younger friend who still has to prove his mettle in the Hong Kong underworld. The friend is eventually manipulated by the gangs to carry out an assassination under conditions that could only prove fatal to him. The hero, unable to dissuade or protect him, simply follows him in a futile act of loyalty and gets shot, too. We seem to find here a link between action and affection similar to what we saw in the hero films. There are, however, a number of differences and complications, seen first of all in the way the film establishes an overall sense of spatial ambiguities and discontinuities that frames and undercuts the conventionalities of the story.

Consider, for example, the first shot of the film. As the credits are being shown, we see on the left-hand side of the screen a mainland Chinese department store with its neon-lit advertisement sign, while on the right, floating in the foreground, are multiple television screens, empty and flickering. In this single shot, two historically distinct spaces occupy one common ground: the physical space of the older kind of commodity – material, located in place, attached to a sign; and the televisual space of information, the new commodity – dematerialized, mobile, and placeless. The film will go on to develop these spatial ambiguities, for example, in its peculiar use of color and slow motion. Color is always either too strong or too weak, and the film looks by turns gaudy or pale, over- or underexposed, too red or too blue. The color is never just right. Similarly, action is so problematic that slowing it down reveals nothing further, certainly not a moral or cognitive point. The more slowly and carefully we look at something, the more puzzlingly it looks back at us, it seems. It is these *irresolutions*, both visual and cognitive, that marks Wong's film as a special kind of film noir: the *neonoir* of a colonial subject caught in the confusions of colonial space (a point I shall return to presently). Violence may always be threatening to erupt, but it is never straightforwardly celebrated as the voluntaristic act of an individual subject, as in John Woo's films; rather, it exists as a ubiquitous and unavoidable dimension of urban space itself, which offers the individual no choice.

When we turn now to the other main part of the story, the love relation that develops between the hero and the heroine, we see how affectivity, too, is shaped by these spatial constraints. The hero moves back and forth throughout the film between lover and friend: from Lantau Island, a quiet undeveloped part of Hong Kong where the heroine lives, to the mean streets of Mongkok where the hero's friend is always in trouble. Scenes of lovemaking are always interrupted by messages of violence in a disconcerting cadence, so much so that one can become fused and confused with the other. For example, Wong shoots the kiss in a phone booth between Maggie Cheung and Andy Lau – one of the most erotic scenes in Hong Kong cinema – in the same way that he shoots the fight scenes: both these scenes erupt suddenly, it is a violence that comes apparently out of nowhere, and both are shot in slow motion. Slow motion, however, is not being used (as it is by John Woo) to romanticize or aestheticize either love or violence, it is used analytically to study, to understand. But analysis by slow motion, like analysis by blowup, leads at a certain point only to a blurring of the image, that is, to bewilderment rather than to understanding. The closer you look, the less there is to see. It is as if for Wong the gangster film, with all its clichés, somehow became an exercise in a hopeless epistemology, the demonstration of a visual aporia, as if every shot had to be closely attended to because things are always surreptitiously passing you by. This is the *déjà disparu*, a reality that is always outpacing our awareness of it, a reality that the film breathlessly tries to catch up with.

What is so remarkable about *As Tears Go By* is the way it manages to construct its images by drawing on and destabilizing the clichés and standard situations of the gangster film. What we notice most about the film – from the opening to the closing sequence where the death of the hero is intercut with one quick shot of a flickering memory of lovemaking – is its visual density. But, as I am suggesting, it is not a visual density that coheres or allows us to map out an intelligible space. Rather, the images disorient by refusing to stabilize. For example, the film ends, as so many in the genre do, with the hero's violent death; but in the final shot, although the hero is dead, the image of him continues to throb on, like a heartbeat, as if the image had acquired a life of its own.

There is one final point to be made, concerning the film's relationship to colonialism – a surprising point, perhaps, because no direct references to the problematic of colonialism or its critique are ever made. The critique is made obliquely in the film's treatment of visuality and in its relation to genre. In visual terms, colonial space might be thought of as working to promote a way of seeing that gives the visible and established the authority of the real. It constructs *a gaze* in which the real appears, and disappears, for a colonial subject. Because Wong's film consistently gives us a form of visuality that problematizes the visible, it can be said to represent and critique such a space. It does this in its use of color and slow motion, but also in the way it produces a general sense of visual overload, seen, for example, in the running together of the fast and the slow; in the absence of transition between the idyllic and the brutal; in the choice of unusual camera angles that disorient, like shots directly from above or below. It is understandable why *As Tears Go By* has often been compared to MTV. But whereas visual overload in MTV usually functions to hold an audience's attention, in Wong's film it functions to suggest that attention itself cannot hold the *déjà disparu*. An oblique address to colonial space can also be read in Wong's particular relation to genre. If the formulaic demands of the genre of the gangster film imply colonization and self-colonization by clichés, and if subverting the formulaic is not viable for a number of reasons (such as the need to get financial support to make films), there is still a third possibility that of doing something else within the genre, of nudging it a little from its stable position and so provoking thought. This is post-coloniality not in the form of an argument; it takes the form of a new practice of the image.

A film of a very different kind that does have an argument is Ann Hui's *Song of the Exile*, which is set in the domestic space of middle-class Hong Kong and focuses on the relation between a mother and daughter. One of the many interesting features of Ann Hui's film is that it takes us away from the largely male concerns of Hong Kong cinema (Wong Kar-wai is not exempt from this charge in his earlier films). *Song of the Exile* begins with the daughter Hueyin receiving an M.A. in media studies in London but failing to get an interview with the BBC (while her British classmate does). She decides to return to Hong Kong to attend her sister's wedding, and there she encounters her mother with whom she has never gotten along. There is a flashback to early days in Macau (lovingly re-created): memories of living with her grandparents, who dream of returning one day to China, of an absent father working in Hong Kong, of a very different mother – quiet, self-effacing, a dutiful daughter-in-law. What has she become now? Just as we thought this was going to be another film – yawn, yawn – about the clash between tradition and modernity, Chinese customs and Western ways, both Hueyin and the audience have a revelation: it turns out that the mother is in fact Japanese, that she met her husband during Japan's last days in Manchuria. All Hueyin's memories of the past and of her mother's behavior are reassessed in light of this knowledge. We have another flash-back to Macau, to a past that looks the same but that is now understood differently. Hueyin realizes for the first time how difficult it must have been for her mother living as an isolated, oppressed subject in Chinese society, set apart by her customs (the grandparents always complained that her food was not hot enough) and by her ignorance of the language, which Hueyin misread as quietness. Within the domestic drama, then, we find a historical allegory of a colonial situation with a Japanese (traditionally, the Hong Kong image of the oppressor) as the oppressed.

The daughter's sentimental and political education continues in the second part of the film when she accompanies her mother to her hometown in Japan. And there it is the daughter's turn to go through the experience of being an alien in a strange country. In one scene she loses her way and wanders into a farm where she picks a tomato to eat. A farmer appears and shouts excitedly at her in Japanese. We know from the subtitles that he is warning her not to eat the vegetable because it has been sprayed with pesticides. She thinks that he is threatening to prosecute her for stealing and runs away. The more the farmer runs after her to warn her, the harder she tries to run. Ignorance of the language makes her believe that she is a criminal. The episode ends happily, though, as they eventually meet the village's English-speaking schoolteacher who explains everything, just as the film itself ends happily with mother and daughter returning together to Hong Kong, having finally achieved some kind of understanding of each other. The mother now regards Hong Kong as her only real home, while Hueyin finds work as a producer at a local television station. In a coda, Hueyin goes to Guangzhou to visit her grandparents who had indeed returned to China, only to become victims of the Cultural Revolution.

In *Song of the Exile*, genre is transcended through the treatment of space and affectivity. We see this first in the presence of a structure that can be identified as the family romance, the fantasy that our parents must be more interesting or worthy than our actual parents. This fantasy about origins is most evident in Hueyin's attitude to her mother in the early part of the film, but it can also be seen in some form in her grandparents' idealization of China and her mother's identification with her native Japan. In the film the personal is political, and understanding one's mother and one's own personal history is the precondition for understanding history and society, specifically Hong Kong history and society. Ann Hui has attempted to link the personal and the political before, for example, in *Starry Is the Night* (1988) about a woman's unhappy love affair with her married university professor and, many years later unbeknownst to her, with the professor's son. In this earlier film, the personal is identified quite weakly with erotic relations with the result that the political point is largely lost in sentimental confusions. *Song of the Exile* has a firmer structure, where the family romance is used as social allegory and functions to show the emotional confusions about 'home' that result from a rapidly changing cultural space. These confusions of the family romance are finally overcome by Hueyin who can be reconciled with her mother, and by the mother herself who can be reconciled with the 'loss' of her Japanese past, and both finally return to Hong Kong as home. The grandparents, on the other hand, who pursue the romance back to China, fail to overcome the past and suffer the consequences of their fantasy.

The film's narrative unfolds in a series of flashbacks, cutting back and forth between past and present. The originality of Ann Hui's use of the technique is that it does not just present to us a past that can elucidate the present through a chronological reshuffling. Rather, we are given a structure that is more spatial than chronological: the flashback technique shows us a past and a present that do not quite mesh, that seem initially to contradict each other, but it is these discrepancies that force a reevaluation of both memory and experience. It is notable that as the film progresses, we begin to see not only flashbacks, but *flashbacks of flashbacks*, as memories themselves are reassessed and finally understood. So while the earlier flashbacks have a nostalgic tone of intense poignancy and puzzlement, it is replaced in the later flashbacks of flashbacks by a general tone of sympathy and understanding, as nostalgia itself is *mise-en-abîme*. In terms both of narrative and technique, the structure then is one of reconciliation, of puzzling experience illuminated by understanding.

The need for understanding is Ann Hui's principal theme. Here is the voice of liberal Hong Kong, which believes that the past and history itself can be changed through the overcoming of misunderstandings and prejudices. Her song of the exile is not a siren's song that leads to rash actions (as Wong Kar-wai's film largely is), but a rational song of reconciliation, a song about the end of exile through understanding. The position it castigates is that of people who hold on stubbornly to a situation that is no longer there, the most striking example being the mother's younger brother, the former war pilot who refuses to accept the fact that the war is over, preferring a life of bitter memories. Yet it is exactly here in the argument for the need for understanding that we find both the film's strength and weakness. It offers hope for understanding, but it does not address with sufficient clarity or take far enough the question of how the cultural space of Hong Kong can be understood or addressed. For example, on one level the film clearly situates Hong Kong in relation to other social-affective spaces – London, Macau, Japan, Manchuria, China – and suggests that Hong Kong as a place can only be constructed out of its shifting relationships with these *elsewheres*. Yet on another level, especially toward the end of the film, a simpler account of Hong Kong as a 'home' that one can come back to, as a definite *somewhere* with its own internalized history, becomes dominant. Understanding, then, becomes based to a certain extent on simplification, both spatial and affective. As a result, despite all its insights (for example, that the grandparents' patriotism is a form of ethnocentricity) and its concern with social and political issues, *Song of the Exile* remains largely just another private story. And the reason for this, it seems to me, is that colonialism is not just a misunderstanding, and explanations alone (as in the pesticide-sprayed tomato scene) cannot make it go away.

There is still the coda to consider, where Hueyin after her Japan experience goes to Guangzhou to visit her dying grandfather. In this short final section, the film's strengths reassert themselves to some extent. This is because it puts aside the need to give an argument about reconciliation to leave us with a number of intensely felt but contradictory images. The first is that of the grandfather lying on his deathbed, put there prematurely by the Red Guards. But at this point, even after firsthand knowledge of some of the harsher realities of Chinese life, he can still say to Hueyin, 'Don't lose hope in China.' This scene is followed by one of the most striking images in the whole film. The grandmother has adopted a mentally disabled child to look after, and it reminds us of the early scenes in Macau when she lavished care on Hueyin. But as she is spoon-feeding him, he suddenly turns on her and literally bites the hand that feeds him. The image is striking because it seems to be not merely an image of ingratitude, but a glimpse of the darker, more inexplicable side of human life that mocks our claims to understand it. Finally, the film ends with two shots almost superimposed on each other: the first, a final flashback to happy days in Macau in the lotus ponds with the doting grandparents; the second, a shot of present-day Guangzhou, busy, energetic, with no time for memories. It is the inclusion of punctums like these, rather than the film's implied argument, that provoke thought and feeling.

Let me turn now to a third film, one of the great successes of the Hong Kong cinema: Stanley Kwan's *Rouge* (1988), which I will be comparing with his 1991 production *Center Stage*. *Rouge* is quite distinct from the two films just discussed, although it has some elements in common with them.

As with Ann Hui's *Song of the Exile*, in *Rouge* the history of Hong Kong as a city is woven into the stories of personal relationships. The film cuts back and forth between Hong Kong in the early 1930s and the late 1980s. As with Wong Kar-wei's *As Tears Go By*, *Rouge* uses genre, in fact, a mixture of popular genres. It has elements of the nostalgia film: the vanished world of the thirties – with its beautiful courtesans, dashing heroes, and baroquely elegant settings – is lovingly re-created. It can be taken as a sentimental story about star-crossed lovers. Fleur, the toast of Shek Tong Tsui (today, a rather shabby quarter of the Western District, but in the thirties the scene of Hong Kong's stylish and expensive local nightlife), falls in love with Chan Chen-bong (also known as Twelve Master), scion of a rich and respectable Chinese business family. The only resolution in the thirties to such a social mismatch is death, and they eventually agree to commit suicide together. This introduces the most clearly generic element into the film, the ghost story. Unable to meet up with Chen-bong in the afterlife, Fleur returns to the world after waiting for more than fifty years to look for him. She places an ad in a newspaper: '3811. Rendezvous at the usual place' ('3811' stands for March 8, 11 pm, the time of their suicide).

But Chen-bong does not show up at the appointed hour. The journalist Yuen who works at the newspaper and his girlfriend Ah Chor, a fellow journalist, decide after some vacillation to help Fleur in her search for Chen-bong.

Kwan's use of the ghost story genre can only be called inspirational. Hong Kong cinema has had a long history of ghost story films ever since the Kuomintang government banned the making of such films together with martial arts epics in 1935 in a campaign against superstition and moral decadence. The genre was given its contemporary form with Ann Hui's *The Spooky Bunch* (1980), which mixed comedy with horror, and Ching Siu-ting's *A Chinese Ghost Story* (1987), which introduced slick special effects. Kwan resorts neither to comedy nor to the use of special effects. Furthermore, even though the screenplay is based on a popular novel by local novelist Lee Bik Wah (who also scripted *Farewell My Concubine*), the film differs from the novel in important respects. Lee Bik Wah's *Rouge* is based on historical and literary sources and appeals to a traditional sense of the supernatural. The film downplays the supernatural in order to emphasize, through linking the figure of the ghost with woman and cinema itself, the even more contradictory dimensions of cultural space in contemporary Hong Kong.

For one thing, as a ghost, Fleur is presented with remarkable restraint (with none of the use of special effects found in popular ghost films). She can do none of the things that ghosts are supposed to do. She is distinguished only by her silk dress (the *cheong-sam*, rarely seen nowadays as daily wear), by certain mannerisms and old forms of expression, and by her formal style of makeup (emphasized in the film's opening shots) – a revenant who has just stepped out of a freeze-frame, 'unchanged for fifty years,' as Ah Chor skeptically puts it (an obvious ironic reference to the Sino-British Joint Declaration and the future of Hong Kong.) The supernatural is suspended in favor of the uncanny, which has quite different spatial implications. Instead of the supernatural, which registers the clear separation and incongruity of this world with the space of an otherworld, we find the mixed, heterogeneous space of the uncanny, where the unfamiliar arises out of the familiar and is a dimension of it: not another space but a space of otherness. The figure of the ghost evokes what David Harvey has called a 'space-time compression.'[12] Fifty years disappear into simultaneity while space in turn becomes heterogeneous and mixed. The result is that two periods of Hong Kong history are brought together in a historical montage. The paradox is that one of the most popular and fantastic of genres is used as a rigorous method of representing the complexities of Hong Kong's cultural space.

One of the striking features of this space caught by the film is a specific and unusual relation between old and new. What we find is not just a mixture of old and new, a point often made about the film, if by 'mixture' is implied that old and new are still distinguishable one from the other, that the present simply includes residues, or ghosts (cf. Henrik Ibsen), from the past. Rather, what we find is a situation where old and new could switch places, and differences begin to blur. Consider once again the ghost as figure. It comes straight out of traditional folklore and can be taken as an example of old-fashioned superstition. (That essentially is how the figure is used in the Lee Bik Wah novel.) But the ghost as figure can also be seen in relation to that most contemporary of phenomena – the *cinematization of space*, where direct observation gives way to the authority of the media image: nothing is more ghostly than the high-definition electronic image. In Paul Virilio's words,

> from now on, we are directly or indirectly witnessing a co-production of sensible reality . . . The direct observation of visible phenomena gives way to a tele-observation in which the observer has no immediate contact with the observed reality . . . the absence of any immediate perception of concrete reality produces a terrible imbalance between the sensible and the intelligible, one which can only result in errors of interpretation.[13]

Fleur is of course neither electronic image nor cyborg, but she shares one characteristic with them: under most circumstances, she is hardly distinguishable from real or living human beings. She may be a creature of the night, but then so are the habitués of the demimonde, just as Arnold Schwarzenegger's Terminator dressed in black leather is indistinguishable from the toughs of Los Angeles. The reversability of ghost and cinematic image parallels the reversability of past and present, knocking history into a strange loop.

What then at first looks like a series of flashbacks that contrasts past and present turns out in fact to be something more original. As in *Song of the Exile*, flashbacks do not just shuffle what in the end can be reconstructed as a linear narrative. In *Rouge* the effect of the cutting back and forth is to establish a *double temporal framework* for all actions, allowing 'before' and 'after' to chase each other. We see some obvious changes and discontinuities: a well-known theater has been replaced by a 7-Eleven, Ti Hung Lau (the pleasure house where Fleur worked) by a kindergarten. But the film also shows us a subtler kind of discontinuity – the discontinuity that appears as continuity. For example, trams and Chinese Opera have both continued to exist from the thirties into the eighties, but their functions, as means of transport or as popular entertainment, have changed. This kind of change within continuity is the most provocative aspect of the film – its uncanny or ghostly aspect. Moreover, it is in such a space that the film places the question of desire. The ghost story becomes a study of affectivity and the way it unfolds in a space of disappearance.

The film is shot in two contrasting cinematic styles. The Hong Kong of the thirties is represented by a camera style that lingers lovingly on every detail to give us a baroque world of wealth, leisure, and decadence, a theatrical world. Chen-bong first meets Fleur at Ti Hung Lau where she is singing a famous passage from a Cantonese opera, and their love develops in a similarly theatrical way. By contrast, the eighties are filmed in a neutral, unmarked, realist, demotic style to give us a mundane world of work, where the journalists Yuen and Ah Chor are too busy at work to have time to think about emotions. Chen-bong presents Fleur with a beautiful locket as a sign of affection; Yuen presents Ah Chor with a practical pair of athletic shoes. Yet once again what is crucial is not the contrast between an old-fashioned decadent world of pleasure and the contemporary realistic world of work and time. There is also a point of crossover, a chiasmus, between the two, situated, for example, in the notion of decadence – which could take different forms. Stanley Kwan has always been interested in the notion of decadence, and he has dealt with the notion in simplified form in his earlier film *Love unto Waste*, but in that film, decadence was no more than a general mood and moral tone. In *Rouge*, however, decadence reveals a complexity that challenges any easy moralizing.

For example, some signs of old-fashioned decadence might be the devotion to pleasure (including the pleasures of Cantonese opera), to opium, or to fine clothes. The world of Cantonese opera (which permeates the film on the soundtrack) may be associated with tradition: we see that Chen-bong's tradition-bound father who vetoed his marriage to Fleur is an aficionado. But opera is also associated with a world of absolutes, where kings can value a beloved wife over a kingdom. Fleur's theatricality combines the obsolete and the absolute in a way that is unfortunately not true of Chen-bong. He serves an apprenticeship in Cantonese opera but, significantly, does not finish it, in the same way that he can smoke opium for pleasure but not die of it. By contrast, for Fleur even clothing itself is coded in the language of tradition and the absolute. There is a scene where Fleur has tea and a tête-à-tête with Chen-bong's mother, hoping to be accepted as a future daughter-in-law. The mother treats her with great courtesy and makes her a 'reasonable' proposition: she would be quite acceptable, even welcome, as a mistress, but not as a wife. She is then asked to model a wedding dress for the intended wife the parents have chosen – in other words, she can 'model' for a wife but cannot be a real wife. It is Fleur's refusal to compromise, to be a surrogate wife, that leads to the suicide. In this decadent world, love can be either a game, negotiable in monetary terms (as in that wonderful scene played with Tse Yin, a veteran of the old Cantonese cinema, where every touch and caress has a price tag), or it can be deadly serious.

On the other hand, the fast-paced world of today is slow in its affective responses. The purposefulness and busyness go together with another kind of decadence: a form of emotional inertia. That is why the love between Fleur and Chen-bong both attracts and appalls the contemporary couple. Their sympathy for Fleur keeps fluctuating. Such passion demands an absolute commitment that they are either unwilling or unable to make. For example, there is one scene that shows Ah Chor and Yuen erotically aroused by their *discussion* of Fleur's affair, and they end up making passionate love. But after the lovemaking she asks him in a voiceover: Will you commit suicide for me? No, he says. And you for me? he asks. No, she replies. The uncompromising nature of passion appears to them to have a sinister side to it. This emerges as we learn the details leading up to the double suicide. Not only did the lovers swallow raw opium together, but Fleur also put sleeping pills in Chen-bong's wine without his knowledge. This makes Ah Chor accuse Fleur of being a murderess, and she drives Fleur from the house. However, on reflection Ah Chor relents, as she realizes that her anger stems from her jealousy of a passion that she lacks: 'It is difficult to be a woman . . . Who among us has her passion?' In contrast to the old lovers, the contemporary lovers, like contemporary Hong Kong society, find it difficult to commit themselves as they flounder in a confusion of values. Fleur's ghostly passion challenges the noncommittal emotional attitudes of Yuen and Ah Chor. They become more and more deeply involved in Fleur's search for Chen-bong because they glimpse that the outcome will affect their own relation to desire. 'We are as anxious to see Twelve Master as you are,' Ah Chor tells Fleur toward the end.

The film, however, does not correlate the space of the old and the new with the moral forms of commitment and compromise. These four terms circulate and produce a number of different permutations. Nor is it a question of a choice of space. This comes out in the ironic ending, where we meet Chen-bong again, the only character who is situated in both spaces. We learn that not only did he survive the suicide attempt; he went on to marry a respectable woman whom he did not love, to squander the family fortune, and to survive into the present as a physical and spiritual wreck, working as a film extra. The implication, therefore, is that even in the most intense love there is misjudgment, error, weakness. The cultivation of personal intensities as a refuge from a morally imperfect world that demands constant compromise cannot avoid contamination from such a world. 'Who wants to die?' Ah Chor asks Fleur, speaking for survival and in defense of Chen-bong – and of herself. But then Chen-bong's survival is also his form of punishment for not keeping faith. One might read the ending as posing a problem about action and conduct in a Hong Kong uncertain about how to deal with its future, a problem that has as yet no resolution.

The other outstanding film by Stanley Kwan is *Center Stage* (1991, a.k.a. *Actress* in the United States, and *Ruan Lingyu* in Chinese). It is a film biography of Ruan, the most charismatic star of the early Chinese cinema that was based in Shanghai, and it follows her life from 1929 when she was only nineteen (but already regarded in film circles as being 'better than Wu Dip,' another legendary actress) to her suicide in 1935, hounded by a former lover and the press. It is, however, film biography of a special kind, and although it seems at first sight a very different kind of film from *Rouge*, with its partial use of documentary methods rather than a ghost story, the two films have a lot in common, particularly as regards the innovative use of genre.

The official details of Ruan's life are well known, and the film recounts them quite faithfully. It is a story of Cinderella in the new age of media. Born in 1910 in Shanghai to parents from Guangdong, Ruan was six when her father died. Her mother went into domestic service with the rich Zhang family, which enabled Ruan to be educated at a famous Shanghai girls' school. At sixteen, she fell in love with the seventh son, Zhang Damin, but parental objections prevented them from being together until the parents died. Subsequently,

Zhang lost the family fortune in poor business deals, and Ruan became an actress and supported the philandering Zhang. She also adopted a daughter. After acting in a number of mediocre films (the prints of which are now lost), she got her first important role in 1929, and a string of popular and critical successes followed. Her private life was less happy. She broke off with the feckless Zhang (who demanded 'alimony' from her) and started living with the business tycoon Tang Jishan, who not only had a wife in the country but also a history of affairs with film actresses. The crisis came in 1935 after Ruan had finished the film *New Woman* with the progressive director Choy Chor Sang. The film was a biography of a woman writer who, abandoned by her husband and unable to make a living from her writing, turned to prostitution to support her child. The film also showed how the yellow tabloids drove her eventually to suicide by printing scandalous reports about her life. This infuriated the Shanghai press, which made sure the film was censored and took every opportunity to attack Ruan, the star. Zhang was paid to publish the story of his life with Ruan, and in his account he also charged her and Tang with adultery. Under constant pressure from Zhang and the press, Ruan finally committed suicide on 8 March 1935 – which also happened to be International Women's Day, as well as the date of Fleur's suicide. She left behind an open 'Letter to the Public,' in response to which Lu Xun wrote an essay that used a quotation from Ruan's letter as his title: 'Gossip Is a Fearful Thing.' The story as it has come down to us is about the tragedy of a beautiful and talented woman destroyed by the power of the press and by a patriarchal society. In his film, Kwan includes a scene where Ruan turns in desperation to the progressive director Choy, who refuses to go away with her because he, too, has a mistress in Shanghai and a wife in the country.

These official details, however, are merely the starting point of the film by Kwan, whose main interest we soon see is not biography but something quite different: the investigation of a legend. The film begins with a number of haunting stills from Ruan's early films, all copies of which have disappeared. This sets the tone and serves to underline from the outset a point made once again by Paul Virilio when, writing about the 'mysterious star system, which becomes essential to the young spectacle industry,' he observed that 'the star is only a spectre of absorption proposed to the gaze of the spectator, *a ghost that you can interview*.'[14] Ruan, the greatest star of all, is still remembered more than fifty years after her suicide: she is, as Maggie Cheung who plays her in the film says, a legend. But the condition of being a legend is a certain ghostliness, as fame is no more than the sum of misunderstandings gathered around a great name (as Rainer Maria Rilke said). The ghost as figure that we first saw in *Rouge* is recapitulated in another modality in *Center Stage* and used to study Ruan Lingyu as legend. (Interestingly enough, both 'ghosts' return after fifty years.)

How then do we go about interviewing a ghost? Drawing on autobiography and personal experience, as Ann Hui did in *Song of the Exile*, is obviously inappropriate. Rather, Kwan introduces a double structure by adopting a quasi-documentary style on top of the fictional film narrative, a structure that parallels the double temporal framework in *Rouge*. Also as in *Rouge* something unusual happens with this structure: the functions assigned to documentary and to fiction film are the reverse of their more usual functions. It is the fictional or narrative part of the work that recounts the known facts of Ruan's life, while it is the documentary part that provides the elements of speculation and exploration. If the 'official story' documents only the stuff of legend into which Ruan herself disappears yet again, then something else must be introduced to disturb this fatal structure. Hence all those interviews with the present-day actresses Maggie Cheung and Carina Lau (who plays Li Lili, Ruan's contemporary) where they compare their own experiences of stardom with those of their predecesors, or all the interviews with Ruan's surviving contemporaries or with her biographers and hagiographers. The point of this kind of documentation is not to establish the facts, which are only too much there, but to interpret them, to speculate about them. The documentary style is not used for greater realism (unlike in the work of Allen Fong); rather, it introduces a certain heteroglossia and allows other voices to be heard: snatches of Cantonese and Mandarin, as well as Stanley Kwan's own voice as interviewer/interrogator.

A large part of *Center Stage* is devoted to showing Maggie Cheung recreating famous scenes from Ruan's films made between 1929 and 1935, where a lot of attention is directed to the craft of acting. For example, we see Cheung as Ruan asking a friend about the painful experience of childbirth and then lying down in the snow to prepare for a scene in a 1929 film about a destitute mother protecting her child in the snow. Or we see Cheung as Ruan in the final deathbed scene of *New Woman*, struggling to get the expression right, being told by the director to draw on her own experiences. These scenes by Cheung filmed in color are then juxtaposed with the performances by Ruan preserved in black and white prints. The point about this procedure does not seem to be to establish the remake as a more or less successful pastiche of the original, or to emphasize the unassailable authority of the archieve. Nor are the reconstructions of Cheung as Ruan preparing for a scene, by connecting the required emotion to her 'real-life experience,' a recommendation of the artistic merits of method acting. Rather, this attention placed on acting and filmmaking makes the following point: in a very real sense *Ruan Lingyu is her acting*. It is not a question, therefore, of looking for a person behind the acting or conversely of identifying the person with the dramatic role: these are merely the most pathetic of fallacies, responsible for creating legend and gossip, turning an actress into a ghost. Rather, it is a way of representing the ghost as an actress.

What *Center Stage* poses, therefore, are the related questions of how to look at Ruan's films today and how to look at film culture in general. But these questions of form arise out of a cultural space where the act of looking itself is both the most developed and the most problematic act of all. Stanley Kwan's obsession with ghostly figures in his two best films turns out to be a method of evoking and representing critically the space of the *déjà disparu*.

Notes

1. Gilles Deleuze, *Cinema I*, trans. Hugh Tomlinson and Barbara Habberjam (Minneapolis: University of Minnesota Press, 1986), 211.
2. Jorge Luis Borges, *Labyrinths*, ed. and trans. Donald A. Yates and James E. Irby (Harmondsworth: Penguin Books, 1970), 169.
3. Paul Fonoroff, 'A Brief History of Hong Kong Cinema,' *Renditions*, 29/30 (Spring and Autumn 1988), 308.
4. Li Cheuk-to, 'A Review of Hong Kong Cinema, 1988–1989,' presented at the ninth Hawaii International Film Festival 1989, East-West Center, Hawaii.
5. Jeffrey Ressner, 'Hong Kong's Flashy Films Battle for American Fans,' *New York Times*, 9 May 1993, 18.
6. Geoffrey O'Brien, 'Blazing Passions,' *New York Review of Books*, 24 September 1992, 38–43.
7. See Walter Benjamin, 'Central Park,' trans. Lloyd Spencer, *New German Critique* 34 (Winter 1985), 42.
8. Quoted in a guest chapter by George S. Semsel, in John Lent, *The Asian Film Industry* (Austin: University of Texas Press, 1990), 28.
9. Quoted in ibid. 113.
10. Paul Virilio, *The Aesthetics of Disappearance*, trans. Philip Beitchman (New York: Semiotext[e], 1991), 20.
11. See I. C. Jarvie, *Window on Hong Kong: A Sociological Study of the Hong Kong Film Industry and Its Audience* (Hong Kong: Centre for Asian Studies, 1977).
12. See David Harvey, *The Condition of Postmodernity* (Cambridge and Oxford: Blackwell, 1990).
13. Paul Virilio, *The Lost Dimension* (New York: Semiotext[e], 1991), 30–1.
14. Virilio, *The Aesthetics of Disappearance*, 54.

6

KUNG FU: NEGOTIATING NATIONALISM AND MODERNITY

Siu Leung Li

Introduction

'Kung fu', as a cultural imaginary consecrated in Hong Kong cinema since the 1970s, was constituted in a flux of nationalism during the historical process whereby China catches up with modernity. More specifically, it is a continuous and paradoxical cultural intervention useful for problematizing 'traditional heritage' in modern life. Partially, it constitutes the Hong Kong imaginary by negotiating the complex and conflicting experience of colonial modernity and post-coloniality.

In kung fu cinema, the restoration of a strong China and of national pride under colonial conditions is often effected through a fetishization of the male kung fu body imagined as an empowering fighting and self-defensive skill. The kung fu imaginary thus becomes a symbolic expression to reassert a Chinese subject in modern times. Yet paradoxically, it has a highly uneasy relation with modernization – if modernity is to be broadly understood as a break with tradition. Representing Chinese cultural essence, the kung fu imaginary is imbued with an underlying self-dismantling operation that denies it own effectiveness in modern life. This ambivalent filmic representation of kung fu as an always already self-negating imaginary problematizes the (re)claiming of a Chinese self and the problem of Hong Kong's self-invention in a 'home in perpetual transit' (Chan 1995: 22). It betrays an 'originary' moment of heterogeneity, an origin of itself as already impurely Chinese. How is 'Chineseness'

From *Cultural Studies* (2001), vol. 15, pp. 515–42.

historically imagined and unimagined by the British-colonized, westernized, capitalist-polluted, culturally-hybrid 'Hong Kong' in relation to its subject formation? Lee (1996: 266) suggests, 'Hong Kong cannot contest any China' because it is itself Chinese, yet '(c)ertainly, Hong Kong's menace to Beijing stems from its cultural otherness'. It is in this 'Hong Kong connection' – kung fu cinema was largely 'made in Hong Kong' – that lies a critical significance of Hong Kong as a defusing hybrid other within the dominant centralizing Chinese ideology, which is itself showing signs of falling apart incited by complex changes imposed upon by global capital over the past two decades.

This paper attends to those kung fu films in which kung fu *per se* is represented as essentially a traditional Chinese martial art using primary hand-to-hand combat, regardless of the degree of authenticity or accuracy in its on-screen depiction. The concern of this paper is the representation of kung fu on film (i.e. kung fu as a discursive construction), not the real-life practice of martial art itself. Focus will be put on those films in which the re(claiming) of 'Chineseness' in the context of 'China/foreign' confrontation and negotiation during the late nineteenth and early twentieth century, is imagined through the (de)construction of the myth of kung fu. It should be noted that 'foreign' (*yang*) is not a simple monolithic entity. At the very least, a western-*foreign (xiyang)* of Euro-America and an eastern-*foreign* (*dongyang*) of Japan is often clearly marked in the Chinese national imagination.

The late Qing-early Republican period (*qingmo-minchu*), a time when China was in imminent danger of being carved up by western powers and post-Meiji Japan, is often seized by kung fu films to provide for them a homely temporal space. But they are not only limited to this historical setting. Some important kung fu movies are set in contemporary times. Bruce Lee's *The Way of the Dragon* (1972) (re-titled *Return of the Dragon* in the USA) is a case in point. It is the story of a country bumpkin from the rural backwater of cosmopolitan British Hong Kong, who is utterly illiterate but equipped with formidable kung fu. He goes to Rome to rescue a female relative's Chinese restaurant from falling prey to a gang-related Italian businessman. Regardless of its contemporary setting, the film builds upon a deep structure of binary opposition: traditional China (intriguingly represented here by diasporic Chinese) versus the modernized west, just like most of the '*qingmo-minchu* kung fu films' do.

As the *qingmo-minchu* kung fu films gradually declined in the early 1980s, there emerged action films in contemporary settings that, for convenience sake, are sometimes labelled 'kung fu-action' or 'contemporary costume kung fu' films. These are often police and gangster dramas or Indiana Jones-type adventures packed with action choreography that demonstrates traces of kung fu. Most of these films (for instance Michelle Yeoh's *Yes, Madam* (1985), *Royal Warriors* (1986) and *Magnificent Warriors* (1987), Jackie Chan's recent hits from the *Police Story* series through *Mr Nice Guy* (1997) to *Rush Hour* (1998) (a Hollywood production), do not fall into the main focus of the present discussion, for their lack of immediately discernible Chinese martial arts as a local tradition, and their substituting more universal action sequences for national kung fu choreography. These films are distanced from the kung fu genre 'proper' and should be understood as a sub-genre that remotely feeds on yet delocalizes and transnationalizes 'kung fu'. They require a separate discussion beyond the scope of this paper.

Empty-hand Fighting in Liminal Space: from Martial to Art

Although the filmic representation of Chinese martial arts dates back to the prewar period, film critics generally agree that:

> Authentic Chinese martial arts (*wushu*) were not represented on screen until as late as the 1950s, when the *Huang Fei-Hong* series began production in the Cantonese film industry of Hong Kong. And it was not until the 1960s and 1970s that the martial arts came to be used as a powerful form of cinematic performance, again, principally in Hong Kong. (Sek 1980: 27–8)

Wong Fei Hung (Huang Feihong)[1] is a historical figure known in folk culture as a *qingmo-minchu* Cantonese kung fu master.[2] Almost ninety episodes of the 'Wong Fei Hung' film series, which feature the actor Kwan Tak Hing in the title role from 1949 to the 1980s, have become one of the major constitutive elements of Hong Kong popular culture. Although there has been a long history of kung fu in cinema, it was during the late 1960s to the late 1970s, the heyday of kung fu film, that it was firmly inscribed in the cultural imaginary. To a great extent, this cultural imaginary was constituted by, and constituting, popular nationalism.

The scene of Chinese kung fu fighters smashing Japanese karateists and western kick-boxers in empty-hand fighting has been a stereotypical cliché for years. The bulk of kung fu films in the 1970s and early 1980s belongs to the *qingmo-minchu* sort. The historical significance is that it is a period of transition from the demise of the Qing Dynasty (1644–1911) to the struggle for the formation of a modern nation, the Republic of China. Bruce Lee's *Fists of Fury* (retitled *China Connection* in the USA) (1972), Jackie Chan's *Drunken Master* (1978) and *Drunken Master 2* (1993), are all set in the early Republican period, while Tsui Hark's radical reinvention of Wong Fei Hung in his six-installment saga *Once Upon a Time in China* (1991–7) relocates the kung fu legend to the last tumultuous days of the imperial dynasty.

Throughout the 1980s and 1990s, although the broad socio-historical background was in general shifted to more 'universal' contemporary settings, it is symbolically significant and not a mere coincidence that the widely acknowledged first 'kung fu film', Jimmy Wang Yu's *The Chinese Boxer* (1970), is set against the backdrop of the early Republican era. The significance lies in the fact that it is a story of Chinese kung fu (very specifically the 'iron palm' style) crushing Japanese karate, set in the historical juncture when Japanese imperialmilitarists invaded the 'sleeping giant', which had just begun to come to terms with its shattered imperial past, and to articulate itself in modern terms while formulating its own nationalism.

Two points should be noted here. First, read in the context of European colonialism in its last phase, the cultural imagination about reviving China by Chinese living in British-Hong Kong has relied on the muscular and masculine[3] body 'accoutered' with traditional Chinese kung fu. Jimmy Wang Yu's 'iron palm' functions as a synecdoche of the invincible male Chinese body. This national imagination through kung fu (as part of a larger discourse of anti-colonialism) was in the beginning operating on gendered principles. It was already and has always been gendered as male.[4] (This is not to say that kung fu heroines do not exist. There have been numerous female kung fu stars of Chinese, Japanese, and western origins).[5]

The question of nation and subject building in the modern *and* colonial context is not straightforward. Jimmy Wang Yu, in fashioning his action-star image, was packaged as a skilled student of karate in real life – he demonstrated crushing tiles on television. Karate was the international *à la mode* martial art at that time. To live by colonial modernity in the 1970s, a Chinese might have to play karate but not the 'Shaolin fist'; that is to say, to be nationalistic and anti-colonial, one's imagination turned to kung fu. Living by this imaginary world was the simultaneous demarcation and collapsing of boundaries. No sooner had differences been discriminated than they were conflated.

Second, unlike swordplay films, the temporal setting of which naturally belongs to the ancient times when the fighting implements were the sword, hand-to-hand fighting kung fu films were in the beginning necessarily caught up in an ambiguously imagined time. Hand-to-hand fighting signals an in-between, heterogeneous, overlapping temporal space in which on the one hand, swords, weapons of the pre-industrial age, were already outdated and largely ineffectual, and on the other hand, firearms, the most efficient killing instruments in the age of modern science and technology, had to be employed sparingly only. While swordplay films verge on the realm of fantasy, kung fu films lean toward the realist mode[6] (the cyber age Hollywood 'kung fu' fantasies of *Mortal Kombat* (1995), *Mortal Kombat 2: Annihilation* (1997), *Street Fighter* (1995) and *The Matrix* (1999) belong to a different category).

This is where the ambiguity of the representation of kung fu lies: it is only in some kind of liminal space in the continuous spectrum between these polarities – ancient/modern, fantasy/realism – that kung fu as a cultural imagination can possibly emerge, and that the heroic bodies can be given seemingly logical and justifiable situations to punch and kick, and thus to reassert the myth of kung fu. However, as Kwai-Cheung Lo points out, a commitment to Hong Kong requires attention to a cultural self-awareness of Hong Kong's in-betweenness, its changing indeterminancy (Lo 1996: 106). Seen in this light, the kung fu imaginary is always already self-negating. The popularity of the kung fu genre perhaps constantly implies the difficulty, if not impossibility, of the representation of kung fu. Modern technology has become the greatest obstacle to a legitimate display of kung fu, even in imaginative forms. Burdened by its own outmoded imperial legacy, China in the first half of the twentieth century did not seem to have produced any technological artifact that could be cherished as a sign of power for the Chinese people to build upon and imagine their national identity and pride. The Japanese have jujitsu, karate (the power of tradition), as well as their (in)famous war machines during World War Two (the power of modernity), arguably consummated in the legendary fighter planes 'Zero'. It is not difficult to see the reason that (Hong Kong-)Chinese people have fallen back predominantly upon the traditional martial art in their cultural imagination to reclaim (at least physical) power and a local/national subjectivity in the modern world, for there has hardly been anything modern to cling on to.

It is such an irony that, according to an anecdote, the legendary kung fu master Huo Yuanjia (1857–1909) once said that martial arts were useless in the modern world:

> (I)f I were born several hundreds years ago, wiping off bandits with spears and sabers, it would be a piece of cake for me to gain high offices. With today's advanced technology and firearms, what's the use of martial arts and heroic courage? (Jin 1969: 148)[7]

Huo always occupies a place in Chinese martial art writing. He has been dramatized in many kung fu films and television dramas, and is exactly the revered mentor of the imagined hero Chen Zhen played by Bruce Lee in *Fist of Fury*. This anecdote reveals that the anxiety of the uselessness of kung fu in the techno-modern world already emerged at the point when modern technology came to China. This anxiety is often repressed in the fantasizing and mythicizing of the power of martial arts especially in the kung fu cinema. But it returns intermittently to haunt us: How is one to represent and to re-place kung fu in the modern world of technology?

In the anecdote, a friend of Huo's provides a simple and straightforward answer that is in tune with the nationalistic sentiments of the time. He consoles Huo:

> It's not right (to think that martial arts are useless). Several hundred years back, all people took the skills of spears and sabers as powerful. You wouldn't be an eminent hero because too many would have the skills. Nowadays our country fellows are sick and weak, I hope that you'll make the most of your skills and spread them to turn sick men into heroes. It's your job. (Jin 1969: 148)

The narrator of the anecdote tells us that 'Huo was thus greatly enlightened and he gathered money to establish the Athletic Club of Essential Martial Arts (*jingwu tiyuhui*) in Shanghai to promote physical education' (Jin 1969: 148).[8] Therefore, Chinese martial arts can at least be useful as a means to strengthen the Chinese body, which is seen by many people (but not all) as a basis for the revival of the feeble country. Huo's friend betrays a contradiction: while trying to convince Huo that he is useful with his martial arts, he also implies and reinstates indirectly that Chinese martial arts are really dying and disappearing, since only a few people are practicing them now, not mentioning the contemporary practitioners' unskillfulness. The irony is that the value of Chinese martial arts and Huo lies in their rarity. And their rarity is a result of their not being in need anymore in a techno-world, as Huo himself paradoxically points out. The fundamental contradiction between kung fu as a traditional fighting skill and the modern weaponry of firearms hangs there. The next question is: what modern space can kung fu effectively and legitimately claim for itself except in sport games, in the military as a supplementary and yet perhaps a shrinking part of training of soldiers, and to the few top martial artists as a lofty ideal of personal spiritual fulfillment and expression? Kung fu as a martial art is becoming more and more contra-modern at a time when even a kind of cyber-techno 'virtual war' has been envisioned. To situate itself in modernity, kung fu has to shift its emphasis from the martial (*wu*) to the art (*shu*).

The biggest embarrassment to the glorified kung fu representation in film is perhaps that firearms have existed and effectively been employed for at least 700 years, not mentioning that gunpowder was invented by the Chinese. When Oliver Cromwell in the mid-seventeenth century made good use of the power of rifles and cannons – as represented in the 1970 British film *Cromwell* – to fight for the redefinition of a nation ruled by the parliament elected by the people rather than submitting itself under King Charles' corrupt dictatorship, what were the Hong Kong people and filmmakers in the 1970s and 80s to do with 'empty-hand' kung fu in their imaginary quest for the anti-colonial national cause at a juncture when the British-Hong Kong Government began to introduce limited regional elections in the 'territory' (a term that had since replaced 'colony' in official colonial discourse)?

If kung fu films failed to reappropriate fragments of glamorous democratic history (something similar to that of *Cromwell*) for colonial Hong Kong in its narration of the imaginary homeland, a radical rereading of the kung fu genre can at least problematize conventional assumptions of monolithic identity, pure origin, and the myth of nation to counteract the reactionary official patriotic discourse in post-handover Hong Kong under the Tung Chee-hwa government. Kung fu films are not to be summarily swept aside as an ineffectual cultural imagination by ridiculing that the genre is all too incredible and easily subject to realist-rationalist dismissal; nor should it be simple-mindedly resolved by a complacent nationalist exultation of the genre as having symbolically redeemed the national pride of the Chinese people. The issue at stake is more complex than that.

The existential space for kung fu film has often to be invented through the formulation of arbitrary generic conventions (meaning that the spectator is not to ask the reason why) and the often crude design of plot to create specific situations for the dominant use of kung fu in fight scenes (meaning that the audience are rarely convinced). Imagine why the opium smuggler Han in Bruce Lee's American film *Enter the Dragon* (1973) totally forbids firearms on his private island? How come that Wong Fei Hung in *Once Upon a Time in China* has the skill and power to 'fire' a bullet using his thumb and middle finger to kill the American slave trader? And Tong Lung (Tang Long, literally 'Chinese dragon') in *The Way of the Dragon* amazingly counters firearms by homemade bamboo darts! Martial arts tournament, as the most glorious and legitimate form of kung fu display in the modern world, is used from time to time as a structural device in kung fu films, with *Enter the Dragon* being paradigmatic. (It is not a coincidence that the whole concept of *Mortal Combat* is conceived upon a once-every-generation martial art tournament on a mystic island between the good and the evil, the mortal and the supernatural, the earth and the Outworld.)

Embedded in a 'twilight zone' between the abandonment of swords and the advance of guns, over and over the kung fu genre has to imagine for itself an existential space which has very weak mimetic basis. A paradox arises for the fact that the uniqueness of this genre simultaneously relies to a great extent on 'accurate and faithful' representations of the 'authentic' performance of kung fu itself on screen, and on the extent to which dangerous stunts in kung fu-action films are to be performed real with no cheating camera work. The order of mimesis and the controlling aura of the authentic are best seen in the works of director Kar Leung Lau (Liu Jialiang) and Jackie Chan. Lau, himself a kung fu player, has gained the special reputation of arguably the most faithful interpreter of kung fu on the silver screen, because of his utmost respect to kung fu as a great cultural tradition. Jackie Chan's own performing of all the daredevil stunts has become his trademark. Chan once said on American television (I give a verbatim transcription here to retain Chan's charismatic style):

> When you watch Jackie Chan movie, no body can do it, very few people can do it. I do the stunts by myself. I think the audience come inside to see me is not the double. Twenty years sixty years later I can sit down to the theater in my home, I can tell the people: Hey, that's me. I don't think a lot of American actors, I don't think they sit down: 'Hey, that's me'. No, that's the double. (Chan, *Good Morning America* 1993)[9]

Kung fu is caught in a dilemma of representation: the traditional and the modern, the mimetic and the non-mimetic modes of discourse are coexistent and coextensive in the filmic imaginary, rendering it more relevant for cultural critics to attend to the incoherence, contradictions and instabilities of its meanings in circulation.

Kung fu films are not totally lacking in awareness of the impossible position of kung fu representations in the flux of modern reason. The very last moment of *The Way of the Dragon* is surprisingly self-reflexive, as film critic Cheng Yu (1984a, 1984b) has pointed out. In the last farewell scene, Tong Lung's friend (played by the comic actor Li Kun), as he sees Tong Lung walking away, gives the movie's last line: 'In this world of sabers and spears, the star of good luck has to be shining high on him wherever he goes'. The Chinese idiom *fuxing gaozhao* (literally 'luck-star-high-shine') is used here, implying that Tong Lung may be just lucky. He is not invincible. Cheng Yu regards this as 'the most human moment with the greatest self-awareness in Bruce Lee's films' (1984a: 22).[10] Tsui Hark's *Once Upon a Time in China* even self-dismantles its own kung fu myth by reiterating in a redemptively sober manner a stock scene that has been ridiculed in many parodies: i.e. the depiction of an indomitable Chinese kung fu fighter killed by western firearms. A variation of this motif of the fundamental 'uselessness' of kung fu in the modern world is represented in Jet Li's *Fist of Legend* (1994; directed by Gordan Chan). The most respected Japanese martial artist Fumio Funakoshi[11] (Yasuaki Kurata) asks Chen Zhen (Jet Li) questions about martial arts before they begin their duel: 'What is the most powerful combat skill?' 'What is the purpose of martial arts?' Chen replies, 'The most powerful combat skill is one that can strike down the enemy in the shortest time. Any skill that wins is the best skill.' 'The one and only one purpose of martial arts is to knock down the opponent.' Funakoshi tells Chen that he is wrong, that the best way to beat your enemy is to use a gun, that the purpose of martial arts is to realize the physical potential of human beings to the greatest limit. This last point is in fact a reiteration of an idea of Bruce Lee's about martial art. In *The Way of the Dragon*, Tong Lung explains to his waiter-friend, who knows no martial arts, that the essence of kung fu is 'to express oneself with no limit to disregard schools and styles'. Bruce Lee also said elsewhere, 'Ultimately martial art means honestly expressing yourself' (*The Pierre Berton Show*). By emphasizing the art and playing down the martial, kung fu seems to have located a possible space within modern reason and logic by re-categorizing itself as an expression of the human body.

The Ambivalence of the Body and the Name: Bruce Lee

Dissatisfied with western critics' elevation of Bruce Lee to cult status my mythicizing his kung fu at the expense of the Asian people's national concern, and arguing against an interpretation that buries Lee's 'nationalistic cause' in 'sub-Mishima psychology' (Teo 1992: 71)[12] and 'narcissism, a code word for homosexual imagery' (Teo 1992: 79), film critic Stephen Teo reinterprets Lee for the Chinese people from a nationalistic stance:

> In *The Way of the Dragon*, before his gladiatorial bout with Chuck Norris in the Roman Colosseum, Lee prepares himself, stretches his muscles, reaches down to his feet, and creaks all his joints. Here is a specimen of superb training, a fighter *all too humanly plausible – not the imagined warrior of an action movie director* (emphasis added). Lee's appeal lies here. A Chinese audience who sees him knows that *Lee has done all Chinese proud* (emphasis added); they all know that his skill is *achievable* (original emphasis), a result of fitness and training and not a given. Lee is a common man hero. (Teo 1992: 70–1)

Teo reads him in terms of 'the cause of Chinese pride' (Teo 1992: 71)[13] and the potentiality of national self-fashioning through rigorous body training. He also emphasizes a 'right' reading of Lee's 'true' aspirations (Teo 1992: 70, 79–80). Two intricately related points need to be addressed here. One is the emphasis on the 'realness' of the on-screen Lee in the figuration of a muscular body; the other is the question of nationalism as an interpretive strategy in cultural politics.

The coexistent and coextensive 'real' and 'less credible' in kung fu representation makes it a prerequisite on the part of the spectator to suspend rationality to a certain extent in order to conceive and receive the already suspended space of kung fu ('empty-hand fighting in liminal space') in the imaginative film world – it is a fictional space within a fictional space. To embrace and enjoy the pleasure of an imagined unitary national identity inscribed in the hero's body – a simultaneously 'all too humanly plausible' and an 'achievable' body – the spectator has to suspend his/her rationality to an extent far beyond the tolerance given to John Woo's not counting Chow Yun Fat's bullets. Suppressing intellect and the incredible in the kung fu genre and foregrounding emotion and the plausible, Teo's nationalist argument is built upon the validity of the 'real' of the kung fu hero on screen ('not the imagined warrior of an action movie director'). It is the attributes of the referent behind the representation – the body and identity of the 'real' Bruce Lee as powerful and 'Chinese' – that have intrinsic empowering values.

What is at stake is exactly how 'real', or how coherent and stable this sign and its referent can possible be in the larger representational context which Lee as the subject has been constitutive of, and in which Lee as the object is being constituted in the discourse in a continual process – from his sudden impact on world cinema in 1970 beginning with *The Big Boss* and his dying young in 1973, to the recent American remake of his legendary career in the 1993 film *Dragon: The Bruce Lee Story* and his final elevation to the Hollywood Walk of Fame in the same year. The latest phase of Lee's re-essentialization as a sign of 'Chinese' and Hong Kong pride was concretized first in the formation of the long overdue Hong Kong Bruce Lee Club in 1995 which reinforced the popular construction of Lee as the transcendental signifier of 'Chinese kung fu', and consummated in 2000 with the four-week Bruce Lee film festival organized by the Hong Kong Film Archive ('The Immortal Bruce Lee: From the Kid to Kung Fu Dragon'), supplemented by a 'Hong Kong Dragon Expo 2000' organized by the Bruce Lee Union and Jun Fan Jeet Kune Do Hong Kong Chapter. Hong Kongers have finally embraced their own hero in full at the turn of the millennium. But Lee as 'a common man *hero*' (emphasis added), as Teo claims him, has meaning only in so far that the notion of 'hero' is understood as a cultural construction reproduced and reinvented in time. The ecstasy of ethno national pride for the Chinese as subalterns relies on the continual reproduction of a heroic myth built upon the subaltern spectators' simultaneous 'hallucination' – the 'seeing what is not there' – of the stability and coherence of the narration of nation, and 'reverse hallucination' – the 'not seeing what is there'[14] – of the elusiveness and incoherence of the imagined nation.

The male kung fu body, which invokes a seemingly unitary Chinese national identity, has its history. The 1960s and 1970s in Hong Kong and Taiwan saw the rise of the so-called 'masculine-macho films' (*yanggang dianying*) (literally *yang* means 'masculine/brightness', the opposite of *yin*, the 'feminine/darkness'; *gang* means 'staunch'). This is mainly attributed to the influential action film director Zhang Che (Chang Che), active from the mid-1960s to the early 80s.[15] He is renowned for his swordplay and kung fu films in which he must depict his romantic hero's tragic death in slow motion, always in the famous mode of *panchang dazhan*, a figuration taken from traditional Chinese opera. It is the convention of depicting the hero with a wounded torso bandaged up to prevent his bowels from spilling out while he slaughters the bad guys in his last moments. Zhang Che has been explicit about his extreme dissatisfaction with the effemination trend in Chinese cinema, as seen in the dominance of actresses, which was a phenomenon, according to him, quite the contrary to Hollywood where men always dominated. He has contributed to turning the tide since the late 1960s by systematically advocating masculine-macho films. His 'most important "contribution" . . . remains the pioneering of a male oriented/dominated ideology in Hong Kong cinema' (Tian 1984: 45). The sociocultural urge for the justification of promoting this violent male-dominated genre was to help re-cultivate masculine strength in the Chinese national character which was said to have become too feminine. In the Eurocentric-Orientalism schema, China was relegated to the subjugated female other. Puccini's operatic representation of the East is revealing: China is Princess Turandot and Japan is Chô-chô the Butterfly. In modern Chinese literature, China has been metaphorically represented as a mother raped thousands of times, or an impotent father, making his son also incapable of sex.[16] Modern China was, to the disappointment of many Chinese people, not a masculine 'real' man. China's response to the challenge of the other has been to emulate the West, to be its equal, to become another 'West', to be and stand up like a 'man' against another man. When the West stereotyped its object of subjugation as female, the kung fu myth advocated, rather than dismantling the uneven hierarchy, the male/female binary and strove to reclaim China as male.

The obsessive display of the muscular male body has been a constant characteristic of Zhang Che's. Almost invariably, and often borders on absurdity, all of his heroes wear costumes exposing their muscular chests regardless of historical accuracy.[17] The ultimate body powerful culminates in Bruce Lee's narcissistic display of his unrivaled naked upper body which is at once wedded with the body of the Chinese nation and 'redeems' the effeminate Chinese man.

Lee's kung fu films, specifically *Fist of Fury* and The *Way of the Dragon*, in many ways (re)produced a naive form of masculine nationalist discourse radiating from his spectacular body. He demonstrated his well-built muscular body indulgently on screen one-and-a-half decades before Sylvester Stallone's

First Blood Part II: Rambo (1985). Flesh itself is not power; body-building is not an end in itself – it is the superb martial arts that give unsurpassed aura to the muscular body to make it a spectacular body and a metaphor for 'the cause of Chinese pride'. While Stallone's Rambo body is empowered by the external addition of hi-tech modern weapons, Lee's body powerful is a result of the internalization of hand-to-hand combat skills of traditional martial arts. And kung fu itself as a Chinese tradition 'naturally' lends itself to the construction of *amour propre* and the invention of the Chinese nation. Stallone and Lee's bodies embody different ideologies respectively: Rambo's a construct of Reaganite cold-war rhetoric; Lee's an imagined collective identity against imperialism and colonization.

The nationalistic narrative of *Fist of Fury* and its mythic representation of kung fu are never coherent enough to underwrite the claim of the body powerful. For what the film tells us is that, after all, it is the semiotic act of un-naming that ultimately exorcises the national humiliation (if it has really been exorcised at all). That explains why many people regard these two scenes in the film classic: (1) Chen Zhen's forcing two Japanese fighters to literally eat the 'words' 'Sick Men of East Asia'; and (2) Chen Zhen's smashing of the wooden sign 'dogs and Chinese are prohibited' put up at the entrance of a park in Shanghai. Chen Zhen never really enters the park after all, and he is finally killed by a blaze of bullets (in a posture of the defiance of death that has become a classic moment in kung fu cinema). However, his death does not negate the nationalistic heroism, for Chen/Lee has presumably already un-named the sick Chinese man. One of the most 'memorable' and actually most-quoted lines (in both forms of parody and homage) from the film – from the mouth of Chen Zhen/Bruce Lee – 'You guys remember well, the people from the Jingwu School are not weaklings' (Mandarin version); 'You guys remember well, Chinese are not sick men' (Cantonese version). This line was transformed into 'I tell you, Chinese are not sick man of East Asia' in Donnie Yen's 1995 thirty-episode TV remake also entitled *Fist of Fury* (Star TV and Asia Television). In either case, the healthiness of the Chinese nation is an absence. It cannot be directly evoked into presence; instead, it has to be defined negatively, by what it is not: 'Chinese are not sick men of East Asia'. From Bruce Lee to Donnie Yen, the outcry of un-naming ('Chinese are not') necessarily and simultaneously re-names that which is to be exorcised ('sick men of East Asia'). A voice has been found, but it is not a voice of naming that strides toward a movement of possession;[18] instead, it is a voice of un-naming that is paradoxically dispossessing and reinscribing the evil at the same time. Lee's outcry intensely and sensationally signifies the paradox of the ultimate exorcising power and sheer ineffectualness of the semiotic act of un-naming, which is presumed in the nationalistic narrative of the discursive field of 'Chen Zhen/Bruce Lee'.

In his self-scripted, self-directed *The Way of the Dragon*, Lee shows a most self-indulgent exhibition of his muscular body in two scenes: his early morning solo practice in the female relative's apartment and the scene of warm-up preparation before the duel with Chuck Norris in the Roman Colosseum. Norris' inordinately hairy and somewhat chubby body is in sharp contrast to Lee's sleek and solid body. It is Lee, a Chinese using Chinese kung fu (as claimed by the film character Tong Lung), overcoming the ultimate alien other, Chuck Norris, an American (the western-foreign other) using Japanese karate (the eastern-foreign other). The film was made at a time when karate was the most popular and most representative of Asian martial arts, to both westerners and Asians alike. Lee's asserted 'Chineseness' is reinforced in his constantly wearing traditional Chinese clothes called *tangzhuang*, or nicknamed after the rise of kung fu film as 'kung fu dress', and his naming of his martial art skills as 'Chinese kung fu'.

Earlier on in the film, in the first combat between Tong Lung/Lee and a group of 'Italian' gangsters in the back alley of his relative's Chinese restaurant, Lee pronounces to those 'foreign devils' (*gweilo*) through a waiter-friend's translation that he is going to show them real Chinese kung fu. He then crushes them using only several seconds. To the common knowledge of many spectators, Lee used his unique blend of combat skill named by himself as 'Jeet Kune Do' (literally 'Tao of the intercepting fist'). The conflation of Jeet Kune Do with traditional Chinese kung fu intentionally by the filmmaker and willingly on the part of the audience is revealing. Lee's own practice of martial arts is highly syncretic. He synthesizes any skill functional and effective, regardless of cultural, national, sectarian boundaries, into his Jeet Kune Do. His practice is probably the example par excellence of cultural hybridity from the realm of martial arts – an attempt to cross boundaries and to resist one single dominant. However, by the blending-hybridizing-syncretizing of any fighting styles into one style – his style – Lee ironically developed a system of his own, with a definitive name. 'Jeet Kune Do' – the non-style becomes a style, the non-hegemonic turns into an iconic overwhelming model to be adored and imitated (although the quintessence of Jeet Kune Do is said to be its inimitability). In any case, Lee's own school of martial arts is apparently not authentically 'Chinese'. Lee was forever propounding his martial arts philosophy of breaking boundaries. 'Chineseness' as identity is represented by hybrid entities. In the fight scene mentioned above, Lee's tongue-in-cheek pompous demonstration of the preparatory posture of some traditional kung fu style before he strikes in his Jeet Kune Do serves only to mark the difference between his style and traditional kung fu. It is again naming that brings an identity ('Chinese' kung fu) into being, and ultimately accomplishes an act (the quest for national pride).

The complex identities in the (self-)representation of 'Bruce Lee' are further constituted in Lee's play on binaries. In *Fist of Fury* and The *Way of the Dragon*, he respectively plays a poorly educated (Chen Zhen) and a simply illiterate character (Tong Lung). In real life, he went to university and studied philosophy. He was articulate and explicit in his anti-Orientalist stance. He said on a talk show, 'I have already made up my mind that in the United States I think something about the oriental, I mean the true oriental, should be shown'

(*The Pierre Berton Show*). But Lee's self-claimed 'Chinese national identity' and exploitation of nationalist sentiments are undercut and exposed by his own already multi-hyphenated and slippery identity – 'American-born-Chinese', 'Chinese-American', 'Hong Kong-Chinese', etc.; and by his boundary-crossing journey. His short life sees a circular back and forth between the US and Hong Kong: born in the 'old golden mountain' (San Francisco), grew up in Hong Kong and went 'back' to the US in his late teens, and again to Hong Kong in search for a career breakthrough in the late 1960s. He died in Hong Kong and was buried for good 'back' in the US (Seattle) – the beginning and the end converge eventually at the same point, leaving behind only intangible traces of a full circle. But, it is, to use Lee's own favourite metaphor, a 'circle with no circumference'. The questions that haunt postcolonials are pressing here: Who is representing whom? On what grounds? On whose terms? By what right? For whom? What/who exactly is being represented?

In interrogating the masculine body and subject formation in Hong Kong, Kwai-Cheung Lo argues that Lee does not fall into the 'Chinese hero' category because of his diverse background and that the 'Chineseness' his filmic image invoked is a distant and void China. His films carry little trace of local Hong Kong culture. All in all Lee's body fails to provide a solid ground to locate a specific Hong Kong identity and even pierces a 'hole' in the conventional signification of the icon (Lo 1996: 110–11). This insightful reading opens up the interpretative space around Lee's body, revealing the hollowness of Hong Kong identity to be 'filled out' by other bodies – animator Yuk Long Wong's body images prove 'the impossibility of a unified subject' while Jackie Chan's 'reveals (the) ambiguity of being both local and international' (Chan Lo 1996: 116). Following this line of critique but taking a slight step back, it seems that Lee's image somewhat prefigures what is to come in Chan and others. What if we 'ground' Bruce Lee's image back to the hole it punched out?

Bruce Lee, while constructing 'Chineseness' in the figure of his empowered muscular body on screen with sentimentally exploitative means, is simultaneously dismantling this icon. Lee's heterogeneity in martial arts and hybrid identity, diasporic journey and metropolitan aura account for the special imaginary link between his figure and Hong Kong, a place colonized, marginalized, hybridized, and yet privileged by a modernity given rise in the ambivalent interaction with the colonizer and western culture. A casual remark by Lee's wife further illustrates the role played by his figure in Hong Kong's self-invention. In recounting Bruce Lee's returning to Hong Kong from the US in 1970 and the fervent welcome given him by the local audience for his fame gained ironically through the ill-fated television series *The Green Hornet*, Linda Lee Cadwell said that Lee was like a 'hometown boy made good'(*Biography*: 'Bruce Lee', 1993). Lee's myth lies not merely in his being a master fighter. More important, the cult hero is an ethnic (Chinese) with a touch of the metropolitan: he philosophizes, theorizes 'Chinese kung fu' in the language of Zen-Buddhism-Taoism, and perhaps more fluent in the empire's language than in his native language. Bruce Lee and Chen Zhen fused into a discursive body that collapses the binaries of literacy/illiteracy, modernity/tradition, and westernization/Chineseness. In retrospect, he was an 'intellectual' traversing the 'third world' and the metropolis. He was inter- and transnational. In the complex process of cultural b(l)ending in the (post)colonial context, a conventional Chinese hero would at once tinted pre-modern, while a local (Hong Kong) hero too provincial and unsophisticated. Lee's image begs to be read as a cosmopolitan postcolonial in the Hong Kong connection, a former 'hometown boy' who carries the aura of the empire's modernity.

Later remakes of the story of Chen Zhen often conflated Bruce Lee and Chen Zhen into their characterizations, resulting in further instability in their subject formation and national imagination. Jet Li's Chen Zhen in *Fist of Legend*, contrary to the poorly educated Chen Zhen created by Bruce Lee, is an overseas student in Japan, attending Kyoto University. But it is so ironic that at the beginning of the film he (accidentally) breaks a fountain pen – a symbol of western modern technology and the power of reading and writing – in the chaos of a victorious fight against Japanese bullies. The intellectual identity fades away gradually after the early part of the film.[19] But Jet Li's characterization is still more complex than Bruce Lee's. Contrary to Lee's glorification of an unquestioned 'Chineseness' as against a constructed otherness, this time around Chen Zhen is depicted as explicitly borrowing the more effective and practical strikes and kicks from karate. He teaches his Chinese fellows the skills of the enemy's martial art. Embracing karate skills and having a Japanese girlfriend (Lee's Chen Zhen is committed to a Chinese woman and Lee himself married an American woman), Jet Li's Chen Zhen loves his country no less that Bruce Lee's, for he can distinguish between 'good' and 'bad' Japanese/foreigners. Blending part of the 'real' Bruce Lee into the characterization, the nationalistic and patriotic rhetoric is reproduced through co-opting instead of excluding heterogeneity. The anti-literacy gesture in the unstable imaginary figure derived from an intellectualism and pretentiousness inscribed in the representation of the persona. The inscription of these two interpenetrating and contradictory representations in one body conflating Bruce Lee/Chen Zhen/Tong Lung has engendered an ostensibly empowered, imaginary national body which is inherently an inconsistent signification.

Transfigurations of a Kung Fu Master: Wong Fei Hung Forever

At the time when Bruce Lee, as Chen Zhen and Tong Lung, was smashing and whamming his Japanese, Russian and American enemies in the utmost fury and bursting nationalistic anger and anguish, the conventional imagination of Wong Fei Hung in 'old Cantonese cinema' in Hong Kong, as an elderly patriarchal figure and folk hero in a self-contained local Chinese space[20] espousing Confucian virtues of righteousness and filiality, was gradually displaced, transfigured and replaced. The climactic moment of transfiguration and rebirth of this Cantonese kung fu figure in a late transitional and (post)colonial Hong Kong context is seen in Tsui Hark's *Once Upon a Time in China*.

Wong Fei Hung is virtually the kung fu master in the history of Hong Kong films, apotheosized by an 'old Cantonese film' series that spanned from 1949–1970, with altogether some eighty episodes made (Yu 1980: 80). The year 1970 has a symbolic significance in the present analysis: it signifies the beginning of an end. When the last episode of this 'old Cantonese' Wong Fei Hung series, entitled *Huang Feihong yongpo liehuozhen* (Wong Fei Hung courageously smashing the blazing battle formation), opened in August of the year, Jimmy Wang Yu's *The Chinese Boxer* – the first 'kung fu film' – was ready to release in December the same year,[21] concluding the year's Hong Kong film output, inaugurating a new 'kung fu film' era, and wrapping up the age of old-fashioned conventional Cantonese *wuda pian* (literally 'martial-art-fighting film'), most aptly represented by the Cantonese Wong Fei Hung series. In the following year came Bruce Lee's *The Big Boss* which started a legend and changed the vicissitude of Hong Kong cinema. The year also sees the temporary demise of Cantonese films for about five years (Yip 1982). Bruce Lee's three kung fu films made in Hong Kong were originally dubbed in Mandarin/Putonghua (see n10 above).

Among the major historical martial arts figures dramatized in kung fu films, Wong Fei Hung, a Cantonese martial artist, seems not to have caught much attention in the Chinese martial art world. His biographical accounts cannot usually be found in common Chinese martial art writings, while Huo Yuanjia, who was active in Tianjin and Shanghai, has often been give much recognition.[22] It is instructive that Wong, at most occupying the marginalia of martial art histories, was reinvented a popular legend by Hong Kong filmmakers in the margins of mainland/stream Chinese culture. It is this marginality as subversion, as well as Wong's being a Cantonese from the southern margin of China, that make this figure an indispensable concern in Hong Kong cultural studies.

Interestingly enough, Wong Fei Hung was intended to be recreated as 'a modernized "Fong Sai Yuk" or "Hung Hei Koon"' (both kung fu heroes in Cantonese folk legends) and a 'modernized heroic figure', to 'save the crisis of *wuxia* film', as Wu Pang (Wu Peng), the original director of the Cantonese series who made a total of fifty-nine episodes, states in his memoirs (Wu 1995: 6). The controlling tropes here are modernization and salvation, a pandemic and stubborn obsession shaping the cultural imaginary of modern China. It is a historical coincidence that this urge to modernize an old genre was proposed at the moment (1949) when the birth of 'new China' was proclaimed and the distancing of colonial Hong Kong from its fatherland entered a long phase. The inception of the Wong Fei Hung myth in Hong Kong popular culture came out of an awareness of the centrality of modern values: rationality and realism. The major characteristic of this series is its reflexive attention to a realistic mode of representation of martial arts emphasizing 'real combat'.[23] Ideologically, the series formulated a stable world of traditional Chinese community with its hierarchical Confucian values – benevolence and filiality are stressed (coincidentally vis-à-vis the sociopolitical upheavals and cultural uprooting in the mainland in the same period). If the series did accomplish its creator's task of saving the *wuxia* film at the turn of 1950 by appealing to rationality, realism, and traditional morality, it ended with the fall of the 'old Cantonese film' era in 1970 in failing to 'modernize' itself once again to catch up with the new technology of kung fu film and the shifting sensibilities of nationalism and colonial identity. To further examine this issue, let me turn to the actor who has been intriguingly conflated, will-nilly, with the filmic character in Hong Kong's imagination.

In the Cantonese 'Wong Fei Hung' series, the actor Kwan Tak Hing (Guan Dexing) (1906–96), who was also skilled in kung fu, played the role of Wong throughout. He had virtually become Wong's reincarnation. After the disappearance of the 'old Cantonese series' in 1970, Kwan reappeared from 1974–81 in four kung fu films playing the character of Wong, often occupying a supporting role in those plots.[24] It is reported that altogether Kwan played Wong Fei Hung in eighty-seven films, and this is noted in the 1994 Guinness Book of Records.[25] Although Jackie Chan plays the young Wong Fei Hung in his 1978 comic-kung fu classic *Drunken Master* and the sequel of 1993, and Jet Li in the first three and the last (also the sixth) of Tsui Hark's *Once Upon a Time in China* saga, Kwan remains in the imagination of most Hong Kong people the one and only 'real' Wong Fei Hung.

Kwan was trained in Cantonese opera in the warrior role-type (*wusheng*) and famous for playing righteous heroes on stage. He has been revered a 'patriotic artist' (*aiguo yiren*) for his resistance against the Japanese invaders during the Second World War and known for his contribution to charity work throughout his life. While Kwan's interpretation of the character of Wong as an embodiment of traditional Chinese values and Confucian morality has been firmly inscribed in the local imagination, and he himself being so patriotic and nationalistic a person, he was nevertheless honored an MBE (Member of the Order of the British Empire) in 1981 by Queen Elizabeth II. He delightfully accepted. The account here is by no means intended to be disrespectful in any way to Kwan; instead, it is taken as an instance pointing to the ironic and paradoxical colonial condition of Hong Kong. It is a further illustration of what Stephen Ching-Kiu Chan called 'a unique form of displaced Hong Kong identity' that has made it possible for Hong Kong people back in the 1950s to '*freely* identify themselves, no so much *with* the colonial government per se . . . as *within* the social imaginary determined consensually by tacit popular acceptance of the existing regime of power' (original emphasis) (Chan 1995: 24). In such a sociopolitical condition overdetermined by 'the Chinese cultural hegemony' and the 'existing British colonial rule' – the 'two antagonistic machineries of identity production historically instituted in our social imaginary', Hong Kong people can collectively and individually desire 'intermittently to become, alternately, "Chinese" and "non-Chinese"' (Chan 1995: 23). In this logic, not only could Kwan (and many other Hong Kong people) live as nationalistic Chinese while accepting OBEs, MBEs, CBEs, JPs, etc., but the Cantonese film world of Wong Fei Hung that Wu Pang and Kwan created in a British colony, set presumably in the last days of the Qing period when historically China was dreadfully threatened by western modernity, can also be represented as safely free of foreign threats. The imaginary of Kwan/Wong is essentially Chinese, self-sufficient, and complacently feeding on its traditional values. Following the supposedly anti-colonial cinematic convention of that time which is contradictory to realism – the Qing people were depicted without a 'pig-tail' – the Wong Fei Hung series manifests and floats in a suspended world of dislocated time frames collapsing the late Qing and the early Republican periods. Possibly a sign of Hong Kong's weak historical consciousness, the series fails to situate itself in historical time and dodges from issues of modernity and modernization with no scruples. Wu Pang's 'modernized Wong Fei Hung' is to be understood in a very limited sense. 'Nationalism' in the enclosed world of the Cantonese Wong Fei Hung series is represented in its promotion and preservation of traditional Chinese morality. In any case, the cozy, homely world where good always prevails over evil, and with only quarrels among Chinese country fellows, has to betray signs of disruption, of the irrepressible confrontation between the self (Chinese, colonized subject) and the other (foreign, colonizer).

In one of the later episodes of the series, the stable 'Chinese' kung fu world of the self is intruded by the alien other, as manifested by the threatening presence of a karateist, who is cheated into evil conspiracy against Wong by the arch villain – variations of this character-type in different episodes have always been played by the famous actor Shek Kin (Shi Jian) who plays Han in *Enter the Dragon*.[26] In this 1968 film entitled *Huang Feihong quanwang zhengba* (Huang Feihong: the boxing championship duel), the karateist challenges Wong with Japanese combat skills, and is defeated by Wong's kung fu. He is also taught a moral lesson in traditional Confucian virtues of benevolence, righteousness, tolerance and forgiveness. It is a classic formulaic structure that Wong Fei Hung (Kwan Tak Hing) almost always gives the arch villain (usually Shek Kin) a chance to repent.

But our reading can hardly end with this simple, traditional formula. There is a further confusion of identity in the characterization of the 'alien' karateist. Although he dresses unmistakably in Japanese costume and his major entrances are punctuated by traditional Japanese music, he is verbally identified by Wong's students as a northern-Chinese. Shoddiness in filmmaking might be the immediate reason for such an 'error'. Nevertheless, the karateist conflates two others in one body. He is a double-other: an other in terms of regional differences of the north-south divide within China, and a non-Chinese other in terms of his foreign combat style.[27]

The traditional imagination of the kung fu world in the 1960s could not possibly turn a complete deaf ear to the encroaching march of the other cultures and values from the 'outside', especially when Hong Kong's economic take-off and subject formation gradually took a significant turn in the same decade (Turner 1995). Wong Fei Hung did respond and attempt 'successfully' in his own world to contain the alien threats by reaffirming and reinforcing the traditional tool and its value – kung fu. But a newly invented vengeance-is-mine type of kung fu hero as exemplarily represented by Chen Zhen and Tong Lung has mostly displaced the traditional tolerance and forgiveness with their furious 'o-cha' punches and kicks. It is in Tsui Hark's *Once Upon a Time in China* – made after the traumatic experience of the 4 June bloody crackdown of the pro-democracy movement in Beijing 1989 and when Hong Kong entered the last years of its handover transition – that the provincial imagination of this traditional kung fu figure and the one-dimensional anti-foreign fury of the Chen Zhen-type were ruptured, diffused and reconfigured in a more complex and imminent condition of (post)coloniality and decolonization. Wong Fei Hung was reinvented once more as a national hero but perplexed by the infusion of modernity into this rapidly changing reality of demising tradition and semi-coloniality. While Bruce Lee's Chen Zhen loses his 'father' (his kung fu mentor Huo Yuanjia), Tong Lung's father is an absence (he only talks about his uncle in Hong Kong), and Kwan Tak Hing/Wong Fei Hung is a 'father', Tsui Hark's Wong Fei Hong has a father but is not one himself. In the 1990s' imagination, he was a man in the process of becoming a father, resituated in an extremely unstable historical moment of China's first modern revolution; a symbolic figure repositioned in a disruptive site of struggle and negotiation intersecting Hong Kong, China and the colonial other as Hong Kong was coming to terms with the return to the fatherland. Was the illegitimate child (the Crown Colony of Hong Kong) not the guilt of an effeminate father (China)?

The circulation of heroic masculinity inherited from the tradition of kung fu films, especially Bruce Lee's wrath and Zhang Che's masculine-macho, takes on a different turn in *Once Upon a Time in China*. Tsui Hark incarnates into the male hero's body the possibilities and potentials of China's yet-to-be-accomplished self-strengthening, putting into question and at once reproducing a masculine nationalist project to confront western encroachment in the rethinking of modern Chinese history. The masculine is recast in Wong as a more pensive hero, with a more intellectual style. The muscular is relocated in the unnamed bodies of Wong's legion of muscular students, who, in their bare torsos, are depicted in a breathtaking ultra-wide shot in the opening credit sequence as practicing kung fu in great spirit and discipline gilded in the early rays of the red sun on a vast beach seemingly stretching to the limit of heaven and earth. In the grand nationalist discourse, China has always aspired to be a strong man.

The theme song of the film borrows its melody from a traditional Cantonese tune *jiangiunling*, which had already been used successfully for decades by the original Wong Fei Hung series as its 'signature tune'. In fact '*jiangiunling*', 'Kwan Tak Hing', and 'Wong Fei Hung' have in the cultural imagination of Hong Kong people become a 'trinity', each of them evokes one and the same 'entity'. The theme song of *Once Upon a Time in China* is entitled 'Men Should Self-Strengthen' (*Nan'er dang ziqiang*) with a set of sentimental yet uplifting new lyrics. This song title also became the original Chinese title for the first sequel, known only as *Once Upon a Time in China 2* in English, which Tsui Hark once said on a radio talk show in 1996[28] was his own most favourite work so far. Apart from its explicit masculinist stance, the interesting circular logic of the lyrics is that the purpose of self-strengthening is to become a great man (*fenfa ziqiang zuo haohan*) and that since men are men they should self-strengthen (*jishi nan'er dang ziqiang*). Therefore, masculinity and the national cause were already (con)fused as one. In addition to the political-allegorical dimension of the *Once Upon a Time* saga as the filmmaker's critique of being Chinese today, its theme song which boosts masculinity in a nationalist undertone has become more politically charged when democratic supporters in Hong Kong began using it annually in rallies protesting the 'June 4 crackdown'. With another set of new lyrics, which are undoubtedly solemn, moving, and dramatic but equally masculinist and nationalist, the song is re-titled 'Memorial to the Great Men' (*Ji haohan*) by the 'Hong Kong Alliance in Support of the Patriotic Democratic Movement in China'. Throughout the entire lyrics, only the male pronoun 'great men' (*haohan*) is used to stand for those who were killed during the 'June 4 crackdown' in Beijing. This elegy was most powerfully heard at the demonstration rally for the release of the Chinese political dissident Wei Jingsheng in December 1995 when the Beijing Government once again unjustly sentenced Wei to another fourteen years. The song was also sung in the June 4 1999 candlelight vigil held at Victoria Park, around 70,000 Hong Kong people gathered,[29] ten years after the suppression.

Political crises in the modern Chinese context seem to be invariably associated with the national cause. The national imagination is obsessively engendered through the reclaiming of masculinity even beyond the filmic world of kung fu. Commenting on Hong Kong people's use of the 'Wong Fei Hung' tune in the June 4 memorial rallies, Xu Jiatuan, former head of the Hong Kong Xinhua News Agency who fled to the USA after the 1989 crackdown, once said that 'this psychological state of using the song to speak out really makes one uncertain whether to mourn or to laugh'(*zhezhong jiege fahui di xintai, zhen shiren tixiaojiefei*). Negotiating between mainland China's hegemony and Britain's colonization, this kind of twisted strategies of political expression – resetting a commercial-sensational-nationalistic song to protest against the fatherland's hegemony – is perhaps the most poignant statement of the compressive absurdity of the transitional and (post)colonial condition of Hong Kong. Adding to this already bitter irony is that this twisted means of expression was validated under the 'patronage' of the colonizer before the handover.

Compared to Bruce Lee's myth of kung fu and nationalistic sentiments, Tsui Hark's heroes are inherently incoherent figures, perplexed by the problem of ethnicity, identity, and cultural self-positioning in unsettling historical moments. Tsui Hark's Wong Fei Hung no longer adheres to or upholds Confucian moral values. He is at a loss in this traumatic transition, losing grip of the traditional values yet not knowing how to adapt to new times. At the same time when the film and its sequels cling on to a masculinist notion of equating men with national strengthening, destabilizing elements are brought into the narrative by Wong's Aunt Thirteenth, a 'westernized' yet 'Chinese' woman who returns home from England. Switching between Victorian dresses and Chinese costumes, Aunt Thirteenth, the feminine, embodying uncertainties and represented as an agent of Europeanized modernization, enchants Wong and drives him to rethink China's situation and its future. This seemingly simple-minded subordinate female character embodies subtle nuances in relation to the film's nationalist discourse.[30] Yet the feminine here is also co-opted into the modern project of progress. When Aunt Thirteenth offers to make a western suite for Wong, he asks, 'Aunt Thirteenth, are foreign countries really that great? Why . . . do we have to emulate others?' The very same 'fact' is (again!) reiterated; she explains, 'They invented the steam engine and many other things. Their science is more advanced than ours. If we don't learn, we'll be left behind.' The eternal game of catching up with the West seems to be, paradoxically, a necessity in the nationalist project on non-West peoples. While Bruce Lee ostensibly sets up oppositions between China and the West, the oppressed and the oppressor, the good and the bad, Tsui Hark resorts to a naive synthesis of the East and the West. In *Once Upon a Time in China 2*, the scene of Wong Fei Hung the Chinese herb doctor and the British-trained medical doctor Sun Yatsen, each using his own medical practice to help the victims in the besieged British embassy, epitomizes the director's idealistic solution to China's catch-up in the uneven game of power in modern history.

A kung fu film by genre, *Once Upon a Time in China* has its unsettling aspects in that it dismantles the kung fu myth that it represents to en-gender the fantasy of a strong and masculine nation. By reiterating that the male Chinese body, however profusely imbued with fabulous Chinese kung fu, is no match for western firearms, this dynamic film seems to be falling back to a hackneyed device. Yet it is exactly at a moment of cliché that rupture is produced. In the film, Yan Zhendong (literally 'vitalizing the East'), a good-natured northerner who has achieved the legendary skill of 'the iron cloth' (meaning that no weapon can penetrate his 'body of steel') is wandering in the southern province of Guangdong, jobless and excluded by southerners as an alien other. The character's status of being subaltern within a subaltern people constitutes a tragic tension that informs the film's reflection on the Chinese national questions. Reminiscent of the older Wong Fei Hung films, he is lured by the local scoundrels to fight against Wong. But Wong the kung fu master does not overcome him this time; the villainous Americans with rifles kill him. His 'body of steel' is perforated like a beehive in a climactic slow motion sequence. Of course the depiction of a seemingly indomitable Chinese kung fu fighter killed effortlessly by gunshots has for a long time been a farcical cliché. It appeared cynically on Hong Kong television gag shows at the height of the kung fu heat in the 1970s and is analogously repeated in Steven Spielberg's *Raiders of the Lost Ark* (1981) in which Indiana Jones in the most inappropriately smug expression shoots dead an Arab swordsman who brandishes his weapon in the most dizzying way. The significance of the reenactment of this motif in *Once Upon a Time in China* is its unexpected serious-mindedness in reiterating a cliché. Yan utters these last words to Wong: 'No matter how great our kung fu is, it is no match for western guns'. It is a dominant characteristic of Tsui Hark to make direct thematic statements in his films which are often to the degree of embarrassment, if not insult, to the audience. That the scene in question is so excessively self-expository and highly self-dismantling has in effect greatly redeemed its preaching stance. This soberly and self-reflexively treated figure in relation to the film's reflection on the predicament of China's self-*re*placement in face of its own cultural degeneration and western imperialism puts it in another category as a sharp contrast to the arrogant and Orientalist travesty in *Raiders*.

KUNG FU: THE 'LEGEND' CONTINUES . . .

Jet Li's *Fist of Legend*, an update of Bruce Lee's *Fist of Fury* after twenty-two years, symbolically acts to reinstate the kung fu legend invoked in the bodies of Huo Yuanjia, Wong Fei Hung, Bruce Lee and Chen Zhen. It conjures the ultimate legend that the Chinese 'spirit of the martial' (*shangwu jingshen*) is indestructible. It is implied that this spiritual quality gives rise to the eternal strength of China as a nation. The arch Japanese villain in the film, General Fujita, states that although Japan has defeated China in military terms, the final conquest of the Chinese people depends on the destruction of this legend. Thus Huo Yuanjia the kung fu icon has to be annihilated by all means. Fujita shares 'wisdom' with General Crassus (Laurence Olivier) in *Spartacus* (1960): 'However, this campaign is not alone to kill Spartacus. It's to kill the legend of Spartacus.' The essence of history making and self-invention seems to rest ultimately in the realm of the discursive and the imaginary. The numerous military defeats of China since 1841 were a signification of its failure on the road to modernity, and accounted for 'Hong Kong' becoming Hong Kong the British Crown Colony. The legend – something that has no 'real' existence – is to symbolically redeem China from this historical disgrace. Bruce Lee's kung fu 'fury' is mythicized to a kung fu 'legend' in late-colonial/transitional Hong Kong with an optimistic twist (Jet Li's Chen Zhen survives and joins the resistance against Japanese militarism). Yet the films' self-reflexivity renders it a self-dismantling fantasy of its own legend of indestructibleness.

The filmic representation of kung fu often envisions a contest between tradition and modernity with a self-denial of modernity caught in a liminal temporal space imagined somewhere in modern history. Jackie Chan and other action stars' transformation of the kung fu genre into action films set against international contemporary backdrops sees the disappearance of 'kung fu' and the emergence of a more universal action choreography that disseminates transnationally. One can at best call it 'kung fu-action'. The trajectory of success of these 'kung fu-action' stars ironically parallels the continuous unveiling of the incoherence of the kung fu imaginary which registers Hong Kong's anxious process of self-invention. The unitary national imagination evoked through the kung fu body only dissembles the impossibility of its own imagination, which seems to be an ineluctable Hong Kong condition. If Hong Kong's colonial history makes the city a troublesome supplement, then the Hong Kong cultural imaginary will always be latently subversive, taking to task delusive forms of unitary national imagination. The latest round of this radical impossibility is manifested in the flux of the desire for internationality in the discursive performance ranging from the Hong Kong SAR Chief Executive Tung Chee-hwa's 1999 Policy Address imagining a 'world-class city' to post-handover big-budget action films aspiring to transnational and global dimensions, e.g. *Who Am I?* (1998), *Hot War* (1998), *Extreme Crisis* (1999), *Gen-X Cops* (1999), *Purple Storm* (1999), *Tokyo Raiders* (2000), *AD 2000* (2000), *Time and Tide* (2000), *Skyline Cruisers* (2000), *Gen-Y Cops* (2000). These films, largely in the footsteps of Hollywood in terms of their scope of perceptions and CG effects, are more often than not imbued with unique Hong Kong 'kung-fu action'. All in all, they are performative acts emerged in the midst of Hong Kong's sudden, intense, post-97 realization of the encroachment of'time and tide' – to allude to Tsui Hark's film of the same title – that Hong Kong is in the process of turning into 'another Chinese city'. The time of the kung fu genre ended coincidentally in the year 1997 with *Once Upon a Time in China and America*, the sixth and last installment of Tsui's Wong Fei Hung saga (produced by Tsui himself and directed by Sammo Hung).[31] If Hong Kong cinema still has the power to explain Hong Kong culture as it had before 1997, it seems that it does not dwell much in the kung fu genre discussed in this paper. For now, the tide has turned to a new 'transnational action' genre exemplified by the films mentioned above. These transnational action films, some of which are very much 'kung fu-action' à la *The Matrix*, can be seen as a further transformation of the contemporary 'kung fu-action' genre that points to a more cosmopolitan Hong Kong culture. We will have to wait and see the next return of the kung fu legend in Hong Kong cinema.

Notes

1. I shall give both the Hong Kong-style Cantonese transliteration and the mainland Chinese pinyin system for names and titles with Cantonese origin, with the pinying appearing in square brackets in the first appearance of the term. All other romanizations are in pinyin except for those personalities who have been commonly known in their English names or other spellings.
2. Wong Fei Hung, according to Yu Mo-Wan, was born in 1847 and died in 1924 (1980: 79). Ho Ng offers slightly different dates: circa 1855–1920 (1993: 147). Zeng (1989: 135) gives the same dates as Ng's.
3. Yvonne Tasker coined the notion 'musculinity' to refer to the action heroines in film and to signify a combination of 'muscularity' and 'masculinity' on the female body: 'That is, some of the qualities associated with masculinity are written over the

muscular female body. "Musculinity" indicates the way in which the signifiers of strength are not limited to male characters' (1993: 149).

4. Related comments can be found in Sek (1980), Rayns (1980, 1984), Cheng (1984a, 1984b).
5. American martial artist Cynthia Rothrock is probably the best known Caucasian woman in kung fu cinema. Recently Malaysian-Hong Kong-Chinese Michelle Yeoh (aka. Michelle Khan) has come into the international spotlight, starring in the Bond film *Tomorrow Never Dies* (1998) and Ang Lee's *Crouching Tiger Hidden Dragon* (2000).
6. Sze Man-hung briefly discusses the relation between *qingmo-minchu* background and the realism of kung fu films (1995: 281–2).
7. The author Jin Enzhong was a martial artist and military man during the Republican era. His own preface dates September 1933. All translations from Chinese are mine.
8. The school was set up in 1910, according to Matsuda (1984: 264). The original Japanese version of Matsuda's book was published in Tokyo in 1979. Today, the Jingwu School has branches in various Asian cities, including Hong Kong and Singapore.
9. Chan talked to Joe Segal in an interview on *Good Morning America* (Feb. 24, 1993).
10. Cheng Yu also points out that this last line in the original Putonghua voice track was later changed in the Cantonese track to: 'Tong Lung deserves people's respect wherever he goes' (1984a: 22). For many years in Hong Kong, only the Cantonese version of *The Way of the Dragon* was available on videotape and on video laser disc. In 1996, the film was released on VCD (video CD) by Mei Ah Laser Disc Co. with both Putonghua and Cantonese voice tracks. DVD versions of all Lee's kung fu films were released in late 1998, with two to three voice tracks and a selection of subtitles in eight or nine languages.
11. The naming of the character as 'Funakoshi' is obviously a deliberate choice, since the 'father' of karate is called Gichi Funakoshi. Coincidentally, he was a contemporary of Huo Yuajia. But when Funakoshi began to spread his karate in Japan in around 1909, Huo was already poisoned to death by a Japanese doctor in Shanghai.
12. A different version of this article appears as the chapter 'Bruce Lee: Narcissus and the Little Dragon' in Teo (1997).
13. The western critic in question here is obviously Tony Rayns (op. cit.). Teo in this article does not quote Rayns directly, but he names him in his 'Bruce Lee' chapter in *Hong Kong Cinema* (1997: 113).
14. Talking about the cultural space of Hong Kong, Ackar Abbas, borrowing from Freud, writes, 'It is as if both locals and expatriates were suffering for a long time from what Freud called "reverse hallucination". As hallucination means seeing what is not there, so reverse hallucination means not seeing what is there' (1993: 2).
15. See Zhang for his personal accounts of his conception and practice of *yanggang dianying* (1989: 51–66).
16. See the poems of Yii Kuang-chung (Yu Guangzhong), 'Qiaoda yue' (Percussion music) and 'Dang wo si shi (When I'm dying). See also Yu Dafu's 1921 novel *Chenlun* (Sinking).
17. Zhang did not regard this shoddiness as important at all. See his response to his critics (Zhang, 1989: 54–7).
18. Susan Bassnett quotes Carlos Fuentes's notion of 'movement of possession' in her discussion of the naming of postcolonial reality in magical realism (1993: 89–90).
19. It is an unfortunate incidence that this film led to a case of 'macho violence'. The incident was on the headlines of many Hong Kong newspapers on 15 August 1995. The night before, a man was wounded outside a video rental shop by a gunshot fired by an off-duty policeman. There was a brawl between the two men who struggled to snatch the newly released laser video disc of *Fist of the Legend*. For details, see *Ming Pao* (15 Aug. 1995: A3).

20. Referring to 'older Cantonese movies', Ackbar Abbas states that 'the local was an ethos of exclusion: it defined a narrow homogeneous social space where foreigners and foreign elements had no place, which is what gives these old movies, when we watch them now, a certain campy quality' (1994: 69). Abbas is here generalizing all 'older Cantonese movies'. It should be noted that it is not infrequent that those Hong Kong people depicted in Cantonese films of the 1950s and 1960s have overseas connections and movements, although mainly with diasporic Chinese communities in south-east Asian locations like Singapore and Malaysia. Some plots of those 'old Cantonese films' are 'tales of two cities' which take place between Hong Kong and overseas locations. There are others that are set in Japan and New York Chinatown. For more information, see *Overseas Chinese Figures in Cinema* (1992).
21. Dates based on *Filmography of Chinese Martial Arts Films* (1980).
22. The biographies of Huo and his son Huo Dong'ge (1895–1956) are featured in Matsuda (1984), Yang (1986: 224–5) and Li *et al.* (1987: 224–5). Huo Yuanjia's biography in Jin is one of the longest in this book (1969: 142–9). All four works give no biographies of Wong Fei Hung. It is interesting to note that Wong's student Lam Sai Wing (Lin Shirong), but not Wong himself, has a brief biography in *Zhonghua wushu cidian*. In a historical work solely devoted to Cantonese martial artists, Wong has a five-line account while Lam's biography occupies one full page (Zeng, 1989: 135–7). The scarcity of extant written information about Wong may account for this last incident.
23. On the cover of the souvenir book of the first Wong Fei Hung film entitled *Huang Feihong zhuan* (The true story of Wong Fei Hung) (1949), we read these phrases following the names of the actors: '*quanbu yinggiao yingma/quanbu zhenjun yanchu*' – meaning 'it's all hard-hitting/it's all actual fighting'. An image of this cover can be found as an inset in *City Entertainment*, 450 (11 July 1996): 16.
24. For a filmography of Kwan Tak Hing, see *City Entertainment*, 450 (11 July 1996): 16.
25. Adding together the thirteen-episode Wong Fei Hung television series that Kwan made in 1976 for Television Broadcasts Co. Ltd. (TVB), there are a total of 100 episodes of Kwan's 'Wong Fei Hung' acting career (Chan, 1996: 14).
26. Rayns has an interesting observation on the final duel in this film in which Shek Kin fights Bruce Lee: 'The fight scene between the two actors, however awkwardly filmed, closes a circle in Chinese cinema lore, linking the conservative traditions of *wuxia pian* of the 1950s with the world-conquering ambitions of the *wuxia pian* of the 1970s. In these terms, the outcome of the fight (the death of the villain) is much less important than the fact that the fight takes place at all' (1984: 29). The '*wuxia*' used by Rayn should more accurately be read as 'kung fu'.
27. The actor playing this ambiguous character is in real life a northerner. In Bruce Lee's *Fist of Fury* he plays a truly Japanese character who is killed by a plummeting samurai sword pierced through his body in a fight against Chen Zhen.
28. In an edition of the talk show *Chengren zhiji* (Adult buddies) on Commercial Radio 1, 11:30 pm to 1:30 am, hosted by filmmaker Manfred Wong.
29. According to the organizer, the Hong Kong Alliance in Support of the Patriotic Democratic Movement in China.
30. Borrowing from Heidegger's concept of *technè*, Kwai-Cheung Lo sees Aunt Thirteenth as 'the embodiment of a dazzling kind of knowledge (which I would like to term *technè* . . .) that keeps presenting and opening itself to Huang and soliciting him to respond in kind' and reads 'their relationship as a possible correlation between man and technology . . . what Aunt Thirteenth represents is the affable, feminine aspect of this threatening technology, which is ultimately accepted along with love, whereas the aggressive, masculine side of technology, represented by the western imperialists and slave traders, has to be expelled and "overcome" ' (1993: 83–4).
31. As the film title suggests, Wong Fei Hung's adventure this time takes place in the American 'wild wild west'. Jackie Chan's latest Hollywood venture *Shanghai Noon*

(2000) follows this structure of 'journey to the West', embedding Chinese kung fu in the American western. Chan's hero has no difficulties dodging bullets from the cowboys and undergoes an initiation: the realization that he is a slave of repressive tradition Chinese values and that emancipation is brought about by Euro-American ideas of freedom. The underlying Orientalism and the editing-oriented action sequence have disappointed a few critics as well as fans back home.

REFERENCES

Abbas, Ackbar (1993) 'The last emporium: verse and cultural space'. *Positions*, 1(1): 1–17.

Abbas, Ackbar (1994) 'The New Hong Kong cinema and the *Déjà Disparu*'. *Discourse*, 16(3): 64–77. Also in Ackbar Abbas (1997) *Hong Kong: Culture and the Politics of Disappearance*. Minnesota: University of Minnesota Press.

Abbas, Ackbar (1996) 'Cultural studies in a postculture', in Cary Nelson and Dilip Parameshwar Gaonkar (eds) *Disciplinarity and Dissent in Cultural Studies*. New York: Routledge.

Bassnett, Susan (1993) *Comparative Literature: A Critical Introduction*. Oxford: Blackwell.

Biography: 'Bruce Lee' (1993) CEL Communications, Inc. and Arts & Entertainment Network.

Chan, Ching-kiu Stephen (1995) 'Future un-imagined'. *Hong Kong Cultural Studies Bulletin*, 4: 20–6.

Chan, Pak Sang (1996) 'Jingdao yidai zongshi Kwan Tak Hing' (In memoriam of the great master Kwan Tak Hing). *City Entertainment*, 450: 14–16.

Cheng, Yu (1984a) 'Anatomy of a legend', in Li Cheuk-to (ed.) *A Study of Hong Kong Cinema in the Seventies*. Hong Kong: Urban Council.

Cheng, Yu (1984b) 'Li Xiaolong: Shenhua huanyuan' (Bruce Lee: unveiling the myth), in Lan Shing-hon (ed.) *A Study of Hong Kong Cinema in the Seventies*. Hong Kong: Urban Council.

'Filmography of Chinese martial arts films' (1980) in *A Study of the Hong Kong Martial Arts Film*. Hong Kong: Urban Council.

Good Morning America (1993) ABC, Feb. 24.

Jin, Enzhong (1969) *Guoshu Mingrenlu* (Records of celebrities in Chinese Martial Arts) (prefaced 1933). Taipei: Hualian chubanshe.

Lee, Gregory B. (1996) *Troubadours, Trumpeters, Troubled Makers: Lyricism, Nationalism, and Hybridity in China and Its Others*. Durham: Duke University Press.

Li, Daojie, Chen, Daoyun and Hu, Jinhuan (eds) (1987) *Zhonghua Wushu Cidian* (A Dictionary of Chinese Martial Arts). Anhui: Renmin Chubanshe.

Liu, Damu (1979) 'Chinese myth and martial arts films: some initial approaches', in Lin Nien-tung (ed.) *Hong Kong Cinema Survey*. Hong Kong: Urban Council.

Lo, Kwai-cheung (1993) 'Once upon a time: technology comes to presence in China'. *Modern Chinese Literature*, 7: 79–95.

Lo, Kwai-cheung (1996) 'Muscles and subjectivity: a short history of the masculine body in Hong Kong popular culture'. *Camera Obsura*, 39: 105–25.

Matsada, Ryuchi (1984) *Zhongguo wushu shiluë* (A concise history of Chinese martial arts) Lu Yan and Yan Hai (trans.) Chengdu: Sichuan Kexue Jishu Chubanshe.

Ng, Ho (1993) *Xianggang Dianying Minsu Xue* (Enthnology of Hong Kong Cinema). Hong Kong: Ci wenhua tang.

Overseas Chinese Figures in Cinema. Law Kar (ed.) (1992) Hong Kong: Urban Council.

Pierre Berton Show (1971) Canadian Broadcasting.

Rayns, Tony (1980) 'Bruce Lee: narcissism and nationalism', in Lau Shing-hon (ed.) *A Study of Hong Kong Martial Arts Films*. Hong Kong: Urban Council.

Rayns, Tony (1984) 'Bruce Lee and other stories', in Li Chenk-to (ed.) *A Study of Hong Kong Cinema in the Seventies*. Hong Kong: Urban Council.

Sek, Kei (1980) 'The development of "martial arts" in Hong Kong Cinema', in Lau Shing-hon (ed.) *A Study of Hong Kong Martial Arts Films*. Hong Kong: Urban Council.

Sze, Man Hung (1995) 'Cong Guan Dexing, Li Xiaolong, he Cheng Long de wuxia pian kan gongchan pian yingxiong xingxiang de zhuanhua' (The transformation of the hero figure in Hong Kong films from Kwan Tak Hing, Bruce Lee, to Jackie Chan), in *Xianggong wenhua yu shehui* (Hong Kong Culture and Society). Hong Kong: Centre of Asian Studies, University of Hong Kong.

Tasker, Yvonne (1993) *Spectacular Bodies: Gender, Genre and the Action Cinema*. London: Routledge.

Teo, Stephen (1992) 'The true way of the dragon: the films of Bruce Lee', in Law Kar (ed.) *Overseas Chinese Figures in Cinema*. Hong Kong: Urban Council.

Teo, Stephen (1997) *Hong Kong Cinema: The Extra Dimension*. London: British Film Institute. Tian, Yan (1984) 'The fallen idol – Zhang Che in retrospect', in Lau Shing-hon (ed.) *A Study of Hong Kong Martial Arts Films*. Hong Kong: Urban Council.

Turner, Matthew (1995) 'Hong Kong sixties/nineties: dissolving the people', in Matthew Turner and Irene Ngan (eds) *Hong Kong Sixties: Designing Identity*. Hong Kong: Hong Kong Arts Centre.

Wu, Peng (Wu Pang) (1995) *Wo Yu Huang Feihong* (Wong Fei Hong and I). Hong Kong: n.p.

Yang, Wuet et al. (eds) (1986) *Jianming Wushu Cidian* (A Concise Martial Arts Dictionary). Harbin: Heilongjiang Renmin Chubanshe.

Yip, Foo Keung (Ye Fuqiang) (1982) 'Liushi niandai Xianggang yueyupian yu shehui bianqian' (Hong Kong Cantonese film and social changes in the 1960s), in Shu Kei (ed.) *Cantonese Cinema Retrospective (1960–69)*. Hong Kong: Urban Council.

Yu, Mo-Wan (1980) 'The prodigious cinema of Huang Fei-Hong: an introduction', in Lau Shing-hon (ed.) *A Study of Hong Kong Martial Arts Films*. Hong Kong: Urban Council.

Zeng, Zhaosheng et al (eds) (1989) *Guangdong Wushushi* (History of Cantonese Martial Arts). Guangdong: Guangdong Renmin Chubanshe.

Zhang, Che (Chang Che) (1989) *Huigu Xianggong Dianying Sanshi Nian* (A Review of Hong Kong Film in the Last Thirty Years). Hong Kong: Joint Publishing Co. Ltd.

7

UNDER 'WESTERN EYES': THE PERSONAL ODYSSEY OF HUANG FEI-HONG IN *ONCE UPON A TIME IN CHINA*

Tony Williams

Rather than being read in exclusively postmodernist terms, Tsui Hark's series Once upon a Time in China *may be understood as a new version of a Hong Kong cinematic discourse involving historical 'interflow.' It deals with dispersion, China's relationship to the outside world, and strategic forms of reintegration designed to strengthen national identitity.*

In Sammo Hung's *Wong Fei Hung Ji Saam* (*West Territory Mighty Lion/Once upon a Time in China and America*, 1997), Master Huang Fei-hong (Jet Li Lian-jie) travels to the Wild West to visit an American branch of the Po Chi Lam Clinic set up by his student Sol. During the journey, he bangs his head against a rock in a turbulent stream and loses his memory. He is rescued by a friendly tribe of Indians. Moments before we see Huang again, an Indian emerges from a tepee proudly announcing the birth of a child. When Huang recovers, he stumbles around in the Indian camp wearing an Indian costume, and his loose unbraided hair is flowing like an Indian's. After using his martial arts prowess to defeat a hostile Indian, who ironically mouths racist American platitudes against the outsider – 'His clothing is different, his skin color is different, his speech is different' – Huang is adopted into the tribe and given the name 'Yellow.' Before this, he attempts to remember events of the recent past. But his vague recollections reveal images reproducing culturally blurred boundaries paralleling his sense of ethnic and geographic displacement. During the recent past of his

From *Cinema Journal*, 40: 1, pp. 3–24.

stagecoach journey through America, Aunt Yee/Thirteenth Aunt/Shishanyi (Rosamund Kwan Chi-lam) had taught him English while Seven/Club Foot (Xong Xin-xin) watched Huang. Club Foot then expresses his yearning for a traditional bowl of Chinese rice rather than Western diarrhea-inducing beans. Huang's memory returns in images that mix his actual national memory with the new experiences he encounters in his unfamiliar new environment. While Yee and Seven repeat their earlier lines, their Indian counterparts inhabit their bodies. The Indian princess (Chrysta Bell Eucht) wears Yee's Western costume and asks Huang, 'What is your name?' Her brother takes Club Foot's position on the stagecoach. Stranded traveler Billy (Jeff Wolfe) is now an Indian, and Huang finally falls from the coach pierced by an Indian lance.

These images form minor incidents in the entire narrative structure of *Once upon a Time in China and America* (1997), the sixth part of Tsui Hark's epic series. However, as Zhang Ailing (Eileen Chang) once remarked, if historical issues may 'be found in life's irrelevance,'[1] significant structures of feeling may appear in visual and sound motifs seemingly marginal to the main narrative. In *Once upon a Time in China and America*, these motifs echo themes that dominate the entire series produced by Tsui Hark, namely, the continuing challenges of historical change and geographic relocation and the need for constant adaptation whenever the Chinese hero finds himself in new situations.

The *Once upon a Time in China* series represents one of the major achievements of 1990s Hong Kong cinema. Focusing on the character of legendary martial artist Huang Fei-hong, the series differs from its predecessors by dealing with issues central to contemporary Hong Kong as it reached the end of one historical epoch and moved toward another. In 1997, Hong Kong lost its status as a British crown colony and became reunified with mainland China.

Although the series is set in the historical past, like most Hong Kong New Wave films, it also looks with foreboding at the implications of reunification as each film was made increasingly closer to the date of that event. By casting mainland Chinese actor Jet Li Lian-jie (who had relocated to Hong Kong) in a role popularly associated from 1949 to 1983 with Cantonese veteran film and television actor Kwan Tak-hing, the series raised questions of continuity and change. Like their fictional counterparts in the series, Hong Kong inhabitants faced problems associated with the new historical era that raised questions about their formerly secure sense of identity. During the late nineteenth and early twentieth centuries, the Chinese people underwent a turbulent series of changes in cultural perspectives and political realignments, increased their contact with Western powers, and were confronted with new technologies. Because of its status as a crown colony, Hong Kong remained relatively free from the challenges facing the motherland. However, this changed in the 1980s and 1990s, when the colony faced a different form of challenge. By focusing on issues faced by the mainland in the historical past, the *Once upon a Time in China* series raised questions that were also relevant to the contemporary population of Hong Kong. Would old values suffice any longer? How would people cope with change and possible loss of identity? Would another form of diaspora, whether mental or geographic, be possible?

The series indirectly suggests some possible resolutions, albeit in a fictional manner. It also works on two levels. First, it deals with the perennial problem of China's relationship to the Western world as perceived by its traditional-minded hero. Huang Fei-hong, who adapts to the turbulent circumstances around him in each part of the series. But, second, it functions as an allegory for the changes the Hong Kong population faced as it moved toward 1997.

Because of censorship, Hong Kong films generally avoided direct representations of political issues, especially one as explosive as reunification. In the light of the 1989 Tiananmen Square massacre, Tsui Hark's series attempted to address issues of change, adaptability, and the possible diaspora facing Hong Kong's people, who were known for settling in different parts of the globe, as well as for being identified with their national homeland. Since the series gradually sees its hero moving in a Western, rather than an Eastern, direction, Part Six naturally locates him in America. Once again, issues concerning the relationship between traditional and modern Western values come to the forefront in Tsui Hark's contribution to this perennial cultural debate.

Many features of the *Once upon a Time in China* series are thus not entirely divorced from the present: dispersion, China's relationship to the outside world, and strategic forms of reintegration designed to strengthen national identity. This latter aspect is crucially important throughout the series. Parts Two and Four argue against xenophobic, isolationist tendencies, which hampered Chinese development in the twentieth century from the Boxer riots (1900) to the mainland Chinese cultural revolution (1965–8). Throughout the series, Hark implicitly argues for a realistic, open-minded appraisal of issues affecting Chinese national identity and the need for change and compromise. It is a message as relevant to the pre-1997 population of Hong Kong as it is to Hark's own fictional reconstruction of Huang Fei-hong, who moves from a position of cultural certainty to confront twentieth-century encroachments affecting his previously secure sense of Chinese identity. In reuniting with the motherland, the formerly lost orphan of Hong Kong faces similar issues of cultural readjustment. Hark attempts to negotiate these problems both allegorically and cinematically by using the figure of Huang Fei-hong as a cultural focus who represents the problematic aspects of cultural identity and the necessity for continual readaptation.

Historical 'Interflow' versus Postmodernist Strategies

Mingyu Yang sees the *Once upon a Time in China* series as a contemporary mythic and allegorical response to the 1997 crisis that marked Hong Kong's return to mainland China.[2] Although Yang notes the historical background that structures each film, he believes each work reflects an ironic carnivalesque postmodernist strategy that blurs history, politics, and fiction and that parodies the traditional concept of the hero played by Jet Li-Lian-jie. Yang notes that several historical, literary, and cultural codes have determined several of the representations of the real Huang Fei-hong (1847–1924), whose actual historical significance has become clouded by myth and legend.[3] Although Yang makes a plausible case for his particular interpretation, the series may be read quite differently. As Stephen Teo has pointed out, certain Hong Kong films might be defined as postmodernist; however, Hong Kong cinema displays its own particular form of postmodernism, which may not parallel Western models regarding the supposedly relative and redundant nature of history. Indeed, it is a postmodernism fully cognizant of the important roles of cultural, historical, and political questions.

Seeing Tsui Hark as one example of this special Hong Kong phenomenon. Teo points out that many causes and effects influenced it, such as 'new wave aesthetics mixed with Cinema City-style slapstick, anxiety over 1997 and the China syndrome, the assertion of Hong Kong's own identity as different from China, and a new sexual awakening arising from an increasing awareness of women's human rights and the decriminalization of homosexuality.'[4] Even the diversely opposite postmodernist films of comedian Stephen Chaio exhibit social and historical features, such as criticism of 'Hongkie' snobbery against mainlanders and the recognition that Hong Kong society 'has successfully sidestepped or leapt over stages of orthodox development.'[5] The version of postmodernity presented in Hong Kong cinema may be more concretely grounded in culturally understood real issues and more historically grounded than its Western counterparts. Indeed, what is regarded as postmodernism in Western terms is not really applicable to the Chinese cultural situation at all.

As Raymond Williams notes in *The Politics of Modernism*, what may appear novel or 'postmodernist' often belongs to familiar patterns of a particular culture or history mistakenly regarded by scholars from another generation as a new theoretical discovery.[6] This is also the case with certain postmodernist definitions of the series *Once upon a Time in China*. As Law Kar notes, from the very beginning of its history, Hong Kong cinema has always engaged in a culturally significant form of 'interflow' between the two geographic locations of America and China. This particular 'interflow' involved several interesting cultural mergers. During the 1930s and 1940s, Chinese personnel worked on Grandview productions in America for exhibition to Chinese audiences. Other aspects 'interflow' involved figures such as the original cinematic Huang Fei-hong, Kwan Tak-hing (1906–96). Law Kar points out that Kwan regularly performed on the West Coast during the 1930s. He returned to America shortly before the Sino-Japanese War and toured with the Dai Guang Ming company. 'In his autobiography, Kwan says that he was taught archery and the use of the whip by Native Americans. He adored Western films and their costumes and remained fond of togging up as a cowboy even into his 70s and 80s.' By incorporating elements of different cultures, Hong Kong cinema exhibits an 'ever-changing identity,' appearing as 'open-minded, eager to experiment in various topics and genres never in a fixed pattern, never stopping.'[7]

Thus, cinematic experiments dealing with pastiche and reintegration were already occurring in the pre-postmodernist era in the recent historical past. Rather than defining Hark's series exclusively according to Western post-modernist parameters involving the blurring of boundaries and pastiche, it is perhaps better to recognize the series as one that takes history seriously. As a work involving 'historical interflow,' the series takes its version of history seriously and does not regard it as a redundant 'grand narrative' according to Jean-François Lyotard's understanding in *The Postmodern Condition*. The series may not be historically accurate, but it does take history seriously within its various fictional structures so as to present messages to audiences facing new historical challenges within their own era. In fact, the series may thus best be seen as a new version of what Law Kar understands to be a significant cultural and historical 'interflow' cinematic discourse characteristic of Hong Kong cinema.

By relating the dilemmas faced by Huang Fei-hong in his various encounters with the Western world to the realization that old conservative traditions are now redundant. Hark uses his reconstruction of a fictional past to comment on contemporary problems. He urges audiences to remember previous past dilemmas and to engage in those specific concepts of adaptability and flexibility so as to cope with new situations, even if it means radical personal change and geographic relocation. Although set in the historical past, the series offers a response to contemporary issues that is not entirely postmodernist in nature but related to Hong Kong's earlier cinematic strategies.

Jet Li as Huang Fei-hong

Tsui Hark commented on Huang Fei-hong that he was a hero who 'had a hard time being a folk hero,' who found it 'painful to carry such a heavy load,' and whose standards 'weren't necessarily correct.'[8] Thus, rather than defining Huang Fei-hong as a postmodernist parody, Hark presents him as a complicated, flawed individual who has to learn from each situation he encounters and discard any traditional 'baggage' that hinders his self-development. When asked about the first film in the series, Hark commented on the complex historical issues facing Huang that the Master's traditional training failed to supply him with appropriate answers to the new cultural, political, and technological problems facing him. For Hark, 'The difference between this film and the others is that there is more emphasis on the Chinese coming to terms with foreign things. In a situation when you must accept something new and you have no idea what that is, you'd be dying for a standard to measure it against.'[9] Unlike Kwan Tak-hing's traditional prototype, Hark's version finds no reliable standards on which Huang Fei-hong may conduct his everyday existence in relation to issues involving Western values.[10]

Hark's conception of Huang Fei-hong is similar to – as well as significantly different from – the original series featuring Kwan Tak-hing. As Héctor

Rodriguez has shown, 'Huang's evolution as a cinematic hero was rooted in the convictions and preferences of the groups and individuals producing and consuming the films, as well as in the institutional context and historical circumstances of their creation and dissemination.'[11] The character played by Jet Li Lian-jie operates according to similar circumstances, several generations later; however, differences between the original series and Hark's conception involve not just the choice of actors but authentic historical concerns. As Rodriguez notes, the original film's 'self-imposed mission was to protect the traditional sources of Cantonese cultural identity from the ravages of time and circumstance,'[12] according to Confucian principles, Kwan Tak-hing's Huang Fei-hong also dominated the original series by virtue of his strong, controlling character:

> Social harmony invariably depended on Huang Fei-hong's capacity to thus educate those around him through the sheer exemplary force of his upright behavior. By illustrating the power of virtue, the plots reaffirmed Confucian conceptions of harmony, civility, and self-containment that marked the protagonist as a civic-minded guardian of the Chinese nation's moral stature and an instrument of social reform.[13]

Several changes occurred in the 1990s. The setting of Hark's series was less local and more international as Western powers threatened Chinese national identity. Furthermore, although historical and industrial factors resulted in the original series having more internal concerns since filming in mainland China was impossible, Hark's series operates on a much broader geographic canvas, with the hero moving throughout China and eventually traveling to America. For example, Part Three uses Forbidden City locations that were off limits to both American and Hong Kong directors until after the Cultural Revolution. Outside historical influences now make remaining in a local community impossible. Jet Li Lian-jie's hero has to move with the times – mentally and geographically – and hence does not have the advantage his predecessor (Kwan Tak-hing) did of relying on a secure sense of cultural stability.

Hark's choice of an actor is also important. Jet Li Lian-jie's Huang is much younger and more adaptable than his predecessor. Kwan usually played Huang as a venerable stern patriarch whose judgment was unquestionable. Student obedience was obligatory – at least during the 1940s and 1950s. In the *Once upon a Time in China* series, Huang often learns from others, such as the Western-educated Aunt Yee, and his students help him out in difficult situations. The only time this ever happened before was in Yuen Woo-ping's *Yung Je Mo Gai* (*Brave No Fear/Dreadnought*, 1981) when naughty devotee Mousy (Yuen Biao) saves Kwan's Huang from the villain by practicing his own kind of laundry kung-fu, which he did not learn from the venerable master. Furthermore, in Yuen Woo-ping's *Lam Sai Wing* (*Benevolent No Enemies/The Magnificent Butcher*, 1979), mischievous student Sammo Hung even mimics his revered teacher, something his more reverent predecessors would have found unthinkable during the 1950s and 1960s. Kwan Tak-hing was associated with Cantonese culture from the beginning of his film career in the 1930s to his final performance in Clifton Ko's *Daa Foo Ji Ga* (*Big Rich Family/It's a Wonderful Life*, 1994). Although Kwan plays the grandfather in a modern family, both his traditional costume and the musical leitmotif associated with his most well known character identify him with Huang Fei-hong.

In contrast, Jet Li Lian-jie is a more flexible and adaptable actor whose persona crosses more cultural and geographic boundaries. Born in mainland China, Jet Li Lian-jie first came to fame when he starred in the first martial arts movie filmed in the People's Republic of China. *Siu Lam Ji* (*Shaolin Temple*, 1982). However, although he had traveled abroad and visited America, his film career did not really take off until Tsui Hark cast him in *Once upon a Time in China*. Jet Li's star persona is thus more adaptable to changing historical and industrial circumstances than Kwan Tak-hing's, as his debut appearance as the villain in *Lethal Weapon* 4 (1998) demonstrates. Such a change in role would have been unimaginable for Kwan Tak-hing. Already undergoing a process of cinematic and cultural transformation in the early 1990s, Li was the ideal actor to embody a fictional character coping with serious historical challenges to his screen character than Kwan Tak-hing, who always remained rooted in the traditional values of Confucius.[14]

Once upon a Time in China as Hark's Version of Historical 'Interflow'

Producer-director Tsui Hark sees the series as embodying a particular type of historical 'interflow' that differs from earlier versions. As a talent educated in America who, like John Woo in *Hard Target* (1993), has recently suffered from the 'curse of Van Damme' in his recent Hollywood cinematic excursions, Hark has also faced problems of cultural diaspora similar to those of his screen hero. Nonetheless, his films take the challenges of historical factors more seriously than the previous films in the series, such as Yuen Woo-ping's *Jui Kuen* (*Drunk Fist/Drunken Monkey in the Tiger's Eyes/Drunken Master*, 1978), which starred Kwan and other figures such as Jackie Chan.[15]

Unlike the earlier films, external historical issues intervene more directly. Parts Two and Three of the series introduce actual historical figures Sun Yat-sen, Lu Hao-dong, Dowager Empress Ci Xi, and Premier Li Hong-zhang, albeit in fictionalized situations. Their roles, however, occupy minor positions in a text that deals with the development of a hero whose progress involves integrating features of Western culture into his persona. Throughout the series, the plot details represent important aspects of Hark's own version of the 'historical interflow' represented by the different era in which he works. They form necessary features of any thorough interpretation of this highly significant series.

The first film raises problems that the other five answer in their own ways. *Wong Fei-Hung* (*Once upon a Time in China*, 1991) begins with a Lion Dance, characteristic of entries belonging to the original Kwan Tak-hing series (1949–70) and to later versions, such as *Dreadnought*. The prologue begins in

1875 with Huang and the actual historical figure of General Liu Yong-fu of the Black Flag Corps watching a Lion Dance performance on his ship, which is anchored off the coast of Fushan. Several ships of different nationalities are nearby. Disturbed by the sound of firecrackers, some French soldiers shoot at the Lion Dance performers before they realize their mistake. The incident prompts Huang to retrieve the lion head before it falls in humiliation. Prior to being sent to Viet Nam to fight the French, General Liu appoints Huang as the martial arts trainer of his corps – a reference to one of the few historical facts we know about the real Huang Fei-hong. Liu says to Huang, 'Foreign ships are anchoring in our docks. Britain has Hong Kong. Portugal has Macao. Russia, Hei long jian.' General Liu also orders his men to dismantle a plaque that reads 'Our Land, Our People.' He now finds the plague disturbing and presents Huang with a fan inscribed with the insulting terms of the Unequal Treaties the Western powers forced on the weak Manchu government as an encouragement to vigilance. After General Liu comments, 'When I return I hope the treaties will be ended,' the film's credits appear and the main narrative begins.

Thus far, the film appears to resemble later mainland nationalistic epics such as Xie Jin's *Yapian Shanzheng* (*The Opium War*, 1997), which was designed to encourage Chinese feelings of solidarity against the Western invaders. As Sam Ho notes, the film 'is marked by a one-dimensional characterization of Westerners,' including 'greedy American slave traders, trigger-happy French soldiers, haughty officials, and hypocritical missionaries.'[16] Of course, not all the Chinese characters are entirely virtious, either. As Rey Chow points out, there is a danger of reading the problematic question of Chinese identity in a one-dimensional manner. The film does a great disservice to the issue's inherent complexity, as well as to China's relationship to the imperialist West. According to Chow, this relationship is 'seldom purely "oppositional" ideologically; on the contrary, the point has always been for China to become as strong as the West, to become the West's equal.'[17] This strategy not only characterizes Law Kar's inclusive definition of Hong Kong cinema but also Tsui Hark's project as a director from the moment he employed George Lucas's Industrial Light and Magic technicians in *Zu, Warriors of the Magic Mountain* (1980).

One of the recurrent characteristics of the first three films is Yee's competence in operating Western technological apparatuses such as a still camera and a primitive movie camera. The series not only develops a romantic relationship between Huang and Aunt Yee, in contrast to the earlier Kwan Tak-hing films, but it also depicts the hero's involvement with a Western-educated heroine who believes in a different set of values and technology. Frequently dressed in Western costume, Yee speaks fluent English as well as Chinese. After living in England for two years, she tells Huang that her heart was always with her people in China. She begins the process of educating Huang about Western technology such as steam engines: 'If we don't learn we'll fall behind,' she says. Eventually, Huang agrees with her ideas: 'Everything will change. China will change with the world.'

Although still affirming his Chinese identity by the end of the film, Huang realizes the need for adaptability – unlike the hypocritical Chinese theater owner who curses Yee behind her back as a 'Chinese pretending to be a *gweilo*.'[18] As Kwai-Cheung Lo remarks, 'She is the embodiment of a dazzling kind of knowledge (that I would like to term as *techne*, not exactly equivalent to technology, though it is always translated as such) that keeps presenting and opening itself to Huang and soliciting him to respond in kind.'[19] Although sometimes deferring to Huang's patriarchal status as a traditional male master, throughout the series Aunt Yee also educates him subtly about the values of Western culture and technology.

In addition to helping Huang realize the superior nature of Western fire-power, she introduces him to Western cuisine and cutlery during the introductory train sequence in Part Two. Unlike her female predecessors in the original series, Aunt Yee plays a highly significant role in helping Huang accommodate his Chinese character to the new challenges of the Western world. She never resembles the usual Hong Kong female cinematic character, who is transplanted back to a past world whose patriarchal values would never allow her presence in the first place; Aunt Yee is much more realistic. Frequently seen in Western costume and operating modern technology, she represents the series' idea of a 'New Woman.' Nevertheless, Aunt Yee also recognizes the restraining nature of the various cultural, historical, and sexual boundaries surrounding her. For example, although she cannot openly express her love for Master Huang like a modern woman, she does lead him away from his rigid patterns of behavior toward more flexible postures much as her classical Hollywood prototypes did for their husbands in films such as *Life with Father* (1947).

Since the entire *Once upon a Time in China* series involves movement from one geographic location to another, it also posits a particular definition of diaspora related to questions of national and cultural identity. Chow defines her project of 'writing diaspora' as 'to *unlearn* that submission to one's ethnicity such as "Chineseness" as the ultimate signified,' as well as negotiating new forms of cultural identity.[20] Such negotiations characterize Huang's development throughout the series. Ugly one-dimensional Westerners certainly appear, but for each such negative character, such as the American slave trader Jackson and the intrusive missionaries of the opening scenes, there are others who contradict the tendency toward overt stereotyping. Indeed, Jackson's Westernized Chinese agents eagerly recruit their unwary countrymen for slave labor in America. Although Huang finds that no Chinese (on whose behalf he actively intervened) will testify against the Shaho gang leader, the Jesuit missionary he earlier spurned saves him from jail by testifying on his behalf. Ironically, during the later attack, the missionary takes the bullet meant for Huang, the bullet fired by Jackson's associate Tiger, in a manner reminiscent of the 'bad' dance hall girl in Hollywood Western movies. Not all *gweilos* are bad!

Problems concerning national identity are brought out in the characters of Huang's students. Butcher Lang/Lin Shirong/Porky (Kent Cheng Juk-si) initially criticizes American-educated, non-Chinese-speaking Bucktooth/Sol (Jackie Cheung Hok-yau) for his lack of ethnic identity, urging him to 'go back to America.' Despite his difficulty in speaking Chinese, however, Sol eventually learns to warn Huang after meticulously practicing his speech beforehand. Although Huang temporarily relapses into anti-Western tirades against both Yee ('Just like a *gweilo*, coming along for trivia') and Sol ('Speak Chinese, you infidel'), he eventually benefits from their help. He learns from Yee that kung-fu is no defense against a bullet and avoids the fate of Master Yim (*Yee Kwan Yan*). Similarly, by rapidly giving alternative coordinate instructions in English, non-martial artist Sol deflects the cannon of Jackson's ship so it doesn't fire on Huang. Sol confuses the American soldiers so much that they end up destroying British Captain Wickens's ship! Neither revered masters nor martial arts experts, the Westernized Yee and Sol intervene during significant moments and use their Western expertise to aid a hero who benefits from that knowledge. After the theater massacre, Huang contemplates a Western gun and bullet. He remarks to Yee, 'You're right. Chinese must change. Fists can't fight guns,' and fires the bullet with his fingers, foreshadowing the strategy he will use against Jackson at the film's climax. Although nationalistic Master Yim realizes this lesson too late – 'We can't fight guns with martial arts' – Huang survives by integrating Western technology into his martial arts repertoire.

Master Yim represents an alter-ego to Huang in several ways. Unlike Huang, Yim stubbornly clings to traditional heroic values that have no relevance in the changing world he inhabits. He never listens to any of the helpful advice Leung Fu offers but ruthlessly dominates his devoted student. His final downfall is both tragic and a warning to any Chinese who refuses to acknowledge signs of changing times. The contrast between these two who represent the different eras of Hong Kong martial arts cinema, is deliberate on director Hark's part. Not only is Master Yim a noble martial artist who compromises himself by joining the Shaho gangsters for money but he also evokes images of earlier cinematic heroes played by Wang Yu (*Duk Bei Do* [*Only Arm Sword/One-Armed Swordsman*, 1967], *Gam Yin Ji* [*Golden Swallow*/aka *The Girl with the Thunderbolt Kick*, 1968], *Wong Hu Men* [*Hammer of God/The Chinese Boxer*, 1970], *Dop Bey Kuan Wan* [*The Chinese Professionals/One-Armed Boxer*, 1971]), who are now anachronistic in the changed universe of *Once upon a Time in China*.

Rumors concerning Wang Yu's supposed links with contemporary Triad gangsters may have inspired this particular casting. Yim tells prospective student Leung Fu/Liang Kuan (Yuen Biao) that it is impossible to make a living as a martial artist. Unlike Huang and Leung, Yim has no secondary profession to support himself. After being fired from his menial theater job, Fu becomes Yim's student until he realizes the extent of his master's corruption. Despite Yim's admonitions of compromise – 'Nothing in this world is justified. Virtue is often found among the lowly. Once we found the school then we can think about justice' – the spectacle of Yim again performing for money in front of a gangster audience finally turns student against master. Both Huang and Yim compromise in certain ways. But Yim's methods reproduce the worst aspects of Western society. Aspiring to be the number-one martial artist in Fushan, Yim dies a miserable death by Western bullets. By contrast, Huang survives and at the climax even wears a Western suit Yee measured for him. Yee even envisages Huang eventually visiting the West, a goal he accomplishes in Part Six of the series.

Wong Fei-Hung Ji Yi (*Man Should Be Self-Sufficient, Once upon a Time in China, Part Two*, 1992) continues the critique of isolationist, nationalistic tendencies. Although Thomas Weisser and Joey O'Bryan tend to see Huang's struggle against the xenophobic White Lotus sect as 'apolitical' and motivated by a 'simplistic (humane?) assist the underdog'[21] credo, the film is more complex. It opens on the White Lotus sect's secret ceremony affirming hostility to foreign influence. Priest Jiugong (Xong Xin-xin) demonstrates his imperviousness to Western bullets, thus seemingly succeeding where Master Yim failed. We later discover, however, that Jiugong's supposed prowess relies on underhanded methods similar to the hidden razor in Yim's pigtail during his second fight with Huang. If Yim counters Huang's affronted comment concerning fair play with 'The world is full of surprises. I must take precautions,' Jiugong appropriates Clint Eastwood's body armor strategy in the climax of *A Fistful of Dollars* (1964). Both Master Yim and Jiugong represent negative directions for any Chinese seeking to cope with the new demands of a highly technological twentieth century and the dangerous results of the one-dimensional thought pattern criticized by Rey Chow. Unlike Huang, neither character will ever 'unlearn' the problematic nature of submission to ethnicity and realize the importance of negotiating new forms of cultural identity in a changing and challenging world.

Ultimately, Hark regards cultural and nationalistic xenophobia as false, underhanded, and retrograde in terms of China's real interests. When Jiugong orders a bonfire of Western artifacts that includes a large clock, an oil painting, a piano, and a Dalmatian, the scene foreshadows the sect's later demonstration outside the British embassy, during which they burn Western-costumed Aunt Yee and her camera in effigy. As Yang notes, the clock becomes a recurrent visual motif throughout the film, contrasting the regressive feelings of the White Lotus sect with a hero who first appears in the film enjoying the benefits of advanced modern technology.[22] Sun Yat-sen and Lu also frequently look at their watches to synchronize their strategy. However, the motif has other meanings in addition to representing the urgent countdown leading to 1997. It both makes a self-reflexive reference to the most meticulously edited film of the series and contrasts the sect's backward desires with Huang's culturally progressive movements, which attempt to reintegrate opposite values. Timing is thus important in more senses than one.

Yang likens the prologue's end dissolve to the speeding train of the credit sequences. When Huang takes Yee's 'steam engine' on a journey to Guangzhou in 1895.

> the dissolve from the burning clock to the speeding train serves to connect the Boxers and the hero, both of whom are superb martial artists. What distinguishes these two is their varying attitudes toward Western culture. The dashed clock in the previous scene implies that the Boxers tend to move backward to the time before the introduction of Western technology and culture into Western society. The hero, on the other hand, is associated with the ever forward progress of Western technology, as he is enjoying the breeze and twilight scenery in the train that also saves him a lot of travel time.[23]

Huang also benefits from the linguistic skills of Sun Yat-sen, who translates a lecture on acupuncture for a group of Western doctors. Although the British ambassador later refuses Huang's offer to tend the wounded Western victims of the sect, Western-educated Sun Yat-sen requests Huang's help when he runs out of anesthetic. Succeeding scenes show Sun's scalpels and Huang's needles jointly undergoing sterilization. Yee then translates Huang's message to the initially reluctant monolingual British ambassador, 'Dr Huang says nothing is more important than saving lives.'

Although Huang never actively supports the failed revolt by Sun and Lu, he realizes the importance of these Western-educated Chinese to the future development of China. Furthermore, the patriotic Huang never approves of genocidal activities against foreigners and missionary-educated Chinese Christian children. In fact, he saves both and elicits a promise from Manchu official Nalan Yuanshu (Donnie Yen Ji-dan) that ensures the children's future safety. Master Huang thus uses Kwan Tak-hing's Confucian principles of fair mindedness and morality for the benefit of individuals outside his Cantonese community group. As in the first film, he uses a Western umbrella against the villains. Huang also ensures that Lu's secret list of rebels will never fall into Manchu hands.

Like Wang Yu, David Chiang Dai-wai's performance as Lu evokes the 1970s era of Hong Kong cinema, when he was a major star of Shaw Brothers films directed by Chang Che. However, although Chiang's character is more positive than Yim's, he does not die a heroic death as in earlier films such as Chang Che's *Bo Sau* (*Kung Fu Vengeance/Vengeance*, 1970), *Chi Ma* (*Dynasty of Blood/Blood Brothers*, 1973), and the Hammer–Shaw Brothers production *The Legend of the Seven Golden Vampires* (1974). Times have changed, and Huang has to ensure Western-educated Sun Yat-sen's safety for his country's future. He has to engage in another climactic battle with yet another alter-ego, Nalan Yuanshu, who also represents a false path for the Chinese people to follow in an increasingly complex world. Although equal in fighting prowess to Huang, Nalan becomes contaminated like Yim. He not only abides by the letter of the law in adhering to a declining Manchu political system but corruptly uses the extremist White Lotus sect to violate the British embassy's diplomatic immunity and cause further bloodshed. Nalan is thus another version of the unacceptable

Chinese hero for the twentieth century and reveals both the challenging wider world to the formerly closed society and the different values with which the hero must come to terms. Naturally, racism and xenophobia are impossible values for Master Huang to follow. Huang Fei-hong not only is patriotic but also is a savior figure for both Westerners and the missionary-educated Chinese children threatened by the White Lotus sect. Although Kwan Tak-hing's character had little if any involvement with the wider Western world. Hark's version reveals the hero as both compassionate and generous toward victims of other racial and cultural groups as well as toward his own people.

Wong Fei-Hung Ji Saam (*Lion King Struggle for Supremacy/Once upon a Time in China, Part Three*, 1993) opens with the Empress Dowager and Premier Li Hong-zhong (a figure condemned by later historians for weakening China by losing territories such as Taiwan) discussing the strategy of using a Lion Dance 'to play off one foreign power against another.' As in the first film's opening prologue, Kwan Tak-hing's beloved Lion Dance now becomes contaminated in a world of political corruption. Yang notes that despite the empress's approval of the use of the Lion Dance to devour the foreigners, 'as the Boxer rebellion broke out in 1900 and the allied troops of eight countries invaded Beijing, it was China that was . . . devoured by eight hungry lions.'[24] Far from uniting the Chinese, the Lion Dance causes disunity, which results in the intervention of Western powers in the next film. Despite Huang's attempt to persuade Premier Li to stop the dance, Li refuses to see him because of his lowly class status and delegates the task to a minor bureaucrat. After the prologue's plot between the claw-ringed empress and the premier, Hark repeats the same transitional device seen in the previous film. The image rapidly changes to show Huang's train traveling to Beijing, suggesting that the corrupt Manchu authorities are as backward as the White Lotus sect.

Part Three shows Yee's affirmative 'steam engine' principle now adopted by Huang's father, Huang Kei-ying, who uses a steam engine 'for more efficient production of medicine' in his Beijing clinic. By this time in the series, Huang Fei-hong realizes the need to learn English, 'to speed up communication with the foreigners.' Although he addresses Yee by her English name, 'Peony,' he faces a rival in the person of Cantonese-speaking Russian consul official Tomansky, who presents her with a movie camera. Tomansky's role in the film combines romantic, historical, and political elements. He is part of a Russian assassination plot to prevent Premier Li from signing away more territory to the Japanese. When he repairs the clinic's steam engine, he argues with Huang over the need for technological developments and his version of historical determinism: 'We cannot escape the changes of history.'

Yee becomes Tomansky's chief antagonist. She prefers Huang and uses the steam vapor from the clinic's engine to take the initiative in kissing her lover, who later breaks with tradition to openly embrace her in front of his associates. Yee also uses Tomansky's gift of a movie camera to photograph Huang's performance. This could be seen as an indirect reference to the future role of movie technology in preserving ancient martial arts techniques. As budding 'director' Fu (Max Mok Siu-chung) comments, 'She can teach others kung fu by movies in the future.' In a scene reversing the traditional master-student relationship, Huang performs for the camera under Fu's direction.

Yee's character also develops added resilience in each part of the series. After becoming a Western-educated damsel in distress in the first film, she uses one of Huang's techniques to throw an assailant off the boat at the end of the second. In Part Six, she rides on horseback and uses Huang's triple shadow-kick technique against hostile Indians. Yee rebuts Tomansky's oppressive historical materialism – 'We can't escape historical changes. The Hans got used to being ruled by the Manchus. You'll find out later that you'll get used to being ruled by Russians' – by articulating statements usually voiced by the hero: 'The Hans will decide our own future.' Her speech complements Huang's condemnation of Premier Li in the concluding scenes. Yee is certainly not Yang's idea of a heroine because she is 'still marginalized by the patriarchal discourse' and simply serves 'the function of perpetuating male heroism' and being 'the object of male looks.'[25]

Part Three also shows Huang reproducing character traits of his predecessor, Kwan Tak-hing. He appeals to corrupt capitalist Chiu Tin Bai by invoking the Confucian values of friendship and politeness, but the gesture is as futile as Kwan's earlier attempts in *Wong Fei-Hung Siu Lam Kuen/Wong Fei-Hung Shaolin Fist* (*The Skyhawk*, 1974). Chiu and his men sarcastically satirize Huang as they leave. By healing Chiu's injured henchman Club Foot (Xong Xin-xin), Huang wins over his opponent through kindness, thus evoking Kwan Tak-hing's earlier gestures toward his usual antagonist, played by Shek Kin. In contrast, the film ends with Huang's openly non-Confucian condemnation of the Manchu government's abuse of the Lion Dance. As Yang notes, his action in tossing back his gold medal is certainly unfilial and an open breach with traditional customs:

> Instead of conforming to the traditional Confucian teaching of hierarchical compliance when a subject should always show obedience to the superior, and the young to the elderly, Huang Feihong courageously speaks to Li Hongzhang. Huang is no more a subject of the Qing Empire since a regime maintained by an older generation has become corrupt and untrustworthy. What makes Huang a real hero now is not his winning of the gold medal for defeating so many competitors with his superb martial arts, as in the old Huang Feihong series, but his will to defy Li Hongzhang and question the purpose of the whole game.[26]

The next two parts of the series reinforce elements in the preceding films. Now played by Zhao Wen-zhou, Huang reverses his geographic direction from south to north by returning to Fushan and (possibly) Hong Kong at the end of Part Five. In *Huang Fei-Hung Ji Sei* (*Once upon a Time in China, Part Four*, 1993), the Western powers, personified by German General Heinlintak, decide to appropriate the Lion Dance for their own purposes. The credit sequences in

Part Four show a lion's head on fire as if in homage to Ringo Lam's 'Fire' films. This time not just any city will be 'on fire,' but Beijing. An honest Manchu official persuades Huang to represent his nation in the new Lion Dance contest. In addition, a female version of the White Lotus sect attacks innocent foreigners. Yee's younger sister, Aunt May/Shisyi (Jean Wong Ching-ying), attempts to protect them, just as Huang did in Part Two. After suffering a racially motivated rebuff by a German female, she appeals to a consoling Father Thomas, a new version of the honest Jesuit missionary from Part One: 'Father, I hope there is a real God to stop the hatred between nations. Otherwise, we cannot escape from the coming disaster.'

Later, Father Thomas actively intervenes by helping Huang escape from prison. His example also influences Red Lotus sect member Su to free herself from xenophobia. She later dies after protecting Westerners, ironically commenting, 'I never imagined I'd die protecting foreigners.'

Although Huang wins the Lion Dance, he receives news that Western armies have invaded Beijing and that the Dowager Empress has fled. After again throwing away his gold medal trophy, Huang draws the same conclusion he did in Part Three: 'We won the competition but lost our country.' He decides to retreat southward 'and prepare for the fight back.'

Although more stylistically and thematically confused than its predecessors. *Wong Fei-Hung Ji Ng Lung Sing Chin Ba* (*Dragon City's Exterminating Tyrant/Once upon a Time in China, Part Five*, 1994) appropriately reproduces changed historical circumstances. Chaos and turmoil dominate China, and fortunate survivors seek passage to Hong Kong. The prologue deals with a confrontation between a petty thief outside South China's Si Kur village and pirate chief Cheng Yuk-lun. Although the thief wards off Cheng with a gun, the pirate uses a spear-and-gun apparatus to kill his adversary. The prologue again sets up a narrative situation that the film must resolve. This time it involves Huang's recourse to Western firearms against a pirate adversary, who represents the final depths of corruption in Chinese society.

Huang and his entourage reach Si Kur, intending to travel to Hong Kong with Yee and Lang. However, they discover a destabilized situation that involves not only pirate terrorism but also court constables, who are reduced to stealing food 'due to government disruption involving nonpayment of salaries after the Allied victory in Beijing.' Pirate chief Cheung Yuk-lun and his sister Ying (Elaine Lui) are the descendants of the 100-year-old former Manchu official, Cheung, who rules the pirate lair like an active version of Grandpa from *The Texas Chainsaw Massacre* (1974). When Huang eventually confronts his aged opponent, he learns that he represents the final degeneration of the Ching Dynasty. Cheung is no longer 'interested in being a magistrate' since 'all the emperors are selfish.' Huang also has to confront a disunited community attempting to come to terms with recent history. Although he decides to work legitimately with the constables, he hears various suggestions ranging from forming an alliance against the foreigners to non-involvement. Huang cautions, 'we can't hinder the development of history.' Part Five thus views old institutional and traditional values as completely bankrupt and futile in dealing with a chaotic historical situation.

Under Western Eyes: Cultural and Geographic Diaspora

The series now explicitly begins to consider questions involving diaspora. It has moved from one Chinese location to another, but now it envisages the hero's eventual relocation not only to Hong Kong but also to a wider world beyond China. The series thus acknowledges a changed Chinese world from the one represented in Parts One, Two, and Three. Whereas previously the Western world operated as an intrusive element in a nationalistic homeland, by Part Five several characters seriously discuss the possibility of relocating elsewhere. Their knowledge of different locations in America, shared by the film's audience – whether in China, Hong Kong, or Taiwan – represents twentieth-century Chinese familiarity with the outside world. The world outside is no longer as threatening as before, thus revealing a different understanding of diaspora than before.

Now, the homeland appears more unstable. When Huang and his men infiltrate the pirate headquarters, they hear comments about an increasingly desirable outside world: 'San Francisco is a nice place,' 'I have property in New York,' and 'Paris is better.' For both heroes and villains, China is increasingly corrupt, Si Kur businessman Tang hoards rice and keeps prices artificially high even after Huang returns the pirate loot. Huang criticizes Tang's speculation as 'more damaging than the pirates. Raised prices will contribute to inflation.' Like his predecessor Chiu Tin Bai in Part Three, Tang is a menace to Chinese community values. Despite his disgust with Tang, Huang saves his life when the hoarded rice goes up in flames. In Part Three, Huang refrained from killing Chiu to save his men from unemployment. Eventually, Huang and his associates decide to leave after they find that the government has sent two warring militia forces to restore law and order.

Several scenes in Part Four show Huang, Fu, Club Foot, and Lang practicing with Western six-guns. This is less a trivial reference to the Western genre than an anticipation of themes to come in Part Six. Huang and his men use Western fire-power to defeat the pirates and enter their lair. Although this sequence appears jokey, it reveals a different picture of Master Huang from that of the first film in the series. By now it appears that Huang Fei-hong has listened to Aunt Yee's ideas about the values of Western technology and has appropriated them into his repertoire. Although still the Chinese hero, he now uses modern devices to pursue his traditional goals of justice.

Once upon a Time in China and America (1997) appears to be a gimmicky attempt to revive a series that waned after its third part, when Jet Li left following a dispute with producer-director-scenarist Tsui Hark. After Hark produced two more films with Zhao Wen-zhao as Huang, the series moved to television before Li and Hark reunited to make a new film helmed by veteran actor, martial arts choreographer, and director Sammo Hung. This film was shot entirely in America. Indeed, John Ford's Monument Valley appears in the opening. However, the decision to move Master Huang to America was not made entirely for commercial or postmodernist pastiche reasons. Nor was it exclusively a veiled reference to the ominous date of July 1, 1997, suggesting that Huang decided to go Hollywood along with John Woo, Chow Yun-Fat, and Michelle Yeoh. In fact, *Once upon a Time in China and America* represents the logical culmination of themes in the preceding film versions but also tackles traditional cultural and historical issues concerning China's involvement with the Western world.

In *Once upon a Time in China and America*, Huang visits Sol's Po Chi Lam clinic in a Western town and encounters problems affecting Chinese communities of the diaspora. The world of Fort Stockton represents another version of the corrupt Western values evident throughout the series. Run by a racially and politically corrupt mayor and a repressive sheriff, Fort Stockton is a town where the Chinese are marginalized, so that it resembles their counterparts' villages in Part One. As in Part One, there are traitors ready to betray the Chinese to corrupt Westerners. However, not all the Westerners are racist. Other marginalized figures extend gestures of friendship, such as the dance hall girls, Sue and Lola, who buy beers for the Chinese before racist forces intervene. Gunfighter Billy represents another version of positive Westerners, similar to the sacrificial Jesuit missionary of Part One and Father Thomas of Part Four, who oppose their society's corrupt values and actively aid the Chinese. In Huang's memory fantasy, Billy's identity becomes racially blurred along with those of Yee and Seven. As Huang develops Western techniques, Billy not only learns martial arts but later joins the Chinese on the gallows as a sacrificial victim of Western racism.

The series charts Huang's development from patriotic, monolingual Chinese hero to a figure who realizes the need for reintegration in the wider world of the twentieth century. Before Huang develops amnesia, he sees Billy about to commit suicide in the desert and moves to rescue him following an English lesson from Yee. To everyone's surprise, Huang leaves the stagecoach interior after spontaneously uttering the word 'Climbing,' which Yee supposedly never taught him. Unlike the earlier films, Huang loses both his identity and his memory until he finally regains it with Seven's aid.

Boundaries become blurred in the series in more than one sense. When Huang rides with Fierce Eagle after his adoption into the tribe, both speak about their respective national identities. Fierce Eagle tells Huang about his tribe's forcible relocation from its original home and his people's desire to return. The still-amnesiac Huang replies, 'At least you know where your roots are. I don't know where I came from.' However, until his memory returns, Huang is at home with a minority group whose cultural and geographic dislocation parallels his own. Huang's involvement with the Indians also parallels Jackie Chan Sing-lung's amnesiac association with a native tribe in Benny Chan's *Ngoh Si Siu* (*Who Am I?*, 1998), as well as his sympathy toward a multiethnic street gang in Stanley Tong's *Hung Faan Kui* (*Red Savage*

Territory/Red Indian Territory/Rumble in the Bronx, 1995). Indeed, it is not unusual for exiled groups to identify with other minorities.[27]

When Huang eventually regains his memory and identity, the process of blurring and diffusion is similar to when he tried to remember the past in the Indian camp. Faced with an amnesiac master, Seven restores Huang's memory by reenacting the fighting techniques of his earlier opponents, Master Yim and Nalan Yuanshu, who represent compromised versions of a Chinese hero Huang previously fought against. Thus, Seven's strategy is not just to restore Huang's memory but to evoke knowledge of the limited nationalistic models of Chinese heroism he once successfully overcame mentally and physically.

The strategy works. As Huang's memory returns, he says, 'This trip to America is just like a dream.' Huang also twice repeats an important speech that emphasizes the importance of integrating Chinese values and learning from the West in this particular diaspora:

> 'You're a long way from home living in a foreign place. The Po Chi Lam was opened for this reason. It is important for people to know who they are. Good healing, strong body, not business. Goods often are worth more than people who become worthless. You must remember who you are. Copy the merits of the foreign people. Compensate for our shortcomings, and shine for the Chinese people. Simply put, you must remember who you are.'

Although Huang affirms essential Chinese values here, he does not approve of rapacious tiger economy capitalism as practiced by Chiu Tin Bai and Tang.

Jet Li's Huang Fei-hong is a younger but more developed version of Kwan Tak-hing's hero. He realizes the importance of integrating opposites in a world affected by both Western capitalism and Chinese diaspora at home and abroad. By moving to America for Part Six, the series not only affirms Law Kar's definition of Hong Kong cinema's characterstic 'interflow' philosophy but it also introduces Rey Chow's 'boundary-crossing' concepts involving the interrogation of Chinese identity and literature. Chow sees a movement from nationalistic to ethnic terms: 'Ethnicity signifies the social experience which is not completed once and for all but which is constituted by a continual, often conflictual, working-out of its grounds . . . it is ethnicity understood in this sense of an unfinished social field that should provide the new terms of criticism as well as reference.'[28]

In its own cinematic way, the *Once upon a Time in China* series attempts to construct a new version of an ethnic Chinese identity by moving beyond constricting definitions of nationhood and geographic boundaries and suggesting new ways to define a Chinese hero. This hero contrasts dramatically with earlier incarnations by Kwan Tak-hing, Jackie Chan, Chan Kwun-tai, Lau Ka-fai, and others. The hero gradually moves from his geographic territory to confront a wider Western world that encroaches on his homeland. He finally visits America, where he reencounters familiar issues of identity, diaspora, and reintegration that appear both in real life and in Hong Kong cinematic representations. Although it features different narrative and geographic situations, the *Once upon a Time in China* series deserves to be viewed as a whole for its examination of the need for cultural change and relocation under changing historical circumstances. Despite the fact that Jet Li's Master Huang visits a country that his venerated predecessor, played by Kwan Tak-hing, never did (at least not in the classic Huang Fei-hong film series), the hero is ultimately at home with both his national identity and the idea that he needs to accommodate himself to a wider world beyond his original homeland.

NOTES

I wish to thank David Desser, Steve Fore, Ange Hwang of the Asian Media Access Center, and the anonymous readers of *Cinema Journal* for their helpful contributions.

1. Zhang Ailing, 'From the Ashes,' trans. Oliver Stunt, *Renditions* 45 (spring 1996): 47. Zhang's actual lines are 'Regardless of whether they are political or philosophical, world views that are too clear-cut are bound to provoke antipathy. Man's *joie de vivre* is solely to be found in life's irrelevancies.'
2. Mingyu Yang, 'China: *Once upon a Time/Hong Kong*: 1997. A Critical Study of Contemporary Hong Kong Martial Arts Films,' Ph.D. dissertation, University of Maryland, 1995.
3. See Yu Mo-Wan, 'The Prodigious Cinema of Huang Fei-Hong: An Introduction,' in Lau Shing-hon, ed., *A Study of the Hong Kong Martial Arts Film* (Hong Kong: Urban Council. 1980), 79–90, and Gene Ching, 'The Kung Fu of Wong Fei-Hong: Hung Gar,' *Hong Kong Film Magazine* 3 (1995): 7–11.
4. Stephen Teo, *Hong Kong Cinema: The Extra Dimensions* (London: British Film Institute, 1997), 246.
5. Ibid.
6. Raymond Williams, *The Politics of Modernism: Against the New Conformists* (London: Verso, 1989), 4, 23–4, 35, 130, 134.
7. Law Kar, 'The American Connection in Early Hong Kong Cinema,' paper presented at Hong Kong Cinema: History, Arts. Identity, 1900–1997, Conference, University of Illinois, Urbana-Champaign, October 11, 1997. See also Héctor Rodríguez. 'Hong Kong Popular Culture as an Interpretive Arena: The Huang Feihong Film Series,' *Screen* 38. no. 1 (spring 1997): 1–24. Rodriguez states that the original series starring Kwan Tak-hing was 'partly a response to the peripheral predicament of modern China in an international arena' (14) and also involved the incorporation of 'narrative norms and situations from popular Hollywood films, especially the Saloon fight characteristic of countless Westerns, transplanted in various Huang Feihong installments to the more indigenous setting of a dim sum restaurant' (3). The previous page contains a photo of Kwan Tak-hing wearing a stylish costume and holding a Western bullwhip. Hong Kong involvement in America thus encompasses the past and present. The late actor Roy Chiao (Kiu Wong), well known for his portrayals of Buddhist monks and honest government officials in King Hu films such as *Hap Nui* (*Chivalrous Woman/A Touch of Zen*, 1971), *Ying Chun Gok Ji Fung Bo* (*Welcome Spring Corner: Storm/The Fate of Lee Khan*, 1974), and *Jung Lit To* (*Righteous Honor Painting/The Valiant Ones*, 1975) frequently undertook missionary work in America. I am grateful to Law Kar for this information.
8. Tsui Hark, '*Once upon a Time in China*,' in *Sixteenth International Hong Kong Film Festival Catalog* (Hong Kong: Urban Council, 1992), 117. For Ng Ho, the *Once upon a Time in China* series represents the third stage in the heroic transformation of Huang Fei-hong. The former scriptwriter for the 1977 television series now

sees him as a 'mock hero' who is 'imbued with a postmodernist predicament . . . faced with the city's corruption an decadence, he is disgusted yet feels impotent to do anything, and even begins to question his own existence.' Ng Ho, 'The Three Heroic Transformations of Huang Feihong,' in *Wong Fei Hung: The Invincible Master* (Hong Kong: Urban Council, 1996), 15. Although parodies certainly exist elsewhere, as in Lee Lik Chi's *Once upon a Time a Hero in China* (1992) and Wong Jing's *Last Hero in China* (1993), Ho's emphasis on the supposed impotence of Hark's hero may be too extreme. Certainly, Huang Fei-hong experiences personal and cultural situations of crisis, but he is always resilient and able to overcome them.

Law Kar takes a different perspective. Although admitting the redundant nature of the original Confucian spirit of Kwan Tak-hing's Huang Fei-hong in a 'self-centered and mercenary society,' Kar makes the following observation: 'The films moral vision and self-contained patriarchal world are also anathema to modern society's seeming preoccupation with freedom and deconstruction. However, one only has to consider their inspirational power on Tsui Hark's radical Huang Fei-hong series of the nineties, or take note of the praise heaped on Kwan Tak Hing when he passed away, to see the enduring power of traditional exemplary models.' Kar, 'Huang Feihong's Family Tree,' in *Wong Feihung: The Invincible Master*, 11.

In this light, it may be premature to close the book on this hero's extraordinary cultural resilience by ending any essay, 'So, Huang Feihong, rest in peace' (15) as Ng Ho does. Finally, Ho sees irony in the scene in which the hero's paper fan bearing the calligraphy 'unfair treaty' becomes damaged in the fire at Baozhilin as expressing a sense of Huang's postmodernist ideological confusion. 'With the fan burnt away, the character for un is gone, leaving only the words "fair treaty" ' (15). However, the ironic nature of the film may reflect the series sense of 'historical interflow,' particularly in regard to how treaties are often rewritten by the winning side. The scene evokes ironic parallels to both breaches by the American government of its many treaties with Native Americans as well as unfair treaties imposed by Western governments on China that were 'fair' according to the perspective of the winners.

9. Hark, '*Once upon a Time in China*,' 117.
10. Such uncertainty begins to appear in the last films featuring Kwan Tak-hing as Huang. See Tony Williams, 'Kwan Tak-hing and the New Generation,' *Asian Cinema* 10, no. 1 (fall 1998): 71–7.
11. Rodriguez, 'Hong Kong Popular Culture,' 2.
12. Ibid. 8.
13. Ibid. 17.
14. For an excellent analysis that takes seriously the treatment of Chinese identity and Western values in the *Once upon a Time in China* series, see Lisa Odham Stokes and Michael Hoover, *City on Fire: Hong Kong Cinema* (London: Verso, 1999), 93–9. For Li's understanding of the flexible nature of his various roles, see Martin Wong and Eric Nakamura, 'Jet Li: The International Weapon,' *Giant Robot* 12 (1998): 46–53.
15. For an informative overview of the entire Wong Fei-hong series, see Kar, *Wong Fei Hung: The Invincible Master*. It contains a filmography of the ninety-nine films that appeared from 1949 to 1995. Unfortunately, not many of the early Kwan Tak-hing films have survived.
16. Sam Ho, 'Equaling the Unequal: Accepting the 1997 Reunion in *Once upon a Time in China*,' unpublished paper, 8.
17. Rey Chow, *Writing Diaspora: Tactics of Intervention in Contemporary Cultural Studies* (Bloomington: Indiana University Press, 1993), 8.
18. The term *gweilo* is a derogatory Cantonese expression for white people that is generally translated as 'white devil.' The term is also used to refer to anyone having mixed American-Chinese parentage, such as Michael Fitzgerald Wong's city cop character in Jamie Luk's *The Case of the Cold Fish* (1995).

19. Kwai-Cheung Lo, '*Once upon a Time*: Technology Comes to Presence in China,' *Modern Chinese Literature* 7 (1993): 83.
20. Chow, *Writing Diaspora*, 25.
21. Thomas Weisser, *Asian Trash Cinema: The Book* (Kingwood, Tex.: ATC/ETC Publications, 1994), 114–15. Joey O'Bryan makes a similar comment in the rough-cut version of the Asian Media Access documentary *The Irresistible Hong Kong Movie Series of Once upon a Time in China*, screened at the Asian Cinema Studies Conference, Trent University, Peterborough, Canada, August 21, 1997.
22. Yang, 'China: Once upon a Time/Hong Kong,' 82.
23. Ibid.
24. Ibid. 89.
25. Ibid. 167.
26. Ibid. 90.
27. The second alternative Cantonese translation of *Hung Faan Kui* draws attention to the American film *Fort Apache, the Bronx* (Daniel Petrie, 1981), whose title deliberately refers to John Ford's classic Western *Fort Apache* (1948). The film obviously sees the multiethnic urban street gang as the modern equivalent of savage Indians who need to recognize their affinities with other minorities to unite against a common oppressor.

    Historical and cinematic precedents do exist for Hong Kong cinema's interest in the Wild West. During 1974, Italian Western actor Lee Van Cleef and Shaw Brothers star Lo Lieh appeared together in Antonio Margheriti's *The Stranger and the Gunfighter.* Chen Lee and Klaus Kinski also starred in Mario Caiano's *My Name Is Shanghai Joe* (1973) and in Bitto Albertini's *The Return of Shanghai Joe* (1974). In 1973, Hong Kong actors Jason Pai-Pico and Po Chih Leo costarred with Italian Western stalwarts William Berger and Donald O'Brien in Yeo Ban Yee's Golden Harvest production, *Kung Fu Brothers in the Wild West*. For an interesting location report from the Bracketville, Texas, set of *Once upon a Time in China and America*, involving crews from Hong Kong, New York, Los Angeles, and Texas, see Clyde V. Gentry III, '*Once upon a Time in China and America*,' *Hong Kong Film Connection* 5, no. 1 (1997): 3–8. Gentry reported spotting a number of Westerns in Sammo Hung's location video collection, such as *For a Few Dollars More* (1965) and *Once upon a Time in the West* (1968).

    The film's treatment of Native Americans deserves a separate study in itself. For relevant information concerning previous cinematic treatments, see Gretchen M. Bataille, *Images of American Indians on Film: An Annotated Bibliography* (New York: Garland, 1985): Michael Hilger, *The American Indian in Film* (Metuchen, N.J.: Scarecrow Press, 1986); *From Savage to Nobleman: Images of Native Americans in Film* (Lanham, MD: Scarecrow Press, 1995); and Ward Churchill, *Fantasies of the Master Race: Literature, Cinema, and the Colonization of American Indians* (San Francisco: City Lights Books, 1998). For problematic issues concerning the representation of Native Americans in *Once upon a Time in China and America*, see Stokes and Hoover, *City on Fire*, 97–8.
28. Chow, *Writing Diaspora*, 143.

SECTION 3
CROSS-CULTURAL CRITICISM AND CHINESE CINEMA

CROSS-CULTURAL CRITICISM AND CHINESE CINEMA

Dimitris Eleftheriotis

Part I of the present *Reader and Guide* concludes with a section dedicated to cross-cultural criticism. The essays included here, by three distinguished scholars in the field (E. Ann Kaplan, Rey Chow and Esther Yau), encapsulate a formative moment of what proved to be one of the most important theoretical debates on how Western critics and theorists relate to cinemas and films from different cultures. This essay will first consider the context within which the three essays emerged: a context of an interesting encounter between, on the one hand, feminist film theory in a moment of revision, and, on the other hand, a vibrant Chinese cinema, which, at the time, held centre stage in international film criticism. Then I will offer a summary of what the collected essays have to say about Chinese cinema and culture, focusing on questions of subjectivity and China's relationship with modernity, as well as comparing and evaluating different propositions on how Chinese cinema should be approached and on the usefulness and role of Western theory in such approaches.

A Context of Change

Esther Yau opens her influential essay (which was first published at the end of 1987) by describing the historical background against which *Yellow Earth* (Chen Kaige, 1984) appeared:

> 1984. China. The wounds of the 'cultural revolution' have been healing for nearly a decade. After the hysterical tides of red flags, the fanatical chanting of political slogans, and militant Mao supporters in khaki green or white shirts and blue slacks paving every inch of Tiananmen Square,

> come the flashy Toshiba billboards for refrigerators and washing machines, the catchy phrases of 'Four Modernisations', and tranquillised consumers in colourful outfits and leather heels crowding the shops of Wangfujing Street. *A context of Change.*[1]

Indeed, the mid-1980s is a period of change in many different respects, all of them relevant to this section. Following the end of the Cultural Revolution in the early 1970s,[2] the deaths of Zhou Enlai and Mao Zedong in 1976 (who were the two most influential leaders of the Chinese Communist Party (CCP) – prime minister and chairman of the Party respectively) and the subsequent struggle with the 'Gang of Four', slow but important changes were introduced in Chinese society and politics. The government, led by Deng Xiaoping, initiated a programme of economic modernisation that gradually embraced in all but name a free-market-economy model, opened the economy up to global processes, and downscaled the all-pervasive presence of the CCP in all aspects of cultural life.

At the same time important changes in the cultural sphere became evident: in 1978 the CCP called for 'a second 100 flowers' to bloom in Chinese art, film and literature.[3] Many films of the late 1970s directly addressed political issues and criticised the oppression of the Cultural Revolution period, as well as interrogating the conventions of socialist realism. The organisation of the film industry (which almost ceased to exist in the 1967–72 period)[4] changed drastically in the early 1980s. As state funding for the industry practically withdrew, studios were allowed to operate with relative autonomy, managing their own budgets, operating in effect in a market economy, with notions of 'profitability' counteracting the previously all-powerful state censorship. Distribution, however, remained controlled by the China Film and Distribution Company until the 1990s.

What became particularly crucial for Western film scholars and critics was the emergence in the mid-1980s of a body of films, now commonly known as 'Fifth Generation' cinema, that was heralded as perhaps the most interesting and challenging – both aesthetically and politically – film 'movement' of the time. Named after a number of young filmmakers (such as Zhang Junzhao, Zhang Yimou, Chen Kaige, Tian Zhuangzhuang, Wu Ziniu, Hu Mei, Zhang Zeming) who graduated from the Beijing Film Academy in the early to mid-1980s, Fifth Generation films appeared in many international film festivals (with *Yellow Earth* initiating the breakthrough in Hong Kong, Hawaii and Locarno; *Red Sorghum* (Zhang Yimou, 1987) winning a Golden Bear in Berlin, and *Farewell My Concubine* (Chen Kaige, 1993) winning prizes in Cannes and being nominated for an Academy Award and also receiving wide commercial distribution in the West). They also attracted intense critical and academic attention.

Academic interest was particularly intense in the USA where, as both Kaplan and Chow detail in their essays, Chinese cinema made an impressive entrance into the curricula of universities as well as in research activity and publications.

It is crucial to locate the three essays that follow within this context of change (in Chinese society, culture and cinema, but also in the discourse of film theory, as we will see shortly), but also of fascination with the 'new' China and its cinema. The term 'cross-cultural criticism' (or analysis) and the debate around its meanings, implications and practice register concerns about the engagement with what seemed to be a rather 'foreign' culture and its products. These concerns were amplified by the uncertainty around the nature of change and the future of the processes of liberalisation and modernisation in China. The global broadcasting of shocking images of the Tiananmen Square massacre in June 1989 obviously fuelled the intense political interest in China.

Almost simultaneously within Anglo-US film studies and theory there was intense anxiety around questions of difference. Challenging the rather monolithic theoretical paradigms associated with 'apparatus theory' (as exemplified in the works of Baudry, Metz, Heath, Doanne, Mulvey and others) and informed by Freudian/Lacanian psychoanalysis, Althusserian Marxism and structuralism and post-structuralism, film theorists and critics concerned with issues of gender, race and ethnicity were forcing a fundamental re-thinking and re-vision of such paradigms. In addition, issues around history, epistemology, politics and aesthetics became absolutely central within debates around modernism and postmodernism, in what was perhaps the most bitterly contested field of critical theory. Clearly, the 1980s was a period of increased sensitivity and anxiety around 'difference' (different histories and historiographies, different subjectivities and subject positions, different representations and systems of representations, ultimately different films) marked by a heightened awareness of one's position and its institutional and cultural peculiarities.

The three essays collected in this *Reader and Guide* bear the marks of the sensitivities, anxieties and uncertainties of the period – they are, in this sense, powerful testimonies to the complex process of approaching a new (and in many ways 'foreign') object of study motivated by fascination but also frustrated by limitations and reservations. Importantly, the essays are written by women and are (substantially if not exclusively) about women in Chinese cinema. They were written (or their writing process was initiated) in the mid to late 1980s and are, in this respect, broadly contemporaneous to debates within feminist film theory around difference.[5] Equally important is the fact that they articulate the shared concern around the appropriateness of Western theory for the study of Chinese cinema in different ways and through the study of different objects.

E. Ann Kaplan identifies the problem as one of lack of knowledge rather than the unsuitability of the theoretical framework, and she proposes an expanded theory that covers the unconscious and the representational practices of the 'Other'. Esther Yau defends the usefulness of Western theory and proposes an approach of rigorous historicism. Rey Chow acknowledges the limitations as well as the pertinence of such theory and proposes a critical engagement that, in the process, re-shapes theory by learning, as it were, from its object of study.

As mentioned above, the three essays focus on different aspects of Chinese cinema: Kaplan concentrates on a comparison between the 1979 film *The Legend of Tian Yun Mountain* (Xie Jin) and the 1986 film *Army Nurse* (Hu Mei), primarily in terms of their representation of women; Yau uses an analysis of the seminal Fifth Generation text *Yellow Earth* in order to propose a historicist methodology and to determine the defining characteristics of the 'context of change'; Chow pays close attention to a non-Chinese film about China, Bernardo Bertolucci's major 1987 box office success *The Last Emperor*, in order to discuss Western ways of looking at China and to describe a 'Westernised' Chinese subjectivity.

The three essays collectively offer a fascinating (and often conflicting) view of the formative stages of cross-cultural criticism and map out some of the crucial questions that still inform the debate. Is cross-cultural criticism possible? In what way should such criticism be undertaken? What is the role of Western theoretical frameworks in such practice? What are the limitations of such paradigms and what might constitute credible alternatives? What can theory learn from engagement with different, unfamiliar texts?

Three Takes on Cross-cultural Criticism

These general, and to some extent abstract, questions arise with specific reference to China, its films and its people in the three essays that follow. A point of departure is clearly the way in which Chinese culture and cinema should be approached. E. Ann Kaplan's essay attempts to deal with the dynamics of a process of 'double exchange' that she identifies as evident at the time: between, on the one hand, the American interest in Chinese films, and on the other, the interest of Chinese scholars in American film theory. She is very careful to define her own position as one of 'self-conscious feminism' and to question her interpretation of the films that she discusses. Crucial for her is the need to listen to and learn more about Chinese filmmakers and cultural practices, in general. However, her sensitivity to cultural difference is undermined by an overwhelming anxiety about (what appears to be for her) the almost impossible task of understanding what she calls 'the Other'. Although her willingness to open up to difference is beyond any doubt, the rhetoric of the essay is startling: 'Cross-cultural analysis, we know, is difficult – fraught with danger. We are forced to read works produced by the Other through the constraints of our own frameworks/theories/ideologies'.[6] Later on in the essay, Chinese films are described as 'Other World films'[7] and, perhaps most worryingly, she concludes:

> Cross-cultural readings are fraught with dangers, as I noted to begin with. Some of the dangers are clear in the assumptions of my readings that I outlined: but how are we to arrive at a method, a theory, for reading texts from Other Worlds until we have first answered some of the questions about how different cultures think about representation; and

> second, until we know more about the unconscious of different cultures as it might pertain to the level of the imaginary and to the terrain of the visual artistic text.[8]

In expressing such fear of the dangers lurking in encounters with 'Other Worlds', Kaplan unintentionally replicates a colonial attitude towards her explorations of Chinese cinema. Importantly such anxiety is twofold: on the one hand, it is about protecting the integrity of the 'difference' of the object of study, and, on the other, it is about the need to enhance the theoretical framework, to make it able to assimilate such 'otherness' in its epistemological scope.

This is very close to what Rey Chow describes as the traditional Western approach to China. She notes in the textual practices of *The Last Emperor* two 'looks' at Yu Pi (the 'last emperor' of the film): an 'erotic look' (invested in the image of the emperor and the imperial *mise en scène* of China), and a 'historical' look (essentially one of classifying and interpreting accurately the eroticised image of China) most evident in the narrative mode of literally interrogating the emperor's past. Chow suggests that the relationship between the two looks is hierarchical, and that the symbolic, interpretative, interrogatory structure frames the imaginary and the erotic one.

It is possible to see Kaplan's anxiety as resulting from the threat that an eroticised, protected 'other' poses for the mastery of an interpretative Western discourse[9] – Chow identifies a similar tendency in Julia Kristeva's book *About Chinese Women*.[10] In addition, Chow's essay challenges Kaplan's argument in terms of the latter's conceptualisation of Chinese culture as existing in total difference from Western cultures. For Chow 'Chinese' and 'Western' do not exist in mutual exclusion but formulate the dialectic on which modern Chinese subjectivity is played out. Importantly, while Kaplan defines the exchange as one between American theory and Chinese films, Chow is interested in a fully interactive relationship that moves beyond the interrogation of 'our' perception of 'other' cultural forms to an analysis of 'other' perceptions of 'our' cultural forms. Rejecting the notion that China stands as 'the Other', she remarks in relation to Kristeva: 'We should ask instead whether the notion that China is absolutely "other" and unknowable is not itself problematic'.[11] Esther Yau's careful and detailed analysis of *Yellow Earth* operates on three different levels which are, nevertheless, interlinked – the strength of her analysis lies in precisely the bringing together of all three:

> a diegetic level (for the construction of and enquiry about cultural and historical meaning), a critical level (for the disowning and fragmentation of the socialist discourses), and a discursive level (for the polyvocal articulations of and about Chinese aesthetics and feudalist patriarchy).[12]

Crucially, Yau suggests that such analysis can succeed through a detailed comparison between the textual and the contextual, identifying historicism as a powerful method for accomplishing such painstaking but clearly possible work. The suggestion here is that what the Western (or any other) scholar needs in order to undertake cross-cultural criticism is a detailed historical knowledge of the context of the films. While clearly such context includes representation and culture-specific articulations of desire, it does not necessarily require a complete knowledge of the 'Other's' psyche.

While both Yau and Chow advise caution in the use and application of theory in this process, they also defend the usefulness (the former indirectly, the latter directly) of such theory. In a sense, what they both propose is a far more dynamic understanding of the changing role of theory than has become rather commonplace now within an increasingly sophisticated and assured discourse of postcolonial criticism. Within such a context the universalising and totalising aspects of 'grand theory' have been repeatedly challenged, while the polarities of 'West' and 'Other' have been undermined by cultural and theoretical 'hybridity'. Homi Bhabha raises some of the political and theoretical questions regarding the role of theory in his essay 'The commitment to theory', in which he concludes:

> the theoretical recognition of the split-space of enunciation may open the way to conceptualising an *inter*national culture, based not on the exoticism of multiculturalism or the *diversity* of cultures, but on the inscription and articulation of culture's *hybridity*. To that end we should remember that it is the 'inter' – the cutting edge of translation and negotiation, the *in-between* space – that carries the burden of the meaning of culture. It makes it possible to begin envisaging national, anti-nationalist histories of the 'people'. And by exploring this Third Space, we may elude the politics of polarity and emerge as the others of our selves.[13]

Clearly cross-cultural criticism/analysis locates itself within (or at) this 'in-between' space in its attempts to formulate an approach (suggested by Bhabha as well as by Yau and Chow) that must find a way to negotiate the 'politics of polarity'. Such an approach is, in theoretical terms, commensurable with what has, to some extent, been the project of a certain kind of 'Western' theory most clearly evidenced in Foucault's attention to discursive constructions of 'otherness', Derrida's deconstruction and postmodernism's attack on universalism. In this context theorisations and analyses of questions of Chinese subjectivity, as well as China's relationship to modernity become crucial 'testing grounds' for competing methodologies.

Kaplan proposes an understanding of Chinese subjectivity as one that places individual identities subservient to collective ones, as formed and imposed by the CCP; she also suggests that China is moving towards modernity, implying that it somehow exists outside it:

> Since Chinese ideology demands the submission of the subject to the State, 'duty' over personal desire, the idea of feminism as an oppositional

> practice is hard to insert. (One could argue that China is, from a Western point of view, still a premodern state: in this case, the idea of a new subjectivity that is linked to new questions about sexual desire and sexual difference could signal the start of the modernism that in the West ushered in bourgeois capitalism.)[14]

She does, however, offer the possibility of 'a new ideology of individualism, perhaps learned partly from exposure to Western cultural products like the Hollywood film'.[15] Yau and Chow reject these formulations of Chinese subjectivity and modernity. The former, in her rigorous historicist approach, traces the tropes of Chinese subjectivity, formulating specific and perhaps peculiar relationships between individual and state, back to a pre-Communist era:

> Ever since the 1920s, the portrayals of individuals in films have been inextricably linked to institutions and do not reach resolution outside the latter. Hence, unlike the classical Hollywood style, homogeneity is not restored through the reconciliation of female desires with male ones, and the ways of looking are not structured according to manipulations of visual pleasure (coding the erotic, specifically) in the language of the Western patriarchal order.[16]

Yau also offers a different formulation of China's relationship to modernity, noting that

> Since the nineteenth century, major historical events in China (wars, national calamities, revolutions, etc) have made four topics crucial to national consciousness – feudalism, subsistence, socialism and modernisation – and discourses are prompted in relation to them in numerous literary and cultural texts.[17]

Chow passionately questions the politics of China's exclusion from modernity (as practised by both Western and Chinese scholars):

> Typically the history of the non-West is divided into the classical/primitive and the 'modern' stages, modern non-Western subjects can be said to be constituted primarily through a sense of loss – the loss of an attributed 'ancient' history with which one 'identifies' but to which one can never return except in the form of fetishism.[18]

She notes such 'fetishism' in the idealised versions of a 'pure' China that only now or very recently starts to discover the West (as witnessed in Kaplan's reference to individualism in Hollywood films). Chow sees the engagement with 'Western' thought and culture as going back a lot longer:

> Unlike what Oriental things still are to many Europeans and Americans, 'Western things' to a Chinese person are never merely dispensable embellishments: their presence has for the past century represented the necessity of fundamental adaptation and acceptance. It is the permanence of

imprints left by the contact with the West that should be remembered even in an ethnic culture's obsession with 'itself'.[19]

The three essays collected here offer a 'close-up' of the formative moment of a very influential debate. In Kaplan's anxiety (motivated by sensitivity and uncertainty) we witness the impact that the fascination with vibrant new and different cinemas had Anglo-American theoretical paradigms. In Chow and Yau, on the other hand, we see the determination to acknowledge difference and to face it with rigorous engagement with the historical context of the 'new', as well as, to question and revise totalising theoretical models.

Notes

1. Esther C. M. Yau, '*Yellow Earth*: Western analysis and a non-Western text', in the present collection, my emphasis.
2. It is important to note that whereas in the 1980s, and in the context of an American discourse, the Cultural Revolution became an unqualified political 'evil', earlier European engagement with it (and Maoism) was far more positive: it influenced not only the politics of the student movement in the 1960s and 1970s but also the approach to cultural politics of *Cahiers du Cinéma* and, distinctly, a certain phase of Jean Luc Godard's films. For a more extensive discussion of such issues, see Sylvia Harvey, *May 68 and Film Culture* (1980), London: BFI.
3. This refers to the original '100 flowers' envisaged in 1956 by Mao Zedong: 'let 100 flowers bloom and 100 schools of thought contend'.
4. Only a handful of films, all revolutionary operas, were produced those years.
5. As evidenced in articles like, for example, Annette Kuhn's 'Women's genres', *Screen*, vol. 25, no. 1, 1984, where she discusses the difference between the concept of social audience and that of spectator, as well as that between soap operas and film melodramas.
6. E. Ann Kaplan, 'Problematizing cross-cultural analysis: the case of women in the recent Chinese cinema', in the present collection.
7. Ibid.
8. Ibid.
9. In her essay Kaplan refers to the possibility of 'erroneous' analyses (which she quickly qualifies in terms of the 'multiplicity of meanings' argument) that might give an indication as to what the fear and the danger might be about.
10. Julia Kristeva (1977), *About Chinese Women*, New York: Urizen Books.
11. Rey Chow, 'Seeing modern China', in the present collection.
12. Esther Yau, '*Yellow Earth*'.
13. Homi K. Bhabha (1994), *The Location of Culture*, London and New York: Routledge, pp. 38–9.
14. Kaplan, 'Problematizing cross-cultural analysis'.
15. Ibid.
16. Yau, '*Yellow Earth*'.
17. Ibid.
18. Chow, 'Seeing Modern China'.
19. Ibid.

8

PROBLEMATIZING CROSS-CULTURAL ANALYSIS: THE CASE OF WOMEN IN THE RECENT CHINESE CINEMA

E. Ann Kaplan

Preamble

The context for this paper is the recent, double-sided phenomenon of an American-Chinese film exchange. On the one hand (and actually initiating the exchange) is the new interest on the part of Chinese film workers of all kinds (not only film students and scholars, but also directors, actresses, critics, script-writers, translators) in contemporary American and European film and film theory, an interest that resulted in certain American scholars being invited to lecture in China; on the other hand (and partly as a result of the invitations) the interest of American scholars in recent Chinese film. Scholars visiting China were not only given a unique chance to see recent Chinese films, but also asked to pronounce judgments on them, which we tended to do in terms of our particular research interests.

So, on the one hand, we have Chinese film scholars turning to American and European film theories to see what might be useful for them, in their writing on both American film and their own cinema; on the other hand, we have some American scholars writing tentative essays on Chinese films. (Those scholars, like Chris Berry, who have lived in China and know the culture and the language are obviously no longer 'tentative.') We have, then, a sort of informal film-culture exchange of a rather unusual kind, precisely because of its relative informality.

What is this exchange yielding so far? On the positive side, first, it is clear that some Chinese students can benefit from theoretical models they find in American

From *Wide Angle* 11: 2, pp. 40–50.

and European theory; they may even benefit from paradigms Americans use in their tentative exploration of recent Chinese films. Second, American scholars have been made aware of a rich and diverse cinema that they barely knew about before, and stimulated to ask new kinds of questions about this cinema.

But the 'exchange' has its problematic sides as well: first, it is becoming clear that there are two distinct audiences for Chinese research – that of the American/European film community, and that of Chinese intellectuals in mainland China. That is, the critical-film discourse within China has certain expectations that do not prevail over here (Chris Berry is currently researching the specific differences). One wonders if Chinese scholars need to learn how to talk about film in one way for an American audience, in another way for a Chinese audience, and what the implications of that is. What exactly are the different critical paradigms?

Second, I am concerned when Chinese scholars assert that American film theorists are merely enacting a new kind of cultural imperialism when they undertake analyses of Chinese films. Is this true? In what senses? What can be done about it?

Third, Chinese scholars sometimes say (in response to an American reading of a Chinese film): 'This is not the *Chinese* way of thinking.' Or 'Chinese do not think that way.' What does this mean? Does it mean that theories develop in very specific national/historical/intellectual contexts that are not readily transferable? Ought we to think of theory in terms of national/cultural issues? If not, how can we take care of questions like those above? It is in the light of this recent, but burgeoning, American-Chinese film exchange (in which I have been personally involved) that the following essay, which touches on a few of the above problems, should be read.

Problematizing Cross-cultural Analysis: the Case of Women in the Recent Chinese Cinema

Cross-cultural analysis, we know, is difficult – fraught with danger. We are forced to read works produced by the Other through the constraints of our own frameworks/theories/ideologies. If this is the case, we must then ask (as has, for example, Gayatri Spivak) what the point of such readings might be.[1] Are such analyses in danger of becoming 'a new form of cultural imperialism, when . . . institutionalized in various college courses on Asian cinema?'[2] Or can we all learn something from such readings?

I will argue that cross-cultural film analyses can be illuminating, and, if clearly positioned, not necessarily 'erroneous.' (Indeed, this word is itself problematic, since it implies that there is a 'correct' reading [i.e., one correct reading], when the whole point of recent theory [especially Bakhtin and deconstruction] has been to show how texts themselves hide their multiple and shifting meanings.) Theorists outside the producing culture might uncover different strands of the multiple meanings than critics of the originating culture just because they bring different frameworks/theories/ideologies to the texts.

I will try to demonstrate a process of interweaving and overlapping cross-cultural readings in a special case study of Hu Mei's *Army Nurse* (1986).

But, before doing this, let me note what I do not have time to do: this in turn permits me to briefly note different kinds and levels of cross-cultural readings that ideally would all be undertaken at the same time, as in Esther Yau's exemplary essay on '*Yellow Earth*: Western Analysis of a Non-Western Text.'[3] In this analysis, Yau reads the 'interweaving and work of four structurally balanced strands on three levels: a diegetic level (for the construction of and inquiry about cultural and historical meanings); a critical level (for the disowning and fragmentation of the socialist discourses), and a discursive level (for the polyvocal articulations of and about Chinese aesthetics and feudalist patriarchy).'

While I will touch on some of these levels briefly, I will focus mainly and deliberately on questions of female desire, sexual difference, and subjectivity. First (and perhaps easiest), I will analyze some representations of women in films by and about Chinese women, from the self-conscious perspective of Western feminism, theories of subjectivity and desire, and finally, of the modernism/postmodernism trajectory. Comparing and contrasting two recent Chinese Films (*The Legend of Tian Yun Mountain* and *Army Nurse*), one directed by a male, the other by a female, will show what such frameworks are able to uncover about the films, while also setting the stage for the following discussions.

But second, I contest (or question) my own readings, which assume that the Chinese cinema arises from the same psychoanalytic desire for replacing the lost object; for introjection, displacement, projection, as we have theorized, produces the desire for cinema in the West. I do this by comparing and contrasting my reading of *Army Nurse* with that of the director, whom I was lucky enough to interview.[4] In my final reading of *her* reading, I hope to raise (but not answer) the following questions: How do non-Western cultures think about representation? Are objectification and fascination with the specular regime part of a universal representational mode or one developed through Western philosophical/intellectual/aesthetic/political traditions? Do non-Western cultures use sound in relation to the image differently than does the dominant Hollywood cinema? Do other cultures, like China, use the cinema for other ends? Finally, I will tentatively set forth what I believe is the best hypothesis in relation to the Chinese cinema.

I: *Comparison of* The Legend of Tian Yun Mountain *(dir. Xie Jin, Shanghai Studio, 1979) and* Army Nurse *(dir. Hu Mei, August 1st Studio, 1986)*

Fredric Jameson's provocative recent statement that all Third World texts are 'necessarily allegorical' provides a useful framework for my discussion, since I want to argue that while Jameson's assertion might fit the first film, it must be qualified for the second. It is misleading to assert that 'even those texts invested with an apparently private or libidinal dynamic . . . necessarily project a political dimension in the form of national allegory.'[5] It is also misleading to say that 'The story of the private individual is always an allegory of the embattled situation of the public third-world culture and society,' at least without adding that many Hollywood films are also blatant 'national allegories.' I will argue that new Chinese films attempt something different than (or in addition to) national allegory, that we find precisely around the issues of female desire and subjectivity.

The issue of 'national allegory' versus 'something else' is inevitably linked to the context within which Other World films are produced, although as is obvious from the case of America, it is not necessary for film studios to be State controlled for them to be ideologically restricted; nor is it necessary that all State produced films are mere 'propaganda.' All film production in China is organized through a series of State run film studios and training academies, where directors, producers, actors/actresses, etc., are employees of the State. The interesting questions here have to do with what film ideas arise, which are accepted for production and make it through the final review process. Interesting also is that the various Chinese studios have all come to have their own special character: they range from the so-called 'experimental' (read 'resisting') Xian Studio to the more conservative Shanghai Studio that made *Tian Yun Mountain*. In order to get her film through the August 1st Studio, Hu Mei had to confront much opposition. Perhaps the fact that there is no opportunity in China for independent production (and therefore, none for explicit alternate cinematic practice in the Western sense) puts the most constraints on filmmakers, and represents the greatest difference from America. In other words, it is not State control of the dominant production that ultimately matters: the State system still requires the concept of 'marketability,' since the State needs people to fill the cinemas as much as does Hollywood, if for different reasons.

As Leo Ou-Fan Lee points out,[6] there are two main legacies for the recent Chinese film as for recent Chinese literature; namely, the humanist social-realist tradition of the 1940s, and second, the revolutionary propagandistic tradition of the Cultural Revolution. Made in 1979, *Tian Yun Mountain* represented a decisive break with the latter tradition, in which films still attacked the old, evil imperialist society and focused on decadence. *Tian Yun*, also set in 1979, offers a severe critique of both the Cultural Revolution and of the earlier anti-rightist campaigns. Its heroine is the new communist youth – energetic, hard-working and committed to correcting the Party's recent errors.

The film self-consciously derides the earlier romantic codes of the fifties generation in favor of the new communist heroine, who has no emotional problems because she has the new 'right' thinking. The older woman's story, narrated to the new heroine, is a standard melodrama, similar to many Hollywood films. The framing story thus comments upon the melodramatic one told by the old party member and that involves the typical melodramatic conflict between ambition and love. The two main messages of the film are

(1) that the Party must not commit the error of condemning good party members because of a slight difference over immediate strategy; and (2) that Party leaders must not allow personal revenge to affect their need to be just.

But there is another message, produced through the reactions of the new heroine to the older woman, which is that such melodramatic love relationships are messy and undesirable. The film thus retains a view of the subject as in the service of the State; problems between subject and State happened because the State made a wrong judgment, not because the relationship between subject and state was wrong. The film embodies the Official Voice in the figure of its Ideal Heroine, who is set off against her conflicted, unhappy and unsuccessful precursors, and in whom we find the film's 'happy ending.' *Tian Yun* insists that the 'happy' woman is the one who is committed to work for the State: or, to put it in psychoanalytic terms, the one who takes the State as her object of desire, or who displaces sexual desire into working for the State.

The newer films, especially those by women directors (and it is those that I will concentrate on here), manifest a new self-conscious split between an evident, but socially forbidden eroticism and romantic love, and the subject's interpellation by the State. The narratives foreground conflict between a sexual desire that is either socially impossible, and/or never spoken, or forever lost; and interpellation by the State, which insists on commitment to 'duty' over erotic, individual desire. (Cf. *Army Nurse, Seasons for Love, Sacrificed Youth, ZhenZhen's Beauty Parlor.*)

Chris Berry has noted that classical Chinese films manifest what he calls 'an anti-individualistic aesthetic, contrary to the Western paradigm.'[7] He argues, interestingly, that the viewing subject is only led (by the cinematic devices) to gender identification at negative points in the text – points of transgression, failure and collapse – which therefore take on negative connotation. In a culture in which, as he notes, individual interest is negatively coded, so any focus in sexual difference (which implies individual interest) must be negative.

But it is precisely here that the films by women directors which I am looking at begin to violate the mandate: the films dare to insert female (and male) desire, and in the way that they do this, they raise the problem of individual interest in a sympathetic manner. The viewing subject is made to identify with the heroine whose desire is made 'impossible' by her obligations to the State. For example, in *Army Nurse*, there is a fantastic scene in which the heroine's desire for one of her male patients is graphically and unambiguously imaged: the camera cuts between the nurse's face – increasingly manifesting sexual arousal – and the man's shoulder with the wound that she is dressing. The bandaging becomes eroticized to an almost unbearable point, as the camera also shows the man's increasing sexual arousal. (Hu Mei told me that this scene had originally been much longer, her studio leadership insisting it be cut.) The nurse and patient never consummate their love, and finally the soldier leaves the hospital. Although the couple have illegally exchanged addresses, the nurse never gets any replies to her letters. Finally, she moves to a better, city hospital; it is time to marry, so a 'suitable' match is found for her by her friends. At the last moment, the nurse refuses to engage in the loveless match, and finally she returns to her old remote Army Hospital position, where at least she has memories of her short happiness.

The entire focus of the film is on the heroine's conflict between love and duty: the filmic devices unambiguously position the spectator in sympathy with the heroine's erotic desire, which we want to be consummated. The film, that is, arguably exposes the constraints that contemporary Chinese culture imposes on sexual expression and fulfilment.

The heroine's personal emptiness is repeated in the other films that I do not have time to analyze here: each of the films contains a key scene in which the heroine's erotic gaze is finally met by the male's returned desire. In each, the desire cannot be expressed or consummated; in all cases, the heroines are left yearning to meet this 'gaze' again – a gaze that is the sign for romantic love and sexual union.

Let me note, briefly, that films by male directors are also preoccupied with the repression of sexual desire, and with the communal codes governing sexual relationships in Chinese life. However, most of the films I saw seemed less about the impossibility of a mutual desire (which is what preoccupies female directors) than about male fantasies of seduction or of revenge on women for men's cultural repression and passive position.[8] For instance, *Girl from Hunan* (dir. Xie Feim, Youth Film Studio, 1984), read in psychoanalytic terms, embodies unconscious male desire for erotic union with the mother – except that one hesitates to label a desire 'unconscious' that is so overtly displayed on the text's surface. Set in a rural community in 1920's China, the film deals with the fate of a fifteen year-old girl forced to marry a six year-old boy. We see the little boy on the one hand sucking on his own mother's breast (the 'couple' live on the family farm belonging to the boy's mother), while at the same time parading his power as husband over his wife, and engaged in semi-erotic play with her. Since the 'wife' is really a kind of surrogate mother to the boy, the scenes are charged with an incestuous eroticism.

Even though the film does indicate the wife's sexual restlessness as she matures (that is, there is some inclusion of her own desire), the seduction scene is almost classically Hollywood in its voyeurism and rendering of the heroine as object of the male gaze. An itinerant farm-worker's lust for the heroine has been established earlier in the film; in each situation, however, the heroine has refused to return the gaze or become complicit with the man's desire. However, in the scene in question, the farmer peeks at her undressing when drenched in a rain storm: gradually becoming aware of his gaze, the film shows the heroine's shy arousal and passive compliance in the intercourse that follows. The scene could be read again as a male fantasy of a female desire always waiting arousal and happy to be satisfied by no matter whom. On the other hand, it could be read (from a Western Feminist perspective) as essentially a rape scene.

On the one hand, then, the film acts out a male fantasy for regression to the infantile state, and for possession of the mother. But the film could also be addressing the contemporary male's unconscious desire for revenge on women for the new-found liberation in the Communist State which insists on parity between the sexes in the public sphere. It is, after all, a parity that contrasts dramatically with the situation in pre-revolutionary China. The revenge is extracted by what amounts, indeed, from a Western Feminist perspective, to a rape. (As Chris Berry recently noted, a similar scene in the highly acclaimed *Red Sorgum* makes the rape much more clear: the new note of an insistence on male machismo in the Chinese film is a cause for concern.)[9]

In fairness to male directors, let me note that at least two films I saw did represent more mutuality in male-female desire: these are *In the Wild Mountains* and *The Old Well*. This latter film, although only seen in its partial, rough cut, had a remarkably erotic scene in which a married man and a single woman, usually extremely controlled about their adulterous fantasies, unleash their desire when they believe that they will not survive their entombment in the old well they are repairing.

Let me now summarize earlier discussions of eroticism in the films by female directors: interpreted through the frameworks of Western feminisms, these films could be said to embody a new awareness of female subjectivity, along with a resistance of interpellation by the State (indeed, the two necessarily go hand in hand). While Western feminists might find the endings of the films retrogressive (that is, we have not been too pleased with narratives that set up desire for the male as the sole end of woman's life), the image of the single woman is itself (as others have pointed out) a new departure in a nation whose social codes translate 'woman' into 'married woman.' I understand that there is not only no social space for the single, professional woman, but also no word to describe her.

The underlying issue for women in China, then, from a Western point of view, would seem not to be entry into the public sphere – the right to work, to equal pay, to equal participation in the work force (issues that preoccupied Western feminists in the sixties and seventies), but a new, as yet not fully articulated, realization about subjectivity. It is this new awareness that haunts the films mentioned in a visual/aural rather than verbal (and explicit) manner. The old concept of self as a construction for/by the State is now pitted against a new ideology of individualism, perhaps learned partly from exposure to Western cultural products like the Hollywood film. Indeed, part of the popularity of the Hollywood films in China may be precisely the resonances they evoke for the Chinese spectator through the representation of a subjectivity he/she is interested in.

Missing from the films (again from a Western feminist perspective) are images of female-female bonding of the kind that would rival heterosexual priorities, and representations of the mother (whether in the form of hypostasization, denigration, or exposure of the mother's positioning): the figure was simply not there in most of the films we saw, and when present represented an unquestioned mother-function position, marginal to the narrative.[10] (A striking exception to this was the representation of Guilan in *In the Wild Mountains* [Yan Xuesu, 1985], who, in the wake of her husband's desertion, manages the farm alone, despite having a young baby to care for, and whose love affair with her husband's brother represents a daring violation of cultural codes.)

It has been said (e.g., by Judith Stacey) that Chinese Communism grafted its repression of subjectivity onto the new State,[11] and that it was able to do this because of the prior centuries of Confucianism. This general repression of subjectivity (male subjectivity was, and is, also repressed) in part accounts for the repression of sexuality in modern China, or its channeling into perverse forms (female foot-binding) in Confucian society. This raises fascinating questions from a Western theoretical standpoint about what a 'feminism' in China might look like, and about links between Western feminisms and a modernism that has still not arguably taken place (and perhaps never should or will take place) in China. The USA feminisms got underway in the sixties through turning bourgeois capitalism's own values on itself. Since Chinese ideology demands the submission of the subject to the State, 'duty' over personal desire, the idea of feminism as an oppositional practice is hard to insert. (One could argue that China is, from a Western point of view, still a premodern state: in this case, the idea of a new subjectivity that is linked to new questions about sexual desire and sexual difference could signal the start of the modernism that in the West ushered in bourgeois capitalism.)

This, if true, would be ironic for Western feminists whose seventies and eighties efforts were aimed ultimately at moving beyond the subjectivities offered in bourgeois capitalism, and who have in any case begun to witness the transmutation of that bourgeois capitalism into its postmodern forms. Western feminisms, in this analysis, confront the challenges (and perhaps possibilities) offered by postmodernism at the very moment that other world nations, like China, begin to move through a modernist feminism.

II: Contesting the Above Analysis: Hu Mei and Army Nurse

On one level, the above analysis assumes that the desire for cinema is a desire either to represent what the *State* desires (i.e., the repression of individuality and its accompanying sexual difference/sexual desire) or to represent directly what the State represses, i.e., sexual difference/desire. The analysis assumes a cultural or political unconscious that finds expression, or in the second case, release, in state films. It also assumes that human subjectivity is constituted through sexual difference – i.e., that, as Juliet Mitchell puts it, 'human subjectivity cannot ultimately exist outside a division between the sexes – one cannot be no sex.'[12] Since this is the case, a nation that does not evidence preoccupation with sexual difference must then be 'repressing' this difference. The fact that the mother is not represented or much discussed anywhere also points to repression of a psychoanalytically central figure in the subject's developing into a 'subject.'

On another level, the analysis attempts to understand Chinese representations in relation to Western feminist readings of Western texts, which in turn rely on certain formulations of what Western feminisms were about.

Finally, the analysis proposes links between certain societal, aesthetic and psychic modes; and sees these constellations as indicating different phases/periods in a nation's history (i.e., premodern, modern, postmodern).

I do not have time to contest all of these assumptions; and merely would suggest that they need careful examination as to their cross-cultural validity. Two small examples will make the point: first, the absence of mother-images has an obvious practical, social level to it, outside of any possible psychoanalytic ones, namely the need of the State to severely limit births due to drastic overpopulation; second, cross-cultural readings are especially problematic in relation to sexuality: would a Chinese audience read the sex scene in *Girl From Hunan* as a rape? How is rape conceptualized in China? Does the definition of rape vary from culture to culture? Is rape acceptable as a representation but not socially? Are we driven to an undesirable relativism in such cross-cultural comparisons?

Since these questions take me too far afield, let me end with noting and commenting on some interesting discrepancies between my above reading of *Army Nurse*, and the director's own comments on the film. Hu Mei first talked about her wish in the film to describe what she felt were specifically female ways of thinking: she noted that women had a less linear way of thinking than men, that women are split, disoriented by the many demands that have always been made on them. Women for her were characterized by a fragmentation and disorientation – a shorter attention span than men – all of which she attributed to conflicting demands.

Now these statements at first seemed to fit into standard Western feminist analyses about the need for women to constantly attend to men – to their husbands at home and then to their bosses at work. But in retrospect, I think Hu Mei was talking about a much older historical situation of women in China as always being only for the Other, only constructed from the place of the Other, unable ever to experience their own desire. She had wanted to convey this sense of her heroine's fragmented, dispersed thinking in a voiceover that would have consisted of unfinished sentences, meaningless phrases, disjointed series of sentences, and so on. But the studio leadership would not permit such a sound track that did not accord with their notion of realist conventions.

I thought these comments were surprisingly in accord with ideas that we associate particularly with French feminisms, and I was struck by that. But Hu Mei went on to provide a completely alternative analysis of what she was trying to do – one which turned the film into a 'national allegory' of the kind Jameson was talking about. She reasoned that there were so many Chinese films, including her own, dealing with female issues and having central female characters, because the female situation could act as an emblem for *all* Chinese peoples' frustrations: for men, too, the pressure of 'consensus' ideology is heavy, but this would be too threatening to deal with directly. The issue of sacrifice and the conflict between individual desire and the demands of the State is dealt with quite safely when put in terms of female love situations. For Hu Mei, it seemed, these narratives embody everyone's frustrations – the impossibility for both men and women to function as individuals – rather than being specifically about sexual difference or female erotic desire. I will comment on this reading in my first 'Ending' that follows:

III: The Endings

It is only fitting that there should be two endings to this paper – one providing the 'ending' as produced through the Western frameworks I began with; the other an ending that addresses the difficulties of cross-cultural textual reading. The first ending might go something like the following:

It seems that there is a new moment in China, and that this is reflected in recent films. It is not by accident that female directors and writers are central in dealing with the change: since women's situation is the more extreme, they are the ones making the strongest demands for subjectivity – for articulation of female desire. In addition, it is clear that the younger women directors, like Hu Mei, relate differently to the State than do the older generation, who lived through the Cultural Revolution. Far more than the older group, this new one is fascinated with America, which they know about primarily through Hollywood films and contact with Hong Kong. Cynical about the revolution, and with no memories of Imperialist China and its horrors, they want modernity, Western goods, and a chance to see America.

From some Western Feminist perspectives, much of this is problematic: we worked hard in the sixties and seventies to rid ourselves of bourgeois subjectivities. Ironically, many of us in the height of things (May 1968), looked to the Chinese Revolution as the model of what could be done – namely, of how a tyrannical order could be overcome and a utopian equality apparently achieved. Kristeva's book *About Chinese Women* embodies some of these idealizations.[13] We responded then to the Chinese revolutionary ideal of commitment to the community, the submersion of self in the collective.

In the eighties, however, Chinese women educated precisely in such values sense something lacking: they want a subjectivity we had identified as linked to bourgeois capitalism and to a modernism that we were attempting to move beyond. From this perspective, one could see Chinese women as working their way through a modernist phase in their assertion of subjectivity. But there seems to be some guilt about the assertion of a specifically *female* subjectivity, *female* desire: this I read from Hu Mei's rather abrupt outlining of an allegorical reading for her and other female directors' films about female desire. We see in operation, again, the difficulty for the Chinese to confront difference (here specifically sexual difference) head on: Hu Mei got concerned about an analysis that seemed to separate males from females – to emphasize specifically *female* frustrations and repressions – and she resorted to an analysis that would apply to *all* the Chinese, that would reassert the collective.

Meanwhile, those of us in America who went through the sixties confront a paradigm shift variously called postmodernism, postindustrialism or New Age Consciousness. Having long ago abandoned the utopian ideal of submersion of self in the collective, we now seem on the brink of a postmodern crisis presaging the impossibility of subjectivity in the old senses. Here then we find a big distance between women in China and in America today.

The second ending might go as follows: cross-cultural readings are fraught with dangers, as I noted to begin with. Some of those dangers are clear in the assumptions of my readings that I outlined: but how are we to arrive at a method, a theory, for reading texts from Other Worlds until we have first answered some of the questions about how different cultures think about representation; and second, until we know more about the unconscious of different cultures as it might pertain to the level of the imaginary and to the terrain of the visual artistic text; and finally, about whether or not the very construction of social 'phases' (feudalism, modernism, postmodernism) is intricately linked to traditions of Western thought, and not relevant to the Chinese situation?

To take but one example from the questions listed here, it seems that gender representations signify on a whole series of levels: for one thing, the gaze is often more mutual than in American films – men's desire imaged as equally frustrated and impossible as that of women; but, further, the entire signifying of sexual relations may stand in as a metaphor (or analog) for the broader political/social/intellectual frustration of both genders. In other words, as Hu Mei indicated, representing woman's unhappiness in film may mask the impossibility for everyone in modern China to give reign to a whole series of desires beyond the sexual.

But we could take the reading even further: if men also suffer from the need to submit to the demands of the State, they are arguably emasculated by their situation. Given the prior phallic order, and given classical Oedipal rivalry with the Father, they may be harmed even more than women. State Communism, in demanding male submission to the Law of the Father with little possibility for obtaining at least some parity with the Father position (as in free-enterprise capitalism), may produce men psychically damaged in deeper ways even than women. In addition, the inability to consummate love hurts them, too, as some recent films stress (see Chen Kaige's *The King of the Children*).

It is, however, hard to be certain about such readings that rely on a perhaps culturally specific concept of the psyche, or about their worth, as I noted at the beginning. The uncertainty exposes the need for more research. If cross-cultural analysis lays bare this need, if it has at least opened up the questions we need to answer, then it will have created the space for beginning a dialogue that may benefit us all.

Notes

1. Gayatri Spivak, *In Other Worlds: Essays in Cultural Politics* (New York and London: Routledge, 1988).

2. Cf. Ma Ning, 'The Textual and Critical Difference of Being Radical: Reconstructing the Chinese Leftist Films of the 1930s.' *Wide Angle*, 11: 2, pp. 22–31.
3. Esther Yau, '*Yellow Earth*: Western Analysis of a Non-western Text,' *Film Quarterly* (Winter 1987–8).
4. Thanks to the kind auspices of Chris Berry, I interviewed Hu Mei when visiting Beijing in Summer 1987.
5. Fredric Jameson, 'Third World Literature in the Era of Multifnational Capitalism,' *Social Text* 15 (Fall 1986).
6. Leo Ou Fan Lee in Chris Berry (ed.) *Perspectives on Chinese Cinema.*
7. Cf. Chris Berry. I am indebted to Berry's pioneering work on women in the Chinese film for my arguments in this paper. See his paper on women in the Chinese film, forthcoming in *Camera Obscura*.
8. Informal discussions with Berry at the Asian Cinema Studies Conference, Athens, Ohio, Fall 1988.
9. Ibid.
10. Cf. Tao Chun in *Country Couple* (Hu Bingliu, 1983): Xiu Chen in *Garlands at the Foot of the Mountain* (Xie Jin, 1984); Qiao Zhen in *Life* (Wu Tianming, 1984).
11. Judith Stacey, *Patriarchy and Socialist Revolution in China* (Berkeley, CA: University of California Press, 1983).
12. Juliet Mitchell, 'The Question of Femininity,' in *The British School of Psychoanalysis: The Independent Tradition* (New Haven and London: Yale University Press, 1986).
13. Julia Kristeva, *About Chinese Women*, trans. Marion Byars Publishers, Ltd. (New York: Urizen Books, 1977).

9

SEEING MODERN CHINA: TOWARD A THEORY OF ETHNIC SPECTATORSHIP

Rey Chow

As contemporary critical discourses become increasingly sensitive to the wide-ranging implications of the term 'other,' one major problem that surfaces is finding ways to articulate subjectivities that are, in the course of their participation in the dominant culture, 'othered' and marginalized. Metaphors and apparatuses of *seeing* become overwhelmingly important ways of talking, simply because 'seeing' carries with it the connotation of a demarcation of ontological boundaries between 'self' and 'other,' whether racial, social, or sexual. However, the most difficult questions surrounding the demarcation of boundaries implied by 'seeing' have to do not with positivistic taxonomic juxtapositions of self-contained identities and traditions in the manner of 'this is you' and 'that is us,' but rather, who is 'seeing' whom, and how? What are the power relationships between the 'subject' and 'object' of the culturally overdetermined 'eye'?

The primacy I accord 'seeing' is an instance of the cultural predicament in which the ethnic subject finds herself. The institutionalized apparatuses of 'seeing' on which I rely for my analyses – cinema, film theory, and the nexus of attitudes and fantasies that have developed around them – are part and parcel of a dominant 'symbolic' whose potent accomplishments are inextricably bound up with its scopophilia. To this extent, the felicity with which my analyses *can* proceed owes itself to the reversal of history that informs the development of theory in the West. This reversal makes available to those who think and write in the West a spaciousness that is necessary for their conceptual

From Rey Chow (1991), *Women and Chinese Modernity: The Politics of Reading Between East and West*, Minneapolis: University of Minnesota Press, pp. 3–33.

mobility, experimentation, and advancement, and that is nonetheless possible only because many others continue to be excluded from the same spaces. The following discussion should be read in this light.

1

During one of the press interviews inaugurating his film *The Last Emperor* in 1987, Bernardo Bertolucci recalls his experience of going to China:

> I went to China because I was looking for fresh air . . . For me it was love at first sight. I loved it. I thought the Chinese were fascinating. They have an innocence. They have a mixture of a people *before* consumerism, *before* something that happened in the West. *Yet in the meantime* they are incredibly sophisticated, elegant and subtle, because they are 4,000 years old. For me the mixture was irresistible.[1]

The registers of time in which the European director organizes China's fascination are hardly innocent. His love for this 'other' culture is inspired at once by the feeling that it exists 'before' or outside his own world, the contemporary world of the consumerist West, and by the feeling that, within its own context, the Chinese culture is highly developed and refined – because, after all, it is '4,000 years old.' In this rather casual and touristy response to China lies a paradoxical conceptual structure that is ethnocentric. By ethnocentric, I do not mean an arrogant dismissal of the other culture as inferior (Bertolucci's enthusiasm disputes this), but – in a way that is at once more complex and more disturbing – how positive, respectful, and admiring feelings for the 'other' can themselves be rooted in un-self-reflexive, culturally coded perspectives.

The story of Pu Yi, as we know, is that of a boy who became China's last emperor at the age of three, who grew up pampered by a court of corrupt eunuchs at a time when China had already become a republic, who collaborated with Japan's invasion of China during the 1930s by agreeing to be emperor of the puppet state Manchukuo, and who, after nearly ten years of 'reeducation' under the Chinese Communist regime in the 1950s, lived the rest of his life as an ordinary citizen in Beijing. For Bertolucci, Pu Yi's story is that of a journey that goes 'from darkness to light.' Pu Yi is a 'great man who becomes little, but also, I think, free.' The way in which positive values are assembled in these remarks is interesting. Situated in a culture that is thought to be 'before' the West and sophisticated in its own way, the story of Pu Yi is also the story of a man's 'liberation.' This assemblage makes one ask: In relation to what is Pu Yi 'free'? What is darkness and what is light? In the most rudimentary manner, the film's colors contradict this notion of a journey 'from darkness to light.' If 'darkness' refers to Pu Yi's imprisonment in China's imperial past and 'light' to his liberation under the Communist regime (those who read Chinese would notice that the wall against which the group activities at the Fushun Detention Center take place is painted with the characters *guangming*, meaning 'light'), why is it that the 'imperial' scenes were shot with such dazzling arrays of phantasmagoric golds and yellows, while the 'Communist' scenes were done in a drab mixture of blues and grays?

Bertolucci's film is an excellent example of a response to modern China that is inscribed at a crossroads of discourses, all of which have to do with 'seeing' China as the other. In demonstrating what some of these discourses are, my discussion necessarily leads into more general problems of Chinese modernity, particularly as these pertain to the formulation of a 'Chinese' subject.

When he describes the differences among the Japanese and Chinese members of his film crew, Bertolucci makes a revealing comment:

> They are very different. The Chinese, of course, are more ancient. But also, the Japanese have this myth of virility. They are more macho. The Chinese are the opposite, more feminine. A bit passive. But passive, as I say, in the way of people when they are so intelligent and so sophisticated they don't need machismo.

He then goes on to describe how Pu Yi's passivity is a kind of 'Oriental dignity' that the West may misunderstand, and so forth. Before we discuss how the equation of the Last Emperor with what is conventionally designated as the 'feminine' quality of passivity is enunciated through the cinematic apparatus, let us consider for a moment what this kind of equation means, what its structural intentions are, and why, even if at a certain level it has a subversive potential, it is highly problematic.

A text that would assist us here, because it shares Bertolucci's idealization of China through the category of the feminine, is Julia Kristeva's *About Chinese Women*.[2] Written at a time when the post-Second World War disillusionment with the liberal West was at its peak in European and American intellectual circles, Kristeva's book should first of all be understood in terms of a *critique* of *Western* discourse, a critique that characterizes all of her works. *About Chinese Women* is primarily a book about the epistemological deficiencies of the West rather than about China. However, Kristeva's critique is complicated by the fact that it is sexualized: China is counterposed to the West not only because it is different, but also because it is, in a way that reminds us of Bertolucci's configuration of it, feminine. In the West, as Kristeva's recapitulation of the creation myth of Adam and Eve shows, woman is merely functional – 'divided from man, made of that very thing which is missing in him' (p. 17). Even though woman has a body, her corporeality is already a sign of her exclusion from the relationship between man and God. Tracing this 'conception' of Western woman through historical as well as mythical sources, Kristeva argues that female sexuality at its most irreducible, that is, physical, level is denied symbolic recognition, and that the sexual difference between man and woman is hence repressed for the more metaphysical fusion between man and God in a monotheistic, patriarchal system. 'China,' on the other hand, organizes sexual difference differently, by a frank admission of genitality. One example of Kristeva's thesis can be found in the way she interprets the Chinese custom of foot binding. This example reveals in an economical way the problems inherent to the idealist preoccupation with another culture in terms of 'femininity.' I want therefore to elaborate on it.

Kristeva reminds us of Freud's observation (in the essay 'Fetishism,' 1927) that foot binding is a symbol of the 'castration of woman,' which, she adds, 'Chinese civilization was unique in admitting' (p. 83). However, Kristeva's appraisal of the Chinese custom goes one step further than Freud's. While the latter sees foot binding as a *variety* of castration, which for him remains the fundamental organizational principle of human civilization, Kristeva emphasizes its specifically feminine significance. Comparing foot binding with circumcision, which she describes as a kind of symbolic castration, she offers the following analysis. Circumcision, which is the equivalent of a prohibitive mark, is made on the body of man. This means that symbolically in the West, it is man who is the recipient of the mark that signifies mutilation, subordination, and hence difference; Western man becomes thus at once man and woman, 'a woman to the father' (p. 26), 'his father's daughter' (p. 85), so to speak. Western woman, in spite of her physical difference, remains in this way uncounted and superfluous. In foot binding, on the other hand, Kristeva sees Chinese culture's understanding of woman's *equal claim* to the symbolic. The custom is a sign of the anxiety that accompanies that understanding, but more important, it is a sign that is conspicuously displayed on the body of woman, which becomes the conscious symbolic bearer of the permanent struggle between man and woman. The gist of Kristeva's reading of China is utopian. Reading *with* her, we would think that the Chinese practice of maiming women's bodies is Chinese society's recognition, rather than denial, of woman's fundamental claim to social power. Anthropologically, the logic that Kristeva follows may be termed 'primitive,' with all the ideological underpinnings of the term at work: the act of wounding another's body, instead of being given the derogative meanings attributed to them by a humanistic perspective, is invested with the kind of meaning that one associates with warfare, antagonism, or even cannibalism in tribal society; the 'cruelty' involved becomes a sign of the way the opponent's worth is acknowledged and reciprocated – with awe.

Kristeva's insights into the Chinese symbolic belong to the same order that Bertolucci, in the remarks I quote at the beginning, marks with the word 'Yet': 'Yet in the meantime they are incredibly sophisticated, elegant and subtle, because they are 4,000 years old.' These are the insights that situate another culture in an ideal time that is marked off taxonomically from 'our' time and that is thus allowed to play with its own sophisticated rhythms. More important, this ideal time in which China is recognized for its 'own' value is much in keeping with the way femininity has been defined in Kristeva's work. First of all, we remember that 'Woman can never be defined.'[3] To define woman as such is to identify with what Kristeva calls 'the time of history' – 'time as project, teleology, linear and projective unfolding, time as departure, progression, and arrival.'[4] Instead, woman for Kristeva is a 'space' that is linked to 'repetition' and 'eternity.' Woman is thus *negative* to the time of history and cannot 'be':[5]

> A woman cannot 'be'; it is something which does not even belong in the order of *being*. It follows that a feminist practice can only be negative, at odds with what already exists so that we may say 'that's not it' and 'that's still not it.' In 'woman' I see something that cannot be represented, something that is not said, something above and beyond nomenclatures and ideologies.[6]

This belief in the 'negative' relation occupied by women to the 'time of history' helps us comprehend the subversive intent behind *About Chinese Women*. Because the existing symbolic order in the West precludes woman in an a priori manner, Kristeva's way of subverting it is by following its logic to the hilt, and by dramatizing woman as totally 'outside,' 'negative,' 'unrepresentable.' Her notion of the *chora*,[7] by which she designates the 'semiotic,' maternal substratum of subjectivity that can be located only negatively, in avant-garde or 'poetic' language, or in the nonrational elements of speech such as rhythm, intonation, and gesture, receives here its further extension through her reading of another culture. The result of this reading is precisely to fantasize that other culture in terms of a timeless 'before,' as we have encountered in Bertolucci's laudatory description of the Chinese as 'a people before consumerism, before something that happened in the West.' Kristeva's rejoinder to Bertolucci can be found in statements like these: '. . . in China . . . The strangeness persists . . . through a highly developed civilization which enters *without complexes* into the modern world, and yet preserves a logic unique to itself that no exoticism can account for' (p. 12; my emphasis). The attributions of a reality that is 'pre-Oedipal' and 'pre-psychoanalytic' (p. 58) to China are what in part prompted Gayatri Spivak's criticism of Kristeva's project, which 'has been, not to *deconstruct* the origin, but rather to *recuperate*, archeologically and formulaically, what she locates as the potential originary space *before* the sign.'[8]

Even though Kristeva sees China in an interesting and, indeed, 'sympathetic' way, there is nothing in her arguments as such that cannot be said without 'China.' What she proposes is not so much learning a lesson from a different culture as a different method of reading from within the West. For, what is claimed to be 'unique' to China is simply understood as the 'negative' or 'repressed' side of Western discourse. In thus othering and feminizing China, is Kristeva not repeating the metaphysics she wants to challenge? Especially since she has so carefully explicated the *superfluous* relation that Western woman has to the symbolic, might we not repeat after her, and say that the triangle Kristeva-the West-China in fact operates the same way as the triangle Man-God-Woman, with the last member in each set of relationships occupying the 'excluded' position? Isn't the Western critic writing negatively from within her symbolic like Western Man in the 'homosexual economy,' being reduced to 'a woman to the father,' 'his father's daughter,' while China, being 'essentially' different, can only be the 'woman' whose materiality/corporeality becomes the sign of her repression?

One way out of this metaphysical impasse is, I think, by going against Kristeva's reading of China as an absolute 'other.' Much as this act of 'othering' China is accompanied with modesty and self-deprecation, which Kristeva underscores by emphasizing the speculative, culture-bound nature of her project, perhaps it is precisely these deeply cultivated gestures of humility that are the heart of the matter here. We should ask instead whether the notion that China is absolutely 'other' and unknowable is not itself problematic. I will cite three examples of Kristeva's unnecessary attribution of 'otherness' to China to illustrate my point.

1. The suggestion that the Chinese language, because it is tonal, preserves an archaic 'psychic stratum' that is 'pre-Oedipal,' 'pre-syntactic,' 'pre-Symbolic' and hence dependent on the 'maternal' (pp. 55–7). To look at Chinese, and for that matter any language, in this manner is to overlook the uses by its speakers, which are precisely what cannot be written off in such terms as 'pre-syntactic' and 'pre-Symbolic.' To put this criticism differently, what is the meaning of an 'archaic' 'psychic stratum' in a culture that Kristeva has herself shown to be 'pre-psychoanalytic'? If 'archaic' and 'pre' are the same, what can China's relevance be other than that of 'primitivism'? And, if a *contemporary* culture is valued for its primitivism, doesn't this mean it is 'outside' our time, confined to its own immobility?
2. Kristeva's idealization of the 'maternal' order in China in terms of an 'empty and peaceful center' (p. 159) – in other words, of what she identifies as *chora*. Kaja Silverman's comments in another context apply equally to Kristeva's treatment of Chinese women as they do to her treatment of 'China': 'By relegating the mother to the interior of the *chora*/womb, Kristeva reduces her to silence.'[9] As my analysis of her reading of foot binding shows, her structural understanding of the 'primitive' logic behind Chinese society's practice of maiming women's bodies leaves the problem of Chinese women's suffering intact. Instead of seeing women in an active discursive role expressing discontent with this practice, her reading says, 'In your suffering, you are the bearers of an archaic truth.' Thus negated, women are refused their place as subjects in the symbolic.[10]
3. Ironically, this refusal goes smoothly with Kristeva's affirmation of another strand of 'otherness' about China: Taoism. In glorifying the 'subversive' and 'liberating' impact Taoism has on Chinese society, Kristeva, like many Westerners who turn to the 'East' for spiritual guidance, must leave aside the consideration that perhaps it is exactly Taoism's equation of the female principle with 'silence' and 'negativity' that traditionally allows its coexistence and collaboration with Confucianism's misogyny. In a culture constructed upon the complicity between these master systems, Chinese women not only are oppressed but also would support their own oppression through the

feelings of spiritual resignation that are dispersed throughout Chinese society on a mundane basis. Kristeva is told this bitter truth by a Chinese woman whom she interviews, but, intent on her own 'materialist' reading of China, she does not want to believe it:

> The mother of three children, of whom the eldest is ten, she studied history for four years at the University and has been working at the museum for the past five years. I ask her:
>
> Wang Chong, for you, is a materialist. What is your definition of a materialist? Wasn't it he who fought against the treatises on the body, and certain Taoist rituals as well? Doesn't the Taoist tradition represent – albeit in mystical form – certain materialist demands against Confucianism?
>
> But my question will remain unanswered, except for her affirmation of 'the complicity between Taoism and Confucianism, two aspects of idealism, both of which are surpassed by Wang Chong'. Surpassed? Or suppressed? (p. 177)

So, as Chinese 'woman' acquires the meanings of the Kristevian materialism that is said to exist in a timeless manner, from ancient to Communist China, *About Chinese Women* repeats, in spite of itself, the historical tradition in which China has been thought of in terms of an 'eternal standstill' since the eighteenth century.[11] By giving that tradition a new reading, Kristeva espouses it again, this time from a feminized, negativized perspective. The seductiveness of this metaphysics of feminizing the other (culture) cannot be overstated. Bertolucci's film gives us a text whose beauty and power depend precisely on such a metaphysics.

2

In one of the early scenes in *The Last Emperor*, after the three-year-old Pu Yi has been installed on the throne, we are shown some of the intimate details of his daily life. The little boy, surrounded by a group of eunuchs who are eager to please him, is seen perching over a miniature model of the Forbidden City. His playmate, one of the eunuchs, takes pains to match the model with 'reality,' emphasizing where His Majesty was crowned, where he lives, where he now is, and so forth. The model therefore functions as an instrument that gives the little boy his 'bearings.' To use the language of contemporary psychoanalytic criticism, we witness in this scene a kind of 'mirror stage' in which a child learns his 'identity' through a representational structure that coheres the present moment of looking with the chaotic, tumultuous events that take place around him. While this profound lesson of self-recognition triggers rings of giggles in little Pu Yi, our attention to it is displaced by another event – the completion of Pu Yi's defecation. Swiftly, one eunuch puts a woven lid over the imperial chamber pot, and the camera, following his movements, shows him delivering this precious item to the imperial doctor, who removes the lid, looks at the feces, smells it, and gives advice on the emperor's diet. Meanwhile Pu Yi is taking his bath, again surrounded by eunuchs who are at once servants, entertainers, respondents to questions, and bearers of the little boy's anal-sadistic tantrums. This series of scenes culminates in the moment when Pu Yi's wet nurse appears at the door. At the sight of her, Pu Yi abandons his play and runs toward her, crying, 'I want to go home, I want to go home.' A eunuch hastens from behind to cover his small naked body with a cloth. This kind of caring, protective gesture from a servant would be repeated a few times during the course of the film, always at a moment when Pu Yi feels utterly deserted.

This series of scenes epitomizes one of the several orders of visualism[12] that are crucial to the film's organization. As emperor, Pu Yi *commands* attention no matter where he is. He is thus the 'center' of a universe that 'belongs' to him. In this respect, 'attention' is one of the many embellishments that accompany the emperor's presence. Be they in the form of colors, objects, or human attendants, embellishments as such have no separate existence of their own, but are always part of the emperor's possessions. This 'attention' is meanwhile a slanted, not direct, gaze: in the scenes where the emperor is about to approach, people stand aside, turn their heads away, or avert their gaze; the eunuchs dare not contradict what the emperor says; people want to kowtow to him even in 1950, when he is no longer emperor. The emperor's position is thus one of dominance, with all the 'phallic' meanings of exclusivity that such a position connotes. As we recall the words of the dying Empress Cixi: no men except the emperor are allowed to stay in the Forbidden City after dark, and 'these other men – they are not real men. They are eunuchs.' However, intersecting this first order of visualism, in which Pu Yi is seen with imperial power, is another, in which Pu Yi is seen as totally passive. 'Commanding' attention becomes indistinguishable from the experience of being watched and followed everywhere. The complexities of this second order of visualism are, as I argue in the following, what constitute the film's 'gaze.'

As Pu Yi cries 'I want to go home, I want to go home,' the fascination of the ubiquitous attention he receives as emperor is transformed and superseded by another meaning – one that reveals 'from within' Pu Yi's lonely condition as a human being. A doubled gaze, then, is at work; the task that Bertolucci sets his camera is that of portraying the absolutely forlon *inner* existence of a man whose outer environment bespeaks the most extraordinary visual splendor. How can the camera do this?

In her discussion of Laura Mulvey's classic essay, 'Visual Pleasure and Narrative Cinema,' Kaja Silverman recalls two representational strategies proposed by Mulvey for neutralizing the anxiety caused by female lack in classical narrative cinema. The first of these strategies 'involves an interrogation calculated to establish either the female subject's guilt or her illness, while the second negotiates her erotic over-investment.'[13] If we substitute the words 'female subject' with 'Pu Yi,' this statement becomes a good description of how the space occupied by Pu Yi vis-à-vis the camera is, in fact, a feminized one. What enables this is the portrayal of him primarily as a child who never grew up, and who is aligned metonymically with the ancient and inarticulate (i.e., temporally and linguistically 'other') world of his mothers.

Instead of being the straightforward inscription of his imperial power, then, the first order of visualism that shows Pu Yi to be the recipient of ubiquitous attention already belongs to what Silverman calls 'erotic over-investment.' Of all the components to this 'over-investment,' the most obvious are, of course, the visible elements of a re-created imperial China: the exotic architecture, the abundance of art objects, the clothes worn by members of the late Manchu court, their peculiar mannerisms, the camel or two resting on the outskirts of the Forbidden City, and the thousands of servants at the service of the emperor. The endowment of museum quality on the filmic images feeds the craving of the eyes. The cinema audience become vicarious tourists in front of whom 'China' is served on a screen. And yet what is interesting about the erotic over-investment is perhaps not the sheer visible display of ethnic imperial plenitude, but the amorous attitude the camera adopts toward such a display. To give one example, in the scene when Pu Yi is practicing calligraphy with his brother Pu Jie, he notices that the latter is wearing yellow. This greatly displeases him, because 'only the emperor can wear yellow.' A verbal confrontation between the two boys follows, which soon becomes a debate over the question of Pu Yi's status as emperor. Pu Jie puts down his trump card: 'You are not the emperor any more.' Our attention to a detail of the sensuous kind – the color yellow – gives way to an awareness of ritual proprieties, but the information pertaining to the ethnic class hierarchy is quickly transformed into the pronouncement of a historical and political *fait accompli*. This transformation, this movement from one kind of attention to another, indicates that the erotic overinvestment of Pu Yi is negotiated by a kind of sympathetic understanding, the understanding that he is the victim of a lavish, elaborate world that is, itself, a historical lie.

Although Pu Yi's perception of the coded meaning of yellow is correct, the environment in which that perception would be of significance has already vanished. At this point, 'erotic over-investment' intersects with the other representational strategy, the 'interrogation calculated to establish either the female subject's guilt or her illness.' The 'sympathetic understanding' that I am speaking about can thus be rewritten as a historical interrogation that shows Pu Yi to be 'ill' or 'deluded'; hence, it follows, we have many suggestions of his entrapment in his dream of being emperor, and of the guilt that he eventually feels. At the same time, however – and this is what makes the film's 'message' highly ambiguous – it is as if the camera refuses to abandon a certain erotic interest in Pu Yi in spite of such historical knowledge. Precisely in its 'sympathetic' attitude toward him, the camera takes over the attention bestowed upon the Last Emperor by other filmic characters and makes it part of *its own trajectory in courting him*. In the scene where Pu Jie is introduced, which precedes the one we are discussing, this courting is orchestrated through a combination of memorable image and memorable sound. We first see a pair of human legs walking toward the prison cell in which Pu Yi is waiting alone, while faintly but audibly, the beat from the film's theme, which we heard once already with the opening credits, prepares us for something important. As Pu Jie enters and the two men's eyes meet, the moment of recognition between brothers is amplified by the music, which now comes to the fore and takes us back to the day when they met each other for the first time as young boys. The forlorn inner condition of a man whose heart is warmed by the renewed closeness of a kinsman is thus not merely 'displayed,' but constructed, interpreted, and interwoven with richly suggestive 'subjective' memory. It is this kind of careful, attentive 'courting' that establishes the second order of visualism and that ultimately accounts for the film's eroticism.

However, having located the eroticism between Pu Yi the feminine, feminized object and the aroused, caressing strokes of Bertolucci's camera, we must add that the latter are figural: they can be felt and heard, but cannot be seen. If Bertolucci's humanistic sympathy for Pu Yi's predicament belongs to a certain historical 'interrogation,' that interrogation must remain *invisible* in the film precisely because it functions as the structuring 'gaze.' As if by a stroke of fate, this gaze finds in Chinese history a 'stand-in' behind which it can hide – the interrogation of Pu Yi by the Chinese Communists.

This other, visible interrogation is in fact what introduces the story of the film, which begins with Pu Yi returning as a prisoner of war from the Soviet Union to China in 1950. The harshness of this interrogation is made apparent from the very beginning, when some fellow prisoners of war, on recognizing Pu Yi, come forward and kowtow to him and are quickly hustled away by others who are wary of the danger involved in such gestures of loyalty to a national traitor. Pu Yi's (fictional) attempt to commit suicide fails. As he wakes up at the slapping of the Fushun jail governor, he asks, 'Where am I?', a question that reminds us of the instruction he received over the miniature model of the Forbidden City decades before. This time his recognition of 'himself' must begin with the loud and cold words, 'The People's Republic of China!' The insensitive and impersonal nature of the interrogation awaiting Pu Yi is obvious. The contrasting lack of sensuality in the scenes in the Fushun Detention Center goes hand in hand with the interrogators who are eager for their famous prisoner's confession. The irony of Bertolucci's direction is subtle: Pu Yi's chief interrogator is played by an actor who reminds one of the young Mao Zedong. There is also the suggestion that the Chinese Communists, apart from coercive terrorizing, understand little about their own history. At the beginning stage of Pu Yi's confession, we are shown a scene in which the jail governor, wanting to find out more about his prisoner's life, turns to the pages of *Twilight in the Forbidden City*, the book written by Pu Yi's Scottish tutor, Reginald Johnston (one-time magistrate of the British Leased Territory of Weihaiwei in Shandong Province), after he returned to England. This scene is remarkable because it shows the elderly Chinese man opening the book in an attempt to know more about recent Chinese history; what he reads, however, becomes the voice of

Johnston narrating events that take us back to the time when he first arrived in Beijing. It is Johnston's voice, then, that the camera follows, and Johnston's account that shapes the elderly Chinese man's understanding of Pu Yi. As Johnston's entry into Pu Yi's life is placed at the point when Pu Yi loses his wet nurse, he is the symbol of the boy's embarkment on a phase of educational 'enlightenment' and his departure from the hallucinatory, decadent, maternal world of breast sucking. In this way, the Chinese Communist interrogation of Pu Yi falls in line with the 'Western' education represented by Johnston. During the interrogation, Johnston's name is invoked at the strategic moment when the jail governor wants Pu Yi to confess to having voluntarily submitted to the Japanese plot to make him emperor of Manchukuo.

The appearance of the Japanese at this point in the film's narrative serves to amplify the utterly passive nature of Pu Yi's political existence. Here, his life as a prisoner – first under the waning Manchu Dynasty, then in the political turmoil of the Chinese Republic, then in Manchukuo, and finally in Communist China – comes together in its multiple layers of 'castration,' to use once again the language of contemporary psychoanalytic criticism. It is here, therefore, that he appears his most handsome and plays his assigned role as 'lack'/the 'castrated' to the full. With his eyes staring dreamily into the distance and the flicker of a smile appearing on his face, he responds to the moralistic charge of his pro-foreignness with an abandoned, easeful matter-of-factness: 'Of course, everything foreign was good . . . especially Wrigley's chewing gum, Bayer aspirin, and cars.' But while Pu Yi's defiance does not go unnoticed, it serves only to fuel the eroticism that has determined the way we look at him all along. These statements from Silverman's description of the film *Gilda* apply equally well to Pu Yi: 'Confession and fetishism do not here work to deflect attention away from female lack to male potency, but to inspire in the viewer (fictional and actual) the desire to have it fully revealed – to have it revealed, moreover, not as a repellent but as a pleasurable sight' (Silverman, p. 231). Hence, Pu Yi's defiance only leads the interrogators to pressure him for more in what increasingly amounts to their sadistic desire to 'have it all' in the name of reform and rehabilitation.

This process of interrogation is conducted over a series of filmic signifiers onto which are displaced the motifs of enlightenment, nationalism, and political progressiveness. As we can see, the interrogative process, like the sensual display of Pu Yi's imperial past, is also directed by a voyeuristic gaze. But with a difference: while the 'imperial' display amounts to a museum aesthetics, the 'interrogation' comes across with a great sense of domination and oppression. As I have already suggested, the most disturbing question is how the Chinese Communist interrogation has been used as a stand-in for the camera's, so that the harshness and cruelty of the act of interrogating can be safely displaced onto the Chinese authorities, while the camera's gaze retains its freedom to roam about the body of the 'other' with its 'sympathetic' humanism. Silverman's observation that 'a gaze within the fiction serves to conceal the controlling gaze outside the fiction'

(Silverman, p. 204) is poignantly relevant in the cross-cultural context of Bertolucci's film. While the Chinese Communist interrogation is shown in an ambivalent light (at best historically necessary, at worst inhumane), the camera is able to sustain its amorous relationship with Pu Yi as a dignified human individual whose truth needs to be protected from the devastation of the interrogators' thirst for facts, thus aesthetically demonstrating what Bertolucci means when he says, 'There is a kind of universal meaning in this figure.' If my reading of Pu Yi as a figure for China-as-woman is at all tenable, then this interested, protective gesture on the part of the European director can be read as an allegory of what Spivak in a different context refers to as 'white men saving brown women from brown men.'[14]

The eroticized relationship between the camera's gaze and the last emperor also means that we cannot confront the issue of femininity in terms of the film's women characters. In the private conversations I had with a couple of female American sinologists, I gathered a favorable response to the women characters, especially the empress, who they thought represents a kind of wisdom and courage that they associate with 'Chinese' women. I think this kind of reading misses the complexities of the cinematic apparatus because it is content with a straightforward correspondence between 'images of women' and 'femininity.' As a result, femininity as the 'space' and 'spectacle' that functions in relation to the camera's gaze into another culture, and the politics that are inscribed therewith, are comfortably bypassed. In actuality, because it is Pu Yi and 'China' who occupy the feminized space in this cinematic structure of eroticism, the women characters are pushed to what I'd call an astructural outside, the 'other' of the other, as it were, that wavers between the ontological statuses of 'nature' and 'hysteria.' The wet nurse, the high consorts of the court, the empress, the Second Consort, and 'Eastern Jewel' all appear as either objects of pleasure or addicts to pleasure, strung together through a narrative that remembers them as gratifying female breasts, partners in sex games, perverse lesbians, and opium smokers. Meanwhile, whenever these women characters think and act with 'courage' and 'wisdom,' their thoughts and acts become indistinguishable from excessiveness if not downright insanity. The empress's contempt for Pu Yi's collaboration with the Japanese in Manchukuo is represented through her 'crazy' behavior at the inaugurating banquet. The film thus corroborates the commonsense feeling that for a woman to make a sensible point, she must first become a spectacle and show herself to be 'out of her mind.' As the bearer of truthful political understanding, the empress survives only as an invalid.

That *The Last Emperor* is a perfect example of how another culture can be 'produced' as a feminized spectacle is confirmed by its reception in Hollywood. The film was nominated for nine Oscars at the sixtieth Academy Awards ceremony and won all nine. A look at the list reveals more specifically what exactly is rewarded: the *making* of the film. The categories included best motion picture, best director, best screenplay adopted from another medium, best cinematography, best art direction, best film editing, best costume, best sound, and best original score. In spite of his excellent performance, John Lone, who plays Pu Yi, was not even nominated for best actor. The question that arises is of course not whether an Oscar is 'genuinely' valuable, but how it is that in a production that seems to be recognized for its excellence in so many respects, the same kind of recognition is not granted its 'players.' The repeated emphases on the 'international' nature of the film's production[15] can hardly disguise the fact that what appear on the screen are mostly what would be identified as 'Chinese' faces enacting a 'Chinese' story/history. My point is not that Hollywood's neglect of the Chinese actors and actresses is a sign of racial discrimination *tout court*; rather, that in this failure to give equal recognition to the film's acting lies perhaps a confusion of the players with what they play. After all, one of the interesting problems about film acting is that the actor/actress straddles the roles of film *maker* and film *image*. Categorically, therefore, acting contains an ambivalence that distinguishes it from other aspects of film production. In the case of a saga like *The Last Emperor*, this ambivalence can only be more pronounced. In turn, we can say that when an actor/actress is given an award for acting, it is an indication that he/she, the actual individual *outside* the film, has done a good job playing a fictional role. An award for acting can thus be looked upon as the film industry's way of distinguishing an actor/actress from a role and of putting him/her on the side of the film 'makers.'

On the other hand, I hope my analysis of Pu Yi and *The Last Emperor* as a feminized space in the structure of Bertolucci's commercialized aesthetics has made it clear by now why it is indeed not surprising that the 'acting' of this film cannot be recognized as 'creative' talent. After all, if this feminized spectacle has grown out of Bertolucci's need for 'fresh air' in the first place, it must remain and can only be rewarded as *his* creation, *his* story. (Bertolucci: 'I am a storyteller, I am not a historian . . . To history I prefer mythology. Because history starts with the truth and goes toward lies. While mythology starts from lies and fantasy and goes toward truth.') What at first sight looks like a sensational advertisement announcing the availability of the film on video cassette and laser videodisc offers an accurate summary of Bertolucci's story: 'Emperor. Playboy. Prisoner. Man.'[16]

3

So far, my reading strategy with regard to *The Last Emperor* has been more or less congruent with the method of dissecting 'narrative cinema and visual pleasure' given to us by Laura Mulvey in her essay of the same title. Mulvey argues that, on the basis of vision, there is a fundamental difference in the classical film between the roles it assigns to men and women. The camera's gaze, associated with scopophilia, is 'masculine,' while images on the screen, in the state of being looked at and thus eroticized, are 'feminine.' Silverman comments: 'This opposition is entirely in keeping with the dominant cultural roles assigned to men and women, since voyeurism is the active or "masculine" form of the scopophilic drive, while exhibitionism is the passive or "feminine" form of the same drive' (Silverman, p. 223). Accordingly, as they look at cinematic images, the spectators identify with the camera's gaze; identification is thus a 'masculinizing' identification that perpetuates the reduction of women to an eroticized image. Although visual pleasure is 'threatening in content' (Mulvey, p. 309) (since, to retrace the logic of Freud's castration complex, it implies male fear and anxiety), it is primarily its function in constructing women as passive and inferior that concerns Mulvey as a feminist.[17]

Mulvey's essay has been controversial since its first publication. Criticisms of her argument converge on what most consider to be its ahistorical theoretical determinism. Fairly recently, Mulvey revised and critiqued her own position, notably in an essay called 'Changes: Thoughts on Myth, Narrative and Historical Experience.'[18] Her self-critique alerts us to the historicity of the *form* in which her original thesis was constructed. Looking at it retrospectively, Mulvey describes the polarization of male and female positions ('active' versus 'passive,' 'spectator' versus 'spectacle,' and so on) as a conceptual typology that, despite its relevance to a particular moment in time, may obstruct further theoretical developments:

> It is as though the very invisibility of abstract ideas attracts a material, metaphoric form. The interest lies in whether the forms of this 'conceptual typology', as I have called it, might affect the formulation of the ideas themselves and their ultimate destiny. Is it possible that the way in which ideas are visualised can, at a certain point, block the process that brings thought into a dialectical relationship with history? . . .
>
> A negative aesthetic can produce an inversion of the meanings and pleasures it confronts, but it risks remaining locked in a dialogue with its adversary . . .
>
> Apart from inversion, shifts in position are hard to envisage. (Mulvey 2, pp. 163, 164, 168)

While I agree with the historical impetus behind Mulvey's self-critique, I find the metaphors that accompany her efforts to decenter her own original argument disturbing. Two examples: 'I feel now that its [her classic essay's] "conceptual typology" contributed in some way to blocking *advance*'; 'negative aesthetics can act as a motor force in the *early phases* of a movement, initiating and expressing the desire for change' (Mulvey 2, pp. 163, 164; my emphases). These metaphors are metaphors of a teleological construction of history, which as a rule emphasizes the immaturity, the rashness even, of 'early' concepts. The rhetorical return to this conventional, almost chronological sense of history is paradoxical in an essay that otherwise offers a very different kind of argument about the historical through the notion of the 'pre-Oedipal.' Citing as an example the way the image of Our Lady of Guadalupe was used as an emblem for political revolt against Spanish rule in Mexico in the early nineteenth century, Mulvey argues for an understanding of the 'pre-Oedipal' that is not in teleological terms: the 'pre-Oedipal' is 'in *transition* to articulated language' (Mulvey 2, p. 167; emphasis in the original); it is not dominant, yet meaningful. Although I would disagree with Mulvey's subscription to the Freudian notion for the same reasons I would with Kristeva's, what is valuable in this part of her argument is not so much the 'pre-Oedipal' per se as *where* she tries to locate it. This is not some exotic past or ancient culture, but 'the rhetoric of the oppressed' – 'a rhetoric that takes on the low side of the polar opposition, in order to turn the world upside down, and stake out *the right to imagine* another' (Mulvey 2, p. 167; emphasis in the original).

To turn the world upside down, to stake out the right to imagine another: these are the tasks we are still faced with. I think Mulvey's original argument should be read in the light of these statements rather than simply against her later attempt to 'historicize' that argument in a more conventional way. What is most productive about her polarization of male and female positions is a radicalness that is often the only means of effecting change. Only when things are *put in the bold*, so to speak, can a thorough dismantling of the habits of seeing be achieved. The perception of the need to be uncompromisingly thorough is itself historical. It is *this* kind of historical perceptiveness that is behind Mulvey's extremely direct, and only thus effective, statement of her original project: 'It is said that analysing pleasure, or beauty, destroys it. That is the intention of this article' (Mulvey, p. 306).

It follows that the most useful aspect of Mulvey's essay lies not so much in the division between masculinity and femininity as 'gaze' and 'image,' as in the conceptual possibilities that inevitably emerge once such a division is so bluntly and crudely crafted. As Mulvey puts it, 'A negation or inversion of dominant codes and conventions can fossilise into a dualistic opposition *or* it can provide a spring-board, a means of testing out the terms of a dialect, an unformed language that can then develop in its own signifying space' (Mulvey 2, pp. 168–9; my emphasis). This 'unformed language' is the language of the oppressed.

In Mulvey's original argument, this language of the oppressed is conceived in visual terms, as part of the state of being-looked-at. This state of being-looked-at is built into the cinematic spectacle itself: 'Going far beyond highlighting a woman's to-be-looked-at-ness, cinema builds the way she is to be looked at into the spectacle itself' (Mulvey, p. 314). What this enables is an understanding of the cinematic image not simply as some pure 'thing' to be perceived, but as what already contains the gaze (the act of gazing) that cannot be seen itself.

We have seen how, in *The Last Emperor*, it is precisely this invisible gaze that directs our paths of identification and nonidentification. It does so by hiding behind other filmic signifiers such as the Chinese imperial order, which bestows *attention* on the emperor to the finest detail, and the Chinese Communist *interrogation* of Pu Yi. What we see on the screen, then, is already something that has been profoundly worked on. For the camera's gaze does not simply 'hide,' but negotiates, mediates, and manipulates; it builds on the 'gazes' that are visibly available on the screen, turning them into occasions for eroticism or humanistic sympathy and in this way 'suturing' the spectators' response.[19]

My use of Mulvey's mode of critique therefore complicates it in two ways. First, I extend the interpretation of image-as-woman to image-as-feminized space, which can be occupied by a man character, Pu Yi, as much as by a woman. Once this is done, 'femininity' as a category is freed up to include fictional constructs that may not be 'women' but that occupy a passive position in regard to the controlling symbolic. At the same time, this use of 'femininity' does not abandon the politics of 'to-be-looked-at-ness,' which, as Mulvey's argument shows, is most readily clarified through women's assigned role in culture.

The second complication is my use of the elements of this cinematic analysis for a polemics of cross-cultural inquiry. The image-as-feminized space raises disturbing questions as to what is involved in the representation of another culture, especially when that representation is seen by members of that culture. Does it call for the 'destruction of visual pleasure' that is the point of Mulvey's critique? Who should destroy it, and how? If not, why not? What are the problems that watching a film like *The Last Emperor* produces – for a Chinese audience? If it is a matter of criticizing Bertolucci for using 'good drama' to 'falsify' Chinese history, one can simply recite historical facts and rechronicle the reality that was not the one of the film.[20] But that precisely is not what matters. What matters is rather how 'history' should be reintroduced materially, as a specific way of reading – not reading 'reality' as such but cultural artifacts such as film and narratives. The task involves not only the formalist analysis of the *producing* apparatus. It also involves rematerializing such formalist analysis with a pregazing – the 'givenness' of subjectivity I indicated in the Preface – that has always already begun.

To rematerialize this pregazing, we need to shift our attention away from the moment of production to the moment of reception. In retrospect, it is the lack of this shift that constitutes the vulnerability in Mulvey's original argument. Given that 'visual pleasure' is indeed the 'evil' of the scopophilic cinematic apparatus, does it mean that the spectator is affected by it in a uniform way? Indeed, the logic of 'Visual Pleasure and Narrative Cinema' would indicate that all spectators are 'masculinized' in reception, since they would be identifying with the camera's gaze. The woman whose ontological status is supposedly that of the image on the screen and who nonetheless also sits in the audience hence poses a very special problem. With what does she really identify? Must she simply become schizophrenic?

In her book *Alice Doesn't: Feminism, Semiotics, Cinema*,[21] Teresa de Lauretis takes up this important question of the female spectator that is left largely unexplored. She does this by supplementing the filmic position of woman as 'visual object' with something else – 'narrative.' De Lauretis argues that the position occupied by 'woman' on the screen is not simply a visible 'image' but a 'narrative image,' a term she borrows from Stephen Heath. The 'narrative image' of woman refers to 'the join of image and story, the interlocking of visual and narrative registers effected by the cinematic of the look' (de Lauretis, p. 140). In cinema as much as in conventional narrative, the female position, 'produced as the end result of narrativization, is the figure of narrative closure, the narrative image in which the film . . . "comes together" (de Lauretis, p. 140). By introducing narrative into the understanding of filmic images, de Lauretis is thus able to distinguish *two* sets of identifying relations for the female spectator. The first, well known to classical film theory, consists of 'the masculine, active, identification with the gaze (the looks of the camera and of the male characters) and the passive, feminine identification with the image (body, landscape)' (de Lauretis, p. 144). The second set of identifying relations is *figural* in nature. It does not consist so much of gazes and looks as it does 'the double identification with the figure of narrative movement, the mythical subject, and with the figure of narrative closure, the narrative image' (de Lauretis, p. 144). Moreover,

> Were it not for the possibility of this second, figural identification, the woman spectator would be stranded between two incommensurable entities, the gaze and the image. Identification, that is, would be either impossible, split beyond any act of suture, or entirely masculine. The figural narrative identification, on the contrary, is double: both figures can and in fact must be identified with at once, for they are inherent in narrativity itself. It is this narrative identification that assures 'the hold of the image,' the anchoring of the subject in the flow of the film's movement. (de Lauretis, p. 144)

In thus supplementing the understanding of filmic images with terms other than those of the visual order alone, de Lauretis accomplishes several things at once. First, by reintroducing the processes of narrative, she revises the film theory that relies heavily on the sexual division based on vision, since that division, as all criticisms of Mulvey's original argument indicate, leads to a rigid polarization between man-as-gaze and woman-as-image. Second, in doing so, she enables a critique of the kind of technical analysis involved in a reading strategy such as Mulvey's while at the same time salvaging and reaffirming the valid political import of Mulvey's project, namely, that women, as the oppressed side of the polarization, must also be understood as *subjects*, not objects, in social discourse. Third, this is possible because the political question of female subjectivity is now posed in different terms: not simply that 'woman is reduced to the image,' but 'woman' is a locus of double identification. It is through a careful discussion of what this 'doubleness' signifies that the 'female spectator' offers the potential of a new means of sociocultural inquiry.

Put in more mundane terms, the paradigm of gaze-as-male and image-as-female breaks down once we think of women who willingly buy tickets to go to the cinema and derive pleasure from the experience. The rejection of the relevance of this experience would result in the kind of denunciation of mass culture that we associate with Adorno and Horkheimer in their classic piece,

'The Culture Industry: Enlightenment as Mass Deception.'[22] It is a rejection because, in spite of often attentive analyses of how the mass culture industry works by subjugating the masses, the experience of the masses is not itself considered a problem except insofar as it is assumed to signify, uniformly, 'stupefaction.' However, if we are to theorize precisely from the perspective of the receiving masses, then the problem is infinitely complicated. As recent studies of popular culture such as Tania Modleski's *Loving with a Vengeance*, Janice Radway's *Reading the Romance*, and Ien Ang's *Watching Dallas* repeatedly indicate, the female viewing/reading subject is elusive, ambivalent, always divided between 'conventional' values and expectations on the one hand, and socially disruptive or destructive tendencies on the other. Central to such conflicts in the processes of reception is the issue of identification, and with it, the problem of pleasure.

Because theoretically the female spectator's position offers an example of a division that is 'irreparable' and 'unsuturable' (de Lauretis, p. 143), film theorists tend to disregard the problem of sexual differentiation in the spectators altogether. This leads to the facile thinking of reception purely in terms of a transcendental or ideal subject, presupposed to be male. Feminist readings such as Mulvey's, also following this thinking but revolting against it, therefore seek to destroy it totally. De Lauretis summarizes this state of affairs with a thoughtful comment about women and pleasure:

> Within the context of the argument, a radical film practice can only constitute itself against the specifications of that cinema, in counterpoint to it, and must set out to destroy the 'satisfaction, pleasure and privilege' it affords. The alternative is brutal, especially for women to whom pleasure and satisfaction, in the cinema and elsewhere, are not easily available. (de Lauretis, p. 60)

Since the need to destroy visual pleasure stems from the belief that what gives pleasure is pure illusion, de Lauretis goes on to suggest that the word 'illusion' be 'dislodged from the particular discursive framework of Mulvey's argument' and be interpreted along the associations given to it by E. H. Gombrich, for whom illusion is a process 'operating not only in representation, visual and otherwise, but in all sensory perception, and a process in fact crucial to any organism's chances of survival' (de Lauretis, p. 61). Readers must turn to de Lauretis's book to realize for themselves the vast implications of this argument based on perception theories. For now, I will limit my discussion to an amplification of 'the particular discursive framework of Mulvey's argument' and of how the notion of 'illusion' may be mobilized and generalized for a *departure* from that framework.

Briefly, I think the discursive framework of Mulvey's essay takes us back to the formulation of 'ideology' advanced by Louis Althusser in his work.[23] Althusser defines ideology in terms of two types of 'apparatuses,' the 'Repressive State Apparatuses' and the 'Ideological State Apparatuses.' While the former work by brute, militant force, the latter, under which Althusser lists churches, public and private schools, the family, the law, the political system, the trade union, the media, and 'cultural' activities such as literature, the arts, and sports (Althusser, p. 143), work by what we might call 'civility.' It is such 'civil' apparatuses that help reproduce the conditions of capitalist production by 'interpellating' individuals into the existing system even as these individuals imagine their actions to be spontaneous and voluntary. Mulvey's essay, I think, draws on this general notion of ideology and localizes it in a specific apparatus, cinema. In this respect, her analysis of the classical narrative film contains two mutually implied equations: first, that between ideology and the masculine gaze; second, that between ideology and falsehood. The critique of cinema as dominated by the masculine gaze is therefore also a critique of ideology as falsehood. And it is, I think, this approach to ideology that de Lauretis means by the 'particular discursive framework of Mulvey's argument.' The notion of 'falsehood' is analogous to that of 'illusion' as defined by *The American Heritage Dictionary*: 'something, as a fantastic plan or desire, that causes an erroneous belief or perception.' Defined this way, 'illusion' calls for its own destruction and, by implication, for the restoration of what is nonillusory. For very understandable reasons, much of the work undertaken in feminism partakes of this anti-illusion tendency, resulting in some extreme cases where a profound lack of interest in or a total disregard of anything related to men is heartily applauded.

Althusser's theory, however, indicates another direction in which feminism and the awareness of 'ideology' can join forces. For this, we need to ponder anew his way of formulating ideology, as 'the *reproduction* of the conditions of production' (Althusser, p. 127; my emphasis). Or, restating it to the same effect, he says:

> Every social formation must reproduce the conditions of its production at the same time as it produces, and in order to be able to produce. It must therefore reproduce:
> 1. the productive forces,
> 2. the *existing relations* of production. (Althusser, p. 128; my emphasis)

What else could be the 'existing relations' of production but the mental attitudes, wishes, sufferings, and fantasies of the individuals involved in the processes of active production? When he discusses the 'reproduction of labor-power,' Althusser includes not only quantifiable value (wages) but also a 'historically variable minimum' – 'needs.' He adds in parentheses that 'Marx noted that English workers need beer while French proletarians need wine' (Althusser, p. 131). Ideology is thus understood by Althusser not really as 'something' that 'causes' a falsified perception, but more as the experience of consumption and reception, as that store of elusive elements that, *apart from* 'wages' and 'surplus value,' enable people to buy, accept, and enjoy what is available in their culture. This understanding of ideology, then, includes the understanding that any reception of culture – however 'passive' and thus 'ideological' – always contains a responsive, performative aspect. However neglected by cultural theorists busy with the criticism of ideology-as-falsehood, this aspect of reception is crucial to the notion of 'illusion' that de Lauretis would like to dislodge from a deeply ingrained, Platonic tradition of criticism and reinvest with the meaning of social survival. As she puts it succinctly:

> The present task of theoretical feminism and of feminist film practice is to articulate the relations of the female subject to representation, meaning, and vision, and is so doing to construct the terms of another frame of reference, another measure of desire. *This cannot be done* by destroying all representational coherence, by denying 'the hold' of the image in order to prevent identification and subject reflection, by voiding perception of any given or preconstructed meanings. (de Lauretis, p. 68; my emphasis)

In a way that echoes de Lauretis, Silverman points out in her discussion of 'suture' the intimate link between suture and 'interpellation' (Silverman, p. 219). Her explanation of suture reminds us of Althusser's analysis of the individual's response to the 'interpellating' call: 'The operation of suture is successful at the moment that the viewing subject says, "Yes, that's me," or "That's what I see"' (Silverman, p. 205). She mentions also that, as viewing subjects, 'we want suture so badly that we'll take it at any price, even with the fullest knowledge of what it entails – passive insertions into pre-existing discursive positions (both mythically potent and mythically impotent); threatened losses and false recoveries; and subordination to the castrating gaze of a symbolic Other' (Silverman, p. 213). These statements serve to emphasize that the task of critiquing processes of ideology, illusion, and suture cannot be performed at the level of pitting reality against falsehood, because in what we think of as 'falsehood' often lies the chance of continued survival, sometimes the only way to come to terms with an existing oppressive condition. This is especially true in the case of the female spectator, as de Lauretis is at pains to demonstrate.

Instead of seeking to 'free' the filmic illusion, de Lauretis restores and redefines its value. She does this by avoiding the tendency in avant-garde film practices to reinscribe materiality *exclusively* in the process of filmmaking. For these practices, by 'roughening' and 'defamiliarizing' the workings of the apparatus (to borrow terms from the Russian Formalists), often demand of the spectator a cool-headed 'detachment' from what they see. Instead, de Lauretis moves toward reinscribing materiality in film watching. Through the writings of Pasolini, she draws attention to the 'translinguistic' function of cinema, showing that cinema 'exceeds the moment of the inscription, the technical apparatus, to become "a dynamics of feelings, affects, passions, ideas" in the moment of reception' (de Lauretis, p. 51). These words, adds de Lauretis, should not be construed as an emphasis on the purely existential or personal, for they point to 'spectatorship as a site of productive relations' (de Lauretis, p. 51).

It is by rearguing the relationship between image and spectator and by foregrounding the cultural components that are specific to an *imaged spectatorship* that a film like *The Last Emperor* can be instrumental in an analysis of modern Chinese subjectivity. Here, once again, I would like to extend the feminist basis of de Lauretis's arguments to a cross-cultural context, by asking how the insights she develops around the female spectator could fruitfully become a way of articulating the ethnic – in this case, Chinese – spectator.

Take this statement: 'Spectators are not, as it were, either in the film text *or* simply outside the film text; rather, we might say, they intersect the film as they are intersected by cinema' (de Lauretis, p. 44). What happens when a Chinese person sees *The Last Emperor?* Is the process comparable to the one described by de Lauretis with regard to the female spectator, who is caught between the feminine (Chinese) image on the screen and the masculine (non-Chinese) gaze of the camera? How does the double, figural identification – with both narrative movement and narrative closure – work?

I cite my mother's response to the film: 'It is remarkable that a foreign devil should be able to make a film like this about China. I'd say, he did a good job!' Instead of being stranded schizophrenically between an identification with Bertolucci's 'gaze' and the projection of herself ('Chinese') as image on the screen, my mother's reaction indicates a successful 'suturing' in the sense of a cohering of disjointed experiences through 'illusion.' As an ethnic spectator, she identifies at once with the narrative movement, the invisible subject that 'tells' the story about modern China, *and* with the narrative image centering on Pu Yi, signifying 'Chinese' history. Even as she highlights the film's non-Chinese making in the phrase 'foreign devil,' the process of identification appears uninterrupted. In fact, one can say that her identification with the narrative image is most successful when she compliments Bertolucci for doing a good job in spite of being a 'foreign devil.' For, although 'foreign devil' is a mark of the awareness of difference, the 'in spite of' attitude points rather to the process in which a seamless interpellative exchange can take place between the spectator and the filmic image. Instead of doubting Bertolucci's version of modern Chinese history, my mother's reaction says, 'Still, that's me, that's us, that's our history. I see it in spite of the hand of the foreign devil.' This response, coming from someone who, while a young girl, was brutalized and abducted by Japanese soldiers in southwest China during the Second World War, is much more complex and more unsettling than the one suggested to me by some of my academic friends who, not surprisingly, criticize the film as an instance of what Edward Said calls 'Orientalism' and thus miss its appeal to many Chinese spectators in Hong Kong, Taiwan, and the People's Republic. I am not applauding the 'Orientalism' that is obviously crucial to the film's structure. However, it seems to me equally important to point out how, much like the female spectator, the ethnic spectator occupies an impossible space that almost predetermines its dismissal from a theoretical reading that is intent on exposing the 'ideologically suspect' technicalities of production only. In such a reading, my mother's response could only be written off as 'unsophisticated,' 'simplistic,' or 'manipulated.'

If, on the other hand, we are to take de Lauretis's discussion of 'illusion' seriously, refusing, that is, to reduce 'illusion' to the polarized opposition between 'truth' and 'illusion,' then the position occupied by the ethnic spectator must be reaffirmed in the inquiry of cultural intercourse. To this position belongs, first, 'historical' awareness: the knowledge of China's imperialized status vis-à-vis the West for the past century or so, and the memories, more recent and more overwhelming, of the millions of rapes and murders, the massacres, and the 'biological experimentations' perpetrated by the Japanese on Chinese soil, in which Pu Yi was undoubtedly chief collaborator in the Northeast. Chinese idioms such as 'foreign devil,' as part of this historical awareness, emphasize – sentimentally and defensively – Chinese people's 'holding their own,' implying by that logic an intuitive distrust of any 'foreigner's' story of Chinese history. But overlapping with the pain of historical awareness is another, equally intense feeling, describable only partly by phrases like 'mesmerization,' 'nostalgia,' and 'a desire to be there, *in* the film.' All these phrases belong to 'illusion' as de Lauretis would understand it, that is, perceptive operations that are, regardless of their so-called falsity, vital to a continual engagement with what is culturally available.

The identification with an ethnic or 'national' history, and the pain and pleasure that this involves, cannot be understood simply in terms of 'nativism.' The spectator is not simply ethnic but *ethnicized*: the recognition of her 'Chineseness' is already part of the process of cross-cultural interpellation that is at work in the larger realm of modern history. To use the words of C. T. Hsia with regard to modern Chinese literature, there is, among many Chinese people, an 'obsession with China.'[24] Why? An answer to this question cannot be given unless we reinsert into the overtones of a collective identity the subjective processes – the desires, fantasies, and sentimentalisms – that are part of a *response* to the solicitous calls, dispersed internationally in multiple ways, to such an identity. In this light, the phrase 'imagined communities' in the title of Benedict Anderson's book is especially thought-provoking.[25] In spite of being a specialist in Southeast Asia, however, Anderson's analysis is surprisingly indifferent to the rise of imagined communities in the non-West as a response to European colonialism. His insights into the origins of imagined communities in Europe – origins that encompass capitalism, technology, and the development of languages – are accompanied by a lack of interest in crucial differences in, say, post-colonial Asia. Take, for instance, this matter-of-fact observation: 'So, as European imperialism smashed its insouciant way around the globe, other civilizations found themselves traumatically confronted by pluralisms which annihilated their sacred genealogies. The Middle Kingdom's marginalization to the Far East is emblematic of this process.'[26] What, we should ask, is the nature of this traumatization and marginalization? The potency of Anderson's two-word phrase – a potency that remains unrealized in his book – lies, I think, not so much in its rapport with the urge in contemporary critical theory to deconstruct centrisms such as 'communities' with their rings of monolithic closure, as in the word 'imagined' as an index to the involved conceptual movements that may or may not coincide with their imagined content.

The word 'imagined' is immensely rich in its suggestions of the process in which the subject is constituted by recognizing, in external objects, that part of herself that has been 'dismembered' for cultural and historical reasons. Within contemporary psychoanalytic theories. Lacan's term '*objet petit a*' (object a), generally interpreted to mean the objects in the life of a subject that are neither fully distinguishable from the self nor clearly apprehensible as other, and which receive their value from the subject's representation of them as missing, would be one way of formulating this process.[27] A more concrete, because visually specific, formulation lies with Freud's theory of fetishism.[28] Central to Freud's theory is that a fetish is a substitute for something that is imagined to be lost or losable; in Freud, that something is the penis. But if we should disengage Freud's theory from its masculinist emphasis on the penis as the paradigm signifier, we would see that what is most interesting about fetishism is the process of loss, substitution, and identification that is at play in the formation of a subject. The fetishist is someone who translates the importance of that part of himself which he fears to be lost/losable into 'its' lack outside himself, a 'lack' that is, moreover, relocalized in another body in multiple ways (e.g., in female hair, feet, breasts, etc.), endowed with a magical power, and thus 'fetishized.' What should be emphasized is that this 'translation' is, in Freud's texts, an imagining process that involves the mutual play between an emotion and a 'sight,' but more precisely a sight-in-recollection. What is seen (the female body) in a first instance (when no neurosis occurs) is remembered in a second instance amid feelings of fear (when the little boy is caught masturbating and threatened to be reported to his father); his 'translation' of these feelings into the female body-as-lack is thus the result of a mental sequence. As such, fetishism is the process of a belated consciousness, a consciousness that comes into itself through memory substitution, and representation. Meanwhile, the 'original' belief in the mother's 'penis' (that is, her complete identification with and indistinguishability from oneself, thus her omnipotence and plenitude) undergoes a twofold change: (1) the knowledge that she does not 'have a penis' is disavowed, and (2) the 'lack' she signifies is repressed and represented in other forms, forms we call 'fetishes.' The original belief, in other words, does not disappear but reappears repeatedly as a wish, which is attached to 'fetishes' in the form of emotions – the emotions of pleasure and of identification.

Removing these formulations of subjectivity from an exclusively psychoanalytic and metaphysical framework, and placing them in modern Chinese history, we see how the experience of 'dismemberment' (or 'castration') can be used to describe what we commonly refer to as 'Westernization' or 'modernization.' Typically, as the history of the non-West is divided into the classical/primitive and the 'modern' stages, modern non-Western subjects can be said to be constituted primarily through a sense of loss – the loss of an attributed 'ancient' history with which one 'identifies' but to which one can never return except in the form of fetishism. The 'object' with which Chinese people are obsessed – 'China' or 'Chineseness' – cannot therefore be seen as an emotional simplism, but must rather be seen as the sign of a belated consciousness and a representation, involving mental processes that are not, as Kristeva would have it, 'pre-psychoanalytic.' We might say that a response such as 'Yes, that's me, that's Chinese' is a fetishizing imagining of a 'China' that never is, but in that response also lies the wish that is the last residue of a protest against that inevitable 'dismemberment' brought about by the imperialistic violence of Westernization.

The point must be emphasized, especially from the position of those that are feminized and ethnicized: these identificatory acts are the sites of productive relations that should be reread with the appropriate degree of complexity. This complexity lies not only in the identification with the ethnic culture, but also in the strong sense of complicity with the 'dismembering' processes that structure those imaginings in the first place. For instance, the Chinese person obsessed with China emotionally is not necessarily one that would dress and live in a 'Chinese' manner, as any superficial acquaintance with 'Westernized' Chinese would reveal. Unlike what Oriental things still are to many Europeans and Americans, 'Western things' to a Chinese person are never merely dispensable embellishments; their presence has for the past century represented the necessity of fundamental adaptation and acceptance. It is the permanence of imprints left by the contact with the West that should be remembered even in an ethnic culture's obsession with 'itself.'

4

In the preceding analysis, I demonstrate the problems pertaining to the ethnic spectator through a specific cultural instance, a film about modern China. I argue that the film, as a technical apparatus, provides the means of redistributing that 'primitive' history to the ethnic subject as 'her own,' but it is the ethnic subject's contradictory response – a historical awareness combined with a pleasurable identification with the film's narrative-imagistic effects – that reveals the full complicity of the cross-cultural exchange. The difficulty of the ethnic, and ethnicized, spectator's position can be shown another way, through the currently prevalent academic attitudes revolving around the study of 'China.'

A few years ago, while attending an Association for Asian Studies meeting, I found myself face-to-face with an American-trained China historian who was lamenting the fact that China was becoming more and more like the West. Among the things that disturbed him the most were the diminishing differences in terms of the technical, cultural, and even linguistic aspects of Chinese life. China's recent development, in other words, makes it more and more impossible to disprove the 'convergence' theory advanced by some social scientists about world modernization. Over the years, many versions of the same concern reveal themselves to me in sinological methodology, usually in the form of an eager emphasis on the uniqueness of Chinese history and a defense of 'China' studies against the 'West.' Depending on the interest of the person, 'sinocentrism' can either take the theoretical position that China's tradition is adequate to itself, or perform, in practice, elaborate reinscriptions and hermeneutical readings of Chinese history/texts. Often, the sinocentric approach to 'China' boils down to an assertion of this kind in the field of literature: if one is studying Chinese texts, one should use 'Chinese' methodologies, not 'Western' ones. To read 'Chinese' texts in terms of 'Western' methodologies is to let the latter distort the former.

These encounters, personal or textual, have been instructive for me in that they make me ask myself: Why is it that these China scholars, who argue for the integrity of China studies, have not struck one chord of enthusiasm in me, a Chinese? What is missing in the dialogue between them and me, when in all likelihood I should feel grateful toward them for defending 'my' culture? It becomes necessary for me to reflect on the nature of their defense of 'Chinese culture,' which I would describe as an idealist preoccupation with 'authentic' originariness. This kind of preoccupation is, of course, not unique to China studies. But in China studies, it runs into specific difficulties. How to strive for authentic originariness, when the history of China in the nineteenth and twentieth centuries is inundated with disruptive contacts with the West? Where could authentic origins possibly come from? In other words, what is 'Chinese'? The concentration on China as 'tradition' is an understandable way out, for as an idea, tradition offers the comfort precisely of adequacy, self-sufficiency, and continuity. It is supported, outside academia, by antique collecting, museums, restaurants, tourism, and the pastime of *chinoiserie*, all of which confirm the existence of a Chinese tradition. What is missing from the preoccupation with tradition and authentic originariness as such is the experience of modern Chinese people who have had to live their lives with the knowledge that it is precisely the notion of a still-intact tradition to which they cannot cling – the experience precisely of being impure, 'Westernized' Chinese and the bearing of *that* experience on their ways of 'seeing' China. Instead of recognizing the reality of this 'ethnic spectator,' much of China studies prefers, methodologically, taxonomic divisions of China into 'premodern' and 'modern,' 'traditional' and 'Westernized' periods, and so forth, even as the fragmented, dispersed, ironic developments of Chinese modernity make the clarity of these conceptual divisions useless. Thus, as is often felt though never directly stated, Chinese from the mainland are more 'authentic' than those who are from, say, Taiwan or Hong Kong, because the latter have been 'Westernized.' A preference for the purity of the original ethnic specimen perhaps? But if so, one would have to follow this kind of logic to its extreme, and ask why sinologists should 'study' China at all, since studying already implies 'othering' and 'alienating' it; and to that effect, how even the most sinocentric of sinologists could possibly justify writing about China in any language other than classical Chinese. Doesn't this state of affairs reenact exactly the problematically bifurcated nature of that nineteenth-century Chinese dictum vis-à-vis the West – *zhongxue wei ti, xixue wei yong* (Chinese learning for fundamental structure, Western learning for practical use)? China historians may criticize the conservatism of this dictum for retarding China's progress into the modern world, but aren't those who opt for a 'sinocentric' approach to China repeating this conservatism themselves?

This problem becomes especially acute as students of Chinese culture attempt to articulate issues in their field by using the tools of 'Western' concepts and theory they have learned. Consider the example of twentieth-century Chinese literature. In his book *Chinese Theories of Literature*, James J. Y. Liu explicitly refrains from discussing this period because it is Westernized:

> I shall not deal with twentieth-century Chinese theories, except those held by purely traditionalist critics, since these have been dominated by one sort of Western influence or another, be it Romanticist, Symbolist, or Marxist, and do not possess the same kind of value and interest as do traditional Chinese theories, which constitute a largely independent source of critical ideas.[29]

The message is loud and clear: twentieth-century Chinese literature is too polluted by the West to merit discussion. On the other hand, however, should one attempt to read modern Chinese literature by means of 'Western' theories, one is, to this day, likely to be slapped in the face with a moralistic and nationalistic disapproval of this kind: 'Why use Western theory on Chinese literature?'

To this extent, de Lauretis's notion of 'imaging' – 'the articulation of meaning to image, language, and sound, and the viewer's subjective engagement in that process' (de Lauretis, p. 46) – is crucial to an understanding of Chinese modernity from the point of view of the Westernized Chinese subject/reader, who is caught between the sinologist's 'gaze' and the 'images' of China that are sewn on the screen of international culture. Between the gaze and the image, the Chinese experience of being 'spectators' to *representations* of 'their' history by various apparatuses is easily erased. China scholars who defend with earnest intent Chinese history's claim to the status of world history help to further the erasure of this spectatorship precisely by their argument for the 'adequacy' of the Chinese tradition, for this argument disregards the quotidian truth with which every Chinese person grows up in the twentieth century, the truth that this 'adequacy' is not so, for 'the world' does not think so. When one has been taught, as a way of survival, the practical necessity of accepting 'the West' and of having good French or English, only to be confronted with the charge, from those who are specialists of one's 'own' culture, that one's methodology of thinking and reading is 'too Westernized,' the politics implied in ethnic spectatorship cannot be more stark and bitter. Such a charge demolishes the only premises on which the ethnic spectator can see and speak – premises that are, by necessity, impure and complicitous. The notion that 'China' is beautiful and adequate to itself, which arises from an act of sentimental fetishizing on the part of the Chinese, becomes for those who are professionally invested a way to justify fencing off disciplinary territories. For a 'Westernized' Chinese spectator/reader, it is impossible to assume an unmediated access to Chinese culture. To use a notion proposed by Yao-chung Li, this spectator/reader is 'in exile';[30] to use a notion proposed by Biddy Martin and Chandra Talpade Mohanty, this spectator/reader is 'not being home.' Exile and homelessness do not mean disappearance. As Martin and Mohanty specify, ' "Not being home" is a matter of realizing that home was an illusion of coherence and safety based on the exclusion of specific histories of oppression and resistance, the repression of differences even within oneself.'[31] If an ethnicized reader does not simply read by affirming Chinese tradition's continuity and adequacy to itself, how might she read? How might the 'Westernized' Chinese spectator be recognized?

In his illuminating study, *Time and the Other: How Anthropology Makes Its Objects*, Johannes Fabian offers many insights that are germane to our discussion. Earlier, I refer to one of them, visualism. Fabian's analysis of 'visualism' is situated in a larger analysis of the uses of time in anthropology, which, as he points out, often denies 'coevalness' or cotemporality between the subjects and objects of an inquiry. This denial occurs at the moment of writing, when anthropologists are away from the field, where they share an immediate present with their objects. The discrepancy between 'field' time and 'writing' time is, once again, encapsulated in Bertolucci's remarks that I quote at the beginning, a discrepancy that is between Bertolucci's 'Yet in the meantime' and 'before.' While a coeval engagement with their objects 'in the field' may reveal their sophistications, anthropologists slip into what Fabian calls 'allochronism' in the process of writing, when shared time is replaced by a more linear, progressive use of time that enables the distinctions between 'primitive' and 'developed' cultures. Allochronism, the casting of the other in another time, goes hand in hand with 'cultural relativism,' a process in which other cultures are territorialized in the name of their central values and vital characteristics:

> Once other cultures are fenced off as culture gardens or, in the terminology of sociological jargon, as boundary-maintaining systems based on shared values; once each culture is perceived as living its Time, it becomes possible and indeed necessary to elevate the interstices between cultures to a methodological status. (Fabian, p. 47)

Sinology and China studies, which have significantly structured the ways we 'see' China in the West, partake of 'cultural relativism' in obvious ways. Typically, 'cultural relativism' works by fostering the distinction between 'classical' and 'modern' China. This is a distinction that shapes the structuring of Kristeva's *About Chinese Women*, in which, 'reflecting a broader Western cultural practice, the "classical" East is studied with primitivistic reverence, even as the "contemporary" East is treated with realpolitical contempt.'[32] The same distinction exists in Bertolucci's 'making' of China; in his film the contrast between the sensuous colors of the 'imperial' scenes and the drabness of the 'Communist' scenes is too sharp not to become emblematic. In different but comparable ways, sinologists who are so much in love with the China of the classical Chinese texts that they refrain from visiting China; who only read the Chinese language silently as pictures but do not speak it; or who, lamenting China's 'convergence' with the rest of the world, emphasize the methodological self-sufficiency of Chinese studies in an attempt to preclude readings of Chinese texts with non-Chinese strategies – these sinologists are also reinforcing and perpetuating the 'allochronism' to which China has been reduced among world cultures.

Furthermore, in universities where the study of China is often part of 'area studies' programs that are made up of political scientists, linguists, anthropologists, geographers, historians, musicologists, as well as literary critics, scholastic territorialization corroborates the bureaucratic. For, once 'China' is fenced off in this way, its 'fate' is left to the grossly uneven distribution of interests and funding between the humanities and the social sciences. While classical Chinese literature can hold on to a well-established, though isolated, tradition of refined textual study, modern Chinese literature, marginalized against classical hermeneutics but also against the data-yielding 'China' of the social scientists, is inevitably deprived of the necessary institutional support that would enable its researchers to experiment with radical theoretical approaches in such a way as to make it accessible and interesting to nonspecialists.

My somewhat personal emphasis on the necessity to change the state of affairs in modern Chinese culture and literature has to do with my feeling that it is in this vastly neglected area that a theory of the ethnic spectator can be most urgently grounded, as Westernized Chinese students come to terms with themselves both as objects and subjects of 'seeing' China. Fabian states:

> Tradition and modernity are not 'opposed' . . . nor are they in 'conflict.' All this is (bad) metaphorical talk. What are opposed, in conflict, in fact, locked in antagonistic struggle, are not the same societies at different stages of development, but different societies facing each other at the same Time. (Fabian, p. 155)

Supplementing the terms of Fabian's analysis with those of our ongoing arguments, we can say that the position of the ethnic spectator is the position of 'different societies facing each other at the same Time,' that is, the position of coevalness.

5

In this chapter I have introduced the problematic of 'seeing' modern China from the point of view of the Westernized Chinese spectator. China exists as an 'other,' feminized space to the West, a space where utopianism and eroticism come into play for various purposes of 'critique.' Kristeva's book about Chinese women shows us how the alluring tactic of 'feminizing' another culture in the attempt to criticize Western discourse actually repeats the mechanisms of that discourse and hence cannot be an alternative to it. 'China' becomes the 'woman' that is superfluous to the relationship between Kristeva the critic and the metaphysical entity of 'the West.' Bertolucci's *The Last Emperor* seems a timely instance illustrating how the feminizing of another culture can be explained cogently in terms of film theory, which casts the problems in a clear light because of cinema's use of visual images. The writings of Mulvey, Silverman, and de Lauretis make it possible for us to see the initially necessary cooperation between feminism and the critique of ideology as falsehood, while indicating what that combination leaves out – the position of the female spectator, whose interpellation by as well as rejection of the screen images is crucial for an understanding of reception as a mode of performative, not merely passive, practice.

Extending the notion of the female spectator, I ask whether we cannot also begin to theorize the position of the ethnic spectator, who is caught, in a cross-cultural context, between the gaze that represents her and the image that is supposed to be her. I argue that it is by acknowledging the contradictory, complicitous reaction to a film like *The Last Emperor* on the part of some Chinese spectators – a reaction that consists in fascination as well as painful historical awareness – that we can reintroduce the elusive space of the ethnic spectator. In the realm of sinology and China studies, I propose, it is the experience of this space that is often dismissed. Instead, the study of China remains caught in the opposition between 'modernity' and 'tradition.' While Westernization is acknowledged as an idea and a fact in history, its materiality as an indelible, subjective part of modern Chinese people's response to their own 'ethnic' identity is consistently disregarded. In thus excluding from its methods of inquiry the position of the ethnic spectator who has never been and will never be purely 'Chinese,' sinology and China studies partake of what Fabian calls 'allochronism,' which is central to 'a nation-centered theory of culture' (Fabian, p. 48). It is only through thinking of the 'other' as sharing our time and speaking to us at the moment of writing that we can find an alternative to allochronism. The position of the feminized, ethnicized spectator, as image as well as gaze, object of ethnography as well as subject in cultural transformations, is a position for which 'coevalness' is inevitable. How might the argument of coevalness affect our reading of China's modernity? What would it mean to include the 'other,' the object of inquiry, in a cotemporal, dialogic confrontation with the critical gaze? How might we read modern Chinese literature other than as a kind of bastardized appendix to classical Chinese and a mediocre apprentice to Western literature? The following chapters of *Women and Chinese Modernity* offer a set of responses to these questions.

Notes

All transcriptions of Chinese are in *pinyin*, except for cases in which a different system, usually the Wade-Giles, was used originally in a quoted text. Translations of Chinese titles that do not exist in English are given in square brackets.

1. Brian Lambert, 'Interview with Bernardo Bertolucci/The Last Emperor,' *Twin Cities Reader*, Wednesday, December 9, 1987, p. 14; my emphases. Other remarks quoted from Bertolucci are taken from the same interview.
2. Trans. Anita Barrows (New York and London: Marion Boyars, 1977, 1986). Page references are given in parentheses in the text.
3. Kristeva, 'Woman Can Never Be Defined,' trans. Marilyn A. August, in Elaine Marks and Isabelle de Courtivron (eds), *New French Feminisms* (New York: Schocken Books, 1981), pp. 137–41.
4. Kristeva, 'Women's Time,' trans. Alice Jardine and Harry Blake, in *Signs: Journal of Women in Culture and Society*, 7, no. 1 (1981), p. 17.
5. 'Women's Time,' p. 17.
6. 'Woman Can Never Be Defined,' p. 137.
7. Kristeva takes this word from Plato, who speaks of 'a chora . . ., receptacle . . ., unnamable, improbable, hybrid, anterior to naming, to the One, to the father, and consequently, maternally connoted.' See 'From One Identity to an Other,' in her *Desire in Language: A Semiotic Approach to Literature and Art*, trans. Thomas Gora, Alice Jardine, and Leon S. Roudiez (New York: Columbia University Press, 1980), p. 133.
8. Spivak 'French Feminism in an International Frame,' in her *In Other Worlds: Essays in Cultural Politics* (New York and London: Methuen, 1987), p. 146; emphases in the original. The attribution of a 'before' to the 'other' is not unique to Kristeva. On his visit to China, Roland Barthes observed this culture with the same kind of fascination. China becomes an object of his hallucination: 'By gently hallucinating China as an object located *outside* any bright color or any strong flavor, any brutal meaning (all this not without a bearing on the relentless parade of the Phallus), I wanted to bring together in a single movement the infinite *feminine* (maternal?) of the object itself, that extraordinary way China, in my eyes, had of overflowing the boundaries of meaning, peacefully and powerfully, and the right to a special discourse, that of a slight deviation, or again a yearning, an appetite for silence – for "wisdom" perhaps . . . This *negative* hallucination is not gratuitous: it is an attempt to respond to the way many Westerners have of hallucinating the People's Republic of China – in a dogmatic mode, violently affirmative/negative or falsely liberal.' See 'Well, And China?', trans. Lee Hildreth, in *Discourse*, 8 (Fall-Winter 1986–7), p. 120; my emphases. Those who are familiar with Barthes's work know that he 'hallucinates' Japan in the same way in *Empire of Signs*, trans. Richard Howard (New York: Hill and Wang, 1982).
9. Silverman, *The Acoustic Mirror: The Female Voice in Psychoanalysis and Cinema* (Bloomington and Indianapolis: Indiana University Press, 1988), p. 112.
10. For a critique of the politics involved in Kristeva's conceptions of femininity, see Ann Rosalind Jones, 'Julia Kristeva on Femininity: The Limits of a Semiotic Politic,' *Feminist Review*, no. 18 (1984), pp. 56–73.
11. For a superb account of the ideologies accompanying the historical depictions of China in the past few hundred years in the West, see Raymond Dawson, *The Chinese Chameleon* (London: Oxford University Press, 1967); Dawson examines the notion of the Chinese as 'a people of eternal standstill' thoroughly in chapter 4.
12. I borrow this term from Johannes Fabian, *Time and the Other: How Anthropology Makes Its Object* (New York: Columbia University Press, 1983), pp. 106–9. Fabian defines visualism as a deeply ingrained ideological tendency in anthropology, which relies for its scientific, 'observational' objectivity on the use of maps, charts, tables, etc. The recommendations for such visual aids 'rest on a corpuscular, atomic theory of knowledge and information. Such a theory in turn encourages quantification and diagrammatic representation so that the ability to "visualize" a culture or society almost becomes synonymous for understanding it. I shall call this tendency visualism.' Visualism 'may take different directions – toward the mathematical-geometric or toward the pictorial-aesthetic.' I return to Fabian's arguments later on

in this chapter; references are indicated in parentheses by 'Fabian' followed by page numbers.

13. Silverman, *The Subject of Semiotics* (New York: Oxford University Press, 1983), p. 225. A reprint of Mulvey's article, originally published in *Screen*, 16, no. 3 (Autumn 1975), can be found in *Movies and Methods*, vol. 2, ed. Bill Nichols (Berkeley and Los Angeles: University of California Press, 1985), pp. 303–15. Hereafter references to Silverman and Mulvey (in Nichols) are indicated in parentheses by their last names followed by page numbers.
14. Spivak, 'Can the Subaltern Speak?', in Larry Grossberg and Cary Nelson (eds), *Marxist Interpretations of Literature and Culture: Limits, Frontiers, Boundaries* (Urbana: University of Illinois Press), pp. 296–7.
15. From the 'Production Notes' attached to the film's compact disc soundtrack: 'The logistics of the production were staggering. *The Last Emperor* brought together people from six nations. Actors came from America, Great Britain, China, Hong Kong and Japan to play the sixty main characters in the story. One-hundred technicians from Italy, twenty from Britain and 150 Chinese worked for six months of shooting to put the film on the screen and 19,000 extras, including soldiers of the People's Liberation Army, appear altogether in the immense crowd scenes. Costume designer James Acheson gathered 9,000 costumers from all over the world.'
16. *Video Review*, August 1988, p. 17.
17. Other feminist critics have produced readings of film that share this concern. See, for instance, Claire Johnston, *Notes on Women's Cinema* (London: Society for Education in Film and Television, 1973), pp. 2–4; Johnston, 'Towards a Feminist Film Practice: Some Theses,' in Nichols (ed.), pp. 315–27; Mary Ann Doane, 'Misrecognition and Identity,' *Cine-Tracts*, 11 (Fall 1980), pp. 28–30; Doane, 'Film and the Masquerade: Theorising the Female Spectator, '*Screen*, 23 (September–October 1982), pp. 74–87.
18. Mulvey, *Visual and Other Pleasures* (Bloomington and Indianapolis: Indiana University Press, 1989), pp. 159–76. (This essay was previously published in *Discourse* in 1985 and *History Workshop Journal* in 1987.) Hereafter references are indicated in parentheses by 'Mulvey 2' followed by page numbers. Mulvey's revisions of her original argument can also be found in 'Afterthoughts on "Visual Pleasure and Narrative Cinema" inspired by *Duel in the Sun*,' *Framework*, 6, nos 15–17 (1981), rpt. in Constance Penley (ed.), *Feminism and Film Theory* (New York: Routledge, Chapman and Hall, 1988), pp. 69–79.
19. For discussions of the term 'suture' in cinema, see Stephen Heath, 'Narrative Space,' in *Screen*, 17, no. 3 (1976), pp. 66–112; 'Notes on Suture,' *Screen*, 18, no. 2 (1977/78), pp. 48–76; Jacques-Alain Miller, 'Suture (Elements of the Logic of the Signifier),' '*Screen*, 18, no. 4 (1977/78), pp. 24–34. Silverman's discussion in her book (pp. 194–236) demonstrates the theoretical connections between suture and discourse, subjectivity, cinema, ideology, and sexual difference.
20. To this end, the reader can turn to, for instance, John K. Fairbank, 'Born Too Late,' *New York Review of Books*, February 18, 1988.
21. (Bloomington: Indiana University Press, 1984). References to this book are indicated in parentheses by 'de Lauretis' followed by page numbers.
22. *Dialectic of Enlightenment*, trans. John Cumming (New York: Continuum, 1987), pp. 120–67.
23. 'Ideology and Ideological State Apparatuses (Notes towards an Investigation),' in his *Lenin and Philosophy and Other Essays*, trans. Ben Brewster (New York and London: Monthly Review Press, 1971). References to this essay are indicated in parentheses by 'Althusser' followed by page numbers.
24. Hsia, 'Obsession with China: The Moral Burden of Modern Chinese Fiction,' in his *A History of Modern Chinese Fiction*, 2nd edn (New Haven: Yale University Press, 1971), pp. 533–4.

25. Anderson, *Imagined Communities: Reflections on the Origin and Spread of Nationalism* (London: Verso and New Left Books, 1983).
26. Ibid. p. 68, note 6.
27. See the chapters 'Tuché and Automaton' and 'From Love to the Libido' in *The Four Fundamental Concepts of Psychoanalysis*, ed. Jacques-Alain Miller, trans. Alan Sheridan (New York and London: Norton, 1981), pp. 53–66; 187–202.
28. See 'Fetishism' and 'Splitting of the Ego in the Defensive Process,' in his *Sexuality and the Psychology of Love*, ed. Philip Rieff (New York: Collier Books, 1963), pp. 214–19; 220–3. The two essays are also in Freud, *The Standard Edition of the Complete Psychological Works*, ed. James Strachey, trans. James Strachey et al. (London: Hogarth Press), vols 21 and 23. See also the section 'Unsuitable Substitutes for the Sexual Object – Fetishism,' in *Three Essays on the Theory of Sexuality*, trans. James Strachey (New York: Basic Books, 1975), pp. 19–21; or Standard Edition, vol. 7.
29. Liu, *Chinese Theories of Literature* (Chicago and London: University of Chicago Press, 1975), p. 5.
30. Li, 'Hermeneutics and Criticism,' in *Chinese Culture Quarterly*, 1, no. 4 (1987), p. 65.
31. Martin and Mohanty, 'Feminist Politics: What's Home Got to Do with It?', in Teresa de Lauretis (ed.), *Feminist Studies/Critical Studies* (Bloomington: Indiana University Press, 1986), p. 196.
32. Spivak, 'French Feminism,' p. 138.

10

YELLOW EARTH: WESTERN ANALYSIS AND A NON-WESTERN TEXT

Esther C. M. Yau

1984. China. The wounds of Cultural Revolution have been healing for nearly a decade. After the hysterical tides of red flags, the fanatical chanting of political slogans, and militant Mao supporters in khaki green or white shirts and blue slacks paving every inch of Tienanmen Square, come the flashy Toshiba billboards for refrigerators and washing machines, the catchy phrases of 'Four Modernizations,' and tranquilized consumers in colorful outfits and leather heels crowding the shops of Wangfujing Street. A context of Change. Yet contradiction prevails. Who are these people flocking to local theaters that posted *First Blood* on their billboards? Are they not the same group that gathered for lessons on anti-spiritual pollution? The Red Book and the pocket calculator are drawn from shirt pockets without haste, just like the old long pipe from the baggy pants of the peasant waiting for the old Master of Heavens to take care of the order of things. In 1984, after the crash of the Gang of Four, when China becomes a phenomenon of the 'post' – a nation fragmented by and suffering from the collapse of faith in the modern, socialist politics and culture, the search for meaning by the perturbed Chinese character begins to occupy the electric shadows of new Chinese cinema.[1]

At the end of 1984, a few Chinese men who were obsessed with their history and culture – all of them had labored in factories and farms during the Cultural Revolution and just graduated from the Beijing Film Academy – quietly completed *Huang Tudi* in a very small production unit, the Guangxi Studio,

From *Film Quarterly* 41: 2, Winter 1987–8, pp. 22–33.

in Southern China. A serious feature that had basically eluded political censorship; *Huang Tudi* (which meant *Yellow Earth*) was soon regarded as the most significant stylistic breakthrough in new Chinese cinema. It won several festival prizes, started major debates at home about filmmaking, and interested international film scholars.[2]

Safely set in the 1930s, *Yellow Earth* tells the story of an encounter between a soldier and some peasants. Despite its ambitious attempt to capture both the richly nourishing and the quietly destructive elements of an ancient civilization already torn apart in the late nineteenth century, the film's story and its use of folksongs/folktale as device and structure is deceptively simple and unpretentious. In fact, the film's conception and its musical mode were originally derived from one of the trite literary screenplays which glorified the peasants and the earlier years of socialist revolution: an Eighth Route Army soldier influenced a peasant girl to struggle away from her feudal family.[3] Such a commonplace narrative of misunderstanding-enlightenment-liberation-trial-triumph or its variations would be just another boring cliché to the audience familiar with socialist myths, while the singing and romance could be a welcome diversion. Dissatisfied with the original story but captivated by the folktale elements, director Chen Kaige and his young classmates – all in their early thirties – scouted the Shaanxi Province in northwestern China for months on foot. Their anthropological observations of the local people and their sub-cultures both enriched and shaped the narrative, cultural, and aesthetic elements in the film.[4] Consequently, they brought onto the international screen a very different version of Chinese people – hardworking, hungry and benevolent peasants who look inactive but whose storage of vitality would be released in their struggles for survival and in their celebration of living. The structure of the original story was kept, but *Yellow Earth* has woven a very troubling picture of Chinese feudal culture in human terms that had never been conjured up so vividly before by urban intellectuals.

The film's narrative: 1937. The socialist revolution has started in western China, but most other areas are still controlled by the Kuomintang. Some Eighth Route Army soldiers are sent to the still 'unliberated' Western highlands of Shaanbei to collect folk tunes for army songs. Film begins. Spring, 1939. An Eighth Route Army soldier, Gu Qing, reaches a village in which a feudal marriage between a young bride and a middle-aged peasant is taking place. Later, the soldier is hosted in the cave home of a middle-aged widower peasant living with his young daughter and son. Gu Qing works in the fields with them and tells them of the social changes brought about by the revolution, which include the army women's chances to become literate and to have freedom of marriage. The peasant's daughter, Cui Ciao, is interested in Gu Qing's stories about life outside the village, and she sings a number of 'sour tunes' about herself. The peasant's son, Han Han, sings a bed-wetting song for Gu Qing, and is taught a revolutionary song in return.[5] The young girl learns that her father has accepted the village matchmaker's arrangement for her betrothal.

Soon, the soldier announces his departure. Before he leaves, the peasant sings him a 'sour tune,' and Cui Ciao privately begs him to take her away to join the army. Gu Qing refuses on grounds of public officers' rules but promises to apply for her and to return to the village once permission is granted. Soon after his departure, Cui Ciao's feudal marriage with a middle-aged peasant takes place. At the army base, Gu Qing watches some peasants drum-dancing to soldiers going off to join the anti-Japanese war. Back in the village, Cui Ciao decides to run away to join the army herself. She disappears crossing the Yellow River while singing the revolutionary song. Another spring comes. There is a drought on the land. As the soldier returns to the village, he sees that a prayer for rain involving all the male peasants is taking place. Fanatic with their prayers, nobody notices Gu Qing's return, except the peasant's young son. In the final shots he rushes to meet the soldier, struggling against the rush of worshippers. End of story.

Yellow Earth poses a number of issues that intrigue both censors and the local audience. The film seems to be ironic: the soldier's failure to bring about any change (whether material or ideological) in the face of invincible feudalism and superstition among the masses transgresses socialist literary standards and rejects the official signifieds. However, such an irony is destabilized or even reversed within the film, in the sequences depicting the vivacious drumdancing by the liberated peasants and the positive reactions of the young generation (i.e., Cui Ciao and Han Han) towards revolution. The censors were highly dissatisfied with the film's 'indulgence with poverty and backwardness, projecting a negative image of the country.' Still, there were no politically offensive sequences to lead to full-scale denunciation and banning.[6] To the audience used to tear-jerking melodramas (in the Chinese case, those of Xie Jin, who is by far the most successful and popular director),[7] *Yellow Earth* has missed most of the opportune moments for dialogue and tension, and is thus unnecessarily opaque and flat. For example, according to typical Chinese melodrama, the scenes where Cui Ciao is forced to marry an older stranger, and the one when her tiny boat disappears from the turbulent Yellow River, would both be exploited as moments for pathos. But here they are treated metonymically: in the first, the rough dark hand extending from offscreen to unveil the red headcloth of the bride is all one sees of her feudalist 'victimizer'; in the second instance, the empty shots of the river simply obscure the question of her death. In both situations, some emotional impact is conveyed vocally, in the first by the frightened breathing of the bride, and in the second by the interruption of her singing. But the cinematic construction is incomplete, creating an uncertainty in meaning and a distancing effect in an audience trained on melodrama and classical editing. Nevertheless, when the film was premiered at the 1985 Hong Kong International Film Festival, it was lauded immediately as 'an outstanding breakthrough,' 'expressing deep sentiments poured onto one's national roots' and 'a bold exploration of film language.' Such an enthusiastic reception modified the derogatory official reaction towards the film (similar to some initial Western reception, but for different political reasons), and in turn prompted the local urbanites to give it some box-office support.[8]

Aesthetically speaking, *Yellow Earth* is a significant instance of a non-Western alternative in recent narrative filmmaking. The static views of distant ravines and slopes of the Loess Plateau resemble a Chinese scroll-painting of the Changan School. Consistent with Chinese art, Chang Imou's cinematography works with a limited range of colors, natural lighting, and a non-perspectival use of filmic space that aspires to a Taoist thought: 'Silent is the Roaring Sound, Formless is the Image Grand.'[9] Centrifugal spatial configurations open up to a consciousness that is not moved by desire but rather by the lack of it – the 'telling' moments are often represented in extreme long shots with little depth when sky and horizon are proportioned to an extreme, leaving a lot of 'emptyspaces' within the frame. The tyranny of (socialist) signifiers and their signifieds is contested in this approach in which classical Chinese painting's representation of nature is deployed to create an appearance of a 'zero' political coding. Indeed, the film's political discourse has little to do with official socialism; rather, it begins with a radical departure from the (imported) mainstream style and (opportunist) priorities of narrative filmmaking in China. One may even suggest that *Yellow Earth* is an 'avant-gardist' attempt by young Chinese filmmakers taking cover under the abstractionist ambiguities of classical Chinese painting.[10]

To filmmakers and scholars, then, *Yellow Earth* raises some intriguing questions: What is the relationship between the aesthetic practice and the political discourse of this film? In what way is the text different from and incommensurable with the master narratives (socialist dogma, mainstream filmmaking, classical editing style, etc.), in what way is it 'already written'(by patriarchy, especially) as an ideological production of that culture and society, and finally, how does this non-Western text elude the logocentric character of Western textual analysis as well as the sweeping historicism of cultural criticism?[11]

This essay will address the above questions by opening up the text of *Yellow Earth* (as many modernist texts have been pried open) with sets of contemporary Western methods of close reading – cine-structuralist, Barthesian post-structuralist, neo-Marxian culturalist, and feminist discursive. This will place *Yellow Earth* among the many parsimoniously plural texts and satisfy the relentless decipherers of signifieds and their curiosity for an oriental text. The following discussion of this text will show that the movement of the narrative and text of *Yellow Earth* involves the interweaving and work of four structurally balanced strands (micro-narratives) on three levels: a diegetic level (for the construction of and inquiry about cultural and historical meaning), a critical level (for the disowning and fragmentation of the socialist discourses), and a discursive level (for the poly-vocal articulations of and about Chinese aesthetics and feudalist patriarchy).[12] In this way, I hope to identify certain premises of Chinese cosmological thinking and philosophy as related in and through this text. In this analytic process, the contextual reading of Chinese culture and political history will show, however, the limitations of textual analysis and hence its critique.[13]

I shall begin with a brief description of the organization of the four narrative strands and their function on both diegetic and critical levels. The Lévi-Straussian structural analysis of myths is initially useful: the peasant father imposes feudal rules on Cui Ciao, the daughter (he marries her off to stabilize the kinship system) and the soldier imposes public officers' rules on her as well (he prevents her from joining the army before securing official approval). Thus, even though the host-guest relationship of the peasant and the soldier mobilizes other pairs of antinomies such as agriculture/warfare, subsistence/revolution, backwardness/modernization, the pattern of binaries breaks down when it comes to religion/politics, since both signify, in Chinese thinking, patriarchal power as a guardian figure. In addition, Han Han, the young male heir in the film, counteracts the establishment (runs in the reverse direction of the praying patriarchs) in the same way Cui Ciao does (rows the boat against the Yellow River currents for her own liberation). Again, the antinomy peasant/soldier is destabilized, as myth is often disassembled in history – that is, the mythic glory of hierarchic dynasties and the revolutionary success of urban militia breaks down when confronted by the historical sensibility of the post-Cultural Revolution period.

There are four terms of description: brother, sister, father, soldier. While there is a relationship of consanguinity and descent, both are complicated by the problematic relation of affinity: Cui Ciao's intimacy with Han Han and their distance from the peasant father is more excessive while romance is taboo and marriage is ritual in the film. The prohibition of incest among family members (Cui Ciao with her brother or father) is transferred to prohibition of romantic involvement between Cui Ciao and the soldier, enforced at the cost of the girl's life.[14] Hence, the textual alignment of patriarchy with sexual repression. However, the film text is not to be confused with an anthropological account. As both Fredric Jameson and Brian Henderson point out, historicism is at work in the complex mode of sign production and in reading.[15] Hence this text would preferably be read with a historical knowledge of the Communist Party's courtship with the peasants and its reconstruction of man [sic] through the construction of socialist manhood – which reserves desire for the perfection of the ideological and economic revolution, while the liberation of women (its success a much-debated topic) becomes an apparatus for the Party's repression of male sexuality, besides being a means for winning a good reputation. Hence the position of contemporary Chinese women, generally speaking, involves a negotiation between patriarchy and socialist feminism in ways more complicated than what one deduces from the Lévi-Straussian analysis of kinship systems.

Now I shall proceed to a more detailed (though non-exhaustive) discussion of what is at work in each of the micro-narratives as narrative strands, as well as the contextual readings relevant to the textual strategies.

First Narrative Strand: the Peasant's Story

The scenes assembled for the first narrative strand have a strong ethnographic nature: the material relation between the Shaanbei peasants and their land is documented through the repetitive activities of ploughing land on bare slopes, getting water every day from the Yellow River ten miles away, tending sheep, cooking, and quiet residence inside the cave home, while marriages and rain prayers are treated with a moderate amount of exotic interest – of the urban Han people looking at their rural counterparts. The peasants are depicted as people of spare words (Cui Ciao's father even sings little: 'What to sing about when [one is] neither happy nor sad?'). They have a practical philosophy (their aphorism: 'friends of wine and meat, spouse of rice and flour') and they show a paternal benevolence (Cui Ciao's father only sings for the soldier for fear that the latter may lose a job if not enough folk tunes were collected). Obviously, anthropological details have been pretty well attended to.

Meaning is assigned according to a historical or even ontological dependence of peasants on their motherly Land and River. This signifying structure is first of all spatially articulated: the Loess landscape with its fascinating ancient face is a silent but major figure both in Chinese painting and in this film. Consistent with the 'high and distant' perspective in scroll painting is the decentered framing with the spatial contemplation of miniaturized peasants as black dots laboring to cross the vast spans of warm yellow land to get to the river or their cave homes.[16] No collective farming appears in this film, and neither planting nor harvesting modify this relationship. The symbolic representation of an ancient agrarian sensibility is condensed in shots that include the bare details of one man, one cow, and one tree within the frame in which the horizon is always set at the upper level and the land, impressive with deep ravines, appears almost flattened. In an inconspicuous way, the Yellow River's meaning is also contemplated: the peasants are nourished by it and are sometimes destroyed by it. A narrative function is attached: this is a place in dire need of reform, and it is also stubbornly resistant. The state of this land and people accounts for the delay of enlightenment or modernity – there is an unquestioning reliance on metaphyical meaning, be it the Old Master of Heavens or the Dragon King of the Sea, but which is tied so closely to the survival of the village. The narrative refusal of and enthusiasm for revolution are motivated: the ideology of survival is a much stronger instinct than the passion for ideals. But to the peasants, the Party could have been one of the rain gods.

There is a vocal part to this cosmological expression as well, articulated dialectically for a critical purpose. We shall attend to three voices: the first, that of the peasant's respect for the land: 'This old yellow earth, it lets you step on it with one foot and then another, turn it over with one plough after another. Can you take that like it does? Shouldn't you respect it?' A classical form of deification borne from a genuine, everyday relationship. Then it is countered by the second, the soldier's voice: 'We collect folk songs – to spread out – to let the public know what we suffering people are sacrificing for, why *we farmers* [my emphasis] need a revolution. 'Gu Qing offers a rational reading of the agrarian beliefs; his statement contains a simple dialectic – the good earth brings only poverty, and the way out is revolution. Yet his statement and his belief is but a modernized form of deification: the revolution and its ultimate signified (the Revolutionary Leader) are offered to replace the mythic beliefs through a (false) identification by the soldier with the peasants ('Our Chairman likes folk songs,' says the soldier). Blind loyalty (of peasants to land) finds homology in, and is renarrativized by, a rational discourse (of soldier to his Leader). The ancient structure of power changes hand here; thereafter, the feudalist circulation of women and socialist liberation of women will also remain homological.

As explicit contradiction between the first two voices remains unresolved, a major clash breaks out in the form of a third voice, which appears in the rain prayer sequence. Assembled in their desiccated land, the hungry peasants chant in one voice: 'Dragon King of the Sea, Saves Tens of Thousands of People, Breezes and Drizzles, Saves Tens of Thousands of People.' Desperation capsuled: the hungry bow fervently to the Heavens, then to their land, and then to their totemic Dragon King of the Sea, in a primitive form of survival instinct. At this moment the soldier appears (his return to the village) from a distance, silent. A 180-degree shot/reverse shot organizes their (non)encounter: a frontal view of the approaching soldier, followed by a rear view of the peasants whose collective blindness repudiates what the soldier signifies (remember his song 'the Communist Party Saves Tens of Thousands of People'). In this summary moment of the people's agony and the film's most searing questioning of the Revolution's potential, the multiple signifieds are produced in and through a mirroring structure: the soldier's failure reflected by the peasants' behavior and the peasants' failure in the soldier's presence.

At the outset, two dialectical relationships are set up explicitly in the text, one against the other: between peasant and nonpeasant, and between peasant and land. The roots of feudalism, through this first narrative strand, are traced to their economic and cultural bases, and are compared in a striking way to Chinese socialism. In this manner, the whole micro-narrative is historicized to suggest reflections on contemporary China's economic and political fiascos. But there is another relationship between the filmic space and the audience's (focal) gaze. The nonperspectival presentation of landscapes in some shots and sequences often leads one's gaze to linear movements within the frame, following the contours of the yellow earth and the occasional appearance and disappearance of human figures in depth on an empty and seemingly flat surface. The land stretches within the frame, both horizontally and vertically, with an overpowering sense of scale and yet without being menacing. In these shots and sequences, the desire of one's gaze is not answered by the classical Western style of suturing, indeed it may even be frustrated.[17] Rather, this desire is dispersed in the decentered movement of the gaze (and shifts in eye level as well) at a centrifugal representation of symbolically limitless space. Such an unfocused spatial consciousness (maintained also by nonclassical editing style) has a dialectical relationship with one's pleasure-seeking consciousness. It frustrates if one looks for phallocentric (or feminist, for that matter) obsessions within an appropriatable space, and it satisfies if one lets the sense of endlessness/emptiness take care of one's desire (i.e., a passage without narrative hold). In these instances, one sees an image without becoming its captive; in other words, one is not just the product of cinematic discourse (of shot/reverse shot, in particular), but still circulates within that discourse almost as 'nonsubject' (i.e., not chained tightly to signification).

Within the text of *Yellow Earth*, one may say, two kinds of pleasures are set up: a hermeneutic movement prompts the organization of cinematic discourse to hold interest, while the Taoist aesthetic contemplation releases that narrative hold from time to time. Most of the moments are assigned meaning and absences of narrative image are filled, though some have evaded meaning in the rationalist sense. When the latter occurs, the rigorous theoretical discourses one uses for deciphering are sometimes gently eluded.

Second Narrative Stand: The Daughter's Story

In as much as the sense of social identity defines the person within Chinese society, individuals in Chinese films are often cast as non-autonomous entities within determining familial, social, and national frameworks. Ever since the 1920s, the portrayals of individuals in films have been inextricably linked to institutions and do not reach resolution outside the latter. Hence, unlike the classical Hollywood style, homogeneity is not restored through the reconciliation of female desires with the male ones, and the ways of looking are not structured according to manipulations of visual pleasure (coding the erotic, specifically) in the language of the Western patriarchal order. With an integration of socialism with Confucian values, film texts after 1949 have often coded the political into both narrative development and visual structures, hence appropriating scopophilia for an asexual idealization. In the post-Cultural Revolution context, then, the critique of such a repressive practice naturally falls on the desexualizing (hence dehumanizing) discourses in the earlier years and their impact on the cultural and human psyche.[18]

The plotting of *Yellow Earth*, following the doomed fate of Cui Ciao the daughter, seems to have integrated the above view of social identity with the recent critique of dehumanizing political discourses. Within the second narrative strand, the exchange of women in paternally arranged marriages is chosen as the signifier of feudalist victimization of women, while the usual clichés of cruel fathers or class villains are replaced by kind paternal figures. The iconic use of feudal marriage ceremonies has become common literary and filmic practice since the 1930s, but compared with other texts, this one is more subtle and complex in its enunciation of sympathy for women.[19] In this regard, we may undertake to identify two sets of homological structures in the text that function for the above purpose. It is through the narrative and cinematic construction of these structures that *Yellow Earth* made its statement on patriarchal power as manifested in cultural, social, and political practices.

The first set of homological structures involves the spatial construction of two marriage processions, each characterized by a montage in close-up of the advancing components (trumpet players, donkey, dowry, the red palanquin and its carriers) in more or less frontal views. In each case, the repetitive and excessive appearance of red, which culturally denotes happiness, fortune, and spontaneity is reversed in its connotative meaning within the dramatic context of the oppressive marriages. More significantly, the absence/presence of Cui Ciao as an intra-diegetic spectator and her look become a lynchpin to that system of signification. In the first marriage sequence, the bride is led from the palanquin to kneel with the groom before the ancestor's plate and then taken to their bedroom. Meanwhile, Cui Ciao as a spectator is referred to three or four times in separate shots, establishing her looking as a significant reading of the movement of the narrative. Yet she is not detached from that narrative at all. Seeing her framed as standing at the doorway where Confucius's code of behavior for women is written, one is constantly reminded that Cui Ciao's inscription will be similarly completed (through marriage) within the Confucian code.[20] Her look identifies her with the scene of marriage, and also relays to the audience her narrative image as a young rural female. The victimizing structure (feudalist patriarchy) and the potential victim (Cui Ciao) are joined through a shot/reverse-shot method, mobilized by her looking which coded the social and the cultural into the signifying system here.

In the second marriage sequence, the similar analysis in close-up of the advancing procession (by a similar editing style) performs an act of recall, which as a transformed version of the first marriage sequence reminds the audience of Cui Ciao's role as the intradiegetic spectator previously. In this instance, however, Cui Ciao is the bride, locked behind the dull black door of the palanquin covered by a dazzlingly red cloth. The big close-up of the palanquin, however, suggests her presence within the shot (hidden), in depth, and going through the process of 'fulfilling' the inscription predicted earlier on for her against her wish for freedom. The palanquin replaces her look but points to her absence/presence. At the same time, Han Han her quiet brother, replaces Cui Ciao as an intra-diegetic spectator looking (almost at us) from the back of the palanquin, figuring her absence and her silence. Han Han as the brother represents an ideal form of male sympathy in that context, yet as the son and heir of a feudal system, he is also potentially responsible for the perpetuation of this victimization. In this manner, the text shifts from a possible statement on class (backwardness of peasants before the Liberation) to a statement of culture (the closed system of patriarchy) to locate the woman's tragedy. With an intertextual understanding of most post-1949 Chinese films presenting feudal marriages, this cultural statement becomes a subtle comment on the (prorevolutionary) textual appropriations of folk rituals for political rhetorics.

The second set of homological structures appears in two pairs of narrative relationships between three characters (between Cui Ciao's father and Cui Ciao, and between Gu Qing the soldier and Cui Ciao) concerning the subject of women's (and Cui Ciao's) fate. Initially, one finds the first relationship a negative one while the second is positive, i.e., the father being feudal but the soldier liberating. This is encapsulated in a dialogue in which the soldier attempts to convince the peasants that women in socialist-administered regions receive education and choose their own husbands, and Cui Ciao's father answers: 'How can that be? We farmers have rules.' However, when one compares the peasants' exchange of women for the survival of the village and the revolutionaries' liberation of women for the promotion of the cause, then one finds both relationships being similarly fixated on woman as the Other in their production of meaning. Such a homology, nevertheless, is assymetrical in presentation. On the one hand, the film is direct about the negative implications of the patrilinear family though without falling into a simple feminist logic (Cui Ciao's father sympathizes with women's tragedy in the sour tune he sings for the soldier). On the other, there is no questioning about the socialist recruitment of women (and Cui Ciao's failure to join the army is regarded as regrettable). The critique falls on another issue: Gu Qing's refusal to take Cui Ciao along with him because 'We public officers have rules, we have to get the leader's approval.' Thus it is nongendered bureaucracy that is at stake here, and not exactly the patriarchal aspects of the feudalist and socialist structures, which can only be identified from an extratextual position.

The suspected drowning of Cui Ciao, then, can be read as the textual negotiation with the symbolic loss of meaning: she is to be punished (by patriarchy, of course) for overturning the peasants' rule (by leaving her marriage), for brushing aside the public officers' rule (by leaving to join the army without permission), and for challenging nature's rule (by crossing the Yellow River when the currents are at their strongest).

When Cui Ciao is alive, the sour tunes she sings fill the film's sound track – musical signifiers narrating the sadness and the beauty of 'yin.' Her death, though tragic, brings into play the all-male spectacles in the text: drum-dancing and rain-prayer sequences each celebrating the strength and attraction of 'yang,' so much suppressed when women's issues were part of the mainstream political mores.[21] Here one detects the 'split interest' of the text in these instances – the nonpolitical assignment of bearers of meaning (rather than the nonsexist) prescribes a masculine rather than feminine perspective of the narrative images of man and woman. That is to say, since the position of men and women in this patriarchal culture has been rearranged for the last three decades, first according to everyone's class background, then with a paternal favoring (as bias and strategy) of women, the text's critique of socialist discourses become its own articulation of a male perspective. In this way, this text does not escape being 'overdetermined' by culture and society, although in some ways by default.

Third Narrative Strand: The Eighth Route Army Soldier's Story

Since the Yenan Forum for writers in 1942, literary writing in China followed a master narrative that privileged class consciousness over individual creativity.[22] In revolutionary realism, character types (and stereotypes) were considered the most effective methods of interpellating the masses during economic or political movements. Literary and filmic discourses on the social being dictate a structure of dichotomies: proletariat/bourgeois, Party members/non-Party members, allies/enemies, peasants/landlords, etc. It was not until 1978 that 'wound literature' gave an ironic bent to the hagiographic mode for Party members and cadres. Still, such writing found shelter in specificity – for example, Xie Jin's *Legend of Tien Yun Mountain* and other adaptations from wound literature were bold in questioning the political persecution of intellectuals during the terrifying decade, unmistakably attributing the causes of people's suffering to the influences of the Gang of Four. Dichotomy, however, was basically maintained even though the introduction of good cadre/bad cadre did cause some reshuffling in the antinomies. Meanwhile, the master narrative remained intact, with authority diminished but the direct questioning of it taboo.[23]

The figure of an Eighth Route Army soldier and Party member in *Yellow Earth*, therefore, was not written without technical caution and political subtleties. A number of alterations to humanize the soldier were made during adaptation which to some extent decentralized his position in the narrative. Nevertheless, the rectitude of a revolutionary perspective and its influence on the peasants were not the least mitigated – that is to say, the third narrative strand sets the three others in motion. Thus, even when the representation of the Party member may be more in line with the popular notion, that is, there is a level of operation that makes socialist interpretation plausible. One may say that with an audience used to being prompted by dialogue and behavior, the figure of Gu Qing does not contest the proper image of a revolutionary military man.

As a signifying structure, the soldier's story functions as (in)difference and as metonymy, which is where the ironic mode works. The figures of that ancient agrarian subculture are no longer the same when Gu Qing, the outsider, enters – they are transformed under the soldier's gaze of bewilderment, which subsequently exerts its critical import. It is the third strand that begins the braiding process among the four and is responsible for the climaxes: the daughter no longer submits to her father's wishes, the son abandons the rain-prayer ceremony. Yet, these changes take place virtually outside Gu Qing's knowledge: he is ignorant of Cui Ciao's dilemma (except about women's fate in a general way) and of the peasants' problem of survival (except in broad terms of their poverty). The Party's political courtship with the peasants is metonymically dealt with here, in the prohibition of romance (as lack of knowledge) between Gu Qing and Cui Ciao, and also powerfully in the last scene of rain prayer which brought into circulation 'hunger' as the peasants' signified (versus the power elite's lack of experience of it) for their rural human-land and marriage relationships. Tension between history and ideology was again condensed, the three to four decades' national history of socialism contesting to little avail the five thousand years' national ideology of subsistence. The peasants' hospitable reception of Gu Qing and Cui Ciao's idealist trust in the Party further reinforce the ironic mode – difference is not a simple dichotomy and often works in the areas least expected. Then, none could go very far: Cui Ciao disappears in the Yellow River, the peasants are dying of drought, while the totemic figure of the Sea Dragon King dominates the scene, lifted by worshippers who want their lives saved. The discourse here is historicist: the cultural and epistemological barriers (of both Party and people) to the capitalist market economy in the 1980s motivates this myth of survival. Yet, it is also historical: the gods, emperors, leaders, all have been sought after by people in disaster, and made disasters by people.

The Fourth Strand: Han Han's Story

A quiet young boy with a blank facial expression. Han Han moves almost inconspicuously as a curious figure in the scenes. One may even ponder a Brechtian address made possible by this marginal but conscious presence. Almost uninscribed by culture, and, to some extent, by the text itself, Han Han has the greatest degree of differentiation (i.e., Han Han = X) and exists to be taken up by the three other narrative strands for signification.[24]

As a peasant's son, Han Han is heir to land, feudalism, and patriarchy. As a brother to Cui Ciao, he is the displaced site of her repressed feminine love and its failure. As a little pal of Gu Qing's he is the first person to learn the song and spirit of revolution. Yet his story is also underdeveloped. In other words, Han Han is neither unconnected nor fixated in the textual generation of meaning. Contrary to the marked positions of other song singers (of either sour tunes or revolutionary songs), Han Han is more ambiguous with his short 'bed wetting song' (which made unrefined jokes with both the Sea Dragon King and the son-in-law) before the soldier recruits his voice for the revolutionary song, which he sings only once. In the scene where he is already made part of the fanatic horde of worshippers, Han Han turns towards the sight of the soldier as the source of possible change in act of individual decision.

However, it is not Han Han the literary figure that escapes inscription. Indeed, pressured by political demands, the textual movement of Han Han is along the trajectory of 'liberation,' though there is no intention of completing it. The circulation of Han Han (as X) along the various narrative strands is, significantly, a production of textual interweaving. When conventional meaning in that society has been fragmented and questioned within the text. Han Han (as a textual figure) functions as the desire for meaning. One may venture to say Han Han is the signifier of that meaning – an insight for history and culture with an urge for change, portrayed as a childish moment before inscription, before meaning is fixed at the level of the political and agrarian institutions. Therefore the silent, blank face, because to speak, to have a facial expression, is to signify, to politicize.

A braid? Perhaps, as one woven by culture in society, and not flaunted as a fetish. Since the nineteenth century, major historical events in China (wars, national calamities, revolutions, etc.) have made four topics crucial to national consciousness: feudalism, subsistence, socialism, and modernization, and discourses are prompted in relation to them in numerous literary and cultural texts. In 1984, when contemporary China struggles with the evil spells of the Cultural Revolution and begins flirting once again with the capitalist market economy, discourses related to the four topics reappear in terms of current issues: will the agrarian mentality of its people prevent China from becoming a modern nation? Will feudal relations persist in spite of the lure of individualist entrepreneurship? Will the country's recent radical economic move (as in the Great Leap Forward) bring another large-scale fiasco? Is the Communist party leadership still competent for the changing 1980s? Will a second Cultural Revolution occur soon? As technology and business turn corporate and global, the answers to these questions can no longer be found in an isolated situation. The China that partakes in the world's market economy no longer operates in an 'ideological context' that is uniquely Chinese (as it had during the Cultural Revolution). Inevitably (and maybe unfortunately), this changing, modernizing 'ideological context' in China also informs the 'avant-gardist' project of *Yellow Earth* which has focused its criticism only on the patriarchal and feudal ideologies of that culture. Arguably, then, *Yellow Earth's* modernist power of critique of Chinese culture and history comes from its subtextual, noncritical proposition of capitalist-democracy as an alternative: it is (also arguably) this grain in the text that attracts the global-intellectual as well.

An historicist reading of texts and contexts is a powerful analytic practice. In the case of *Yellow Earth*, such a reading enables one to relate the film's textual strategies to the specific political and cultural context, while at the same time exposing some of the text's symptoms. However, there still remains a need to locate *Yellow Earth*'s difference from other interesting Chinese films made during the same period. Wu Tianming's *Life* (1984), for example, deals with the disparity between intellectual and agrarian life as an important subcultural dichotomy in Chinese identity and boldly pits individual motivation against class issues. Again, such a film is possible in China only in the 1980s. Yet, one may argue that discursive constraints are not fully watertight in their operations. With respect to *Yellow Earth*, there is a presence of a certain 'negative dialectics' that seems to run counter to its grain of modernist activities and does not yield to an historicist reading. It is, again, the simple Taoist philosophy which (dis)empowers the text by (non)affirming speaking and looking: 'Silent is the Roaring Sound, Formless is the Image Grand.' There are many such instances in the film: when the human voice is absent and nobody looks, history and culture are present in these moments of power(lessness) of the text. With this philosophy, perhaps, we may be able to contemplate the power(lessness) of our reading of the text.

Notes

1. For detailed discussions of the conflicts and contradictions involved in recent political and economic formulations of Chinese socialism, see Bill Brugger (ed.), *Chinese Marxism in Flux, 1978–84, Essays on Epistemology, Ideology and Political Economy*. New York: M. E. Sharpc, 1985.
2. In 1985, *Yellow Earth* won five festival prizes – in China, Hawaii, Nantes, Spain and Locarno. This film's impact on film-makers and critics in China and Hong Kong was documented in *Talking About Huang Tudi*, Chen Kaiyen (ed.), Beijing: China Film Press, 1986. For an English discussion, refer to Tony Rayns's discussion of the dissident 'Fifth Generation' of young PRC directors, and also his review of *Yellow Earth* in the BFI *Monthly Film Bulletin*, 10/1986.
3. A number of melodramatic and political clichés in the original essay *Echoes of the Deep Ravine* were dropped in Chen Kaige's adaptation into the screenplay titled *Silent Is the Ancient Plain*. The impressive color tones of the first work print inspired the film's final title *Yellow Earth*.
4. According to director Chen Kaige, Cui Ciao's father in the film is close to a *vérité* version of a local peasant he met during the walking reconnaissance of Shaanzi Province, and the bachelor singer in the first marriage sequence was also a local recruit. Yet, according to official views, the film's representation of peasants was ethnocentric and derogatory. One may understand this disparity by noting that Chinese socialism has always favored a more progressive image of peasants.
5. 'Xintinyou,' the folk songs sung in the northern Shaanxi region, provide a rich form for metaphoric expressions and direct telling of the singers' sentiments.
6. The first film completed by a group of Beijing Film Academy '82 graduates, *One and Eight* (*Yige He Bage*, 1984) was directed by Zhang Jun Zhao. Cinematographer Chang Imou's contribution was already regarded as the major reason for the film's aesthetic excellence. However, the film's entire ending was altered due to censorship and it was still banned from circulation. *Yellow Earth* also has several censorship problems but with its ambiguities it has better luck with the Film Bureau.
7. Examples from Xie Jin's most popular films include *The Red Detachment of Women* (1961) in which a serf girl reacted positively to a soldier's influence and turned herself into a brave red soldier, and *Legend of the Tienyun Mountain* (1978) in which two women were emotionally entangled with a persecuted rightist intellectual. Xie Jin has successfully dealt with topical issues in melodramatic form snot with classical style which made most of his works tear-jerking successes in China.
8. According to Tony Rayns, the triumph of *Yellow Earth* in film festivals prompted the official accusation of its bad influence on local aspirations to 'compete with the ideology of the bourgeoisie at foreign film festivals.' On the other hand, it is the film's international reputation that silenced established filmmakers and officials.
9. Originally from Lao Tzu's *Dao De Jing*. This Taoist concept of representation was developed in two seminal discussions on Chinese aesthetics, 'On the Origins and Bases of Chinese and Western Painting Techniques' (written in 1949) by Zhong Baihua and collected in Zhong's *A Stroll in Aesthetics*, Shanghai: The People's Press, 1981, pp. 80–113.
10. Some of the principles of Chinese spatial representation had been taken up by the West for interrogation of its own norms, e.g., Beijing Opera by Brechtian theater, and hence what is classical for one cultural system can be appropriated for avant-gardist reasons in another. Here, I would quickly add (with reference to Edward Said's discussion on 'Traveling Theory' in *The World, the Text and the Critic*) that while critical consciousness is the issue, classical Chinese painting as the borrowed theory itself is not free of institutional limitations in the local context. On the other hand, the aestheticization of nature in *Yellow Earth* could also be quickly seized by Western audiences for sentimentalized retreats to a pre-industrial corner of the world.

11. Culturalist or neo-Marxist criticisms of mass culture focus mostly on sign systems produced within bourgeois capitalism. In general, hardcore propaganda is taken to be characteristic of socialist sign systems, which is a gross simplification of the complicated mediations and processes at work in those economies and cultures. With reference to China, a more complicated view of socialist mass cultures is called for, and Bill Brugger's *Chinese Marxism in Flux* can be read along with Victor F. S. Sit (ed.), *Commercial Laws and Business Regulations of the PRC, 1949–1983* (London: Macmillan, 1983) to see that utilitarian individualism, for example, is functional within recent Chinese economic discourses.
12. For substantial discussions of the interweaving of Confucianism, socialism and patriarchy in contemporary China, see Richard Madsen, *Morality and Power in a Chinese Village* (Berkeley: University of California Press, 1984) and Judith Stacey, *Patriarchy and Socialist Revolution in China* (Berkeley: University of California Press, 1983).
13. Refer to Said's discussion of Derrida's and Foucault's approach to texts in 'Criticism Between Culture and System.' *The World, the Text and the Critic*, pp. 183–225.
14. The largely asexual representation of revolutionary characters was a major practice in the Revolutionary Model Plays, the only films made during 1970–3. In the post-Cultural Revolution era, the hagiographic mode of representation was debated as suppression of 'true human character' in literary and film circles.
15. Both Brian Henderson's '*The Searchers:* An American Dilemma' (Bill Nichols (ed.), *Movies and Methods* vol. II, p. 429–49) and Fredric Jameson's *The Political Unconscious* (Ithaca: Cornell University Press, 1981) have informed the historicist reading of this essay. I am also thankful to Nick Browne of UCLA who introduced me to them and gave valuable advice, and to David James of Occidental College for his inspiring comments.
16. The term 'Chinese westerns' was used recently in China to describe films that took to northwestern China for location shooting (e.g., Tin Zhuangzhuang's *On the Hunting Ground*, 1984). Yet, while the American frontier appealed to the immigrants' evolutionist expansion of social and political organization over inanimate nature (according to Frederick J. Turner), the Chinese west evoked a non-aggressive self-reflection: or according to Wang Wei, 'The sage, harboring the Tao, responds to eternal objects; the wise man, purifying his emotions, savors the images of things.'
17. While I agree with Heath's critique of Oudart-Dayan's definition of 'suturing' in filmic discourse as 'narrow,' I still refer here, for the sake of convenience, to the privileged example of shot/reverse-shot as the suturing approach to spatial articulation.
18. In this respect, Laura Mulvey's 'Visual Pleasure and Narrative Cinema' would not be relevant to many Chinese films, and especially not to those made during the Cultural Revolution which prohibited erotic codes in its representation of women.
19. One may suggest, in terms of Teresa DeLauretis's 'Desire in Narrative' in *Alice Doesn't* (Bloomington: Indiana University Press, 1984), pp. 139–46), that there are instances in which the girl in *Yellow Earth* moves as 'mythical subject' in narrative while men became her topoi; the marriage sequence and the river-crossing sequence are arguable examples.
20. The four Chinese characters in the shot are 'San Cong Si Dè,' meaning 'three obediences and four virtues.' The 'three obediences' for a Chinese woman are obedience to her father at home, to her husband after marriage, and to her son in her widowhood.
21. 'Yin,' the female element; 'Yang,' the male element. These two elements in Chinese cosmology involve symbolic systems and economies present both in the male and the female gender.
22. 'Talks at the Yanan Forum on Literature and Art,' *Mao Zedong on Literature and Art*, Beijing Foreign Language Press, 1977.

23. Recently, the citing of Mao's 'Talks at the Yanan Forum' as the standard of literary and artistic creation in China is usually indicative of a tightened literary policy. In 1987, with the 'anti-bourgeois liberalization' movement, China celebrated the forty-fifth anniversary of the 'Talks.'
24. This concept is taken from Gilles Deleuze's 'A Quoi Reconnaît-on le Structuralisme?' (1973). Han Han's name in Chinese means simple and lacking the ability to talk well.

PART II
FRAMEWORKS OF STUDY

SECTION 4
NATIONAL CINEMA: THE CASE OF TURKEY

Dimitris Eleftheriotis, 'Turkish national cinema'
Nezih Erdoğan, 'Narratives of resistance: national identity and ambivalence in the Turkish melodrama between 1965 and 1975'
Ahmet Gürata, 'Translating modernity: remakes in Turkish cinema'
Nezih Erdoğan, 'Mute bodies, disembodied voices: notes on sound in Turkish popular cinema'

TURKISH NATIONAL CINEMA

Dimitris Eleftheriotis

Introduction

Turkish cinema, approached in this chapter as 'national cinema', powerfully foregrounds a number of crucial issues implicated in the study of both national and Asian cinemas. The pedagogical importance of the study of Turkish cinema within the present *Reader and Guide* lies precisely in its problematic nature as a critical category, and in its ability to pose a number of fundamental questions such as, for example: is Turkish cinema Asian cinema? Is Turkish cinema an epistemological given or a category under construction? What does the 'national' refer to in the designation Turkish national cinema?

The three essays (one by Ahmet Gürata and two by Nezih Erdoğan) included in this section not only offer illuminating insights into the history of Turkish cinema, but are also exemplary for their rigorous critiques of essentialist, purist understandings of 'national cinema'. In this sense they constitute valuable testimony to the committed and often painful struggle of numerous film historians, critics and theorists to increase our knowledge of neglected cinematic traditions, while simultaneously resisting the restrictions and reductions posed by the discursive category of 'national cinema'. This essay briefly considers some of the issues arising from the inclusion of Turkish cinema in this *Reader* on Asian cinemas, then it outlines the key themes of the three essays that follow; finally it looks at the discursive restrictions imposed on writers by the discursive category 'national, cinema', and identifies some of the ways in which each one of these essays negotiates and challenges these constraints.

Prima facie it seems paradoxical to include Turkey, its cinema and its films in a study of Asian cinemas. In political terms Turkey is an important member of NATO, a political and military alliance defending the West from the 'threats' of the East (initially understood as communist Europe but now interpreted in broader terms) – in fact, Turkey is often seen as the West's final frontier. Turkey has been a member (albeit troublesome) of the Council of Europe since August 1949 and, perhaps more importantly, is preparing to initiate negotiations with a view to becoming a full member of the European Union. As the heated debate surrounding EU accession indicates, Turkey's position is more ambiguous in cultural terms,[1] and it is often perceived as perhaps a nation-state 'in between' East and West rather than as the West's final frontier. While, for example, Istanbul is instantly recognisable as a seminal European civil and cultural landmark, Anatolia has been the object of often outrageously orientalist imagery of European origin. And while Turkish songs compete in the Eurovision Song Contest and Turkish football teams play in the various UEFA competitions, a powerful racist perception of Turkish *Gastarbeiter* as cultural and racial others, rather than fellow European cosmopolitan citizens, remains disturbingly commonplace.

Turkey's uncomfortable and ambivalent positioning as an Asian (or alternatively European) country offers a glimpse of the fundamentally problematic nature of constructing objects of study relying on (in themselves dubious) geographic designations. Many of the geographically designated Asian countries demonstrate a series of characteristics typical of the discursive modality and imagery of the so-called West: from the world-leading technology of East Asia to the futuristic cityscapes of Kuala Lumpur, Singapore and Shanghai, and from Turkey's NATO membership to Japan's G8 status, boundaries are proven to be as fragile and imaginary as the arbitrary designations of East and West. Furthermore, diasporic communities around the world (and, remarkably so, Turkish German filmmakers) are transforming through their cultural interventions our perceptions of geographic boundaries, rigid binaries and pure nations, challenging in the process all certainties surrounding Eurocentric notions of identity.

Turkish history in the twentieth century, in its persistent negotiation with the West, demonstrates certain important themes that can also be observed (albeit in sometimes very different articulations and temporalities) in the histories of other Asian countries such as Japan, Korea and Taiwan. Most prominent of these themes is the determination to maintain a strong engagement with Western sociopolitical, cultural and techno-scientific ideas, forms of social organisation, and models of economic development. Turkey is, in this sense, typical of numerous nation-states and cultures occupying 'in-between' discursive spaces.

Turkey as a modern, secular nation-state was established in 1923 under the political leadership of Kemal Atatürk who became the first president of the Republic. Atatürk's legacy has been the systematic and all-pervasive programme of Westernisation that in many ways constituted a powerful imagination of the cultural destiny of the new nation.[2] However, as the numerous military coups and social upheavals demonstrate, the new Western-aspiring national imagination did not decisively defeat traditional views of social life and organisation. In fact, the history of Turkey since 1923 is marked by multiple and particularly intense struggles around the meaning, the content and the form of what constitutes the imagination of the nation.

Turkish Cinema

> It was decided [that] a major new television drama about Atatürk would be commissioned to celebrate the hundredth anniversary of his birth . . . no one had thought a Turk could be equal to the challenge of playing this blond, blue-eyed westward-looking national hero. The predominant view was that great national films called for great international stars like Laurence Olivier, Curt Jurgens and Charlton Heston. (Orhan Pamuk, *Snow*)[3]

The position of cinema within such a sociopolitical context is particularly interesting, as it seems to encapsulate some of the key contradictions and hegemonic struggles of Turkish society. As is also the case with most countries in the world, cinema in Turkey was perceived in its early years as a quintessentially Western cultural form, the product and ultimate demonstration of the power of the accelerated industrialisation and the technological and scientific achievements of countries such as France, the USA and the UK. Countering this Western 'essence' of cinema was the ability of the medium to reach significant numbers of the population of this vast country and, perhaps more importantly, to offer powerful representations of Turkish life that became popular with wide audiences.

The three essays that follow focus on the 1950s, 1960s and 1970s, the period when the Turkish film industry reached unprecedented heights of productivity and popularity. Each one of the essays identifies and explores key contradictions in films of the period as well as in the critical discourses around national cinema. Ahmet Gürata and Nezih Erdoğan approach national cinema with great caution, recognising that such a category is as imagined as that of the nation. They both identify aspects of Turkish cinema that cannot be assimilated within an essentialist nationalist discourse. For both of them, what makes Turkish cinema distinct is not a unique thematic and aesthetic identity, but instead the particular and multiple ways in which Turkish cultural traditions interact with hegemonic aspects of colonial and neo-colonial discourse: Gürata explicitly addresses the widely spread phenomenon of remakes, adaptations and spin-offs, and Erdoğan traces, through close textual analysis, the fundamental ideological contradictions in the cinema of the period.

Significantly all three essays identify popular cinema, widely known in Turkey as Yeşilçam,[4] as particularly crucial for approaching questions of national identity and national cinema. By directing their investigation outside the limits of elite or high culture, they are able to resist rather simplistic notions of national identity and cinema, expressed in statements such as the following by Yusuf Kaplan:

> A nation has to develop its own cinematography, its own film language, by relying on its visual culture, narrative traditions, and capacity for artistic experiments. Turkish filmmakers have proved that they are beginning to discover a distinctive way of story-telling which will enable them to create a truly national cinema.[5]

On the contrary, Erdoğan asserts 'I will examine the dynamics by which Turkish popular cinema describes a national identity, and I will attempt to demonstrate how the specificity of this identity can be seen in the very way it mimics and resists others.'[6] His determination is echoed by Gürata who sees in the hybrid nature of remakes a useful conceptual tool in approaching national cinema as the process of 'reinterpretation and negotiation of the historical and social forces of modernism in Turkey'.[7]

In his 1998 essay Erdoğan demonstrates how Yeşilçam melodramas register and work with the profoundly ambivalent relationship between Turkish and Western identities. He notes that, in their articulation of desire, the melodramas of the period negotiate a multitude of fundamental social tensions organised around a number of key binaries such as lower/upper class, rural/urban, Eastern/Western, and are riddled with contradictions resulting from the difficulty (if not impossibility) of resolving them. He uses the example of the 1970 film *Karagözlüm* to investigate some of the above binaries. What makes the film an interesting case study is the way in which it identifies and places in conflict important and readily recognisable cultural traditions: Western classical music, Turkish traditional music and Hollywood cinema. In a particularly pertinent dream-sequence the hero of the film finds himself both the subject and the object of a fantasy of Hollywood which Erdoğan sees as emblematic of the fundamental ambivalence of Turkish identity and Turkish cinema: '*Karagözlüm* offers us a dual set of relationships which reveal the actual fantasy of the colonized – to share the colonizer's fantasy.'[8]

In an essay published four years later, Erdoğan focuses on a distinctive technical and aesthetic characteristic of Yeşilçam, the use of dubbing (or post-production recording of sound) as a way of recording film dialogue. Dubbing has been greatly criticised as a technologically 'abnormal', even backward practice that also demonstrates serious aesthetic 'flaws' in terms of the lack of 'credibility', 'naturalness' and 'sincerity' that it entails. Erdoğan notes that such criticism aligns, in a peculiar way, New Turkish cinema[9] with the aesthetic and ideological values of Hollywood, especially around notions of 'realism'. In defence of Yeşilçam sound-recording practices, the essay rejects any notion of intrinsic technological and aesthetic superiority that synchronous sound might have, and proposes that dubbing must be understood not as a negative category but as a way of articulating different relationships between vision and sound, body and voice. Significantly, Erdoğan suggests that the practice of dubbing, while not conforming to Western aesthetic and ideological standards, does belong to a well-established Turkish tradition of 'anti-illusionist' cultural forms such as '*Karagöz* (shadow play) . . . *Orta Oyunu* (a form of theatre inspired by the *commedia dell' arte*), and *Meddah*, a one-man show in which the performer deliberately interrupts his story with irrelevant issues.'[10] Furthermore, revisiting the theme of ambivalence explored in the earlier essay, Erdoğan considers two contrasting theoretical frameworks dealing with the disjuncture between body and voice that dubbing entails. On the one hand, he considers theorisations of the apparatus, within which voice is described as perfectly mapped on the body of the actor, an embodied voice that enables narrative transparency and unifies the viewing experience. In contrast to that, dubbing as practised by Yeşilçam offers a disembodied voice that Erdoğan links to a specifically Islamic theology[11] in which voice takes priority over bodies as 'logos that penetrates all bodies'. The two different theoretical frameworks suggest different ways in which the (fundamentally Western) cinematic apparatus functions. While in Hollywood cinema the specific body/voice articulation supports the technological and cultural embodiment of patriarchal power, in Yeşilçam such power is questioned by the disengagement of voice and body. Erdoğan explores the dynamics of such disengagement by considering two different narrative trends in Turkish films of the 1970s: 'blind men "seeing" the voice', and 'blind women "hearing" the sight'. Such gendered narratives are marked with ambivalence as they question the patriarchal power inherent in the apparatus, while at the same time resolving themselves in a typical apparatus fashion by re-unifying body, sight and voice.

Gürata explores the ambivalent representations of women in Turkish adaptations as emblematic of the deep ambivalence around the process of modernisation that initiated in the 1920s. The basic conflict is between a modern, emancipated model of womanhood that modernisation promises, and the traditional mother figure that patriarchal society demands. While generalising this conflict as one of the particular modes in which Turkish cinema 'negotiates' modernity, Gürata also considers specific ways in which such conflict surfaces in specific films. Adaptations of Hollywood melodramas offer clear examples of how such negotiation becomes concrete as they demonstrate the particular ways in which narratives around female characters have been transformed by the Turkish versions in order to preserve a system of honour that upholds Turkish patriarchy. In Gürata's as well as in Erdoğan's work the defining characteristics of a national cinema are not sought in a few privileged examples that offer clear manifestations of a pure, unified and totally distinctive Turkish essence: on the contrary, they seek them in the multiple modalities of numerous popular but profoundly impure films, genres and narrative strands. For both Gürata and Erdoğan, the distinctiveness of Turkish cinema and identity is to be found in its particular engagement and negotiation with international forms and traditions. Negotiation, however, is not just a useful way of theorising the relationship between Yeşilçam and Western cinema, but also encapsulates the dynamics of the discursive activity involved in the production of critical/theoretical work on marginal or marginalised national cinemas within the theoretical paradigm/hegemonic canon of Anglo-US film theory. The final section of this essay will attempt a mapping of the discursive characteristics of such an encounter.

The Discursive Restrictions of 'National Cinema'

There are several shared discursive characteristics that are demonstrated in scholarly writing on national cinemas, and which seem to transcend national or cultural specificity. In the following pages I will explore how such discursive limitations/negotiations surface in the context of national cinemas marginalised in Anglo-US theory with specific reference to the three essays included in this *Reader and Guide*.

However, it is worth noting first that theoretical paradigms and canons are in themselves under constant flux and revision – as a result the discursive limitations imposed on the study of national cinemas are also constantly reviewed and renegotiated. Important in that respect is a sense of a 'critical mass' of writing on a specific national cinema, a threshold that when reached and surpassed enables the production of work liberated from the 'burden of representation' that limits earlier attempts at theorising certain national cinemas. Particularly interesting, in the context of the present volume, are the cinemas of Hong Kong, Japan, India and China. These seem to have established themselves firmly as objects of study and research in the field, in marked opposition to Turkish national cinema, on which there is little critical/theoretical work in English. Indeed, Anglo-US academics seem to have had little exposure to Turkish films, with notable exemptions such as the films of Yilmaz Güney, of Nuri Bilge Ceylan (with *Uzak* on general release in the UK in 2004) or the diasporic films of Fatih Akin.

Writing within a context of inadequate exposure to the history of a national cinema imposes the first discursive limitation on critics/theorists. In order for a specific investigation into a certain aspect of national cinema to be meaningful to readers largely unaware of its characteristics, writers are often forced to dedicate lengthy passages to provide sketchy and (almost inevitably) reductive outlines of the history of the relevant national cinema.[12] Almost two thirds of Erdoğan's 1998 essay is dedicated to the introduction of a pertinent context for his topic; almost as lengthy is Gürata's similar mapping of the field, which he feels obliged to offer before he is able to move on to discuss specific forms of adaptation. It is interesting to note that Erdoğan's second essay is able to proceed to the core argument by relying on work that had been published in the four years separating the two essays, as well as on his own earlier work.

A heuristic way to negotiate such restraint is the proposal by some critics of an important moment of 'origin', an incident or a film from early history that seems to concisely encapsulate the main characteristics of a national cinema. Typical here is the introduction of Erdoğan's 1998 essay, in which the film *Mürebbiye*, 'one of the first Turkish feature films', is used as a 'shorthand' for the ambivalent relationship between Turkish cinema and the West. While this is an effective and often intelligent way of dealing with discursive restraints, it can inadvertently lead to the creation of a rather arbitrary national canon of films. It also exposes writers to accusations of reduction, and invites numerous counter-examples of 'moments of origin' contradicting those asserted by the writer.

A different way to deal with the same problem is to focus on a specific genre either because it appears to be particularly important in terms of popularity/familiarity with national (and sometimes international) audiences or because its study facilitates particularly effective discussions of key aspects of a national cinema. Once again, the danger is 'canon formation', which tends to equate whole national cinemas with a specific genre (or limited genres): for example, Hong Kong and martial arts films or India and Hindi melodramas. Crucially all three essays included in the present volume focus mainly on melodramas. Such choice is by no means arbitrary in terms of the importance of the genre within the given national context; it is worth noting however, that melodramas emerge as a genre regularly surfacing in discussions of national cinemas. The privileged status of melodrama can be perhaps explained by the ability of the specific genre to mediate between individual identities and social institutions and structures, and in that respect it provides access to key questions of national culture and identity.

An important implication of the 'burden of representation' issue is the pressure placed on critics/theorists to balance the political necessity to represent to a foreign public a 'valued' aspect of national cinema with the epistemological demands of the object of study. This leaves critics in a doubly vulnerable position, pressurised to either 'advertise' a national cinema or become subjected to accusations of 'devaluing' its artistic achievements. Particularly commendable, in this context, is the determination of both Erdoğan and Gürata to focus their scholarly work on films of the 'popular' rather than of the 'high art' variety. Their emphasis on popular films goes against national critical consensus which, as Erdoğan notes, sees 'Yeşilçam as the first obstacle to be tackled'.

Of additional difficulty is the consideration of hybrid forms (such as co-productions, adaptations, or texts that clearly engage with foreign forms) as part of a critical discourse on national cinema. Such forms are traditionally excluded from national cinemas studies as being either too complicated or too contaminating of the hegemonic understanding of the 'national' as 'essential' and 'pure'. Particularly admirable here is Gürata's proposition that remakes offer privileged insights into (rather than obfuscate) an understanding of the dynamics of Turkish national cinema.

A discursive difficulty of fundamental importance is the production of work on national cinemas within the aegis of an Anglo-US theoretical paradigm. The development of such a paradigm is closely linked with the study of certain types of films (overwhelmingly Hollywood-produced or European art movies) which are markedly different from those produced within different contexts. The applicability of such theory becomes a key issue that the critics/writers have to negotiate. What often emerges through such encounters is the development of alternative theoretical approaches inspired by local/national contexts. Such alternatives not only offer more culturally sensitive ways of approaching the object of study, but they can also initiate much needed theoretical revisions of the Anglo-US paradigm.

The two Erdoğan essays offer an interesting example of the dynamic evolution of his approach, which can be traced through first the adaptation and then the rejection of a theoretical idea of clear Anglo-US origins. In both essays the writer deals with questions of realism and illusionism (notions that are central to the apparatus-related theorisations of the 1970s) as he attempts to theorise Yeşilçam's all-pervasive 'anti-illusionism'. In the first essay this is explained in the following terms: 'Yeşilçam was a hybrid cinema: it produced a cinematic discourse blending Hollywood-style realism with an unintentional Brechtian alienation effect.'[13] The turn to Brecht is doubly uncomfortable: not only because 'alienation' seems to be an imported, out-of-context concept, but also because if alienation is 'unintentional', there is little theoretical usefulness in describing Yeşilçam in such terms. In the 2002 essay Erdoğan deals with the same issue in a far more convincing and rigorous way, articulating a position that is particularly useful both in terms of its explicatory power and its cultural specificity. The anti-illusionism of Yeşilçam is explained as belonging to a long-established popular tradition of 'anti-illusionist' cultural forms, as well as in terms of an alternative theology. It is important to note this particular case not as a sign of intellectual weakness but as emblematic of the struggle against the discursive restraints imposed on the writer and the resourceful way in which such restrictions and limitations are negotiated.

Closely associated with the theoretical hegemony exercised by a discourse inspired by Hollywood cinema or European art cinema is the normative position that the aesthetic practices of such cinemas occupy. There is considerable pressure, perpetuated by critics such as David Bordwell,[14] to approach national cinemas as conscious (and almost by default failed) imitations of Hollywood aesthetic conventions and techniques. It is particularly admirable, therefore, that both Gürata and Erdoğan brilliantly defend the aesthetic peculiarities of Turkish cinema: the overwhelming reliance of the industry on remakes, for the former, and the practice of dubbing, for the latter, are approached not as structural or technical inferiorities but as culturally meaningful and perfectly justifiable acts of choice.

It is clear, then, that critics, theorists and historians of marginalised national cinemas find themselves in positions similar to those assigned to Turkish national cinema by our two contributors: involved in a process of negotiation, mediating between the specificities of their national cinema and the universalism of Anglo-US theory. It is no surprise, finally, that such writers turn to post colonial criticism and theoretical work as particularly pertinent theoretical discourses. The emphasis on 'in-between-ness', mimicry and ambivalence that characterises such discourse, offers a valuable tool in the attempt to navigate around the discursive limitations of 'national cinema'.

Notes

1. See, for example, *The Guardian*'s special report on Friday, 5 November 2004: 'The West is ready for the EU. The East is lost in the past: Much of Turkey is still a world away from Europe, culturally and economically'.
2. Atatürk's centrality cannot be overstated: his political imagination not only gave birth to modern Turkey but still anchors the nationalist discourse. A clear indication of this is the fact that Atatürk is an assumed name, replacing his birth name of Kemal Mustafa Pasha and meaning 'father of the Turks'.
3. Orhan Pamuk (2004), *Snow*, London: Faber & Faber, p. 194.
4. Yeşilçam translates as 'Green Pine', the name of the street in Istanbul where many movie businesses were located in the 1950s.
5. Yusuf Kaplan (1977), 'Turkish cinema' in Geoffrey Nowell-Smith (ed.), *The Oxford History of World Cinema*, Oxford and New York: Oxford University Press, p. 661.
6. Nezih Erdoğan, 'Narratives of resistance: national identity and ambivalence in the Turkish melodrama between 1965 and 1975', reprinted in this collection.
7. Ahmet Gürata, 'Translating modernity: remakes in Turkish cinema', reprinted in this collection.
8. Erdoğan, 'Narratives of resistance'.
9. Erdoğan sees New Turkish cinema as developing in clear opposition to Yeşilçam and as a form of 'art cinema' also standing in opposition to Hollywood. In terms of sound-recording practices, Erdoğan notes a significant break from dubbing, initiating in 1996 and defining the practices of New Turkish cinema.
10. Nezih Erdoğan, 'Mute bodies, disembodied voices: notes on sound in Turkish popular cinema', reprinted in this collection.
11. He contrasts this to the use of disembodied voice in Hollywood as theorised by Mary Ann Doane ('The voice in the cinema: articulation of body and space', in Phil Rosen (ed.), *Narrative, Apparatus and Ideology*, New York: Columbia University Press, 1986).
12. A common trend in international film studies conferences is to group all 'national cinemas' papers in one or more panels, irrespective of their methodological or theoretical differences or even their subject. Presumably the 'potted history' that they all seem to have to provide offers enough common ground to justify such groupings.
13. Erdoğan, 'Narratives of resistance'.
14. See, for example, David Bordwell (1987), *Narration in the Fiction Film*, London: Methuen.

11

NARRATIVES OF RESISTANCE: NATIONAL IDENTITY AND AMBIVALENCE IN THE TURKISH MELODRAMA BETWEEN 1965 AND 1975

Nezih Erdoğan

National Cinema and an Identity in Crisis

One of the first Turkish feature films, *Mürebbiye/The Tutor* (Ahmet Fehim, 1919)[1] was banned by the allied forces which had occupied Istanbul just after World War I. It was adapted from Hüseyin Rahmi Gürpinar's novel of the same title, published in 1898. *Mürebbiye* tells the story of a French woman who seduces the members of a snobbish family she works for. Apparently the text was meant to give a comical illustration of the upper classes' infatuation with French culture. But the film was released in the context of the occupation of Istanbul by the allied forces, and by then the focus was on the corrupt French tutor who, more or less, represented Western woman. Domestic film circles read *Mürebbiye* as Turkish cinema's 'silent resistance' to occupation.[2] What is more interesting is that the censor for the allied forces banned the film on the same grounds.

Woman as the site of production of meaning is one of the issues that I will discuss in this essay. For now, I would like to point out that the expression 'silent resistance' is somewhat problematic here. To the Turkish eye, the cinema was a Western form of entertainment right from the start. Sigmund Weinberg, a Polish Jew of Romanian nationality, launched the first regular public screenings in Istanbul in 1896. These were Lumière shorts, *L'arrivée d'un train en gare de la Ciotat* (1895) among them. Weinberg also made some documentaries and was reputed to be an 'expert' in cinematography. Soon, companies such as Lumière, Pathé, Gaumont and Ciné Théâtrale d'Orient began to distribute French,

From *Screen*, 39: 3, pp. 257–71.

American, German and Danish films. In the beginning, the audience of these films consisted mostly of the non-Muslim minorities who lived in Pera (now Beyoğlu), a district of Istanbul marked by a Western life style. D. Henri screened films in a pub named 'Sponeck'; Matalon, another Jew, in the 'Lüksemburg Buildings'; and Camdon, probably a Lumière man, in 'Varyete Theatre' – all places with Western names. In addition, publicity was printed in French, German, Armenian and Greek but not in Turkish. Pera was posed as an object of desire for the Muslim upper class and, partly, for the intellegentsia at a time of modernization fuelled by Western-oriented policies, and the cinema seems to have served as the latest desiring machine – the films that were shown presented glamorous scenes from various European centres, and filmgoing itself had the charm of being a Western-style ritual.[3]

Mürebbiye is not the only example of a national cinema that produces a discourse of resistance while a general perception of cinema itself was already constructed entirely in Western terms. And it is not surprising that, as far as national cinemas are concerned, any formulation of resistance is overshadowed by images of mimicry. Turkish popular cinema, Yeşilçam, whose death was announced in the early 1980s, had been frequently criticized for imitating other cinemas, and repeating other films.[4] Back in 1968, the film magazine *Yeni Sinema* (*New Cinema*) noted that more than half of the 250 films made that year were adaptations – plagiarisms, to be more precise – of foreign box-office successes.[5] Given this fact, one can easily deduce an identity crisis, but what are we to make of an identity which is in permanent crisis? And what kind of national identity can be formed from a cinema renowned for its failures rather than its successes, or for its endless efforts to mimic others rather than to produce films that are 'Turkish to the core'?

In this essay I will examine the dynamics by which Turkish popular cinema describes a national identity, and I will attempt to demonstrate how the specificity of this identity can be seen in the very way it mimics and resists others. Cinema, as a desiring machine, produces a discourse which operates on a social level, involving psychical processes with subject effects. I will argue that these psychical processes are characterized by ambivalence (for example, mimicry and resistance) which provides a ground for the 'identity in crisis' I refer to above. In this respect, I will make use of post-colonial theory, particularly its formulation of the ambivalent nature of colonial discourse and the way it operates on the social unconscious. However, I am not going to offer an analysis of colonial discourse as such, rather I will focus on 'the discourse of the national identity as derivative of colonial discourse' as articulated by Yeşilçam.[6] Indeed, Turkish popular cinema is one popular site where such an 'identity in crisis' has been experienced for decades.

My study covers the period when commercial cinema enjoyed its heyday – that is, between the mid 1960s and mid 1970s – producing an average of 200 films per year. *Konfeksiyon* films, as they were called, were made in a rush to meet a continuously increasing demand.[7] Not only did they entertain the domestic audience, they also became very popular in other Middle Eastern countries, such as Iran, Iraq and Egypt. Production declined dramatically after the 1980s, and today only about ten Turkish films reach the movie theatres each year. This is primarily due to the US film distribution companies that now control exhibition mechanisms in Turkey, and secondly to the gap between the audience and the inaccessible discourse of current Turkish films, many of which follow the conventions of European art cinema. The new Turkish cinema has lost its audience to television channels which repeatedly show old popular films – the frequency of commercial breaks suggests that these films still appeal to a mass audience, still contribute to popular imagery.

Turkish Popular Cinema: A Field of Tensions

The first three decades of Turkish cinema were marked by the domination of a single man, Muhsin Ertuğrul, who was, and is still, widely criticized for transferring the stylistic devices of theatre to cinema. This period came to an end in 1953, when a number of filmmakers initiated a somewhat different practice. Ayşe Şasa, a veteran scriptwriter, calls this the period of the 'illiterates', in that they were neither aware of, nor interested in, the artistic possibilities of the cinema. Craftsmen of rural and lumpen origin now ruled Yeşilçam. They did not hide their commercial interest in the films from which they made big profits. Şasa maintains that the period of the 'illiterates' in Turkish cinema was undervalued because of its low-quality films: its potential of growing a genuine cinematic 'seed' was underestimated, as was 'the poetry that was hidden in this artless authenticity'.[8]

The mid 1960s witnessed the beginning of a debate about national identity in Turkish cinema. A group of writers from various branches of literature gathered around the film magazine *Yeni Sinema*, and founded the Turkish cinematheque (with some help from Henri Langlois). They argued that a national cinema with international concerns was impossible within Yeşilçam, which was associated with worn-out formulas, plagiarism, escapism and exploitation. While *Yeni Sinema* published interviews with film directors such as Godard, Renoir and Antonioni, and translations from theoretical works examining cinema in relation to other arts, screenings organized by the cinematheque gave a particular audience access to canons of European art cinema. When one looks back at this scene, one can see a programme aiming at an art cinema. If, in Europe, art cinema developed as a resistance to the increasing domination of Hollywood, in Turkey, Yeşilçam appeared as the first obstacle to be tackled; alternative modes of production were sought, and festivals and competitions held to promote short films.[9]

When the Asiatic mode of production championed by the novelist Kemal Tahir became a popular issue in the late 1960s, a close friend of his, the then film critic and promising film director Halit Refiğ, elaborated a concept of national cinema: films are made by money coming *from* the people, so they must be made *for* the people, one way or another. Since it is impossible to reach the people of Turkey via Western forms, a cinema which considers the people's characteristics and needs must be developed within Yeşilçam, which already has formed its audience. Refiğ insisted that Yeşilçam relied less on a capitalist mode of production than on a labour-intensive one, and urged film writers and producers not to turn their backs on it. He used ironic language when he criticized the elitist approach of the cinematheque group:

> To sum up, cinema [according to the group of cinematheque] is a universal art. The criteria for the evaluation of this art are provided by the West. To be able to make a good film, one must do whatever a Western filmmaker would do. There is no point in taking an interest in Turkish films as they do not subscribe to Western criteria . . . and one must fight to have the Turkish audience develop a sympathy for and to love films coming from the West.[10]

In 1967 the major film directors of the time refused to respond to a questionnaire on the role of criticism prepared by *Yeni Sinema*, and that was the end of relations between filmmakers and the cinematheque.[11] Here is a list of keywords which represent the two cinemas (one of which was only a programme then).

New Cinema	**Yeşilçam**
Western	domestic
art cinema	popular cinema
model: European art cinema	model: Hollywood
to create	to produce
auteur policy	star system
alternative modes of production	capitalist mode of production
festivals, competitions	production–distribution–exhibition

Inevitably, the sharp conflict in this set of oppositions was occasionally resolved by some directors. Yilmaz Güney, for instance, produced popular, commercially successful films which were also hailed by the cinematheque group. At the beginning of the 1980s, New Cinema began to introduce its first films to the domestic audience (and to international film circles), but it could not get out of the domain of Yeşilçam entirely. At first *Yeni Sinema* attempted to win over some established directors, Lütfi Akad and Yilmaz Güney among them. Then came a generation of young filmmakers who tried hard to differentiate their films from those of popular cinema: although they made these films in Yeşilçam, they sought recognition from international art cinema institutions. In Yeşilçam, stars were used to brand the film product; the New Cinema directors also worked with stars but, following auteur policy, the director was inscribed as the 'creator' of the film. Audiences began to read authorial credits, such as 'an Ali Özgentürk film', 'an Ömer Kavur film'. In addition, the New Cinema assumed the point of view of European art cinema (which includes the

European audience) in that it produced representations of Turkey either as an 'impenetrable other' (*Hazal, Bedrana, Kumal/The Concubine*) or as a fantasmatic Western country (*Piano Piano Bacaksiz/Piano Piano My Little Boy, Seni Seviyorum Rosa/I Love You Rosa, Yengeç Sepeti/The Crab Basket, Gizli Yüz/The Secret Face*). It is interesting to note that a British film critic, reporting from an Istanbul Film Festival in 1992, describes the latter films as 'pretentious allegories drawing on influences from Bunuel to Bergman'.[12]

The mid 1970s witnessed television and sociopolitical catastrophe pushing Yeşilçam into another crisis, while New Cinema continued to seek its audience by way of international festivals and other such events. Thomas Elsaesser makes a similar observation about German cinema in the early 1980s:

> the Germans are beginning to love their own cinema because it has been endorsed, confirmed and benevolently looked at by someone else: for the German cinema to exist, it first had to be seen by non-Germans. It enacts, as a national cinema now in explicitly economic and cultural terms, yet another form of self-estranged exhibitionism.[13]

To echo Elsaesser in a slightly different context, for Turkish art cinema to exist, it had to be 'endorsed, confirmed and benevolently looked at' by some one else. But unlike German cinema, with a few exceptions it never enjoyed such recognition. What was expected from German cinema was, for instance, the sophisticated, self-reflexive films of Fassbinder. This has not been the case for Turkish cinema: *Susuz Yaz/The Dry Summer* (Metin Erksan) and *Yol* (Yilmaz Güney), which won prizes at major festivals, both illustrate the harsh circumstances of rural life stricken with poverty, absurd moral values, oppressed individuals, and so on. Roy Armes's comment on the relationship between the Third-World cinema and intelligentsia is relevant here:

> But the processes of their education and the advent of national independence will have made them very aware that they cannot become Western filmmakers. Hence they will tend to prove their identity by plunging deeply into local tradition, myth and folklore. The result is all too often an ambiguous cinema which is too complex in form for local audiences and too esoteric in substance for Western spectators.[14]

That 'they cannot become Western filmmakers' needs further elaboration. I want to demonstrate that fetishism and, relatedly, fantasy complicate things further. Indeed, Turkish film directors are very well aware that they cannot become Western filmmakers, but the fetishistic disavowal of difference keeps them moving in the same direction (to adapt the famous 'I know very well but nevertheless . . .', 'I am very well aware that I cannot become a Western filmmaker, but nevertheless . . .'). The problem is not in knowing but in doing, as Slavoj Žižek maintains:

> They know very well how things really are, but still they are doing it as if they did not know. The illusion is therefore double: it consists in

> overlooking the illusion which is structuring our real, effective relationship to reality. And this overlooked, unconscious illusion is what may be called the, ideological fantasy.[15]

Turkish art cinema deserves a more detailed analysis, but I want now to return to Yeşilçam and to demonstrate that the dissemination of colonial discourse is not exclusive to New Cinema. I will concentrate upon melodrama as a popular genre which plays on desire, providing us with invaluable insight into the ambivalent nature of national identity.

The Identities of Melodrama

As Thomas Elsaesser observes, family melodrama,

> dealing largely with the same Oedipal themes of emotional and moral identity, more often records the failure of the protagonist to act in a way that could shape the events and influence the emotional environment, let alone change the stifling social milieu. The world is closed, and the characters are acted upon, and each other's sole referent, there is no world outside to be acted on, no reality that could be defined or assumed unambiguously.[16]

Steve Neale notes that 'melodramas are marked by chance happenings, coincidences, missed meetings, sudden conversions, last minute rescues and revelations, *deus ex machina* endings'.[17] Melodrama, in short, is perfectly suited to Yeşilçam, which sticks to narrative traditions inspired by legends, fairy tales and epopees (rather than by, say, tragedy, which emphasizes the inner conflicts and transformations of its characters). While, in its beginnings, Western melodrama recorded the 'struggle of a morally and emotionally emancipated bourgeois consciousness against the remnants of feudalism',[18] Yeşilçam exploits melodrama in articulating the desires aroused not only by class conflict but also by rural/urban and eastern/western oppositions. Immigration from rural areas to big cities is still a social phenomenon with significant economic and cultural consequences. The possibilities of crossing from one class to another and from village to big city provide the ground upon which melodrama plays and activates its machinery of desire. Hence the formulation: lower class/rural = East/local culture vs upper class/urban = West/foreign culture.

The Yeşilçam melodrama repeatedly returns to the 'boy meets girl' plot: they unite, they split, they reunite. In one particular variation, the boy from the urban upper class and the girl from the lower class have an affair and then the boy leaves the girl. The girl finds him again, but learns that he no longer wants her. She comes back in disguise (urban, rich, sophisticated) and the boy, having failed to recognize her, falls in love. This time the girl takes her revenge and leaves him. In the end, her identity is revealed and the boy learns his lesson. The upper class, which is fixed as the object of desire here, is encoded with its Western attributes.[19] Luxurious American cars, blondes wearing revealing dresses, crazy parties and whisky all connote moral corruption, and construct an iconography of the West.[20] This is in sharp contrast with the virtues (simplicity, loyalty, correctness and chastity) of the woman from the rural area/lower class. In a recurrent plot, the heroine is raped/seduced and immediately deserted by a man whom she already loves. She has a baby and brings it up under reduced circumstances, and then somehow becomes rich. Towards the finale, having come to appreciate the heroine's virtues, the long-lost lover, now father, returns, but the heroine's pride delays the reunion (*Sana Dönmeyeceğim/I Will Never Return To You, Ayşem/Ayşe Mine, Kinali Yapincak/Golden Red Grape*). In *Dağdan Inme/Came Down From The Mountains* the male hero is struck by the appearance of an extremely attractive woman he meets at a party. She is actually a villager, desperately in love with him. *Taşra Kizi/The Girl From The Province* tells the story of a girl who comes to Istanbul from a small town. She moves into the house of an old family friend, who turns out to be her father. This film, like many others, exemplifies how melodrama resolves conflict using the Father figure (as father, police chief, judge, boss) as its agent.[21] In many instances the authoritarian Father plays the benefactor, and sides with the girl against the spoiled son. There are, of course, some contradictory variations (for example, the rich father making friends with two young men who turn out to be his daughters' boyfriends). Variations, however, do not negate the argument that the Father regulates the economy of desire and power. The message, which is of course addressed to the lower-class/rural subject, is that the upper class will be able to survive only if the lower class helps. Possibilities of identification in these films are a matter of justifying the audience's (especially female audience's) desire for, and wish to be desired by, the upper class. Yeşilçam melodramas thus offered a sense of legitimacy to the squatters who had migrated from rural areas.

Plagiarism, of which Yeşilçam has often been accused, is by no means a simple issue. The technical and stylistic devices of Yeşilçam differ radically from those of Hollywood and European cinema. Lighting, colour, dubbing, dialogue, shooting practices, point-of-view shots and editing create a very specific cinematic discourse in even the most faithful of adaptations. In trying to meet a demand for 200 films a year, production practices had to run at great speed and thus by default a visual tradition of shadowplays, miniatures, and so on was revived. To save time and money, shot/reverse-shot and other point-of-view shots were avoided as much as possible. This meant the domination of front shots: characters mostly performed facing the camera and did not turn their backs to it. This made full identification impossible and gave way to empathy instead. When a Hollywood film shows a box, it says 'This is a box'. Yeşilçam, on the other hand, attempted to achieve the same statement but could not help saying 'This is supposed to be a box, but actually it is only an image which represents a box'. Yeşilçam was a hybrid cinema: it produced a cinematic discourse blending Hollywood-style realism with an unintentional Brechtian alienation effect.

Characters who were never depicted as individuals, and who could not act but were 'acted upon', reinforced the melodramatic effect. Given such circumstances, it is not difficult to see why split identities have always been convincing for, and appealing to, the audience. The Yeşilçam character can trick her lover into believing that she is someone else, taking on various successive identities. What was once a poor, uneducated girl with a strong accent can instantly become an attractive, sophisticated lady of manners. A girl from the lower class can adapt herself to the rules of the high society she has just joined without any trouble. These are, of course, narrative reproductions of Pygmalion and Cinderella. If we can hazard that splittings are mobilized by presenting the upper class/West to the lower class/East as an object of desire and identification, then splitting is a symptom which betrays Yeşilçam own conception of national identity. Ambivalence (narcissism/aggression), identification and fantasy are the basic terms of the logic of this conception. Splitting, as a matter of fact, provides the ground for ambivalent psychical positionings of the subject in relation to its object of desire, and transition from one identity to another takes place in the realm of fantasy: after the poor young girl is discovered by the owner of a night club, she quickly becomes a rich and famous singer. The huge efforts required to achieve success (private education from a non-Muslim instructor, music lessons, training, rehearsals) are either shown in a rapid succession of scenes or ignored entirely.

Apollo, Molotov Cocktail and 'The Favourite of Maharajah'

Now I want to examine a film which, I believe, focuses the problem of national identity as derivative of colonial discourse. *Karagözlüm/My Dark Eyed One* (Atif Yilmaz, 1970) is not a typical or normal melodrama; even its plot is different from the ones I have so far described. Rather it is a limit-text, which stands at the margins of the logic of melodrama, and this is why I think it is capable of representing Yeşilçam melodrama perfectly.

Azize (Türkan Şoray) is a fisherman's daughter who enjoys singing while she works in the fish market. She happens to meet Kenan (Kadir Inanir), an idealist composer who disdains all kinds of music but Western classical. Teasing him for his pretentious cultural preference she names him 'Chopin'. As in the case of many melodramas, Azize is then discovered by the owner of a music-hall, and becomes a famous singer, finding herself in an entirely different network of sociocultural and economic relations. Kenan, having failed to find a decent job, begins work as a waiter at the same place. They eventually fall in love. Kenan drops classical music in favour of composing popular songs for Azize ('Lretire from Chopinhood'). He mails his work anonymously to her, never revealing his identity. Two Hollywood producers who happen to hear her singing one night offer to co-star Azize with Rock Hudson in a film ('The Favourite of Maharajah') on the condition that she will bring her 'unknown composer' along with her to Hollywood. She is delighted with the idea that she will enjoy world-wide fame, but her mysterious, hitherto unknown composer (Kenan disguised as an old man) shows up, and not only declines the offer but also accuses her of 'being adrift in a Hollywood dream'. He deserts Azize and gets engaged to Semra, the daughter of a rich family. Azize, having discovered that 'one who wants to have everything, loses what she already has', quits her job and goes back to selling fish. But, in the end, Kenan reappears and they are reunited.

The film is very quick to establish the opposition of East/popular culture and West/elite culture. In the scene following the opening, Kenan's close friend, Orhan, advises him to drop 'this *kefere* [infidel's] music which is a pain in the neck' and perform his art for a larger audience in order to make a fortune from his talent. Once Azize starts working at the music-hall she cannot enjoy the new life she is expected to lead. When the vacuum cleaner goes dead in a power cut, she and her assistant happily use brooms. They are almost embarrassed to use mechanical appliances for any kind of housework that can be done manually. Technology not only marks a class conflict here, it also serves as an icon for a Western lifestyle.

But the dream sequence is most significant since it reveals the 'intention of the text'. In order to go to Hollywood Azize has to locate her unknown composer, but Kenan is none too happy with her enthusiasm, and is reluctant to give away his secret. As he tries to make his mind up he falls asleep and has a dream. In the dream we see the chamber of the maharajah. Azize enters the scene and begins to dance in front of a man whom we are not allowed to see. Then Kenan sneaks into the chamber through the back door, and becomes furious when he sees Azize dancing for someone else. In response, Azize puts out her tongue in mockery. But what strikes Kenan most is that right behind Azize, accompanying her on the flute, he sees himself, dressed in Indian clothes. Kenan produces a bomb (a molotov cocktail) from the pocket of his coat and throws it right into the middle of the chamber. The bomb explodes and Kenan awakes. He has made his decision: he will not let Azize go to Hollywood.

When Kenan detonates the bomb we do not see any damage done: we do not see the palace falling into pieces, we do not see anybody killed, and we do not hear any screams. We see only a smoke-screen and then, in closeup, Kenan awakening in dismay. What has broken down is not the content of the dream but the fantasy screen itself.

As Mahmut Mutman stresses, colonial discourse and orientalism play on sexual difference. Psychic processes (fantasy, castration, fetishism, aggression) which mobilize the discourse, enable the re-presentation of Woman as a cultural construct: 'Muslim woman stands where the political, the economic and the cultural "values" meet: her culturally specific embodiment is the commodity that is exchanged with other commodities'.[22] Which applies to *both* sides (colonized and colonizer) of colonial discourse. In Turkish, *anavatan* and *anayurt*, which might be translated as 'motherland' and 'mother country', are terms which explain how Woman comes to represent values attached to the concept of nationhood. And this is precisely what *Karagözlüm* does through the agency of Kenan: Chopin/the unknown composer is asked to trade Azize for a brilliant career (she dances to his music). Azize, an Arabic word in origin, means 'dear' or 'beloved' in Turkish and can easily be associated with the common usage *Aziz Vatan* (beloved country). The molotov cocktail was an icon of the militant Left in the 1970s, frequently used in demonstrations against the growing US hegemony. It was considered an unsophisticated, cheap, easy-to-produce, easy-to-use combat weapon, a suitable device for a 'people at war with imperialism'. What seems problematic to my analysis at this point is that Kenan's dream actually serves as a screen onto which 'Hollywood' projects its fantasy. It is also the very dream Kenan refers to when he accuses Azize of being adrift in a Hollywood dream.

Through his music, Kenan fixes his beloved as an object of desire, and then exhibits her body (that is, hands her over) to Hollywood. More importantly, the splittings of Kenan verify the ambivalence of colonial discourse: there is a Kenan (the flute player) who accompanies Azize with his music, a Kenan (the white male hero) who is struck by what is going on in the scene and explodes the bomb, and finally a Kenan who dreams all of this. I suggest that the dream sequence forms the kernel of the entire film. The splittings that take place within it are parallel to the diegetic ones: the flute player is the unknown composer, now unmasked, the one who bombs the palace is the waiter, and the one who dreams is a Kenan who retired from 'Chopinhood' in favour of Azize. But who is the maharajah? Although we see very little of him, he is a pivotal figure around which the rest of the characters revolve. Motionless, he is watching Azize dancing. It seems he controls the space with his gaze. He can see Azize and the flute player and vice versa. He cannot see the waiter (or the audience), and although the waiter cannot see his face he is very well aware of his presence. So the maharajah is also a borderline separating the waiter and the audience from Azize and the flute player. The audience identifies first with the dreaming Kenan and then with the waiter. When Kenan throws the bomb, he not only puts an end to the dream, but also to the voyeuristic pleasure of the maharajah. The audience of the exotic films of Hollywood shares the erotic experiences of the Oriental despot and then identifies with the white male hero who bursts into the palace and takes the girl away from him. In this connection, the explosion has a double effect which brings us back to the problem of split identities: Kenan-tears apart the fantasy screen of 'Hollywood', yet identifies with it by playing the white male hero who is already a part of this same fantasy. Therefore, *Karagözlüm* offers us a dual set of relationships which reveal the actual fantasy of the colonized – to share the colonizer's fantasy. This is made possible by a subtle reversal: the narrative switches positions and the colonized becomes someone other than Kenan. Aggression takes place elsewhere; neither the word 'maharajah' nor the setting is Turkish, but it is still Oriental.

Azize and her father ride to the fish market on a shabby motorcycle they have named Apollo. If we go back to 1970, the production date of this film, we can see the reference to the US moon landing. To name an old motorcycle after

Apollo is a parody intended as mockery, but as Fredric Jameson emphasizes in a different context, 'the parodist has to have some secret sympathy for the original' and 'there remains somewhere behind all parody the feeling that there is a . . . norm'.[23] And *Karagözlüm* re-establishes Western norms by illustrating cultural deviations. Throughout the film we hear three sorts of music, representing three levels of culture: classical Western music (Kenan – the norm), traditional Turkish popular music (Azize – the settlement) and popular dance music (Semra – the corrupt).[24] Kenan has to sacrifice classical music (the norm) for Azize and the values she represents (the popular); when he thinks he has lost her to Hollywood, he decides to marry Semra (the corrupt).

My observation is supported by another film. In *Sana Tapivorum/I Worship You* (Aram Gülyüz, 1970), Ayşe (Zeynep Değirmencioğlu) studies ballet at a dance school. In order to meet her expenses, her mother works as a singer in a night club, which utterly embarrasses Ayşe. When the rumour is spread that her mother is more or less a prostitute, Ayşe is cut by her classmates and teachers. She drops out of school under pressure and, at the same time, she is informed that her mother is dangerously ill. The doctors tell her that she will die unless she is sent to Switzerland for an operation. Ayşe is desperate because she cannot afford to pay for the operation. Her mother's boss offers her money, but she would have to dance in his night club in return. When Ayşe refuses the offer furiously, he asks ironically whether her body is more sacred than her mother's life, remarking that her mother did the same thing in order to be able to pay her tuition fees, upon which Ayşe agrees to start working in the night club. Ayşe's classmates and teachers appreciate the sacrifice she has made for her mother and decide to help her. In the meantime, Ayşe locates her long-lost father, who was once a famous brain surgeon and is now an alcoholic, and after a climactic speech she persuades him to do the operation. In the final scene we see Ayşe taking the leading role in a ballet performance and all the characters in the audience, especially the owner of the night club regretfully weeping. Her body, as in many Yeşilçam melodramas, is a metaphor for postponement and sacrifice. Once again, Woman provides the ground for an exchange of values. The body which represents the cultural values of the dance school (the norm) is not more sacred than the Mother. It must be sacrificed for the Mother and submitted to the night club. Only then will the Mother survive and the Father assume his identity.

'Pay It to the Waiter!'

As I have tried to demonstrate, colonial discourse and its derivatives operate in a vast area, and neither nationalism nor any other sort of anti-Western practice can easily avoid reproducing them. For Yeşilçam, the moment of colonial discourse is the moment of transgressing the boundaries it has defined. Yeşilçam depicts the West perjoratively; however, it supresses the fact that the social class which represents the West is represented in fantasmatic scenes where everything can be vindicated and thus desired unashamedly.

One must, nevertheless, not forget that Yeşilçam melodrama stages a real ambivalence in the sense that reversals work both ways. It imposes the cultural values attached to national identity as necessary and temporary deviations. One must conform to them for now so as to acquire the norm (that is the West) in the future. To be able to be Chopin one day, one must be a waiter or an unknown composer now – because Azize is at stake; to be able to go back to the dance school one day, one must work in a night club – because mother is ill and money is required for the operation.

When the Hollywood producers burst into Azize's dressing room to meet her, the owner of the music-hall cannot figure out what they want. 'They want the bill', Azize guesses, and points to Kenan, who happens to be there. 'Pay it to the waiter', she suggests. Kenan's intervention prevents Azize from going to Hollywood, so Hollywood does pay the bill to Yeşilçam in a way. Yeşilçam seems determined to demand a payment, only it cannot avoid reproducing colonial discourse once again, since it fixes national identity precisely in this problematic moment.

Notes

An earlier version of this essay was presented at the Theory, Culture and Society Conference, Berlin, August 1995. I wish to thank Mahmut Mutman and Stephanie Donald for their comments.

1. The large majority of the films cited in this essay were not released in English-speaking countries. I am, however, adding my own English translation of the original titles to give an idea of their content.
2. Nijat Özön, *Fuat Uzkinay* (Istanbul: TSD, 1970) cited in Giovanni Scognamillo, *Türk Sinema Tarihi* 1896–1986 (Istanbul: Metis, 1987), p. 28.
3. Nilgün Abisel gives a detailed account of how intellectuals debated the tension between foreign films and cultural identity in her work *Türk Sinemask Uzerine Yazilar* (Ankara: Image, 1994)
4. Yeşilçam is a street in Istanbul where film production companies gathered until a decade ago. It also denotes a specific system of production-distribution-exhibition that dominated the Turkish cinema between the late 1950s and mid 1980s.
5. Ikilem Yanliş konunca', *Yent Sinema*, nos 19/20 (June/July 1968), p. 3.
6. I borrow this expression from the title of a book by Partha Chaterjee. *Nationalist Thought and Colonial World: a Detivative Discourse* (Minneapolis: University of Minnesota Press, 1993).
7. Daytime 'women only' screenings were part of a strategy developed by the movie theatres to regulate this demand.
8. Ayşe Şasa, *Yeşilçam Günlüğü* (Istanbul: Dergah, 1993), p. 30.
9. Ece Ayhan, a famous poet, evaluated the contributors to a short film competition: 'This Young Generation of honour has chosen to work away from Yeşilçam in order not to fall prey to it'. 'Simurg', *Yeni Sinema*, nos 19/20 (June/July 1968), p. 10.
10. Halit Refiğ, *Ulusal Sinema Kavgasi* (Istanbul: Hareket, 1971), p. 47.
11. 'We refuse to collaborate with the Turkish cinematheque and its publication *Yeni Sinema* for their hostility to the Turkish cinema in general and Turkish filmmakers in particular'. Memduh Ün, Atil Yilmaz, Metin Erksan, Lütfi Akad, Duygu Sagiroglu, Alp Zeki Heper, Osman Seden, Halit Refiğ, *Yeni Sinema*, no 4 (July 1967), p. 34.
12. John Gillet, *Sight and Sound*, vol. 2, no. 4 (1992), p. 5.
13. Thomas Elsaesser, 'Primary identification and the historical subject: Fassbinder and Germany', *Cine-Tracts*, vol. 3, no. 3 (1980), p. 52.

14. Roy Armes, 'Twelve propositions on the inaccesibility of third world cinema', in Christine Woodhead (ed.), *Turkish Cinema: an Introduction* (London: Turkish Area Study Group Publications, 1989), p. 7.
15. Slavoj Žižek, *The Sublime Object of Ideology* (New York and London: Verso, 1989), pp. 32–3.
16. Thomas Elsaesser, 'Tales of sound and fury: observations on the family melodrama', in Bill Nichols (ed.), *Movies and Methods*, Volume II (London: University of California Press, 1985), p. 177.
17. Steve Neale, 'Melodrama and tears', *Screen*, vol. 27, no. 6 (1986), p. 6.
18. Elsaesser, 'Tales of sound and fury', p. 168.
19. At this point Yeşilçam gets closer to Indian melodrama. Ravi Vasudevan gives an instance of a female character who was sentenced to death for murdering a man but thinks she is already guilty 'of having adopted customs alien to their land' (*Andaz/A Sense of Proportion* [Mehboob Khan, 1949]). 'The melodramatic mode and the commercial Hindi cinema: notes on film history, narrative and performance in the 1950s', *Screen*, vol. 30, no. 3 (1989), pp. 41–4.
20. Mehmet Açar notes that the innocent girl is always offered a Western drink, often whisky, when she is to be seduced. 'Felakete çeyrek kala', *Sinema* (February 1996), p. 88.
21. I thank Mahmut Mutman for drawing my attention to this issue.
22. Mahmut Mutman, 'Pictures from alar: shooting the middle east', *Inscriptions*, no. 6 (1992), p. 15.
23. Fredric Jameson, 'Postmodernism and consumer society', in Hal Foster (ed.), *Anti-aesthetic: Essays on Postmodern Culture* (Port Townsend: Bay Press, 1986), pp. 113–14.
24. It must be noted that *Karagözlüm* borrows its title from a popular song, like many other Turkish films.

12

TRANSLATING MODERNITY: REMAKES IN TURKISH CINEMA

Ahmet Gürata

The Turkish film industry, which had grown rapidly in the 1950s, became by the 1960s one of the largest film-producing national industries, with an average annual production of 200 movies. In 1972, just before the economic crisis that affected the movie industry severely, Turkey ranked third among the major film-producing countries, with 301 movies. Almost 90 per cent of these movies, however, were remakes, adaptations or spin-offs (Scognamillo 1973: 68). In other words, they were based on novels, plays, films and even film reviews or publicity materials of foreign origin. Furthermore, in most cases the source material for these adaptations and remakes was not credited. As in literature, the notion of plagiarism in Turkey was not identical with that prevalent in the West. So how can we define these films?

While both adaptation and remake are usually defined by their legally sanctioned use of material (whose rights the filmmakers should have purchased), in Turkey that was not the case. Veteran script-writer Bülent Oran, who wrote over 300 scripts throughout his career, remembers that there were all sorts of sources and thousands of books available for free, 'for example, a Harold Robbins novel, that Hollywood would be willing to pay millions for, was sold for 20 liras' (Oran 1973: 17). Furthermore, the appropriation of material whose sources (filmic or non-filmic) are almost impossible to identify, rendered proper legal procedures unnecessary for the filmmakers.

Different understandings of remakes might be an appropriate starting point in order to account for their popularity in Turkey. First of all, a remake may aim at paying tribute to an earlier film. This could take various forms, from 'unwavering idealisation' to 'unalloyed negativity' (Eberwein 1998: 18). For example, director Aram Gülyüz, whose movie *Gariban* (1966) is a remake of René Clair's *La Porte des Lilas* (1956), states that his version was merely a sign of appreciation:

> I shot this movie by copying each sequence of the original; and I am proud of it. Other producers and directors are doing the same thing, but hiding it. Why be ashamed of it? On the contrary, it is an honour to imitate such masterpieces. Are those painters who replicated *La Jaconde* ashamed of it? No one asks for royalties or rights, so why should one hide it? If we hide it, then it would be stealing. But if we reveal the fact then this would be an indication of our appreciation. (cited by Scognamillo 1966: 29)

However, beyond the motives of imitation and homage, there were also economic imperatives underlying remakes. By recycling some of the films to which they hold the rights, studios save money (Eberwein 1998: 18) and are encouraged by the earlier success of a particular movie. In some cases, there lies a basic intuition that the audience will continue to buy a particular story in its new incarnation because the underlying fable is still compelling (Braudy 1998: 328). Nevertheless, all these explanations were based on the assumption that the studios would acquire the property rights of the earlier films that they want to recycle. In Turkey it was not necessary to reserve such rights. As explained above, thanks to the lack of any legal procedures, Turkish filmmakers could get away with their remake strategy.

As for the latter assumption of remake as a pre-sold property, it would be interesting to compare the dates of release for the original films and their remakes. Most of the remakes were shot in 1960–75, whereas the 'originals' are from the 1940s and 1950s. Usually, there is a gap of ten to twenty years between the two releases. Furthermore, there was a transformation in the socio-economic structure of the audiences in Turkey between 1930 and 1960. International films, with few exceptions, were screened in first-run movie theatres, while Turkish films were distributed widely everywhere. Thus, it is unlikely that the same audiences saw the original and the remake. In fact, one can argue that they appealed to two distinct socially and economically constructed audience groups. Scriptwriter Bülent Oran's comments on Turkish remakes also support this latter point. Oran thinks earlier releases were much more appropriate for remaking, because '1940s movies are much closer to our audience's tastes in terms of plot and worldview. Not only the filmmakers, but the level of society and the worldview, are forty years behind Europe. Those melodramas that made them cry may be ridiculed today, but not here in Turkey' (1973: 18–19).

On the other hand, producer Nusret İkbal suggests that the movie industry was not able to support a domestic production of over 200 films a year, in terms of script writing:

> The number of original movies are very few. We plagiarise photography, artifice, mise-en-scène as well as the plots of foreign movies. Earlier, Turkish

> cinema imitated German and Arab films, now we are dealing with cheap imitations of American, Italian and French cinema. And we describe this as 'influence'. This is rather deceptive. However, everyone has to plagiarise, while we are producing 150 movies each year. In these circumstances no single filmmaker can create an original piece. Because s/he lacks both time and creativity. (cited by Özgüç 1965: 13)

For him, the motive behind remakes is the assembly-line production system that limits the time and effort spend on each production. However, as some writers suggest, there is not much difference between writing an original script and re-writing the script of an earlier film, in terms of creative energy and cost. According to Oran, the latter was even more difficult to create:

> I don't like literary adaptations. Although they seem unconstrained, they have lots of disadvantages. Remaking a movie . . . appears to be very easy. In fact, that is the most difficult and risky [of all the scenarios]. The reason for this is the difference between the sensations, worldview and understanding. (1973: 17)

As Oran suggests, remaking a movie in a culturally different context involves a lot of problems. There are a number of issues to be concerned, such as moral codes and cultural values. For example, the filming of *The Postman Always Rings Twice* was halted as the movie involved an extra-marital relationship (Scognamillo 1973: 67). Therefore, it is quite doubtful whether remakes involve less creative effort or are more cost-effective compared with original films.

This discussion of definitions and possible motives for remakes cannot fully explain the phenomenon in Turkish context. So what might be the functions that remakes tend to serve? In order to answer this question, one has to emphasise the hybrid nature of these films. In this respect, it might be helpful to use the metaphor of translation to explore the remake as a cross-cultural interpretation, and, to explore initially the parallels between remakes and literary translations.

Between Two Worlds

The first literary translations of European literature appeared in the nineteenth century in the Ottoman Empire. They were considered as one of the means of closing the cultural and technical gap between the Empire and Europe. Significantly, the first literary texts appearing in Ottoman Turkish were popular French plays, starting with Moliére's *Le Médecin Malgré Lui* (1813). In 1862, two novels, Fénelon's *Aventures de Télémaque* and Victor Hugo's *Les Misérables*, appeared in Turkish. The influence of these literary forms on Ottoman literature is evident in the dominant technique of translation: naturalisation. This took many forms, from paraphrasing to abridgement. Usually the story was transposed into an Ottoman milieu, and the characters made to behave in accordance with locally acceptable customs. This technique was described as 'translation in accordance with Turkish customs and morals' (*Türk adat ve ahlakina tatbikan tercüme*), as translator Ahmet Vefik Pasha puts it (cited by Özön and Dürder 1967: 5). These free translations also took extensive liberties, from basic omissions to adding parts or changing the title. Some novels were condensed into much smaller volumes. And, in some cases, the form of the original works was transformed into verse. Generally, the classical or syllabic verse of traditional poetry was used for plays or novels.[1]

The 'naturalisations' in these translations went so far that the differences between original works/authorship (*telif*) and translations (*tercüme*) were not easy to identify in Ottoman literature. In fact, when the adaptation took the form of creative writing, the publishers neglected to make any mention of the original author. And it is no coincidence that some of these translators were also the pioneers of Ottoman literature. Their aim was to achieve what Fredric Jameson describes as a compromise between the abstract formal patterns of Western novel construction and the raw material of local social experience. This formal compromise, supported by translations from Western European literature, 'was highly unstable as form and content cannot always be welded together seamlessly' (Jameson 1993: xiii). The main reason for this compositional paradox is the contrast between irreconcilable elements.

This paradox can be defined as a 'cultural schizophrenia', according to Daryush Shayegan. Criticising Foucalt's argument in *The Order of Things* (1970) that there is never more than one episteme defining the possible conditions for all knowledge in a given culture at a given moment, Shayegan describes a context where epistemes can coexist. He argues that two different historical *epistemes*, one affecting psychic, emotional behaviour and atavistic attitudes, the other shaping the modern ideas which come from outside, can in fact coexist at a given moment, but at the cost of reciprocal deformation:

> Between them lies a *caesural fault*: a split which is especially crippling because it divides the being into two unequal segments which cannot communicate except on the most elementary level, as there is no bridge to facilitate harmonious internal dialogue. This is not to say that they have no contact, however. Indeed it is precisely where they meet that all kind of distortions arise, as the two *epistemes*, like reflecting screens facing one another, become disfigured by the mutual scrambling of their images. (1992: 72)

Such distortions are most evident in the form of literary narratives of the late Ottoman and early Republican period in Turkey. However, it might be wrong to define this coexistence as a form of deformation as Shayegan puts it. On the contrary, paradoxical intermingling of these two epistemes can appropriately be considered as a productive survival strategy.[2] To understand this compositional paradox, we could look at Franco Moretti's work, which further elaborates Jameson's formulation. Instead of a binary relationship between Western formal pattern and local content, Moretti proposes a triangular scheme: foreign *plot*, local *characters* and local *narrative voice* (this is somewhat an adaptation of foreign form). According to Moretti, it is precisely in this third dimension that the novels seem to be most unstable: 'the narrator is the pole of comment, of explanation, of evaluation, and when foreign "formal patterns" (or actual foreign presence for that matter) make characters behave in strange ways, then of course comment becomes uneasy – garrulous, erratic, rudderless' (2000: 65).

The Ottoman and early Turkish literatures also reflect this instability in their style. The reason for this peculiarity lies in the narrator's intention of recasting new ideas to their society. As Jale Parla comments:

> behind the inclination towards renovation stood a dominant and dominating Ottoman ideology that recast the new ideas into a mould fit for the Ottoman society. The mould, however, was supposed to hold two different epistemologies that rested on irreconcilable axioms. It was inevitable that this mould would crack and literature, in one way or another, reflects the cracks. (cited by Moretti 2000: 62)

In this sense, the translation of foreign models, or the hybridisation of what Moretti defines as foreign *plot*, local *characters* and local *narrative voice*, can be described as a form negotiation of various discourses on modernity and modernisation.

Negotiating the Modern

Şerif Mardin, in his study of Turkish modernisation through Ottoman novels, identifies a number of problems raised by social and political change. The most important of these problems is what Mardin describes as 'super or over-westernisation'. This problem is best exemplified in Bihruz Bey, the archetypal Western fop in Recaizade Mahmut Ekrem's (1846–1913) *Araba Sevdasi* (Aspirations for Horse-Drawn Carriages) (1895). The novel satirises the superficial veneer of Westernization, which a new class has adopted in Turkey after the passing of the edict of *Tanzimat* reform of 1839. Bihruz Bey, who sacrifices his father's fortune to his compulsion for lovely horse-drawn carriages, like his Russian counterpart Oblomov, suffers from lack of identity and of roots. His most striking attitude is his infatuation with the material aspects of Western civilisation (Mardin 1974: 406–9).

As Mardin notes, Bihruz Bey types reappear in Turkish literature as individuals to be made fun of or despised: 'Over and over again the same figures, whether comical or tragic, appear as traitors to their culture, whose example is to be shunned' (1974: 411–2). It would be wrong to consider the 'Bihruz Bey syndrome' as an anti-modern stance. In literature and film the syndrome had a more instrumental function for the purposes of social mobilisation. The critique of over-Westernisation was used to support a line of modernism more in consort with traditional values. In this context, the traditional terms – often represented by the country – were used to ridicule the superficiality and stupidity of over-Westernisation. Not surprisingly, the conflicts between traditional and modern values and lifestyles are resolved in the modern environment, rather than through the restoration of a traditional order. For example, in *Sürtük* (Ertem Eğilmez, 1965) – remade by the same director in 1970 – a film that is inspired by *Love Me or Leave Me* (Charles Vidor, 1955), the Pygmalion-like educators of the film's heroine are ridiculed for their Western manners. However, it is only by completing these courses that the heroine could make her entry into the city and become successful.

This idea of a 'less radical version of modernity' is best exemplified in Ziya Gökalp's distinction between 'culture' and 'civilization'. In *The Principles of Turkism* (1923), which became a sort of blueprint for the Turkish revolution, Gökalp praises the material civilisation of Europe while opposing its non-material aspects. In order to formulate this, drawing on the ideas of the German sociologist Tönnies, he made a distinction between culture (*hars*), 'the set of values and habits current within a community', and civilization (*medeniyet*), 'a rational, international system of knowledge, science and technology'. He believed that the road to salvation lay in replacing this civilisation with a modern European one, while holding to Turkish culture (Zürcher 1993: 136).[3] In this approach, instead of 'all that is solid melting into air', a cultural continuity in the form of negotiation or resistance is predicted. Rather than discussing the model's attainability, I would like to concentrate on the ways in which the policies based on these interpretations negotiated modernity, and the hybrid forms produced as a result of this process. This negotiation might be summarised as a synthesis between the rational and humanist aspects of the West and the non-degenerated values of the East, as Sevda Şener suggests in her study of twentieth-century Turkish theatre (1971). In the context of remake, it involves the reconstruction of certain cultural practices and mores, as well as resistance to social atomisation or separation.

Modernity and Women

The clash between modern and traditional values is often symbolised in the figure of women in Turkish literature and cinema. In this tradition, which has its roots in nineteenth-century Western literature, the female characters became ideal bearers of the corruption and decay that modernisation creates. Although the representation of women has changed through the years, this connotation remained largely intact. The clash of generations and the immorality of women following Western ways were the most popular themes in twentieth-century literature. Together with these, the decline of authority and the growth of sexual immorality continued to provide a central focus for writers and readers of novels and short stories into the 1930s (Duben and Behar 1991: 199). In the nationalist novels of the 1920s and 1930s, an alternative female character emerged in the form of a self-sacrificing 'comrade-woman' who is also an asexual sister-in-arms (Kandiyoti 1989: 149). Yet women's immoral behaviour was still considered a significant threat.

In contrast with these models, remakes offered a new type of woman who is sexually attractive yet virtuous. In classical French melodrama, unlike American melodrama, the heroine need not be a virgin (Brooks 1995 [1976]: 32). When the genre was appropriated by American filmmakers in the early twentieth century, virginity became a central theme. It was only in 1940s that the issue fell from the agenda for the desiring heroines of Hollywood movies. In this sense, Turkish remakes were much closer to the early American melodrama. For example, in *Mildred Pierce* (Michael Curtis, 1945), Veda Pierce blackmails Mrs Forester by saying that she is carrying Ted's baby. On the other hand, in the Turkish remake of the film, *Şoför Nebahat ve Kizi* (Nebahat the Taxi Driver and her Daughter, Süreyya Duru, 1964), her counterpart Hülya had to obey stricter rules. She warns her rich boyfriend that only after marriage they can have a sexual relationship. And when she sleeps with her mother's boyfriend, her mother thinks she can marry no one but him, in order to save her honour.

The concept of adultery is evaluated differently in Turkish remakes. Scriptwriter Bülent Oran describes the rules of the film industry in detail:

> The woman [in Turkish cinema] could only love one man. She could only sleep with that one man. No one can touch her. If this rule is broken, the film will fail to make any money . . . In foreign films, women's excessive behaviour, extra-marital relationships, walking hand-in-hand with another man are tolerated. When it comes to Turkish films things are different. For example, in one of my scripts [*Dağlar Kizi Reyhan* (Metin Erksan, 1969), which is a take on *Love Me or Leave Me* (Charles Vidor, 1955)], we portrayed a music hall owner: an evil and cruel man. He fell for the lover of the hero. By hiding some cannabis in his clothes, he got him arrested. Finally, he married the girl. That is all fine . . . For the spectators the ending is quite certain: The hero will be released and reunite with the heroine. However, there is something wrong: in a movie, no Turkish guy could marry a woman who had sex with another man. Therefore, on the first night of their marriage, the heroine acted boldly and said: 'You bought me. You can have my body [by force], but not my soul'. So what did that evil man do? He said: 'I'll never touch you against your own will', and slept in another room. And this has gone on for some ten years until the hero is released. Obviously, this is quite illogical . . . However, the spectator accepts it, as it is morally right . . . This 'logic of the illogical' is characteristic of Turkish cinema. (Oran 1973: 24)

The 'logic of the illogical', explained by Oran, is a significant feature of the remakes. Although Mildred married Monte Beragon, Nebahat remained single in the remade version. She went out for dinner with her business partner Cengiz, but there was no implication of a sexual relationship between them. Otherwise, it would be impossible for her to remarry her ex-husband. Even widows cannot remarry in Turkish film. Therefore, it is quite significant that the Turkish filmmakers had not attempted to remake Douglas Sirk's *All That Heaven*

Allows (1954) and *Magnificent Obsession* (1953). Although, in Hollywood melodrama, it is only man who survives adultery, by stepping outside the boundaries of marriage (Doane 1987: 119–20), adultery is prohibited for men as well in Turkish cinema. In *Şoför Nebahat ve Kizi*, Nebahat never forgives her husband, who committed adultery, and he is portrayed as suffering for this crime.

To sum up, the Western melodramatic binarism between virginal/maternal innocence and fallen woman is often ambiguously combined in a single character: the heroine. The heroine of the Turkish remakes is able to protect her virginal innocence under all conditions, even if she is forced to marry someone else than her lover. The heroine earns her living as a singer when she is fallen and separated from her family. Despite a number of persistent suitors, she would never break her vow of chastity. Once the misunderstanding between the hero and heroine is cleared up, they reunite. In the end, the heroine, who was economically liberated, is unconvincingly resigned to her position as mother and housewife. And she is no longer an object of the male gaze as a singer.

On the other hand, the excessive behaviour of women associated with over-Westernisation is usually symbolised by showing off, excessive make-up and accessories, gambling, drinking alcohol, balls, partying and new dances (Parla 1993: 83–5; and Şener 1971: 17–18). A typical example of this criticism is found in party scenes and the contrast between traditional and Western music in Turkish films. The music accompanying these films is usually the traditional Ottoman-Turkish music (or a modernised version of it), while the degenerate rich kids are often portrayed partying with pop or rock music. In the same way, gambling and alcohol connote the negative aspects of Westernisation.

Communalism versus Individualism: Politics and Love

In 1940s and 1950s Hollywood melodrama, the rise of capitalist society is represented by the disappearance of traditional patriarchal authority, especially by the absent father. This absence triggers a hostile competition between the individual characters. This phenomenon of competitive individualism as historical development was closely linked to the transition from traditional to modern urban society (Singer 2001: 138). Social atomisation brought the destruction of patriarchal authority and communalism.

On the other hand, family and community/district (*mahalle*) were considered as the moral foundation stones of the Ottoman and Turkish societies. They had complementary functions, as historian İlber Ortayli suggests: 'The Ottoman community was linked organically with the family. Events such as birth, marriage and death concerned the whole community and invoked solidarity' (2000: 28). Therefore, the rise of individualism was seen as a threat to the social order in Turkey:

> Individualism, as the late nineteenth-century Ottomans first came to know it, whether in love or in politics, was the expression of a rejection

> of the past, and of the shackles of repressive family, community and authority. However, in the intense nationalistic years beginning with the young Turk period [early twentieth century], it also came to be associated with anti-nationalism, moral corruption and even treason. (Duben and Behar 1991: 94)

The effects and conceived threats of transition from a communalistic type of society to competitive individualism were also apparent in remakes. A 'corporatist solidarity' – suggested by Ziya Gökalp – between the members of a family, workplace or district (*mahalle*) was defended against the individualistic social morals of modern society. The characters are often portrayed within their local community and receive support from their circle of friends when in need. Overall, the characters of the remakes appear to be much more contented than in the desiring heroines of American melodrama.

Supporting communal values in their social life, the characters of the Turkish remakes take a different stand when it comes to love. Marriages in the film take the form of individual choice, that of love between two individuals. Although the consent of families was crucial, it was the couples that took the decision and made the necessary arrangements.[4] However, in real life marriage based on a mutual arrangement between the bride and the groom was particular to urban culture, and a rarity in Turkey. As Duben and Behar state, in early twentieth-century Istanbul, although some sort of love relationship under the guidance and sponsorship of families was becoming more widespread, the *idea* of love carried an implicit threat to family (1991: 246). According to a study carried out in 1985–9, marriages based on mutual arrangement formed only 4.8 per cent of the total marriages, while 48.1 per cent of the couples opted for arranged marriages based on viewing the bride, and 28.4 per cent knew each other through friends and relatives (cited by Tekeli 1995: 9). Therefore, the so-called love-marriages and the portrayal of emancipated women in films should be read as the product of conflicting factors and tendencies. On the one hand, these films were a social reflection of what was taking place in 1960s Turkey, especially in an urban environment. On the other hand, as in the case of love-marriages, melodrama served as a female wish-fulfilment fantasy. Finally, such representations also registered growing anxieties created by social transformations. That is quite clear in the reconstruction of patriarchal authority in films. In the end, the love-marriage never brings individual freedom: all the female characters give up their careers when they marry.

Spaces of Modernity

The physical space of classical Hollywood melodrama is the bourgeois home, sanctified by patriarchal laws. In the European vein of melodrama, at the opposite of this ideal private sphere there exist the dance hall, the music hall and nightclub, where the 'fallen women' are projected as the object of the male gaze. As Ana Lopez defined with reference to Mexican melodrama, the nightclub is a barely tolerated social space. It is 'nevertheless the part of the patriarchal public sphere where the personal – and issues of female subjectivity, emotion, identity, and desire – finds its most complex articulation' (2000: 511). This public space, though rarely featured in classical Hollywood, has a significant function in Turkish melodrama. Here, as an equivalent to nightclubs, we can identify two different types of space with distinct narrative functions. The first and more 'respectable' type is the *gazino* (music hall), which caters for family audiences. The *pavyon* (nightclub) is for predominantly male customers. Here, the female performers also serve as *consommatrices*. Similarly, sexuality, which is not systematically excluded from the narrative, appears in two different forms. The first and most widespread kind of sexuality is in the form of the heroine's performance on the *gazino* stage. While accomplishing the primary purpose of the pleasure of performance, *gazino* scenes also provide an unintentionally liberating release that the heroine achieves. The second and more erotic type of sexuality appears as a kind of violence and threat to narrative stability. This is most apparent in *pavyon* performances or in party scenes. The music featured in the former is 'traditional', whereas 'Western' dance music accompanies scenes in the latter version.

Interestingly, in Turkish melodramas when the heroines are separated from their families, they become performers instead of taking menial jobs. Their 'rise to stardom' is often achieved quite easily. As performers on stage they can also transgress socially accepted definitions of femininity, with the transgression presented as a form of sacrifice they had to bear. Once they are reunited with their family, the briefly liberated heroines return back home. In the family environment, work is set against maternity. Obviously, this 'rise to stardom' plot is both a wish-fulfilment fantasy and a narrative requirement for foregrounding musical performance.[5]

Another typical modern setting of Turkish melodramas was the home. It should be noted that all these remakes were produced and set in the cosmopolitan city of Istanbul, and thus tended to depict a modern and upper-crust environment. In these films, sets and furnishing are emphasised to such an extent that the codes of realism become secondary. This excessive luxury resembles the 1930s Italian 'white telephone' films. That genre, which took its name from the 'white telephones' which the characters use to talk to each other, catered for the modern taste for window-shopping. As Laura Nucci, an Italian actress of the period, pointed out, the art deco set designs corresponded less to actual interior designs of homes than to a popular view of modernity (cited by Hay 1987: 39). In Turkish cinema, this modern and art deco sensibility was symbolised by a number of residences on the banks of the Bosphorus, which were used over and over again in a number of films in the 1960s. These modern houses offered a fantasy space for the viewers.

Remake and National Cinema

The idea of national cinema has long been shaped by the dominant conception of culture as a unified entity. Since Siegfried Kracauer's seminal work on German cinema, *From Caligari to Hitler* (1947), national cinemas are often evaluated in a context isolated from their mixed nature and cross-cultural or transnational disclosure. The cultural imperialism thesis, which emerged in the face of growing Hollywood domination in the world film market, questioned this confined notion of national film industries. Emphasising the cultural and economic impact of US film imports on national cinema, the cultural imperialism thesis championed an authentic cinematic expression as opposed to the threat of globalisation. However, by condemning the 'cultural imperialism' in the audio-visual field, it also assumed a unified notion of national culture, whose essence could, and should be, reflected by the creators of film. Furthermore, by focusing mainly on 'acclaimed' cinematic works and particular auteurs, national cinema studies often overlooked popular and mainstream works, which have much wider national appeal, as well as the diversity of cultural strands. In this process, inevitably, binary oppositions are established between high culture and mass culture, or between major and minor works. In most of these studies, the national cinema is proclaimed as a unique identity and a stable set of meanings, identifying a hegemonising, mythologising process, as Andrew Higson describes (1989: 37).

Analysing the intertextual and hybrid nature of the remakes, this study aims at offering a distinct approach for the study of national cinema. The most significant element of the remake is the reinterpretation and negotiation of historical and social forces of modernism in Turkey. While offering something like a homogenised picture of cultural and moral characteristics of urban Turkey, these films mobilised a resistance against some of the values depicted in original films. Asserting a localised version of modernity as opposed to the evolutionary and universalistic content of Westernisation, the remakes can be best conceptualised in the framework of 'multiple or alternative modernities'.

Characterised by complexity, ambiguity and incompleteness in sociologist Johann P. Arnason's work (1993, 1997), the project of modernity is interpreted differently by different actors in different countries. These different routes and forms offer new insights into film studies by bringing to critical attention the variety of ways in which international films has been translated into alternative forms. As I have tried to demonstrate, this process of translation in Turkish cinema involves a defence of communalistic and patriarchal values from the threat of social atomisation and modern social relations. This 'less radical version of modernity' asserts a differentiation between 'culture' (the set of values and habits current within a community) and 'civilisation' (a rational, international system of knowledge, science and technology). Praising the material civilisation of the West, the Turkish approach opposes its non-material aspects. The hybrid product of this synthesis is quite apparent in the way in which remade movies reflect the transmutation and negotiation of the dominant model of modernity.

Notes

1. Translators appropriated similar practices of domestication during the French and English Enlightenment, and later elsewhere. For example in Egypt, free transposition of the foreign literature was not called 'translation' (*tarjama*), but 'adaptation' (*iqtibas*), 'arabization' (*tar'ib*) or even 'egyptianization' (*tamsir*) (Jacqemond 1992, and Cachia 1990). In China, a common way of tampering was to paraphrase the whole novel to make it a story with Chinese characters and Chinese background. Also dynamic motifs are retained while static ones were left out, making Western novels sketchy and speedy, and more like Chinese traditional fiction (Zhao 1995: 229–30).
2. I owe this idea to Nezih Erdoğan's comments on Shayegan's work.
3. There are significant similarities between Gökalp's model and Partha Chatterjee's differentiation between the material – the domain of the economy and statecraft, of science and technology – and the spiritual, an 'inner' domain bearing the 'essential' marks of cultural identity. Chatterjee argues that in this latter domain the nation can remain sovereign, even when the state is in the hands of the colonial power (1993: 5–6).
4. According to a research by Emine Demiray, 75 per cent of the couples marry for love in Turkish films produced between 1960 and 1970. The decision of marriage is usually taken jointly by the couples; only 17 per cent of the couples have arranged marriages (Demiray 1994: 43).
5. In Turkish melodrama – as is the case in Indian and Egyptian melodramas – the music is foregrounded as a form of spectacle. This overemphasis on music is apparent in the situating of major characters, especially women, in the role of singer. But here verisimilitude is of central importance, as the characters never burst into song in their ordinary environment and social reality cannot be magically transformed via music.

Bibliography

Arnason, Johann P. (1993), *The Future That Failed: Origins and Destinies of the Soviet Model*, London: Routledge.

Arnason, Johann P. (1997), *Social Theory and Japanese Experience: The Dual Civilization*, London: Kegan Paul International.

Braudy, Leo (1998), 'Afterword: rethinking remakes', in Andrew Horton and Stuart Y. McDougal (eds), *Play it Again, Sam: Retakes on Remakes*, Berkeley: University of California Press, pp. 327–34.

Brooks, Peter (1995 [1976]), *The Melodramatic Imagination: Balzac, Henry James, Melodrama, and the Mode of Excess*, New Haven/London: Yale University Press.

Cachia, Pierre (1990), *An Overview of Modern Arabic Literature*, Edinburgh: Edinburgh University Press.

Chatterjee, Partha (1993), *The Nation and Its Fragments: Colonial and Postcolonial Histories*, Princeton, New Jersey: Princeton University Press.

Demiray, Emine (1994), 'Türk Filmlerinde Nasil Evleniyorlar', *25. Kare* 7, 41–4.

Doane, Marry Ann (1987), *The Desire to Desire: The Woman's Film of the 1940s*, London: Macmillan.

Duben, Alan and Cem Behar (1991), *Istanbul Households: Marriage, Family and Fertility 1880–1940*, Cambridge: Cambridge University Press.

Eberwein, Robert (1998), 'Remakes and cultural studies', in Andrew Horton and Stuart Y. McDougal (eds), *Play it Again, Sam: Retakes on Remakes*, Berkeley: University of California Press, pp. 15–33.

Foucault, Michel (1970), *The Order of Things: An Archaeology of the Human Sciences*, London: Tavistock Publishing.

Hay, James (1987), *Popular Film Culture in Fascist Italy: The Passing of the Rex*, Bloomington and Indianapolis: Indiana University Press.

Higson, Andrew (1989), 'The concept of national cinema', *Screen* 30 (4), 36–46.

Jacquemond, Richard (1992), 'Translation and cultural hegemony: the case of French-Arabic translation', in Lawrence Venuti (ed.), *Rethinking Translation: Discourse, Subjectivity, Ideology*, London and New York: Routledge, pp. 139–58.
Jameson, Fredric (1993), 'In the mirror of alternate modernities', in Karatani Kojin, *Origins of Modern Japanese Literature*, Durham and London: Duke University Press, 1993.
Kandiyoti, Deniz (1989), 'Women as metaphor: the Turkish novel from the Tanzimat to the Republic', in Kenneth Brown (eds), *Urban Crisis and Social Movements in the Middle East*, Paris: L'Harmattan, pp. 140–52.
Kracauer, Siegfried (1947), *From Caligari to Hitler*, Princeton: University of Princeton Press.
Lopez, Ana M. (2000), 'Tears and desire: woman and melodrama in the "Old" Mexican cinema', in E. Ann Kaplan (ed.), *Feminism and Film*, Oxford: Oxford University Press, pp. 505–20.
Mardin, Şerif (1974), 'Super Westernization in urban life in the Ottoman Empire in the last quarter of the nineteenth century', in Peter Benedict, Erol Tümertekin and Fatma Mansur (eds), *Turkey: Geographic and Social Perspectives*, Leiden: E. J. Brill, pp. 403–46.
Mazdon, Lucy (2000), *Encore Hollywood: Remaking French Cinema*, London: BFI.
Moretti, Franco (2000), 'Conjectures on world literature', *New Left Review* (second series) 1, 54–68.
Oran, Bülent (1973), 'Senaryo Yazari Bülent Oran'la Bir Konuşma', *Yedinci Sanat* 3, 15–26.
Ortayli, İlber (2000), *Osmanli Toplumunda Aile*, Istanbul: Pan Yayincilik.
Özön, M. Nihat and Baha Dürder (1967), *Türk Tiyatrosu Ansiklopedisi*, Istanbul: Remzi Kitabevi.
Özgüç, Agah (1965), 'Türk Sinemasinda Kleptomani Devam Eoliyor', *Ses* 21, 10–13.
Parla, Jale (1993 [1990]), *Babalar ve Oğullar: Tanzimat Romaninin Epistemolojik Temelleri*, Istanbul: İletişim Yayinlari.
Scognamillo, Giovanni (1966), 'Türk Sinemasinda Yabanci Etkiler', *Yeni Sinema* 3, 28–32.
Scognamillo, Giovanni (1973), 'Türk Sinemasinda Yabanci Uyarlamalar-1', *Yedinci Sanat* 9, 61–73.
Shayegan, Daryush (1992), *Cultural Schizophrenia: Islamic Societies Confronting the West*, trans. John Howe, London: Saqi Books.
Singer, Ben (2001), *Melodrama and Modernity: Early Sensational Cinema and Its Contexts*, New York: Columbia University Press.
Şener, Sevda (1971), *Çağdaş Türk Tiyatrosunda Ahlak, Ekonomi, Kültür Sorunlari*, Ankara: A.Ü. DTCF Yayinlari.
Tekeli, Şirin (1995), 'Introduction: women in Turkey in the 1980s', in Şirin Tekeli (ed.), *Women in Modern Turkish Society: A Reader*, London: Zed Books.
Viviani, Christian (1987), 'Who is without sin? The maternal melodrama in American film, 1930–39', in Christine Gledhill (ed.), *Home is Where the Heart Is: Studies in Melodrama and the Woman's Film*, London: BFI, pp. 83–99.
Zhao, Henry Y. H. (1995), *The Uneasy Narrator: Chinese Fiction From the Traditional to the Modern*, Oxford: Oxford University Press.
Zürcher, Erik J. (1993), *Turkey: A Modern History*, London: I. B. Tauris & Co.

13

MUTE BODIES, DISEMBODIED VOICES: NOTES ON SOUND IN TURKISH POPULAR CINEMA

Nezih Erdoğan

A Paradigmatic Shift

In 1997, veteran film star Tanju Gürsu won the award for best male actor at the Antalya Golden Orange Film Festival for his role in *Köpekler Adası/Isle of Dogs* (Halit Refiğ, 1997). The jury's decision provoked heated debate because Gürsu's character had been post-dubbed by another film and theatre actor, Müşfik Kenter. It was questioned whether an actor who borrowed someone else's voice should be honoured with such an award. In connection with this, a newspaper published a series of interviews with various well-known personalities, who expressed a range of opinions on the matter. Burçak Evren, film historian and critic, claimed that dubbing 'prevented film from naturalness and it became something artificial'. The young film director Mustafa Altioklar emphasized the concept of 'credibility': 'When a film is post-dubbed it is no longer convincing – hence the lack of sincerity. When you shoot the film with sound the player feels the magic more easily.' Şener Şen, the star of Yeşilçam, the mainstream cinema of the 1960s and 1970s, and now superstar of the New Turkish Cinema, referred to the difficulties of dubbing: 'The player forgets the feelings of that particular moment of the shoot and during the dubbing he tries hard to remember them'. Altioklar argued further that: 'Cinema is 50 per cent sight and 50 per cent sound; ignoring the sound means we start filming with only the remaining fifty per cent'.[1] This chimes with the claim made by the television celebrity Cem Özer, that 'the Yeşilçam actor is 60 per cent absent from the cinema'.

From *Screen*, 43: 3, pp. 233–49.

Dubbing, which was standard practice for Yeşilçam, is central to the debates about sound in the emerging New Turkish Cinema. It is a practice which seems unlikely to survive the shift to a new paradigm in which the keywords are 'credibility', 'naturalness' and 'sincerity' – a clear break from Yeşilçam's mode of representation. Although New Turkish Cinema does not seek to disown the heritage of its predecessor entirely, Yeşilçam's conventional use of sound seems to have been abandoned.

The mid 1980s witnessed an attempt at a radical break with Yeşilçam. A number of filmmakers tried their hands at new themes and styles which, roughly speaking, reflected the changing role of women, an increasingly liberal economic policy, the growing interest in various sorts of self-reflexive fiction, and the stylistic influence of television commercials and pop videos. In the latter, I am referring particularly to a visual style which, for example, avoided the flat lighting, highly saturated colour and minimal camera movement favoured by Yeşilçam.[2] In contrast, New Turkish Cinema tended to play on high-key and low-key lighting, chiaroscuro and use of a travelling camera. It was not until 1996, however, that the filmmakers took the final step: one by one they dropped post-dubbing and started shooting with sound. The audience thus saw for the first time the famous Dolby Digital train precede a Turkish film, *Eşkiya/The Bandit* (Yavuz Turgul, 1995), which quickly became a blockbuster. *Eşkiya* was a Eurimages film, welcomed by the film writers for being as technically flawless as any Hollywood film. Yavuz Turgul, who used to write screenplays for the late Ertem Eğilmez (a director of stereotypical melodramas), did not try to disguise the film's Yeşilçam roots. A documentary on the making of the film shows him on set, lecturing on how Yeşilçam is too easily condemned for its limitations when it should in fact be taken seriously. Indeed, *Eşkiya* addresses issues that Yeşilçam had raised again and again: money versus love, love versus paternal responsibility, dedication versus individual freedom, all boiling down to redemption and sacrifice. Some recent popular films, for example *Ağir Roman/Cholera Street* (Mustafa Altioklar, 1997), *Dar Alanda Kisa Paslaşmalar/Offside* (Serdar Akar, 2000), *Hemşo/Compatriot* (Ömer Uğur, 2000), and even a very successful television serial, *Ikinci Bahar/Second Spring* (dir. Türkan Derya, tx 2000–2001, designed by Turgul) seem to have taken a similar tack. However, this thematic continuity is overshadowed by some of the practices adopted by New Turkish Cinema; in addition to shooting with sound, the tendency to construct 'genuine' characters (as against the non-psychological types of Yeşilçam) yielded an altogether different mode of representation. As I will try to demonstrate, the actor's body is the site of this difference.

The criticism levelled against dubbing overlooks the fact that auditory practices are socially constructed and their terms can be challenged by the same values they have adopted. One need only recall the account given by Michel Chion of a Frenchman who travelled to Britain in 1929 to attend the screening of a talking film for the first time. Although the film was perfectly synchronized, he wrote later, 'it was extremely annoying for it strengthened the audience's demand for credibility'. 'But we now know how the film sound developed', says Chion, 'along the lines of establishing tolerances, approximations.'[3] Tolerances may negate and even replace each other, and what is regarded as annoying today may be tolerated tomorrow or vice versa. By tolerance I am referring to a function of the audiovisual contract mutually conceived by the cinematic institution and the viewing subject. In this essay I will discuss some aspects of this contract in its relation to the body as constituted by Yeşilçam. For the sake of convenience, I will limit my essay to two main issues: first, understanding the practice of dubbing in a framework given by the cinematic apparatus which embodies the configurations of the voice and the body; second, 'loss of sight', a recurrent theme in melodrama which becomes symptomatic in its play on characters' sensory perception. These issues demand closer analysis in relation to the development of diverse sound practices.

In discussing this, I want to consider Tom Levin's elaboration of the powers of apparatus. Originating from a conversation between Martin Heidegger and a Japanese philosopher who insistently argues that Western technology appropriates practices of the 'other' into the structure of its own cinematic inscription, Levin refers to Theodor Adorno's and Hanns Eisler's contention that no matter how radical and innovative these practices may be, 'they are ultimately put in an apparatus which spits them out again in a digestive, blunted, and conventionalised form'.[4] What he implies is that apparatus is something like a box which takes in cinematic practices, gives them a form of its own and then spits them out. This topography collapses right away, because any kind of practice is plausible only in terms of its apparatus. As James Lastra states in his criticism of Levin's argument: 'there is no identifiable "thing" which can be put in apparatus, because there is no thing-to-be represented outside the goals of the very act of representing'.[5] It is, of course, crucial to note that Lastra is not arguing that apparatus grants diverse sound practices a right to existence, but rather that sound can be designed, produced and thus 'heard' only in reference to, and within the confines of, the apparatus. Similarly, my premiss is that Yeşilçam was able to produce a sort of resistance (not in the form of negation but of negotiation) to the cinematic apparatus from within.[6] In order to grasp the nature and potential of Yeşilçam's resistance, I will try to show how it oscillated between non-illusionism and classical realism. Thus, while Yeşilçam operated with the codes of realism, the operation itself always failed to meet the requirements of a fully-fledged realist text. Indeed it might be asked if Yeşilçam, as a commercial cinema which is today best known for its naivete, bears a striking resemblance to Brechtian alienation effects.[7] However, instead of hastily appropriating Yeşilçam into Brechtian terms, I would rather draw attention to the tradition of Turkish non-illusionism it inherited. This includes *Karagöz* (shadow play), which uses two-dimensional cut-out figures, *Orta Oyunu* (a form of theatre largely inspired by the *commedia dell' arte*), whose cast consists of comic types, and *Meddah*, a one-man show in which the performer deliberately interrupts his story with irrelevant issues. These are entertainment forms all extinct today, but their residual traces can be found in Yeşilçam's narrative and stylistic devices.

Dubbing: a Contested History

Mikhail Yampolsky, in his study of dubbing as taken up by Antonin Artaud and Jorge Borges, refers to a story by Isak Dinesen where the facial features of a child are flattened after he uncannily begins to sing with the voice of a 'possessive' female singer. Taking this as a metaphor for dubbing, Yampolsky argues that 'dubbing can be described as the intrusion of foreign acoustical matter into the body, causing deformities on the surface of the body that can be defined as the "events" of dubbing. "Events" in this case are the changes occuring on the visible surface.'[8] Although Yampolsky is discussing the case of well-known French actors dubbing US films, he concludes in general that when a body borrows a voice there will be a price to pay. That is, the body is vulnerable to the operations of the voice which will force changes, the most drastic being that the body collapses into a surface. Fatih Özgüven's novel *Esrarengiz Bay Kartaloğlu/Mysterious Mr Eagleton* offers an experience of reading identical to that of dubbing a film. The text contains instructions for voicing passages, looped dialogues following one another, and speech seems to gain a life of its own, independent of the characters suffering the indeterminacies of their own reality. At a certain point, the text gives away the crux of the matter: the hero, Vecit Kartaloğlu, is on a sea voyage and chatting with a female traveller about a prewar US film which tells the story of a recently divorced couple. Kartaloğlu found the film bizarre, because it was dubbed 'with a most savage Mediterranean dialect' which did not match the female character. He observes:

> then anything that the story strove to impose was smashed to smithereens and vanished. It was not a game of desire, do you understand, hers was a genuine desire which did not fit into the plot, all the while I watched it, I kept saying if only she stopped being a clown. For her voice was saying something else, she was torn between her story and her voice.[9]

Similarly, Thomas Elsaesser, in his classic essay on melodrama provides this assessment: 'dubbing makes the best picture visually flat and dramatically out of sync: it destroys the flow on which coherence of the illusionist spectacle is built'.[10] In the following, I will investigate how Yeşilçam negotiates these perceived difficulties.

Many film scholars are surprised to learn that dubbing had not always been standard practice in Turkish Cinema. In the early 1930s Kemal Film, a pioneering film company, hired a German sound technician to build it a studio. In 1932 its contract director, Muhsin Ertuğrul, made the first commercial talking film, *Bir Millet Uyaniyor/A Nation Awakening*. However, a decade later the producers of *Dertli Pinar/The Troubled Spring* (Faruk Kenç, 1943), who did not want to wait for the arrival of some equipment that had been sent to Germany for maintenance, started shooting without sound. Screenwriter Bülent Oran remembers:

> Silent shooting is easier and more feasible. It saves time and thus cuts down the production costs. Also, it offers the possibility of casting good-looking actors with bad diction. In addition to that, the prompter saves the players from wasting their time by memorizing their lines. That is, to cut a long story short, it offered many advantages.[11]

Until then the existing sound studios were used for dubbing foreign-language films. Interestingly, dubbing was already recognized as part of what made foreign films enjoyable. Among the first dubbing directors were Ferdi Tayfur, who 'gave his voice to' Laurel and Hardy and the Marx Brothers, his sister Adalet Cimcoz, who ran an art gallery, and Nazim Hikmet, an internationally renowned poet who had to flee to Moscow because of his Communist leanings.[12] Turkish audiences still have vivid memories of Tayfur's improvizations in the studio, playing not only with the characters' lines but also with their accents, creating alternative, and more familiar, identities for them than those originally conceived. To his Turkish fans, for example, Groucho Marx was known as Arşak Palabiyikyan, an Armenian name referring to his bushy moustache. So, in its early years, dubbing did not merely serve as translation from a foreign language into Turkish; it was also the means by which adaptations and imitations were assimilated, creating identifiable characters and plots for the audience.[13]

Obviously, conversion to post-dubbing cannot be explained solely by a studio's impatiénce over a faulty piece of machinery, rather it can be seen as an anticipation of the shape of things to come. The indigenous film business was given a premature spur, first by tax cuts, then by migration within Turkey from rural areas to big cities. Along with radio, cinema became the leading entertainment form in this period (television took over much later, in the 1970s), and by the early 1960s the growing demand for indigenous films caught producers off guard. The film industry made a number of hasty rearrangements in order to speed up production: flat lighting, fewer camera setups and more remakes (to save on screenwriting time), all of which gave way to a specific form of narration. Given the circumstances, it seems inevitable that Yeşilçam would have to convert to dubbing. It brought with it not only a degree of flexibility, but also a shorter production period, shifting the actors' load onto the sound studios.

There were only a few actors who dubbed themselves.[14] Most were prevented from doing so by the unsuitability of their accent or diction, or by tight schedules. Instead, sound studios hired 'dubbing artists', mostly theatre actors. Dubbing was an extra job for which they were paid well, and a theatrical background meant they generally spoke distinctly and intelligibly. Each film was dubbed in three to five sessions, each lasting three hours.[15] The film was divided into segments and the actors were scheduled accordingly, with the dubbers who were not voicing lead characters often taking on more than one lesser character each.[16] Each segment was looped and played repeatedly while the actors studied the lip movements, if necessary made alterations to the dialogue, and then rehearsed the scene. When the dubbing director felt that they were ready, she/he gave a cue to start recording. During the recording, with the text in their hands, the actors gathered around the microphone and usually maintained the same distance from it regardless of how the players were positioned in relation to the camera. Thus the distance between onscreen actors and the camera and between dubbing actors and the microphone did not cohere: the former varied, while the latter usually remained unchanged; the point of audition was oblivious to both shooting scale and the positions of the actors onscreen.

This may not have been an altogether pleasant situation for the actors. In 1965 Cüneyt Arkin, at the beginning of a brilliant acting career, wrote that to rely too heavily on dubbing during the shooting ruined an actor's performance. He suggested that due to lack of rehearsal time or from carelessness, the actor would not be able to appropriate the dialogue for herself/himself and often feared that the lines would not be given in good time. However, she/he trusted that all these mistakes would be repaired in that magic place, the sound studio: 'The actor, then, trying to get rid of her/his line at once, rolls up the words and does not care to convey their meanings'.[17] For example, we could envisage a scene in which two characters are having a conversation. Since the players would only be able to have a quick glance through the screenplay and would not know what they were supposed to say, they would need a prompt to read out their lines for them. The prompt – usually the scriptgirl – sometimes had to hide behind a couch or under a table to avoid being caught on camera. She occupied a space within the diegesis of the film, yet was always invisible. For the actors onscreen it is the prompt who initiates and controls their speech: the first player repeats to the second player what she has just heard from the prompt. The second player does not listen to her but to the prompt, who is now reading out his lines. This means that on the sonic level, the body of the Yeşilçam screen actor is a waiting body; waiting and anxious to hear what is to come from a place other than that represented visually onscreen. The discrepancy between the visual and the aural is divisive in both its reception and its delivery of speech. The film actually represents two voices which come simultaneously from different sources – one from the player in the space of the profilmic event and the other from the prompt who, whilst present, is deliberately absented from the visual field. This is further complicated by the fact that during the screening the audience hears neither of the two; it receives the voices and sounds from the sound studio.

Yeşilçam is prone to other discontinuities and failures. Lipsynch, for example, may collapse at anytime; on many occasions the audience will see the actor opening her/his mouth with no voice to accompany it, and speech will be heard after the mouth is shut. Another technical failure is the distortion of the first syllable of words. Such an error may cause an exclamation required at a climactic moment (for example, 'Hayir! Olamaz!'/'No, that's impossible!') to be unintentionally hilarious ('N'ayir! N'olamaz!'/'No! N'at's n'impossible!'). Another more consistent discrepancy can be observed in the process of reverberation. As I have already mentioned, the reverberation or audible placing of the actors produced in the soundtrack does not mirror the space of the imagetrack in the way we expect today. An example would be the cliche of two lovers meeting on a hill with a view of the sea and the city of Istanbul: even when the bodies are clearly placed outdoors, 'their' voices come from an interior. Ambient sound is scarcely used – no wind blowing, no waves breaking, no birds chirping – music compensates for everything. If sound-effects were used, they were mostly produced in the studio; if there was time to search the archives for suitable sources, then stock material was used. From this perspective, the soundtrack of Yeşilçam appears extremely impoverished. Take, for instance, the opening scenes of *Sürtük/Streetwalker* (Ertem Eğilmez, 1970): we see Ekrem (Ekrem Bora), a tough owner of a chain of music halls, and his men in a car on their way to bust a night club. On the soundtrack we hear jazz music which is apparently non-diegetic. On reaching the club the men beat up a bodyguard who stands in their way and enter, pushing through a crowd dancing to the same music, which has now become diegetic. Aside from music, the soundtrack contains only footsteps and the sounds of intermittent fighting between Ekrem's men and the guards. The sound-effects thus function only as 'images of sounds' and are not intended to produce a reality effect. A final significant discrepancy relates to singing, which also functions in a curious manner. This is especially important, for Yeşilçam as a genre is dominated by melodrama. Many of the films exploit singing both for its entertainment value and to enable a twist in the narrative. A common plot follows a poor female character who becomes a famous singer. In *Hayatim Sana Feda/This Life Devoted to You* (Muzaffer Aslan, 1970) – a film which I will discuss in detail later – the star, Türkar Şoray, is dubbed by Adalet Cimcoz. However, when she begins to sing, we hear the voice of Lale Belkis, another well-known actor and singer. To us the screen actor's body, commuting between voices, is possessed twice, for narrative (speech) and for non-narrative (musical performance) purposes.[18]

Michel Chion repeatedly stresses that sound is vococentric, that '*the presence of a human voice structures the sonic space that contains it*'.[19] I want to argue that Yeşilçam may have taken this to its extreme. Speech in Yeşilçam, whilst cueing the flow of the action, can be seen to switch bodies 'on' and 'off'. In *Sürtük*, for example, Ekrem and Suzan, an aging singer in decline, go to a low-class night club. Suzan has a row with the singer, Naciye (Hülya Koçyiğit), whom she despises openly. To teach Suzan a lesson Ekrem decides to make Naciye a star, and the following day buys her new clothes and takes her to his house where Suzan is waiting for him. First we see Suzan from Ekrem's point of view, then the POV is dispossessed and Ekrem and Naciye enter from the right. The camera centres up to show Ekrem, Suzan, Naciye, the housemaid and the chauffeur. Failing to recognize Naciye in her new clothes, Suzan rises and starts walking across the frame, pauses briefly to fondle Ekrem's shoulder (a desperate attempt to signify possession), then stops by Naciye. Trying to control herself, she turns to Ekrem and asks: 'Who is this doll? A foreign artiste?' Ekrem replies 'Don't you recognize her? You called her a "streetwalker" last night.' The scene's frontality (with all the players in line facing the camera), establishes a curious hierarchy: the main characters are in the centre and the rest in the periphery. They stand motionless and seem unaffected by what is happening around them until they begin to speak. Even the object of their verbal exchange, Naciye, awaits her turn to be activated. Later, Ekrem seeks someone to teach Naciye how to sing. He finds Ferdi (Göksel Arsoy), a piano player working in one of his music halls, and sends for him. We see Ferdi waiting in Ekrem's study, sitting in an armchair looking downwards. Ekrem appears at the door behind where he is sitting, enters the room, steps towards Ferdi and taps him on the shoulder, saying 'Hello, welcome!' It is only at this point that Ferdi acknowledges the presence of Ekrem. His body can now be activated in Ekrem's direction and thus inserted into the flow of the scene.[20]

Rick Altman suggests how the image – or, to be more precise, the body – may serve as an alibi for the voice onscreen. He argues that sound in cinema is like a ventriloquist who 'uses' the body, that is, manipulating it as if it were a puppet. Trying to conceal the fact that the voice comes from the loudspeakers placed behind the screen, the players move their lips and the audience is led to – and wants to – believe that its source is someone within the diegesis of the film.[21] Thus, an impression of reality is maintained and the audience is protected from the uncanny effect of the voice coming from a non-human source (the speakers). Altman's analogy may be extended further: the practice of dubbing as described above suggests that in Yeşilçam, it may appear as if all the puppets are 'spoken' by the same ventriloquist. This is very much in accordance with the traditional shadow play, *Karagöz*, which was dethroned by cinema. The *Karagöz* master (*hayali*) speaks through the mouths of all the types, each with a different accent, and even produces the musical score as well as the sound effects (mostly by the help of a *def*, a kind of tambourine with cymbals). What are the implications of this?

In a discussion of what happened to the body with the coming of sound, Stephen Heath draws on the observation by Jean-Luc Godard and Jean-Pierre Gorin that when the cinema began to speak, every actor began to speak the same thing. He argues:

> Evidently there is a strong homogenization and idealization of the silent cinema here that needs resisting and analyzing, but the point remains valid that the sound cinema is the development of a powerful standard of the body and of the voice as hold of the body in image . . . In the silent cinema, the body is always pulling towards an emphasis, an exaggeration, a burlesque (the term of an intractable existence); in the sound cinema,

> the body is smoothed out, given over to that contract of thought described by Godard-Gorin, with the voice as the medium, the expression, of a homogenous thinking subject – actor and spectator – of film.[22]

Although Heath is writing of sound cinema in general, his observations are insightful. Does Yeşilçam allow for or produce a thinking subject? Do the actors all speak the same thing? I would argue that, as far as the dubbing described above is concerned, they do not speak at all. Their bodies are given over not to homogenous thinking subjects but to Logos expressing itself through voices that were only slackly attached to bodies. Hence Yeşilçam is like the shadow-play master whose voice remains the same by way of the differences it produces. It might well be suggested that the voice *in* Yeşilçam is the voice *of* Yeşilçam; the utterances are instances of Logos which dictates its moral universe and orchestrates the unfolding narrative. An analysis of the scripts may confirm this. Onat Kutlar, in his criticism of Yeşilçam screenplays, argues that speech is, in effect, mostly redundant, for it simply describes the action, and the language itself is not colloquial, ultimately producing a kind of cinema which is not 'alive'.[23] Thus an actor in Yeşilçam, I maintain, is 'be-spoken'. This is why almost all of the dialogue, instead of functioning as the indices of a character's interior psychological situation, transform all the characters into a set of statements. Does this therefore suggest that speech in these instances takes more or less the form of a voiceover? For although bodies are seemingly assigned to speech, the soundtrack, and particularly the sound of the voice, fails to conceal the fact that it (and thus Logos) simply uses bodies as a vehicle for its mediation. The voice is thus disembodied, and this disembodied voice creates/comes from a theocentric space. In an endnote to her article on the articulation of body and sound in cinema, Mary Ann Doane points to these theological implications of the disembodied voice:

> Two kinds of 'voices without bodies' immediately suggest themselves – one theological the other scientific (two poles which, it might be added, are not ideologically unrelated): (1) the voice of God incarnated in the Word; (2) the artificial voice of a computer. Neither seems to be capable of representation outside a certain anthropomorphism, however. God is pictured, in fact, as having a quite specific body – that of a male patriarchal figure.[24]

Whilst Western culture allows for a visual representation of God, endowing Him with a male, patriarchal body, the voiceover nonetheless gains its theological status thanks to its disembodiment. Leaving aside the ambiguity that arises from the possibilities of representing God, I want to reiterate with Doane that in the classical cinema the use of voiceover can reveal the relationship between sexual difference and its theological implications.

Doane's arguments, however, are related to a specific cultural heritage and belief system. In contrast, Yeşilçam originates from a very different conception of reality and the relationship between various domains of Being. Islam, not unlike some eastern doctrines such as Tibetean Buddhism and Taoism, devised a conception of Being – Allah – which escapes any kind of figurative representation, let alone anthropomorphism. If we leave aside the symbolism of esoteric teachings (such as Sufism) which can mostly be traced in literary texts, it is clear that personification, and therefore spatio-temporalization, of Allah is strictly avoided. Seyyid Hussein Nasr argues:

> Islamic aniconism, which removes the possibility of the concretization of the Divine Presence (*hudur*) in an icon or image, is a powerful factor in intensifying the spiritual significance of the void in the Muslim mind . . . God and His revelation are not identified with any particular place, time or object. Hence His Presence is ubiquitous. He is everywhere, in whichever direction one turns, as the Quranic verse, 'Whithersoever ye turn, there is the face of God' (II: 115), affirms.[25]

Obviously, all this is not to say that space-time is devoid of divinity, for everything serves as a sign-vehicle of the Divine. The dichotomy of the embodied voice/disembodied voice, in so far as it reserves a specific place for God as the disembodied voice or Logos, is based on Christian theology which, as Doane argues, eventually issued a patriarchal figure, whereas Islam strictly rejects attributing a body to Allah. Hence in Islam Logos may penetrate all bodies. I think this may provide us with clues as to how voiceover functions differently in Yeşilçam: having diffused the 'Divine Presence' throughout the soundtrack, voiceover proper and voiceover as travesty of dialogue eventually blur the border between what we may perceive as diegetic and nondiegetic, thus making it impossible to identify the male voice alone with the attributes of the apparatus.

Blind Men 'Seeing' the Voice

The play between the voice and the body may be still more complicated, however. The voice may be seen to establish a character, but then transcend it by restoring the distance between audience and character onscreen. This may be understood through 'loss of sight', an often ridiculed theme which is very common in Turkish melodrama. I will argue that this subgenre may serve as an object-lesson for my purposes in this essay.

In his essay on Indian melodrama, a genre which heavily influenced Turkish cinema, Ravi Vasudevan argues that the man's loss of sight connotes his indifference to the woman's desire.[26] Indeed, in *Aşk Mahudesi/Goddess of Love* (Nejat Saydam, 1969), for example, former lovers Leyla (Türkan Şoray) and Ekrem (Cüneyt Arkin) encounter each other in a music hall. Leyla does not know that Ekrem has had an accident and has lost his sight. Ekrem shivers, and when his companion asks him what happened he replies that he felt the presence of someone he knew. Leyla looks at him but he does not return her gaze. Her heart broken, she leaves. Thus it may be suggested that his loss of sight makes him indifferent to, and unaware of, her desire. However, the theme of the blind man in Turkish cinema requires a broader scope that enables a discussion of body–voice split. The incidents and coincidences – blindness being the most prominent – devised by Yeşilçam are carefully planned and controlled by the logic which also governs the construction of cinematic bodies. Sightlessness provides clues about the psychic mechanisms at work in Yeşilçam's approach to voice and body. When the characters are or become blind, desire is not only made possible but also mediated by the voice which is disembodied not for the audience but for the character in the diegesis of the film. This involves an investment in the diegetic/character and nondiegetic/audience (op)positions.

Both men and women may be subject to a deprivation of this kind, but economy of sexual difference dictates a specific plot for each sex. In *Feride* (Metin Erksan, 1971),[27] *Aşk Mahudesi* and *Adim Anmayacağim/I Shan't Recall Your Name* (Orhan Elmas, 1971), the man, having split up with his woman, loses his sight. For instance, *Feride* tells the story of Kemal (Engin Çaglar) who sees his wife, Feride (Emel Sayin), in the arms of another man and thinks he is dishonoured. In fact, the man has set them up, but no matter how hard Feride tries to explain the situation, Kemal will not listen and sends her away in disgrace. Left in the house with a collaborator in the deception, Füruzan (Lale Belkis, the archetypal wicked blonde), Kemal proceeds to lose all his money in a desperate card game. When Füruzan realizes that she will not now be able to enjoy his wealth she walks out. Then Kemal loses his sight as a result of heavy drinking. He retires to a modest house and lives in isolation, but one day he meets, in a nearby park, a little girl whose charm returns the joy of life to him. She is, of course, his daughter by Feride, who is now a famous singer. Feride comes to his house in search of the child and they meet again. She manages to overcome the shock of seeing him and easily convinces Kemal, who shows his horror and disgust upon hearing her voice, that she is not Feride but someone else.[28] She begins to visit him regularly and they start an 'innocent' affair which lasts until Kemal regains his sight thanks to a successful operation. Feride disappears again but, in the end, the child renuites them.

Adim Anmayacağim follows the same plot with a slight variation: Gül (Hülya Koçyiğit) returns home as a nurse to look after Engin (Cüneyt Arkin). Neither he nor their grown-up daughter, Oya, recognize her. Engin falls in love with Gül and decides to have the operation to cure his blindness ('I want to look at you until I am gratified!').[29] Just as Gül is about to disappear out of the fear that Engin would expel her again if he saw her, she learns that the man who destroyed her marriage is now after their daughter. Indeed the man drugs Oya and attempts to rape her. Gül follows them and saves Oya but has to kill the man. In court she does not even defend herself but, having learned that she is sacrificing her life for the honour of the family, Engin appears as a lawyer and 'proclaims' the truth. When he tells the judge and the audience the sad story of Gül, their sympathy stands in for the verdict and the narrative jumps to her immediate release and the reunion of the family. It is significant here that the space of the Law is where all misunderstanding and conflict are resolved. As already discussed, *Aşk Mahudesi* deviates from this plot but still conforms to the same structure. Ekrem and Leyla fall in love and decide to marry. However, a jealous ex-fiancee convinces Leyla that she has caused the suicide of Ekrem's brother. She unwillingly leaves Ekrem on the pretext of her desire for a singing career. When Ekrem learns that she actually loves him, he rushes to her home but crashes his car on the way. He loses his sight but pride prevents him from letting her know this. They run into each other on a few occasions, but since Leyla does not know that he is blind she thinks Ekrem is refusing to acknowledge her presence/appearance and thus her desire. In the end, however, she learns the truth and they are reunited.

All three plots position the woman as the victim of a third party. The male protagonist's rejection of the woman is repayed by a split in his perception of the world. The disappearance of the woman coincides with the man's loss of sight and sometimes his property, thus exposing castration as a necessary ordeal. He is blinded by what he has seen (because he has believed in the truth of what he apparently 'sees') and thus fails to 'see' what the woman is really saying. The voice attached to the female body is now a waste of words and the body is established as the site which negates the desire of the man and the family that legitimates his desire. Anything that her body will now emit, vocally such as explanations and excuses, or physically such as another body (a baby), is discarded as waste, if not abject. Only then may the woman return as the voice. Her voice is thus worth listening to only when it is detached from its 'material' source, that is, her body. The proximity of the protagonists may vary: in *Feride* and *Adim Anmayacağim* they are within each other's reach, whereas in *Aşk Mahudesi*, Ekrem can hear Leyla's singing only via loud speakers placed outside the music hall. In different contexts the woman's voice represents both closure and disclosure, revealing an ambivalent attitude towards the female voice. So while Ekrem can listen to Leyla singing, which stands in for her presence, Engin cannot endure Gül's voice coming from the radio; agitated, he yells to have it turned off. Yet both types of reaction arguably derive from the same psychic structure: the mother's voice is substituted for the umbilical cord, but at the same time it evokes the painful memory of rupture.[30]

The audience's identification with the male character is understood in narrative terms as the sharing of the same information about a given situation. At the moment of crisis this position shifts to one of empathy; the audience knows more than the character does, and does not approve of his attitude, yet will still side with him. While the audience is almost always given an omniscient view, the pathos of melodrama lies in the flaws in the distribution of information. Empathy returns to a position of identification only when the male character begins to 'see', which also returns the voice to the body of the female character. This is why the audience feels so frustrated when the character cannot see what it sees – that the voice which is divine to the male character is in fact coming from the body he condemned as disgraceful.

Blind Women 'Hearing' the Sight

Women lose their sight, too. They are either already blind when the film opens (*Üç Arkadaş/Three Comrades* [Memduh Ün, 1958, 1971], *Serseri/The Tramp* [O. Nuri Ergün, 1959]) or lose their sight very early on (*Hayatim Sana Feda*).[31] Therefore, unlike the men who pay for their misunderstandings, women's loss coincides only with the initial narrative thrust. And while men begin to see in the finale, women's acquisition of sight, instead of concluding the film, gives the narrative a final push: the beloved one is still to be attained. The woman has to choose the right man from several who claim the same identity, and has to return the male voice, which is the source of her desire, to the originary body. The emblematic film here is *Üç Arkadaş*. It features Muhterem Nur as a blind girl who earns a living by selling safety pins on the street. Three musicians, all male, seeing that she is vulnerable to the dangers of the big city, take her to their ramshackle house. Here they construct a make-believe world for her, convincing her that she is living with successful musicians in a luxurious villa. They find the money necessary for an operation to cure her blindness, but the moment she regains her sight they disappear. She goes on to become a famous singer and starts to search for them. On finding the house where they used to live, she realizes she had become a part of, and target for, their fiction. Even the portrait which they had told her was of an aristocratic ancestor turns out to be a kitsch painting of an ape. In the end she finds them by following the distant sound of their voices.

Hayatim Sana Feda, meanwhile, tells the story of Zeynep (Türkan Şoray), who loses her sight in a car accident. Harun (Cüneyt Arkin), who is responsible for the accident, tries to help Zeynep financially only to find that she is too proud to accept such an offer and is full of hatred for the man who caused her loss of sight. Zeynep finds a job as a singer in a music hall, whose owner agrees to employ her on the condition that the audience must not realize that she is blind. In order for her to act as if she could see, his authorial voice maps the space of her performance, with the microphone (the 'phallus') in the centre: 'First find the microphone', he instructs, 'it will be your guide on the stage. Then five steps to the right and then five to the left. That is all.' Thus Zeynep's body becomes a spectacle for the audience in reference to the microphone which mediates her voice and serves as her anchor on stage. But Zeynep's desire will jeopardize this illusion. Harun introduces himself as a blind musician and soon they fall in love. One night, after she has sung one of Harun's songs, her awareness of his presence in the audience endangers the power of the microphone (as phallus), and she fails to locate it and loses her balance. Surprisingly, Zeynep's desire is not punished and the accident does not have serious consequences. Harun provides the money for an operation and, once Zeynep can see, he disappears and then reappears in the guise of a music tycoon, Kemal, who is willing to make her a star. Kemal proposes to her and she accepts, but this fails to make him happy. Kemal feels betrayed and swears to take revenge on behalf of his 'true' self, Harun. But the day before their marriage, Zeynep, while singing, has a vision of Harun (whose face is obscured) and realizes that she is still in love with him. She confesses to Kemal that she cannot marry him, upon which he reveals his true identity.

Another film, *Serseri* runs against this formula and offers a radically different positioning of the woman. Kazim (Sadri Alişik), a poor fisherman, finds a homeless blind girl, Zeynep (Sema Özcan), on the beach where he keeps his boat. He takes her to his cabin and begins to look after her. In this case it is Zeynep who offers Kazim a reading of his world which she cannot see. 'My body has become all eyes', she says, 'I can see with my everything except my eyes.' Kazim begins to see things from her angle ('It is me who has been blind until now'), and having fallen in love with her decides to try everything possible to help her regain her sight. He steals money for an operation and when in hospital the bandage is removed from Zeynep's eyes, the camera turns away from her and looks out of the window to show the police arresting Kazim. He asks a close friend to impersonate him and marry her, but the 'embodiment' of Kazim's voice fails to convince Zeynep: 'You are not him', she protests, 'I saw him with my ears'. She visits him in the jail, but Kazim rejects her saying he is not the Kazim that she knew. The guard looking over Kazim's shoulder – as representative of the Law – intervenes: 'There is no Kazim here but you'.

Since the voice is always the medium of truth – although it reserves a right to fiction – it belongs to a higher order in the hierarchy of Being. However, as I have tried to demonstrate, this does not mean that Yeşilçam aims to establish the Cartesian body–soul duality. In connection with this, a Sufi source gives an eloquent illustration of a change in the body of the prophet Joseph, Jacob's eleventh son. Having shed all his wordly desires and personal attributes, the appearance of Joseph undergoes a radical transformation: 'His body is not wrapped around flesh but Divine Love, thus his skin becomes transparent; when he eats, one can see the colour of the food going down his throat, and when he drinks it is possible to see the flow of the drink'. Curiously, the text does not stop there: 'Looking at the soles of his feet, one can see his face.'[32] I cannot give an exhaustive account of all the implications of this story. I must be content with saying that this, obviously, does not suggest a rejection of the body in favour of spirituality, that is, a split between 'body' and 'soul'. On the contrary, Divine Love penetrates Joseph's body, releasing its parts from the hierarchy (head/feet, heaven/earth) into which they were initially inscribed. By the same token, by giving the body to the service of Logos and frequently by denying the characters the 'look', and therefore the sight of the body (particularly the body of the other), Yeşilçam appears to have separated the two domains. Ultimately, however, the body–soul duality is resolved, since it is made clear that there has to be a body in the first place, for it is the body which makes the mediation of voice, and thus truth, possible.

NOTES

I would like to thank Lewis Keir Johnson and Zafer Aracagök for their helpful comments and suggestions.

1. Zarife Öztürk, 'Türk sinemasi "ses" diyor'/'Turkish cinema claims sound'. *Radikal*, 23 October 1997, p. 18.
2. For an account of transition from Yeşilçam to New Turkish Cinema, see the entry, 'Turkish cinema, by Nezih Erdoğan and Deniz Göktürk' in Oliver Leaman (ed.), *Companion Encyclopedia of Middle Eastern and North African Film* (London and New York: Routledge, 2001), pp. 537–9.
3. Michel Chion, *The Voice in Cinema*, trans. Claudia Gorbman (New York: Columbia Press, 1999), p. 131.
4. Tom Levin, 'The acoustic dimension: notes on cinema sound', *Screen*, vol. 25, no. 3 (1984), p. 67.
5. James Lastra, 'Reading, writing and representing sound', in Rick Altman (ed.), *Sound Theory, Sound Practice* (London: Routledge, 1992), p. 75.
6. For this conception of resistance to apparatus I am indebted to Çetin Sankartal.
7. For a discussion of this, see Kezban Güleryuz, 'Sinema ve türksel gerçeklik'/'Cinema and the Turkish way of reality', *Yeni Türkiye*, nos 23/24 (1998), pp. 3156–7.
8. Mikhail Yampolsky, 'Voice devoured: Artaud and Borges on dubbing, trans. Larry P. Joseph, *October*, no. 64 (Spring 1993). p. 62.
9. *Esrarengiz Bay Kartaloğlu/Mysterious Mr Eagleton* (Istanbul: Can, 1990), p. 83 (translation mine).
10. Thomas Elsaesser, 'Tales of sound and fury: observations on the family melodrama', in Bill Nichols (ed.), *Movies and Methods*, Volume II (Berkeley, CA: University of California Press, 1985), p. 173.
11. 'Yeşilçam nasil doğdu, nasil büyüdü, nasil öldü ve yaşasin yeni sinema'/'How Yeşilçam was born, how it grew, how it died and long live new cinema', in Süleyma Murat Dinçer (ed.), *Türk Sinemasi Üzerine Düşünceler/Thinking on Turkish Cinema* (Ankara: Doruk, 1996), p. 281.
12. See Cimcoz's memories on the early years of dubbing: 'Sözlendirme anilan'/ 'Memories of dubbing', *Yeni Sinema*, nos 19/20 (June–July, 1968), pp. 40–42.
13. By imitation I refer to *taklid*, the traditional theatre actor's impersonation of a person or, to be more precise, a type.
14. Following Richard Dyer, who finds the usage of 'actress' as degrading to female players, I use 'actor' and sometimes 'player' for both sexes.
15. Erman Şener gives a detailed account of dubbing process in his 'Sözlendirme sorunu'/'The problem of dubbing', *Yeni Sinema*, nos 19/20 (June–July 1968), pp. 36–7.
16. Although this was true generally for the dubbing of extras, sometimes they went so far as to dub the leads as well. Hayn Caner, in his memoirs proudly reveals that in *Ağlayan Melek/The Weeping Angel* (Safa Onal, 1970), a very talented 'dubbing artiste', Jeyan Mahfi Tözüm, dubbed both the heroine, Türkan Şoray, and her friend Dya Peri in the same scene. *'Yeşilçam' Filmlen/'Yeşilçam' Films* (Istanbul: Vizyon, 1995), p. 12.
17. 'Türk sinemasinda oyun ve oyunculuk'/'Play and playing in Turkish cinema', *Sinema 65* (August 1965), pp. 24–5.
18. It must be noted that this does not hold true for the cases in which an established singer plays the lead.
19. Chion, *The Voice in Cinema*, p. 5 (emphasis in original).
20. Since the main characters do the most of the talking and they are more likely to be shown in two-shots than in crowded ones, this observation is more accurate with minor characters.

21. Rick Altman, 'Moving lips cinema as ventriloquism', *Yale French Studies*, no. 60 (1980), pp. 76–8.
22. Stephen Health, *Questions of Cinema* (London: Macmillan, 1985), p. 191.
23. Onat Kutlar, 'Türk sinemasynda konuşmalar üzerine bazi aykin notlar'/'Counter arguments on speech in Turkish cinema', *Yeni Sinema*, no. 9 (August 1967). pp. 17–18.
24. Mary Ann Doane, 'The voice in the cinema: articulation of body and space', in Phil Rosen (ed.), *Narrative, Apparatus and Ideology* (New York: Columbia University Press, 1986), p. 347, fn. 2.
25. Seyyid Hussein Nasr, *Islamic Art and Spirituality* (New York: State University of New York Press, 1987), p. 187.
26. Ravi Vasudevan, 'Melodramatic mode and the commercial Hindi cinema: notes on film history, narrative and performance in the 1950s', *Screen*, vol. 30, no. 3 (1989), p. 36.
27. For a detailed analysis of *Feride*, see Elif Rongen-Kaynakçi, '*Feride*, a Yeşilçam melodrama: Turkish popular cinema and the construction of cultural identity', unpublished MA thesis, University of Amsterdam, 1997.
28. In such encounters, the men recover from the shock and readily believe that they have mistaken the voice for the voice of the women they had sent away.
29. While the sense of sight can always be regained, either the character cannot afford the operation, or she/he simply does not wish to see again.
30. For an account of this, see Chion, *The Voice in Cinema*, pp. 61–2.
31. Which confirms Freud's castration scenario.
32. Zeynep Sayin, 'Bati'da ve doğu'da bedenin temsilinde haysiyet ve zillet ll'/'Integrity and vileness in the representation of body in the West and in the East', *Defter*, no. 40 (Summer 2000), p. 221.

SECTION 5
GENRE CRITICISM AND POPULAR INDIAN CINEMA

GENRE CRITICISM AND POPULAR INDIAN CINEMA

Dimitris Eleftheriotis

This section contains four essays that discuss in detailed and insightful ways the textual peculiarities of popular Indian films, while at the same time paying close attention to the ways in which they address their audiences. Their usefulness for the student of Indian cinema extends beyond the descriptive and analytical to the historical. Not only do the four essays collectively offer an account of changing textual practices and modes of address from the 1940s to the present but they also provide evidence of the evolution of critical work on popular Indian cinema. From Thomas's pioneering 1985 essay, through Vasudevan's ground-breaking argument a decade later, to the more recent works of Gopalan and Garwood, the four contributions that follow trace the assertion, identification and exploration of the significance of the textual and spectatorial peculiarities of popular Indian cinema.

Re-framing Genre Criticism

Crucially the essays included here define their analyses in the context of (or in conversation with) genre criticism. Working within such a critical framework presents the writers with clear advantages but it also poses problems. Some of the general difficulties with the concept of genre and the critical practice attached to it are by now well established: the arbitrary and empiricist way in which classificatory categories are produced, the impossibility of defining 'pure' genres, the difficulty in accounting for both hybridity and change have been carefully considered by theorists such as Rick Altman and Steve Neale.[1]

On the other hand, there are considerable advantages in the ways in which genre criticism has historically defined and analysed its object of study.

Of crucial value to the study of film are the close links, enabled by the concept of genre, between specific formal aspects of films (narrative structures, themes and patterns, types of performance, editing, soundtrack, mise-en-scène), the sociohistorical context of films (through the examination of iconography, the cultural/historical referent or the myth-making processes in genres), the conditions, methods and strategies of the film industry, and audience expectations and pleasures. It is this ability of genre, as a critical category in film studies, to cover and link 'multiple concerns' that makes the approach particularly useful.[2]

Nevertheless, there are also considerable difficulties when a genre approach is adopted for the study of non-Hollywood films and cinemas. With a handful of notable exceptions,[3] the theoretical work produced addresses either specific Hollywood genres, or genre in general but in the context of Hollywood cinema. As a result, generic characteristics attached to specific Hollywood genres become normative, universalising and often prescriptive categories. It is evident that an application of genre criticism for the study of popular Indian cinema needs to re-define the frame of reference of such criticism within a specific national context. It is not surprising, then, that the essays included in this section revisit issues discussed in the previous section on national cinema: genre criticism in specific national contexts unavoidably addresses questions of methodology and re-evaluates the appropriateness of the theoretical framework.

A starting point for Thomas, Vasudevan and Gopalan is the negotiation of the place that a generic approach to Indian cinema occupies within a discourse of genre criticism. Thomas's essay is almost emblematic of the difficulties of such negotiation, not in terms of its substance of argument but in terms of its discursive positioning in a 1985 special issue of *Screen* themed around 'other cinemas, other criticisms', which groups together authors, approaches and cinemas with little affinity to each other apart from their proclaimed 'otherness'. Thomas not only protests against the label of 'other' attached to Indian cinema but also makes a strong argument for asserting the distinctiveness of such cinema in terms of specific textual and contextual characteristics. Her essay represents a corrective move attempting to address Indian cinema in its own terms (by relying heavily on the views of Indian critics and filmmakers) and in the process arguing for a culture-specific genre approach. Thomas also clarifies that generic classifications within the context of Indian cinema are radically different from those associated with Hollywood; the terms 'comedy', 'musical' and 'melodrama' are almost meaningless as ways of distinguishing between kinds of Indian cinema since most films will have aspects of all these genres. She points out that classifications such as 'social' (which Vasudevan considers in detail in his essay), 'family social', 'devotional', 'stunt' and 'multi-starrer' are more commonly used and more relevant for the Indian context.

Vasudevan's essay also expresses scepticism towards Anglo-American critical categories: firstly by considering and subsequently rejecting the designation 'third cinema' as appropriate to Indian cinema, and secondly by pointing out that commercial cinema in India negotiates a 'national space' in opposition to the norms of Hollywood.

Gopalan's essay (an introduction to her monograph on Indian cinema) clarifies that her objective is to identify and analyse conventions unique to Indian cinema (what she calls a 'constellation of interruptions') but also suggests that such an approach leads to an inevitable process of theoretical revision:

> just as popular Indian films rewrite certain dominant genre principles, film theory, too, needs to undergo revisions in order to read adequately the differing structuring of anticipation and pleasure in this cinema that also has a global application and circulation.[4]

The re-definition of the frame of reference and the critical engagement with genre criticism of the above authors (and of course many others) enables Garwood to address the textual specificities of *Hum Saath Saath Hain* (Sooraj Barjatya, 1999) and propose a thesis regarding its mode of address that is firmly located within the context of scholarship on Indian cinema.

The four essays included in the present *Reader and Guide* collectively offer detailed descriptions of the textual characteristics of popular Indian cinema, paying particular attention to audience positions, viewing experiences and the changing context of production, distribution and exhibition of Indian films.

Textual Characteristics

Before proceeding any further it is important to note that the term 'Indian cinema' is a rather problematic umbrella term that actually refers to a rather fragmented and varied object. Indian films are produced in a variety of different industrial and cultural contexts, in more than forty languages (with Hindi, Bengali, Malayalam, Kannada, Marathi, Tamil, Telugu, Gujarati and Marathi being the most popular) and in several regions.

The essays that follow focus primarily on Hindi films, a choice perhaps explained by the hegemonic position that Hindi cinema occupies within India. Ravi Vasudevan's essay directly addresses the ways in which that hegemonic position is textually and contextually constructed. The four essays collectively cover various aspects of about sixty years of Indian cinema, as well as offering a sense of how scholarship on Indian cinema has developed in the past twenty years.

In her discussion of the textual specificities of popular Indian films Thomas stresses the value of repetition that is placed on them by audiences. Echoing Gürata's positive evaluation of remakes in Turkish cinema discussed in the previous chapter, Thomas suggests that the similarity of story-lines between films is something that both audiences and filmmakers are aware of, and, in opposition to critical consensus, it is potentially a source of pleasure rather than boredom. In fact, predictable narratives function only as pretexts, as opportunities to explore emotions and to display spectacles. The emphasis in Indian popular films lies more in the 'how' you tell a story rather than 'what' it is about. The success of the usually multi-stranded narratives depends on the delicate balance between narrative and spectacle or emotion.

This is a notion that Ravi Vasudevan elaborates further, by proposing an analogy between popular Indian films and what Tom Gunning, in his analysis of early cinema, describes as a 'cinema of attractions': a cinematic mode marked by the importance of displaying various attractions (foreign views, magical tricks, spectacular events, technological capabilities of the apparatus) rather than a preoccupation with overarching narrative cohesion.[5] Such an analogy is further reinforced by Thomas's suggestion that popular Indian films are characterised by a relaxed attitude to realism, operating within distinctive but loose conventions of verisimilitude, which are in themselves often exceeded within the films' musical numbers and other spectacular attractions.

Indian films usually demonstrate an awareness of their use of narrative as a pretext for the display of narrative and emotion. Three of the essays collected here identify self-reflexivity as a prominent characteristic of popular Indian cinema: Thomas in the specific analysis of *Naseeb* (Manmohan Desai, 1981), Gopalan in the discussion of cinephilia as a common theme of many films, and Garwood in terms of the re-formatting of songs and performances in *Hum Saath Saath Hain*. It is interesting to compare the self-reflexivity of Indian films (structured around their specific conventions of verisimilitude) to the 'unrealistic' use of dubbing in Turkish cinema discussed in the previous chapter. It is important to reiterate in this context that these different ways of approaching the textual practices of films are not perceived by the authors as being in any way inferior to the normative Hollywood ones; recognition and positive evaluation of difference resists the classification of such cinematic forms as 'other'.

Equally reminiscent of the approach adopted in the previous chapter is Vasudevan's emphasis on negotiation in his detailed exploration of the textual characteristics of the 'social' films of the 1950s. More specifically, Vasudevan explores the relationship between tableau and movement, as well as structures of looking that construct the male body as an object of sacred devotion. He convincingly argues that the tension – firstly between the aesthetics of stasis and frontality and that of dynamic mobility, and secondly between the structures of looking that construct male characters as both subjects and objects of the look – are not only constitutive components of the textuality of the films but also represent a negotiation between traditional and modern cultural values and codes.

Vasudevan, Thomas and Garwood note the importance of kinship relations and family conflict as narrative themes informing the plots of many popular Indian films: in the 'social' films of the 1950s, in *Naseeb* and *Hum Saath Saath Hain*, respectively. It is no surprise, then, that across a variety of different genres melodramatic tropes are omnipresent. However, as Vasudevan points out, the Indian appropriation of such tropes is distinctly different from those described in 'Euro-American theoretical mappings', most importantly in terms of its ambivalent attitude towards the secularism of melodrama:

> a melodramatic narrative and dramaturgy is also employed in Indian film genres such as the mythological and devotional, not only in post-sacred genres such as the social. To further confound the secular dimensions of melodrama, even in the Bombay 'social', the genre of the modern day, women often employ a traditional Hindu idiom deifying the husband.[6]

Gopalan, on the other hand, identifies the distinctiveness of contemporary Indian films by exploring a constellation of interruptions (intervals, censorship, numbers) that bring together contextual and textual aspects of popular Indian cinema, linking the films with the culturally specific form of their reception.

As discussed earlier, it is precisely this connection between texts and audiences that is particularly valuable within a 'genre' approach, and I shall now shift focus to attend to the ways in which the four essays address several aspects of the viewing experience of popular Indian films.

Audiences

The authors of the following four essays are anxious to refute critical designations of the audience of popular Indian films as naïve and childlike; as Vasudevan notes in the context of the 1950s: 'In these accounts, the spectator of the popular film emerges as an immature, indeed infantile, figure, one bereft of the rationalist imperatives required for the Nehru era's project of national construction.'[7] Thomas describes audiences as involved, reactive and noisy, addressed in a way that is clearly different from that of 'much Western cinema'. This happens primarily through affect, as films are experienced as a succession of 'moods' with overarching narratives holding very loosely together the different 'modes of affect'. In the context of *Naseeb*, Thomas notes that the textual practices of the film demand sophisticated knowledgeable audiences that need to be won over:

> *Naseeb* is undoubtedly unusual in taking the self-reflexive and self-parodic elements inherent in much Hindi cinema so far, but the fact that it is acceptable is significant. Despite what middle-class critics imply, it is clear, if one experiences an Indian audience irreverently clapping, booing and laughing with the films, that they know perfectly well that the films are 'ridiculous', 'unreal' and offer impossible solutions, and that pleasure arises in spite of – and probably because of – this knowledge.[8]

Gopalan's work on interruptions is informed and motivated by a cinephilia that is defined as both personal (the author's own intimate relationship with the films) and a characteristic of the relationship between popular Indian films and their audiences (cinephilia is a structure that informs the viewing experience and the text). In her theorisation, audiences (as well as films and their filmmakers) are understood as knowledgeable cinephiles whose appreciation of the 'details' of films causes moments of interruption, for example by paying homage to a song, film style or star.

Vasudevan and Garwood (and to some extent, Gopalan) deal in detail with specific interactions between the structures of national and international film markets, textual practices and ways in which spectators are addressed: Vasudevan in the context of Hindi films in the 1940s and 1950s, Garwood and Gopalan in the contemporary or recent context.

Vasudevan's essay focuses mainly on an analysis of the Indian market, paying particular attention to the formation of a national market for Bombay films that is linked to their dominance since the 1950s. Given the strength of regional identities in India, the hegemony of Bombay cinema is of particular political and theoretical significance: not only in terms of an overarching Hindu identity which, constructed as pan-Indian, suppresses other regional identities, but also because of the crucial questions raised about the textual and contextual construction of such hegemony.

As discussed earlier, Vasudevan explores the textual peculiarities of the 'social' films of the 1950s as a negotiation between traditional and modern codes and identifies in this process a re-articulation of traditional authority around an overarching middle-class, Hindu identity:

> In the Hindi social film, instead of a fantasy of upward mobility, a democratising downward spiral is set in motion, the hero being precipitated into a life of destitution and crime. The circling back, the recovery of identity, is then tied to a normalization of social experience, a recovery of the reassuring coordinates of social privilege.
>
> As a result, in line with dominant ideological currents in the wake of independence, the social film of the 1950s expanded the terms of social reference, urged an empathy towards social deprivation and invited a vicarious identification with such states. But the recovery of the hero at the conclusion finally underlines the middle-class identity that structures the narrative.[9]

Vasudevan also links such a process to specific changes in the film industry in the 1940s that asserted an offscreen dominance of Hindu actors and filmmakers. Vasudevan notes the popularity of Indian films in the 1950s in much broader international markets, not only in traditional places of Indian immigration (East Asia, Mauritius, the Middle East, South-east Asia, Northern Africa) but also 'in the countries of the former Soviet Union and China'. His tentative explanation for such popularity is that there are similarities between such transitional societies and India as they move from traditional to modern social structures, a transition registered, as we have seen, in the textual practices of the films.

Lalitha Gopalan notes a series of important changes in the Indian film industry and the national and international market since the 1970s: the increasing number and importance of films in languages other than Hindustani, the confidence of the industry vis-à-vis the perceived threat of Hollywood (as the relaxation of protectionist policies suggests), the growth of the video, DVD and satellite markets offering additional support rather than competition to the industry, and technological improvements offering new attractions to audiences. Crucially Gopalan suggests that recent and contemporary popular Indian films appear to address international as well as national audiences:

> The more conventional representation of the world in Indian popular cinema – song and dance sequences set in foreign locales – is not only spruced up to arouse the spectator's interests in tourism, but also aggressively participates in the movement of global capital. These sequences not only bring the world home, but also acknowledge a loyal audience abroad that wishes to see its own stories of migrations and displacement written into these films.[10]

This is a concept that Ian Garwood further explores through his specific discussion of NRI (Non-resident Indian) audiences in relation to recent films. Garwood notes the increasing importance of the North American and British markets for the Indian film industry and, through close textual analysis of the status of the song and dance sequences in *Hum Saath Saath Hain*, he identifies two different ways in which NRI audiences are addressed in the so-called 'NRI romance' genre:

> The NRI romance relies on the display of 'traditional' Indian music culture to court a diasporic audience as *citizens*. But, in keeping with its project to appeal to its audience also as particular kinds of *consumers*, it subjects these traditions to a process of repackaging and reformatting. The musical number is expected to stir deep patriotic feeling in its ideal spectator, at the same time as it is pushed forward aggressively as a particular kind of commodity, as if in a shop-window display.[11]

Garwood further suggests that there exists a hierarchical relationship between the two modes of address, with the values and identities attached to the consumer framing those of the citizen. Read in tandem with Vasudevan's essay, such an argument constructs a historical trajectory that outlines some of the key hegemonic struggles around identity within popular Indian cinema: while in the 1940s and 1950s an overarching Hindu identity becomes privileged on a national level through the negotiation of the tradition/modernisation binary, in more recent times, and through the particular articulation of a local/global dynamic, a consumerist identity appears to emerge above that of citizenship.

Notes

1. For a more detailed critique of genre criticism, see Rick Altman (1999), *Film/Genre*, London: BFI, and Steve Neale, 'Question of genre', *Screen*, vol. 31, no. 1, 1990.
2. For a further consideration of this view on genre criticism, see Altman, *Film/Genre*, pp. 14–15.

3. See Christopher Frayling (1981), *Spaghetti Westerns: Cowboys and Europeans from Karl May to Sergio Leone*, London: Routledge; Marcia Landy (1991), *British Genres: Cinema and Society, 1930–1960*, Princeton: Princeton University Press.
4. Lalitha Gopalan (2002), 'Introduction: "Hum Aapke Hain Koun?" – cinephilia and Indian films', *Cinema of Interruptions: Action Genres in Contemporary Indian Cinema*, London: BFI, reprinted in this collection.
5. Tom Gunning (1986), 'The cinema of attraction: early film, its spectator and the avant-garde', *Wide Angle*, vol. 8, nos 3–4.
6. Ravi Vasudevan (1995), 'Addressing the spectator of a "third world" national cinema: the Bombay "social" film of the 1940s and 1950s', *Screen*, vol. 36, no. 4, reprinted in this collection.
7. Ibid.
8. Rosie Thomas (1985), 'Indian cinema: pleasures and popularity', *Screen*, vol. 26, nos 3–4, reprinted in this collection.
9. Vasudevan, 'Addressing the spectator'.
10. Gopalan, 'Introduction: "Hum Aapke Hain Koun?"'.
11. Ian Garwood, 'Shifting pitch: The Bollywood song sequence in the Anglo-American market', in the present collection.

14

INDIAN CINEMA: PLEASURES AND POPULARITY

Rosie Thomas

> The pseudo-intellectuals here try to copy Westerners. We think we're better than Westerners – they can't make films for the Indian audience.
>
> (Bombay filmmaker)

Discussion of Indian popular cinema as 'other' cinema is immediately problematic. There is no disputing that, within the context of First World culture and society, this cinema has always been marginalised, if not ignored completely. It has been defined primarily through its 'otherness' or 'difference' from First World cinema, and consumption of it in the West, whether by Asians or non-Asians, is something of an assertion: one has chosen to view an 'alternative' type of cinema. However, this is a cinema which, in the Indian context, is an overridingly dominant, mainstream form, and is itself opposed by an 'Other': the 'new', 'parallel', 'art' (or often simply 'other') cinema which ranges from the work of Satyajit Ray, Shyam Benegal and various regional filmmakers, to Mani Kaul's 'avant-garde' or Anand Patwardhan's 'agitational' political practice. In these terms Indian popular cinema is neither alternative nor a minority form. Moreover, in a global context, by virtue of its sheer volume of output, the Indian entertainment cinema still dominates world film production, and its films are distributed throughout large areas of the Third World (including non-Hindustani-speaking areas and even parts of the Soviet Union), where they are frequently consumed more avidly than both Hollywood and indigenous 'alternative' or political cinemas. Such preference suggests that these films are

From *Screen*, 26: 3–4, pp. 116–32.

seen to be offering something positively different from Hollywood, and in fact, largely because it has always had its own vast distribution markets, Indian cinema has, throughout its long history,[1] evolved as a form which has resisted the cultural imperialism of Hollywood. This is not, of course, to say that it has been 'uninfluenced' by Hollywood: the form has undergone continual change and there has been both inspiration and assimilation from Hollywood and elsewhere, but thematically and structurally, Indian cinema has remained remarkably distinctive.

Corresponding to this diversity of contexts, each constructing Indian popular cinema as a different object, has been considerable confusion of critical and evaluative perspectives. This article will examine the ways in which this cinema has been discussed by critics in India and abroad, and will suggest that, as a first step, the terms of reference of the Indian popular cinema itself should be brought into the picture. It attempts to do this, using material from discussions with Bombay filmmakers[2] about what, for them, constitutes 'good' and 'bad' Hindi cinema in the 1970s and 80s.[3] Points will be illustrated through the example of one very popular, and at the time of release generally lauded, film, *Naseeb* (1981 *Destiny*),[4] whose producer/director, Manmohan Desai, is Bombay's most consistently commercially successful filmmaker. It will be suggested that, while First World critical evaluation outside these terms of reference is, at best, irrelevant and also often racist, to impose a theoretical framework developed in the West – particularly one concerned with examining textual operations and the mechanisms of pleasure – does allow useful questions to be asked, as well as opening up the ethnocentrism of these debates.

The most striking aspect of First World discourse on Indian popular cinema must be its arrogant silence. Until home video killed the market in the 80s, the films had been in regular distribution in Britain for over thirty years, yet ghettoised in immigrant areas, unseen and unspoken by most non-Asians. Even in 1980, when the first Bombay film (*Amar Akbar Anthony*) was shown on British television, it passed more or less unnoticed: the BBC not only programmed it early one Sunday morning, without even troubling to list it with other films on the *Radio Times* film preview page, but pruned it of all its songs and much narrative, including most of the first two reels, which are, not surprisingly, crucial to making any sense of the film. Although the situation has begun to change over the past two years, largely through the initiative of Channel Four's two seasons of Indian entertainment cinema, the traditional attitude remains one of complacent ignorance. Clichés abound: the films are regularly said to be nightmarishly lengthy, second-rate copies of Hollywood trash, to be dismissed with patronising amusement or facetious quips. British television documentaries have a long tradition in perpetuating these attitudes, for the baroque surface of the Hindi film, particularly if taken out of context, makes for automatic comedy. Even *Time Out*'s TV section recently announced *Gunga Jumna* (a classic of Indian cinema, but obviously unpreviewed) with the smug throwaway: 'Sounds turgid, but who knows?'[5].

Where popular Indian films have been taken at all seriously, it has either been to subject them to impertinent criticism according to the canons of dominant Western filmmaking:

> *Mother India* is a rambling tale of personal woe, narrated episodically in unsuitably pretty Technicolour.[6]

or to congratulate them patronisingly:

> All told, a disarmingly enthusiastic piece of Eastern spectacle, exaggerated in presentation and acting, exotic, and yet charmingly naive . . .[7]

They have generally been looked at as 'a stupendous curiosity' – even, in the 50s, as an ethnographic lesson, a way to:

> get to close grips with a handful of (India's) inhabitants. That Indians make the same faces as we do when they fall in love astounds me beyond measure . . .[8]

But the most general theme since the 1960s has been unfavourable comparison with the Indian art cinema:

> It all goes to prove once again that Satyajit Ray is the exception who proves the rule of Indian film-making.[9]

As Indian art cinema is comparatively well known and enthusiastically received in the West, and much conforms to conventions made familiar within European art cinema, Western audience assumptions about film form can remain unchallenged. In fact, the art films serve mostly to confirm the 'inadequacy' of popular cinema to match what are presumed to be universal standards of 'good' cinema – and even of 'art'. Western critics are perhaps not completely to blame, for they take their cues from the Indian upper-middle class intelligentsia and government cultural bodies, who have a long tradition of conniving at this denunciation and, somewhat ironically, themselves insist on evaluating the popular films according to the canons of European and Hollywood filmmaking. One commonly hears complaints about the films' 'lack of realism', about the preposterous 'singing and dancing and running round trees', and that the films are 'all the same' and simply 'copy Hollywood'. To dislike such films is, of course, their privilege. What is disturbing is the tone of defensive apology to the West and the shamefaced disavowal of what is undoubtedly a central feature of modern Indian culture. Thus, for example, Satish Bahadur, comparing popular cinema unfavourably with Satyajit Ray's *Pather Panchali* (which 'was a work of art . . . an organic form'), refers to its 'immaturity' and asserts:

> The heavily painted men and women with exaggerated theatrical gestures and speech, the artificial-looking houses and huts and the painted trees and skies in the films of this tradition are less truthful statements of the reality of India . . .[10]

Even Rangoonwalla, who has devoted considerable energy to compiling much of the published material available on Indian cinema, dismisses the work of the 1970s as 'a very dark period, with a silly absurd kind of escapism rearing its head,'[11] and he is tolerant of popular cinema only if it attempts 'sensible themes'.

One of the central platforms for this kind of criticism is the English language 'quality' press. Week after week, the Indian *Sunday Times* and *Sunday Express* produce jokey review columns which score easy points off the apparent inanities of Hindi cinema. Typical is a *Sunday Times* feature entitled 'Not Only Vulgar but Imitative', which skims through all the critical clichés: absurd stories, poor imitations of Hollywood, lack of originality, and finally the myth of a golden age – of the *1960s* (sic) – when commercial films were 'gentle, warm-hearted, innocent'. Most significant is the fact that the article appeared – by no coincidence – in precisely the week that Bombay was full of Western delegates to the annual film festival. It makes no bones about its intended audience, to whom it defers:

> not surprisingly the West cares little for these films. All that they stand for is exotica, vulgarity and absurdity . . .[12]

Naseeb was, of course, received within this tradition. The *Sunday Express* review was captioned: 'Mindless Boring Melange', and, for example, described a central scene – in fact one that was spectacularly self-parodic, in which many top stars and filmmakers make 'Guest Appearances' at a party – as:

> a 'homage' to . . . all those who have, in the past thirty years, brought the Hindi film down to its present state of total garish mediocrity. In fact, the film encapsulates the entire history of our sub-standard 'entertainment' – elephantine capers . . . the manufactured emotion, the brutalism in talk and acting, the utterly 'gauche' dances . . .[13]

The tone is echoed throughout the popular English-language (hence middle-class) press, and even among regular (middle-class) film-goers there appears to be huge resistance to admitting to finding pleasure in the form. Thus letters to film gossip magazines ran:

> Want to make *Naseeb*? Don't bother about a story or screenplay. You can do without both. Instead rope in almost the entire industry . . . Throw in the entire works: revolving restaurant, London locales, and outfits which even a five year old would be embarrassed to wear to a fancy dress competition. Now, sit back, relax, and watch the cash pour in.[14]
>
> Manmohan Desai's concept of entertainment still revolves around the lost and found theme, with a lot of improbabilities and inanities thrown in . . . But how long can such films continue to click at the box-office? Soon audiences are bound to come to their senses.[15]

There are also, of course, more serious and considered critical positions within India, notably of the politically conscious who argue, quite cogently, that

Hindi cinema is capitalist, sexist, exploitative, 'escapist' mystification, politically and aesthetically reactionary, and moreover that its control of distribution networks blocks opportunities for more radical practitioners. It should, of course, be remembered that what may be pertinent criticism within India may be irrelevant – or racist – in the West, and apparently similar criticisms may have different meanings, uses and effects in different contexts. However, two central objections to all the criticisms do stand out. One is the insistence on evaluating Hindi cinema in terms of filmmaking practices which it has itself rejected, a blanket refusal to allow its own terms of reference to be heard. The second is the reluctance to acknowledge and deal with the fact that Hindi cinema clearly gives enormous pleasure to vast pan-Indian (and Third World) audiences. In view of this, such supercilious criticism does no more than wish the films away. Dismissing them as 'escapism' neither explains them in any useful way, nor offers any basis for political strategy, for it allows no space for questions about the specifics of the audiences' relationship to their so-called 'escapist' fare. What seems to be needed is an analysis which takes seriously both the films and the pleasures they offer, and which attempts to unravel their mode of operation.

Clearly, a body of 'film theory' developed in the West may mislead if it is used to squash Hindi cinema into Western filmmaking categories, particularly if it brutalises or denies the meanings and understandings of participants. Thus, for example, Hollywood genre classification is quite inappropriate to Hindi cinema and, although almost every Hindi film contains elements of the 'musical', 'comedy' and 'melodrama', to refer to the films in any of these ways imposes a significant distortion. Certainly no Indian filmmaker would normally use such classifications. Important distinctions are marked instead by terms such as 'social', 'family social', 'devotional', 'stunt' or even 'multi-starrer' (terms hard to gloss quickly for a Western readership). However, the *concept* of genre, in its broadest sense – as structuring principles of expectation and convention, around which individual films mark repetitions and differences[16] – does appear to be potentially useful in opening up questions about Hindi cinema's distinctive form. In the first place, it moves immediately beyond the tired rantings about Hindi cinema's 'repetitiveness' and 'lack of originality' – although, on this point, some of the Bombay filmmakers are in fact many steps ahead of their so-called 'intellectual' critics:

> People seem to like the same thing again and again, so I repeat it . . . but you always have to give them something different too . . . There can be no such thing as a 'formula film' – if there were, everybody would be making nothing but hits . . .[17]

Secondly, it points to questions about narrative structure, modes of address and conventions of verisimilitude that, at the least, help organise description which can take Indian cinema's own terms of reference into account and from which further questions about spectatorship and pleasure become possible. The rest of this article attempts to illustrate such an approach.

Contrary to common 'intellectual' assumptions within India, the Indian mass audience is ruthlessly discriminating: over 85 per cent of films released in the last two years have not made profits,[18] and these have included films with the biggest budgets and most publicity 'hype'. There is a clear sense among audiences of 'good' and 'bad' films, and the filmmakers, committed as they are to 'pleasing' audiences, make it their business to understand, and internalise, these assessments. While the yardstick of commercial success is of course central – for filmmakers a 'good' film is ultimately one that makes money – they do also have a working model of (what they believe to be) the essential ingredients of a 'good' film and the 'right' way to put these together. This model evolves largely through the informal, but obsessive, post-mortems which follow films whose box-office careers confound expectations, and is undergoing continual, if gradual, redefinition and refinement.

Bombay filmmakers repeatedly stress that they are aiming to make films which differ in both format and content from Western films, that there is a definite skill to making films for the Indian audience, that this audience has specific needs and expectations, and that to compare Hindi films to those of the West, or of the Indian 'art' cinema, is irrelevant. Their statements imply both a sense of the tyranny of this audience and a recognition of the importance of a class link between filmmaker and audience. The example of the barely educated Mehboob Khan, whose cult classic *Mother India* (1957) still draws full houses today, is often cited proudly – buttressed by assertions that his film is 'of our soil', 'full of real Indian emotions' – and by that token inaccessible to the emotionally retarded, if not totally cold-blooded, West.[19]

Whatever the critics' clichés may suggest, no successful Bombay filmmaker ever simply 'copies' Western films. Of course, most borrow openly both story ideas and sometimes complete sequences from foreign cinemas, but borrowings must always be integrated with Indian filmmaking conventions if the film is to work with the Indian audience: no close copy of Hollywood has ever been a hit.[20] Filmmakers say that the essence of 'Indianisation' lies in: (1) the way that the storyline is developed; (2) the crucial necessity for 'emotion' (Western films are often referred to as 'cold'); and (3) the skilful blending and integration of songs, dances, fights and other 'entertainment values' within the body of the film. There is also the more obvious 'Indianisation' of values and other content, including reference to aspects of Indian life with which audiences will identify, particularly religion and patriotism. It is, for example, generally believed that science fiction would be outside the cultural reference of the Indian audience, and censorship restrictions mean that films about war, or overtly about national or international politics, risk being banned.

The filmmakers' terms of reference often emerge most clearly when discussing a film which is judged a 'failure'. A trade press review[21] of *Desh Premee* (1982 *Patriot*), one of Manmohan Desai's few unsuccessful films, particularly revealing.

> *Desh Premee* has all the ingredients that make a film a hit, yet every aspect is markedly defective. Firstly, the story has a plot and incidents but the narration is so unskilled that it does not sustain interest. There is no grip to the story. The situations are neither melodramatic, nor do they occur spontaneously, but look forced and contrived. Secondly, the music side is not as strong as the film demands. All songs are good average, but not one song can be declared a superhit. Thirdly, emotional appeal is lacking. Although there are a few scenes which try to arouse feelings, they fail to hit their objective. Fourthly, production values are average, considering the producer. The traditional grandeur of Manmohan Desai is missing, as are technical values.
>
> *Desh Premee* has no sex appeal. The romantic part is too short. Comedy scenes and melodramatic scenes are missing . . . [My precis: the stars' roles are not properly justified . . . several appear for too short a time . . . action, thrills and background music are only average . . .]
>
> Several of the scenes look like repetitions from many old hits and there is no dose of originality in the film . . . Although every formula film is basically unrealistic and far from the truths of life, everything can still be presented with acceptable realism and logic. But in this film there are several 'unbelievables' even with normal cinematic licence granted. This is not expected from any seasoned film-maker.[22]

Particularly interesting is the order in which defects are listed: the screenplay is recognised to be crucial, the music (i.e. the songs) of almost equal importance, 'emotional appeal' a significant third, and fourth are production values, or expensive spectacle. A 'dose of originality' and 'acceptable realism and logic' are additional points of general importance. Big stars are a decided advantage (viz. 'the ingredients that make a film a hit'), but cannot in themselves save a film – particularly if not exploited adequately, and in contrast, *Naseeb* on its release had been particularly praised for 'Assembling the biggest starcast ever (and) . . . justifying each and all of them.'[23]

Two themes emerge from this review: firstly that of the expected narrative movement and mode of address, and secondly, the question of verisimilitude.

Narrative

Indian filmmakers often insist that screenplay and direction are crucial and the storyline only the crudest vehicle from which to wring 'emotion' and onto which to append spectacle.

> It's much more difficult to write a screenplay for *Naseeb* than for a Western or 'art' film, where you have a straight storyline. A commercial Hindi film has to have sub-plots and gags, and keep its audience involved with no story or logic.[24]

The assertion that Hindi films have 'no story' is sometimes confusing to those unfamiliar with the genre. 'Who cares who gets the story credits? Everyone knows our films have no stories', and, in fact, the story credits are often farmed out to accommodating friends or relatives for 'tax adjustment' purposes. However, Hindi cinema has by no means broken the hallowed bounds of narrative convention, and the most immediately striking thing about *Naseeb* is the fiendishly complex convolutions of this multi-stranded and very long succession of events, which nevertheless culminate in an exemplarily neat resolution. What is meant by 'no story' is, first, that the storyline will be almost totally predictable to the Indian audience, being a repetition, or rather, an unmistakable transformation, of many other Hindi films, and second, that it will be recognised by them as a 'ridiculous' pretext for spectacle and emotion. Films which really have 'no story' (i.e. non-narrative), or are 'just a slice of life', or have the comparatively single-stranded narratives of many contemporary Western films, are considered unlikely to be successful.

> The difference between Hindi and Western films is like that between an epic and a short story.[25]

Not only is a film expected to be two-and-a-half to three hours long, but it is usual for the plot to span at least two generations, beginning with the main protagonists' births or childhoods and jumping twenty or so years (often in a single shot) to the action of the present. There is of course good evidence that Hindi films have evolved from village traditions of epic narration, and the dramas and the characters, as well as the structure, of the mythological epics are regularly and openly drawn upon. Filmmakers often insist that: 'Every film can be traced back to these stories', and even that 'There are only two stories in the world, the *Ramayana* and the *Mahabharat*.'[26] In fact, it is the form and movement of the narrative that tends to distinguish the Hindi film, the crux of this being that the balance between narrative development and spectacular or emotional excess is rather different.

As the *Trade Guide* review implies, audiences expect to be addressed in an ordered succession of modes. *Desh Premee* had failed allegedly because, among other reasons, there was no comedy, no melodrama, too little 'romance' and no 'emotion', while *Naseeb* had earlier been commended because 'everything' was there:

> balancing beautifully the story, the plot, the screenplay, the dialogue and dramatic situations . . . (and) providing properly the thrills, the action, boxing, chasing and other modes . . .[27]

Filmmakers talk about 'blending the *masalas*[28] in proper proportions' as one might discuss cookery, and (defensive stances for the benefit of Westerners or 'intellectuals' notwithstanding), they have a clear perception that these elements, including the inexcusably maligned songs and dances, are an important part of the work of the film, which is to achieve an overall balance of 'flavours'. Clearly, something of a commercial motivation is at work here (one puts in 'something for everybody'), but it is also considered very important that one does not 'just shove these things in', for, it is said, 'the audience always knows if you do'.

Naseeb's narrative movement is by way of swift juxtaposition of cameo scenes of spectacular – or humorous – impact, rather than steady development of drama. Clearly, as in all mainstream cinema, Hindi films work to offer the viewer a position of coherence and mastery, both through narrative closure and by providing a focus for identification within the film (in *Naseeb* this is a male hero with, as will be argued below, a particularly reassuring mastery of potent phantasy). However, spectacular and emotional excess will invariably be privileged over linear narrative development. The spectator is expected to be involved not primarily through anticipation of *what* will happen next, but through *how* it will happen and affective involvement in the happening: excitement, thrill, fear, envy, wonder, not to mention the eroticism which lies behind the desire for spectacle itself. While many Hindi films depend essentially on emotional drama (although with spectacle always of importance), *Naseeb* is primarily about spectacle – with song and dance, locations, costumes, fights and 'thrills' (or stunts), most of Bombay's top stars, and sets which range from a luxury glass mansion to a baroque revolving restaurant and a fanciful 'London' casino. 'If the story is weak, you have to be a showman and show the public everything,'[29] says Desai. But unregulated, uncontained spectacle, however novel, interesting and pleasurable, always risks losing its audience's involvement (e.g. *Trade Guide*'s: 'The narration is so unskilled that it does not sustain interest'). *Naseeb* depends on two strategies to avoid this. One is its skill at swift transition between well balanced 'modes' of spectacle, the other the strength and reassuring familiarity of the narrative, which is, in fact, structured by discourses which are deeply rooted in Indian social life and in the unconscious (and in this its relationship with Indian mythological and folk narrative becomes particularly apparent).

Briefly, the story of *Naseeb* concerns the friendships, love affairs, family reunions and fights between the (adult) children of four men who won a lottery ticket together and fell out over division of the spoils. Any attempt at succinct summary of the intricacies of this extraordinarily convoluted plot and its characters' relationships is doomed to failure – nor is it strictly relevant. It is probably enough to point out that the story is built around three chestnuts of Hindi cinema which were particularly popular in the late 1970s/'80s, the themes being: (1) 'lost and found' (parents and children are separated and reunited years later following revelation of mistaken identities); (2) '*dostana*' (two male friends fall in love with the same woman and the one who discovers this sacrifices his love – and often life – for the male friendship or *dostana*); and (3) revenge (villains get their just deserts at the hands of the heroes they wronged). Analysis of the narrative suggests that the discourses which structure it are those of kinship (the blood relationship and bonds expressed in its idiom), 'duty' and social obligation, solidarity, trust, and also a metaphysical discourse of 'fate' or 'destiny' and human impotence in the face of this. Order, or equilibrium, is presented as a state in which humans live in harmony with fate, respecting social obligations and ties of friendship or family. Disruption of this order is the result of selfish greed, fate (or human meddling in fate) and (hetero)-sexual desire.

The narrative is built upon a simple opposition between good/morality and evil/decadence, and connotations of 'traditional' and 'Indian' are appended to morality, which is an ideal of social relations which includes respect for kinship and friendship obligations, destiny, patriotism and religion (and religious tolerance) as well as controlled sexuality. Evil or decadence is broadly categorised as 'non-traditional' and 'Western', although the West is not so much a place, or even a culture, as an emblem of exotic, decadent otherness, signified by whisky, bikinis, an uncontrolled sexuality and what is seen as lack of 'respect' for elders and betters, and (from men) towards womanhood.

Filmmakers are quite aware of building their narratives around terms of an opposition so basic that audiences cannot easily avoid immersion:

> Kinship emotion in India is very strong – so this element always works – that's what 'lost and found' is about. It doesn't work so well with educated audiences who go several days without seeing their families, but it works with B and C grade audiences who get worried if they don't see a family member by 6.30 p.m., whose family members are an important part of themselves and their experience of the world.[30]

However, the films also appear to deal with these basic family relationships at a much deeper level, and what appears to be highly charged imagery, which is not organised into conscious narrative coherence, regularly erupts in these films. Thus, for example, *Naseeb* boasts a scene whose parallels with the Oedipal scenario are hard to ignore, in which the father and 'good' son/hero, unaware of their blood relationship, are locked in mortal combat – the father wielding a knife above his prostrate son. Just as one is about to kill the other, the hero's foster mother, who had fallen and lost consciousness, revives, appears at the top of the stairs with a bleeding wound on her head prominently bandaged, and shrieks. The action freezes, mistaken identities are explained, and the son agrees to follow his father into combat with the villains. For this encounter the father hands over to him a special ring, bearing the mark of Hindu religion (the sacred symbol OM), which protects him in a succession of fights and later becomes the mechanism by which he escapes, on a rope, from a burning tower in which the villains (that which is not socialised) meet gory deaths. In fact, somewhat bizarrely, the film can be read as a narrative of masculine psychic development (the emergence of the sexed subject within the social order), with the early scenes of anarchic sexuality followed by an Oedipal crisis and a subsequent drama of sons following the Father into the Symbolic Order.

To point to the kind of reading that a very literal psychoanalysis produces is not to advocate reducing *Naseeb* – or psychoanalysis – to this. However, it does raise interesting questions about the relevance of psychoanalysis in the Indian context and, in fact, the greatest problem is not how to *apply* such concepts, but whether one can *ignore* patternings which obtrude in so implausibly striking a manner. Although few films order their imagery in so fortuitously neat a diachrony, its potency and overtness is not unusual, and what a letter-writer can dismiss as nothing but 'the lost and found theme with a lot of improbabilities and inanities thrown in' can be very far from inane in the context of the spectator's own phantasy.

VERISIMILITUDE

Beyond the basic suspension of disbelief on which cinema depends, any genre evolves and institutionalises its own conventions, which allow credibility to become unproblematic within certain parameters.[31] Compared with the conventions of much Western cinema, Hindi films appear to have patently preposterous narratives, overblown dialogue (frequently evaluated by filmmakers on whether or not it is 'clap-worthy'), exaggeratedly stylised acting, and to show disregard for psychological characterisation, history, geography, and even, sometimes, camera placement rules.[32]

Tolerance of overt phantasy has always been high in Hindi cinema, with little need to anchor the material in what Western conventions might recognise as a discourse of 'realism', and slippage between registers does not have to be marked or rationalised. The most obvious example is the song sequences, which are much less commonly 'justified' within the story (for example, introduced as stage performances by the fictional characters) than in Hollywood musicals. Hindi film songs are usually tightly integrated, through words and mood, within the *flow* of the film – 'In my films, if you miss a song, you have missed an important link between one part of the narration and the next'[33] – and misguided attempts to doctor Hindi films for Western audiences by cutting out the songs are always fatal. However, the song sequences (often also dream sequences) do permit excesses of phantasy which are more problematic elsewhere in the film, for they specifically allow that continuities of time and place be disregarded, that heroines may change saris between shots and the scenery skip continents between – verses, whenever the interests of spectacle or mood require it.

Although Hindi film phantasy needs comparatively slight authenticating strategies, *Naseeb* does negotiate the terrain with care, and this is undoubtedly one of its strengths. In fact the viewer is immersed gradually, as the film moves through three phases: an initial mode bordering on 'social realism', a second period of self-reflexivity and parody, and a final phase in which dream imagery and logic are unproblematic. Particularly interesting are the middle scenes, which make self-conscious and sophisticated play with the ambiguity between registers. Thus, for example, in the party song mentioned above 'real' Bombay film stars appear, as themselves, at a film party located firmly within *Naseeb*'s fiction, and, throughout, the central hero's romance is presented largely as a parody of Hindi cinema clichés, with him actually commenting, after a dazzling display of kung-fu skills to rescue his pop-singer girl-friend from rapacious thugs: 'It's just like a Hindi film'. Later, when he finds her modelling for a throat pastille advertising film on the beach, he 'mistakes' the film scenario for 'reality' and, as the director yells 'Start camera' and a crew member runs into frame with a microphone, the hero (speaking to camera in both the film and the film within the film) begins a flowery proposal of marriage in the style of Hindi film dialogue.

Naseeb is undoubtedly unusual in taking the self-reflexive and self-parodic elements inherent in much Hindi cinema so far, but the fact that it *is* acceptable is significant. Despite what middle-class critics imply, it is clear, if one experiences an Indian audience irreverently clapping, booing and laughing with the films, that they know perfectly well that the films are 'ridiculous', 'unreal' and offer impossible solutions, and that pleasure arises in spite of – and probably because of – this knowledge.

However, this is not to say that 'anything goes': as the *Trade Guide* review implied, there is a firm sense of 'acceptable realism and logic', beyond which material is rejected as 'unbelievable'. In fact, the criteria of verisimilitude in Hindi cinema appear to refer primarily to a film's skill in manipulating the rules of the film's moral universe, and one is more likely to hear accusations of 'unbelievability' if the codes of, for example, ideal kinship behaviour are ineptly transgressed (i.e. a son kills his mother; or a father knowingly and callously causes his son to suffer), than if the hero is a superman who singlehandedly knocks out a dozen burly henchmen and then bursts into song.

Any rigorous discussion of the conventions of verisimilitude and the apparent tolerance of 'non-realism' in Hindi cinema would have to consider much wider issues, including concepts and conventions of 'realism' in Indian culture generally. However, even examination of the cinematic heritage on which *Naseeb* draws is suggestive and, significantly, Manmohan Desai and two of his writers learned their craft as apprentices in the Wadia studios, producers of the two most popular genres in Indian filmmaking history, the 'mythologicals' and the stunt films. Although mythologicals were generally considered to be of higher status ('the Brahmin of film genres'), filmmakers recognised their overlap ('mythologicals were just special effect and stunt films which happened to be about gods rather than men'), for both were primarily moral stories with displays of magical happenings, supermen and gods. On the other hand, the influence of Hollywood cannot be ignored, from James Bond, whose idiom inflects many recent films, to the phenomenal impact of Douglas Fairbanks in the 1920s (when *Thief of Baghdad* was the decade's most popular film),[34] or of Charlie Chaplin, who was as big a star in India as elsewhere. Echoes can be found of all these traditions in *Naseeb*.

The Spectator

It would appear that the spectator-subject of Hindi cinema is positioned rather differently from that of much Western cinema. In fact, even on the most overt level, Indian cinema audience behaviour is distinctive: involvement in the films is intense and audiences clap, sing, recite familiar dialogue with the actors, throw coins at the screen (in appreciation of spectacle), 'tut tut' at emotionally moving scenes, cry openly and laugh and jeer knowingly. Moreover, it is expected that audiences will see a film they like several times, and so-called 'repeat value' is deliberately built into a production by the filmmakers, who believe that the keys to this are primarily the stars, music, spectacle, emotion and dialogue – this last having a greater significance than in Western cinema.[35]

What seems to emerge in Hindi cinema is an emphasis on emotion and spectacle rather than tight narrative, on *how* things will happen rather than *what* will happen next, on a succession of modes rather than linear denouement, on familiarity and repeated viewings rather than 'originality' and novelty, on a moral disordering to be (temporarily) resolved rather than an enigma to be solved. The spectator is addressed and moved through the films primarily via affect, although this is structured and contained by narratives whose power and insistence derives from their very familiarity, coupled with the fact that they are deeply rooted (in the psyche and in traditional mythology).

Whether, and how, one can relate the 'spectator-subject' of the films to the Indian 'social audience'[36] is not immediately clear, although certain comparisons with other discourses within India through which subjectivity is lived are suggestive. For example, it has been suggested[37] that Hindu caste, kinship and religious 'ideologies', in particular beliefs in destiny and *Karma*, position a decentred, less individuated social subject. One can also point to specific cultural traditions of performance and entertainment which must be of direct relevance, notably the forms on which early cinema drew, from the performances of the professional story-tellers and village dramatisations of the mythological epics, to the excesses of spectacle ('vulgar' and 'garish' according to contemporary critics) of the late nineteenth and early twentieth century Urdu Parsee theatre with its indulgent adaptations of Shakespeare and Victorian melodrama. Beyond this, one must remember that Sanskrit philosophy boasts a coherent theory of aesthetics which bears no relation to Aristotelian aesthetics and, rejecting the unities of time and place and the dramatic development of narrative, the theory of *rasa* (flavours/moods) is concerned with moving the spectator through the text in an ordered succession of modes of affect (*rasa*), by means of highly stylised devices. All Indian classical drama, dance and music draw on this aesthetic.

Of course, most present-day filmmakers make no conscious reference to this heritage and, for example, the privileging of spectacle and music can be accounted for in many other ways, not least the pragmatic one that, to make money, the films need to appeal across wide linguistic and cultural divides within India itself. 'Tradition' cannot be used to provide too neat an 'explanation' of the present form – apart from anything else, Indian cultural 'tradition' is a heterogeneous assimilation of Sanskritic, Islamic, Judeo-Christian and many other influences, and could be selectively drawn upon to 'explain' almost any present form. Moreover, invoking tradition also holds dangers of uncritically romanticising the present form as exotically 'other' and ignoring its diverse influences and constant evolution. Its role should rather be seen as one of a framework of terms of reference within which certain developments have been stifled, others allowed to evolve unproblematically, and which can be used to throw light on the different possibilities of forms of address which might be expected or tolerated by an Indian audience.

This article has attempted to examine Indian popular cinema's 'terms of reference' by placing it within a number of contexts: primarily that of the filmmakers' own descriptions of their films and generic expectations, but also briefly that of audiences, and of earlier and co-existing cultural forms and traditions. There is, of course, the problem of the infinite regress of context: no description of conditions and discourses could ever be 'adequate' to contextualising Indian cinema. But any criticism which ignores the specificity of the textual operations and pleasures of Indian popular cinema will remain caught up in the confusion and condescension which marked British responses to the London release of *Aan* in 1952:

> But having proved themselves masters of every cliché in the Western cinema, its remarkable producers should have a look around home and make an Indian film.[38]

Notes

1. The first Indian feature film, a mythological, D. G. Phalke's *Raja Harischandra*, was released in 1913.
2. This refers here primarily to those employed in the film industry as producers, directors, writers and distributors.
3. Films produced in the Hindustani language (and primarily in Bombay) account for less than 20 per cent of pan-Indian film production. However, they alone are distributed throughout the country and, having the biggest budgets, stars and hence prestige, influence almost all regional language filmmaking.
4. *Naseeb*'s box-office returns rank with those of three other films as the highest of 1981. It is one of the most expensive 'multi-starrers' ever produced in India (distribution rights sold for a little over £2 million in total).
5. Geoff Andrew in *Time Out*, August 2–8, 1984.
6. James Green, in the *Observer*, March 26, 1961, referring to *Mother India*.
7. 'ER' in the *Monthly Film Bulletin*, September 1952, vol. 19, no. 224, referring to *Aan*.
8. Virginia Graham in *The Spectator*, July 18, 1952, referring to *Aan*.
9. *Monthly Film Bulletin*, August 1963, vol. 20, no. 355, referring to *Gunga Jumna*.
10. A. Vasudev and P. Lenglet (eds), *Indian Superbazaar*, Vikas, Delhi, 1983, p. 112.
11. F. Rangoonwalla, *Indian Cinema Past and Present*, Clarion, Delhi, 1983.
12. Khalid Mohamed in *Times of India*, 'Sunday Review', January 8, 1984.
13. *Sunday Express*, May 3, 1981.
14. Iqbal Masud in *Cine Blitz*, July 1981.
15. *Star and Style*, November 13, 1981.
16. Stephen Neale, *Genre* London, British Film Institute, 1980.
17. Manmohan Desai, in interview with the author, May 1981.

18. *Trade Guide*, January 5, 1985. Video piracy has had a particularly harsh effect on the Bombay film industry. However, even in the late 70s it is alleged that only 10 per cent of releases made 'sizeable' profits (*Report of the Working Group on National Film Policy*, Ministry of Information and Broadcasting, May 1980, p. 17).
19. It has, in fact, been generally well received in the West and is the only Indian film ever to have won an Oscar nomination (Best Foreign Film, 1958).
20. Where European and Hollywood cinemas have drawn upon literary traditions for their story ideas, Hindi cinema has primarily looked to other films for basic stories to adapt. Inspiration from Hollywood is often integrated with storylines from the Indian mythological epics, e.g. a recent proposal 'for a cross between *The Omen* and the *Mahabharat*'. The only virtual frame-to-frame remakes of Hollywood films (*Khoon Khoon* of *Dirty Harry* and *Manoranjan* of *Irma La Douce*) flopped disastrously. So did *Man Pasand*, based closely on *My Fair Lady*, a failure which the BBC ignored in its dismissive documentary on the film in 1982.
21. There are two weekly Bombay trade papers, *Trade Guide* and *Film Information*. Their reviews are generally respected in the film industry (unlike all other press reviews, especially the Sunday critics') and do in fact have a good record in predicting subsequent box-office performance.
22. *Trade Guide*, Special Edition, April 2, 1982 (with slight stylistic adaptations).
23. *Trade Guide*, May 3, 1981.
24. K. K. Shukla, screenplay writer of *Naseeb*, in interview with the author, April 1981.
25. Javed Akhtar, screenplay writer, in interview with the author, February 1981.
26. The two key mythological epics of India.
27. *Trade Guide*, May 3, 1981.
28. Literally, spices.
29. Manmohan Desai, quoted in *Bombay* magazine, April 22, 1981.
30. K. K. Shukla, screenplay writer, in interview with the author, May 1981.
31. Stephen Neale, op cit.
32. Camera placement rules can be disregarded, particularly in action (fight) scenes, which seem to be allowed something of the non-continuity conventions of song sequences.
33. Raj Kapoor, filmmaker, in interview on *Visions*, Channel Four, February 1983.
34. E. Barnouw and S. Krishnaswami, *Indian Film*, Oxford University Press, 1980, p. 47.
35. Audiences often talk of dialogue as a central draw, and books and records of film dialogue sell sometimes better than collections of film music.
36. Annette Kuhn, 'Women's Genres', *Screen*, January–February 1984, vol. 25, no. 1, p. 23.
37. L. Dumont, *Homo Hierarchicus*, London, Weidenfeld and Nicolson, 1970.
38. Unreferenced in BFI microfiche collection of *Aan* reviews in UK newspapers, 1952.

15

ADDRESSING THE SPECTATOR OF A 'THIRD WORLD' NATIONAL CINEMA: THE BOMBAY 'SOCIAL' FILM OF THE 1940S AND 1950S

Ravi S. Vasudevan

Recent discussions of cinema and national identity in the 'third world' context have tended, by and large, to cluster around the concept of a 'third cinema'. Here the focus has been on recovering or reinventing 'national' aesthetic and narrative traditions against the homogenizing impulses of Hollywood in its domination over markets and normative standards. One of the hallmarks of third cinema theory has been its firmly unchauvinist approach to the 'national'. In its references to wider international aesthetic practices, and especially to modernist drives, third cinema asserts but problematizes the boundaries between nation and other. In the process, it also explores the ways in which the suppressed internal others of the nation, whether of class, sub- or counter-nationality, ethnic group or gender, can find a voice.[1]

A substantial lacuna in this project has been any sustained understanding of the domestic commercial cinema in the 'third world'. This is important because in countries such as India the commercial film has, since the dawn of the 'talkies', successfully marginalized Hollywood's position in the domestic market. This is not to claim that it has functioned within an entirely self-referential autarchy. The Bombay cinema stylistically integrated aspects of the world 'standard', and has also been influential in certain foreign markets. But it constitutes something like a 'nation space' against the dominant norms of Hollywood, and so ironically fulfils aspects of the role which the avant-garde third cinema proclaims as its own. Clearly, the difference in language cannot be the major explanation for this autonomy, for other national cinemas have

From *Screen*, vol. 36: 4, pp. 305–24.

succumbed to the rule of the Hollywood film. Instead, it is in the peculiarities of the Indian commercial film as an entertainment form that we may find the explanation for its ascendency over the home market.

The formation of a national market for the Bombay cinema was a multi-layered phenomenon. Bombay became ascendent in the home market only in the 1950s. Earlier, Pune in Maharashtra and Calcutta in Bengal were important centres of film production, catering to the Marathi and Bengali speaking 'regional' audience as well as to the Hindi audience which is the largest linguistic market in the country. While these regional markets continued to exist, Bombay became the main focus of national film production. This ascendency was curtailed by the emergence of important industries in Tamilnadu, Andhra Pradesh and Kerala, producing films in Tamil, Telugu and Malayalam. From the 1980s, these centres produced as many, and often more, films than Bombay.[2] There has been a certain equivalence in the narrative form of these cinemas, but each region contributed its distinctive features to the commercial film. In the Tamil and Telugu cases the cinema also has a strong link with the politics of regional and ethnic identity.

The achievement of the commercial cinema has had ambivalent implications for the social and political constitution of its spectator. All of these cinemas are involved in constructing a certain abstraction of national identity; by national identity I mean here not only the pan-Indian one, but also regional constructions of national identity. This process of abstraction suppresses other identities, either through stereotyping or through absence. The Bombay cinema has a special role here, because it positions other national/ethnic/religious and social identities (it has largely avoided representing the crucial question of caste) in stereotypical ways under an overarching north Indian, majoritarian Hindu identity. The stereotypes of the 'southerner' (or 'Madrasi', a term which dismissively collapses the entire southern region), the Bengali, the Parsi, the Muslim, the Sikh and the Christian occupy the subordinate positions in this universe. Bombay crystallized as the key centre for the production of national fictions just at the moment that the new state came into existence, so its construction of the national narrative carries a particular force.[3]

Indian commercial cinema has exerted an international presence in countries of Indian immigration as in East Africa, Mauritius, the Middle East and South East Asia, but also in a significant swathe of Northern Africa.[4] It has also been popular in the countries of the former Soviet Union and China. Such a sphere of influence makes one think of a certain arc of narrative form separate from, if overlapping at points with, the larger hegemony exercised by Hollywood. From the description of the cultural 'peculiarities' of the Bombay cinema which follows, one could speculate whether its narrative form has a special resonance in 'transitional' societies. The diegetic world of this cinema is primarily governed by the logic of kinship relations, and its plot driven by family conflict. The system of dramaturgy is a melodramatic one, displaying the characteristic ensemble of manichaeism, bipolarity, the privileging of the moral over the psychological, and the deployment of coincidence. And the relationship between narrative, performance sequence and action spectacle is loosely structured in the fashion of a cinema of attractions.[5] In addition to these features, the system of narration incorporates Hollywood codes of continuity editing in a fitful, unsystematic fashion, relies heavily on visual forms such as the tableau and inducts stable cultural codes of looking of a more archaic sort. Aspects of this picture echo the form of early Euro-American cinema, indicating that what appeared as a fairly abbreviated moment in the history of Western cinema has defined the long-term character of this influential cinema of 'another world'. What is required here is a comparative account of narrative forms in 'transitional' societies which might set out a different story of the cinema than the dominant Euro-American one.

In this paper I want to isolate certain aspects of this way of framing the Bombay cinema, focusing in particular on how the spectator of the 'national film' is addressed. I conceive of this as 'an analysis, even if rudimentary, of the position of the spectator within his/her cultural context, within certain large representational and belief systems'.[6] I am using examples from the 1940s and 1950s Hindi social film – the genre used to address the problems of modern life – to explain how the cinema invited the spectator to assume an identity defined along the axis of gender, class and nationhood. I want to do this primarily by identifying the way in which filmic visual culture and narrative form impinge on and shape the subjectivity of the spectator. For a large part of this paper, I will be concerned with the textual constitution of the spectator, but in the final section I will outline the dimensions of a historically significant spectatorial position that developed in the 1940s. I will focus on the way in which prevailing anxieties about the definition of a national identity at the time of the country's independence were reflected in offscreen discourses about actors and directors and how they influenced filmic reception. The popular cinema was involved in mapping a symbolic space which envisaged the national formation as being grounded in certain hierarchies. Here, I lay particular emphasis on the relations between the majority Hindu group and the minority Muslim as it was relayed through film narratives and offscreen discourses.

A Dominant Paradigm

Before turning to visual and narrative analysis, I want briefly to summarize some of the conventional viewpoints about the commercial film in India and the nature of its spectator. The dominant view is that of a tradition of film criticism associated with Satyajit Ray and the Calcutta Film Society in the 1950s. This school of criticism, which has proved influential in subsequent mainstream film criticism, assailed the popular cinema for its derivativeness from the sensational aspects of the US cinema, the melodramatic externality and stereotyping of its characters, and especially for its failure to focus on the psychology of human interaction. In these accounts, the spectator of the popular film emerges as an immature, indeed infantile, figure, one bereft of the rationalist imperatives required for the Nehru era's project of national construction.[7]

Recent analyses of the popular cinemas in the 'non-Western' world suggest to me that the melodramatic mode has, with various indigenous modifications, been a characteristic form of narrative and dramaturgy in societies undergoing the transition to modernity.[8] 'National' criticisms of this prevalent mode have taken the particular form that I have just specified, and have had both developmentalist and democratic components. The implication was that, insofar as the melodramatic mode was grounded in an anti-individualist ethos, it would undercut the rational, critical outlook required for the development of a just, dynamic and independent nation.[9]

In the Indian case, this premise of modern film criticism has been taken in rather different directions. The critic Chidananda Das Gupta emerges from the dominant tradition, being one of the founder members of the Calcutta Film Society. His recent book, *The Painted Face*,[10] argues that the commercial film catered to a spectator who had not severed his ties from the countryside and so had a traditional or pre-modern relationship to the image, one which incapacitated him or her from distinguishing between image and reality.[11] Das Gupta also argues that the pre-rationalist spectator was responsive to Bombay cinema's focus on family travails and identity, a focus which displaces attention from the larger social domain. He describes the spectator caught up in the psychic trauma brought about by threatened loss of the mother and the struggle for adult identity as adolescent and self-absorbed or 'totalist'.[12] We have echoes here of the realist criticism of the 1950s in its reference to the spectator of the commercial film as infantile. There is a class component to the psychological paradigm, in which the uprooted, lumpen and working class are regarded as the main audience for the Bombay film. Such a conception of the spectator ultimately has political implications. Das Gupta sees this social and psychic configuration reflecting the gullible mentality that enabled the rise to power of the actor-politicians of the south, M. G. Ramachandran and N. T. Rama Rao.[13] The naive spectator actually believed his screen idols to be capable of the prowess they displayed onscreen. In Das Gupta's view, the rational outlook required for the development of a modern nation state is still lacking, and the popular cinema provides us with an index of the cognitive impairment of the majority of the Indian people.

This psychological and social characterization of the premodern spectator is pervasive, even if it is not used to the same ends as Das Gupta's. The social psychologist Ashish Nandy, while working outside (and, indeed, against) the realist tradition, shares some of its assumptions about the psychological address of the commercial film.[14] Nandy argues that the personality as expressed in Indian culture differed from that conceived by modern Western culture. There are two features in his conception of the psychical difference between pre-modern and modern forms in film narratives. For him, the dominant spectator of the popular cinema, caught in 'traditional' arenas of life and work, is quite remote from the outlook of the modern middle class; as such, this spectator is attracted to a narrative which ritually neutralizes the discomfiting features of social change, those modern thought patterns and practices which have to be adopted for reasons of survival. Regressing into a submissive familial frame of reference provides one narrative route for the traumatized spectator. But there is a second, contestatory psychic trajectory. Nandy suggests that Indian culture was defined by androgynous elements which provided the most fertile form of resisting colonial, and more broadly modern, paradigms of progress. He embraces the cultural indices of a subjectivity which is not governed by the rationalist psychology and reality orientation of that contested other. In this sense he valorizes that which Das Gupta sees as a drawback.

So a psychical matrix for understanding the address of the commercial Bombay film to its spectator, echoing in some respects the realist criticism of the 1950s, has been extended into the more explicitly psychoanalytical interpretations of spectatorial dispositions and cognitive capacities. Ironically, these premises are shared both by those critical of the commercial film and its spectator for their lack of reality orientation, and those who valorize Indian culture's resistance to modern forms of consciousness. These arguments in turn support different visions of how the relationship between psychology, class and society/nation can give rise to different dynamics of social transformation.

The popular cinema is much more complicated than these criticisms allow. Greater attention has to be paid to the relationship between family and society, between the private and the public, and especially the relations of power within which this subjectivity is produced. For instance, a marked feature of these formulations is the absence of any understanding of patriarchy, of the gendered authority which I will argue is central to understanding the sociopolitical vision of the popular film. Film studies in India will have to engage with the terms of identity offered by the cinema, its fantasy scenarios and its norms of authority and responsibility instead of insisting that an 'adult' identity is non-negotiable or, in certain countercultural readings, undesirable. Above all, it will have to look at these questions as ones of cinematic narration.

An Indian Melodrama

On the issue of personality construction and its implications for social transformation, a useful point of departure is the elaborate Euro–American theoretical mapping of melodramatic modes of theatre and fiction. It is worth recalling that British theatre exercised considerable influence on the development of the nineteenth-century Indian urban theatre.[15] In Peter Brooks's work,[16] melodrama emerged in the nineteenth century as a form which spoke of a post-sacred universe in which the certainties of traditional meaning and hierarchical authority had been displaced. The melodramatic narrative constantly makes an effort to recover this lost security, but meaning comes to be increasingly founded in the personality. Characters take on essential, psychic resonances corresponding to family identities and work out forbidden conflicts and desires. The family is then positioned as the new locus of meaning. The spectator is addressed through the most basic registers of experience, with the narratives focusing on primal triggers of desire and anxiety. In the process, the social dimension is not displaced, but collapses into the familial and, indeed, the family itself becomes a microcosm of the social level. Melodramatic narratives therefore tend to represent the most significant characters of social life as key familial figures, father, mother and child. It would be a mistake then to categorize these narratives as bounded by the psychic universe of the inward, family-fixated adolescent. That would be to reduce the universe constructed by film narratives to their foundational address.

However, a melodramatic narrative and dramaturgy is also employed in Indian film genres such as the mythological and devotional, not only in post-sacred genres such as the social. To further confound the secular dimensions of melodrama, even in the Bombay 'social', the genre of the modern day, women often employ a traditional Hindu idiom deifying the husband. What implications does this have for melodrama as a so-called post-sacred form?

Narrative structures and strategies are rather more complicated than these religious idioms would suggest. The sociologist Veena Das, in her article on the popular mythological film *Jai Santoshi Ma/Hail Santoshi Ma* (Vijay Sharma, 1975),[17] and the art critic Geeta Kapur, in her analysis of the 'devotional', *Sant Tukaram* (Fatehlal and Damle, 1936),[18] show that the invocation of the sacred is continuous with the reference to non-sacred space, that of the family drama and everyday activity. And Anuradha Kapur's account of the urban Indian Parsi theatre suggests that the discourse of the sacred was subordinated to an emerging discourse of the real through the adoption of realist representational strategies. In her analysis, the representation of the godly through the frontal mode of representation and direct address characteristic of ritual forms is complicated by the integration of these modes into the lateral movement of characters and by features of continuity narrative. The face of the god is in turn stripped of the ornamental features highlighted in ritual drama, and his human incarnation underlined.[19]

As far as the female devotional idiom in socials is concerned, it can paper over the powerful chasms which films open up within the ideology of masculine authority and female submission.[20] The case of the female devotee especially suggests the ambiguities which may lie beneath the invocation of male sacred authority. Feminist critics have noted that it is possible to interpret the female devotional tradition as primarily emphasizing female desire, a strategy which both circumvents patriarchy and reformulates it.[21]

In all these cases, therefore, a complication of the sacred or an outward movement into the secular form is observable. We could say that a melodramatic tendency of failed or uncertain resacralization is also at work here. An Indian melodrama, both as a phenomenon having a direct genealogy with its Western counterparts, as well as a larger cultural enterprise concerning the formation of new subjectivities, therefore has a definite existence and historical function. The concept of melodrama, straddling various types of representation and subjectivity, in which sacred and secular, the mythical and the real coexist, will help us get away from a definition of these terms as mutually exclusive. It is the *relay* between the familial, the social and the sacred in the Indian cinema's constitution of its diegetic world which complicates any straightforward rendering of the psyche of the Indian spectator.

Further specifications and distinctions about the spectator need to be made in terms of generic address. While D. G. Phalke inaugurated the popular cinema with the mythological genre, new genres very quickly emerged. These included the costume film, or the 'historical', the spectacular stunt or action-dominated film, the devotional film about the relationship between deity and devotee and, finally, the social film. Our knowledge about the terms in which the industry addressed spectators through genre, and the way spectators received genres, are as yet rudimentary. But a 1950s essay by an industry observer noted that stunt, mythological and costume films would attract a working-class audience.[22] The film industry used two hypotheses to evaluate their audience. Firstly, that the plebeian spectators would delight in spectacle and visceral impact, uncluttered by ideas and social content. Secondly, that such an audience was also susceptible to a religious and moral rhetoric, indicated by their enjoyment of the mythological film. In the industry's view, therefore, the lower-class audience was motivated by visceral or motor-oriented pleasures and moral imperatives. Their susceptibility to the veracity of the image was not an issue in this discussion on attracting an audience.

On the other hand, the film industry understood the devotional and social films, with their emphasis on social criticism, to be the favoured genres of the middle class. However, by the 1950s, the industry reformulated its understanding of genre and audience appeal. After the collapse of the major studios – Bombay Talkies, Prabhat, New Theatres – the new, speculative climate of the industry encouraged an eye for the quick profit and therefore the drive for a larger audience. This encouraged the induction of the sensational attractions of action, spectacle and dance into the social film, a process explained as a lure for the mass audience.

Industry observers clearly believed the changes in the social film to be quite superficial, the genre label being used to legitimize a cobbling together of sensational attractions. And, indeed, there is something inflationary about a large number of films released in the period 1949–51 being called 'socials'. The label of the social film perhaps gave a certain legitimacy to the cinematic entertainment put together in a slapdash way. However, I will argue that these films did offer a redefinition of social identity for the spectator; the mass audiences earlier conceived of as being attracted only by sensation and themes of moral affirmation were now being solicited by an omnibus form which also included a rationalist discourse as part of its 'attractions'.[23]

Many of the formulations of the dominant paradigm refer to the cinema after the 1950s. Writers such as Das Gupta and Nandy believe that the 1950s was a transitional period between the popular culture and mixed social audience of the 1930s and 1940s and the mass audience emerging from the 1960s.

However, I would suggest that the cinema of the 1950s already prefigures some of the dominant methods of the subsequent period, especially in its deployment of a rhetoric of traditional morality and identity to bind its imagining of social transformation. Perhaps it is the focus of these writers on the overt rhetoric of popular narratives that has obscured a certain dynamic in the constitution of the subject which displays dispositions other than the straightforwardly 'traditional'.

Visual Codes of Narration (I): Iconicity, Frontality and the Tableau Frame

Let me now turn to the issue of visual address. For the purposes of identifying the processes of cinematic narration, we have to turn to the Indian cinema's initial formation: a phase, from 1913, in which it not only absorbed religious and mythological narratives, but also certain modes of address. An aesthetics of frontality and iconicity has been noted for Indian films in certain phases and genres by Ashish Rajadhyaksha[24] and Geeta Kapur.[25] This aesthetic arises from mass visual culture, in instances ranging from the relationship between deity and devotee, to the enactment of religious tableaux and their representation in popular artworks such as calendars and posters. When I refer to the iconic mode, I use the term not in its precise semiotic sense, to identify a relation of resemblance, but as a category derived from Indian art-historical writing that has been employed to identify a meaningful condensation of image. The term has been used to situate the articulation of the mythic within painting, theatre and cinema, and could be conceived of as cultural work which seeks to bind a multi-layered dynamic into a unitary image. In Geeta Kapur's definition, the iconic is 'an image into which symbolic meanings converge and in which moreover they achieve stasis'.[26]

Frontal planes in cinematic composition are used to relay this work of condensation and also to group characters and objects in the space of the tableau, a visual figure which, in the Indian context, can be traced to Indian urban theatre's interactions with British melodrama in the nineteenth century. In Peter Brooks's formulation, the tableau in melodrama gives the 'spectator the opportunity to see meanings represented, emotions and moral states rendered in clear visible signs'.[27] And Barthes has noted that it is

> a pure cut-out segment with clearly defined edges, irreversible and incorruptible; everything that surrounds it is banished into nothingness, remains unnamed, while everything that it admits within its field is promoted into essence, into light, into view . . . [it] is intellectual, it has something to say (something moral, social) but is also says it knows how this must be done.[28]

In Barthes's argument, the tableau has a temporal dimension to it, a 'pregnant moment' caught between past and future.[29] To my mind, these observations suggest both the highly controlled work involved in the construction of the tableau and also its inbuilt possibilities of dynamization. Its constitution of a frozen dynamic implicitly suggests the possibilities of change. This means that deployment of the tableau frame does not invariably mean indifference to the problem of offscreen space. Dissections of the tableau, cut-ins to closer views on the scene, the use of looks offscreen and character movements in and out of frame serve to complicate the tableau, fulfilling the promise of its reorganization.

I will illustrate the dynamic employment of the frontal, iconic mode, and of tableau framing in a sequence from Mehboob Khan's saga of peasant life, *Mother India* (1957). This segment presents, and then upsets, a pair of relatively stable iconic instances. The mother-in-law, Sundar Chachi, is centred through a number of tableau shots taken from different angles to highlight her authority in the village just after she has staged a spectacular wedding for her son. This representation of Sundar Chachi takes place in the courtyard of her house. The other instance is of the newly-wedded daughter-in-law Radha, shown inside the house, as she submissively massages her husband's feet, a classic image of the devout Hindu wife.[30] The two instances are destabilized because of the information that the wedding has forced Sundar Chachi to mortgage the family land. The information diminishes her standing, causing her to leave the gathering and enter her house. Simultaneously, it also undermines Radha's iconic placement as submissive, devout wife. As she overhears the information, the camera tracks in to closeup, eliminating the husband from our view; she looks up and away, offscreen left, presumably towards the source of the information. As the larger space of the scene, the actual relationship between the inside and the outside, remains unspecified, the relationship is suggested by her look offscreen left. The likelihood of this positioning is further strengthened when Sundar Chachi enters the house and, looking in the direction of offscreen right, confesses that she has indeed mortgaged her land. The final shot, a repetition of Radha's look offscreen left, binds the two characters through an eyeline match. The women are narrativized out of their static, iconic position through narrative processes of knowledge circulation and character movement, and by the deployment of Hollywood codes of offscreen sound and eyeline match.

This deployment of tableau and icon is regularly observable in the popular cinema, even if their dispersal and reorganization is not always rendered by such a systematic deployment of the codes of continuity editing. In another, fairly systematic instance, from *Andazl Style* (Mehboob Khan, 1949) I have suggested that the particular combination of character-centred continuity narration with the tableau plays off individual and socially coded orientations to the narrative event. The continuity codes highlight individual movement and awareness, and the tableau condenses the space of the social code. Instead of invoking themes of individual/society and modernity/tradition, I argue that such combinations present the spectator with shifting frames of visual knowledge, different sensoria of the subject.[31] Indeed, rather than attach specific forms of subjectivity to specific modes of representation in a schematic way, I believe that there are instances when certain socially and ritually coded relationships are relayed through what is, after all, the mythicized individuation of the continuity mode. Central here is a particular discourse of the image and the look in indigenous conventions.

Visual Codes of Narration (II): Looking

While visual codes deriving from mass visual culture are open to the dynamization of the sort I have described, they continue to retain a certain integrity of function, especially in the reproduction of authority structures. For example, hierarchies of power may develop around the image of a character. This character image becomes the authoritative focal point of a scene, occupying a certain privileged position which structures space as a force field of power. In contrast to formulations about looking which have become commonplace in the analysis of Hollywood cinema, the figure looked at is not necessarily subject to control but may in fact be the repository of authority. As Lawrence Babb[32] and Diana Eck[33] in their studies of looking in Hinduism have suggested, the operative terms here are *darsan dena* and *darsan lena*, the power to give the look, the privilege of receiving it. However, there may be other functions of looking in play, as when tension arises around the question of who bears authority. The look of the patriarch is privileged in such narrative moves. In a host of 1950s work, from *Awara/The Vagabond* (Raj Kapoor, 1951), *Baazi/The Wager* (Guru Dutt, 1951), *Aar Paar/Heads or Tails* (Guru Dutt, 1954) through the later work of Guru Dutt in *Pyaasa/The Thirsty One* (1957) and *Sahib, bibi aur ghulam/King, Queen, Jack* (Abrar Alvi/Guru Dutt, 1963), the patriarchal gaze is highlighted as a dark, controlling one, seeking to arrest the shift in the coordinates of desire and authority.

In terms of visual address, the residual traces of sacralization are still observable in the reposing of authority in the male image. The family narrative that underpins the Hindi cinema resorts to a transaction of authority around this image. The patriarch gives way to the son, his successor, at the story's conclusion. This male figure's authority is placed in position by the direction of a devotional female regard.

I will cite an example from *Devdas* (Bimal Roy, 1955), a film based on a well-known Bengali novel by Sarat Chandra Chatterjee. Devdas, the son of a powerful landed family, is prohibited from marrying the girl he desires, Parvati, because of status differences. He is a classic renouncer figure of the type favoured in Indian storytelling, a figure who is unable, or refuses, to conform to the demands of society, and wastes away in the contemplation of that which he could never gain. I want to refer to a scene which employs continuity conventions to the highly 'traditional' end of deifying the male as object of desire. The sequence deals with Devdas's visit to Parvati's house, and indicates a strategy of narration whereby Parvati's point of view is used to underline the desirability and the authority exercised by Devdas's image. In this sequence, Parvati finds her grandmother and mother in the courtyard discussing Devdas's arrival from the city and the fact that he has not yet called upon them. Devdas, offscreen, calls from outside the door. From this moment, Parvati's auditory and visual attention dominates the narration. Before we can see Devdas entering the house, we withdraw with Parvati to her room upstairs, and listen to the conversation taking place below along with her. Devdas announces that he will go to see Parvati himself. In anticipation of Devdas's arrival, Parvati hurriedly starts lighting a *diya*, a devotional lamp, and the melody of a *kirtan*, a traditional devotional song expressing Radha's longing for Krishna, is played. We hear the sound of Devdas's footfall on the stairs, and Parvati's anxiety to light the lamp before Devdas enters her room is caught by a suspenseful intercutting between her lighting of the lamp and shots of the empty doorway. The doorframe in this sequence suggests the shrine in which the divine idol is housed. Devdas's entry is shown in a highly deifying way; first his feet are shown in the doorway, followed by a cut to the lighted lamp. Finally his face is revealed. There follows a cut to Parvati, suggesting that this is the order through which she has seen Devdas's arrival. As she looks at him, in a classical point of view arrangement, conch shells, traditional accompaniment to the act of worship, are sounded. The future husband as deity, object of the worshipful gaze, is established by the narration's deployment of Parvati's point of view. Her lighting of the devotional lamp and the extra-diegetic sound of the *kirtan*, and conch-shells underline the devotional nature of the woman's relationship to the male image. Guru Dutt would use the doorframe to similar effect at the climax of *Pyaasa* and the *kirtan* from *Devdas* is used again on that occasion.

I have already suggested that filmic narration is subject to ambivalence in relaying the image of masculine authority through a desiring female look. Within the *bhakti* or devotional tradition, the female devotee's energy is channelled directly into the worship of the deity, without the mediation of the priest. However, the Lord still remains a remote figure, making of the devotional act a somewhat excessive one, concentrating greater attention on the devotee than the devotional object.[34] Another implication of this arrangement is that we are being invited to identify with the romantically unfulfilled woman character, a problematic position, perhaps, in terms of the gendering of spectatorship.

We need to retain a constant sense of the way the dominant tropes of narration are complicated by such features of excess. However, I still think it is necessary to acknowledge the framework of masculine authority within which female desire is finally held. And I suggest that we need to go back to the tableau and the framework of seeing provided by an iconic frontality to understand the ways in which the elaboration of filmic narration is determined by these imperatives.

In *Pyaasa* there is a scene in which the poet–hero, Vijay, refers to the prostitute, Gulab, as his wife in order to protect her from a policeman who is pursuing her. The prostitute is unaccustomed to such a respectful address, especially one suggestive of intimate ties to a man she loves, and is thrown into a sensual haze. Vijay ascends a stairway to the terrace of a building where he will pass the night. Gulab sees a troupe of devotional folk singers, *Bauls*, performing a song, *Aaj sajan mohe ang laga lo* (Take me in your arms today, O beloved), and follows Vijay up the stairs. The *baul* song is used to express Gulab's desire, and cutting and camera movement closely follow its rhythms. The scene is structured by these relations of desire, which are simultaneously relations of distance, as the woman follows, looks at and almost touches the man she loves (who is entirely unaware of all this) but finally withdraws and flees as she believes herself unworthy of him.

The relation between devotee and object of devotion determines the space of this scene, it remains the structuring element in the extension and constraining of space. The relationship here is not that of the iconic frontality of traditional worship. The desired one is not framed in this way, for continuity codes dominate the scenic construction. Even in the scene I have cited from *Devdas*, continuity codes construct space and it is a shot/reverse shot relationship which defines the ultimate moment of looking. Nevertheless, if we think of the male icon as the crucial figure towards and from which the narration moves, we can see how a 'traditional' marker of authority and desire is the anchor to the spatializing of narrative. We have here something akin to a tableau constructed over a series of shots, its constituent elements – Gulab, Vijay and the performers – being ranged in a relatively consistent spatial relationship to each other. From the point of view of the male spectator, what is being underwritten is not, or not only, the subordinate position in the act of looking, it is a moment which uses looking to relay his own desirability to him.

The Sociopolitical Referent

The relaying of patriarchal authority through reorganized tableaux, the transfer of the authoritative image from one character to another and the presence of an empowering female look, present the essential visual–narrational transaction. In this sense there is a certain rearticulation of traditional authority and hierarchies of the visual culture into the narrational procedures of the cinema. Hollywood codes of narration, oriented to generate linear narrative trajectories motivated by character point of view and action are employed. But what is of interest is that they are used to 'enshrine' the male character in the female look as I have described, or to route the male character back to an original family identity. This latter narrative trajectory is widely observable in the series of popular crime films of the 1950s, such as *Awara, Baazi, Aar Paar* and *CID* (Raj Khosla, 1956). This circularity has something to do with the particular structures of the family narrative in the 1940s and 1950s. Something akin to a Freudian family romance was at work, in which the fantasy that the child has parents other than those who bring him up is played out. In the Hindi social film, instead of a fantasy of upward mobility, a democratizing downward spiral is set in motion, the hero being precipitated into a life of destitution and crime. The circling back, the recovery of identity, is then tied to a normalization of social experience, a recovery of the reassuring coordinates of social privilege.[35]

As a result, in line with dominant ideological currents in the wake of independence, the social film of the 1950s expanded the terms of social reference, urged an empathy towards social deprivation and invited a vicarious identification with such states. But the recovery of the hero at the conclusion finally underlines the middle-class identity that structures the narrative. However, certain shifts are observable in the nature of family narrative and the recovery of identity. In socials of the 1940s such as *Kangan/The Bracelet* (Franz Osten, 1940) and *Kismet*, there is a proper reconciliation between son and father, and a type of joint family structure seems to be back in place. By the 1950s, however, the hero's recovery of identity and social position does not result in reconciliation with the father, but the positing of a new family space. This nuclear family is formed in alignment with the state, as if politics and personality were allied in a common project of transformation.

Indeed, while I have tried to suggest the ways the popular film seeks to integrate new forms of subjectivity into more conventional tropes, it is important that we retain the signs, however fragmentary, of other subjectivities in play, whether these express the drives of individualized perception, of an assertive masculinity, or the recovery of the popular conventions of female devotion. I have suggested elsewhere, in a study of *Andaz*, that the popular cinema of this period drew upon Hollywood narrative conventions in order to highlight the enigmatic dimensions of its female character's desires. The film was notable for its use of hallucinations and dreams to define the heroine in terms of an ambivalent psychology and as agent of a transgressive but involuntary sexuality. Such conventions were drawn upon to be contained and disavowed. A nationalist modernizing imperative had to symbolically contain those ideologically fraught aspects of modernity that derived from transformations in the social position and sexual outlook of women. The result was a fascinatingly perverse and incoherent text, one whose ideological achievements are complicated by the subjectivities it draws upon.[36]

A 'National' Spectator

The terms of cinematic narration I have sketched here are rather different from the notions of spectatorship which have emerged from that model of the successful commodity cinema, Hollywood. Historians and theoreticians of the US cinema have underlined the importance of continuity editing in binding or suturing the spectator into the space of the fiction. The undercutting of direct address and the binding of the spectator into a hermetic universe onscreen heightens the individual psychic address and sidelines the space of the auditorium as a social and collective viewing space. This very rich historiography and textual analysis[37] speaks of the fraught process through which US cinema's bourgeois address came into being. This work describes how social and ethnic peculiarities were addressed in the relation between early cinema and its viewers. The process by which the cinema took over and came to develop its own entertainment space was a process of the formation of a national market in which the spectator had to be addressed in the broadest, non-ethnic, socially universal terms. Of course, what was actually happening was that a dominant white Anglo-Saxon norm came to be projected as universal. Along with this process, there developed the guidelines for the construction of a universal spectator placed not in the auditorium but as an imaginary figure enmeshed in the very process of narration.

The mixed address of the Hindi cinema, along with the song and dance sequences and comic skits which open up within the commercial film, suggests a rather different relationship of reception. Indeed, it recalls the notion of a 'cinema of attractions', a term developed by Tom Gunning to theorize the appeal of early Euro–American cinema.[38] In contrast to the Hollywood mode of continuity cinema or narrative integration, Gunning argues that early cinema was exhibitionist. The character's look into the camera indicated an indifference to the realist illusion that the story tells itself without mediation. The films displayed a greater interest in relaying a series of views and sensations to their audience rather than following a linear narrative logic. These elements were to be increasingly transcended in the Hollywood cinema's abstraction of the spectator as individuated consumer of its self-enclosed fictional world. In the process, the audience, earlier understood to be composed of workers and immigrants, was 'civilized' into appreciating the bourgeois virtues of a concentrated, logical, character-based narrative development.[39]

Elements of this formulation of a cinema of attractions are clearly applicable to the Bombay film. But the Bombay cinema too was engaged in creating standard, universalizing reference points. To understand the processes by which the Hindi cinema acquired certain acceptable 'national' standards, we have to be able to identify how it took over certain widespread narrational norms from the past. But alongside this, we also need to examine how it was involved in constructing certain overarching cultural norms that suppressed the representation of marginal currents in Indian narrative and aesthetic traditions.

Research into the urban theatre of the nineteenth century will provide one point of entry into the understanding of the process by which narrational norms were transmitted to the cinema. This theatre presaged the cinema in its negotiation of Western form, of technology, of narrative, even of a notion of entertainment time.[40] But it was also reputedly a great indigenizer, appropriating other traditions into Indian narrative trajectories. One narrational function that was carried from the theatre was that of a narratorial position external to the story, reminiscent of the *sutradhar* or narrator of traditional theatre. The comic, or *vidushak*, also left his mark as one of the staple figures of the commercial cinema.[41] Here he sometimes plays the role of a narrator external to the main narrative and is often engaged in a relationship of direct address to the audience. There is a certain didacticism involved in his functions. In a more commonplace function, it is the very absurdity of the comic figure, quite obviously opposed to the larger-than-life attraction of the hero, which invites a less flattering point of identification for the audience, and thereby a certain narratorial distance towards the story. Further, in the very superfluity of his functions, we could say that the comic was the spokesman within the story for a different order of storytelling, one which celebrates the disaggregative relationship to narrative.

But the main repository of such a narratorial externality to the main story and its process of narration is what I would term the 'narrational song'. This is enacted by a source other than any of the fictional characters. Through such a song, we are offered an insight into the emotional attitude of individual characters and the wider cultural and even mythic significance of certain actions and events. For example, when Devdas leaves Parvati in Bimal Roy's *Devdas*, Parvati listens to *Baul* singers as they sing of Radha's sorrow at Krishna's departure. This is a direct representation of her mood, but in addition to emotional attitudes, the song also represents a highly conventionalized cultural idiom.

The embedding of such cultural idioms offers us a stance, quite ritualistic in its intelligibility, towards the development of the narrative. We are both inside and outside the story, tied at one moment to the seamless flow of a character-based narration from within, in the next attuned to a culturally familiar stance from without. This may not be a simple, normative move on the part of the narration; indeed, we may be offered a critical view on narrative development. Significantly, such culturally familiar narratorial stances are sometimes separate from the space of the fiction. Not only are they performed by characters otherwise superfluous to the main storyline, there is often also an actual disjunction between the space of the story and that of the narrator. In this sense, the narrational song can be identified with the properties of the extra-fictional music used on the soundtrack. They both inhabit a space outside the fiction and alert us to a certain point of view or emotional disposition which we find culturally intelligible.

The disaggregation of address in Hindi cinema, such as is found in the external narrator and the comic and musical sequence, therefore integrates with a recognizable set of conventions. Further, the Bombay cinema also generates an enlarged and standardized identity across these divergent points of address. This can be located in this cinema's construction of masculine authority and its privileging of a symbolic Hindu identity. The outlines of such a masculine subjectivity were accompanied by a sharper delineation of sexual difference than that within the original cultural idiom. The androgynous aspects of Krishna's sexual identity are marginalized by fixing the male position as the object of sensual female regard and devotion.[42] For all the richness of its ambiguous use of female desire and its unconventional articulation of the hero's masculinity. Guru Dutt's *Pyaasa* is quite clear about the imperative of fixing a masculine locus of authority in its conclusion. Perhaps we have here a symbolic nationalist reformulation of culture in the cinema, undercutting the space for marginal discourses, and seeking to control ambiguity in the relationship between gender and power. Historians such as Uma Chakravarty have shown how this takes place in revisions of the Ramayana,[43] and Patricia Uberoi has suggested that a similar process, aligned to high-caste images of women as subordinate, self-effacing and motherly, took place in the culture of the calendar print.[44] These patterns may help us identify the universalizing ambition of the Hindi cinema, despite its disaggregative features. The scope of universalization lies not merely in the subordination of all elements to narrative, but in ensuring that multiple and tangential tracks never exceed the limits of the dominant address. This implies that the concept of the cinema of attractions needs to be rethought when it becomes the characteristic, long-term feature of a national commodity cinema.

Identifying a Contextual Address to the Spectator

In the last part of this paper, I want to refer to a more historically specific address through which a symbolic identity was negotiated by the cinema. I will argue that, although the language of the Bombay cinema is Hindustani and therefore the product of cultural interaction between Muslim and Hindu culture, the spectator of the commercial cinema is primarily positioned in relation to the overarching Hindu symbolic identity relayed through the cinema. This is effected through the types of cultural address which I have described, through narrational song, gender idiom and modes of visual address. The strongly Hindu cultural connotation of these features is so pervasive that it is invariably thought of as the norm, rather than as a historically specific project for spectatorial identification. In the early 1940s, however, the industry became much more self-conscious about its market, and how it was to be addressed. In making this observation I am merely sketching out certain guidelines for research rather than laying out the definite time scale and the range of resources used to put together the symbolic narrative of the Hindu nation. Preliminary findings suggest the importance of this line of enquiry.

In 1937, the All India League for Censorship, a private body, was set up to lobby for stringent measures in regard to what was perceived to be an anti-Hindu dimension in the film industry.[45] It claimed that the industry was dominated by Muslims and Parsis who wanted to show the Hindus 'in a bad light'. Muslim actors and Muslim characters were used, it declared, to offer a contrast with Hindu characters, portrayed as venal, effete and oppressive. The League evidently assumed that the government of Bombay, led by the Indian National Congress, would be responsive to their demand that certain films be banned for their so-called anti-Hindu features. Such expectations were belied by K. M. Munshi, Home Minister in the Bombay Government, who dismissed the League as bigoted. Indeed, this was how the League must have appeared at the time. But their charges do bring to light the fact that certain offscreen information, that is, the religious identity of producers, directors and actors, was being related to the onscreen narrative, and in fact was seen to constitute a critical social and political level of the narrative.

It is against this background that we should situate the as yet rudimentary information which suggests that in the next decade the industry itself was coming to project an address to its market which clearly apprehended and sought to circumvent Hindu alienation. Syed Hasan Manto, who had written scripts for Hindi films, recalled that he was pressurized to leave his job in the early 1940s because he was a Muslim. Indeed, Bombay Talkies, the studio for which Manto worked from 1946 to 1948, came under threat from Hindu extremists who demanded that the studio's Muslim employees be sacked.[46] At a more symbolic level, a process seems to have been inaugurated by which the roles of hero and heroine, which normally remain outside the purview of stereotypes associated with other characters, had to be played by actors with Hindu names. In 1943, when Yusuf Khan was inducted as a male lead by Devika Rani at Bombay Talkies, his name was changed, as is well known, to Dilip Kumar. In the actor's account, the change was quite incidental.[47] But we have information about other Muslim actors and actresses who underwent name changes, such as Mahzabin, who became Meena Kumar,[48] and Nawab, who became Nimmi;[49] and, in 1950 a struggling actor, Hamid Ali Khan changed his name to Ajit on the advice of the director, K. Amarnath.[50] I am sure that this short list is but the beginning of a much longer one, and an oral history might uncover something akin to a parallel universe of concealed identities. The transaction involved seems to have been purely symbolic. Evidence from film periodicals suggests that the true identity of such actors was mostly well known, and yet an abnegation of identity was undertaken in the development of the star personality. It is as if the screen, constituting an imaginary nation space, required the fulfilment of certain criteria before the actor/actress could acquire a symbolic eligibility.

Following in the tracks of the Hindu communal censorship League of 1937, *Filmindia*, the sensationalist film periodical edited by Baburao Patel, showed that a bodily sense of communal difference had come to inflect a certain reception of film images. *Filmindia*, incensed in 1949 when demonstrations prevented the screening of *Barsaat/Monsoon* (Raj Kapoor, 1949) in Pakistan,[51] was delighted to see two Muslim actresses, Nimmi and Nargis, kiss the feet of Premnath and Raj Kapoor in the latter's *Barsaat*. In an ironic aside, the gossip columns of the periodical suggested that, to balance this act of submission, a Muslim director such as Kardar should now arrange to have a Hindu actress kiss Dilip Kumar's feet. Clearly, it was understood that such an inversion was not a likely scenario, and a vicarious pleasure was being taken in this symbolic triumph.[52] How much of these offscreen discourses actually went into the structuring of onscreen narratives? It seems to me no coincidence that in the same year in which *Filmindia* carried this dark communal reception of *Barsaat*, in *Andaz*, a film by a Muslim director Mehboob, Nargis should again be seeking to touch Raj Kapoor's feet, desperate to demonstrate her virtue as a true Indian wife, and to clear herself of charges of being involved with Dilip Kumar. The image of the star is not just reiterated in this interweaving of on- and offscreen narratives; there is an active working out and resolution of the transgressive features which have come to be attached to him/her. For example, speculations about Nargis's family background and suspicions of her chastity following her affair with Raj Kapoor seemed to repetitively feed into, and be resolved within, a host of films from *Andaz* to *Bewafa/Faithless* (M. L. Anand, 1952), *Laajwanti/Woman of Honour* (Rajinder Suri, 1957) and *Mother India*.[53]

The way in which this symbolic space was charted out by the Hindi commercial cinema is comparable to the way in which the white hero became the norm for the US commercial cinema and, preeminently, his WASP version. In both cases, the ideological construction of this space appears to be neatly effaced, but the discourses surrounding the films clearly indicate that this was not so.

In this symbolic space, the minorities too can have a presence, usually as subordinate ally of the Hindu hero. But we must not forget the specific address the industry made to the Muslim community in the form of the Muslim social film. Unfortunately, I have not seen enough of these to be able to situate them adequately within or against the grain of Hindu nationhood. *Elaan/Announcement* (Mehboob Khan, 1948) falls into this category, and it clearly urges the Muslim community to emulate its educated sections and pursue the path of modernization. Perhaps the pejorative and ideologically loaded implication of this specific address was that the wider society, comprising the Hindus, had already made this advance.

Conclusion

I have suggested that we must situate the whole project of the Hindi commercial cinema in its cultural context, that of a mass visual culture which displays certain rules of address, composition and placement. Through the deciphering of this system, we shall be able to understand the position given to the spectator, the types of identity he or she is offered. This starting point will enable us to hold on to the historical spectator as he/she is moved through regimes of subjectivity set up by generic and social address, and by the integration of a new dynamic of narration from the Hollywood cinema. In citing these imperatives of analysis, I seek to problematize a dominant paradigm in Indian criticism. This has focused on the particular familial rhetoric of the popular cinema to suggest that its address disavows the 'real' and reflects significant cognitive and political dispositions in its spectator. In a word, this is a disposition which seeks to counter a rational outlook, seen by the popular cinema's critics as the basis of a modern society and nation state; in certain anti-modern interpretations, such failings may actually constitute a virtue.

In contrast, in my reading of cinematic narratives, we can observe the refashioning of the spectator in accordance with certain new compulsions, a streamlining of narrative form around the drives of individualized characters. Instead of an unqualified assimilation of such drives, the transformation is held within a culturally familiar visual economy centred on a transaction around the image of male authority. But there are always excessive aspects to this process of cultural 'domestication', and we need to retain a sense, however fragmentary, of the range of subjectivities which are called into play by the negotiatory features of narrative construction.

The Hindi cinema displays a disaggregative address in its structures, quite in contrast to the narrative integrity and spectatorial enmeshing of another successful commodity cinema, that of Hollywood's classical narrative cinema. However, I have argued that despite this a coherence can be discerned in the limits set by dominant discourses to otherwise diverse narrative and performative strands. Even disaggregation, I have suggested, has certain binding features in the way it articulates the spectator to earlier practices of narration and to many points of cultural institution and investment. In other words, it performs a symbolic remapping of identity and suppresses other more complicated traditions of gender, of Hinduism and other forms of culture. It is through this process of standardization that the cinema constitutes an enlarged, transcendent identity for its spectator.

Finally, I have suggested that, from the 1940s, contextual information gleaned from discourses about the cinema indicated that such a 'national' project was yoked to constructions of the Indian nation as one dominated by the Hindu, and was arrived at through symbolic transactions of offscreen identity and onscreen narrative.

Notes

Versions of this paper were presented at the Nehru Memorial Museum and Library, New Delhi, Department of Film and Television Studies, University of Amsterdam, and the *Screen* Studies Conference, June 1994. I thank Radhika Singha and Thomas Elsaesser for their comments, and the Indian Council for Historical Research, the British Council, Delhi, and the *Screen* Studies Conference organizers for enabling me to attend the *Screen* conference.

1. For a representative selection of articles, see Jim Pines and Paul Willemen (eds), *Questions of Third Cinema* (London: British Film Institute, 1989).
2. For the standard account, see E. Barnouw and S. Krishnaswamy, *Indian Film* (London and New York: Oxford University Press, 1980); also Manjunath Pendakur, 'India', in John A. Lent (ed.), *The Asian Film Industry* (London: Christopher Helm, 1990), p. 231.
3. For reflections on the subordinating implications of Bombay's national cinema, see my 'Dislocations: the cinematic imagining of a new society in 1950s India, *Oxford Literary Review*, vol. 16 (1994).
4. M. B. Bilimona, 'Foreign markets for Indian films'. *Indian Talkie, 1931–56* (Bombay: Film Federation of India, 1956), pp. 53–4. A substantial deposit of Indian films distributed by Wapar France, an agency which catered to North African markets, are in the French film archives at Bots d'Archy. For the importance of Indian film imports to Indonesia and Burma, see Lent, *The Asian Film Industry*. pp. 202, 223; and for patterns of Indian film exports at the end of the 1980s, see Pendakur, 'India', p. 240. The Hindi film's contribution to the general sense of subordination of local products in North Africa and the Middle East is indicated in the observation that 'none of these cinemas [from Morocco to Kuwait] is doing well . . . markets are flooded with Rambos, Karate films, Hindu [sic.] musicals and Egyptian films' Lisbeth Malkmus, The "new Egyptian cinema" ', *Cineaste*, vol. 16. no. 3 (1988), p. 30.
5. The term comes from Tom Gunning, 'The cinema of attraction: early film, its spectator and the avant-garde', *Wide Angle*, vol. 8, nos 3–4 (1986). There is a more elaborate discussion of this term in relation to the Bombay cinema later in this

paper. For reflections on other 'attraction' based cinemas see Laleen Jayamanne. 'Sri Lankan family melodrama: a cinema of primitive attractions', *Screen*, vol. 33, no. 2 (1992), pp. 145–53; and Gerard Fouquet, 'Of genres and savours in Thai film', *Cinemaya*, no. 6 (1989–90), pp. 4–9.

6. Nick Browne. 'The spectator of American symbolic forms: re-reading John Ford's *Young Mr Lincoln', Film Reader*, part 5 (1979), pp. 180–8.
7. For an exploration of this influential critical tradition, see my 'Shifting codes, dissolving identities: the Hindi social film of the 1950s as popular culture', *Journal of Art and Ideas*, nos 23–4 (1993), pp. 51–85.
8. See the collection of essays in Wimal Dissanayake (ed.), *Melodrama and Asian Cinema* (Cambridge: Cambridge University Press, 1993).
9. For example, Mitsushiro Yoshimoto's account of the postwar domestic criticism of Japanese cinema, 'Melodrama, post-modernism and Japanese cinema' in Dissanayake (ed.), *Melodrama and Asian Cinema*, pp. 101–26, especially pp. 110–11. Thus where late nineteenth-century Europe's discourses about melodrama helped institute a hegemonic class culture, in the context of developing societies, the 'failures' of melodrama are regarded within the imperatives of establishing a modern national configuration. For the class implications of the European context, see Christine Gledhill, *Home is Where the Heart Is: Melodrama and the Woman's Film* (London: British Film Institute, 1987), Introduction.
10. Chidananda Das Gupta, *The Painted Face* (New Delhi: Rolly Books, 1991).
11. Das Gupta, 'Seeing is believing', in *The Painted Face*, pp. 35–44.
12. Das Gupta, 'City and village, and 'The Oedipal hero', in *The Painted Face*, pp. 45–58, 70–106.
13. Das Gupta, 'The painted face of Indian politics', in *The Painted Face*, pp. 199–247.
14. All references are to Ashish Nandy, 'The intelligent film critic's guide to the Indian cinema', *Deep Focus*, vol. 1. nos 1–3 (1987–8); reprinted in Nandy, *The Savage Freud and Other Essays on Possible and Retrievable Selves* (Delhi: Oxford University Press, 1995).
15. See R. K. Yagnik, *The Indian Theatre: Its Origins and Later Development under European Influence, with Special Reference to Western India* (London: Allen and Unwin, 1933), pp. 92–117, for accounts of the influence of British melodrama on Indian urban theatre.
16. Peter Brooks, *The Melodramatic Imagination: Balzac, Henry James, Melodrama and the Mode of Excess* (1976) (New York: Columbia University Press, 1985).
17. Veena Das, 'The mythological film and its framework of meaning: an analysis of *Jai Santoshi Ma', India International Centre Quarterly*, vol. 8, no. 1 (1981), pp. 43–56.
18. Geeta Kapur, 'Mythic material in Indian cinema', *Journal of Arts and Ideas*, nos 14–15 (1987), pp. 79–107.
19. Anuradha Kapur, 'The representation of gods and heroes: parsi mythological drama of the early twentieth century', *Journal of Arts and Ideas*, nos 23–4 (1993), pp. 85–107.
20. See my ' "You cannot live in society and ignore it" nationhood and female modernity in *Andaz* (Mehboob Khan, 1949)', *Contributions to Indian Sociology* (forthcoming).
21. Kumkum Sangari has noted the following effects of the female devotional voice: 'The orthodox triadic relation between wife, husband and god is broken. The wife no longer gets her salvation through her "godlike" husband . . . *Bhakti* offers direct salvation. The intermediary position now belongs not to the human husband or the Brahmin priest but to the female devotional voice. This voice, obsessed with the relationships between men and women, continues to negotiate the triadic relationship – it simultaneously transgresses and reformulates patriarchal ideologies.' Sangari, 'Mirabai and the spiritual economy of Bhakti', *Economic and Political Weekly*, vol. 25, no. 28 (1990).

22. All references are to Barnouw and Krishnaswamy, 'The Hindi film', in *Indian Talkie*, p. 81.
23. The reasons for the restructuring of the 'social' film are complex. Artists associated with the Indian People's Theatre Association (IPTA), which had ties with the Communist Party of India, had started working in the film industry from the 1940s. Amongst these were the actor Balraj Sahni, the director Bimal Roy and the scriptwriter K. A. Abbas. The latter was involved in *Awara/The Vagabond* (Raj Kapoor, 1951), a film representative of the new drive to combine a social reform perspective with ornate spectacle. However, the years after independence were characterized by a broader ideological investment in discourses of social justice associated with the image of the new state and the ideology of its first prime minister, Jawaharlal Nehru.
24. Ashish Rajadhyaksha, 'The Phalke era: conflict of traditional form and modern technology', *Journal of Art and Ideas*, nos 14–15 (1987), pp. 47–78.
25. Kapur, 'Mythic material in Indian cinema'.
26. Ibid. p. 82.
27. Brooks, *The Melodramatic Imagination*, p. 62.
28. Roland Barthes, 'Diderot, Brecht, Eisenstein', in Stephen Heath (ed. and trans.), *Image, Music, Text* (London: Fontana, 1982), p. 70.
29. Ibid.
30. See a panel from the eighteenth-century Hindu text analysed by Julia Leslie, *The Perfect Wife: the Orthodox Hindu Woman According to the Stridharmapaddhati of Tryambakayajvan* (Delhi: Oxford University Press, 1989), for an example of this tradition.
31. Vasudevan, 'Shifting codes, dissolving identities', pp. 61–5.
32. Lawrence A. Babb, 'Glancing: visual interaction in Hinduism', *Journal of Anthropological Research*, vol. 37. no. 4 (1981), pp. 387–401.
33. Diana Eck, *Seeing the Divine Image in India* (Chambersburg: Anima Books, 1981).
34. Sangari, 'Mirabai and the spiritual economy of Bhakti'.
35. For an elaboration of this narrative structure, see my 'Dislocations'.
36. Vasudevan, 'You cannot live in society – and ignore it'.
37. See Miriam Hansen, *Babel and Babylon: Spectatorship in American Silent Cinema* (Cambridge, MA: Harvard University Press, 1991); and Thomas Elsaesser (ed.), *Early Cinema: Space-Frame-Narrative* (London: British Film Institute, 1990).
38. Gunning, 'The cinema of attraction'.
39. Hansen, *Babel and Babylon*, chapters 1 and 2.
40. A. Yusuf Ali, 'The modern Hindustani drama'. *Transactoins of the Royal Society of Literature*, vol. 35 (1917), pp. 89–90.
41. For an account of the *sutradhar* and the *vidushak*, see M. L. Varadpande, *Traditions of Indian Theatre* (New Delhi: Abhinav Publications, 1978), pp. 84–5; also David Shulman, *The king and the Clown in South Indian Myth and Poetry* (Princeton: Princeton University Press, 1985).
42. This can be seen as part of an epochal refashioning of Krishna, suggestively presented in Nandy, 'The intelligent film critic's guide'.
43. Uma Chakravarty, 'The development of the Sita myth: a case study of women in myth and literature', *Samya Shakti*, vol. 1, no. 1 (1983), pp. 68–75; also Paula Richman (ed.), *Many Ramayanas: the Diversity of a Narrative Tradition in South Asia* (Delhi: Oxford University Press, 1992).
44. Patricia Uberor, 'Feminine identity and national ethos in Indian calendar art', *Economic and Political Weekly*, women's studies section, vol. 25, no. 28 (1990), pp. 41–8.
45. All references are taken from Bombay, Home Department, Political file no. 313/1940. Maharashtra State Archives.
46. See the introduction to Saadat Hasan Manto *Kingdom's End and Other Stories*, trans. Khalid Hasan (London Verso Books, 1987).

47. *Filmfare*, 26 April 1957, p. 77
48. *Filmfare*, 17 October 1952, p. 19.
49. *Filmfare*, 28 November 1952, p. 18.
50. Ajit, interviewed by Anjali Joshi, *Sunday Observer*, Delhi, 16 December 1991. For some ideas about the onscreen ramifications of Hamid Ali Khan's change of name, see my 'Dislocations'.
51. *Filmindia*, April 1950, p. 13.
52. *Filmindia*, May 1950, p. 18.
53. For further reflections about Nargis's career, see Rosie Thomas, 'Sanctity and scandal in *Mother India*', *Quarterly Review of Film and Video*, vol. 11, no. 3 (1989), pp. 11–30; and Vasudevan, 'You cannot live in society – and ignore it'.

16

'HUM AAPKE HAIN KOUN?' – CINEPHILIA AND INDIAN FILMS

Lalitha Gopalan

Consider a scene from Ram Gopal Varma's Hindi film *Rangeela/Colourful* (1995). Muna walks into the film studio to apologise for his uncouth behaviour at the movie theatre the previous evening. He sees Mili practising her dance moves and cannot fathom her stories of studio grandeur emanating from this ordinary, dark space. She rises to his challenge: the lights beam on her, music streams in, and Mili gyrates to 'Jo mangta hai'/'What you want'. Dumbstruck, Muna imagines joining Mili in a song and dance sequence that includes a virtual journey through New York and Hyderabad. In short, Muna falls hopelessly in love with Mili. Until this moment, the film insists on a bantering relationship strengthened by their mutual love for films: he is a ticket tout outside Bombay film theatres; she, a chorus girl in a Hindi film. Each is trying to get closer to the magic of cinema. Occurring in the first half of the film, as seasoned viewers of the Hindi film love story, we expect him to run into troubled waters, thus delaying his union with Mili. As he struggles to confess his love, to get what he wants (jo mangta hai), a triangular economy of desire unfolds: the hero of the film within the film, Kamal, also falls in love with Mili when he watches her practise dance on the beach. Unlike Muna, Kamal is motivated in his desire for Mili by her exuberance outside the studio. In a fortunate turn of events, Kamal recommends Mili to replace the heroine in his film. They finally produce their film, and the audience declares Kamal and Mili a successful pair on the screen. Intimidated by their success, Muna flees Bombay, assuming that Mili's rise to

From Lalitha Gopalan (2002), *Cinema of Interruptions*, London: BFI, pp. 1–33.

stardom squeezes him out of her life. However, Mili, with Kamal's help, tracks him down. In the final moments of the film, she confesses her love for Muna.

Their union remains credible within the film's own internal logic favouring cinephilia over filmmaking, a preference dictating the difference between Muna's and Kamal's desire for Mili. Even as the film struggles to preserve Muna's love as independent of Mili's meteoric rise to stardom, we *know* that it orchestrated his love from the point of view of a film-going fan, a cinephile, and only later as somebody outside the play of light and sound. He falls in love with Mili's image in the studio, the film star, not his pal on the streets. Mili, on the other hand, expresses her desire only at the very end of the film, but her unstated reasons and indecisiveness drive the narrative logic of the love story. In other words, we wait eagerly for Mili to decide between her star-struck devotion for Kamal and her love for films that leads her to Muna. The film implies that Kamal loses because of his inability to participate in the correct triangulation – he loves only Mili, whereas Mili's first love is the cinema. It is Muna and Mili's love for cinema that dictates their love story, the preferred triangulation in the film.[1]

Rangeela, like Varma's other films, summons cinephilia, reminding us that both filmmakers and viewers share complicity – their films can 'read' our desire as much as we can marshal our critical machinery to read their creations. Obviously, *Rangeela* is not a first in this genre: Ketan Mehta's comic film *Hero Hiralal* (1988) revolves around an auto rickshaw driver's obsession with a film star; casting Kamal Haasan in four different roles, Singeetham Srinivasa Rao's Tamil film *Michael Madan Kama Rajan* (1990) plays with thematic and visual conventions in Tamil cinema; and Ram Gopal Varma's *Daud/Run* (1997) uses the caper to highlight the frustrations of a hermeneutic reading of Indian popular films. Reading back our insights to us, analysing stereotypical endings and stock details, these films showcase a cinema that can confidently parody its own conditions of production while fine-tuning certain genre tendencies. Parading conventions as comic interventions – the wet sari, the sad and loving mother, song and dance sequence – each of these films strikes an ironic posture that, as critics, we are reluctant to accord the commercial industry. Even Sooraj Barjatya's Hindi film *Hum Aapke Hain Koun . . . !/Who Am I to You . . . !* (1994), a smash hit advertising itself as wholesome family entertainment with fourteen songs, does not shy away from a comment on spectatorship.[2] The opening credit sequence has both leads, Madhuri Dixit and Salman Khan, looking straight at us and singing 'Hum aapke hain koun?'/'Who am I to you?'; asking us to reflect on our relationship to cinema, the film draws us into a triangular economy of desire, making us an integral part of its love story.[3]

We can fully appreciate the verve of these films if we recall that in each filmic instance they maintain a respectful distance from Indian cinema's tragic tale of filmmaking narrated in Guru Dutt's *Kagaz Ke Phool* (1959), in which the hero as film director suffers a tortured relationship to both filmmaking and love. Dutt's film interpolates us as voyeurs looking at the unfolding narrative of doom, a relationship to the screen ideally suited to reaffirming the negative potential of cinema. In sharp contrast, the playful and ironic commentary on filmmaking cited in the above films depends on our familiarity with cinematic conventions, familiarity cultivated through our long relationship with Indian popular cinema. More often than not, by calling attention to our viewing habits within the diegesis and naming it love, contemporary Indian films have closed the gap between the screen and spectator. Whether or not we accede to the proposal of love and familiarity from the screen, these films signify a confidence in filmmaking we have not been privy to for the past twenty-five years.

This confidence signals changes in aesthetic, technical, and reception conditions, simultaneously nudging us to acknowledge a shift in our critical engagement with cinema. To account for the changing conditions of production and conditions satisfactorily, between the screen and the spectator, we should read popular Indian films from the point of view of a cinephiliac, one that is based on an ambivalent relationship to cinema: love and hate.

Whereas cinephilia colours the selection of genre films in this book, the task of this introductory chapter is to map the theoretical and methodological issues implicit in my reading of films. Starting with the place of cinephilia in film theory, I move to consider the different changes in production and reception of Indian films, both locally and globally, that inspire the love of this cinema. Encouraged by its ability to entertain beyond national boundaries, this book places popular Indian cinema within a global system of popular cinema to account for its simultaneous tendency to assert national and local cinematic conventions, and also to abide by dominant genre principles.

Identifying the strength of certain conventions unique to Indian cinema as a *constellation of interruptions* allows us to consider national styles of filmmaking even as Hollywood films assert their global dominance. By bearing in mind this constellation of interruptions, we should reconsider the direct importation of film theory as ideal reading strategies for Indian films, even though they have been productive in understanding the structure of pleasure and anticipation of Hollywood genre films. The introduction, in short, suggests that, just as popular Indian films rewrite certain dominant genre principles, film theory, too, needs to undergo revisions in order to read adequately the different structuring of anticipation and pleasure in this cinema that also has a global application and circulation.

Even the most casual tourist in India resorts to hyperbole to describe the potency of this cinema that produces 1,000 films in more than twelve languages each year. For instance, in his travelogue *Video Nights in Kathmandu*, Pico Iyer declares in a significant synecdoche that spills over its own rhetoric, 'Indian movies were India, only more so.'[4] Other writers, such as Salman Rushdie, Alan Sealy, and Farrukh Dhondy, have used various aspects of Indian film culture to spin fabulous narratives of success and failure, stardom and political life, love and villainy.[5] For the uninitiated, most commentators will list implausible twists and turns in plots, excessive melodrama, loud song and dance sequences, and lengthy narrative as having tremendous mass appeal, but little critical value. However, the films cited above belie such judgments and are symptoms of seismic changes between cinema and society that have seeped into the ways in which we read, think, and write about Indian cinema, thus initiating our love affair with it.

However expansive the influence of cinema, Indian filmmakers are acutely aware that most films fail at the box office. Their financial anxieties have increased in recent years with the rise of adjacent entertainment industries that threaten to diminish the power of films, even if cinema as an institution is not waning in the public imagination. Trade papers from the 1980s record the industry's fears of the growing video industry that many believed would eventually discourage audiences from going to theatres. Nevertheless, the arrival of video shops in India also exposed the film-going public to world cinemas, an opportunity previously afforded only by film festivals and film societies. Suddenly films from other parts of Asia, Europe, and America were easily available to the film buff. Filmmakers were also very much part of this video-watching public, freely quoting and borrowing cinematic styles: for instance, director Ram Gopal Varma started his career as a video-shop owner. While a section of the urban rich retreated to their homes, trade papers reported an increase in film attendance in small towns and villages. Instead of assuming that one mode of watching would give way to the next evolutionary stage, we now find films coexisting alongside a robust video economy and satellite or cable television. Ironically, both cable television and video shops are also responsible for creating nostalgia for older films. Together, these different visual media have changed reception conditions by generating an audience that has developed a taste for global-style action films while simultaneously a cherishing a fondness for the particularities of Indian cinema.

In addition to video and satellite saturation of the visual field, American films (sometimes dubbed in Hindi) started reappearing in Indian theatres after a new agreement was signed between the Government of India and Motion Picture Producers and Distributors of America, Inc. (MPPDA) in April 1985, ending the trade embargo that began in 1971.[6] Initially, Indian filmmakers protested against this invasion, but slowly reconciled themselves to their presence after recognising that American films did not pose a threat to Indian film distribution.[7] Occasionally we find characters in Indian films taking potshots at American cinema: in Ram Gopal Varma's *Satya* (1998), protagonists purposely misread *Jurassic Park* (1993) as a horror film starring lizards; in Tamil films, cross-linguistic puns abound around James Cameron's *Titanic* (1997). These playful engagements with American culture confidently acknowledge that Indian cinema audiences belong to a virtual global economy where films from different production sites exist at the *same level* – a democratisation of global cinephilia. Perhaps I am exaggerating the dominance of Indian cinema, but the confidence of some Indian filmmakers does hold out hope for unsettling the inequalities of the global marketplace where we are all too aware of American films unilaterally expanding into newer territories.

While economic liberalisation opened Indian markets to a range of television programmes and videos, it also facilitated, however slowly, access to state-of-the-art film technology for filmmakers. Within the industry there were discernible changes in the production process. According to Manmohan Shetty, who runs a film processing business, Adlabs, a sea change occurred in 1978 when Kodak introduced a negative film that could be processed at high ambient temperatures (105°F), improving colour resolution.[8] At about the same time, professionally trained technicians in editing, cinematography, and lighting began entering the commercial industry from film institutes in Pune and Chennai (Madras), vastly improving the quality of film production, as well as increasing its cost. Manjunath Pendakur notes that the rising costs of film production since the 1980s not only includes huge salaries for film stars, but also higher wages for directors and technicians.[9] Audiences seem attuned to these changes on screen: in Chennai, the crowds become hysterical when cinematographer P. C. Sriram's name runs across the screen; directors have fan-supported websites competing with those of movie stars.

The profusion of filmmaking talent strengthened the Malayalam, Tamil, and Telugu industries. Since 1979, film production in Tamil and Telugu continued to keep pace with Hindi films, each producing about 140 films annually.[10] Increased production from regional industries has weakened the stranglehold of Hindi films as the largest commercial industry in the nation, while improvements in dubbing facilities have ensured a national audience for Tamil and Telugu films. Additionally, filmmakers from the south such as S. Shankar, Sashilal Nair, Priyadarshan, Mani Ratnam, and Ram Gopal Varma have been making inroads into the Hindi film industry, once a prerogative of female stars.[11] The migration of directors also means that narratives focusing on national themes – inter-communal love story, war, and terrorism – are no longer a prerogative of Hindi cinema, but also surface in regional cinemas. Concurrently, narratives in Hindi films have receded from national secular themes addressing an urban audience, dabbling instead with regional stories resonating with preoccupations of the Hindi belt: Rajputs, Biharis, and Punjabis now crowd the Hindi film screen.

Technical and aesthetic improvements in mainstream Indian cinema remind us that commercial filmmakers benefited from narrative experiments introduced by independent filmmakers in the 1970s. Consciously setting themselves apart from commercial cinema, films by Adoor Gopalkrishnan, G. Aravindan, Mrinal Sen, Girish Kasarvalli, Kumar Shahini, and Mani Kaul focused on social and political antagonisms to narrate their tales of disappointment with the post-colonial state while also conveying hopes for a different society.[12] Screened at film societies or special shows in large movie theatres, their films drew the urban elite to cinemas and shaped film-viewing habits by encouraging the audience to focus more intently on the screen. A substantial number of commercial films made in the late 1980s borrowed from these filmmaking practices while continuing to improve on conventions of entertainment. Not unlike independent cinema, we now find directors gaining currency as auteurs in commercial cinema, controlling the production of their films and characterising them with a unique cinematic style. In turn, the National Film Development Corporation (NFDC, the state body that finances independent films) started producing films that liberally incorporated mainstream stories and stars.

Further, Indian films have, on occasion, internationalised the production process: S. Shankar's Tamil film *Kaadalan/Lover* (1994), for example, had its special effects enhanced in a Hong Kong film studio. Critics rightly focus on the film's playful commentary on upper-caste hegemony and its attendant economies of taste, but we cannot ignore how globalisation of the production process also influences the narrative of caste contestations.[13] The more conventional representation of the world in Indian popular cinema – song and dance sequences set in foreign locales – is not only spruced up to arouse the spectator's interests in tourism, but also aggressively participates in the movement of global capital. These sequences not only bring the world home, but also acknowledge a loyal audience abroad that wishes to see its own stories of migrations and displacement written into these films. A number of Hindi films – *Pardes* (1997), *Dilwale Dulhaniya Le Jayange* (1995), *Dil to Pagal Hai* (1998), *Kuch Kuch Hota Hai* (1998) – index an audience straggling between national identities, harbouring longings for an original home, or possessing the capital for tourism. Considered together, these narrative and production details place the viewer of Indian films in a global cinematic economy, finally catching up with a long history of global reception.

Since Independence, Indian films have travelled to the former Soviet Union, Latin America, Africa, and Southeast Asia, entertaining audiences whose personal histories have few ties with the subcontinent.[14] Sometimes, these travel routes are visible on video copies – Arabic subtitles on Hindi films, Malay on Tamil films – telling us of a global set of viewers who watch other national cinemas besides Hollywood. More recently, *Newsweek* reported that Japan is spellbound by Tamil films, especially those starring Rajnikanth, because 'Indian films are filled with the classical entertainment movies used to offer.'[15]

Although Indian films now enjoy a crossover audience, extra-filmic events nudge us towards other readings of popular films. It is now commonplace to find the loyal Indian diaspora cultivating appreciation by sponsoring stage shows of film stars, events that read popular films as star-studded texts. However, it is filmmakers in the diaspora who have been openly engaging with, and in the process teaching us a lesson or two in, defamiliarising Indian film conventions. In both Srinivas Krishna's Canadian production *Masala* (1992) and Gurinder Chadda's British film *Bhaji on the Beach* (1994), we find lengthy quotations from Indian cinema: protagonists express desire by resorting to song and dance sequences. Inserted in films working with small budgets and relying on art-house distribution, such sequences serve as fabulous strands expressing immigration fantasies born out of travel and displacement. In a more abrupt manner,

Rachid Bouchareb's French–Algerian film *My Family's Honour* (1997) uses Hindi film songs on the soundtrack and even splices an entire musical number from *Hum Kisise Kum Nahin/We Are Number One* (1977) into its narrative on North African immigrants living in France. Displaying no diegetic link to the narrative, the jarring disjunction of this sequence conveys the disruption brought about through immigration and displacement in Bouchareb's film. Terry Zwigoff's *Ghost World* (2000), narrating traumas of the summer after high school, opens with a song and dance sequence, 'Jab jaan pechachan'/'When we got to know each other' from *Gumnaam* (1965), intercutting with the main narrative. The feverish cabaret and twist number offers the bored teenager the requisite degree of exotic abandon. Baz Luhrmann confesses to not only having seen Indian popular films, but also being mesmerised enough to deploy several song and dance sequences in his film *Moulin Rouge* (2000). Benny Torathi's Israeli film *Desparado Piazza*, also called *Piazza of Dreams* (2000), splices in a song sequence from *Sangam* (1964) to map a different history of migration for ethnic Jews.[16] All these films celebrate these interruptions as a way of accounting for cinephilia even when the protagonists have to adjust to arduous conditions imposed through transnational migration, ennui-ridden teenagers, or a courtesan's love story. These unexpected sites of reception allow us to see, from without, how Indian films are available for a wide range of readings, including camp and cult possibilities, based on their multi-plot narratives and multiple disruptions.

Within India, critical writing on cinema has blossomed in the past two decades, reporting a serious, sometimes cinephiliac, relationship to films. Published from Bangalore, *Deep Focus* combines interviews with directors from different parts of the world, film reviews, and lengthy critical pieces. *Cinemaya*, based in Delhi, follows the festival schedule in Asia, brings its readers news of the latest films and interviews with directors, and addresses a pan-Asian audience from Turkey to Japan. These two magazines locate Indian cinema, both popular and alternative, and its audience within a global network of cinematic styles.

The short-lived *Splice* was published from Calcutta with an exclusive focus on alternative cinematic practices, and it explored the correspondences between avant-garde practices in India and those in the former Soviet republics. For a brief time *Splice* was an integral part of a thriving film scene in Calcutta, which now includes a film archive at Nandan and a brand-new film studies department at Jadavpur University. The *Journal of Moving Images* from the Department of Film Studies at Jadavpur addresses an emerging academic audience in India. *Lensight*, published by the Film and Television Institute of India (FTII) in Pune, addresses itself to filmmakers with reports on state-of-the art lab processing techniques, editing equipment, and cameras, and also carries lengthy interviews with filmmakers on their craft. Although pitched exclusively at filmmakers, *Lensight* carries a wealth of information on sociological conditions of production that are not widely available to a film critic.

Finally, the publication of *Encyclopaedia of Indian Cinema* (1994, revised edition 1999) stamped the scholarly seal of approval on Indian cinema. Expansive in its scope, Ashish Rajadhyaksha and Paul Willemen's opus strings together biographies, film lists, and plot summaries, providing a road map on different features of Indian cinema from genres to independent film movements and regional cinemas. Considered together, these publications both expanded and variegated the scope of cinephilia in India beyond the standard fanzines celebrating the star system.

These disparate details form the bedrock of material changes in the production and reception of Indian popular cinema. Spelling out these details undercuts a series of archaic oppositions that we find steadfastly held in film studies: between national and international cinemas, overlooking alternative routes of film distribution; between Hollywood and other national cinemas, casting the latter as bad copies instead of examining them as a rejoinder to a hegemonic cinema; between national and regional cinemas, placing Hindi cinema at the helm of the national imaginary and ignoring a simultaneous move towards regional nationalisms; between national and global audiences, by not anticipating audiences that also endow Indian popular cinema with meaning that exceeds its own intended horizon of address; between art and commercial cinema, repeating a high-modernist division between high and low cultures without admitting to a more variegated terrain of taste. Naming these mobile processes speaks to a post-colonial condition that according to Stuart Hall marks a 'critical interruption into that whole grand historiographical narrative which, in liberal historiography and Weberian historical sociology, as much as in the dominant traditions of Western Marxism, gave this global dimension a subordinate presence in a story which could essentially be told from within European parameters'.[17] In other words, this book reads popular Indian films as an interruption in film theory, a film theory that, although generated from engagements exclusively with Euro-American cinemas, assumes a transregional durability.

Sholay and Reading Strategies

More than any of the above material conditions effecting our relationship to the screen, Ramesh Sippy's *Sholay/Flames* (1975) was a landmark in Indian cinema, for ever changing the production and reception of popular cinema in the past twenty-five years. Coinciding with the state of emergency declared by Prime Minister Indira Gandhi in 1975, *Sholay* was emblematic of a number of films feeding off what political theorists refer to as a crisis of legitimacy of the Indian state.[18] Film critics, media activists, and film scholars agree that the unrest in civil society marked by communal riots, police brutality, violent secessionist movements, and assaults against women and minorities seeped into film narratives.[19] Stacked with gangsters, avenging women, brutal police, and corrupt politicians, these films resolve their narratives through vigilante actions that repeatedly undercut the authority of the state.[20] Activist organisations such as Delhi's Media Advocacy Group argue that representations of brutality in contemporary commercial cinema have a direct and reinforcing effect on the level of violence in civil society.[21]

However, *Sholay*'s iconic status exceeds a mimetic relationship to reality, drawing in large part from its reconfiguration of the Western.[22] Mixing a host of conventions from Indian popular cinema such as song and dance sequences, *Sholay* successfully produced an Indian riposte to the classic American Western. Fans of this cult film extensively quote Salim Khan and Javed Akhtar's script back to the screen; rumours abound on the existent variations of the closing sequence; and overnight the actor Amjad Khan, playing the villain Gabbar Singh, became one of the most popular stars of the film. Anupama Chopra's book *Sholay: The Making of a Classic* – required reading for a fan – revives cinephiliac obsession with this film by journeying to the origins of production.

The film also spurred the first psychoanalytical critique of popular Indian cinema. In a much neglected essay, Madan Gopal Singh evaluates the tremendous success of this film by picking one scene as a symptom of the changing relationship between screen and spectator: the 'Mehbooba! Mehbooba!' song and dance sequence.[23] According to him, in this sequence the camera gropes the dancer's body and, by extension, provides us a point of view that was hitherto unavailable in popular Hindi cinema. Singh uses voyeurism as a conceptual tool to describe the altered relationship between screen and spectator in the film, an idea that draws extensively from certain cinematic principles found in Hollywood – omniscient narration, continuity editing, internally coherent narrative, and the ideal spectator's identification with the camera – leading to the argument that the camera's groping mechanism fragments the female dancer's body and generates viewing pleasure. But he glosses over the fact that song and dance sequences explicitly distract the viewer from narrative flow and contradict the conventions of continuity editing. Overtly exhibitionistic, song and dance sequences break the codes of realism on which psychoanalytical voyeurism relies.[24] Nevertheless, Singh's cryptic formulation prods us to consider how even the most superficial and entertaining song and dance sequences carry an ideological charge, heightening our viewing pleasure.[25]

Singh's essay also tells another story, a story of the intellectual context of his critical engagement with Hindi films. Originally published in the Left avant-garde *Journal of Arts and Ideas*, Singh's essay echoes the opinions of alternative filmmakers such as Kumar Shahini, Mani Kaul, and John Abraham, who were both writing and making a different kind of narrative cinema. Accounting for the hegemonic potential of Hindi commercial cinema, especially its ability to throttle radical filmmaking, Singh bemoans the loss of freshly minted student filmmakers from the Film and Television Institute of India (FTII) to the commercial industry, a move, he argues, that turns them into technicians of special effects. Whereas *Sholay* affords Singh the occasion to critically assess the ideological manifestations of the consumerist cinema, his theoretical speculations helped shape an entire generation of film theorists working on Indian cinema.[26]

In sharp contrast to Singh's critical essay, *Sholay* is a revered master text of success for filmmakers: Ram Gopal Varma confesses to knowing every shot of two of his favourite films – *Sholay* and *The Godfather* (1972); more recently, Rajkumar Santoshi allegedly watched *Sholay* every morning while shooting his own *China Gate* (1999).[27] *Sholay* is the legendary source that spurred an entire generation of filmmakers to borrow from globally circulating genres, yet also to reincorporate conventions from Indian popular cinema with great aplomb.[28] Spawning a number of B films throughout the 1980s, the full impact of Sippy's innovative cinematic style on popular Indian cinema – accommodating Indian cinematic conventions within a Hollywood genre – was fully developed a decade later by J. P. Dutta, Mani Ratnam, Mukul Anand, Ram Gopal Varma, Rajkumar Santoshi, and Shekhar Kapur.

These divergent readings of *Sholay* demonstrate a gap between critics writing on popular Indian cinema and filmmakers. Simply put, critics tend to take a moralistic view of mainstream cinema, seeing very little of the 'popular' in them, whereas commercial filmmakers see themselves as entertainers and regard critics as elitists whose opinions rarely count in the workings of the industry.[29] This stand-off between critics and commercial filmmakers is as old as the practice of narrative cinema itself and has little new to add to debates on the differences between highbrow and lowbrow, mass and popular cultures, which as cultural critics we have learned to make and then unmake. In the end we have settled on 'popular culture' as the most viable concept that absorbs the paradoxes of our trade: we can read resistance in its form, even as we continue to be mesmerised by it.[30] This rather tenuous definition seems vastly superior to the polarised definitions of cultural taste that plague readings of Indian films. There is no doubt that we learn a great deal from vigilant readings of cinema's hegemonic influence that reveal its power to affirm ethnic stereotyping, sexism, and jingoism, and caution us against being taken in by its dazzling surface. But all too often we tend to pay little attention to questions of pleasure. Inasmuch as we assume that commercial films maintain the status quo, suppressing all radical possibilities in their viewers, we must also admit that filmmakers are constantly inviting us to return to the movies through novel cinematic approaches.

Cinephilia and Film Theory

Cinephilia, as Paul Willemen reminds us, suffers from considerable neglect in film theory, even though it once dominated the writings and films of the French *nouvelle vague* directors.[31] What distinguishes cinephilia from its more lofty cousin, film criticism, is its attention to a system of signs beyond the central narrative – gestures from actors, *mise en scène* details, and even throw-away shots – that the obsessive film-viewer reads as special signals from the filmmaker. Suggesting that the eclectic use of psychoanalysis was one of the reasons cinephilia has a shifting presence in film theory, Willemen speculates:

> Even though the recourse to psychoanalysis did allow the questions of cinephilia to be addressed, the importation of psychoanalytic terminology

> was a costly business both for film theory and for psychoanalytic theory. The cost was erasure of concepts such as transference and resistance from both theoretical discourses. Since the practice of psychoanalysis is inconceivable without these two terms, the psychoanalytical theory mobilized by and for film theory was seriously flawed, to say the least. On the other hand, the absence of these two key concepts allowed critics freely to delegate their neuroses to the films where they would be 'read'. In effect, this reduced the films to the reader's screen memories. Since then, the relation between psychoanalysis and film theory has been reversed: instead of using random bits of psychoanalytic theory to generate readings of films, now bits of films are used to introduce readers to psychoanalytic theory. (p. 225)

Willemen does not offer a clear definition of cinephilia, but his discussion on the discourse of cinephilia proposes at least a proper name to grasp the incoherence of 'loving cinema'. Several ideas, associations, and relationships that crop up in Willemen's discussion I find particularly instructive for my own reading of Indian cinema.

> Cinephilia doesn't do anything other than designate something which resists, which escapes existing networks of critical discourse and theoretical frameworks. What is this thing that keeps cropping up in all these different forms and keeps being called cinephilia? (p. 231)
>
> Cinephilia being designated in cinema is an activation of complicity. Cinephilia is a component of a film culture which is then recycled in the film and which therefore bonds viewer and film in a particular moment of complicity. (p. 241)
>
> Actually the cinephiliac moment is my preferred description because of its overtones of necrophilia, of relating to something that is dead, past, but alive in memory. So there is a kind of necrophilia involved, and I don't mean that negatively. (p. 227)
>
> It's a theory premised on notions of revelation, on the notion of excess . . . So it is no accident, indeed, from what is highly necessary, that cinephilia should operate particularly strongly in relation to a form of cinema that is perceived as being highly coded, highly commercial, formalized, and ritualized. For it is only there that the moment of revelations or excess, a dimension other than what is being programmed, becomes noticeable. (pp. 237–8)

Describing cinephilia variously as resistance, complicity, necrophilia, and excess, Willemen prescribes it as an antidote to the usual theoretical practice of subsuming, even smothering, films under a formal theoretical edifice. In tandem with Willemen's formulation, discussion of cinephilia or its death has filled the pages of film criticism: Susan Sontag's essay lamenting the death of cinema; French film journals *Vertigo* and *Cahiers du cinéma* devoted complete issues to cinephilia; *Film Quarterly* used the genre of letters between Jonathan Rosenbaum and a group of younger critics to generate discussions on cinephilia.[32] Christine Keathley glides through these discussions foregrounding the overlaps and incommensurable links between film theory and cinephilia.[33] What these essays capture is a disenchantment with certain strands of film theory that repudiate the love of films as a primary condition; reading symptoms has overtaken the love-struck moments that brought many of us to film studies. A glance at critical work in film studies in the past two decades confirms Willemen's and his fellow travellers' suspicions of waning cinephilia; thankfully, there are a couple of exceptions that deserve mention. Even if these writers do not completely incorporate ideas of transference, they provide us with tools to help us grapple with our complicity when analysing films we love but rarely admit to in our writing. Richard Dyer's essays time and again address various contradictory reasons for studying popular culture, by insisting that we cannot spend our time imagining why it is pleasurable to 'others' if we do not understand how we as critics may find popular culture pleasurable.[34] Not forgetting the Frankfurt School's warnings that dazzling entertainment reels us into pure appearances, Dyer walks a tightrope between critical positions to suggest that we crack the common-sense assertion that it is 'only entertainment':

> Yet entertainment offers certain pleasures not others, proposes that we find such-and-such delightful, teaches us enjoyment – including the enjoyment of unruly delight. It works with the desires that circulate in a given society at a given time, neither wholly constructing those desires nor merely reflecting desires produced elsewhere; it plays a major role in the social construction of happiness. We have to understand it itself, neither take it as given nor assume that behind it lies something more important. (p. 7)

Dyer's assertion that we consider entertainment *qua* entertainment bears an uncanny resemblance to the more negative dismissal of cinema as 'pure appearances', but with a difference. Incisively using Gramsci's concept of 'common sense', Dyer leads us to de-familiarise the obvious aspects of entertainment, whose meaning appears settled, before using his critical scalpel.

Admitting that we as critics are very much subjects of entertainment also echoes in Sharon Willis's readings of race and gender in contemporary Hollywood film.[35] In *High Contrast*, she argues that films rely on the visibility of race and gender, categories resonating with our own theoretical preoccupations with difference:

> So powerful is our cultural wish to believe that differences give themselves to sight that the cinema is able to capitalize, both ideologically and financially, on the fascination that dazzling visual contrasts exercise upon us. At the same time, *as films read our social field*, they may both mobilize and contain the conflict, uneasiness, and overwrought affect that so often accompany the confrontation of differences in everyday practices.

> Cinema seems to borrow and channel these energies through a volatile affective range, from terror, panic, shock, and anxiety to titillation, thrills, excitement, fascination, pleasure, and comfort, while it proliferates representations of social difference as a central or peripheral spectacle. (p. 1. My emphasis)

Both Dyer and Willis not only demonstrate a dialectical relationship between viewer and screen, but also uncover our complicity in the circuits of pleasure generated by mass culture – a contrast from the usual refrain that popular cinema numbs, leaving us few options of resistance. Their positions extend Willemen's cinephilia by suggesting that our investments in popular cinema can yield changes in the public sphere through more watchful yet playful reading strategies. In all three positions we find a marked tendency towards seizing filmic details and revealing symptoms in our cultural imaginary, whether racist, sexist, or, more positively, queer possibilities. In an analogous fashion, Roger Cardinal argues for pausing over peripheral detail in films, a mode of looking associated with 'non-literacy':[36]

> The mobile eye which darts from point to point will tend to clutch at fortuitous detail (the chicken) or to collect empathetic impressions of touch sensations (the bare feet in the dust) . . . The act of pausing over the peripheral detail can have more than trivial implications . . . the whole screen is acknowledged as a surface which is, so to speak, *detailed all over*, like a mosaic, available to the gaze as an even field of rippling potency and plenitude. (pp. 124, 126)

In a not so dissimilar manner, Naomi Schor elegantly argues in *Reading in Detail* that reading details betrays an investment in the ornamental, the useless, and, by extension, the feminine, even if details are routinely recruited to serve realism.[37] Reading details emerges as a space of memory for the reader as she travels through various intertextual details triggered by an image. Schor asserts that, despite the rather long association between detail and femininity, reading details is very much a feminist project.

> If today the detail and wider semantic field it commands enjoys an undisputed legitimacy, it is because the dominant paradigms of patriarchy have been largely eroded. Eroded, but not eradicated. By reversing the terms of the oppositions and the values of the hierarchies, we remain, of course, prisoners of the paradigms, only just barely able to dream a universe where the categories of *general* and *particular, mass* and *detail*, and *masculine* and *feminine* would no longer order our thinking and our seeing. (p. 4)

These critical positions suggest in a roundabout way that cinephiliac readings – the fetishisation of details – open film texts to other scenes of contestations in public life towards which master theoretical tools broadly gesture in their proclamations of progressive and regressive meanings of films. Willemen's insight into the symbiosis between cinephilia and 'highly commercial' cinema, in particular, instructs my own reading of contemporary Indian popular films, where one of the pleasures of working on contemporary Indian cinema surfaces when films read our desires back to us, both regressive and Utopian.

Undoubtedly this relationship to Indian films emerges from my own location in American academic life, where on the one hand I am constantly translating Indian films into the established paradigms of film theory and, on the other, circumscribing a discrete theoretical domain for reading Indian cinema. But the translations are far from perfect. At film conferences in America, for instance, one finds a polite interest in Indian cinema – alternative or popular – but little enthusiasm. The same small clutch of listeners migrate from one international panel to another – Russian, Italian, Chinese, Indian, Iranian – with hordes of American film scholars crowding into auditoriums for papers on the latest Hollywood blockbuster. In spite of film studies' self-representation as a marginal field, there is no doubt that the dominant American imaginary, where its own interests are at the centre, influences my colleagues who find *difference* in international cinema a difficult idea to come to terms with. All too often as students of Indian cinema, we spend too much time imparting basic information to an audience whose standard question begins: 'Although I have not seen an Indian film . . .' Unlike my colleagues in the field, my students are more open to international films, more agreeable to expanding their film taste beyond the canon of genre films. In all honesty, however, unequal power dynamics in the classroom cannot be entirely discounted as a proximate cause for their enthusiasm. Yet there are limits to their cosmopolitan film taste. For instance, in my course on postwar Westerns, I decided to show Ramesh Sippy's *Sholay*. My students were already well prepared for international responses to the American Western and had only recently discussed Paul Smith's essay on Sergio Leone. But they seemed rudely shocked by Sippy's film. Leaving aside the problem of a bad video copy, the students were indignant that they had to watch such a long film. Whereas some of them were genuinely interested in a different national cinema, others were not keen on going down this politically correct route, complaining that it did not merit the attention that they accorded even to kung fu films. Since we had not seen the singing cowboy Westerns, singing in a Western, especially two men singing to each other, was the last straw for them. I had no choice but to confess that this film changed my viewing experience when I was a teenager growing up in India with an ambivalent relationship to popular cinema. Having internalised a middle-class disdain for popular cinema, I did not care for it, but seeing *Sholay* changed all that. It was not pedagogical authority that changed their attitude to the film, but rather a peek into my cinephiliac obsessions as well as my nostalgia infused with diasporic longings for Indian cinema. Instead of disabling me, admitting to enjoying Indian cinema a long time ago sharpened my reading of differences between films instead of seeing them as an amorphous form of mass culture the ideological content of which is transparent. We ended our class discussion with a renewed interest in Christian Metz's famous formulation:[38]

> To be a theoretician of the cinema, one should ideally no longer love the cinema and yet still love it: to have loved it a lot and only have detached oneself from it by taking it up again from the other end, taking it as the target for the same scopic drive which made one love it. (p. 15)

Genre and Interruptions

Sholay exemplified the possibility of very deftly combining dominant genre principles developed in Hollywood films with conventions particular to Indian cinema. Recasting the linear trajectory of genre films to include several local cinematic conventions, Indian popular films often render the former illegible to the outsider. For example, my students' initial reaction to *Sholay* was based on how song and dance sequences distracted them from the structuring of anticipation in a Western, rather than on asking how the film rewrites the genre so as to shore up our investments in a linear narrative. What I am suggesting is that it seems presumptuous to think that, when Hollywood genres are appropriated by other national cinemas, we should find a straightforward application of dominant genre principles instead of reading how local contexts of production and reception intervene and prevail over genre. The end product of this encounter between global and local features can, at times, be read as a subordinate response to Hollywood, a strategy forwarded by Paul Smith in his reading of Leone's 'spaghetti Westerns', or we can simply read them as a riposte that simultaneously reveals how Hollywood genres are also built around certain national cinematic styles.

Some clarification of the concept of film genre is in order before I launch into the particularities of Indian cinema. Identified as a narrative form developed by classical Hollywood commercial cinema, film theorists have developed a barrage of theoretical and methodological tools to understand the narrative structure, cinematic specificity, and viewer's relationship to genre films. For instance, cinematic genres are differentiated by iconography: frontier landscapes in a Western, city spaces in gangster films. At other times, we understand how genre verisimilitude derives from details in the *mise en scène*: monsters in horror films and horses in a Western. Genre theory continues to benefit from psychoanalytical theories by allowing us to see how our viewing pleasures are dictated by a structuring of repetition and difference in films. Research on advertising and distribution practices of Hollywood films reveals that film producers were deeply involved in using genre categories to target and consolidate their audience: women's films, summer action films, etc. Instead of considering genre in either–or terms, Steve Neale suggests we see genre films as a dynamic among the industry, films, and viewers to better understand cinema as a modern commodity form.[39] In his book on American genre films and theory, Rick Altman proposes that, far from being particular, Hollywood films are constructed as multiple, overlapping genres to reach a wider audience.[40] Discrete genres as a predilection of critics only surfaces after the fact. Whatever particular features film critics or filmmakers deploy to differentiate one genre from another or see multiple genres in one film, American genre films broadly obey certain cinematic principles perfected in classical Hollywood cinema that frame the unfolding narrative: continuity editing, omniscient narration, internally coherent diegesis, and character-motivated plot.

In contrast to the internally coherent narrative form generated by Hollywood genre films, genres in Indian popular cinema display a set of features that are akin to pre-classical cinema, especially several extra-diegetic sequences or sequences of attractions. Instead of concluding that these films stage the underdeveloped aspects of capitalism in the Indian economy, a different set of concerns nurtures this narrative form, including a desire to domesticate cinematic technology and develop a national cinematic style. For instance, writing on Dadasaheb Phalke's *Raja Harishchandra* (1913), Ashish Rajadhyaksha argues that the prevalence of frontal address in this film points to how narrative strategies in early cinema borrowed from painting, theatre, and traditional arts lured the viewer into this new technological apparatus. In a similar vein, Geeta Kapur suggests through her reading of *Sant Tukaram* (Damle/Fattelal, Marathi, 1936) that frontal address in this 'saint film' was a calculated move by the filmmakers to draw in viewers accustomed to watching theatre, while the sequence of miracles mandatory in a saint film highlighted cinema's ability to produce magic. Both Kapur and Rajadhyaksha alert us to how cinema in India developed in a whirl of anti-colonial struggles that included an impulse to forge an independent cultural form by both reinterpreting tradition and making technology developed in the West indigenous.

Besides the direct address, other features of Indian popular cinema similarly undercut the hermetic universe developed in Hollywood films by interrupting it with song and dance sequences, comedy tracks, and multi-plot narratives. Spectacular, at times excessive, the elaboration of these attractions in this cinema has invited critics to dub them 'masala films' – a culinary term that seeks to define a medley of narrative strands in popular cinema. Naming the films made in the 1950s and 1960s as the 'feudal family romance', Madhava Prasad argues that this super genre asserts its dominance through narrative strategies of annexations whenever new sub-genres emerge.[41] In short, Prasad suggests that instead of discrete genres, a megalomaniac genre cannibalises the formation of sub-genres. In a more generous tone, Ravi Vasudevan sees popular Hindi film as a discontinuous form that includes attractions such as song and dance sequences and comedic sub-plots.[42] Instead of skipping over these moments that either break the diegetic universe or disrupt the linear trajectory of the narrative, we must simply face the fact that the most persistent narrative form found in Indian popular cinema includes several interruptions bearing a more or less systematic relationship to the narrative. In other words, we should start to heed production details that concentrate on how Indian filmmakers expend considerable energy experimenting with the choreography and location of these sequences, and in the process acknowledge how our viewing pleasure arises from these interruptions and the novel ways in which a popular film strings together these sequences.

Identifying these interruptions encourages us to start in the reverse direction, that is, by exploring how these films experiment as well as strengthen Indian cinematic conventions, rather than mulling over how these films are derived from Hollywood genres. Moreover, attending to these interruptions throws light on how the concept of a national cinematic style emerges at the conjuncture of state interests in quality cinema, the film industry's interests in profits, and the global circulation of popular cinemas. To account for how these disparate interests in production and reception shape the textual make-up of popular films, this book looks at three different kinds of interruptions that brand the narrative form of Indian cinema: song and dance sequences, the interval, and censorship.

Song and Dance Sequences

One of the most common and popular features of Indian films are its song and dance sequences. According to Barnow and Krishnaswamy, Indian talkies always had songs: the first sound feature, Ardeshir Irani's *Alam Ara/Beauty of the World* (1931), had more than seven songs; another early Hindi film had forty songs; and, not to be outdone, a Tamil film had sixty.[43] By the 1950s, 'the film song had become a key to successful film promotion'.[44] Filmmakers continue to release audio tracks before the film's release, and it is widely believed that those sales alone can recover the production costs of a movie.[45] Music directors, choreographers, and singers receive awards, and these sequences often outlast the film's own story in the popular memory. Over the years, commercial filmmakers have tried experimenting with their absence with varying commercial success: K. A. Abbas's *Munna/Lost Child* (1954), the Tamil film *Antha Nal/That Day* (1954), B. R. Chopra's *Ittefaq* (1969), P. C. Sriram's *Kurudhippunal/River of Blood* (1995), and Ram Gopal Varma's *Kaun/Who?* (1998) are some examples. But, as song and dance sequences guarantee a definite income, it has been difficult to dispense with them altogether. Song and dance sequences traverse radio and television, independently of the films themselves, a phenomenon encouraging critics to rush to the conclusion that they are inserted into films only as entertaining spectacles with tangential links to the narrative.

In contrast to these assumptions that promote their extra-diegetic relationship to the narrative, or dismiss them as 'sequences of attractions' reminiscent of early cinema, song and dance sequences deserve another look, differentiating their relationship to the diegesis: delaying the development of the plot, distracting us from the other scenes of the narrative through spatial and temporal disjunctions, and bearing an integral link to the plot. Even in one film, there can be different articulations of these sequences, thus complicating the idea of a single diegesis or the value of the extra-diegetic. The lack of uniform temporal sequencing across different films alerts us to consider genre differences and auteur signatures inflecting the choreography of song and dance sequences.

In addition to attending to the ways in which song and dance interrupt the narrative in various ways, the iconography of these sequences of attractions calls our attention to other interests that bolster a spectator's interests in Indian cinema. For instance, the abrupt cut to exotic locations sparks the tourist interests of the viewer, and similarly the object-laden *mise en scène* endorses consumerism. Not unlike the commercial imperative towards product placement in contemporary American cinema, song and dance sequences draw in a whole host of adjacent economies such as tourism and consumerism that are not so easily compartmentalised in Indian cinema.

INTERVAL

The 'Interval' is the ten-minute break in every Indian popular film after eighty minutes of film screening. Lights are turned on, the projector is turned off, and viewers step out of the theatre to smoke a cigarette, eat a snack, or visit the restroom. Unlike the strong imprint of song and dance sequences in the filmgoing experience, the location of the interval remains an elusive detail in the memory of even the most avid film viewer. It is simply seen as a brief respite from the long screening. Trade papers, however, make passing references to which halves of the film were more, or less, interesting.

The interval weighs in as a crucial punctuation, adjusting both opening and closing strategies of the film – in effect, producing two opening and closing sequences in every Indian film. As with the song and dance sequences, I suggest the interval is not randomly located, but is regulated by genre constraints and directorial style. Breaking the spell of the dark auditorium, the interval reminds us of early cinema's exhibition practices when a film was one of many instalments of the evening's entertainment. In its current form, the interval is a cinematic device that organises the dose of cinematic attractions mandatory in Indian cinema as well as serving as a punctuation mark that continually directs our anticipation in surprising ways by opening and closing certain narrative strands.

Both song and dance sequences and the interval attune us to their structural function in popular Indian films, particularly their play on spatial and temporal disjunctions. Their articulation in specific texts highlights how films imbibe both global and local conventions: genre films adjust to song and dance sequences, and the interval doubles the structuring of anticipation and pleasure found in genre films. In each case, they call attention to interruptions in the convention of the linear narrative with a single diegesis dominant in Hollywood or other commercial industries, with their attendant assumptions of realist codes.[46] The ideal spectator of film theory, cloistered from adjacent consumer economies surfaces as a phantom figure in Indian popular cinema; the Indian spectator, in contrast, travels several circuits of pleasures generated by a multi-diegetic narrative.[47]

Censorship

In addition to these two kinds of interruptions, viewers of Indian films are aware that the state monitors the relationship between cinema and society most visibly through film censorship. The most glaring manifestation of state intervention in film production is the Board of Censors' certificate that precedes each film. This inaugural moment of every film publicly released in India, imported or indigenous, informs the spectator that the film has been approved by the state and carries with it traces of censored cuts. Although a carry-over from the colonial period, the post-colonial state, too, perceives films as having a tremendous influence over its citizenry and thus directs its regulations towards the production and control of 'quality' films.[48] However, instead of seeing censorship as *post facto* interference from the state, I suggest that filmmakers spend considerable energy in incorporating censorship regulations *during* filmmaking, in an attempt to pre-empt sweeping cuts that would drastically effect the flow of the narrative. Moreover, over the years, the relationship between the state and the film industry reveals a spectrum of negotiations – from an obedient nationalism to a flagrant flouting of regulations – that fuels the production of images on the screen.

Although the obscenity codes governing Indian cinema address a wide range of issues affecting both image and dialogue, in practice the object of greatest scrutiny is the female body. I use the term *coitus interruptus* to exemplify the different ways in which the film industry negotiates the code to finally produce the female body on screen. This is not a gratuitous evocation of contraception, but rather a play on the structural similarity between two mechanisms – contraceptive regulations and censorship – suggesting how the state isolates the female body as the prime site of control and regulation in the public sphere. Among the several manifestations of *coitus interruptus*, the withdrawal-of-the-camera technique is instantly recognisable in various Indian films: the camera withdraws just before a steamy love scene ensues, and the film replaces it with extra-diegetic shots of waterfalls, flowers, thunder, lightning, and tropical storms. The varying configurations and recurrent use of *coitus interruptus* demonstrate how the film industry, despite its laments about state control, has been preoccupied with the withdrawal-of-the-camera technique as a crucial source of surplus pleasure. With its focus on dodging censorship prescription as well as maintaining its interest in the female body on screen, *coitus interruptus*, as a cinematic convention, captures an intimate and tense relationship between the state and the film industry predicated on attempts, however contradictory, to align the *national* subject with the film spectator. Far from perfectly aligning with the interests of the state and the film industry, the viewer is drawn into a fetishistic scenario where she or he oscillates between a cinephiliac mourning over lost footage on the one hand and, on the other, acknowledges that the state employs patriarchal laws to produce limits on seeing.

I maintain, however, that these sequences of attractions do not completely override attempts to construct an internally coherent narrative, as some critics have implied. Song and dance sequences are not randomly strung together in the Indian films I look at, but both block and propel the narrative in crucial ways. The interval, the halfway stopping point, obviously upsets the image of the dream chamber, but by not acknowledging its presence we fail to see it as a punctuation that binds and disperses narrative energies in Indian popular cinema. Censorship regulates representations on screen, but the innovative sequences that are inserted as replacements afford not only a commentary on the relationship between the state and the film industry, but also on the contours of the extra-diegetic. Just as continuity in classical Hollywood narrative offers us both pleasure and anger, in this cinema, too, we find pleasures *in* these interruptions and not *despite* them. Indian cinema is marked by *interrupted pleasures*.

These interruptions do not carry equal weight across the terrain of popular cinema. Depending on directorial style or genre pressures, each film measures these interruptions differently in such a way as to suggest a *hierarchy* of interruptions. For instance, song and dance sequences are better elaborated in a love story than in a gangster genre. In a Mani Ratnam film, irrespective of the genre, we expect an elaborate choreography of song and dance sequences, flattening the temporal disjunctions of other interruptions.

Although the presence of numerous interruptions warrants Madhava Prasad's claim that Hindi cinema, at least in the 1950s, took the shape of the 'supergenre' that absorbed any hint of a reformist tendency, I would suggest that a characteristic feature of contemporary popular cinema in India has been its ability to balance strict genre features with the conventions of attractions peculiar to this cinema. In the process, the structuring of anticipation and pleasure in Hollywood genre films is rewritten. For instance, *Sholay* revises the Western by mixing a series of local features: song and dance sequences, the interval, censorship, and the idea of a 'multi-starrer'. Ram Gopal Varma's *Satya* (1998) elaborates on the interrelationship between the globally circulating gangster genre and local conventions, fully aware that its audience is habituated to global television and video programmes. In contrast to the typical ensemble found in the multi-starrer, Varma raided television and regional cinema for its actors. The most significant detail that haunts the public reception of the film is the relevance of the song and dance sequences. Apparently, Bharat Shah, the producer, did not approve of the initial rough cut, which had no songs; the final version has four songs developing the romantic sub-plot, as well as celebrating the fraternity of gang members.

Filmmakers are constantly at work finessing the alchemy of conventions and at times generating a commentary on the sequencing of these codes. Parthepan's Tamil film *Housefull* (1999), for instance, remarks on the function of these interruptions. The plot involves a bomb scare at a movie theatre in Madurai. The police and the bomb squad try to surreptitiously control the situation by asking the projectionist to keep the audience's attention on the screen, thus preventing them from leaving the theatre. Complying with the police request, the projectionist skips two crucial reels – one with song and dance sequences, which he claims will bring the men out in large numbers; the other, which marks the interval, will open the floodgates for the entire audience. While the audience in the film is transfixed on the unfolding story of the film within a film, our film also responds to the police dictate: although we have a clearly defined 'Intermission', the film has dispensed with song and dance sequences. At one level, Parthepan's film comments on the rash of bombings that mark Indian public life by intimidating the Utopian community of moviegoers – people from different communities, classes, and religions – that venture to see a film at a movie house aptly called the 'Bharat Theatres'. Yet what I find compelling about the film is its ability to articulate police work as a method to discipline the narrative – bombs and attractions are managed simultaneously. *Housefull* exemplifies the conditions of contemporary film production: a film leaning towards an internally coherent narrative yet continuously commenting on its textual production, and at the same time maintaining the intermission as a local condition of reception. These examples reveal how we cannot simply import one theoretical paradigm over others to account for non-Hollywood narrative styles, but must work through the ways in which they address a spectator who is at the crossroads of several intersecting cinematic styles.

The peculiar conditions of Indian commercial film narrative are constantly shifting, undoing our assumptions concerning some of its constituent elements. Defying making sense by importing reading strategies inspired from classical, early, or contemporary American cinema, contemporary Indian cinema compels us to employ several of these theoretical positions simultaneously to read *one* film. Despite being far removed from the central engine of capitalism and its accompanying realist narrative, Indian cinema mimics, copies, and rewrites these forms while simultaneously maintaining a local quotient of attractions. In a curious twist in the history of appropriation and application of film theory across national cinemas, certain ontological questions surrounding narrative cinema – questions that Eisenstein raised in his famous essay on 'montage of attractions' – find a fertile ground in contemporary Indian cinema.[49] Amalgamating different interruptions in Indian popular cinema also bears an uncanny resemblance to Peter Wollen's conceptualisation of the 'multi-diegesis' in Jean-Luc Godard's *Vent d'Est/Wind from the East* (1969), a film that he claims undoes the narrative conventions of both Hollywood and Soviet films.[50] We might be hard-pressed to see an immediate link between an overtly avant-garde practice and popular Indian cinema, but, not unlike Wollen, viewers of Indian films do see its digressions and interruptions as intrinsic to enjoying and understanding these films, as well as the place of intense ideological struggles.

Film Theory and Interruptions

Although suggesting that only a cinephiliac relationship to Indian cinema reveals a constellation of conventions peculiar to that cinema, I do not wish to overstate the case for the privileged point of view of the native viewer who implicitly knows all the plots and their temporal sequences. Such a claim overlooks how film-viewing habits are also shaped by globally circulating genres and that one does not have to be a connoisseur of Indian popular cinema to understand the narrative logic of this cinema. In fact, a film buff familiar with both pre-classical and avant-garde cinemas in America will recognise, with little difficulty, this cinema's difference from Hollywood, as well as its points of contact.

At the same time, I believe that a simple transposition of film theory developed through readings of Hollywood films cannot adequately account for local features. Instead of putting forward a separate theoretical paradigm for reading Indian cinema, I suggest calibrating film theory through a reading of *interruptions* in Indian films, thus rupturing the provincialism surrounding film theory and, in the process, rejuvenating it. In turn, certain aspects of film theory are ideally suited to cracking the ideological underpinnings of this cinema that appear so obvious to the familiar viewer. Inasmuch as this book dwells on interruptions and principles of continuity in Indian cinema, it equally seeks correspondences with film theory by investigating particular disruptive moments that have periodically shifted the terms of debate.

Film theory, especially the semiotic and psychoanalytical paradigms of the 1970s, argues that classical Hollywood films seem particularly pliable to conceptualisations of fetishism and scopophilia, given their impulse towards an internally coherent narrative where we are encouraged to identify with the cinematic apparatus while sitting in a dark room. These near-perfect conditions of film viewing wedded to the studio system do not hold up so well even when transported to early cinema in the same region. For instance, Tom Gunning describes early narrative cinema as a series of several 'attractions' loosely strung together – a far cry from an internally coherent narrative typified in classical Hollywood narrative.[51] He speculates that traces of these attractions later surface in underground cinema, which by intention works against conventions of mainstream narrative cinema. Similarly, Miriam Hansen reminds us that recalling early cinema tempers the notion of the ideal spectator that psychoanalytical film theory depends upon; in the process, she encourages us to consider the historical conditions shaping film viewing.[52]

To the credit of psychoanalytical film theory, it should be pointed out that Christian Metz did raise the issue of exhibitionism in his essay on 'two kinds of voyeurism', but for the most part film theorists have ignored narrative cinema's overt attempts to create spectacles by preferring to focus on conventions of realism.[53] Laura Mulvey's classic essay 'Visual Pleasure and Narrative Cinema' raises a number of issues concerning sexual difference, but we often overlook one of the crucial insights of her work: the moments of *disruption* in classical Hollywood that we have habituated ourselves not to notice, in particular the excessive focus on a woman's body that often breaks the diegesis.[54] Mulvey identifies a particular tendency in narrative cinema to fetishise parts of a woman's body in excess of narrative needs, a process that merits our naming those moments as *spectacle*. In other words, Mulvey's essay should have urged us to look for other ideologically charged disruptions – the focus on coloured bodies for comic relief, on ethnic faces for stereotypes of fear and loathing – instead of exclusively salvaging conventions of realism in cinema. What I am suggesting is that, before the onset of critical work on early cinema there were moments in psychoanalytical film theory that cast doubts on the internally coherent realist narrative, but this was a road not taken until film historians started marshalling empirical evidence from another period to remind us that questions of spectatorship need to be located within historical contexts of reception.

Critical work on early cinema is not the only challenge to a film theory developed by coupling semiotics and psychoanalysis. Increasingly, we find work on contemporary Hollywood springing from a dissatisfaction with premises of ideal spectatorship. Timothy Corrigan's *A Cinema without Walls* exemplifies this trend by alerting us to changing reception conditions, including 'the media politics of the Vietnam war, the restructuring of the movie industry through conglomerate takeovers, the widespread effect of technologies such as the VCR, and the contemporary fascination with different kinds of nostalgia'.[55] Commenting on the collapse of the fixed walls of the movie theatre (Plato's cave or 'dream chamber' in film theory), he suggests that 'audiences remove images from their own authentic and authoritative place within culture and disperse their significance across the heterogeneous activity that now defines them'.[56] Corrigan remarks on the links between fragmented audiences and post-studio production conditions:

> As a powerful revision of Baudrillard's 'mirror of production' model, the fluidity and unpredictability of the international marker has made, it would seem, the structures of production less and less determinant, and so force films increasingly *to anticipate the volatility of their reception as a textual determinant* (p. 23, my emphasis)

According to Corrigan, in contrast to Euro-American cinema's preoccupation with classical notions of an integrated film text, which generated an industry of readers who expended critical energy in deciphering the secret of the text, we now confront 'illegible films' that test the limits of 'intelligibility and interpretation'. He suggests that, in opposition to the concentrated reader, it may be more useful to use Walter Benjamin and Siegfried Kracauer's conception of the distracted viewer to understand contemporary conditions of film reception that 'have changed so significantly that models of interpretative legibility, from newspapers to scholarly journals, seem to find themselves frequently befuddled' (p. 61). Corrigan extends this idea to formulate new reading strategies for cinema:

> At both the operatic spectacles of the theaters and the home spectacles of the VCRs, audiences now watch movies according to a *glance aesthetic*

> rather than a *gaze aesthetic*: movies and spectators are indeed 'closer' than ever before (in Benjamin's sense) but it is a closeness that encourages viewers to casually test and measure a film as part of a domestic or public environment rather than become part of a concentrated reading. (p. 62)

What writers since Corrigan have been describing and analysing as the textual and financial shape of 'New Hollywood' is intimately tied to large shifts in global capitalism. For instance, Murray Smith observes areas that financial, technical, and aesthetic issues appear to both confirm and undo any deterministic reading of this beast called 'New Hollywood':[57]

> Since the 1960s, there has been a proliferation of terms designating more-or-less fundamental shifts in the nature – and thus the appropriate periodization – of Hollywood cinema: the New Hollywood, the New New Hollywood, post-classicism, and more indirectly, post-Fordism and postmodernism. (p. 3)

Critics largely agree that, in the post-studio era, the American film industry is fuelled by finances from elsewhere; that the global spread of financing may lead to a similar multinational dispersal of post-production facilities so that an 'American' film product is no longer viable; and, finally, that the collapse of national-oligopoly studio structures appears to have inflected film narratives in such a way that we find, as Corrigan suggests, fragmented narratives where rules of continuity and closure are no longer dominant.

Corrigan's formulation ultimately remains absorbed with changes within Euro-American cinema. Similarly, critical work on early cinema and pre-classical spectatorship interrogates the dominance of psychoanalytical models based on narrative coherence and ideal spectatorship, yet scholars draw their examples largely from American cinema, a feature no doubt rising from a widely held assumption that various experiments with narrative structuring were fully worked out in Hollywood films. This unacknowledged focus on one national cinema has allowed critics either to assume an easy migration of theory across different national cinemas on the one hand or, in a gesture coloured by cultural relativism, to cast other national cinemas within a different sociological framework while preserving theoretical insights arising from textual operations as a prerogative of American cinema.

There has been little effort by critics to locate the extraordinary details of New Hollywood in relationship to other national cinemas, an effort that may have revealed that most national cinemas, particularly the Indian, have never had an elaborate studio system, but continue to operate in what Janet Staiger describes as the 'unit package system'.[58] From its inception, the economics of the Indian film industry never replicated the production conditions of the American movie industry, but instead relied on loan sharks, the personal capital of filmmakers, and illicit or 'black' money.[59] Actually, the volatile conditions of the post-Vietnam American cinema cited by Corrigan have already been a feature of

Indian cinema for over fifty years and have particular textual manifestations that are recognisable through various *interruptions*, as discussed above. The fragmentary narrative cited as a unique feature of New Hollywood has long been a cinematic style in Indian popular cinema, which invented the 'multi-starrer', a concept that Justin Wyatt identifies as the 'high concept' of the post-studio era in America.[60] What I am suggesting is that whereas the technical, economic, and aesthetic dominance of Hollywood is now common sense, its changing economic conditions and aesthetic styles may have more in common with less 'integrated' film industries elsewhere. In other words, in studying Indian popular cinema we are not simply looking for faithful or deviant versions of Hollywood as a nostalgic desire for a refurbished cinema emergent from a different spatial location; rather, we should see them as an opportunity to explore a global exchange of narrative styles. There is no doubt that the globalisation of capital throws up points of contact between different national cinemas that previously we would have found to be either unimaginable or only secured through a narrative of imperialism. These national manifestations of dominant genre principles call attention to postmodern or transnational aesthetics of disruptions and discontinuities in a master narrative. I have used the words global and local to describe the formation and reconfiguration of genre conventions in Indian cinema; however, in postmodern writings, the nation is often a receding figure overshadowed by a 'transnational imaginary' – a term coined by Rob Wilson and Wimal Dissanayake:[61]

> What we would variously track as the 'transnational imaginary' comprises the *as-yet-unfigured* horizon of contemporary cultural production by which national spaces/identities of political allegiance and economic regulation are being undone and imagined communities of modernity are being reshaped at the macropolitical (global) and micropolitical (cultural) levels of everyday existence. (p. 6)

Offering a more cynical reading of these new arrangements, Henry Jenkins and Dirk Eitzen argue that dominant sectors of global capitalism always refashion themselves to avert total collapse.[62] Considering these different positions, I would add that the movement of global capital does not erase local conventions even if at times it coalesces around the figure of the nation.

. . .

The selection of films in this book [*Cinema of Interruptions*] illustrates the links between local and global cinematic styles, a selection infused by cinephilia rather than by a hyperrational methodology of inclusion.[63] Not only are these films ideally suited to exploring the tension between local and global cinematic styles as a particular mode of double articulation, but they also demonstrate a confidence in filmmaking that is most visible in the strengthening of local conventions even as they overtly engage with the structuring of anticipation and pleasure found in genre films. Highlighting Indian cinema's indirectness, in-between-ness, its propensity for digression and interruptions, the book modulates reading strategies inflected by psychoanalysis and narratology, moulding them to sharpen our understanding of this cinema. Through close readings of films, each chapter of the book explores the ways in which interruptions are yoked to the structuring of global genres and how my own reading strategies inherited from film theory accommodate local difference.

. . .

By choosing action genres, *Cinema of Interruptions* not only engages with the thematic preoccupations of violence in films, but also with how these films enunciate violence textually.[64] It celebrates various experiments in interruptions, directorial styles, and ongoing dialogue between different local cinemas. Hopefully, it will support the flourishing, of different cinematic practices in India. My investigation interrogates the constituents of narrative cinema, which is far from settled. In doing so, I resuscitate André Bazin's query 'What is cinema?' and respond by saying that it is inextricably linked to our Utopian imaginings, it stages the most anxious impulses of our psychic and social life, and it gives us hope for a better world. At the same time, the book also supplants Bazin's paternal query by responding to a more prescient question posed by the opening credits of Sooraj Barjatya's film, 'Hum aapke hain koun?'/'Who am I to you?'

Notes

1. René Girard (1972), *Desire, Deceit, and the Novel: Self and Other in Literary Structure*, tr. Yvonne Freccero, Baltimore: Johns Hopkins University Press.
2. The artist M. F. Hussain saw the film over forty times just to see actress Madhuri Dixit perform the 'Devar ho to aaisa' dance number.
3. I wish to thank Ravi Vasudevan for drawing my attention to this meaning.
4. Pico Iyer (1988), *Video Nights in Kathmandu: Reports from the Not-So-Far East*, New York: Knopf.
5. Salman Rushdie (1988), *The Satanic Verses*, London and New York, Viking; Alan Sealy (1990), *Hero*, Delhi: Viking India Ltd; Farrukh Dhondy (1990), *Bombay Duck*, London: Cape.
6. Manjunath Pendakur (1985), 'Dynamics of Cultural Policy Making: The US Film Industry in India', *Journal of Communication*, Autumn, pp. 52–72; Manjunath Pendakur (1990), 'India', in John A. Lent (ed.), *The Asian Film Industry*, Austin: Texas University Press.
7. Personal conversation with P. C. Sriram, September 1995.
8. Manmohan Shetty (1994), 'Trends in Film Processing', *Lensight*, vol. III, no. 4, October.
9. Pendakur, 1985.
10. Film production in 1979: 113 in Hindi; 139 in Tamil; and 131 in Telugu. In 1995: 157 in Hindi; 165 in Tamil; and 168 in Telugu. Figures are from Ashish Rajadhyaksha and Paul Willemen (eds) (1999), *Encyclopaedia of Indian Cinema*, London: BFI (rev. edn).
11. Anupama Chopra (1997), 'Southern Invasion', *India Today*, 13 October, pp. 38–40.

12. For a comprehensive evaluation of alternative filmmakers, see John W. Hood (2000), *The Essential Mystery*, New Delhi: Orient Longman.
13. On *Kaadalan*, see Vivek Dhareshwar and Tejaswini Niranjana (1996), '*Kaadalan* and the Politics of Resignification: Fashion, Violence, and the Body', *Journal of Arts and Ideas*, 29, January.
14. Conversation with O. P. Dutta, April 1999. Dutta tells of the 1950s and 1960s when the Soviets would purchase a number of films, but Indian filmmakers never kept track of these exhibitions or purchases. On viewing Indian films in Nigeria, see Brian Larkin (1997), 'Indian Films and Nigerian Lovers: Media and the Creation of Parallel Modernities', *Africa*, vol. 67, no. 3, pp. 406–40.
15. *Newsweek International*, 10 May 1999. My thanks to Tejaswini Ganti for posting this article.
16. I wish to thank Haim Bresheeth for this wonderful example from Israeli cinema.
17. Stuart Hall (1996), 'When Was "Post-Colonial"? Thinking at the Limit', in Iain Chambers and Lidia Curti (eds), *The Post-Colonial Question: Common Skies, Divided Horizons*, London: Routledge.
18. Achin Vanaik (1991), *The Painful Transition*, New York: Verso.
19. Veena Das (1992), 'Introduction', in Veena Das (ed.), *Mirrors of Violence: Communities and Survivors in South Asia*, Delhi: Oxford University Press.
20. Firoze Rangoonwala (1993), 'The Age of Violence', *Illustrated Weekly of India*, 4–10 September, pp. 27–9; Rashmi Doriaswamy (1995), 'Hindi Commercial Cinema: Changing Narrative Strategies', in Aruna Vasudev (ed.), *Frames of Mind: Reflections on Indian Cinema*, New Delhi: UBS.
21. Media Advocacy Group and National Commission for Women (n.d.), *People's Perception: Obscenity and Violence on the Screen*, New Delhi; The Media Advocacy Group and National Commission for Women (1993), *A Gender Perspective for the Electronic Media*, March, New Delhi. I wish to thank Roopal Oza for alerting me to these reports.
22. Ken Wlaschin (1976), 'Birth of the "Curry" Western: Bombay 1976', *Film and Filming*, April, vol. 22, no. 7, pp. 20–3. Touted as a 'curry Western' by film critic Ken Wlaschin, reviewing the Film Festival in 1976, Sippy's film fits quite easily into revisionist Westerns such as spaghetti Westerns.
23. Madan Gopal Singh (1983), 'Technique as an Ideological Weapon', in Aruna Vasudev and Phillipe Lenglet (eds), *Indian Cinema Superbazaar*, Delhi: Vikas.
24. Judith Mayne (1993), *Cinema and Spectatorship*, London: Routledge. Mayne provides a splendid and sympathetic critique of the ideal spectator in psychoanalysis.
25. Although Singh's formulation has critical value, I should like to question his reading of the song: a close analysis of the scene shows that the camera does not actively grope the dancer's body even though it fragments her body. Attributing movement to a phantom camera, Singh may be implicitly admitting to being taken in by the entertaining song and dance number!
26. Rashmi Doraiswamy and Aruna Vasudev – the author of the best book on Indian censorship – floated the film journal *Cinemaya* with the explicit intention of expanding interest in Asian cinema from an Asian location.
27. Interview with Naseeruddin Shah, *Filmfare*, May 1998.
28. *Sholay* emerges as the first important film in the life of several young stars in a survey conducted by *Filmfare*, June 1999.
29. Rosie Thomas (1985), 'Indian Cinema: Pleasures and Popularity', *Screen*, vol. 26, nos 3/4, was one of the first to propose that the popular film industry be taken seriously, on its 'own terms'.
30. Colin McCabe (1986), 'Defining Popular Culture', in McCabe (ed.), *High Theory/ Low Culture: Analyzing Popular Television and Film*, New York: St Martin's Press.
31. Paul Willemen (1994), 'Through the Glass Darkly: Cinephilia Reconsidered', in *Looks and Frictions: Essays in Cultural Studies and Film Theory*, Bloomington: Indiana University Press.

32. Susan Sontag (1996), 'The Decay of Cinema', *New York Times Magazine*, 25 February, pp. 60–1; *Vertigo*, no. 10 (1988); *Cahiers du cinéma*, no. 498 (1998), *Film Quarterly*, Fall (1998). Peter Wollen (2001), 'An Alphabet of Cinema', *New Left Review* (Second Series), vol. 12, November/December, pp. 115–33 – part polemic, part eulogy, Wollen offers a delightful yet moving tribute to cinema in the form of first principles and cannot help proclaiming that the letter 'C' stands for cinephilia.
33. Christine Keathley (2000), 'The Cinephiliac Moment', *Framework Online*, no. 42.
34. Richard Dyer (1992), *Only Entertainment*, London and New York: Routledge.
35. Sharon Willis (1998), *High Contrast*, Durham, NC: Duke University Press.
36. Roger Cardinal (1986), 'Pausing over Peripheral Detail', *Framework*, nos 30/31, pp. 112–30.
37. Naomi Schor (1987), *Reading in Detail: Aesthetics and the Feminine*, New York: Methuen.
38. Christian Metz (1982), *The Imaginary Signifier: Psychoanalysis and the Cinema*, tr. Celia Britton, Annwyl Williams, Ben Brewester, and Alfred Guzzetti, Bloomington: Indiana University Press.
39. Stephen Neale (1992), *Genre*, London: BFI (rev. edn); Stephen Neale (2000), *Genre and Hollywood*, London and New York: Routledge.
40. Rick Altman (1999), *Film/Genre*, London: BFI.
41. M. Madhava Prasad (1998), *Ideology of the Hindi Film: A Historical Construction*, Delhi: Oxford University Press.
42. Ravi S. Vasudevan (1995), 'Addressing the Spectator of a "Third-World" National Cinema: The Bombay Social Film of the 1940s and 1950s', *Screen*, vol. 36, no. 4.
43. Erik Barnow and S. Krishnaswamy (1980), *Indian Film*, New York: Oxford University Press, p. 69.
44. Barnow and Krishnaswamy, p. 157.
45. American film producers have also started to see the commercial viability of soundtracks. Music stores now exclusively stack a separate section with movie soundtracks.
46. See Judith Mayne (1993), *Cinema and Spectatorship*, for a splendid exegesis on the cultural context of Hollywood production and its preferred spectator.
47. Peter Wollen uses 'multi-diegesis' to describe Jean-Luc Godard's film *Vent d'Est*, arguing that Godard is responding to both Hollywood and Mosfilm narratives, characterised by a single diegesis, by producing a film with multi-diegesis.
48. See Aruna Vasudev's (1978) ground-breaking book *Liberty and Licence in Indian Cinema*, Delhi: Vikas; Kobita Sarkar (1982), *You Can't Please Everyone: Film Censorship, the Inside Story*, Bombay: IBH; CLRI (1982), *The Indian Cinematograph Code*, Hyderabad, AP: Cinematograph Laws Research Institute.
49. Sergei M. Eisenstein, 'The Montage of Film Attractions', in Peter Lehman (ed.) (1997), *Defining Cinema*, New Brunswick: Rutgers University Press.
50. Peter Wollen (1982), 'Godard and Counter Cinema: *Vent d'est*', in *Readings and Writings: Semiotic Counter-Strategies*, London: Verso.
51. Tom Gunning (1990), ' "Primitive" Cinema: A Frame-Up? Or the Trick's on Us', in Thomas Elsaesser and Adam Barker (eds), *Early Cinema: Space, Frame, Narrative*, London: BFI, pp. 95–103; Tom Gunning (1990), 'Non-Continuity, Continuity, Discontinuity: A Theory of Genres in Early Films', in Elsaesser and Barker (eds), *Early Cinema*, pp. 86–94.
52. Miriam Hansen (1991), *Babel and Babylon: Spectatorship in American Silent Film*, Cambridge, Mass: Harvard University Press.
53. Christian Metz (1985), 'Story/Discourse: Notes on Two Kinds of Voyeurism', in Bill Nichols (ed.), *Movies and Methods*, Berkeley: University of California Press.
54. Laura Mulvey (1975), 'Visual Pleasure and Narrative Cinema', *Screen*, vol. 16, no. 3.
55. Timothy Corrigan (1991), *A Cinema without Walls: Movies and Culture after Vietnam*, New Brunswick: Rutgers University Press, p. 4.

56. Corrigan, p. 7.
57. Murray Smith (1997), 'Theses on the Philosophy of Hollywood History', in Steve Neale and Murray Smith (eds), *Contemporary Hollywood Cinema*, London: Routledge.
58. Janet Staiger (1985), 'The Hollywood Mode of Production', in David Bordwell, Janet Staiger, and Kristin Thompson, *Classical Hollywood Cinema: Film Style and Mode of Production to 1960*, New York: Columbia University Press.
59. M. A. Oomen and K. V. Joseph (1991), *Economics of Indian Cinema*, New Delhi: IBH.
60. Justin Wyatt (1994), *High Concept: Movies and Marketing in Hollywood*, Austin: University of Texas Press.
61. Rob Wilson and Wimal Dissanayake (1996), 'Introduction: Tracking the Global/Local', in Rob Wilson and Wimal Dissanayake (eds), *Global/Local: Cultural Production and the Transnational Imaginary*, Durham, NC: Duke University Press.
62. Henry Jenkins (1995), 'Historical Poetics,' in Joanne Hollows and Mark Jankovich (eds), *Approaches to Popular Film*, Manchester: Manchester University Press, 1995; Dirk Eitzen (1991), 'Evolution, Functionalism, and the Study of American Cinema', *The Velvet Light Trap*, vol. 28, Fall, pp. 82–3.
63. I do want to add a note of caution that not all popular films in India contain articulations of local and global, several films made in Tamil, Telugu, and Hindi remain removed from global signifying systems.
64. Critical work on violence in South Asia by Veena Das and Valentine Daniel has been crucial to my understanding of the relationship between cinematic representations, narratives of violence, and the eruption of violence in the public sphere. See Veena Das (ed.) (1992), *Mirrors of Violence: Communities, Riots and Survivors in South Asia*, Delhi: Oxford University Press; Valentine Daniel (1998), *Charred Lullabies: Chapters in an Anthropography of Violence*, Berkeley: University of California Press.

17

SHIFTING PITCH: THE BOLLYWOOD SONG SEQUENCE IN THE ANGLO-AMERICAN MARKET

Ian Garwood

Bollywood's New Markets

On the occasion of the 2004 Cannes Film Festival, the trade magazine *Variety* produced a special supplement focusing on the Mumbai film industry (henceforth referred to as Bollywood). Its lead article concerned the increasing export potential of Bollywood movies, and it opened in a manner commensurate with much journalistic writing on the subject:

> In the past decade, the non-resident Indian (NRI) has assumed God-like status in the Mumbai film industry. The Indian diaspora, one of the fastest growing communities in the world, is conservatively estimated at 20 million.
>
> For these Indians, scattered from New Zealand to North America, Hindi films are the umbilical chord that ties them to the motherland.
>
> Second-generation teenagers, who can't speak the language, read subtitles. Hindi movies are a global glue binding disparate peoples with their songs, stars and unabashed melodrama.
>
> The Bollywood export market, worth an estimated $20 million, is roughly divided into the UK (40 per cent), US (30 per cent) and the rest of the world (30 per cent). While the UK brings in more theatrical revenues, the US is bigger for home entertainment.[1]

Four elements of this passage are significant, in terms of the way they illustrate a popular rhetoric around the cultural and commercial function of Bollywood movies targeted at non-resident Indians (NRIs). Firstly, there is the hyberbolic description of the market value of non-resident Indians themselves, valued as 'gods' for the increased earning potential they offer to Bollywood in relation to their counterparts living within Indian borders. Secondly, the article makes the familiar assertion that these movies serve an important cultural role for their diasporic audience, as a vehicle through which NRIs may connect imaginatively with traditional 'Indian' culture, thereby confirming themselves to be part of a wider global Indian community. Thirdly, there is a conventional recital of the films' perceived unique selling points ('songs, stars and unabashed melodrama'). Finally, the passage breaks down the proportion each overseas market occupies in relation to exported Bollywood movies, noting the financial importance of the UK and US to this market, above all others.

Bollywood movies have always found a market outside India,[2] but the emergence of the UK and the US as the most commercially lucrative export territories is a recent development. This has occurred in the context of a general drive, especially from the early 1990s, to reform India's economy in the mould of Western liberal capitalism. In the context of the Bollywood film industry, institutional measures have dramatically increased the flow of trade, in both directions, between Indian and Western markets.[3] The bestowing of official status upon the film industry by the Indian government in 2000 encouraged further the interaction of Bollywood with global finance and markets, as it allowed producers to secure loans from the state bank for the first time, and made the industry more attractive to multinational corporations. Thus, *Variety* was able to report that 2003 had been the most profitable year ever for Bollywood in the export market, even though the previous year had seen the industry suffer its worst losses for a decade on the domestic front.[4]

Since *Hum Aapke Hain Koun*! (Sooraj R. Barjatya) heralded an era of international 'superhits' in 1994, a number of films have found favour with the NRI-audience in the UK and US markets. In the decade following *Hum Aapke Hain Koun*!'s breakthrough success, these films have been overwhelmingly located within the genre of the family romance, to the extent that the 'NRI romance' has become an accepted genre classification in journalistic discourse.[5] The most commercially successful NRI romances include *Dilwale Dulhaniya Le Jayenge* (Aditya Chopra, 1995), *Kuch Kuch Hota Hai* (Karan Johar, 1998), *Kabhi Khushi Kabhie Gham* (Karan Johar, 2001), *Kal Ho Na Ho* (Nikhil Advani, 2003), and *Chalte Chalte* (Aziz Mirza, 2003). Each have courted their audience through a distinctive set of narrative themes, which Ravinder Kaur describes as:

> family values, moral superiority, true (unpolluted) love, the sacrifice of individual desires for greater good of the family/community, and the struggle and victory of the Indian Diaspora in preserving their cultural universe through Indian rites of passages in an alien environment.[6]

The insistence with which the NRI romance pursues these themes suggests that, on one level, the films are offering their viewers a chance to participate imaginatively in a particular type of Indian *citizenship*. They celebrate an 'Indian-specific' national identity, with which NRIs are encouraged to identify: a national identity expressed through the seductive spectacle of everyday ceremony, religious ritual, and emphasis on traditionally 'Indian' family values that is repeated from film to film.

Anthony C. Alessandrini has identified another significant trend in the NRI romance in addition to the courting of viewers as citizens: the seduction of the audience through the rituals of 'capitalist consumption'.[7] Referring specifically to *Hum Aapke Hain Koun!*, Alessandrini argues that it

> is an ideal film in the context of India's recent move to a policy of economic 'liberalization', for, like this policy, it promises an endless flow of goods and effortless prosperity – represented in the film by the taken-for-granted affluence of the two families and the huge amounts of food (including Cadbury bars and Pepsi) that are consumed continuously.[8]

So, a consistent strategy of these films has been to flatter their viewers' competencies as consumers as well as citizens: the NRI romance concentrates almost exclusively on characters from the affluent middle class, whose wealth is evidenced as much by their accumulation of Western-style consumer goods, involvement in international business, or actual experience of living in the West, as it is by the signs of a more traditionally prosperous Indian lifestyle.

My particular interest is in the way the musical number helps to court the NRI viewer in this dual role: as both citizen and consumer. It is significant, I think, that the *Variety* article lists 'songs' as the first element in its description of the Bollywood formula. The song sequence is a crucial part of the branding of Bollywood in Western film territories, the single most identifiable element that marks its territory from its Hollywood counterparts.

It is my suggestion that the musical number in the NRI romance is marked, quite self-consciously, by its responsibilities in helping to carry the Bollywood 'brand' to new international markets. As a way of focusing this argument, I am going to use the example of the song sequences of *Hum Saath Saath Hain* (Sooraj R. Barjatya), a superhit from 1999, made by the same team responsible for *Hum Aapke Hain Koun!*. *Hum Saath Saath Hain* (*HSSH*) uses different representational strategies in its musical sequences, depending on whether they are set in urban or rural spaces. The city-set numbers display an *excessively* artificial aesthetic which reinforces their status as commodities, and which refers them to an international NRI audience in particular. The spectating position offered to the NRI viewer in relation to the song sequences involves a certain type of distance, even as the numbers are also presented as a vehicle to transport the viewer 'home' in their imaginations to India.

'Preserving' the Song Sequence in *HSSH*

The film follows the various romances of the sons and daughter of an affluent businessman living in an unnamed city, which I assume to be Mumbai. The father trains his sons in the family business, but his chief desire is that the family remain united: the movie's tagline, 'the family that prays together, stays together', displays the film's traditionalist credentials. Midway through the film, the action moves away from the city to the family's ancestral home, in the village of Rampur, where the father is building an electricity plant, to be overseen by his sons.

The moment when the unnamed urban metropolis meets the rural idyll of Rampur is a musical one. The family, together with the new and prospective partners of the three brothers, are sitting around in their city home, watching an old black and white home movie of their upbringing in Rampur. The black and white film shows a number of the assembled characters in earlier days, and settles on two musical performances: the first featuring Vivek, the oldest brother, as a child, teaching a group of younger children the English alphabet through the song 'ABCDEFGHI'; the second a duet between Vinod, the youngest son, and Sapna, his childhood friend (and in the present day prospective girlfriend), entitled 'Maiyaa Yashoda'. For this number, Vinod and Sapna are dressed in regal costume and are miming the song on a small stage, with their delighted family around them, and with a playback singer providing the vocals for Sapna to the side of the performing space.

The songs featured in the home movies summon a response in the on-screen audience watching them: they struggle to identify and then make jokes about their younger selves and, significantly, sing along with the 'ABCDEFGHI' number; the songs also return later in the film as full blown musical sequences, which are performed by the grown-up characters who had enacted them as children in the home movie sequence.

What interests me in this sequence is the self-conscious presentation of its musical numbers as *filmed* performances. I am also interested in the way musical and visual material is reformatted, repeated and imitated – in the space of the sequence and through the film as a whole. I want now to unpack the various repetitions, reformattings and acts of impersonation that take place, before arguing for the contradictory readings that such self-conscious presentation of its musical material may encourage.

If the home movie is regarded as containing the 'original' musical performances, the first reformatting that takes place is a visual one: we are made to see the black and white, small-screen footage as part of a broader canvas, that is to say the wide-screen, colour image through which we see the film as a whole unfold. This produces a sense that the original black and white image is being archived: preserved within the frame of the contemporary wide-screen, colour image to which the viewer is otherwise exposed. I think this sense of the musical number as something that is being self-consciously preserved, indicates a wider tendency in the NRI romance, a point I will expand upon later in this essay.

As well as presenting the original performance in a frame within a frame, a process of reformatting, the sequence also rhymes character movement within the colour footage with movement within the black and white footage – a process of imitation. In this excerpt, we see the grown-up characters nodding their heads from side to side to the tune of the first song; this same head movement is the very next thing we see from their childhood counterparts, as the film cuts back to the black and white footage. This process of imitation between colour and black and white footage is taken up more extensively later on, when the grown-up Sapna and Vinod perform, in full colour, the 'Maiyaa Yashoda' routine we see in the black and white home movie.

This process of repetition and imitation is just as evident on the soundtrack. Most obviously, the grown-up characters sing along to the voices of their younger selves during 'ABCDEFGHI'. But there is also a type of *mimicry* going on within the confines of the home movie screen during the 'Maiyaa Yashoda' number: the original performance features Vinod and Sapna as children, with Sapna *miming* to a song being performed by a female singer sitting beside the stage; the sensation of a mimed performance is exacerbated by the experience of hearing an adult voice coming out of a child's mouth.

Behind these overt layers of imitation and mimicry is a more latent one: the voice of the singer we see to the side of the stage is dubbed, according to Bollywood convention, by a credited playback singer. So we are seeing Sapna as a child miming along to an on-screen singer, who is, in turn, being voiced by an invisible playback singer. A different configuration of mimer and mimee appears when the grown-up Sapna sings the same song to the grown-up Vinod in the full-blown musical sequence later on. At this point, the actress playing the grown-up Sapna, Karisma Kapoor, is being dubbed by the same playback singer who had provided the original vocals in the black and white footage. The viewer is now asked to accept that the voice that had belonged to the stage-side singer in the black and white home movie, is magically transferred to the grown-up Sapna the moment she breaks in to song.

Citizenship Through Music in *HSSH*

Two possibilities come to mind when considering the significance of these various visual and musical acts of repetition and mimicry, each plotting a contradictory path to the other. Firstly, the repetitions and acts of mimicry could be viewed as typical of the Bollywood movie and the musical number's special place within it. After all, the 'repeat value' of the soundtrack – be it dialogue or music – is something that has often been prized by viewers of Bollywood movies. The early part of this sequence, where the grown-up family join in with the 'ABCDEFGHI' song being performed in the home movie, could be viewed in this light: as simply a home-spun representation of the sing-a-long culture that has long been associated with the Bollywood film viewing experience.

It is also commonly noted that musical performance is part of everyday life in India, to a unique extent. Film songs are routinely sung out of their original contexts; religious festivals and other kinds of ceremonial occasions offer wide scope for an array of different types of musical performance. In the sequence under discussion, we see song and dance as an integral part of everyday family life: both in terms of the show being put on in the black and white footage, clearly a special family occasion, and in the use the same family make of the recording of it as a bonding musical experience when they play back the footage fifteen years later.

So, there is a sense that this sequence is simply a reflection of the everyday experience of music in traditional Indian culture: an experience that is founded on repetition – whether it be the ritualistic quality of the ceremonial song and dance, or the repetition of favourite songs on special occasions – and also on mimicry, witnessed by the singing back to the screen we see represented in this sequence, and the happy acceptance of the convention of the playback singer that allows the same voice to be connected with different on-screen bodies in the Bollywood movie, without the pleasure of the musical spectacle being disrupted.

This explanation suggests a retention of the status quo. The NRI romance is doing what Bollywood movies have always done: drawing on India's rich tradition of musical performance on the one hand, as a pretext for launching into a spectacular song and dance number; and adding to the repertoire of memorable film songs that feed into that traditional culture on the other. The reports that songs from the first blockbuster NRI romance, *Hum Aapke Hain Koun!*, immediately became staples at real-life Indian weddings tend to support the idea that these films' musical numbers are feeding off and feeding into a vibrant traditional Indian culture.

Returning to my original suggestion that the NRI romance constructs its ideal viewer as both a citizen and as a consumer, the musical number – cast in the role I have provisionally outlined – would seem to allow the viewer the chance to identify themselves with the first term in that description: as a truly 'Indian' *citizen*, who affiliates with the traditions of musical performance – be they ceremonial traditions or cinematic ones – put on show in the films.

Urban Song Sequences in *HSSH*

But, what about the courting of the viewer also as a *consumer*? A spectator not just attuned to 'Indian' traditions, but also keyed in to the global consumer culture in which the Indian government, especially since the early 1990s, so clearly desires to take part? My second explanation for the emphasis on repetition and mimicry in the sequence discussed from *Hum Saath Saath Hain* takes account of the appeal to the consumerist side of the ideal viewer of the NRI romance.

In many of the romances, the emergence of India as a player in the powerful Western commercial markets is demonstrated by the presence of lead characters who migrate freely between Western territories and India, conducting business on a global scale, whilst remaining true to their 'Indian' roots.[9]

In *Hum Saath Saath Hain*, the acts of migration are less expansive, but their significance is just the same: the mobility of the lead family here is between an urban commercial centre within India, and an underdeveloped rural village. The father's ambition is to adhere to traditional Indian family values – the family that prays together, stays together – whilst also engaging in free enterprise: raising the capital to set up an electricity plant in the village of his childhood, as a small contribution to the modernisation of his country, within the context of a liberalised, consumer-orientated economy.

The musical sequences in the film are played out differently, depending on whether they take place in urban or rural environments. All the musical performances are marked by a self-awareness and acceptance of artifice typical of the Bollywood movie. But within this context, the urban song and dance sequences are coded as far more staged than the rural ones.

There is a distinct difference between the organisation of *mise en scène* in the city-set musical numbers and the rural ones. The numbers of the first third of the film, set around the family's city home, are marked by a very definite division between the foreground – where the main characters sing and dance – and the background, which is typically characterised by a severe flatness and absence of musical performance. In fact, the credit sequence, which features the main characters performing the title number, is played out against an entirely blank backdrop. The next number, 'Yeh To Sach Hai', a tribute from the sons and daughter of the family to their parents, is performed at the very front of a stage that has colourful cardboard cut-outs of musical instruments at its rear. The two-dimensional quality of the backdrop is exacerbated by the appearance of a large black and white photo of the sons and daughter as small children: like the cardboard instruments, this photo acts as a 'flat' representation of three-dimensional objects.

Of all the city-set musical numbers, 'Yeh To Sach Hai' contains the greatest sense of flow between performing and audience spaces, as the performers often move away from the stage to interact with their parents who are watching the tribute to them. However, even at these moments, the distinction between foreground performance and static backdrop is reconfigured, as the parents become part of the performing line, behind which the rest of the audience looks on respectfully. Even when, towards the end of the number, the audience begins to dance around the main performers, the film rarely allows a view that sees the leading characters encircled: instead the camera consistently reframes the action tightly around the lead performers so that the circling movement remains intimated rather than fully displayed.

The next number, the exuberant song and dance performed just before the eldest son Vivek's wedding ceremony, reproduces the strategy of restricting any sense of dynamic interaction to the performers and the overt subjects of the song (Vivek and his bride Sadhana). Otherwise, the extravagant dance routines are filmed from a predominantly frontal position, with a large group of spectators forming the backdrop some way behind them.

The wedding-party scene after the ceremony constitutes the longest musical sequence of the city-set section of the film. Here the distinction between performers in the foreground and a static, flattened background is registered, as in the earlier tribute song to the parents, by the theatrical backdrops against which the staged performance is set. The artificiality of the background is multiplied by the series of (impossibly quick) scene changes that take place during the course of the number. In addition, any sense of dynamism between the performers and audience is reduced to cutaways to the characters who are being addressed in the song (which is led by Vinod and Sapna imitating members of their family, as a way of introducing Vivek's new wife to them).

Rural Song Sequences in *HSSH*

After the black and white home movie sequence, the action moves to the rural setting of Rampur. In contrast to the city-set musical numbers, the three song sequences set in a rural environment are more integrated into their natural surroundings, with a far more extensive interplay between foreground and background performance. Characters wander through the landscape and are touched by it, rather than simply performing in front of it. In the first sequence, the bus journey which takes the family from the city to the countryside, this interaction is exemplified by Vinod singing the 'ABCDEFGHI' song whilst hanging off the side of the bus, leaning towards the verge of the hill they are traversing, with mountain mist surrounding him. In addition, this moment is immediately followed by Vinod back in the bus, singing the next line: the two different performing spaces, the outside and inside of the bus, exist here in a state of seamless connection, unlike the strict demarcation of performing space characteristic of the earlier city-set musical numbers.

The penultimate number, 'Mhare Hiwada Mein', initially set on an elephant tour of various exotic locations around Rampur, features musical performance on both foreground and background planes, rather than restricting the singing and dancing to the foreground as in the city-set sequences. Expansive, deeply focused shots show rows of dancers performing towards the very back of the frame as the main characters perform in front. As the sequence narrows its focus on the relationships between the middle son Prem and his fiancée Preeti, as well as youngest son Vinod and Sapna, the performers appear unexpectedly from behind architectural features in the middle of the frame – this again contrasts with the emphasis on foreground musical performance in the earlier city-set sequences.

Finally, the reprise of 'Mayaii Yashoda', first seen in the home movie footage, moves from the kind of frontally framed performance reminiscent of the earlier sequences, to one where the performers interact more and more with the audience (to the extent that the position of Vinod as performer or audience addressee becomes indistinct). The sequence also resolves itself as a performance in the round, rather than as one presented in proscenium style, as dancers and audience members alike link hands and whirl around in a series of circles. The camera cranes up to give the viewer a full view of these circular patterns, in contrast to the finale of the city-set 'Yeh To Sach Hai', which, as I have discussed, remains focused on its leading performers at the front of the frame, despite the intimation that they too are encircled by the audience by the end of the number.

THE 'SUPERIOR' URBAN PERSPECTIVE OF *HSSH*

In the film, the urban is associated with modernisation, the positive drive towards a Westernised consumer culture; the rural village is associated with tradition – it provides the ancestral home of a family for whom traditional family values mean so much. For the viewer to be addressed effectively as a citizen consumer, the urban and rural spheres – and their associated values – *should* carry equal weight: affiliation to 'Indian-specific' tradition, that is to say citizenship, should go hand in hand with modernising aspirations, that is to say consumerism.

However, the framing procedures of the musical numbers do not indicate that this balancing act is achieved in *Hum Saath Saath Hain*. Ultimately, the rural experience is framed only within the perspective of the urban. The more 'natural' interactive qualities of the village-set song sequences are only apparent because they are set against the more obviously artificial strategies of musical display, demonstrated by a sharp distinction between foreground and background, that have been established in the city-set song sequences.

The urban demonstrates the ability to frame 'natural' musical experience, represented by the rural, within its own, more artificial, discourse. The home movie sequence is crucial in indicating this. It introduces two of the three songs that will subsequently be heard in full-blown versions in the village section of the film. The manner of this introduction demonstrates the urban's ability to place the rural experience within a particular frame. In this process, the 'naturalness' of the song performances is distorted. The original performance of the children singing 'ABCDEFGHI' and 'Mayaii Yashoda' is literally robbed of its colour. The more integrated, three-dimensional quality of this original performance of 'Mayaii Yashoda', which is shown to take place with the audience around every side of the stage, is flattened, as it is projected on to the two-dimensional home movie screen. Interaction between the musical performers and their audience *does* take place, as the grown-up family sing along to their youthful selves. However, this interaction only takes place at one remove: the safe distance between foreground and background, and flattening of the performing space, typical of the earlier city-set song sequences, is reasserted.

Ravi S. Vasudevan, amongst others, has identified an 'aesthetics of frontality' and the tableau[10] as key to the visual codes of narration of a range of Indian films (his particular focus is on the Bombay 'social' film of the 1940s and 1950s). The tableau suggests initially a static type of framing in which meanings are highly condensed, but, for Vasudevan, this sense of stasis is always subject to a potential movement:

> These observations [of Roland Barthes on the tableau] suggest both the highly controlled work involved in the construction of the tableau and also its inbuilt possibilities of dynamization. Its constitution of a frozen dynamic implicitly suggests the possibilities of change. This means that deployment of the tableau frame does not invariably mean indifference to

> the problem of offscreen space. Dissections of the tableau, cut-ins to closer views on the scene, the use of looks offscreen and character movements in and out of frame serve to complicate the tableau, fulfilling the promise of its reorganization.[11]

In relation to the Bombay 'social' film, Vasudevan suggests that the dynamic motor for the reorganisation of the tableau is the structuring of vision around the establishment of patriarchal authority.[12]

The structuring principle behind the different kinds of framings in the musical sequences of *Hum Saath Saath Hain* appears to me to derive from other sources. The more static, frontal compositions of the urban musical sequences derive what dynamism they have from a mapping out of the strong familial ties between the characters: the cutaways from the frontal framings of the actual singing and dancing performers inevitably direct the viewer towards the family member whose virtues are being extolled by the song. In this sense, the song and dance sequences act to court the spectator as an Indian citizen, offering the spectacle of frontal framings being reorganised to affirm the solidity of traditionally 'Indian' family roles.

However, the contrast between the emphasis on frontal framings and static tableau compositions in the urban sections and the more interactive performing spaces of the rural musical sequences suggests another principle governing the film's musical-visual economy: that is to say, the contrast bespeaks a heightened awareness of the commodity value of the musical number itself, as part of the branding of the NRI romance in its newly important Western markets.

For this newly courted sector of the international audience, that is to say the UK and US markets, the musical number of the Bollywood movie is simultaneously a point of nostalgia and of novelty: nostalgia because it forms part of the Indian tradition to which the films encourage the NRI-audience to connect (courting them as citizens); and novelty, because the routine interruption of the narrative through song-and-dance is a formula which does not exist in the dominant filmmaking cultures of the US or the UK (thus constituting one of the unique selling points of Bollywood for the viewers in their role as consumers).

HSSH as Metaphor for the NRI Viewing Experience

The characters' viewing of the home movie footage in *Hum Saath Saath Hain* encapsulates the musical number's dual courting of its NRI-audience: the on-screen urban-dwelling audience represent the surrogates of the off-screen NRI-viewer. As a metaphor for NRI consumption of Bollywood movies, this sequence proposes the NRI viewer to be self-consciously different to a particular version of the 'typical' spectator of popular Indian cinema. Ravi Vasudevan summarises Chidananda Das Gupta's description of this 'typical' viewer in this way:

> [Gupta] argues that the commercial film catered to a spectator who had not severed his ties from the countryside and so had a traditional or pre-modern

> relationship to the image, one which incapacitated him or her from distinguishing between image and reality.[13]

Whatever problems there may be with the assumptions behind this assessment of the 'typical' spectator of popular Indian movies, it is significant that *Hum Saath Saath Hain* explicitly presents its characters involved in an act of spectatorship which frames musical performance as a distanced *image* (black and white rather than colour, in the past rather than present, with the grown-up characters struggling at first to recognise themselves from their childhood images). As such the scene proposes a superior urban perspective on the traditional song-and-dance sequence which mirrors that of a more 'sophisticated' and 'distanced' NRI-consumer, who has chosen to engage with a Bollywood text amongst all the choices in popular entertainment available in their particular market.[14]

So my first explanation for the repetitions and mimicry within the home movie sequence proposed that these were in fact traditional qualities with which the NRI romance seeks to affiliate itself: allowing, in particular, the NRI audience to experience a feeling of citizenship in relation to India, despite their geographical dislocation from the country itself.

My second explanation suggests that the self-conscious reformatting of musical material in the sequence actually indicates a different, more mediated relationship to traditional Indian music culture, or at least, to its traditional film music culture. It is noticeable that, when the film returns to the city for the last third of its duration, there are no significant song sequences. It is as if the film has exhausted its own possibilities in terms of spectacular musical expression: the 'flatness' and lack of dynamism of the early song sequences would not be suitable for the more melodramatic action of the closing scenes, in which the family threatens to fall apart. Yet, there is also no question of importing the more 'natural' interactive strategies of staging associated with the rural musical sequences: as the home movie scenes show, these natural performances fall foul to contaminating influences as soon as they reach city limits.

The success of the NRI romance, along with the more general infiltration of an identifiably Bollywood aesthetic in commercial Western cinema, does offer a powerful example of contra-flow: the penetration of non-Western cultural forms into Western markets, as opposed to the more commonly told story of the West's economic and cultural incursions into other territories. However, *Hum Saath Saath Hain* suggests that the Bollywood musical number does not emerge unscathed from such a transaction. The NRI romance relies on the display of 'traditional' Indian music culture to court a diasporic audience as *citizens*. But, in keeping with its project to appeal to its audience also as particular kinds of *consumers*, it subjects these traditions to a process of repackaging and reformatting. The musical number is expected to stir deep patriotic feeling in its ideal spectator, at the same time as it is pushed forward aggressively as a particular kind of commodity, as if in a shop-window display.

The aggression with which the NRI romance courts its international audience through the song sequence could be interpreted as a form of cultural anxiety. Indeed, commentators have suggested that the 'genre' is in danger of exhausting itself, and a small number of films have adopted a different strategy to court the NRI market: that is to say, they have eschewed the song sequence entirely in favour of a representational scheme that is more in keeping with the conventions of mainstream Western filmmaking.[15] The highly self-conscious presentation of the city-set musical numbers in *Hum Saath Saath Hain*, together with its retreat in to musical silence in its final third, demonstrates how the tensions between the forces of tradition and those of the market can exert a visible and audible pressure on films designed for previously underexploited international territories.

Notes

1. Anupama Chopra, 'Passage from India: Bollywood filmmakers cater to subcontinental diaspora', *Variety*, 13 May 2004, p. A1.
2. Ravi S. Vasudevan summarises these traditional markets as East Africa, Mauritius, the Middle East, South-east Asia, Northern Africa, the former Soviet Union and China; see Ravi S. Vasudevan, 'Addressing the spectator of a "third world" national cinema: the Bombay "social" film of the 1940s and 1950s', reprinted in this collection.
3. Both Ravinder Kaur and Anthony C. Alessandrini describe some of these measures in the articles cited below
4. *Variety*, 'Passage from India', p. A1.
5. The currency of the term in contemporary critical discourse is demonstrated by a 2005 article in *The Hindustan Times* entitled 'Is the NRI romance dead?', which provides an overview of the 'genre', whilst also predicting its demise: http://www.hindustantimes.com/news/181_1271029,00110003.htm, 8 March 2005.
6. Ravinder Kaur, 'Viewing the West through Bollywood: a celluloid Occident in the making', *Contemporary South Asia*, 11: 2, 2002, pp. 199–209, pp. 200–1.
7. Anthony C. Alessandrini, '"My heart's Indian for All That": Bollywood film between home and diaspora', *Diaspora*, 10: 3, 2001, pp. 315–40, p. 324.
8. Ibid. p. 324.
9. All the NRI romances mentioned in this essay feature at least one character who lives in, or travels to, a Western territory.
10. Ravi S. Vasudevan, 'Addressing the spectator of a "third world" national cinema'.
11. Ibid.
12. Ibid.
13. Ibid.
14. Of course, it is not just NRI viewers who engage with these films; nor is it the case that viewers in India have less choice over what they view. However, this chapter is focused on the way *HSSH* seems to make *particular* efforts to provide a textual construction of the NRI spectator.
15. The article in *The Hindustan Times*, referenced above, indicates this tendency to question the sustainability of the NRI romance formula. In this instance, the international success of the songless Bollywood drama *Black* (Sanjay Leela Bhansali, 2005) is taken as a sign of the NRI romance's imminent demise.

SECTION 6
QUESTIONS OF AUTHORSHIP AND TAIWANESE CINEMA

FILM AUTHORSHIP AND TAIWANESE CINEMA

Gary Needham and I-Fen Wu

ISSUES OF AUTHORSHIP

Gary Needham

This section examines film authorship in relation to Taiwanese cinema with specific reference, in this Introduction to the section, to the emergence and context of the Taiwanese New Cinema or New Wave. All three chapters presented here explore in their own way the centrality of authorship; they do so not just a framework for discussing the various talents of individual directors, Hou Hsiao-Hsien, Edward Yang, and Ang Lee, but as a necessary device for exploring a range of contexts and responses from urban alienation to transnationalism. These chapters also reveal how authorship – while perhaps exhausted in debates about dominant, canonical and popular cinemas such as classical Hollywood and European art cinema – is still in other, particularly non-Western contexts, a valuable interpretive framework for negotiating and mediating sociocultural and national experiences.

Taiwanese cinema as an object of study and film criticism, in an international framework, is solely defined by a now well-known roster of established film directors. Likewise, in Taiwan itself the attempt to invigorate the declining film industry in the early 1980s was kick-started by government investment in a generation of young up-and-coming directors. In order to help the reader to grasp the relationship between authorship and Taiwanese cinema, we feel it necessary to outline the Taiwanese New Cinema as a contextual background for understanding the rise to international recognition of Hou Hsiao-Hsien and Edward Yang.

It is now well known that the practice of *auteur* criticism is an approach that entails an almost contradictory position, a double bind of scepticism and celebration, both knowledge and ignorance. It appears as commonsense and obvious, and makes it virtually impossible to avoid the common practice of attaching names to texts, since it is almost always a matter of convention of everyday discussion, presentation and organisation. However uneasy the function of the author may be within the range of theoretically informed frameworks of authorship, one still bestows a value on the name and naming of each author, with a degree of reluctance and acceptance both in reading and writing about them academically and organising and classifying of texts for study and research. This is, in more detail, what James Naremore refers to as 'the paradoxical "survival of the author" in contemporary film criticism'.[1] In the following analyses of three Taiwanese film directors, the authors highlight the importance of each individual 'brand' and the discursive foundations upon which such individuals become synonymous with certain frameworks from film criticism and post-colonialism, cultural exchange and urban alienation, and transnational working practices. One of the questions to be answered in this Introduction and followed through in the three chapters is why and how Taiwanese cinema – more specifically the first and second waves of Taiwanese cinema – have been reduced, not unproblematically, to a handful of canonised names: Hou Hsiao-hsien, Edward Yang and Ang Lee (and one would be able to now extend this argument to Tsai Ming-Liang). It must also be stressed that this is a predominately Western selection, engineered by film festivals and critics – as it usually is – that rarely includes equally important directors like Wu Nien-Chen.

In many instances authorship, as a critical practice, often tells us less about cinema, and even less about Taiwanese cinema, than it does about the function of criticism itself as an institutional and ideological apparatus imposing and shaping the meaning of texts and influencing their reception. It is not unfair to even suggest that the 'discovery' of Asian directors by Western critical apparatuses, whether through fandom and appreciation or academic studies, has been the equivalent of a kind of excavation process with all the colonial meanings such an accusation implies. The critic or fan as archaeologist, whether it is the academic pursuit of the so-called modernist visionaries of Japanese cinema or the British martial-arts film fans' adoration of Hong Kong's Shaw Brothers, excavate texts and directors like treasures whose value lies in their very otherness and relative obscurity to the average multiplex cinemagoer outside Asia. This is an issue we explore in more detail in our essay on Japanese cinema, which as a national cinema has historically occupied the central position of otherness more than any of the other Asian cinemas.

Authorship as a debate has significant historical value. It has been central to the development of film studies, as well as cinephilia and film criticism. We do still produce a type of discourse that implicitly stresses the importance of the director, if not as the romantic figure of those early auteurist studies, at least as an organising principle. We do impose on the named creative individual various degrees of influence in the production of a film's meaning, a unifying anchorage for our discussions and analysis of style and theme. Authorship is, therefore, one of the major points of reference in discussing the artistic qualities of film, and it is also shared with industrial and promotional practices and in general the more pedestrian thinking about films in everyday life. For example, we usually include the director's name after films in course documents and in the referencing of film titles filmographically.

Like the concepts of genre and national cinema, the idea of the author is one of the most accepted and practical ways of organising groups of films. In international industry practice, authorship and genre, along with stardom, are still the primary means to promote the majority of films, whether they are Japanese horrors, Indian westerns, or Hollywood romantic comedies. The director remains the figure, along with the star, who mediates between the industry and the public as a representative, a spokesperson for the film in promotional interviews, and often as the source of the film's preferred meaning. More recently, with the emergence of DVDs, such figures have an increased presence as disembodied voices fixing the reading of a film on the many audio commentary tracks and additional extras available in the digital format, as part of what Catherine Grant has referred to as the 'increasing reificatory and commodifying processes of contemporary auteurism'.[2]

Given its place in the history of film criticism and film studies, authorship is, by all accounts, one of the most fully documented debates, and therefore we feel no need to flesh it out in too much detail here.[3] As a critical practice, authorship came to the fore through the writing in *Cahiers du Cinéma* in the 1950s. The *Cahiers* collective were important in their rallying for the seriousness of cinema as an art form. Establishing the figure of the auteur in the 1950s, particularly those working in the Hollywood studio system and on B movies, *Cahiers* found meaning in the thematic and stylistic patterns of particular directors' bodies of work that could be attributed to such individuals' resistance to (Hollywood) cinema's material and industrial base. Therefore, establishing the figure of the cinematic author could legitimate the position of cinema as an art form rather than an industrial one. Even by the late 1960s Geoffrey Nowell-Smith, a once staunch proponent of structuralist *auteur* analysis, could view the authorship debate with hindsight, as illustrated in the following concise definition from his book on Italian director Luchino Visconti:

> The so-called *auteur* theory can be understood in three ways: as a set of empirical assertions to the effect that every detail of a film is the direct and sole responsibility of the author, who is the director; as a standard value, according to which every film that is a *film d'auteur* is good, and every film that is not bad; and as a principle of method, which provides a basis for a more scientific form of criticism that has existed hitherto.[4]

Nowell-Smith discounts the first two ways in favour of the third for his *auteur* study of Luchino Visconti. The 'scientific approach' to cinema influenced by the popularity of Lévi-Strauss and structuralism was in itself a necessary stepping-stone in further establishing film studies as a legitimate academic discipline. However, later theoretical interventions in the 1970s influenced by the so-called

'French theory' or 'screen theory' accepted that the author was only one cog within a larger machine turning with the interconnected wheels of both industry and ideology. James Naremore suggests that authorship persists because it simply does not have a satisfactory theoretical or methodological foundation. He asks:

> Why is it possible that so many sophisticated critics, exploring quite different problems, can continue to be interested in individual artists? The answer is that the decision to write about specific directors, producers, writers, or actors doesn't *in itself* involve a commitment to theory, a method, a formal taxonomy, or even a politics.[5] (emphasis in original)

While Naremore is correct in suggesting that the validity of authorship rests on its tangible relationship to theoretical and methodological rigour, he is incorrect in assuming that *auteur* criticism is politically barren particularly when positioned against Asian cinemas' struggle to localise and nationalise simultaneously as a challenge to Hollywood's hegemonic position in their region and to the more troubling issue of colonial history.

But what about the *auteurs* of the Asian cinemas? The reputations of directors of Asian cinemas were established initially in the context of the postwar interest and fascination with Japanese cinema that was outlined in the first section of the book. Those Japanese directors, while identified as 'artists', were certainly not considered to be part of the development of the authorship debate, which was fundamentally between Hollywood cinema and European art cinema: a transatlantic rather than a transpacific dialogue between the magazines *Cahiers du Cinéma* in France, *Movie* in the UK, and the American film critic Andrew Sarris in the USA, also writing in *Film Culture*. One only needs to think of Sarris' denigration that 'American directors are generally superior to *foreign* directors' (my emphasis).[6] Yet there is a huge oversight here since one of the first fully sustained analyses of any director was Donald Richie's *The Films of Akira Kurosawa*, published in 1965, the same year as the other landmark *auteur* study, Robin Wood's *Hitchcock's Films*.[7] It was not that directors like Kurosawa, Mizoguchi and, later, Oshima and Ozu were not considered in auteurist terms but rather that they were treated as separate from it. They were bracketed off from the debate much like Asian cinema has been bracketed off and excluded from the dominant trends in film studies because, as we argue, many of the concepts and theories cannot account for the non-Western text or at best have a destabilising effect that requires a sensitive and complex working-out.

As recently as the early 1990s, with few exceptions, the concept of the author has made it easy to discuss Asian films without having any specialist knowledge of the institutions and ideologies that have shaped them. The author functions here at its simplest as a brand name, a unifying strategy. The simplicity of emphasis on style and thematic consistency means the critic who privileges these aspects of the unifying brand-name function of the director is able to negate the specific cultural forces and contextual parameters that form part of the film's meaning and cultural base, and can instead perceive the film as the director's signature staging. A good example here would be the work of John Woo. Typically, such approaches also avoid questions of the national and the generic. As I suggest in the article on Hou Hsiao-Hsien, the Taiwanese director's construction by critics as being like the Japanese Ozu Yasujiro has completely overlooked both the history of Japanese colonialism in Taiwan and the practical aspects of Hou's shooting on location with non-professional actors. Furthermore, the limited approaches in this aspect of auteurism not only avoid any consideration of popular Asian cinema's industrial base but also of the cultural base of film production, genres and reception. As Pidduck suggests in her chapter on Ang Lee, one needs to account for the new precedents of transnational and cross-cultural networks in which Asian cinemas, directors and audiences now find themselves situated.

In this respect, the study of Hong Kong cinema is leading the way, for example in the recent book-length studies of individual films and directors in *The New Hong Kong Cinema* series which illustrates a marked inherent connection between authorship, identity, post-colonialism, globalisation and transnational reception.[8] Authorship is no longer the limiting domain of the cinephile's appreciation or the industry's promotional mediator but, rather, an active source of dialogue with the larger regional and cultural concerns of Asia. This is central to an understanding of the politics of authorship and Taiwanese cinema in relation to historical representation and the anti-essentialist Taiwanese identities that are intrinsic to the films of Hou Hsiao-hsien and Edward Yang.

One of the reasons why authorship is important for Asian cinemas is that it challenges the privileged position that both Hollywood and European art cinema have occupied in criticism and popular opinion vis-à-vis authorship. This is particularly true of Taiwanese cinema which occupies a fairly marginal position even within the study of Asian cinemas simply because it is often subsumed under the all-encompassing rubric of Chinese cinema. Taiwanese cinema's presence in English-language studies is marked by several inclusions in books on Chinese cinema and it is rarely treated as autonomous from it. This certainly belies the harsh reality of the recent situation concerning post-nationalist Taiwan's complex relationship with China and its nation-state status. Therefore, as the following sketch of Taiwanese New Cinema illustrates, Taiwanese cinema needs its *auteurs* as bastions of Taiwan's uniqueness and difference from the larger essentialising tendencies of a core Chinese cinema because, as James Naremore so incisively suggests, 'marginalised social groups can declare their solidarity and create a collective identity by adopting authors as cultural heroes'.[9]

The question of the appropriateness of the function of authorship in Asian cinemas also needs to account for the agency of the director as someone with the lived experiences of, for example, colonialism or diasporic identification. Such an approach shifts the emphasis from the director who occupies the romanticised position equal to a creative role; instead, following Michel Foucault, it would consider 'the name of the author' as a discourse around which the director is a filter for various lived experiences. In other words, recognising the social and cultural experiences that shape texts through the agency of the director is a crucial strategy for minor and marginal cinemas. As Wu argues in her chapter on Edward Yang's *Taipei Story*, the directors of the New Cinema were central in addressing the structural changes in postwar Taiwan, which transformed it from an agricultural society to an industrial one, and their effects on the Taiwanese cultural and national landscape. Authorship has never been a concept that is particularly sensitive to lived experiences that go beyond the textual level. The following chapters seek to challenge the banality of authorship's many contemporary manifestations by focusing on not just the creativity but the agency of individual directors situated as they are between the struggles over tradition and modernity, the national and transnational, the colonial and the post-colonial, and the local and global.

THE TAIWANESE NEW CINEMA

I-Feu Wu

The Taiwanese New Cinema first appeared in the early 1980s. Differing from other New Waves, such as the French cinema of the late 1950s, the beginning of the New Cinema in Taiwan did not burst out through a strong sense of innovation; rather, the impetus that led to its development was the threatening power of the Hong Kong film industry. Hong Kong had gradually developed a series of commercial strategies that imitated the classical Hollywood studio system of vertical integration and promotion. The Mandarin Hong Kong films of the Shaw Brothers and MP and GI (Motion Pictures and General Industries, later renamed Cathay after its parent company) studios were aggressively promoted star vehicles supported through vast networks of distribution and exhibition. Hong Kong's studio film production, designed to be a cultural commodity, has thus successfully expanded its domination over the film industries of other Asian countries in the region since the 1970s.[10] Under pressure from the success of Hong Kong cinema, Taiwanese film production was losing dominance not only in South-east Asia, but also in Taiwan itself, completely losing its market to Hong Kong film production.[11] Meanwhile, audiences had grown tired of the dogmatic inflexibility of the local cinema, which was laden with romantic cliché and repetitious melodramas about traditional moral values, and also found it cheaper and more convenient to watch films at home. Thus, the other important cause of the deterioration of Taiwan's film industry was the popularity of home videos. It was evident that

Taiwan's film production was severely challenged by confrontations with the commercial Hong Kong cinema and the introduction of home video.

In order to compete with the commercial Hong Kong cinema, the Taiwanese government's Information Office took responsibility for restructuring Taiwan's film industry. From 1983, the Taipei International Film Festival has been held annually, and has provided the opportunity to screen international art films, to enable financial support to promote Taiwanese films at international film festivals, and to garner a new generation of local film critics who were given a chance to develop their criticism. That in turn led to Taiwanese films being perceived as cultural products of significant value rather than commercial entertainment forms. Meanwhile, the government's Central Motion Pictures Corporation (CMPC) was forced to seek ways to innovate the film industry. The first new idea to be introduced was support for young, talented directors. Although the CMPC's ambition was to promote Taiwanese cinema, the New Cinema seemed to emerge slowly in the first three years. There were no particular feature films to characterise this movement until 1982, when the four-part portmanteau film *In Our Time/Kuangyin de kushih* was made under CMPC supervision.

In Our Time is generally regarded as the starting point of the New Cinema, in that its narrative style and structure differed from previous films. The four young directors, who had been trained either in Taiwan or abroad, broke new ground by representing the social changes in Taiwanese society from the 1950s to the 1980s. Because of the different narrative structure and unprecedented approach to social transformation, *In Our Time* refreshed the audiences interested in local cinema and drew the attention of film critics who announced the arrival of Taiwanese New Cinema. Yet the New Cinema did not really become commercially successful until a year later when *Growing Up/Hsiao-Bi de kushih* (1983) and *The Sandwich Man/Erzi de da wan'ou* (1983) were received with both box-office and critical success. *Growing Up* depicts a story in which a local Taiwanese girl marries a Chinese mainlander, and it shows how their child, Hsiao-Bi, copes with family problems and experiences the difficulties of Taiwan's social transformation. *Sandwich Man*, which is composed of three episodes directed by Hou Hsiao-Hsien, Wan Ren and Tseng Chuang-Hsiang, presents the bitter taste of lower-class life and the post-colonial mentality of 1960s Taiwan. Because of their commercial success and critical acclaim, *Grow Up* and *Sandwich Man* are regarded as the significant milestones of the New Cinema.

Although New Cinema had established its style as a reflection of social reality, its development was still limited by strict censorship. As a government institution, the CMPC had to support the New Cinema in order to save Taiwan's film industry, but it simultaneously constrained it through censorship regulation. Before martial law was lifted and the restrictions on the media were liberated in 1987, censorship was driven by political propaganda; for example, language could not contain too much Taiwanese dialect, and the subject matter could not confront political issues head-on. In fact, after *Sandwich Man* was shot, the CMPC found it hard to release the film because of the issues it dealt with: the poverty of labour workers and Taiwan's dependent development under Japanese and US power, which were regarded as dark sides of society, and could hardly pass censorship regulation. Eventually, though reluctantly, accepting the young directors' claim for the function of film as beginning to explore and question the reality of everyday life, the CMPC had conflicts with the three directors when *Sandwich Man* was shot. However, the success that *Sandwich Man* achieved at the box office loosened the strict censorship policies, gradually allowing the CMPC to be more flexible more supportive of new directors and their individual styles.

The New Cinema filmmakers stressed the significance of realism for historical representation, using films as a way of examining contemporary society. They advocated that a film should entail a more realistic relationship with common people's lives, which should neither be idealised nor deliberately distorted. For this reason, most of the New Cinema filmmakers employed a static camera, and avoided techniques that emphasised dramatic force such as close-ups and rapid cutting, in order to evoke a true-to-life atmosphere. The extensive use of long takes, long shots and deep focus by the New Wave filmmakers recalls the type of realism that Bazin privileged as the closest equivalent to human perceptions in real life. These stylistic devices have become characteristic of the New Cinema, serving as both the filmmakers' and the movement's signature. By seeing style as the expression of the personal vision of its directors, the New Cinema has come to be internationally recognised for that. This has enabled the Taiwanese New Cinema to be received as a cinema of *auteurs*, not only through specific stylistic tendencies but also through the fact that such tendencies have a long association with the *auteur* cinema *par excellence*: European art cinema. This latter association is fleshed out in Wu's chapter in its discussion of the relationship between Edward Yang and Michelangelo Antonioni.

Most of the Taiwanese New Cinema directors are around the same age, and were born after 1945, the era when Taiwan moved from Japanese colonisation to Chiang Kai-Shek's Chinese nationalist regime. The directors had experienced almost the same social changes and economic developments through the 1950s to the 1970s, and these were highly relevant to the issues that the New Cinema dealt with in the 1980s. Under the military dictatorship of the nationalist government, which blamed its fiasco in the Chinese Civil War on communist rebellion and insisted on the military retrieval of mainland China, the postwar generation grew up in an unstable political situation, with anti-communist ideology imposed upon them through education. The military dictatorship, in the name of democracy against communism, played a historical role, disciplining postwar society until the 1970s, when Taiwan had begun economic development. The economic take-off in the 1960s led to changes in social structure, and made possible Taiwan's political transformation. Industrialisation in the 1960s not only brought rapid economic growth to Taiwan, but also accelerated its modernisation, from an industrial developed country in the 1970s into a multinational capitalist society in the 1980s. Aware of this rapid socioeconomic transformation changing Taiwan's political, cultural and social landscape, the New Wave directors were keen to represent the past and to portray contemporary social conditions. The materials they deal with clearly articulate a set of historical narratives, implicitly linked to their concern with the distorted and irrational sense of historical identity propagated through official channels. In this respect, the fracturing of history has gradually taken shape through filmic representation, in the sense that historical identity has been questioned by the filmmakers' concern with the representation of historical reality. Addressing significant historical events, New Cinema not only narrates the experiences of the past, but also questions the notion of any core national identity through the historical narrative. If, as Robert Burgoyne suggests, 'the interrogation of history is a stage in the search for identity', then historical representation within the New Cinema does lead to the exploration and reconsideration of the complexity of Taiwan's national and cultural identities.'[12]

New Cinema's concerns with national history and national identity have led it to be recognised by Taiwanese film critics as a national cinema. On the other hand, New Cinema is rarely popular at a national level, with the exception of a few films, such as Hou Hsiao-Hsien's *Sandwich Man* and *A City of Sadness* (1989). New Cinema rarely achieved national success after *Sandwich Man*, partly because the issues it addresses are more serious than entertaining, partly because its narrative styles are hard to follow, unlike in the film productions the audience are used to watching, in which a clear story-line is developed, famous stars are cast, and the editing follows a linear narrative. Nevertheless, New Cinema has remained a critically decisive moment in the history of Taiwanese cinema and has sustained its presence in international film culture. This is traced in multiple ways through the following three chapters on Hou Hsiao-Hsien, Edward Yang and Ang Lee.[13]

Notes

1. James Naremore (1990), 'Authorship and the cultural politics of film criticism', *Film Quarterly*, vol. 44, no. 1, Fall, p. 14.
2. Catherine Grant (2000), 'www.auteur.com?', *Screen*, vol. 41, no. 1, Spring, p. 101.
3. John Caughie (ed.) (1981), *Theories of Authorship*, London: British Film Institute, 1981.
4. Geoffrey Nowell-Smith (1967), *Luchino Visconti*, London: Secker and Warburg, pp. 9–10.
5. James Naremore (1990), 'Authorship and the cultural politics of film criticism', *Film Quarterly*, vol. 44, no. 1, Fall, p. 21.
6. Andrew Sarris (1981), 'Notes on the auteur theory' [extract], in John Caughie (ed.), *Theories of Authorship*, London: British Film Institute, p. 64.
7. Donald Richie (1965), *The Films of Akira Kurosawa*, Berkeley: University of California Press; Robin Wood (1965), *Hitchcock's Films*, London & New York: Zwemmer & A. S. Barnes.
8. Books currently in this series from Hong Kong University Press include Wimal Dissanayake (2003), *Wong Kar-Wai's* Ashes of Time; Jeremy Tambling (2003),

Wong Kar-Wai's Happy Together; Karen Fang (2004), *John Woo's* A Better Tomorrow; and Andrew Schroeder (2004), *Tsui Harl's* Zu Warrioirs of the Magic Mountain.

9. James Naremore (1990), 'Authorship and the cultural politics of film criticism'.
10. Taiwanese films were popular in Hong Kong. However, with the success of Bruce Lee's kung fu films that emerged in the early 1970s, the Hong Kong film industry has become the leading one in Asia. In contrast with the success of Hong Kong cinema, Taiwan's film industry has declined. According to statistics, Taiwan produced 189 films in 1968, but twenty-five years later in 1994, only twenty-three were made. Only in two periods (1972–82 and 1986–9), during which Hong Kong films were boycotted by Taiwanese film distributors, did Taiwanese films have the chance of being accepted by local audiences. It is suggested that Taiwan's film industry is strongly eclipsed by that of Hong Kong (Li Ding-Tzann (1996), 'Marginal empire: the case of Hong Kong's film industry, with Hollywood and colonial Japan compared', in *Taiwan, A Radical Quarterly in Social Studies*, no. 21, January, Taipei, p. 145. Li's article shares some points with L. K. Leung's thesis, 'The evolution of Hong Kong as a regional movie production and export centre', masters thesis, Hong Kong: The Chinese University of Hong Kong, 1993).
11. In the 1970s, Taiwan produced 2,150 narrative films, averaging 215 films a year, and acting as the major film exporters in South-east Asia. But in 1991, among 484 films released in Taiwan, 211 films were Chinese features, and only thirty-three of those were locally made. These statistics show that foreign films monopolise Taiwan's film market, with Hong Kong films providing nearly 40 per cent, and local films less than 10 per cent. See Shen Shiao-Yin (1995), 'Permutations of the foreign/er: a study of the works of Edward Yang, Stan Lai, Chang Yi, and Hou Hsiao-Hsien' Ph. D. thesis, Ithaca: Cornell University.
12. Robert Burgoyne (1996), 'Modernism and the narrative of nation in *JFK*', in Vivian Sobchack (ed.), *The Persistence of History*, London: Routledge, p. 19.
13. For example, Edward Yang's *Taipei's Story* (1985) was released for only four days, and was then forced to close because of its miserable box office performance. See Huang Jien-Yeh (1994), *The Films of Edward Yang*, Taipei: Yuan-Liu Publications, pp. 123–4.

18

OZU AND THE COLONIAL ENCOUNTER IN HOU HSIAO-HSIEN

Gary Needham

International recognition of Hou Hsiao-Hsien came halfway through his career when he won the Golden Lion prize at the Venice Film Festival in 1989 for *City of Sadness/Beiqing chengshi*. It is unfortunate that before *City of Sadness* Hou was only known to the very few who had the chance to catch some of his remarkable films such as *A Summer at Grandpa's/Dong Dong de jaiqi* (1984) and *A Time to Live and a Time to Die/Tongnian wangshi* (1985) screened at film festivals and on very limited runs at metropolitan art cinemas. For example, *A Summer at Grandpa's* was screened at film festivals in Cannes, Edinburgh, Rotterdam, Sydney, and Pesaro, to name but a few. Many of these earlier films were never picked up for wider distribution in English-language film markets outside Asia than, say, the films of the Chinese Fifth Generation filmmakers which played centre court during this period of 'discovery'.[1] Without downplaying the praise at the time for *A Time to Live and a Time to Die*, it was with the award of the Golden Lion at Venice that Hou really began circulating as a name, a festival-winning sanctioned name in world cinema, and yet *City of Sadness* was in retrospect a halfway turning-point in his career, both in terms of the consolidation of his authorial style and the extent of his ambitions. After the critical success of *City of Sadness*, many English-language film magazines and journals begun to take a more serious and sustained interest in Hou and his Taiwanese contemporaries like Edward Yang. It was at this crucial point of international recognition in 1989 that a critical investigation and attempt to define Hou's style, his vision and his place in the pantheon of world cinema *auteurs*, as seen from a particular perspective, really began. A minor critical industry started, from key articles in *Sight and Sound* to smaller write-ups in arts and culture sections in newspapers and magazines. It is not that Hou was completely absent from any English-language film criticism before 1989 – Tony Rayns had written an informative piece in Monthly Film Bulletin in 1988 based on several film festival interviews – but rather that Hou and the Taiwanese cinema to which he belonged were seen as extremely minor, if not completely overlooked, in the period in which Taiwanese cinema was flourishing.[2] Taiwanese cinema, as the Introduction to this section suggests, is either relegated to being part of 'Chinese cinema' and peripheral to mainland productions, or in the case of Hou to being an *auteur* often divorced from his sociohistorical and cultural context.

It is from this point of emergence in the discourse of world cinema and the critical apparatus that supports it that I wish to examine how Hou Hsiao-Hsien was constructed in relation to other film directors that came before him, in terms of film criticism, what this form of criticism suggests and why was Hou sometimes seen as nothing short of the reincarnation of Ozu Yasujiro. In contradistinction to this definition of an Ozu-like Hou, other critics and scholars, and Hou himself, have sought more recently to trace his stylistic lineage through an attention to his similarities with a range of specifically Chinese aesthetic practices. This essay then is an attempt to try and locate the Taiwanese film director Hou, if there is such a thing, and to place his reputation within a particular moment of film criticism. I hope to sort out Hou's position as a Taiwanese director caught in a deluge of critical struggles and contradictory definitions, colonial histories and post-colonial identity, Japanese influences and Chinese aesthetics. This chapter will challenge the construction of an Ozu-like Hou before *City of Sadness* through his most praised work from that period, *A Time to Live and a Time to Die*.

An Ozu-like Hou?

The uneasy predicament of definition created through film criticism and colonial encounter, in which Hou is positioned between Taiwan and Japan then subsequently China, is also a position that has changed since 1989, the year of *City of Sadness*'s international recognition. 1989 is also the year in which Hou apparently saw his first film by Ozu. Ozu has become one of many reference points in Hou's later career where, for example, scenes from Ozu's *Late Spring/Banshun* (1949) appear on television in *Good Men, Good Women/Hao nan hao nu* (1995). This chapter is concerned with the period before one can credibly establish connections of authorial influence on Hou by Ozu. It is also the period of Hou's career, before *City of Sadness*, where the most insistent formal and thematic consistencies between the two directors have been forged *de facto*. It is also worth pointing out that it would be fruitless to negate absolutely any connection between the two directors after 1989, even where influence might or might not be concerned; rather, one needs to point out the ways in which criticism works in its dealings with authorship when it comes to Asian cinemas. Recently Hou, along with other established world cinema figures

Wim Wenders and Aki Kurasmaki, was asked by Shochiku, Ozu's home studio, if they could direct an episode each in a portmanteau Ozu tribute film. Hou preferred to do an entire feature-length film rather than contribute to a portmanteau film with other directors. The result of this singular project was developed into the Shochiku-produced *Café Lumiere/Kohi Jikou* (2004). It has premiered on Ozu's 100th birthday on 12 December 2003 in Japan, and officially released across Asia late in 2004, and it featured one of Japan's most distinguished young contemporary actors, Tadanobu Asano, in the leading role. This was not the first time Hou was connected to Ozu after 1989, for in 1993 he contributed to a Shochiku documentary, *Talking with Ozu*, in which several directors were asked to reflect on the Japanese director.[3]

The habit of constructing an Ozu-like Hou is practised even by the most diligent of post-colonial critics who have fallen in to an all-too-easy association between the two directors when discussing the formal and thematic elements of Hou's earlier films. What is important here is that the association between the two directors is consolidated with reference and analysis to the films made before Ozu even figured in the mind of Hou. It is these earlier films, which are the cornerstones of the Taiwanese New Cinema, that have often been the focus of criticism and analysis of the Ozu-like Hou, films such as *A Time to Live and a Time to Die*.

Two career-overview English-language essays on Hou that appeared after *City of Sadness* and are clearly motivated by its success (one in *Sight and Sound* (UK), the other in *Film Comment* (US)) are good examples of the Ozu-Hou association that appears closely after the release of *City of Sadness* and makes *de facto* judgements about the early films, most notably *A Summer at Grandpa's* and *A Time to Live and a Time to Die*.[4] Alan Stanbrook, writing in *Sight and Sound*, suggests the following:

> The opening scene, a prelude in which newly graduated children sing farewell to their old school, works in the same way as the emotional climax of *Tokyo Story*, in which the daughter glances at the watch just given her by her aunt . . .[5]

And:

> The early sequences, depicting the repatriation of the occupying Japanese after 1945, *even look Japanese*. The beautiful scene which is shot in the same way by an Ozu or a Mizoguchi in the 1950s. And it's not just a matter of influence. Hou has always maintained that the Ozu flavour many have found in his work is coincidental because at the time it was first remarked upon, he had never seen an Ozu film. Perhaps: but Ozu, after all, was part of the Japanese cultural heritage and for more than fifty years Taiwanese life was imbued with it.[6] (my emphasis)

Every flourish of style that is Hou's becomes mediated through the then more critically-prestigious *auteurs* of Japanese cinema by association despite

Stanbrook's acknowledgement that he is aware that Hou had never even seen any Ozu films up to that point. Stanbrook's choice is blatantly picked from the Western critical canon – *Tokyo Story/Tokyo Monogatari* (1953) being among the *Sight and Sound* critics' top ten films of all time – and even more so, Stanbrook softens the harsh reality of colonialism as something as innocent as cultural heritage.

Typically, Asian filmmakers are positioned far down the line of influences, behind filmmakers whose genesis is usually not Asian. For example, Edward Yang is continually likened to the Italian modernist director Michelangelo Antonioni. While this particular example of Hou has a more localised web of influence, it still demonstrates the need for criticism to posit such a continuum of influence and association in order to make sense of difference which, often more than not, is traced back to the postwar French and Italian art cinemas. Casual references by Asian filmmakers to European cinema are usually taken up as a grand statement of their bowing in the shadow of a greater influence and heritage that unfortunately gives weight to the Eurocentric impulses of many critics and even scholars. Therefore, homogenising difference in the case of Hou or, in Yang's case, constructing his origin in the more prestigious Italian art cinema (although Yang himself has stated his inspiration as being a mixture of New German Cinema politics and the Hong Kong New Wave) does not serve to highlight the historical and cultural specificity of Taiwanese cinema but rather its position in the discursive constructs of art cinema and world cinema.

Similarly, following Stanbrook, Godfrey Cheshire writing in the US publication *Film Comment* about *A Time to Live and a Time to Die* has this to say:

> The techniques and the spirit behind them strongly recall Ozu, although Hou is said never to have seen an Ozu film until after he made *A Time to Live*. If true, this provides an intriguing indication of a *common impulse among oriental filmmakers* determined to develop styles both individually and culturally their own.[7] (my emphasis)

The struggle for definition in Chesire's essay ranges from references not only to Ozu and Chinese arts but, demonstrating his Eurocentrism, also to Proust and Fassbinder, only making matters more confusing as Hou's originality becomes lost in a mire of European, Japanese and Chinese points of reference. However, this question of definition is in some ways consolidated later with the suggestion that Hou's 'greatest affinity should be to a Japanese' which is, to no great surprise, Ozu. This Hou-Ozu association has become routine to the point that even film critics sensitive to non-Western cinemas have succumbed to its influence. Wimal Dissanayake and Kwok Kan-Tam, in their introductory text *New Chinese Cinema*, devote a chapter to Hou where the director is referred to as having an 'Ozu-like patience and meditativeness, particularly such as the elder Japanese director demonstrated in his *Tokyo Story*'.[8] And, again, with reference to *A Time to Live and a Time to Die*, they write 'Like Yasujiro Ozu before him, Hou allows his camera to meditate on a location before and after the action has taken place in a way that provokes deeper reflection'.[9] This last quote makes specific reference to the empty spaces or shots that have their genesis in the formal analysis of Ozu by Paul Schrader, Noel Burch and David Bordwell: the so-called 'pillow shots' described by Burch that have been problematically interpreted as an aesthetic embodiment of Zen transcendentalism.[10] These studies of Ozu were marked by an interest in Ozu's breaking of the codes of the classical paradigm. David Bordwell and Kristin Thompson's groundbreaking 1976 article in *Screen* foregrounds issues relating to space, continuity and motivation which have become the standard examples of the analysis of Ozu's 'difference' and, more often than not, the definition of his authorship. Ozu was seen to break with the convention of the 180-degree rule, which preserves background unity and screen direction, by favouring a filming space of 360 degrees. He also shoots from a low camera position and includes specific shots of objects such as vases and exterior shots of telegraph poles, gardens and laundry lines which are used for transition between one scene and the next and appear to have no narrative motivation within a classical narrative economy. Even a basic knowledge of Japanese cinema would reveal that these are aspects specific to Ozu as an *auteur* and are not representative of Japanese cinema as a whole. Ozu's style was his particular way of conceiving through cinema an ontological domestic space that would reflect seating positions (low camera placement) and spatial relations between people (360-degree filming space) in differentiated backgrounds made up of *shoji* screens and walls. One must remember that traditional Japanese houses, like those depicted in Ozu's films, could be altered to make larger rooms or create more rooms through moveable screens. Thus domestic space is changeable and not fixed. In her study of indexical relations and psychological perceptions of space in Japan, Jane Bachnik has pointed out that the clear distinction between inside and outside relations (known as *uchi* and *soto*)[11] is not a clear dichotomy: domestic space is not as fixed as it is might be elsewhere and privacy can be intuitive rather than governed by closed doors and permanent concrete walls. Therefore, it is important to stress that the praxis of lived space and how to conceive of it cinematically is not the same for Taiwan as it is for Japan and not the same for Ozu as it is for Hou. If one associates the two directors in this way, it homogenises both the ontological spaces of Japan and Taiwan and the narrative spaces constructed by each director in order to reflect their own experience and approach to space, domestic or otherwise.

While many critics and scholars are wont to point out that Hou had not seen any Ozu films, there seems to be no ability to resist such an all-too-easy association. For the record, Hou has on more than one occasion told the many interviewers who have broached this idea of the Ozu influence that he is doing something altogether different in both theme and style. Throughout the last ten years Hou has in fact increasingly made a point of aligning himself with Chinese aesthetics, although the Ozu project for Shochiku, *Café Lumiere*, complicates any attempt to pigeonhole a director who has also stressed his desire to make a *wuxia* film (swordplay martial arts) following his contemporaries Ang Lee and Zhang Yimou's success in that popular genre.

One can speculate on the reasons for this Ozu-Hou association as being rooted in three problem areas. The first problem is simply the inability of critics who are able to deal with Hou's fundamental difference. The difference of his style, the use of the long take, the elliptical narrative structure, the unmotivated shots all make for difficult critical engagement. Therefore, it is much easier to simply connect Hou with another director or even a film movement. Those directors who have already been established or sanctioned with degrees of critical legitimacy, Ozu and Mizoguchi for example, make for an easier critical review or analytical essay than thinking afresh about style or considering the multiple contexts and influences shaping any particular film. Hou has even been associated with François Truffaut and Jean-Luc Godard, as well as keeping the candle burning for Neo-realism. The latter association with neo-realism is probably due to the fleeting scenes from Luchino Visconti's *Rocco and his Brothers/Rocco e i suoi fratelli* (1960) showing in the local cinema in *The Boy's from Fengkuei/Fenggui lai de ren* (1983). This moment is less about intertextuality than it is about illustrating a particular historical context when the Taiwanese government imported select European films as part of a trade and cultural relations initiative.

The second problem is the attempt by Western critics to find a film language that would be the Asian equivalent to the classical paradigm that was consolidated during the Hollywood studio period – in other words, to find the formal paradigm of the other as the standard practice of film criticism as latent orientalism. Narrative economy, continuity and identification aside, the classical paradigm functions as the yardstick or the norm with which all other modes of filmmaking are compared, or attempt to challenge, or redefine. The classical paradigm is practical since it is a standard practice of narrative economy and temporal and spatial continuity of popular cinemas the world over from Godzilla to Bollywood and Turkish melodrama. But it is also monolithic in that its hegemonic status constructs everything else as art cinema or experimentation, and it acts fundamentally as a discourse of othering all non-Western modes of filmmaking that do not conform to the popular model. This suggests that all other attempts to conceive of time and space are deviations from the norm even though the classical paradigm is most effective as a finely tuned perversion of time and space itself and is the solicitation of an absolute form of identification in suture because of it. Even more so, contemporary Hollywood filmmaking and increasingly media-literate audiences are wont to deal with more formally complex texts that challenge older modes of film form rooted in such formal economies as well as the increasing incorporation and appropriation of cinema aesthetics from Hong Kong, Japan and elsewhere.

Finding similarities between Hou and Ozu smoothes out the differences between the two directors and any question of cultural, ethnic or national specificity and identity. It is the ongoing attempt, both latent and manifest, to define a film language or style, albeit without a proper context, that can be seen to represent a fictive and localised 'oriental cinema', whether it is valued and celebrated or devalued vis-à-vis a more global Hollywood that occupies and maintains its position as the norm.

The third problem, and the one most likely to suggest at first glance a direct link to Ozu, is the use of locations that bear the signs of the Japanese colonial period in Taiwan. The architecture and design of many of the buildings and houses that appear in Hou's films are from the period of colonisation and the enforced Japanisation of Taiwan. It is this visual link that has potentially stressed, at first glance, the connection between Ozu and Hou since the houses are architecturally similar in Japan and Taiwan during this period. It is also the most offensive oversight to associate the style of Hou's films with Ozu when the real connection is one of colonisation and Japanese imperialism in Taiwan. Even Hou himself makes a point of illustrating this most recently in an interview in *Cineaste* where he says that 'You have to remember that, during this time, people in the Taiwanese countryside lived in Japanese-style houses. What can I do about that? People have said that I was imitating Ozu, but this is simply what Taiwanese houses look like.'[12] This practice is typical of an insensitive film criticism out of touch with historical reality when one considers the complex colonial history in the first half of the nineteenth century when Japan occupied Taiwan between 1895 and 1945. It is worth noting that Japan is more or less written out of most of the histories of colonialism simply because it was not European and therefore not situated in the centre/periphery relationship so central to our understanding of colonialism as expansion from a European centre. Post-colonial studies is a narrative of Europe and its others, of Africa and India, therefore it is all too easy to overlook the internal colonial struggles in East and South-east Asia. Hence, it never really occurred to anyone that it might be an issue to suggest a Japanese cultural influence on a Taiwanese film director as actually being about colonialism and not about cinema and authorship. Japan is an aberration in terms of colonialism for not being European. Post-colonial literatures likewise almost never include Taiwan, and film criticism rarely accounts for colonialism when it comes to authorship, genre and formal analysis.

Taiwan was occupied by Japan for fifty years, and the process of enforced Japanisation was implemented to transform Taiwan and its people in to imperial subjects loyal to the Japanese emperor. The Japanese also instituted an assimilation-policy programme that in turn led to Japanese being made the official language of government and education in Taiwan. There was also a name-changing programme, the building of Japanese shrines and monuments, the implementation of Japanese design and architecture in both public and private spheres, and other processes of cultural change affecting the practices of everyday life. However, attitudes past and present to the period of Japanese colonisation are mixed as a result of the transformative effects that brought about processes of modernity which at the time exceeded those of its Chinese neighbours. As Leo Ching has illustrated, the desire for modernity in Taiwan was inextricably bound up with the process of Japanisation, so there is not a clear-cut opposition between a victimised Taiwan and bad imperial Japan.[13] When Japan was defeated at the end of the World War Two in 1945, Taiwan was ceded by the US to Chiang Kai-Shek's Chinese nationalists (the KMT) as opposed to being granted its own autonomy. Almost immediately a systemised erasure and reversal of Japanisation by the KMT would attempt to Sinicise Taiwan by changing names and places, razing to the ground Japanese temples and statues, and making Mandarin the official language of the island.

It is this complex historical change of colonisation under both the Japanese and Chinese, the coming in to being of hybrid identities, linguistic diversity, enforced Japanisation and subsequent Sinicisation, diasporas and natives, modernity and transformation, and overall in-between-ness that are the building blocks of contemporary Taiwan and the hallmark of its post-coloniality. They are the basis of many themes explored not only by Hou Hsiao-Hsien and the Taiwanese New Cinema, but also by the nativist regional literature (*Xiangtu wenxue*) before them that was to influence and transform the local cinema as it had done with literature.

A Time to Live and a Time to Die

A Time to Live and a Time to Die was Hou's seventh feature after *That's the Way She Strolls Around /Juishi liuliu de ta* (1981), *The Naughty Wind /Feng'er tita cai* (1982), *The Green, Green Grass of Home /Zai na hepan qing cao qing* (1982), *The Boy's from Fengkuei* (1983), *A Summer at Grandpa's* (1984), and the title episode from the portmanteau film *The Sandwich Man/Erzi de da wan'ou* (1983) that launched the Taiwanese New Cinema. The Mandarin title of *A Time to Live and a Time to Die*, *Tongnian wangshi*, is literally translated as 'the past things of youth', a title better suited to a film about memory, specifically the memory of Hou's youth and of his father. The English-language title also recalls the name of a Douglas Sirk film, *A Time to Love and a Time to Die* (1959), which again suggests an altogether new direction in the spiralling web of connections that frame Hou as being anything but himself.

A Time to Live and a Time to Die was shot on location at the house of Hou's childhood and therefore bears some traces of authenticity in its attempt to frame both a particular historical period and a personal experience, hence the voiceover of the director himself at the start of the film: 'This film comprises some memories from my childhood, particularly impressions of my father.' One must also remember how important memory is to the formation of identity in post-colonial contexts.

A Time to Live and a Time to Die is typical of the New Taiwanese Cinema in exploring identity through memory and nostalgia much in the same way that memory and nostalgia are central to a post-colonial Hong Kong cinema. The story is of Ah-Hsiao, the character we are to assume is Hou's alter ego, and his family who have moved from the Chinese mainland after the defeat of the nationalists by the communists. Ah-Hsiao's father lives with the hope of return one day. The rites-of-passage story charts ten years of Ah-Hsiao's life through his experience of loss, both of his father and mother and later his grandmother. The personal experiences of growing up in a Chinese family in Taiwan are played against the context of the warring struggles between China and Taiwan. Ah-Hsiao is drawn more to his new home in Taiwan than to his parents' longing for return to the mainland. Hou frames the historical changes happening in Taiwan against the personal tragedy of Ah-Hsiao's loss and the subsequent 'birth' of Ah-Hsiao as a man, as a modern Taiwanese and culturally hybrid individual.

An examination of two scenes from the film, the opening scene and the scene of the father's death, are intended to illustrate Hou's differences from Ozu, pointing towards a more author-specific definition of Hou's style through editing and cinematography as well as revealing the extent to which colonialism is apparent in a close-reading of the *mise en scène*.

A Time to Live and a Time to Die opens with a close-up shot of a plaque outside a house – it reads in Chinese 'Residence of the Gaoxing District Administration' – as the voiceover of the director begins to narrate the real story of how his father came to Taiwan from China. As the voiceover continues, we begin to see through a sequence of six proceeding shots the space of the home and the fiction unfold. The second shot, which lingers, is of an empty room with recognisable Japanese *tatami* flooring and *shoji* screens; the next shot is an empty bamboo chair at a desk; the next shot has the father sitting at the bamboo chair, indicating a temporal ellipsis has occurred; and the subsequent shots reveal the occupants from a long shot outside the house where two boys are playing and from a medium shot of the back area and kitchen where the sister and mother can be seen preparing food. These shots establish the main focus of the film as the home and the family but they also reveal in their staging of *mise en scène* the family living in the wake of Japanese colonialism and at the start of Chinese occupation of which they themselves constitute its diaspora. The shots which are presented to us do not merely represent the home but reveal in their very fragments the competing aesthetics and historical shift from Japanese to Chinese occupation. The foregrounding in the second shot of the film of the *tatami* floor and the *shoji* screens of the main room serve as reminders that this house was once the occupancy of middle-class Japanese residents. The home is now occupied by a Chinese family of a lower class than the previous residents and it has been adapted through extension and rebuilding of the Japanese space to accommodate what one must assume is a larger family and one more concerned with the creation of a suitable home for their temporary exile than with the sentiment behind Japanese aesthetics. The father's bamboo chair, as is later revealed, represents his belief in returning, to the mainland and therefore his resistance to invest in higher-cost long-term furnishings. The hybrid nature of the space, with its mixture of recognisable Japanese aesthetics and functional ramshackle corrugated iron roof, bamboo furniture, and stone kitchen, indicates the clash between the period of Japanese colonisation and the later, assumed temporary occupation by Chinese nationalists as mentioned above. Therefore, the *mise en scène* of domestic space constructed in these opening shots functions as a palimpsest as Japan is rewritten over by China, literally in the erasure of Japan through a Sinicisation programme (razing buildings and temples, renaming streets, changing the official language) but also figuratively through the mundane nature of what is being represented, a family home of Chinese exiles. However, a third rewriting of this space presented to us occurs in the voiceover of the director who in fact authorises such a space as the one of his own memory. The opening scene opens up multiple positions for thinking about both memory, historical context and authorship as it intersects through what is otherwise the banality of domestic space bearing the traces of colonial legacy, Chinese exile, and personal recollection.

These opening shots also indicate where the potential for reading an aspect of the Ozu influence might be found. There can be no other reason than that of the presence in the mise en scène of the *tatami* floor and the paper screens. Their appearance here is a colonial reminder rather than some lineage of authorial influence or 'common impulse among Oriental filmmakers' as Cheshire suggests. To suggest Ozu as an influence here is the critics' own rewriting of that space beyond both authorial intention and history. Throughout both *A Time to Live and a Time to Die* and the earlier *A Summer at Grandpa's* the houses of the protagonists are both previous domiciles of Japanese residents and as such bear the tradition of a Japanese aesthetic through their interior's geometrisation of space. This assumption of an Ozu-like Hou is based on how the film looks at a superficial level.

In the sequence midway through the film that depicts the father's death and the family's reaction, an examination of the shot duration and editing in relation to Ozu illustrates the difference between the two directors and works towards outlining Hou's style in this particular period.

The scene of the father's death in the film is a dramatic turn for the protagonists, particularly Ah-Hsiao and his mother, and a rare moment of emotional excess in the film. We learn that the father's distancing of himself from the family was out of his love to protect them from catching the tuberculosis that he himself was dying from. The visual pattern of the space in this scene again reveals the Japanese aesthetic that works here to foreground spatial divisions betweens different planes of action and to indicate the camera placement as one of initial detachment from the heightened drama. During the scenes in which the family grieves around the father's bed the duration of the shots and the camera placement is worth remarking on. The camera's placement is from an anterior position of detachment, almost voyeuristic as the paper screen works to mask the frame and suggest the camera's hidden presence as being outside the unfolding drama. The next shot is a jump-cut forward in space to the middle plane of the drama to become part of the family's intimate moment of grief. The camera cuts in to the action to get closer to the drama rather than occupying a different position within the space as Ozu would more than likely do. Ozu is a master of cutting and redefining space and therefore places great emphasis on editing processes, whereas Hou prefers to preserve the natural order of space through editing restraint, long takes, and strategies of camera placement that all suggest a detached observation in as real a time as possible for the event being filmed. Hou prefers to keep his camera in one place and avoids alternating shot lengths and shot reverse-shot structures. For example, in *The Boy's of Fengkuei* we are always positioned at great distant from the action during the important scenes of violence in a camera placement that is at once both detached and voyeuristic. However, *The Boy's of Fengkuei* contains more of a range of devices than later films and does not place any great emphasis on the defining long take, thus making it difficult to form generalisations about consistency of style. This scene of grief in *A Time to Live and a Time to Die* is uncomfortable for the spectator because the camera holds back from allowing us access to the appropriate space of intimacy and character identification through a distance from the action. It is also a shot of an unbearably long duration. Hou reluctantly gets close to the drama of this scene, the most emotionally fraught scene in the film, and yet he causes the spectator a good deal of stress in doing so. It is an equally effective counter-strategy to the affective language of melodrama that so depends on the close-up reaction of faces and an overwrought musical score to cue the spectator. Hou achieves his dramatic power through the resistance to such commonplace generic strategies. The emotional intensity of this scene also stands in contra-distinction to Ozu and his penchant for downplaying or even sublimating and eliding the potential for heightened emotional drama. What can only be described as a painfully long and hysterical outburst of grief in Hou's film would be absolutely unthinkable in Ozu and it would undermine the Japanese director's authorial command of his drama. Comparing the two scenes of grief, the one described above from *A Time to Live and a Time to Die* and the death of the mother in *Tokyo Story*, reveals two directors at opposite ends of the spectrum in their choice of film style, staging of bereavement drama and its emotional impact on the spectator.

The Long Take and the Search for a Chinese Aesthetic

What Hou is challenging, whether consciously or unconsciously – and this is a central tenet of the New Taiwanese Cinema as a whole – was the popular forms of both Hollywood and Hong Kong cinema that were staple viewing for local audiences. He is seeking to address issues pertinent to Taiwan, and to find a film language distinctive enough to reinforce its localisation, a new style based, on the one hand, on with a resistance to the transparency and affective manipulation of emotions and, on the other, to the tense rhythmic editing patterns and distinctive organisation of time and space evident in Hong Kong film genres. Hong Kong's own localisation in contemporary films and gravitation to a mythical China in its period films, and Hollywood as an exotic occidental fantasy were simply not adequate enough forms to respond to the changes in Taiwan and the resurgence and construction of a specifically Taiwanese identity. Probably the most distinctive aspect of Hou's style and of other Taiwanese New Cinema, for example Wan Ren's *Ah Fei* (1983), is the extensive use of the long take. Hou's most sustained use of the long take is in *Flowers of Shanghai/hai shang hua* (1998) which is composed solely of thirty-nine long takes. Likewise, Tsai Ming-Liang has taken the long take to its limits in continuing the legacy of one of the New Cinema's defining aspects and making both an authorial statement and a continuation of a specifically Taiwanese aesthetic in films such as *Vive L'amour/Aiqing wansui* (1994) and *Goodbye, Dragon Inn.*

Hou's concern with the long take again reveals his difference from Ozu not just in style but in intent. What needs to be stressed here is that the long-take in Hou is concerned with what is taking place *within* the shot and not with the relations *between* the shot. This is the fundamental difference between Hou's use of the long take and that of other filmmakers who on occasion employ such a device. The shot in Hou can be autonomous and sustains itself rather than in relation to the preceding or proceeding shots. While it would be wrong to suggest that this accounts for everything Hou has made, it nonetheless seems to indicate a defining aspect of his authorship especially during the New Wave period. This particular use of the long take stands in opposition to the largely held formal definition of the long take from Brian Henderson's influential essay where he argues that the long take is 'not in itself a principle of construction' but rather an essential way of 'building sequences' and therefore tied to the shot relations of editing.[14] Hou has explained how the long take also developed out of working with friends and non-professional actors who could not shadow act in their reverse shots. It is important to bear in mind then that the development of the long take and also the long shot are as much to do with finding a local style and the development of an authorial style as it was initially a practical response to non-professional actors. As Hou explains:

> When I began making movies, I was fond of getting close friends to act in them . . . I would deliberately put the camera quite a distance away and not move it. Hence I had to find the right angle for every scene so that the camera could take in as much situations and people as I wanted. Because of this decision, I am very respectful of the objective space I am shooting.[15]

Later on in the next paragraph from this interview, conducted around the time of *The Puppetmaster/Xi meng rensheng* in 1993, Hou further suggests:

> Sometimes my actors would leave the frame, but I still won't change my shot, hence you get an empty shot on the screen. Here I am utilising a concept from Chinese painting – *liu-pai* (literally, 'to leave a whiteness') which means that even after the character has left the frame, or even when you have a unexplained space outside the frame – though it is empty and imagined, the audience must join together with me and complete the shot.[16]

Both Hou himself and recent scholarship on Hou are taking the director in a different direction from the Ozu pigeonhole that has framed him for many years. His move towards the development of a more mature and sustained engagement with a Chinese aesthetic influence is becoming frequently foregrounded. It provides a new and more convincing context for the development of his authorial style. Both Ni Zhen and Berenice Reynaud illustrate this draw towards Chinese traditions in their analysis of *City of Sadness*.[17] Ni Zhen groups Hou and the directors of the Chinese Fifth Generation together in suggesting a shared aesthetic heritage among Chinese filmmakers based on a specifically Chinese cinematic signification derived from the multi-focal perspectives of Classical Chinese painting. He also positions Hou within a history defined by the influences of Fei Mu and the Chinese avant-garde. In his description of what he calls 'temporal blanks' and 'empty shots', Ni provides a model of Chinese spectatorship based on the formal structure of both Chen Kaige and Hou Hsiao-Hsien's style that neatly resists the suturing effect of shot reverse shots and Renaissance perspective central to the 'global style' of the classical paradigm. While this sophisticated alternative to classical spectatorship extends the definition of the impact of Hou's style by placing him within a China-centric artistic heritage, one must still be careful of placing Hou within a general category of Chinese cinema that would similarly prioritise sameness rather than difference among the Chinese-language cinemas. Beyond signification, as Chris Berry's analysis of *City of Sadness* illustrates, language dialect and register in Hou's films 'marks the difference denied by China' through the multiplicity of dialects that resists any attempt to establish a core Chinese identity through language standardisation.[18] This emphasis on linguistic diversity and the mutual unintelligibility of language is central also to Wu Nien-Chen's *Buddha Bless America/Tuipin tienguo* (1996) and the marking out of power relationships and identities through language between the different racial and ethnic groups in postwar Taiwan. While Hou's films acknowledge degrees of Chinese-ness, one must remember that the original project of the New Cinema and the nativist literature was its concern with distinctive and new forms of identity, hybrid or otherwise, that would correspond to what it means to be a Taiwanese vis-à-vis more essentialist Chinese identities, Han-centrism, and Western hegemony. It might be useful, then, following Hamid Naficy, to consider the Taiwanese New Wave as quite literally, and metaphorically, an accented cinema, a cinema that speaks *with* an accent rather than *without* through both form and dialogue.[19]

What Hou has talked about most recently at length in the journal *Positions* is the profound influence that Mainland Chinese novelist Shen Congwen (1902–88) has had on his way of thinking about his approach and development of authorial style since *The Boys from Fengkuei*.[20] Through his objective style Shen Congwen provided Hou with the right strategy for developing his own detached narrational style. Shen often deals with provocative issues such as execution that interviewer Michael Berry suggests are rendered in a way that he 'might as well be describing a family dinner'.[21] One can see how this influence would have shaped both the approach to the scenes of violence in *The Boys from Fengkuei* and the family trauma in *A Time to Live and a Time to Die* described above.

WHO'S HOU?

The detached observational style that Hou has employed through his distanced and fixed camera placement and his preference for the long take have been developed out of a number of possible paths the director has taken over the years. From his attempt to get around non-professional actors' lack of experience in the early films to the search for both a distinctive Taiwanese film, language and a unique authorial voice have opened up multiple ways of understanding the author named Hou Hsiao-Hsien. Film criticism has often clutched at straws in order to pin down the director, whether specifically through Ozu Yasujiro or more generally with the search for a common Asian film language. These approaches both overlook the colonial history of Taiwan and in themselves enact a neo-colonial viewpoint that constructs positions of otherness. More recent shifts towards negotiating a Chinese influence on the director are more solid in their approach and are supported by the director himself. However, these must also be understood within the larger sociocultural context of the Taiwan/China relationship, one that is fraught with a great deal of complexity and tension. Therefore, one must not simply reproduce Hou as simply another Chinese filmmaker to be grouped alongside Zhang Yimou or Chen Kaige. Hou is a filmmaker at once Taiwanese and unique. As *Café Lumiere* demonstrates, Hou is unpredictable, contradictory and ever changing, and with his 'Japanese film' he seeks to tell us more about Taiwan than Japan and hopefully lays the ghost of Ozu which has forever nagged him as a frame of reference.[22] If anything, *Café Lumiere* reveals to us through Hou's vision of Tokyo, lingering shots of tempura restaurants and character silences, a reversal of what Ozu might have looked like if Hou had influenced him.

NOTES

1. In the UK the ICA (Institute for Contemporary Arts) in London was responsible for programming and introducing to audiences the work of both Hou Hsiao-Hsien and the Chinese Fifth Generation filmmakers.
2. Tony Rayns (1988), 'The Sandwich Man', *Monthly Film Bulletin* vol. 55, no. 653.
3. The other directors include Wim Wenders, Stanley Kwan, Aki Kurasmaki, Claire Denis, Paul Schrader, and Lindsay Anderson.
4. Alan Stanbrook (1990), 'The worlds of Hou Hsiao-Hsien', *Sight and Sound*, 59: 2, and Godfrey Cheshire, 'Time Span: The cinema of Hou Hsiao-Hsien', *Film Comment*, Nov/Dec 1993.
5. Alan Stanbrook (1990), 'The worlds of Hou Hsiao-Hsien'.
6. Ibid.
7. Godfrey Cheshire (1993), 'Time span: The cinema of Hou Hsiao-Hsien', *Film Comment*, Nov/Dec, p. 58.
8. Wimal Dissanayake and Kwok-Kan Tam (1998), *New Chinese Cinema*, Hong Kong: Oxford University Press, p. 47.

9. Ibid. p. 49.
10. Paul Schrader (1976), *Transcendental Style in Film*, New York: Da Capo Press; David Bordwell and Kristin Thompson (1976), 'Space and narrative in the films of Ozu', *Screen* vol. 17, no. 10; Noel Burch (1979), *To the Distant Observer*, London: Scholar Press.
11. Jane Bachnik and Charles J. Jr. Quinn (eds) (1994), *Situated Meaning*, Princeton: Princeton University Press.
12. Lee Ellickson (2002), 'Preparing to live in the present: An interview with Hou Hsiao-Hsien', *Cineaste*, vol. 27, no. 4, p. 19.
13. Leo T. S. Ching (2001), *Becoming 'Japanese': Colonial Taiwan and the Politics of Identity Formation*, Berkeley: University of California Press.
14. Brian Henderson (1976), 'The long take', in Bill Nichols (ed.), *Movies and Methods* vol. 1, Berkeley: University of California Press.
15. Alice Ou (ed.) (1993), *Taiwan Films*, Taipei: Variety Publishing, p. 346.
16. Alice Ou (ed.) (1993), *Taiwan Films*, p. 347.
17. Berenice Reynaud (2002), *A City of Sadness,* London: British Film Institute; Ni Zhen (1994), 'Classical Chinese painting and cinematographic signification', in David Desser and Linda C. Erlich (ed.), *Cinematic Landscapes*, Austin: University of Texas Press.
18. Chris Berry (1994), 'A nation t(w/o)o: Chinese cinema(s) and nationhood(s)', in Wimal Dissanayake (ed.), *Colonialism and Nationalism in Asian Cinema*, Bloomington and Indianapolis: Indiana University Press.
19. Hamid Naficy (2001), *An Accented Cinema: Exilic and Diasporic Filmmaking*, Princeton: Princeton University Press.
20. Michael Berry (2003), 'Words and images: A conversation with Hou Hsiao-Hsien and Chu T'ien-Wen, *Positions: East West Culture Critique*, Durham: Duke University Press.
21. Ibid. p. 690.
22. For a discussion of *Café Lumiere* in relation to contemporary Taiwanese politics, see Hou Hsiao-Hsien, Chu Tien-Hsin, Tang Nuo, and Hsia Chu-Joe (2004), 'Tensions in Taiwan', *New Left Review*, no. 28, July/August.

19

TOKYO LOVE STORY AND NY BAGELS: EAST-WEST CULTURAL ENCOUNTER IN EDWARD YANG'S *TAIPEI STORY*

I-Fen Wu

Apart from Hou Hsiao-Hsien, who is generally regarded as the most important figure of Taiwanese New Cinema, Edward Yang De-Ch'ang is the other master of the New Wave. Yang started to establish his filmmaking career when he was invited to make the second episode of *In Our Time/Kuangyin de sushih* (1982), and he is remarkable in addressing Taiwan's socioeconomic restructuring from an agricultural to a modernised and capitalist society. His films are consistently concerned with the social and personal problems that confront the middle class in the increasingly urbanised, US-influenced Taipei. Strikingly different from Hou's style and subject matter, Yang's utilisation of detached camera shots, long takes and discontinuity editing in capturing the alienated urban life in Taipei is regarded as similar to the modernist aesthetic art of European director, Michelangelo Antonioni.[1] Before returning to Taiwan and becoming a filmmaker, Yang had worked for years as a computer technician in the USA and his long-time experience of living abroad gave him a sharp observational position on cultural incompatibility between East and West. His films *Taipei Story/Qingmei zhuma* (1985) and *A One and A Two/Yiyi* (2000) offer another dimension of viewing Taiwan's high-tech, capitalist society, as a contrast with Hou's approach to the American cultural impact on modern Taiwan.[2]

Among Yang's early films *Taipei Story* probably stands out as the most profound depiction of the cultural conflicts that Taiwanese society has confronted since the country's modernisation. This film displays the rich cultural context of modern society, providing a sharp insight on the incompatibility between traditional and foreign cultures. *Taipei Story* is about the urban life of 1980s Taipei. It precisely presents the essential loneliness of individual human beings living in a metropolis in which the changes of cultural landscape and the class structure divided by economic development relentlessly alienate people. Ah-Jean is a senior business assistant in an international corporation in Taipei. She is in her early thirties, financially independent, and has just bought an apartment with a mortgage. Trusted by her boss, Jean is promoted every year and never expects her life to change, until one day the corporation is taken over, her boss leaves for America, and she is told to quit. Around the same time, her boyfriend, Ah-Long, with whom she grew up, returns from the United States to carry on the family business, after his family all emigrated to the United States. Ah-Long used to play junior baseball and has been very much involved in this sport. Jean frequently goes to the pub with her friends to kill time, whereas Ah-Long prefers karaoke and playing cards with his friends; they do not see each other often. One day, Jean is extremely angry with Ah-Long because he lends their money, which they are saving for their emigration to the United States, to her father, and she is later irritated to learn that Ah-Long has met Ah-Kwan, his ex-lover, in Tokyo, when he changed plane there. Ah-Long moves out, and Jean invites her younger sister, Ah-Lin, a lay-about who hangs around with her friends, to live with her. A friend of Lin is drawn to Jean and frequently finds chances to get close to her. One evening, Jean sees him expecting her downstairs. Hesitating, she eventually makes a phone call to Ah-Long, asking him to escort her home. Ah-Long has a fight with the young boy, who unexpectedly stabs Long and flees on his motorcycle. Ah-Long dies on the street.

Edward Yang's films are always self-consciously concerned with the difficulties of adapting to a changing environment, and are particularly interested in exploring the social dynamics of the middle class. It seems to Yang that the bourgeois class displays the most explicit and detailed impulses through which to examine a contemporary society, as middle-class people apparently confront the spread of a dominant ideology of foreign culture and experience the process of a transforming Taiwan. Therefore, most of Yang's films are about middle-class people, and their specific focus is normally on independent but sensitive women.

In *Taipei Story*, Ah-Jean, instinctive and smart like most of the female characters in Yang's film, is a profile of a contemporary bourgeois woman who is successful in her career but emotionally empty. To the music of J. Bach's *Cello Suites*, the opening credits dissolve as the camera slowly wanders through Jean's apartment, panning over images that give a portrait of middle-class life: a bourgeois-style living room, modern electric appliances, and many pairs of sunglasses. Jean comes into shot as she is choosing some sunglasses and looking at herself in the mirror. This expressive use of sunglasses continues through the film and implies that Jean self-consciously disguises herself to be tough and strong, as if it can prevent her loneliness and insecurity being seen. When she learns the news from the new executive that she is to be laid off, she calmly leaves her job but puts her sunglasses on to hide her frustration right after she walks out of the lobby; after discovering that Ah-Long is still seeing his ex-lover, she frequently wears her sunglasses whenever she goes out, even though it is not necessary. Jean seems truly frightened for her security, which in a way reflects on her longing for Ah-Long's company and her wish to emigrate to the United States. The day she leaves her job and comes back late in the evening, Ah-Long is sitting in their bedroom watching a baseball game. He turns around to give Jean a glance, but says nothing, and then turns back to watch TV. Jean comes near to him, putting her head on his shoulder, and softly complains: 'You didn't ask why I came back so late.' This is an expression of emotional loneliness rather than merely female dependency on a man, for Jean wishes that Ah-Long could understand and give her support.

Jean does not allow her fragility to reveal itself in front of her friends, even though she is truly lonely and deeply insecure in her own mind. She frequently spends time with her friends in the pub, listening to their jokes and laughing till she cries; or else she joins her sister's friends, having fun at their party until midnight. But she becomes a different person whenever she goes to her parents' home, where she is taciturn in the face of her father's non-stop nagging. In the scene in which she helps her mother to prepare for dinner, her father, who is eating and talking with Ah-Long at the table, drops his spoon on the floor. With no intention of picking it up, he grabs Jean's and continues eating his dinner. Jean picks up the spoon and is annoyed with her father's selfishness, but remains silent and eventually returns to the kitchen where her mother is cooking quietly. For Jean, the house in which she grew up is a world that is completely patriarchal, in the selfish and dominant chauvinist way in which both her mother and herself are physically and mentally abused by the father. It is possible to say that it may not be the glittering urban life that draws Jean to work in Taipei, but rather her fear of living under the shadow of her father's selfishness and physical violence, as well as of her mother's traditional fatalism.

In contrast with Jean, who is inclined towards westernisation, Ah-Long seems quite the opposite. Unlike Jean, Ah-Long is not attracted to American culture and is not very interested in moving to the United States. The director portrays Ah-Long as an alternative to the emptiness of modern urban life, considering the problem of cultural conflicts through Ah-Long's self-questioning of his identity. The representation of Ah-Long in the film is as emotionally simple and straightforward, as being generous and loyal to his friends. For example, when Jean's father seeks financial help from him, he lends him money that is intended for a business investment with his brother-in-law, regardless of the fact that his budget is tight. When he pops into the house of his childhood friend, Ah-Kim, and learns that his wife is gambling with the neighbours while neglecting her children, he is furious enough to take her home, ignoring her shouting in the street. Ah-Long is the kind of thoughtful person who would listen to Ah-Kim's complaints about his tough life, and sensitively feel responsible for supporting him with some money. His thoughtfulness is also reflected in his respect for the elder generation–for instance, his childhood baseball coach, whom he frequently visits, and accompanies to instruct children playing baseball.

Perhaps because of his remembrance of the past and his lack of interest in modern cultural dynamics, Ah-Long is distanced from Jean and her friends. When invited to join Jean and her friends in a pub, Ah-Long is apparently tense as his temperament is strikingly different from the others. His uneasiness is explicitly revealed by his stiff facial expression, and it is soon clear to Jean as he shows no interest in their conversation, and later to Jean's friends as he is asked by one of them to play darts. When he loses four rounds and is about to start the next one, Jean's friend teases him with a provocative manner: 'Didn't you used to play baseball?' This taunt is hurtful to Ah-Long in the sense that his past, of which he is proud, is being humiliated. Ah-Long strikes this man in the face in response, pointing out that he simply lives in his past glory and memory, and does not bother about the changes to the world. Ah-Long's fight with Jean's friend here is closely related to the concern that Yang has been exploring in the relationship between the individual and urbanisation. In *Taipei Story*, it seems that people cannot avoid being evaluated in the contemporary society, in which people are judged by what they have rather than how they are, and that inevitably makes the relationship between people become superficially business-like.

On the one hand, the Ah-Long character is a narcissist living in his own world: he is not aware that the environment, which he used to know, has changed. As Kwan says, he remains unchanged, and appears to be an idealist who always thinks that he can help his friends to sort out their problems, trying to retrieve a hopeless situation by himself, but is totally oblivious to the fact that the world has moved on, and that people can barely remain the same in these circumstances. On the other hand, he is a character created to be critical of the changes in the sociocultural landscape, whose trajectory as portrayed in the film leads to the discovery of the hidden problems within 1980s urbanised Taipei. Yang's observation of the contemporary cultural landscape is expressed in his delicate exploration of the relationship between Jean and Ah-Long. In *Taipei Story*, Yang ambitiously expands his approach to the potential crisis brought about by the processes of urbanisation, the issue he continues to deal with in his later films, and he wants to make explicit the link between urbanisation and the alienation of human relationships, not only by the complicated relationships between the central characters but also by how he represents city spaces.

Architecture is often framed by Yang's camera shots as a visual means of exploring the cultural pattern of Taipei City. Yang also frames Jean and Ah-Long within different kinds of architecture throughout the film, offering visual interpretations of their relationship. For example, Jean is frequently placed within her bourgeois apartment and the pub in the East District of Taipei, while Ah-Long is either doing business in Di-Hua street or playing cards in a karaoke pub;[3] Jean does not behave spontaneously at her parents' home in the West End, and neither does Ah-Long when he is with Jean in the East District pub. The differences between them are visually revealed in a variety of city spaces, foregrounding their potential alienation from each other. Yang seems to consciously frame his camera shots with doors and windows, forming a visual stylisation and foregrounding the images presented. In the opening scene, when Jean takes Ah-Long to see her new apartment, both of them stand in front of the window looking out over the park. The huge window is framed visually to separate them, but it also implies an unseen split in their superficially stable relationship. Their alienated relationship is suggested by similar frames throughout the film, and an unbridgeable gap between them obviously exists on the visual level. When Ah-Long is waiting for Jean in his car, the noise of the rush-hour traffic seems to swallow the whole city. Jean does not hear Ah-Long until she sees him waiting for her on the other side of the street; she tries to approach him but is stopped many times by the heavy traffic. On one level, the rushing vehicles represent urbanised Taipei as a busy, noisy city at the peak of an economic boom, in which people are indifferent, worrying more about losing time than consideration for others. On a more specific level, the busy traffic is like a river, forming a visual, haunting effect to separate Ah-Long and Jean, that again points to the gap that always comes between them.

Although Yang has stated that he was not influenced by Michelangelo Antonioni, the narrative of *Taipei Story* is similar to that of Antonioni's *L'eclisse* (1962), in which the subtle feeling depicted in the relationship between Piero (Alain Delon) and Vittoria (Monica Vitti) is similar to that of Yang's between Jean and Ah-Long. Taiwanese film critics have sensed that Yang's films, especially the early ones, have been strongly influenced by Antonioni's style – primarily an expression of alienation with steady but precise cinematic language – and they regard the rhythm and style of *Taipei Story* as being close to *L'eclisse*. In *L'eclisse*, Antonioni includes some particular objects in the film frame as symbols that add power to the film's narrative, and lead the viewer to find more than what the art designer has put there. According to Biarese and Tassone, the immense, visually striking pillar which is always framed between Piero and Vittoria at the stock market has a symbolic meaning: 'it [the column] is not there by accident, or for its beauty, like the columns in certain Renaissance Annunciation's . . . Between Piero and Vittoria there will always be an obstacle, the stock market.'[4]

Antonioni's interpretation of Piero and Vittoria's relationship relies very much on visual suggestion, which is particularly based on Vittoria's feeling and emotion, implying that neither of them, in fact, really loves the other, and that the differences between them make their relationship almost impossible to continue. The target of Antonioni's social and political critique in *L'eclisse* relies on the differences between Piero and Vittoria that he explores. Piero's mercenary values and extremely practical personality are emphasised in order to portray a bourgeois society in early 1960s Italy, in which people are irrationally driven to make a fortune through the stock market but are largely indifferent to their personal relationships; for example, Piero abandons his girlfriend shortly after meeting Vittoria.[5] When the stock market collapses, Vittoria asks where does all the money go and what are these people going to do, whereas Piero is quiet, and seems to be used to the frenetic intensity of the situation. It is true that, as Biarese and Tassone point out, between Piero and Vittoria there is not just a huge column, but a whole stock market. Or, perhaps, it is not just a stock market between them, but their different values towards relationships, society and life.

Likewise, what affects Jean and Ah-Long's relationship is their differing perception about life and the future. Ah-Long never wants to emigrate to the United States which, for him, is a cruel and mercenary world, as he hears from his brother-in-law that he once shot a black man for fun, and how the Taiwanese use cash to buy luxury villas in the white people's residential district. Only once does he express a wish to live there, when he has fought with Jean's friend in the pub. But his motivation for emigration is rather a passive excuse to escape from this society which has quickly changed towards the indifferent, a place where he is not allowed to look back upon his glory. But Jean's emigration to America is not a temporary run-away plan, but a long-term expectation constructed on the foundation of her imagination about the United States. It thus becomes understandable that what is between Jean and Ah-Long is definitely not Kwan, whose existence often makes Jean feel that she is to lose Ah-Long, but their different expectations towards what they want. Ah-Long seems more genuinely alive when doing things relevant to baseball, things that allow him to escape into the past. Apparently, neither of them is keen to share each other's life sphere, which is acknowledged in the scene when Ah-Long hears of Jean's unemployment: he pets her but simultaneously pays attention to the baseball game on TV, which ironically shows that there is always something between them, whether it is palpable or not. And Yang's repetitive location shots through the film – in which the simple pub is contrasted with the karaoke bar, the skyscrapers in the East District with the architecture of Di-Hua street in the West End – as well as urban middle-class apartments and the baseball ground all visually mark different spheres of life. They have a cultural implication towards urbanisation that, under the reshaping of multicultural influences, the contemporary urban culture appears polarised, as the urban spaces have developed to be modern and traditional, new and old.

As C. J. Hamelink sees the explicit connection between the processes of cultural synchronisation and the spread of capitalism, it seems to be inevitable that cultural homogenisation will be an unprecedented feature of global modernity, which in a sense means that the diversity and richness of global culture is threatened.[6] It is certainly hard to conclude whether cultural homogenisation could be a 'destructive process' causing the diversity of cultural systems to wane, as it could possibly be a cultural convergence that contributes to the enrichment of other cultures and communities.[7] On the other hand, cultural homogenisation does play an important role in changing other cultural systems into an adaptive mechanism through the interplay of transnational corporations, largely American ones; these are the major players in the spread of capitalism as well as in the process of urbanisation in developing areas, simply restructuring different cultural practices within a single cultural pattern which, in a sense, is a kind of colonisation of other cultural identities.[8]

On the one hand, cultural homogenisation is perceived as threatening to erase the diversity of global culture while, on the other, it is widely received as a popular culture that has moved the world towards uniform products, world brands: 'an ideal from the multinational capitalist's point of view.'[9] Those people who have been brought up under the influence of a traditional culture and later experienced the impact of foreign culture, for instance Jean and Ah-Long, might have confronted the problem of cultural conflicts. By contrast, the younger generation, like Jean's sister Lin, has trouble identifying with the features of national culture since they have been blurred by the imposition of multinational culture – Lin completely identifies with the culture of 'world brands' – which collapses the borders of national cultural identity. There is a scene in *Taipei Story* in which Lin is talking enthusiastically to her grandmother about how wonderful the shops are in Shinjuku district, and how much she wants to shop there.[10] Her excitement about Japanese culture, responded to by her grandmother's silence, is an example illustrating that contemporary young people's sense of culture is built on the culture of commodities that constitutes a weakening of national culture. As shown in the film, most famous world brands like Pepsi and Fuji, which are consumed and seen everywhere in Taipei City, successfully cross the cultural boundaries of their target markets, and transform themselves from mere commercial commodities to become the landscape in every country, regardless of individual cultures and lifestyles.

It can hardly be denied that the material-cultural effects of consumerism arising from the development of global capitalism may lead to an obsession with the culture of commodities, and an extreme materialism that will make modern people more selfish and less aware of other people's needs. Ah-Long's brother in-law, who never appears in *Taipei Story*, does not answer Ah-Long's phone calls when he learns that the latter needs his financial help; Jean's architect friend tells her in a flat tone that he cannot distinguish which buildings are his, as all of them in Taipei look so similar. It seems that people in *Taipei Story* are either completely obsessed with buying and possessing things as a way to reduce their anxiety towards the pressures of school and society, or numb to the development of affluent consumerism. While the conveniences of capitalist modernity are fully enjoyed in a contemporary society, its reverse aspects should be simultaneously considered as they suggest that modern people's sense of morality is trapped in materialism. The contradictions in capitalist modernity are not simply caused by the differentiation of the sphere of consumption from other social spheres, but also by the adaptation of the socio-cultural structure to other different systems. The point raised earlier with regard to the portrayal of Jean's different personality in different city spaces is emphasised at the end of the film when Ah-Long is dying on the street, where a discarded TV is showing a baseball match. Ah-Long, in a sense, is like the old TV disposed on the street, becoming out of date and not belonging to this modern city. His death could be explained as a final release from the memory of his past, as well as from the social constraints that he has such difficulties in overcoming. Ah-Long's tragedy is in a sense Yang's pertinent allegory of urban Taipei in which the transcultural space is expanding while the interconnectedness of people is fading out.

Notes

1. Kwok-Kan Tam and Wimal Dissanayake (1998), *New Chinese Cinema*, Oxford: Oxford University Press, p. 65. Yang said that, among Antonioni's films, he had only seen *L'Avventura*, and did not find it very inspiring; see Huang Jien-Yeh (1995), *The Films of Edward Yang*, Taipei, Yuang-liu publication, p. 29.
2. *Taipei Story* is Yang's third film, but his first one to focus extremely upon modern Taipei City. His first film is one of the episodes in *In Our Time*; the second is *That Day, on the Beach/Hai tan de yi tian* (1983), a story about two women's transformation as a mirror of Taiwan's change. After *Taipei Story*, *Terrorizer/Kong bu fen zi* (1986) is a film that started to bring him a wider audience in the West. In 1991, he filmed *A Brighter Summer Day/Gu ling jie shao nian sha zen shi jian*, which is based on a real story that happened in the 1960s about a teenager homicide. It is probable that this film is Yang's memory of the era he grew up, as *A Time to Live, A Time to Die* is for Hou Hsiao-Hsien. Afterwards *A Confucian Confusion/Du li shi dai* was shot in 1994, in which Yang came back to his focus on metropolitan culture, also a consistent theme in his next film, *Mahjong/Ma jiang* (1996). His recent film *A One and A Two/Yiyi* (2000) is a panoramic, multi-strand slice of Taiwanese city life, which won him the award of best director at the Cannes Film Festival.
3. Di-Hua Street is located near Taipei City's West End, which was constructed long before the Japanese colonial era. Taipei's West End used to be a busy business centre in northern Taiwan since the Chinese immigrants moved to Taiwan in the seventeenth century. Geographically near to the convergence of the Tamshui River and Taiwan Strait, the West End area developed as a business centre and most of the importation and exportation business had to be through Di-Hua Street. Therefore, Di-Hua Street has been famous for the wholesale business. It is still a popular shopping area, in particular for the Chinese New Year. Di-Hua Street is also renowned for its history and architecture. The architectural characteristics of Di-Hua Street are its corridor on the ground floor, and the special access into the house, which was a common style of Taiwanese houses until the 1970s, when the Taiwanese started living in apartments. In the early 1990s, the Taiwanese government reported the old condition of Di-Hua Street and proposed to reconstruct it, which incurred a strong rejection among historians. The government eventually gave up the plan for reconstruction partly because its proposal was not agreed by the Taiwanese congress, and partly because it was threatened by the idea that the Japanese would not mind buying and importing a deconstructed Di-Hua Street to Japan to show Japanese people the historical profile of Taiwan during the Japanese colonial era. As for the East District, this refers to the east part of Taipei City, an area mainly known for fashion and entertainment, which has been developed as a centre of the younger generation, and has gradually replaced the West End since the 1980s.
4. Cesare Biarese and Aldo Tassone (1985), *I film di Michelangelo Antonioni*, Rome: Gremese Editore, p. 115. Quoted in Peter Brunette (1998), *The Films of Michelangelo Antonioni*, Cambridge: Cambridge University Press, p. 77.
5. Brunette, *The Films of Michelangelo Antonioni*, p. 82.
6. John Tomlinson (1991), *Cultural Imperialism*, Baltimore: Johns Hopkins University Press, pp. 108–13. Tomlinson refers to C. J. Hamelink (1983), *Cultural*

Autonomy in Global Communications, New York: Longman, as an example to elaborate his discussion of multinational capitalism and cultural homogenisation.
7. Tomlinson, *Cultural Imperialism*, p. 110.
8. Ibid. pp. 113–14.
9. Ibid.
10. Shinjuku is an area in Tokyo renowned for shopping and fashion.

20

THE TRANSNATIONAL CINEMA OF ANG LEE

Julianne Pidduck

With his diverse transnational filmography, Ang Lee has distinguished himself as the most versatile and commercially successful *auteur* of the New Taiwanese cinema. Alongside Stan Lai's *Peach Blossom Land/Anliang taohua yuan* (1993) and *The Red Lotus Society/Feixia a da* (1994) and Tsai Ming-liang's *The River/Helui* (1997), Lee's films can be grouped within a 'second wave' of New Taiwanese Cinema characterised by fluid identities and urban sensibilities. For Zhang Yingjin, these filmmakers perceive 'new Taiwanese identities as conditioned less by an idealized projection of the native soil than by the incessant *flow* of capital, commodity, desire and traffic, which constantly transgress boundaries of all kinds – spatial, temporal, cultural, ethnic, moral and sexual'.[1] This account is suggestive for understanding Lee's cinematic exploration of personal identity (sexuality, gender, generation) within a 'diasporic' Chinese milieu, and within other cultural and historical contexts of displacement and social change.

Since the international success of his second feature *The Wedding Banquet/Hsi yen* (1993), Lee's career has been characterised by different types of border-crossing: he has worked across diverse industrial and cultural production contexts, employing Chinese and Western popular genres to address both Asian and Western audiences. Lee's career was launched by a trilogy of Taiwanese/American family comedy-dramas *Pushing Hands/Tui shou* (1991), *The Wedding Banquet, and Eat Drink Man Woman/Yin shi nan nu* (1994). Subsequently, Lee directed four 'period' literary adaptations from diverse cultural and historical settings: Regency England (*Sense and Sensibility*, 1995), 1970s American suburbia (*The Ice Storm*, 1997), the American Civil War (*Ride with the Devil*, 1998) and early nineteenth-century China (*Crouching Tiger, Hidden Dragon/Wo hu cang long*, 1999). More recently, Lee directed a little-known gangster film *The Hire: Chosen* (2001) and the comic-book adaptation *Hulk* (2003); *Brokeback Mountain*, a revisionist western set in the 1970s, is scheduled for release in 2005.

Lee's profile as a cosmopolitan and adaptable director places him within an emergent category of 'branded' and bankable Asian directors alongside John Woo, Zhang Yimou, Jackie Chan, Wong Kar-Wai, Shekhar Kapur, Chen Kaige and Takeshi Kitano. While many Asian filmmakers (including Taiwanese New Wave directors Hou Hsaio-hsien, Edward Yang and Tsai Ming-liang) have found Western critical acclaim through the art cinema circuit, Lee has specialised in popular genre films, a choice that has afforded him comparably broader audiences in Asia, North America and Europe.

While critical scholarship has all but demolished the idea of authorship as an 'organizing consciousness' within a body of work, this idea persists strongly within popular and industry discourses. This chapter will examine recurrent themes and stylistic elements of Lee's films alongside his deliberate construction as an *auteur*. This case study is particularly interesting because Lee's chameleon-like adaptability confounds self-evident categories of 'Taiwanese' or 'Chinese' cinema and authorship.

The 'Father Knows Best' Trilogy

Lee established his reputation with a trio of family melodramas, *Pushing Hands*, *The Wedding Banquet* and *Eat Drink Man Woman*. Known as the 'father knows best' trilogy, these films establish themes that have come to be associated with Lee's oeuvre as a whole: family and 'coming-of-age' social dramas, intergenerational and cross-cultural conflicts, and tensions between cultural tradition and modernisation. Deftly combining dramatic and comedic elements, the films achieved box-office success and critical acclaim in Taiwan and abroad. The success of Lee's early films stands out within a failing Taiwanese national cinema of the 1990s that struggled to compete with Hong Kong and American popular films. Indeed, Lee's career was jumpstarted with a prize for the script of *Pushing Hands*, a prize awarded in conjunction with Taiwanese state subsidies developed in 1989/1990 to support outstanding screenplays and to enhance distribution and exhibition.[2] Already a resident in the US, Lee received state support for his initial three films from the CMPC and the Government Information Office (GIO).

Like the careers of his contemporaries of the Taiwanese New Cinema, Lee's career has been shaped by the powerful forces of Western capital, markets and critics. Lee has gradually been constructed (and has contributed to constructing himself) as a cinematic *auteur* within the framework of transnational film production and marketing. This discourse of authorship follows a Western romantic vision where artistic works bear the imprint of the author's 'personal vision'. As M. H. Abrams writes, this approach seeks to 'isolate and explain the special quality of a work by reference to the special quality of the character, life, lineage and milieu of its author'.[3] Frequently cited in the films' promotional materials and press coverage, the concept of the director's experience as central to the meaning of the text applies best to Lee's initial three films, where he is credited as co-writer and director.

Born and educated in Taiwan, Lee studied theatre at the Taiwan Academy of Art for three years, emigrating to the US in 1977 to study theatre and later film at New York University. The experience of the emigrant son figures centrally in his first two films, *Pushing Hands* and *The Wedding Banquet*. Each narrative chronicles elderly Chinese parents who visit their son who has moved to the US, with the drama stemming from clashes between traditional Chinese and modern and/or 'Western' values. In interviews, Lee often discusses his conservative mainland Chinese father[4] who strongly disapproved of his non-traditional career choice, and versions of this oedipal drama can be recognised in the 'father knows best' trilogy. Each features a traditional and enigmatic mainland Chinese father figure played by Sihung Lung.

Best known of Lee's early films, particularly among Western audiences, is *The Wedding Banquet*. With a modest budget of US$1 million, the film was nominated for Best Foreign Language Film at the Academy Awards and grossed almost $26.3 million worldwide.[5] The film begins with Wai Tung Gao (Winston Chao), a young gay Taiwanese man who shares an affluent, urban, gay lifestyle with his lover Simon (Mitchell Lichtenstein) in New York City. Concealing his personal life from his family, Wai Tung finds himself under constant pressure from his elderly Taiwanese parents to marry and produce an heir. To make peace, the son arranges a marriage of convenience with a young Chinese woman, Wei-wei (May Chin), who is seeking a green card. The deception reaches another level of absurdity as the groom's non-English-speaking father General Gao (Lung) and Mrs Gao (Ah Lei Gua) arrive in New York for the wedding banquet, the film's centrepiece.

In a drunken romp during their wedding night, Wai Tung impregnates his new wife, providing by chance the heir that his parents had so desperately hoped for. Subsequently, relations between Wai Tung and his lover Simon deteriorate as they try to maintain a heterosexual charade for Wai Tung's parents. In a final twist, however, Simon discovers that General Gao understands English after all, and that he has seen through the sham all along. Acknowledging Simon as his son-in-law with a birthday gift of money, Wai Tung's father emerges as an omnipotent patriarchal figure who has patiently and cleverly orchestrated his traditional aspirations for his son.

For Wei Ming Dariotis and Eileen Fung, the structuring tension between traditional Chinese culture and the influence of Western modernity evident in *The Wedding Banquet* is a recurring theme within Lee's films.

> Lee's work illustrates the inevitable conflicts and negotiations between individuals bound by familial and societal obligations. These familial and

> social dramas are often set in scenes where the infiltration of Westernization is in direct conflict with orthodox Chinese ideologies . . . Lee's films consistently negotiate among cultures, nations, generations, and genders – illustrating the repressive as well as revitalizing forces of Chinese traditions in the intersection of the residual past and emerging future.[6]

This suggestive reading implies a slightly different model of authorship, where an *auteur's* oeuvre does not flow directly from the director's experience or personality, but rather can be read through recurring underlying themes and signature stylistic motifs.[7] Within the dominant logic of American and European film criticism, this claim elevates specific filmmakers above the mundane industrial status of *metteur en scène* to *auteur*.

Much of the appeal of the 'father knows best' trilogy arises from the charisma of Lung's father characters who are pitted against the forces of modernisation and Westernisation. In *Eat Drink Man Woman*, for instance, Lung plays Tao Chu, Taiwan's greatest chef, who acts as a single father to three daughters. With Taiwanese culinary arts in decline, Chu suffers from depression, symptomatically losing his sense of taste. Here, the preparation and consumption of sumptuous cuisine become the narrative and philosophical focus. Food preparation, display and consumption as important anchoring elements in Chinese cultural tradition and daily life also arise in *Pushing Hands* (with the cooking classes at the Chinese community centre) and in the climax of *The Wedding Banquet*. These films follow a relatively functional narrative cinematic style, but one emergent stylistic feature emerges with Lee's careful attention to the material details and textures of everyday life: food preparation, martial arts or dinner etiquette.

Eat Drink Man Woman foregrounds generational conflicts between the traditional father and his three young daughters, where Chu insists on preparing elaborate meals for his daughters who have difficulty eating the food. Food operates as a metaphor for love, and the comedy-drama chronicles complex familial relationships and budding romances across three generations. As with *The Wedding Banquet*, *Eat Drink Man Woman* ends with a surprise revelation by the enigmatic Chu, and several romances come to fruition. The film's attention to the art of Chinese cuisine signals Lee's sustained attention to the value of tradition – and its (literally) 'indigestible' elements.

Within this trilogy, the father figures exemplify Lee's interest in Chinese traditional culture as 'something that is highly versatile and adaptive'.[8] *Pushing Hands* opens with an extended lyrical sequence where the elderly tai chi master performs his art in an American living room. Chu's tai chi is intercut with shots of a white American woman (later revealed to be the old man's daughter-in-law Martha) working at her computer. This wordless intercutting establishes the film's central conflict between the traditional Chinese patriarch and the modern American woman writer who resents her father-in-law's protracted visit. Chu's technique of 'pushing hands' emerges within the film as a metaphor for a distinctively Chinese strategy of coping with change and conflict, 'a way of keeping balance while unbalancing your opponent'. The historical resonance of this strategy becomes clear as Chu's story unfolds: like Lee's own father he has been forced to flee mainland China for Taiwan after violent persecution by the communists.

With these plotlines, Lee has come under fire from some critics for deploying exotic motifs such as martial arts, the Asian gay theme or Chinese gourmet food to attract Western viewers.[9] Dariotis and Fung suggest that in his first three films Lee 'plays with, and sometimes reproduces, the stereotypes based on . . . binary oppositions'; for instance, the plot-line of *The Wedding Banquet* pits ' "East" versus "West," old and young, female versus male'.[10] Although each work initially highlights the younger characters' modern and/or Western perspectives, in each case it is the will, the wisdom or the suffering of the father figure that is ultimately vindicated – hence the trilogy's 'father knows best' label. With this emphasis on father-son relationships in *Pushing Hands* and *The Wedding Banquet*, the leading female characters Martha Chu (Deb Snyder), Mrs Gao and Wei Wei are either underdeveloped or caricatured. Ultimately, Dariotis and Fung suggest that Lee's first three films attempt 'to restore the patriarchal order so as to recuperate the dislocated familial and societal harmony'.[11]

Playing with stereotypes, Lee's use of 'Chinese' motifs is crucial to his strategic development as an Asian director recognised in the West. In his own account of his cross-cultural practice, Lee uses the metaphor of Chinese restaurants in the US: 'The westerners begin Chinese food by trying Sweet and Sour Chicken. After a while, they will be able to taste more authentic food. The more Chinese restaurants we have here in the US, the easier we are able to find green onion and tofu in our nearby local supermarket.'[12]

Collaborative Authorship

Eat Drink Man Woman and *Crouching Tiger, Hidden Dragon* are the films where Lee most directly employs Taiwanese and Chinese identities and mythologies. Intriguingly, however, the lead writer on both of these films was Lee's longstanding American collaborator, James Schamus. Lee's partnership with Schamus and his production company Good Machine brings into relief current pragmatic transnational practices of film authorship. In the late 1980s, the aspiring director approached the independent American production company Good Machine with *Pushing Hands*, a choice that has been crucial to the development of Lee's international profile. Established in 1991 by Schamus and Ted Hope, Good Machine (along with Miramax, The Shooting Gallery and October Films) played an important role in the 1990s rise of American independent film. The company has produced key films by Todd Solondz, Todd Haynes and Hal Hartley, as by well as the bankable Lee.[13]

The Western box-office appeal of *The Wedding Banquet* and *Eat Drink Man Woman* was undoubtedly facilitated by the renewed market for international art cinema associated with Miramax (*Mediterraneo*, 1991; *Belle Epoque*, 1992; *Il postino*, 1994; and the 'Fifth Generation' Chinese films by Chen Kaige and

Zhang Yimou). Returning to Lee's metaphor of the Chinese restaurant, the device of ethnic food as spectacle in *Eat Drink Man Woman* coincides with the culinary narrative of the 1992 Mexican film *Like Water for Chocolate* (or indeed the 1987 Danish film *Babette's Feast*). In keeping with new Taiwanese identities associated with 'the incessant *flow* of capital, commodity, desire and traffic', Lee's career development under the auspices of Good Machine reflects a pragmatic understanding of emergent Western desire for (certain modes of) alterity in cultural consumption.

Schamus has collaborated extensively with Lee throughout his career, sharing credits on all of his films, either as writer or producer. Shedding light on the hybrid American/Asian poetics of Lee's films, this partnership problematises traditional concepts of authorship as projecting a 'unifying consciousness'. For instance, Schamus recounts how he struggled with the script for *Eat Drink Man Woman*, never having visited Taiwan; Lee consistently rejected early drafts as culturally inauthentic. It was only when Schamus rewrote the film 'as if it was just one gigantic sloppy Jewish [American] family' that Lee accepted the script as believably 'Chinese'.[14] Written in English, the script of *Eat Drink Man Woman* was subsequently translated into Mandarin. Described by Shamus as 'transcultural ping pong', this process was repeated with *Crouching Tiger, Hidden Dragon*, where English and Chinese drafts were shuttled back and forth between Shamus and the Taiwanese writer Wang Hui Ling.

Lee's collaboration with Schamus has been crucial to his entire filmography, yet the Taiwanese director is consistently promoted as the primary talent. A key player in the American film industry, Schamus describes Good Machine's strategy of working over a long period of time with particular directors because 'in the low-budget world, the writer-director is the key figure in terms of marketing'.[15] Shamus's account suggests yet another understanding of film authorship 'as a *commercial* strategy for organizing audience reception, as a critical concept bound to distribution and marketing aims that identify and address the potential cult status of an auteur'.[16] Yet this deliberate *commercial* construction of the director as individual genius is at odds with the consortial and pragmatic practices of film production. Already, in Lee's most identifiably autobiographical films, there is a shared labour of production and writing. With Lee's subsequent projects, this consortial practice is increasingly associated with transnational 'assemblages' of capital, cast, crew and subject-matter.

These transnational practices of authorship can be usefully reformulated within Arjun Appadurai's 'global cultural economy'. Appadurai posits a new social role for the imagination as 'a form of negotiation between sites of agency ("individuals") and globally defined fields of possibility'.[17] The global cultural economy is described as a 'complex, overlapping, disjunctive order' constituted by five dimensions of global cultural flow: ethnoscapes, mediascapes, technoscapes, finanscapes and ideoscapes.[18] In relation to Lee's transnational filmography, Appadurai's model is suggestive in tracking the complex flows of capital (finanscapes), creative personnel and audiences (ethnoscapes), genres, myths and narratives (ideoscapes and mediascapes). In this context, we might rethink cinematic authorship as a 'navigation [of these landscapes] by agents who both experience and constitute larger formations'.[19]

Sense and Sensibility, Lee's first Anglo-American mainstream project, exemplifies his ability to direct culturally and industrially diverse productions, an adaptability that will characterise much of his career. Lee shares authorial credits on the film with Emma Thompson, who won the Academy Award for her screenplay. *Sense and Sensibility*'s crew and cast (including Merchant-Ivory veterans Thompson, Hugh Grant and a fleet of superb British character actors) epitomise the industrial machinery and creative expertise of established (national) genres. Here, the artistic imprint of the director is difficult to isolate.

Lee's ability to direct family and intergenerational melodrama is central to his subtle authorial signature, and a perceptive review credits Lee as 'an artist of family and society' whose inaugural trilogy's 'mastery of the visual dynamics of interior spaces and their psychic pressures' stands him in good stead for the Austen adaptation.[20] Yet what is the contribution of veteran British cinematographer Michael Coulter (who helped to create the claustrophobic interiors of Terence Davies's *The Long Day Closes* (1992))? Meanwhile, the film's interiors draws heavily from the Dutch seventeenth-century painter Vermeer, while the film's landscapes borrow from English painters Constable and Turner – even a Mizoguchi citation creeps in with a scene of reed-gathering by the water.[21] Intrinsic to postmodern mediascapes, this collage of intertextual citation further displaces the imprint of authorship across different cultural and historical sites.

This process of transnational genre production culminates in *Crouching Tiger, Hidden Dragon*. An exceptional pan-Chinese and international project, this mythic *wuxia pan* (Chinese swordfighting movie) incorporated creative personnel and funding from mainland China, Hong Kong, Taiwan and the US.[22] Like *Sense and Sensibility*, it could be seen to be multiply-'authored': Schamus's and Wang's screenplay adapting Wang Du Lu's 1940s epic novel; the cinematography of Hong Kong veteran Peter Pau (*The Killer/Di xue shuang xiong*, 1989, and *Swordsman/Xiaoao jianghu*, 1990);[23] martial arts sequences by Hong Kong director and fight choreographer Yuen Wo-ping who has famously brought his expertise to Western audiences through *The Matrix* (1999) and *Kill Bill* (2003). Christina Klein foregrounds Yuen's 'auteurist' contribution to *Crouching Tiger* through his method of choreographing 'the action *and* the cinematography of each shot . . . composing the next shot so that it flowed seamlessly . . . essentially editing each fight scene in the camera'.[24]

The film score was written by mainland Chinese classical composer Tan Dun with the theme performed by Paris-born, US-educated world-class cellist Yo-Yo Ma. According to Tan, this cello theme 'became the bridge between high and low [culture], east and west, and between the world instruments and the Western instruments'.[25] The bridging function of the music is emblematic of *Crouching Tiger*'s profile as a pan-Chinese or even diasporic production.

Significantly, Lee has described this project as 'a personal "homecoming of sorts," '[26] and the film's talented pan-Chinese cast and crew enacts a mythic 'imagined China'. Set during the classical Qing dynasty, featuring locations suggesting Shanghai or Beijing or iconic Chinese landscapes such as the Gobi Desert and the Taklamakan Plateau, *Crouching Tiger* is steeped in traditional signifiers of Chineseness. Yet, like Lee's 'father knows best' trilogy, *Crouching Tiger* is ambivalent in its adjudication between 'essential'/'traditional' or modern/'diasporic' elements of Chinese identity.

For instance, Lee decided to produce the film in Mandarin (rather than the Cantonese used in the Hong Kong *kung fu* films associated initially with Bruce Lee). This decision marks an homage to what he sees as the roots of the *wuxia genre* in Hong Kong Mandarin-language productions of the mid-1960s and 1970s.[27] This choice led to practical difficulties, given that among the lead players only Zhang Ziyi spoke fluent Mandarin; Chang Chen (Lo 'Dark Cloud') spoke with a Taiwanese accent, while Hong Kong actor Chow and Malaysian actress Yeoh delivered their lines phonetically. Although Lee's strategy evokes Mandarin as the authentic Chinese language of myth, the film's uneven linguistic flow led to a mixed reception among Mandarin speakers worldwide.

Issues of language and perceived cultural 'inauthenticity' affected the film's reception in mainland China where box-office figures were poor in contrast with record-breaking attendance in Singapore, Malaysia and Taiwan. A Shanghai journalist offers one account of the film's lukewarm mainland reception, wryly applauding its 'wonderful demonstration of the irrelevance of gravity, but here in Shanghai we were very unimpressed by the story and the fight scenes. "Produced to meet foreigner tastes" is the most common opinion of it here'.[28] As Klein points out, 'while globalization may have made it easier for media texts to cross the supposed East-West divide, it has not erased the divisions within the Chinese diaspora itself'.[29]

Writing from a diasporic Chinese perspective, Ien Ang critiques the hegemony of mainland China as the site of 'authentic' or 'essential' Chineseness, notably an 'epic relationship which invests the homeland myth with its power'.[30] For Ang, this essentialist and static vision of Chineseness overshadows the diversity and fluidity of Chinese diasporic experience. It is worth noting that in the wake of *Crouching Tiger*'s international success, Zhang Yimou has directed two subsequent epics *Hero/Ying xiong* (2002) and *House of Flying Daggers/Shi mian mai fu* (2004). It is this mythic account of China projected compellingly through the epic *wuxia* form for both Asian and Western audiences that is so powerful, and potentially so problematic. A profitable foray into static myths of Chinese national identity for global consumption, this vision stands at a great remove from the contemporary urban settings and identities addressed in the second wave of the New Taiwanese cinema – or indeed in the specific post-colonial Taiwanese history of *The Puppetmaster* or *City of Sadness*. Yet, returning to the specificity of Lee's cinematic vision, *Crouching Tiger* takes up themes recurring across his filmography: tensions between tradition and modernisation, and the complex registers of gender identity and sexual desire.

THE OUTSIDER'S VISION: FAMILY AND INTERGENERATIONAL CONFLICTS

Lee's core strength as a director arises from an ability to handle the subtle emotional registers of melodrama. At the still centre of even his 'epic' and 'action-centred' works are carefully-drawn dynamics of family strife and romantic yearning. The dramatic cornerstone of *Crouching Tiger* arises from the repressed desires of Li Mubai (Chow) and Yu Shu Lien (Yeoh); their lifelong unrequited desire is forbidden by strict codes (*jianghu*) of honour and loyalty. Their sexual repression and longing contrast sharply with the younger couple's passionate romance, and especially the rebellion of the younger woman, Jen Yu (Zhang), against the conventions of bourgeois femininity. The famous flying combat scene in the bamboo between Li and Jen dramatises a sexual tension and rivalry between the heroic patriarchal figure and the young, female upstart who has stolen his 'sword'. The irreverent Jen who defies the patriarchal codes of the *jianghu* has been described as a proto-feminist heroine, but other critics point to the narrative closure of tradition, where Jen ultimately takes her own life as punishment for her transgression.[31] This latter reading corresponds to feminist critiques of the patriarchal and traditional elements in the 'father knows best' trilogy.

This precise attention to the dynamics of desire recurs in Lee's diverse Anglo-American period adaptations. Amidst a torrent of vigilante raids and thundering hooves in *Ride with the Devil*, Jake Roedel's (Toby Maguire) palpable yearning for the young widow Sue Lee (Jewel) highlights the awkwardness of the sexual 'coming of age' ritual. Youthful sexuality is also central to *The Ice Storm*, where the children's awkward gropings are juxtaposed with their parents' confused sexual antics in the context of the American sexual revolution. In turn, *Sense and Sensibility* poignantly portrays a family of women living in genteel poverty, drawing out the rivalry between the passionate Marianne (Kate Winslet) and her 'sensible' older sister Eleanor (Emma Thompson).

Even in *Hulk*, easily the most maverick of Lee's films, Bruce Banner's (Eric Bana) traumatic childhood experience of domestic violence figures centrally in his alter ego's explosions of rage. Like the 'father knows best' trilogy, this comic book narrative rests on an oedipal struggle between the afflicted son and his father the evil scientist. The treatment of landscape is a stylistic element that links *Hulk* with Lee's other films. American desert scenes in *Hulk* recall the stunning expanse of the Gobi Desert in *Crouching Tiger*. In fact, from *The Ice Storm's* attention to the changing seasons culminating in the deadly glitter of the ice storm, Lee incorporates the natural environment as an expressive cinematic element in dynamic relation with the characters and storyline.

As Lee went on from *Crouching Tiger* to *Hulk*, critics emphasised the variation within his oeuvre rather than its common points. After all, Austen's

Georgian middle England, the American Civil War, 1970s American suburbia – or indeed feudal China – are all remote to a Taiwanese/American experience. Western media commentaries often marvel at the filmmaker's extraordinary adaptability, but it is worth noting that the same scrutiny is not applied to Western *auteurs* such as Bernardo Bertolucci (*The Last Emperor*, 1987; *Little Buddha*, 1993) or Jean-Jacques Annaud (*L'Amant/The Lover*, 1992; *Seven Years in Tibet*, 1997) who turn to 'Asian' subject-matter – or indeed Anglo-American *auteurs* who venture into the distant past of period adaptation. Lee himself insists that this adaptability arises from a lifelong 'outsider' status:

> I'm not a native Taiwanese, so we're alien in a way in Taiwan today, with the native Taiwanese pushing for independence. But when we go back to China, we're Taiwanese. Then, I live in the States; I'm a sort of foreigner everywhere . . . Of course, I identify with Chinese culture because that was my upbringing, but that becomes very abstract; it's the idea of China.[32]

If the 'idea of China' on a broad canvas is the subject of *Crouching Tiger*, with *Hulk*, Lee (a longtime US resident) delves into the belly of the beast of American popular culture. Here, Lee is perhaps furthest from his preferred subject-matter of cross-cultural melodrama, but it is interesting to note that it was Lee himself who provided the physical prototype for Hulk's bodily movements. Hulk was produced in the wake of the 9/11 attacks on New York and it was released around the time of the invasion of Iraq. Some commentators have seen Hulk's righteous rage with the terrifying awakening of America as the 'sleeping giant'.[33] Yet on another reading, the green Hulk – imprinted with Lee's own bodily movements – could also be seen as an alien or outsider relentlessly pursued by the American military. Framed in part from an outsider's perspective, the hapless Hulk's terrible pursuit across the desert by military jets and helicopters evokes another one-sided vista of desert warfare.[34]

Notes

1. Zhang Yingjin (2004), *Chinese National Cinema*, London: Routledge, pp. 278–9.
2. Ibid. p. 274.
3. M. H. Abrams (1981), 'Literature as a revelation of personality', in J. Caughie (ed.), *Theories of Authorship: A Reader*, London: Routledge, p. 19.
4. See, for instance, Chris Berry (1993), 'Taiwanese melodrama returns with a twist in *The Wedding Banquet*', *Cinemaya* 21, p. 54.
5. Brooke Comer (1995), '*Eat Drink Man Woman*: a feast for the eyes', *American Cinematographer* 76(1), January, p. 62.
6. Wei Ming Dariotis and Eileen Fung (1997), 'Breaking the soy sauce jar: diaspora and displacement in the films of Ang Lee', in Sheldon Hsaio-peng Lu (ed.), *Transnational Chinese Cinemas*, p. 187.
7. See John Caughie (1981), 'Auteurism', in Caughie (ed.), *Theories of Authorship*, p. 12.
8. Dariotis and Fung, 'Breaking the soy sauce jar', p. 189.
9. Pei-Chi Chung (2000), 'Asian filmmakers moving into Hollywood: genre regulation and auteur aesthetics', *Asian Cinema* 11(1), Spring/Summer, p. 39.
10. Dariotis and Fung, 'Breaking the soy sauce jar', p. 201.

11. Ibid. p. 217.
12. Lee, cited in Chung, 'Asian filmmakers moving into Hollywood'.
13. Rebecca Traister (2003), 'Crouching budget, hidden profits: James Schamus, Columbia professor, bets $137 million on Ang Lee epic', *New York Observer*, 23 June, p. 1, electronic version: http://www.findarticles.com/p/articles/mi_m0ICQ/ is_2003_June_34/ai_104461704/print, accessed 28 November 2004.
14. Schamus, interviewed in the *South Bank Show*'s television profile of Ang Lee (ITV, 13 July 2003).
15. Comer, '*Eat Drink Man Woman*', p. 63.
16. Timothy Corrigan (1991), *A Cinema without Walls: Movies and Culture After Vietnam*, New Brunswick, NJ: Rutgers University Press, p. 103.
17. Arjun Appadurai (1993), 'Disjuncture and difference in the global economy', in Bruce Robins (ed.), *The Phantom Public Sphere*, University of Minnesota Press, p. 274.
18. Ibid. p. 275.
19. Ibid. p. 276.
20. David Lyons (1996), 'Passionate precision: *Sense and Sensibility*', *Film Comment* 32(1), January/February, p. 40.
21. Ibid. p. 41.
22. For details on the film's co-production arrangements, see Philip Kemp (2000), 'Stealth and duty', *Sight and Sound*, December, p. 15.
23. For a discussion of Pau's cinematography, see David E. Williams (2001), 'High-flying adventure', *American Cinematographer* 82(1), January, pp. 54–77.
24. Christina Klein (2004), '*Crouching Tiger, Hidden Dragon*: a diasporic reading', in *Cinema Journal* 43(4), Summer, pp. 27–8. For a discussion of Yuen's distinctive use of horizontal, vertical and 'performance' space for fight scenes, see Klein, pp. 28–30.
25. Rudy Koppl (2001), 'Tan Dun: scoring Ang Lee's dream of China', *Music from the Movies* 31/32, Winter, p. 47.
26. Lee, cited in Klein, '*Crouching Tiger, Hidden Dragon*', p. 22.
27. For instance, *Crouching Tiger* draws heavily from King Hu's 1962 film *A Touch of Zen.*
28. May May (2001), 'Catching the trade winds', *Vertigo* 2(1), Spring, p. 9.
29. See Klein, '*Crouching Tiger, Hidden Dragon*', p. 37. For a discussion of language and reception, see pp. 36–7.
30. Ien Ang (2001), *On Not Speaking Chinese: Living Between Asia and the West*, London: Routledge, p. 33.
31. For an incisive discussion of the film's gender politics, see Kenneth Chan (2004), 'The global return of the *Wu Xia Pan* (Chinese sword-fighting movie): Ang Lee's *Crouching Tiger, Hidden Dragon*', *Cinema Journal* 43(4), Summer, pp. 9–14.
32. Zhang Yingjin, *Chinese National Cinema*, p. 54.
33. See the 2003 *South Bank Show* documentary about Ang Lee.
34. Thanks to Gary Needham for suggesting this point, and for his other helpful comments on this chapter.

SECTION 7
STARDOM: THE CASE OF BRUCE LEE

BRUCE LEE: STARDOM AND IDENTITY

Dimitris Eleftheriotis and Gary Needham

This section considers closely Bruce Lee, perhaps the most famous star ever to emerge outside the Hollywood star system. In this introductory essay we will focus on two important aspects of Bruce Lee as a star. Firstly we will examine certain instabilities in his star image arising from a number of key factors: the incommensurability of Lee's short career and his legendary status; the interaction between national cinematic and cultural values and forms and international systems of film production, circulation and marketing; and the international cinematic and cultural context of the period. In the second part of the essay we will address questions of identity and masculinity.

THE 'LEGEND OF BRUCE LEE'

Dimitris Eleftheriotis

What is perhaps the most startling aspect about Bruce Lee's star image is that it is based on a very limited number of films and a very short career. In fact one can convincingly argue that his legendary status comes almost exclusively from four films that he starred in, all made within a two-year period, 1971–3.

Bruce Lee was born in San Francisco in 1940 and shortly after that moved to Hong Kong, where he worked in the film industry mainly in minor roles and as a child actor. He returned to San Francisco in 1959, and perhaps his most notable involvement with film there was as the stereotypically 'oriental' Kato, the sidekick of the crime fighter Green Hornet (played by Van Williams) in the eponymous TV series.[1]

Prior to his 'second coming' to Hong Kong, this was his only significant claim to fame (apart from several guest appearances as a martial arts expert in a few films and TV series), together with a role that he actually never got: that of Kwai Chang Caine in the TV series *Kung Fu* (ABC, 1972–5); the part eventually went to David Carradine. Ironically, the popularity of the series was a major contributing factor in familiarising international audiences with martial arts films.

Lee returned to Hong Kong in 1971 and he was offered the leading role in *The Big Boss/Tong saan daai fong* (Wei Lo, 1971), a film produced by Golden Harvest productions, a company set up by the former Shaw Brothers manager Raymond Chow. He also starred in *The Fist of Fury/Jing wu men* (Wei Lo, 1972), also a Golden Harvest production. The two films made Lee into a big national/regional star and his next film was written, produced and directed by him. *Way of the Dragon/Meng long guojiang* (Bruce Lee, 1972) was a significant turning point in his career as it deliberately targeted broader international markets and led to the 1973 co-production with Warner Brothers, *Enter the Dragon* (Robert Clouse, 1973). Bruce Lee died in June 1973 when the film was at the stage of post-production.

In many ways Bruce Lee was 'always, already' a legend, at least for European and American audiences. His first film to be widely released in the international market was, paradoxically, the last film that he ever made, *Enter the Dragon*. As far as many cinema-goers around the world were concerned, his name became famous only after his death. An additional contributing factor has always been the difficulty of establishing with accuracy what films he appeared in and even the titles of his films: for example, *The Big Boss* is also known as *Fists of Fury*, a title perilously close to that of his second film. In fact, the vast majority of European and American audiences watched his films in the 1970s in almost reverse chronological order, starting with the American co-production and eventually concluding with the two smaller Hong Kong films.

The confusion was further fuelled by marketing strategies that advertised films starring Bruce Lee well after his death – *Game of Death* (Robert Clouse, 1978) is the best-known example of the various 'official' posthumous films. This particular film tried to capitalise on wild speculations regarding the circumstances and even the reality of Bruce Lee's death by organising its plot around a martial arts movie actor (played by Bruce Lee) who 'fakes' his own death as a way of defending himself against his enemies. Furthermore, in the 1970s and 1980s a number of Hong Kong actors appeared with names almost identical to Lee (such as Bruce Li and Bruce Le), starring in a number of films that were often marketed in national/international markets as 'authentic' Bruce Lee films.

It is obvious, then, that the legendary status that Bruce Lee enjoys has, at least partly, been facilitated by the impossibility for European and American audiences of engaging with him as a star at any level that can go, even slightly, beyond mythical opacity. His life and death, the ambiguities and uncertainties around his film career and his films, as well as profound instabilities of his star image, meant that Bruce Lee entered the consciousness of international film audiences not as a 'real' actor and star but as a 'legend'.

Many of the instabilities and ambiguities arose from the attempts to present and market Bruce Lee (in many ways a 'national' star *par excellence*) as an international star. The three essays collected here explore in different ways some of the challenges posed for international producers and distributors by Bruce Lee's masculine and national identity. Leon Hunt's essay traces the specific context of popular and film culture that shaped the American 'understanding' of Bruce Lee in *Enter the Dragon.* As Hunt argues, Robert Clouse's direction tried (and in many ways he succeeded) to forcefully alter Bruce Lee's style of performance and to provide diegetic ways of fixing a contextual frame of reference for Lee's character that could make him more accessible to American (and other Western) audiences:

> Director Robert Clouse rather notoriously claimed that he had to 'kick the strut' out of Lee to make him palatable for international audiences, citing a gesture well known to fans of his Hong Kong films – 'he slid his thumb across his nose like the way they used to do in American gangster movies of the 30s'.[2]

Hunt also discusses the importance of martial arts themes and stories in the comic books of the time, and the reliance of the producers of *Enter the Dragon* on the iconic potential of mythical figures such as Fu Manchu.

We can trace some of the instabilities and uncertainties around the marketing of Bruce Lee through the study of trailers for *Way of the Dragon*, made available in a 'Special Collector's Edition' DVD of the film, packaged and distributed in the UK by Medusa Communications and Marketing. More specifically, we will consider the 1972 original theatrical trailer, the 1974 UK premiere release theatrical trailer, and the 2000 UK promotional trailer for the DVD.

Just under four minutes long, the original trailer suggests a rather uncertain approach to marketing the film. A number of different aspects of the film are selectively presented in this trailer. It opens with an aesthetic 'trademark' of the martial arts genre, a rapid zoom out from Lee's eyes, followed by a series of fighting scenes involving Lee, with superimposed titles emphasising the fact that this is a film produced, written, directed by, and starring Bruce Lee.

While such an opening seems to suggest a clear desire to market Bruce Lee as a martial arts genius in total control of the film, the trailer then shifts to a brief scene in which the criminal boss is informed that their opponents are helped by 'just one man' but one that 'knows Chinese kung fu', leading to the exclamation/question 'Kung fu?' Responding to the question, the trailer proceeds, through a rapid series of fighting scenes, to offer a description of what Lee's special martial abilities are and what they can achieve. This seems to indicate uncertainty as to whether international audiences were at that moment familiar with Lee's technique and indeed with Lee himself.

The shots that follow offer another dimension to the uncertainty about the marketing strategy. The trailer provides a number of scenes that reference different generic registers: the travel film, comedy, romance, sexploitation films, and action thriller, all of which were particularly profitable low-budget genres in the international market of the late 1960s and early 1970s.[3] Such a strategy for marketing the film indicates two possibly conflicting objectives on the part of the producers and distributors. On the one hand, it demonstrates a desire to place the film within an identifiable generic framework, and at the same time to locate the 'new genre' itself within a pantheon of popular genres. On the other hand, it betrays an indirect but clear recognition that such a type of film might be unfamiliar to international audiences and it tries to account for such an eventuality by proposing a series of 'fallback' generic options. The trailer concludes with a long series of fighting scenes with a privileged place given to Lee's famous Colosseum fight against Chuck Norris.

The 1974 trailer (two and a half minutes long) demonstrates a more assured way of marketing the film. The shots that make up the short film are almost exclusively fighting scenes showcasing different fights and the fighting style of Bruce Lee. The trailer works with a dubbed version of the film and uses a voiceover highlighting the unique selling points of the film ('the ultimate *Way of the Dragon*'): 'Starring Bruce Lee conquering evil in Rome and using all his fighting skills in this authentic martial arts adventure'. The need to emphasise 'authenticity' indicates the need to differentiate the 'product' from competing 'imitations and fakes', as well as the confidence to aggressively promote Bruce Lee as the 'real thing'.

Way of the Dragon is presented as a serious, authentic martial arts film, by now an established and recognisable generic 'brand'. The trailer clearly tries to capitalise on the unprecedented popularity of martial arts in European and American culture at the time, by defining some of the other actors as recognised athletes: 'co-starring some of the world's greatest fighters; Chuck Norris, seven times World Karate Champion; Robert Wall, the 1971 number one karate professional, Wong In-Sik, Korean Master of Aikido'. It appears to be the case that by June 1974, when the UK trailer was released, the marketability of both the martial arts genre and of Bruce Lee's star image is well established and audiences are assumed to be very familiar with both of them. Once again, the Colosseum fight features heavily, with the last third of the trailer dedicated to it and accompanied by the commentary: 'Action, thrills, excitement . . . revived in the Colosseum in a very different way . . . the *Way of the Dragon*!'

The 2000 promotional trailer for the DVD treats Bruce Lee and the film as being truly legendary.[4] The trailer, which is eighty seconds long, divides neatly into three parts of almost equal length. The first consists of spectacular, state-of-the-art graphics of the letters making up Bruce Lee's name as well as images of slowed-down action of the Colosseum fight between Lee and Norris. The letters are golden and slightly transparent, allowing parts of the image to become visible shades. The heroic music that accompanies the trailer is interrupted by enhanced 'body' sounds that give the (already slowed-down) action a hyper-real quality. The second part of the trailer consists of fighting scenes edited to the fast beat of the film's main musical theme, while the final part replicates the first part of the trailer in its slow motion, music and sound effects with the titles inviting us to 'experience the legend'.

The trailer, then, seems to follow a format within which the film and its star are placed in an archive, bracketed by the mythologising first and last segments, with the graphics literally over-writing Bruce Lee's performing body. While this is certainly a marketing strategy that aims to display the technical potential of the new format (DVD), it also capitalises on Bruce Lee's (by now) unambiguous status as a film legend. Graphically and suggestively in this trailer, Bruce Lee's body and performance, as well as his film, are deemed almost immaterial, of secondary importance, fading away in the face of a legend.

It is interesting to consider briefly the Colosseum scene, as it occupies a privileged position in all three trailers. In the 1972 trailer the Colosseum is primarily an extension of the location, with Rome offering a cosmopolitan and marketable setting for the film; in the 1974 trailer the Colosseum becomes the suitable setting for a memorable martial arts display, performed by the world's leading fighters; in the 2000 version, however, the Colosseum becomes home of the legend – no longer just an attractive location, nor the perfect set for the film's narrative and spectacle, but the natural mythical setting for the legend of Bruce Lee.

ENCOUNTERS WITH THE DRAGON

Gary Needham

The Colosseum becomes a crucial site in securing the type of masculinity that Bruce Lee comes to represent through the way his body is displayed, raced and nationalised. This operates in *Way of the Dragon* through the encounters Bruce Lee's character Tang Lung has with his own body and with the characters of Chuck Norris and Mr Ho. Bruce Lee's encounter with a range of masculinities in *Way of the Dragon* works towards bringing about and fixing the meaning of his body through relations of ethnicity, race, sexuality and nationality. This occurs through three key encounters in the film. An analysis of these three encounters draws out many of the key concerns mobilised around Bruce Lee as a particular identity situated in relation to genre and other identities.

Encounter One: Himself

Early on in *Way of the Dragon*, Bruce Lee's character Tang Lung catches the attention of an attractive Italian woman (Malisa Longo) while sitting nonchalantly in a Roman piazza.[5] They strike up a quick friendship based on looks and gestures, and she leads Tang Lung back to her apartment. While the Italian woman slips away, Tang Lung begins practicing martial arts in the mirror, admiring his body's flexibility and musculature in a moment of spectacle and narcissism. We might also assume that this martial arts warm-up is physical preparation for the sexual encounter about to happen, particularly since Lee's body is coded in terms of an erotic visual display. The woman appears back in a few minutes, topless, and Tang Lung quickly flees her apartment in a panic. In short, he is defeated at some level by the nakedness and sexuality of the female body, unprepared as he is for this type of challenge.

There are a number of possible ways to read this scene. It places the character of Tang Lung outside the circuit of sexual desire in the narrative, yet, on the other hand, his body is coded through conventions of erotic display. He is sexually immature and unaware of the seductive power of his own body as an object of someone else's desire. However, while desire for the opposite sex is unthinkable, the real desire of the character Bruce Lee portrays is positioned through the seduction of his own body reflected in the mirror. It is a moment of pure narcissism on the part of the character. Of course, narcissism is a cliché often used to rendered homosexuality as the fatalistic desire for sameness. This reading is fairly dependent upon Western conceptions of identity and desire (narcissism, for example); however, we must also take into consideration the multiple sites of reading a star's body that inform its reception.

A second way to read this scene is through the generic conventions of masculinity in the martial arts film. Familiarity with the Hong Kong martial arts films that precede those of Bruce Lee reveals the extent to which Lee's films stick to many of the conventions of masculinity informed by the concepts of *wen* and *wu*. In their book *The Politics of Chinese Language and Culture*, Hodge and Louie explain how masculine ideals were often constructed around ideological types referred to as *wen* and *wu*. Historically, a man's trajectory in life would lead him towards one of those types. The basic opposition between the two ideological types is between the scholar and the warrior but more important is the way in which the *wen-wu* complex informs the relationships between men and women. The *wen* type of masculinity was scholarly, intellectual, literary, 'soft' and able to foster heterosexual relationships. The *wu* type of masculinity was active, physical, military, 'hard' and invested in platonic but deeply emotive relationships with the same sex and the rejection of the opposite sex. As they explain:

> The *wen-wu* complex was designed to both legitimate and control men's powers and desires. The element of control operated differently in the two terms. The discipline built in the acquisition of *wen* qualities was so

> extensive that it did not need special emphasis in the ideological scheme . . . The ideology of *wu* not only emphasised the different skills to be acquired by training and disciplining the body, it included an insistent puritanical asceticism. In this ideology the *wu* hero shows his masculinity by rejecting the allure of women.[6]

Throughout the Hong Kong martial arts films of the 1960s and 1970s that paved the way for Bruce Lee, women are continuously rejected, marginalised and sidelined, and, in the most extreme cases, absent altogether. In fact, women who seduce men are often revealed to be on the side of evil and corruption. When a martial hero falls for a woman, it usually signals the onslaught of tragedy. While not all martial arts films are entirely prescriptive to *wu* ideologies, there were several female martial arts stars like Cheng Pei-pei for example; it is a dominant tendency, especially in the films of pioneering director Zhang Cheh who deliberately engineered the cinematic cult of *yanggang* (staunch masculinity) throughout his long career.[7]

Therefore, we can read Bruce Lee as continuing the tradition of *wu* masculinity archetypes. The scene in which he rejects the advances of a woman is integral in upholding the ideological construction of the *wu* form of masculinity.

Encounter Two: Mr Ho

The second encounter that Lee's character is faced with is the wicked and effeminate Mr Ho who, unlike the Italian woman, is also Chinese. Mr Ho is explicitly coded as homosexual through his gestures, speech and flamboyant clothing. Mr Ho's clothing becomes central to his opposition with the other Chinese men in the film who wear simple clothing and have no concern for fashion and style. Mr Ho is also in charge of a group of Italian henchmen who push for protection money at the Chinese restaurant where Tang Lung is a family guest. Mr Ho's Chinese identity is contaminated through his alignment with the Italian mafia and his overt homosexuality. Obviously his corruption is to be understood as an extension of his sexual identity, but we can also suggest that his rejection of Chinese masculine comradeship in favour of the Italian mafia is linked to his transformation through a type of identity contamination brought about through misplaced allegiances. Mr Ho's severing of his relationship to China has perverted his identity and he has become an evil and decadent queen.

Mr Ho is not the real nemesis in *Way of the Dragon* but he exists to help regulate and repress the location of a more authentic queerness and homoeroticism that exists in the text. His character also enables Tang Lung's specular relationship with his own body to remain unquestioned in terms of it being a narcissistic homo-erotic fascination. Mr Ho buffers any queerness in the text by being the homosexual villain who works to define the heterosexuality of everyone else and to distract any traces of desire and tension between men that could be read in exclusively sexual terms. On the other hand,

Mr Ho is a more modern incarnation of the evil eunuch, also a staple of period martial arts films.

This is not the end of the queerness of Bruce Lee by any account. Nguyen Tan Hoang writes about the gay Asian-American porn star Brandon Lee (also the name of Lee's son) in terms of his active masculinity (Asian men are conventional passive bodies in gay porn) and the intertextual citations of Bruce Lee in his performance. Nguyen Tan Hoang links the body of Bruce Lee and Brandon Lee within an economy of stardom in which white American men, straight and gay, admire the image and the power of the Chinese masculine bodies of both Lees 'within a visual economy where Asian men are seen as physically powerful, energetic, graceful, and sensual'.[8] He reveals the similarities between the two genres, the male identifications and desires for both Bruce Lee and Brandon Lee, and the way in which the two stars are paired off against a range of opponents/partners in a play of racially coded contests of power and male bodily display.

Encounter Three: Chuck Norris

The final encounter in the Colosseum is crucial in determining the racial and national dimensions of Bruce Lee's identity as a contest of power and bodily display. The set-up of the final fight in the film between Bruce Lee and Chuck Norris is established through the Colosseum as the historical site of masculine violence and contest. This scene also employs several stylistic devices of the duel appropriated from Western films, a genre also associated with male violence. These continuities in some sense naturalise the relationship between masculinity and violence as a timeless essence of male identity.

As the two men warm up, a gesture of civility, the spectator is treated to the lithe musculature and perfection of Bruce Lee's body. In contrast, when Chuck Norris removes his top after Bruce Lee, we are instantly faced with an entirely different corporeality. Norris is nothing short of grotesque. His body is revealed as unsightly, through having too much hair and too much fat. His body is entirely abject in relation to the standards set by Lee's physique. This is a rare moment in which the white male body is made other through its relation to the Chinese male body. In isolation, there is nothing definitively abject about Norris's body but when positioned against Lee's it takes on a significance that racially codes whiteness as otherness.

Furthermore, Chuck Norris is marked by another level of impurity as the white man who is an expert in Japanese karate. Norris is once removed from the alignment between race and culture. The characters that Lee portrays in his films perpetually reinforce essentialist identities that exclude any permutations of difference. Norris as the defeated karate expert also represents a thinly-veiled anti-Japanese sentiment (Chinese kung fu is better than Japanese karate) that follows on from the openly anti-Japanese theme of *Fist of Fury*. In fact, many of Bruce Lee's films mobilise fairly problematic ideas around race and national identity from anti-assimilation to outright xenophobia. These problematic sentiments become re-coded through Lee's stardom, in terms of a Chinese-Hong Kong nationalism and pride, and through the exclusion of other identities, for example, women and queers. As with many other male stars of Hong Kong cinema (Wang Yu, Ti Lung, David Chiang) the male Chinese body comes to represent an interface between stardom and national identity. It also challenges the discourses of orientalism, racism and the stereotypes of the 'yellow peril' (*Fu Manchu, Ming the Merciless*) and the 'sick man of China'.

However, the reality of Lee's short-lived personal career and shifting meaning of his stardom outlined in the first half of this introduction reveal the differences and contradictions of stardom. Bruce Lee, the legend of cinema and icon of Chinese nationalism, is also Bruce Lee the man born in San Francisco who married Linda Emery in a Seattle church.

Notes

1. The thirty-episode series was aired in 1966–7 on ABC television.
2. Leon Hunt, 'Han's island revisited: *Enter the Dragon* as transnational cult film', reprinted in this collection; Hunt also traces how popular fiction figures such as Fu Manchu inform the context of Lee's reception.
3. Particularly European productions and co-productions spearheaded by Italian and French films.
4. *Enter the Dragon* spearheads a series of collector's DVDs under the title 'Legends of Hong Kong'.
5. Malisa Longo was a fairly well known 'beauty' of European genre films, particularly soft-core sex films like *Emanuelle binaca e nera* (Adalberto Albertini, 1976) and *Miranda* (Tinto Brass, 1985).
6. Bob Hodge and Kam Louie (1998), *The Politics and Chinese Language and Culture: The Art of Reading Dragons*, London: Routledge, p. 124.
7. Chang Cheh (2003), *Chang Cheh: A Memoir*, Hong Kong: Hong Kong Film Archive.
8. Nguyen Tan Hoang (2004), 'The resurrection of Brandon Lee: the making of a gay Asian American porn star', in Linda Williams (ed.), *Porn Studies*, Durham: Duke University Press, p. 228.

21

BRUCE LEE: NARCISSUS AND THE LITTLE DRAGON

Stephen Teo

No other figure in Hong Kong cinema has done as much to bring East and West together in a common sharing of culture as Bruce Lee in his short lifetime. In him, Hong Kong cinema found its most forceful ambassador; an Asian role model espousing aspects of an Eastern culture who found receptive minds in the West. The only other examples of such a phenomenon that come to mind are figures from Japanese cinema such as Sessue Hayakawa or Toshiro Mifune, but they never enjoyed popular success on Lee's scale. Lee's success was based on the action choreography of his unique kung fu style – which he dubbed *Jeet Kune Do* or 'The Art of the Intercepting Fist'. However, his international success harboured aspects other than the purely physical dimensions of his art which cannot so readily be adopted by other cultures. His death in 1973 spawned a legend and the world-wide scale of the cult which developed suggests that there was something universal about his figure. Lee is all things to all men, but just what are these things?

The *mise en scène* of Lee's films is a superior example of what American reviewers dismissively call 'chop-socky' films, and there is a decidedly ironic side to his success in the West, since an anti-Western sentiment is more than apparent in his persona. In his short career, Bruce Lee stood for something that in the 90s is hardly deemed politically correct: Chinese nationalism as a way of feeling pride in one's identity. Lee had experienced his share of racial prejudice as an immigrant in the US and it was perhaps natural that he would incorporate the

From Stephen Teo (1997), *Hong Kong Cinema*, London: BFI, pp. 110–21.

theme of pride and anti-racism in his movies. But he went further, overlaying what was essentially a humanist reaction against racism with a Chinese nationalist sentiment.

Nationalism is a potent theme in the work of both old and new Hong Kong directors, from social-realist Cantonese melodramas to Mandarin historical epics, and from martial arts films to new wave works. Bruce Lee's work accentuates it even more than usual, stirring the hearts of Chinese audiences everywhere while foreign critics talk of jingoism and chauvinism. Americans, though, may see in it the reaction of a Chinese immigrant struggling against racism and attempting to assert the right to be American. Lee, the ardent nationalist, was after all an American citizen. But the nationalistic theme in his films has nothing to do with his adoptive country.

Lee's Chinese nationalism cannot be easily dismissed if one wishes to appreciate fully his appeal to Chinese audiences. The nationalism Lee's films invoked is better understood as an abstract kind of cultural nationalism, manifesting itself as an emotional wish among Chinese people living outside China to identify with China and things Chinese, even though they may not have been born there or speak its national language or dialects. They wish to affirm themselves and fulfil their cultural aspirations by identifying with the 'mother culture', producing a rather abstract and apolitical type of nationalism. The historical formation of this rather exceptional form of nationalism is complex and deeply rooted. Briefly, and roughly, Chinese dynastic rule regarded China as the centre of the universe, the heart of the Heavenly Kingdom. In its terminology, *tianxia* signified both the Chinese Empire and the world as a whole, with its myriad people. Alongside this concept, the notion of *guo* designated a localised political unit, a specific part of the Empire or, in modern terminology, of the world. According to Confucian orthodoxy, *tianxia* designated a civilisational value, whereas *guo* referred to a regime of power, to what the West would regard as a state government or, since the Empire was also the world, with regional government. Chinese nationalism focuses on the moral and cultural aspects of Chinese civilisation, on *tianxia*. Questions of international relations and of political power structures related to the regulation of *guo*, including the specifics of the rise or fall of a particular ruling house, and to the regulation amongst different *guo*. It is with this dichotomy that Chinese nationalist thought entered the 20th century. It did not attach itself to any particular form of state government, partly because there was no effective state. Instead, Chinese nationalism remobilised seventeenth-century cultural philosophies relating to the achievement of the people's general well-being, and tried to combine that with the achievement of an economic modernity that would allow China to take its place as an equal amongst nation-states. It is this particular discourse which was formalised into a nationalist ideology by Sun Yat-sen and his chief ideologue, Dai Jitao, as well as by the founders of the Communist Party in China. The consequences of this intellectual and political history are still acutely present in contemporary forms of Chinese notions of identity and 'self-strengthening': a pride in a culturalist version of *tianxia* combined with a fairly sceptical attitude towards regimes of national state power. This ideology is particularly suited to a diasporic people since it allows them to remain distant from 'their' state while retaining pride in the cultural values allegedly embodied in their tradition which is, as all traditions are, highly portable.

The degree of multicultural tolerance in countries with sizeable Chinese minorities determines the interpretation and indeed the intensity of such a cultural nationalism. For instance, in certain Southeast Asian countries, this may amount to a 'cultural chauvinism' in the light of anti-Chinese discrimination. In this essay, cultural nationalism is understood as a culturally positive, politically abstract phenomenon emerging from *tianxia* and hitting Hong Kong cinema around the late 50s in the context of the Cold War and its Yellow-Peril rhetoric rather than as a byproduct of the successful Communist Revolution (regarded with the scepticism befitting any *guo*).

Hong Kong film directors and writers readily delved into Chinese myths, legends and history to find themes and motifs on which to base their films and scripts. They were in a unique position to show abstract loyalty to China, unlike their counterparts in China itself or in Taiwan, which required its citizens to treat the island as the real China. Hong Kong is not a country, so that to speak of a Hong Kong nationalism would be a contradiction in terms. Its residents' dislike of communism and, in recent years, its distrust of Britain produced a nationalism based not on support for a particular regime or political ideology, but on a cultural ideal which, ironically, is rooted in *tianxia*, a residue of the Heavenly Kingdom.

One sign of Chinese communities expressing such an abstract nationalism is their ready identification with Chinese screen characters, especially when, as in some Southeast Asian countries, local political factors make it difficult for audiences to express their nationalistic feeling. In addition, the traditional apathy of overseas Chinese towards politics plays a key role in fostering this abstract nationalism. It has come to characterise the thinking of many overseas Chinese who do not call China their home, but view China as *zuguo* or motherland, the repository of one's cultural identity, the land of one's ancestors and the source of myths and legends which imbue the process of growing up, wherever. In later chapters, the abstract nationalism of contemporary Hong Kong directors such as Tsui Hark, Ann Hui and Yim Ho will be discussed in the context of the so-called new wave's 'China syndrome' in the mid-80s. Hong Kong's China syndrome belies the contemporary political equation of Chinese nationalism with the communist regime in China. On the contrary, it asserts Hong Kong's identity as a separate cultural, social and political entity not to be confused with China. However, this has not always been the case.

In the immediate post-war years, Hong Kong took in scores of Chinese refugees, including filmmakers, fleeing the civil war and, later, the communist regime. Political feelings concerning the situation in China ran high. Hong Kong cinema was divided along left–right lines, with production companies being identified by their political affiliations to the Chinese Communist Party or to the KMT. Authorities in China and Taiwan wooed filmmakers in Hong Kong and encouraged them to fight for Chinese hearts and minds. Whether any of these filmmakers were card-carrying members of political parties was immaterial to the prevailing mood of partisan nationalism. Left-wing studios such as Great Wall, Fenghuang and Long Ma, were clearly oriented towards the communist regime. Other companies, such as Yonghua and the Asia Film Company, received financial aid from Taiwanese and American sources.[1]

Towards the late 50s, Shaw Brothers and the MP and GI studios consolidated their hold on the film market and initiated a more glamorous studio era. The competition between these two major studios, each with their own roster of contract stars and directors, benefited both the industry and the audiences. The studio era coincided with the isolation from the world scene of a China that was also fast becoming a superpower, but the struggle between the left–right factions of the early 50s was abandoned in favour of the provision of glossy and escapist entertainment.

The two studios specialised in producing historical epics and romances, stories of concubines or emperors who either saved collapsing dynasties or wrecked them. Such films purveyed the notion of abstract nationalism (or cultural nationalism) to audiences in the region. In the 70s, the films of Bruce Lee inherited that tradition. Kung fu films were particularly conducive to nationalism of the abstract kind. Its martial heroes shared a Masonic-like background harking back to traditions laid down by venerable Shaolin monks and their disciples who make vows to fight the foreign Manchus and restore the Chinese Ming Dynasty. A kung fu fighter was seen as a person who fought for a cause, seeking to restore power and dignity to the Chinese race. The motto was that Chinese people should lift their heads rather than bow in shame and subjugation to foreigners (*ditou* in Chinese). The fact that China was for many years drawn, quartered and occupied by foreigners added to the Chinese inferiority complex. The anti-*ditou* syndrome informs Bruce Lee's nationalist spirit.

The case of Bruce Lee is of particular interest because his international appeal does not appear to contradict his forthright insistence on his Chineseness. Western admirers of Lee view him differently from his Eastern admirers, and the difference revolves around his nationalism. To many Western viewers, Lee's nationalism is a non-starter. American admirers of Lee's cult dwell in his art as a reaction against racism, as in Rob Cohen's appealing but over-simplified film biography of the actor, *Dragon: The Bruce Lee Story* (1993), where white racism against Asian migrants in America features as a strong motif. As for other details in the actor's philosophical make-up, Lee (played by Hawaiian actor Jason Scott Lee, no relation) is shown adhering to Chinese superstition, bound by some kind of fatal destiny which could be warded off by *bagua* emblems. Lee is consumed by nightmares in which he constantly battles an armour-clad knight obviously symbolising Death. In a climactic scene at the end, Lee fights the Death-knight in a Chinese cemetery (where his own grave is located), more as an attempt to divert the attention of Death from his son, Brandon, who died in an accident on a film set in 1993. Nationalism, where it features as part of the man's character-building framework, concerns Lee's struggle to win the public admission that Asians can be Americans too. But it is still Lee's kung fu style and methods which attract and make up the most important components of his philosophy, as seen in *Dragon.* Another component is Lee's sex appeal and magnetic personality, which draws Western audiences to him irrespective of the xenophobic streak in his Hong Kong films.

The English critic Tony Rayns has argued that Lee's narcissism is a trait which distinguishes him more than his nationalism.[2] To the West, Lee is a narcissistic hero who makes Asian culture more accessible. To the East, he is a nationalistic hero who has internationalised some aspects of Asian culture. Both views appear antithetical. Narcissism may well be one aspect of Lee's character through which an international audience gains access to eastern motives and behaviour, but it does not fully explain his appeal to a Chinese audience. For them, Lee's narcissism is a manifestation of the anti-*ditou* factor that galvanises characters into action in kung fu movies. Lee is literally putting his bravest face (and body) forward in order to show that the Chinese need no longer be weaklings. The physical art of kung fu entails the exertion of power and physique. Narcissism then ties in with Lee's urge to 'show face' (*biaomian*) as opposed to 'lose face' (*diaolian*).

Chinese audiences take pride in the image Lee projects as a superb fighting specimen of manhood who derives his status from 'traditional' skills. They are aware that his kung fu skills are not the result of supernatural strength or special effects. They know from versions and legends of Chinese history that this skill is achievable, a result of fitness and rigorous training. This principle of counting on one's own physical skills has been followed by other martial arts stars such as Jacky Chan. A scene in *The Way of the Dragon* illustrates the first principle of discipline and training in kung fu: before his gladiatorial bout with Chuck Norris in the Roman Coliseum, Lee warms up physically, stretches his muscles, creaks all his joints, reaches for his feet. Lee shows himself to be a specimen of thorough training, a true-to-life fighter and not the imaginary creation of an action movie director.

But Lee is more than a superb fighter, his kung fu skills more than physical brawn. His will to succeed, the philosophy of his kung fu, had to do with what influenced his return to Hong Kong from the United States to start his short but sensational career as a kung fu star. The legend of his return to Hong Kong (the story of his disappointment in losing the role of Kwai-chang/Caine in the Hollywood *Kung Fu* television series and the realisation that prejudice still ruled in the film capital) gave a special, classic status to the first three movies he made in the territory. Chinese audiences who see Lee in these films know that he has done all Chinese proud by using his skills in the service of a cause that inspires Chinese people to assert their identity and culture and never to bow their heads in shame (*ditou*) or lose face (*diaolian*).

The Big Boss/ Tang Shan Daxiong (1971), Lee's first movie produced by a Hong Kong studio (Golden Harvest) after his failure to establish himself in Hollywood, is on the surface a simple and undemanding action picture. Lee plays Cheng Chiu-on, a new migrant in a Thai town who joins a group of other overseas Chinese workers employed in an ice factory. The plot develops around the disappearance of Cheng's buddies and his subsequent investigations. He comes into conflict with the factory's boss (Han Yingjie) who had in fact killed Cheng's buddies because they discovered his drug trafficking activities. Acting with a spontaneous but disciplined style, Lee etches out a character who is defined by action. However, Cheng is not a mere cypher for Lee's kung fu skills. He is a fully-rounded character who can evoke empathy in the audience's hearts with minimal interpretation from Lee. Cheng resorts to action only through the trigger of conscience. He wears around his neck a jade amulet his mother had given him as a reminder that his kung fu skills should not be abused. Only when one of the thugs pulls off the chain and breaks the amulet does Cheng put his kung fu skills to use. Cheng is a character compelled to action for a reason. He fights for a cause. For better or worse, that cause is based on racial awareness, on the quest to make the Chinese character a dignified, respected and honoured figure. *The Big Boss* gains significance through Lee's propagation of such a cause.

In his next film, *Fist of Fury/Jingwu Men* (1972), Lee makes his strongest statement for the cause. It gives Lee his most substantial role, that of a young patriotic student named Chen Zhen who avenges the death of his master and redeems the honour of his martial arts school. The school is the Jingwu Men (or school of the most refined martial arts), located in the Japanese concession of Shanghai. Huo Yuanjia, the master, has been murdered by rival Japanese martial artists. During his memorial service, the Japanese launch a challenge to the Jingwu Men. Through a Chinese lackey-interpreter, they insult Huo's followers, brandishing a plaque with the words 'Sick Man of East Asia' and daring any member to fight them. Chen Zhen takes up the challenge, infiltrates the Japanese school and single-handedly defeats them.

In the role of Chen Zhen, Lee sheds the country bumpkin persona seen in *The Big Boss*. Chen Zhen has attained the rank of fifth disciple. With the death of his master, he alone among the school's students is willing to put his kung fu skills to work. In so doing, he risks abusing the ideals of the school which stresses that martial arts must only be put to the service of one's country and not for other bellicose reasons. The provocations of the Japanese prove too much for Chen and goad him into action. Part of the fascination of *Fist of Fury* lies in watching Chen harness his anger so as to release it in the form of powerful and deadly kung fu strokes, kicks, punches: a true marriage of action and intention executed with grace, simplicity and style. Chen's dilemma lies in the realisation that he could easily abuse his kung fu skills for the purpose of revenge, blood-letting and pure fun. Ironically, it is through such 'abuse' that

Chen Zhen's sense of justice is satisfied. The film ends with Chen Zhen's arrest by the Shanghai police; but, taunted by the crowd of foreigners outside the gate who demand colonial justice, Chen runs towards them, leaping and flinging himself at the foreigners as they fire pistols at him. The image of the leap is frozen and Chen Zhen becomes a martyr, dying for a nationalistic cause. If evidence is needed to substantiate the nationalism which inspires Lee's characters, it is this final freeze-frame. Chen Zhen is also shown reacting against the semi-colonial subjugation of China: in addition to the Sick Man of East Asia' sign hurled at the Jingwu Men disciples, Chen Zhen takes issue with the 'No Dogs and Chinese' sign stuck in front of the gates of the city park. He destroys the sign after beating several Japanese who suggest that they would bring Chen into the park if he got down and crawled on all fours like a dog.

The anti-foreign bias in Lee's nationalism, most explicitly stated in *Fist of Fury*, can be dismissed as naked xenophobia, or acknowledged as the legitimate anger of a subjugated colonial and lowly Asian immigrant. Lee's feelings about his own experiences as an Asian immigrant in America undoubtedly seeped through. The nationalist motif in Lee's films is substantially a personal exorcism, a kind of retribution which Lee metes out to foreigners for their prejudices; it drives Lee's characters into action and puts Lee's kung fu talent to use. But it has been argued that such personal motivation diffuses the nationalist motif, leaving room for a psychological counter-argument in the form of Lee's narcissism.

Such a counter-argument is put forth by some critics in assessing *The Way of the Dragon*. It is, in their eyes, Lee's most narcissistic film. Lee's character, Tang Lung, goes to Rome to protect a Chinese restaurant threatened by a syndicate which has set its sights on the land on which the restaurant was built. After thwarting the first crude attempts to terrorise the owners into submission, Tang Lung must deal with professional fighter-killers hired by the syndicate. The film's biggest set-piece takes place in the Roman Coliseum where an American martial artist (played by Chuck Norris, Lee's sparring partner in the US) and Tang Lung fight to the death like the gladiators of ancient Rome.

The first work to be directed and scripted by Bruce Lee, *The Way of the Dragon* is, sadly, a flawed and transitional work which must now remain as Lee's testament, a reminder of themes which could have developed further and with more assurance and confidence had he lived. Up to this production, Bruce Lee had not only continuously espoused the art of Chinese kung fu, he had also dealt with the theme of the Chinese immigrant who must face discrimination and oppression: double blows to the pride and dignity of the Chinese character as they put roots in foreign lands. The character of Tang Lung is reprised from the immigrant persona previously seen in *The Big Boss*. The character is really part bumpkin, part martial arts master-philosopher. We see more of the former while the latter is relatively undeveloped. Unfortunately, the bumpkin persona takes over and transforms Lee's previous heroic figure into a parody. Signs of self-mockery can be detected in scenes such as those in the Roman Coliseum set-piece where Tang Lung rips body hair off the American's chest and blows it off the palm of his hand. Lee becomes a cult figure more at home in a cartoon comic. The parodic, almost camp, image of Lee probably originated from the famous scene in *The Big Boss* where a perfect image of a man is imprinted on a wooden wall after Lee has punched him through it.

Lee's indulgence in playing the bumpkin does not stand him in good stead with Western critics who will be put off by the grossness and crass naïvety of his character, because it strikes so close to home. This bumpkin easily reminds Westerners of the infamously rude Chinese waiters in Chinese restaurants all over Europe. On top of this negative image is Tang Lung's buffoonery. The first shot in *The Way of the Dragon* is a close-up of a tense and nervous Tang Lung. As the camera pulls back, we see why: he is in Rome's international airport surrounded by foreigners and stared at by a middle-aged European lady. Next, he goes to the restaurant and, unable to speak English or Italian, can only point to the menu, unaware of what he is ordering. Later, he is picked up by a prostitute. Not realising her real identity, he goes to her apartment. There, in front of a mirror, he practices kung fu (a scene held up by critics pushing the narcissistic line as a classic illustration of Lee's cinematic narcissism) before noticing the now naked prostitute, which is when he realises what her profession is.

The image of the bumpkin is emphasised at the expense of Lee's nationalism. We do not see much of Lee's master-fighter persona dealing with the cause. Tang Lung is a bumpkin who is skilled in kung fu rather than a kung fu master who comes from humble origins. The 'narcissism' scene of Tang Lung practising kung fu naked to the waist has become a major icon in Lee's myth. There is a camp quality to this scene which makes it memorable. But it forms only a brief segment in the whole film and actually ends with self-deprecating humour: as Tang Lung wraps up his exercise, he notices the poster of a naked couple embracing each other; quickly he puts palms together, shakes his head and closes his eyes as if to murmur a prayer. Other equally memorable scenes in *The Way of the Dragon* tend to be overlooked. One such is the mime scene where Tang Lung confronts the boss of the syndicate. His lack of English means that he cannot verbally warn the boss to lay off. He mimes it all out, with clenched fists, body movements, grunts and scowls, overcoming his verbal shortcomings and conveying a clear message to the enemy. The fight scenes too are among Lee's most graceful. Although a flawed work, *The Way of the Dragon* crystallises all the important motifs seen in previous Lee films. His bumpkin-master fighter persona is a welded character which falls short of a new heroic persona because of the implicit caricature. Alas, Lee died before he could develop this persona further in more representative works.

Lee's last completed work was *Enter the Dragon* (1973), a co-production between Hollywood-based producers and Lee's Hong Kong backers, with guaranteed international distribution by Warner Brothers. This is surely an important work in Lee's career as it shows Lee at a certain disadvantage in the hands of Western filmmakers. For precisely the same reason, not a few Western 'experts' on Lee consider it a minor work. Even when judged a superior work by the standards of the kung fu action genre, *Enter the Dragon* is really an uneasy amalgamation of antithetical East–West sentiments. It conveys the West's antipathy towards Lee's nationalism, and it shows a sullen and sulking Lee forced to submit to the West's perception of him as a mere action hero. Lee's strong personality still comes through as he performs a clichéd characterisation of the reserved, inscrutable and humourless Oriental hero so often seen in Hollywood movies. With the exception of an expository sequence before the opening credits introducing Lee's character (also called Lee), and putting his inheritance of the illustrious Shaolin kung fu tradition into perspective, the character has no significance beyond the purely mechanical. The theme of Chinese pride and honour *vis-à-vis* the prejudices and humiliations of foreigners, so starkly seen in Lee's Hong Kong productions, is only occasionally put forward. It is Lee's natural dignity and force of character which convey the message.

As the film opens, Lee is fighting in a practice session before a Shaolin high priest. Lee has reached the pinnacle of the Shaolin school of martial arts. The priest reminds him of the Shaolin precepts for mental preparedness: 'The enemy is only an illusion; the real enemy lies within oneself; he leaves and joins with the self.' Lee comprehends immediately: 'The self is abstract. To fight the enemy is a game; I play this game seriously.' Unlike Lee, the filmmakers do not quite grasp the spiritual message. Whereas his Hong Kong movies such as *Fist of Fury* show Lee struggling with his inner self to exorcise the enemy within, all the better to fight a righteous cause without, *Enter the Dragon* only capitalises on the outer struggle. Together with Americans Roper and Williams (played by John Saxon and Jim Kelly, respectively), Lee goes to the island fortress ruled by an errant Shaolin disciple named Han (played by Cantonese villain Sek Kin). Nominally there to take part in a martial arts competition held once every three years, Lee is actually on a secret mission to collect evidence against Han's criminal operations and to bring him to task for betraying the Shaolin principles. Lee succeeds magnificently. With the help of Roper, he destroys the fortress. The compulsory duel scene between Han and Lee is set in a hall of mirrors. Lee is reminded of the principle that the 'enemy is an illusion'. With this in mind, he overcomes Han, who, in contrast, counted on gimmickry: his amputated right fist is armoured with weapons such as a talon and a steel hand.

Aesthetically, the Chineseness of *Enter the Dragon* does not integrate well with the Western sense of narrative decorum. From a Hong Kong perspective, the film moves slowly for a kung fu action movie, spending too much time on introducing characters. There is too much of a tendency to neatness. It is the kind of filmmaking that some critics may call 'literate' as opposed to the 'illiterate' slam-bang style of Hong Kong movies. But its literacy has nothing to do with a real understanding of the themes which Bruce Lee stood for.

The film does provide Lee with his only chance in any of his works to expound on the spiritual principles of kung fu: it briefly shows him inheriting the mantle of kung fu from a Shaolin high priest (played by Roy Chiao) who practises the illusory-self principle (a scene cut from most international release prints). He then passes on the inheritance to a younger disciple, to whom he intones: 'Emotional content, always remember, emotional content!' Lee's performance in *Enter the Dragon* is his least interesting, a casualty of the Western filmmakers' demand for superficial decorum at the expense of character interpretation. Although the action sequences are finely choreographed by Lee, they appear academic. Seen today, Lee's presence in *Enter the Dragon* imparts a strange feeling. His 'serious' demeanour hints at a premonition of death. Clearly Lee could not fully express himself, finding satisfaction only in action – his shrieks, wails and cries are his most eloquent among all his movies.

Lee's improvised action choreography may have earned him the title of postmodern hero in Western eyes. But his kung fu, part of the generic tradition of Chinese action movies, is innovative and exotic compared to the fisticuffs and armaments of Western-style action scenes. So too is the element of narcissism if this is defined as the tendency of heroes to strike a pose in kung fu stance to evoke masculine sexuality. If narcissism is taken to mean homoeroticism, male bonding, *covert* homosexuality – then all these are part of the tradition of martial arts–kung fu films, particularly evident in the films of Zhang Che in the late 60s and 70s.

The West has tended to see an Eastern hero such as Lee as a camp figure who appeared in star vehicles designed to pander to the public's taste for action. Serious critics charge that Lee's movies do not amount to narrative wholes, and that they are only relevant or interesting because of the actor's presence and his skilful display of kung fu (a critical position which some critics also hold on Hong Kong cinema in general). What is not clear is whether some Western critics offer a thesis of narcissism as a counter argument to Hong Kong critics' focus on nationalism in Lee's movies, or whether their attempts to rationalise Eastern culture has brought forth a claim of narcissism to explain concepts such as nationalism and Lee's stand against racial prejudice.

The cult of Bruce Lee propagated after his death has resulted in blatant exploitation of his name and personality. Imitators sprung up sporting names like Bruce Le, Bruce Ly and Bruce Lai. Lee's own studio, Golden Harvest, was responsible for the travesty *Game of Death/Siwang Youxi* (1979), a film claimed to be Lee's last. The film credits Lee as lead actor, screenwriter and co-martial arts director, when in fact, these credits refer to only ten minutes of genuine Lee footage in the whole 102-minute running time of the film. The rest was directed by an American, Robert Clouse, Lee's director in *Enter the Dragon*, with new action sequences co-ordinated by Sammo Hung and choreographed by Yuan Biao. Clouse's film deals with a character named Billy Lo, a martial arts movie star who finds himself the target of an enlistment drive by an international crime syndicate. Billy Lo is played by a Bruce Lee lookalike, while his co-stars are grizzled Hollywood supporting actors Gig Young, Hugh O'Brian and Dean Jagger. The film cuts together out-takes, clips and inserts of the real Lee compiled from *The Way of the Dragon* and an undisclosed ten-minute sequence shot by

Lee for his next production after *Enter the Dragon*. These incredible ten minutes show Lee entering a pagoda and on each level, encountering a protector whom he must subdue in order to continue up to the next level. On the second level, Lee's opponent is seven-foot tall Hakim, played by basketball star Kareem Abdul Jabbar, in line with Lee's practice of using former students and genuine martial arts professionals as actors in his pictures.

Both the Eastern and Western minders of Lee's cult showed their inability to understand Lee's legacy. *Game of Death* is a barely adequate action picture which hardly knows how to handle Lee's screen persona – whether to treat him as myth, common man hero, superhero or master fighter. Needless to say, it gives no mention to Lee's real concerns and themes, not even in the film's most inspired moment: the allusion to the last shot of *Fist of Fury* in which Lee's character turns martyr for a nationalistic cause. During the shoot for a new movie, Lo is required to leap towards a hostile crowd aiming pistols at him. He is shot by a real bullet fired by an assassin planted among the extras, a scene which now assumes some poignancy since it is reminiscent of the circumstances surrounding the death of Lee's son, Brandon. Wounded in the face, Lo is taken to hospital and survives with nary a mark. He is persuaded by a journalist friend (Gig Young) to play dead. Lo's 'death' is reported in the press, giving the filmmakers a chance to insert footage of Bruce Lee's actual funeral ceremony including a brief glimpse of him lying in the coffin.

The crucial freeze-frame image of the last leap in *Fist of Fury*, with its attendant philosophy, is squandered in the interest of a false tribute to Lee. The result is parody, exacerbated by the attempt to integrate his image into the narrative. One may well ask how Lee's admirers perceive the star after his death. Clouse obviously sees him in mechanical, stylistic terms, as an action star, and pays no heed to his nationalist consciousness or his spiritual kung fu philosophy. The cult worship of Lee seems unable to cope with all that, and more's the pity. With his death, Lee became an object, even a fetish.

This chapter which deals with nationalism as an important theme of Hong Kong cinema seeks to put the concept of nationalism in its right perspective. Lee's nationalism, and that of many other Hong Kong directors and actors, is of the popcorn variety, a lowbrow version of nationalism which appeals most to home-grown audiences. The common-man Chinese hero who is both physical and philosophical is unique in Hong Kong cinema and Bruce Lee was the only star who could have created the prototype. Furthermore, his films offer interesting subjects for analysis in terms of style versus content, demonstrating how the two either integrate or fall apart if one aspect is overemphasised.

To see Lee as a mere kung fu martial artist without taking into account his nationalist sentiments is to perceive Lee as Narcissus gazing in a mirror: the image reflected is an illusion without substance. It ignores the symbolism of the dragon in Lee's Chinese name, Li Xiaolong, which means Li, the Little Dragon. When the dragon looks in the mirror, it sees not Narcissus but the Chinese masses looking back. This is the substance behind the reflective theory of Hong Kong cinema – that it mirrors the aspirations of Hong Kong people, and reflects their psychological mind-set and behaviour. This is also the substance behind Lee's narcissism. With death, Lee achieved true mythic status, allowing him to be all things to all men: Narcissus gazing in the mirror or Little Dragon exhorting the Chinese to stand up and be counted. Lee achieved the distinction of being both Narcissus and Little Dragon, straddling East and West.

Notes

1. For left–right divide in the Hong Kong film industry and the rise of the two majors, Shaw Brothers and MP and GI, see Chapters 1 and 5 of Stephen Teo, *Hong Kong Cinema* respectively.
2. Tony Rayns, 'Bruce Lee: Narcissism and Nationalism', *A Study of the Hong Kong Martial Arts Film*, HKIFF catalogue, 1980.

22

HAN'S ISLAND REVISITED: *ENTER THE DRAGON* AS TRANSNATIONAL CULT FILM

Leon Hunt

> This 'unique' dragon (the Chinese, the spiritual, etc.) is not one of those Won Ton Kung Fu flicks from H.K. . . . (the title) *Enter the Dragon* suggests the emergence (the entrance) of someone (a personality) that is of quality. (Bruce Lee)[1]

Hong Kong in Action

For fans of 'Hong Kong action', 1998 was a key year. Jackie Chan, the biggest star in Asia, finally 'arrived' in Hollywood with the Top 10 hit *Rush Hour* (Brett Ratner, US 1998). Chow Yun Fat and Jet Li made Hollywood debuts in *The Replacement Killers* (Antoine Fuqua, US 1998) and *Lethal Weapon 4* (Richard Donner, US 1998), respectively; Michelle Yeoh had just beaten them to it as a 'Bond Girl' in *Tomorrow Never Dies* (Roger Spottiswoode, US/UK 1997). But for an older generation of fans, the restoration of Bruce Lee's *Enter the Dragon* (Robert Clouse, HK/US 1973) was the key event, and a reminder of an earlier 'crossover', from cult to mainstream, from East to West. While *The Replacement Killers* has been described as 'a film which competently integrates the best levels of American and Hong Kong action cinema . . . an example of an original transnational film',[2] *Enter the Dragon* was arguably the first transnational Chinese-American action film.

Enter the Dragon takes place on an island – Han's Island was mooted as a title – an island, appropriately, of uncertain nationality. At one level, this seems like a reference to Hong Kong, given that Han's Island rests partly in British

From Xavier Mendik and Graeme Harper (eds) (2000), *Unruly Pleasures*, Guildford: FAB Press.

waters. But what Hong Kong and *Enter the Dragon* share is a similar sense of hybridity, of uncertain ownership and cultural affiliation. The film is most frequently damned as inauthentic, neither one thing nor the other – too cheap and tacky for Hollywood, too cynical and prepackaged for Hong Kong. According to Stephen Teo, its 'Chineseness . . . does not integrate well with the Western sense of narrative decorum',[3] as though this hybridity was doomed from the start. Tony Rayns, meanwhile, represents the orthodox view that it attempts to 'crossbreed a Sax Rohmer revival . . . with the most thoroughly discredited aspects of the James Bond ethic',[4] later concluding that it was 'better forgotten'.[5] *Enter the Dragon* has, of course, not been forgotten – it's a key reference point for kung fu/'China'/Hong Kong imprinting themselves on the Western popular imaginary. Moreover, the gleeful hybridity of recent Hong Kong cinema – Kevin Costner's *The Bodyguard* (Mick Jackson, US 1992), remixed to accommodate Jet Li's kung fu skills, becomes *Bodyguard From Beijing* (Yuen Kwai, HK 1994), for example – does much to problematise these lurking implications of 'pure' national cinemas. Nevertheless, the film's enduring appeal seems a predominantly Western (and Japanese) phenomenon. It was less successful in Hong Kong than early Lee films like *Fist of Fury* (Lo Wei, HK 1972) and *Way of the Dragon* (Bruce Lee, HK 1972). 'Rarely, if ever,' Bey Logan suggests, 'has one film with one star loomed like such a colossus over a genre',[6] but he admits that the comparison is with other American Martial Arts films. Elsewhere, he acknowledges that Lee's long term influence on Hong Kong cinema was 'negligible' and that the 'big Chinese hits released the year after his death . . . look pretty much as they would had Bruce never returned to Hong Kong'.[7] I do want to suggest, however, both that there's rather more 'Hong Kong cinema' in *Enter* than tends to be acknowledged and that, in any case, Western fans (who may also include diasporic Chinese) have some right to Bruce Lee's crossover film – Lee was himself a transnational, trans-Pacific. If *Enter* is heavily contested – breakthrough or sellout? – that's because Lee is, too.

What makes the film's Hong Kong-ness problematic is the slippery, shifting sense of what constitutes 'Hong Kong', not only as a colonial or post-colonial space, but also a marketable, international cinematic commodity. By the 1970s, Hong Kong itself was a comparative representational absence, not least from Hong Kong cinema. Ackbar Abbas has argued that prior to the emergence of the 'New Wave' (Tsui Hark, Ann Hui) in the late 1970s and the signing of the 1984 Joint Declaration returning Hong Kong to China, 'stories about Hong Kong always turned into stories about somewhere else, as if Hong Kong culture were somehow not a subject'.[8] It was impending reunification which enabled Hong Kong to see itself 'with new eyes', discovering 'itself as a subject'[9] – most critics operate on the implicit agreement that Shaw Brothers, Bruce Lee and Chang Cheh's Shaolin cycle barely belong to the same national cinema as John Woo, Tsui Hark and Wong Kar-Wai. Meanwhile, Western representations of the city traditionally presented a socio-geographically unspecific 'exotic' space akin to Sternberg's Shanghai or Morocco,[10] or, by the time of *The World of Suzy Wong*

(Richard Quine, US/UK 1960), 'an approximation of late 19th century Paris, a city of some seedy exoticism and dubious charm'.[11] The novelisation of *Enter the Dragon* finds Williams (Jim Kelly) 'digging the Suzie Wongs' and observing that 'the miniskirt had caught up to Hong Kong'.[12] *Enter the Dragon* adheres to the image of Hong Kong as a space of transit, 'a doorway, a point in between'[13] – by implication, in between China and the West. Lee (Bruce Lee), Roper (John Saxon) and Williams pass through on their way to Han's island, Williams pausing to reconfigure it as a universalized ghetto ('the same all over the world'). Kung fu put Hong Kong cinema on the international market, but the genre itself seemed to signify an abstracted 'China' rather than the island itself.

Early '70s kung fu was Mandarin-language (in a predominantly Cantonese-speaking city), made by studios and talents largely transplanted from Shanghai and with visible influences (and technical expertise) from Japanese samurai films. Japan – often vilified in the '70s films – remains a key influence, only now the reference point is manga/anime rather than samurais and judo sagas. The 'new' Hong Kong action cinema, by contrast, was neon-lit, cosmopolitan, hi-tech and awesomely cool – predominantly, a cinema of hair gel and shades, not pigtails and nunchakus. Hong Kong cinema may have 'found itself', but authenticity didn't come into it – according to Abbas, this new sensibility was 'posited on the imminence of disappearance', a disappearance manifested in terms of ephemera, speed and abstraction.[14] Hybridity is just one expression of this – John Woo, for example, has described the gangster society of his films as 'a hybrid of all the worlds of all the films I loved, an imaginary place recreated from the (American) gangster films I saw when I was young'.[15] This suggests a type of transnational dreaming, a useful idea for rethinking *Enter the Dragon*. Admittedly, the film rests more on the West dreaming about the 'Orient', but Lee's presence and influence complicates the image-flow.

Director Robert Clouse rather notoriously claimed that he had to 'kick the strut' out of Lee to make him palatable for international audiences, citing a gesture well known to fans of his Hong Kong films – 'he slid his thumb across his nose like they used to do in American gangster movies of the '30s'.[16] Chow Yun Fat, too, seems to have been 'de-strutted' for *The Replacement Killers*. But when Clouse extracts his foot from his mouth – a style of kung fu much practiced by Western filmmakers – he describes 'the new Bruce Lee' as a 'mosaic'.[17] He has clothes, in particular, in mind – a combination of 'beautiful silk Chinese suits' and ('70s fashions permitting) sharp Western tailoring (shades of the debonair Chow). If this suggests a rather culturally polarised wardrobe, one might also mention the tight, black jump-suit Lee wears in the underground cavern scenes which suggests a less geographically overdetermined generic space.

Blurring the Boundaries of Cult Status

In Sheldon Hsiao-peng Lu's anthology *Transnational Chinese Cinemas*, transnationalism describes not only the way contemporary global capitalism operates, but the blurring of national cinematic boundaries through international markets, foreign investment and co-productions. Lu demonstrates that Chinese cinemas were transnational from the start – the first Chinese feature, *The Difficult Couple* (1913), was made by a US company based in China and there were abortive plans in the 1930s to build an 'Oriental Hollywood' in Shanghai. This scenario is now much more pronounced, both because of the tripartite terrain of 'Chinese cinema' (Mainland, Hong Kong, Taiwan) and because all three are part of the global market. In addition, Hong Kong and other émigrés are creating a 'nascent Chinese American film . . . a transpacific, transnational Chinese film culture'.[18] The book includes persuasive accounts of both John Woo and Jackie Chan as transnational Chinese figures,[19] but Lee is little more than a footnote, despite the fact that he anticipates both men. Like Chan, Lee was employed as a performer of action; like Woo, he was employed as an orchestrator of action – he choreographed (some might say directed) the fight scenes in *Enter the Dragon*. Like Chan (but unlike Woo), Lee brought other Chinese talent into his 'crossover' film – eagle-eyed aficionados like to spot Chan himself, Samo Hung, Yuen Biao, Yuen Wah (Lee's acrobatic stunt double) and Lam Ching-ying amongst *Enter*'s stunt team.

The film was a co-production between Warners' subsidiary Sequoia and Golden Harvest's Concorde (Lee and Raymond Chow), written and directed by Americans with a predominantly Chinese crew – it's Lee's input on script and direction which partially qualifies this distinction between primary (American) and secondary (Chinese) labour. Warner Brothers were the prime movers in the Western incorporation of kung fu, and of Lee, who had already had a less than happy experience with them over what was to become *Kung Fu* (ABC 1972–5). More importantly, Warners had picked up Shaw Brothers' *King Boxer/Five Fingers of Death* (Cheng Chang-Ho, HK 1972) for distribution and had an unexpected hit with it (the film outgrossed the first two Lee films in Britain and the US). Clouse attributes this initiative to Warners' head of Asian distribution, Richard Ma, who had spotted an Orientalist fad in the making with Nixon's visit to China and the popularity of Chinese food.[20] *Enter*, it seems, was partly a way of squeezing Run Run Shaw out of any further deals, but there's also a sense of 'conquering' the genre just as martial arts had come to the West via American excursions into South-East Asia.

Even so, the signs of caution were visible – Rayns refers sniffily to 'American "stars" of the calibre of John Saxon',[21] and his equal billing with Lee gives us some sense of what Warners thought of their Chinese leading man. Nevertheless, Saxon is an interesting transnational figure in his own right, as fans of Italian exploitation would no doubt testify – a minor character actor at best in the US, Saxon has often shone for directors like Mario Bava, Dario Argento and Antonio Margheriti. Add a touch of blaxploitation in the irresistible figure of Jim Kelly ('I'll be too busy lookin' good!') and it's little wonder that *Enter* is one of the quintessential cult films. This second-guessing of different audiences now seems very modern and astute. Lalo Schifrin's score joins the trans-generic dots, deploying blaxploitation motifs (wah-wah guitar) alongside echoes of his own *Mission Impossible* score and the sort of 'Oriental' themes only found in the West. Hong Kong soundtracks did their 'sampling' rather more directly, mixing snatches of, say, Isaac Hayes' *Theme From Shaft* with selected Morricone or John Barry. Kung fu has remained central to the hip-hop soundscape, from Wu Tang Clan samples to the 'shapes' thrown on the dance floor.

Enter the Dragon was the most successful of Hong Kong's international co-productions, but it wasn't the only one. The '70s 'chop sockies' are often compared with spaghetti westerns – the baroque room Wang Yu rigs up to defeat *The Master of the Flying Guillotine* (Wang Yu, HK 1976) before depositing him in a ready-made coffin is especially reminiscent of an Italian Sabata film. However, Italian co-productions like *Blood Money* (Antonio Margheriti, HK/It 1974) did neither genre any favours. *The Man From Hong Kong* (Brian Trenchard-Smith and Wang Yu, HK/Australia 1975) anticipates kung fu's '80s excursions into gritty urban thrillers and has impressive choreography by Samo Hung. *The Legend of the Seven Golden Vampires* (Roy Ward Baker, HK/GB 1974), a co-production between Shaw Brothers and Hammer Films, also has impressive choreographic credentials – Lau Kar Leung and Tang Chia – and provides a particularly illuminating comparison with *Enter the Dragon*.

Kitsch, Comics and Comparisons

Enter the Dragon has Vietnam at least partly on its mind – its two American heroes are vets, the narrative 'goal' is the securing of an island of uncertain territorial ownership and neither Saxon nor Kelly fully grasp the codes or agendas underlining the struggle. *The Legend of the Seven Golden Vampires* is more overtly colonialist. The film opens with a marvellous representation of two genres merging. Kah, High Priest of the Seven Golden Vampires, travels from China to Transylvania to seek the aid of Dracula in restoring the cult to its former glory. The Count is uncooperative by nature but tired of languishing in 'this miserable place', and so he 'possesses' Kah's body and leaves for China. Thereafter, Kah speaks with Dracula's voice, but a flamboyant gesture is accompanied by an unmistakable 'swish' on the soundtrack to represent these two genres inhabiting one body. Subsequently, however, the film is about two white Europeans – Dracula and Peter Cushing's Van Helsing – performing a kind of mythological colonization. We first meet Van Helsing as he delivers a lecture on ancient Chinese legends to a frankly sceptical audience at Chungking University. Naturally, the Prof knows better. As he travels into the cursed village of Ping Kwei, he experiences a 'been here before feeling', an anticipation of what's around the next corner – in other words, for this colonizer of the Orient's imaginary, China's mysteries are already 'known'. Van Helsing teams up with Hsu Tien-an, his brothers and his sister (Shih Szu). 'My brothers would die in your defence,' Hsu Tien-an promises Van Helsing rather unwisely, because that's pretty much what transpires. Kung fu is explicitly played out as a spectacle for a (diegetic) white Western gaze – 'it was the most fantastic display – I've never seen anything like it.' Van Helsing tells Chiang rather condescendingly after one battle. *Enter the Dragon* seems to begin similarly – Lee 'performs' for the gaze of British emissary Braithwaite, who arrives at the Shaolin Temple to employ him. But at least Lee has his own agendas – when Braithwaite says that 'we' would like him to attend Han's tournament, Lee replies sardonically, 'We, Mr Braithwaite?'

Lee plays a (former?) Shaolin monk employed to take part in a martial arts tournament while gathering information on a heroin and prostitution ring on a secluded island – the island's mastermind is Mr Han (Shek Kin), a renegade Shaolin. Lee is one of three heroes, but the only one with clearly defined goals – revenge (Han is indirectly responsible for his sister's death), honour (less clear in the 'unrestored' version) and what is usually seen as a colonial/colonised policing of the 'Orient'. Roper (Saxon) is a gambler, a devil-may-care, white American smoothie – he arrives with dozens of suitcases, all of them presumably containing polo-neck sweaters. Williams's (Kelly's) hair puts the 'afro' into Afro-American – he's defined through Black Power and Hendrix posters, hassles with racist cops, an inexhaustible sexual appetite, plenty of 'strut' and most of the best lines. The tournament proceeds; Lee gathers evidence. In his first bout, he's pitted against his sister's killer, Oharra (Bob Wall, Lee's favourite punchbag), and takes the opportunity to humiliate and then kill him. Han mistakes Williams for the island prowler and kills him, using one of a selection of deadly artificial hands – he's rather more taken with Roper and offers him a job. As Roper seemingly wavers, Lee works his way through the island caverns and numerous guards before being captured. Roper refuses to fight Lee and they team up against more of Han's guards. Han tries out some more of his lethal hands – bear claw and a hand of knives – but the wounds just make Lee more photogenic. Only a hall of mirrors delays Han's defeat and he's left impaled on a spear.

'Man, you come right out of a comic book!' Kelly says to Han – oh, how the reviewers jumped on that line! – and he's almost right. But, as most writers point out, Sax Rohmer and Ian Fleming got there first. At one level, it's almost as though the price of Lee embodying the Chinese Superman – he'd never been so invincible before – was a Yellow Peril villain. It's more likely, though, that the film had to work with some of the representations it already knew – representations which still had some mythic power. Rohmer's *Fu Manchu* novels had been reprinted by Pyramid books in the US in the 1960s, and their success was a factor in Harry Alan Towers' series of films starring Christopher Lee (1965–8). Marvel Comics had made a deal with Rohmer's estate to base a comic around the character, but were initially unable to find a suitable format. The kung fu 'craze' evidently provided the impetus for such a format, because in December 1973, *Special Marvel Edition* number 15 featured Fu Manchu's oedipally heroic son, Shang Chi, Master of Kung Fu. Shang Chi was a hit – by issue 17, the comic was retitled *Master of Kung Fu* and ran continuously until 1983. Its most immediate influences were Bond, *Nick Fury Agent of S.H.I.E.L.D*, and *Where Eagles Dare*, but by issue 31, *Enter the Dragon* was exerting a visible influence – island fortresses, international drug rackets, whirling nunchakus and a bare-chested, pouting hero. Like his TV counterpart, David Carradine's Kwai Chang Caine, Shang Chi was of mixed race – also a recurring device in American kung fu paperbacks – and portrayed as a lethal, philosophically-minded hippy (he later developed an alarming taste for Fleetwood Mac). Trained in seclusion – like an inverted Shaolin Temple – Shang Chi is initially his father's assassin. But Nayland Smith 'turns' him, and, like Lee, he defects to the British secret service.

Fu Manchu – pre-Republic, let alone pre-Mao – remains committed to restoring the Manchu (Quing) Dynasty, inhabiting an invisible, mobile 'China', a ' "China" which no longer exists . . . except as a construct . . . carefully hidden inside an otherwise innocent office building'.[22] The Manchus figure prominently in the kung fu genre – the Quing Dynasty, during which they ruled the Han Chinese, often figures as a way of addressing colonialism (or, more recently, reunification), with Shaolin heroes like Fong Sai Yuk cast as rebellious Ming patriots. But in the Western imaginary, Manchurian corruption formed half of a binary opposite in representing China – either incorrigible, decadent tyrants or passive, easily colonised, sheep (see Han's 'refuse found in waterfront bars' in *Enter*). Such exotic villains had even colonised outer space in the form of Flash Gordon's Ming the Merciless (Manchu, Ming, Han – the dynastic signifiers are all too consistent).

Fu Manchu was already a nostalgic figure when he first appeared in 1913 – Nayland Smith first set eyes on him in 1911, the year Sun Yat Sen saw off the Quing Dynasty for good. What seems to be going on in the early '70s – against the backdrop of Nixon and Vietnam – is a renegotiation of what 'Chinese culture' signified in the West, a resetting of boundaries around who could be incorporated (martial artists, 'mystics') and who couldn't ('inscrutable' hardliners – i.e. communists). Western kung fu heroes were positioned between races, like Caine and Shang Chi, or between cultures, like Lee. But kung fu itself could easily inhabit the same cultural imaginary as the Yellow Peril – an excess of civilisation and culture, a decadent refinement of violence. Certainly they recombine in Jet Li's Wah Sing Ku in *Lethal Weapon 4*.

But Fu Manchu himself is something of an interracial paradox; on the one hand, 'the yellow peril incarnate', 'the cruel cunning of an entire Eastern race, accumulated in one giant intellect', but also 'tall, lean and feline, high-shouldered, with a brow like Shakespeare and a face like Satan'.[23] That's a potent set of signifiers – feminine, European, a fallen angel. Dr No, too, is a fallen angel – named in negation of his father – and of more literal mixed race. Han, of course, has 'fallen' from the genre's key prelapsarian space, the Shaolin Temple – renegade 'White Eyebrow' monk Bai Mei, who aided the destruction of the temple, was a later mainstay of Shaolin-themed kung fu films. Shek Kin's voice was dubbed by actor Keye Luke, Kung Fu's blind father figure, Master Po, as though to underline the inverted Shaolin patriarch. Shek himself was a reminder of another generic father. Cantonese folk hero Wong Fei Hung was played by Kwan Tak-hing in seventy-five films between 1949 and 1970, with Shek often cast as the villain. Rayns parallels the series' run with Bruce Lee's days as a 'punk . . . looking for fights',[24] as though there was always an Oedipal connection waiting to be made. But what's most striking about Han is that his Fleming-like taste for cats is overridden by his taste for Nietzschean epigrams. 'We are unique, gentlemen', he tells his invited warriors, 'In that we create ourselves . . . We forge our bodies in the fires of our will'. Later, he holds forth to Roper on the inseparability of culture and strength – 'it is strength that makes all other values possible . . . Who knows what delicate wonders have died out of the world for want of the will to survive?' This Will to Power doesn't seem to have been an accident. Writer Michael Allin apparently saw him as 'a combination of Richard Nixon and director John Milius'.[25]

Eastern West

Both the '70s and the '90s Hong Kong crossovers were preceded by dubbed exports. In the '70s, such exports constituted an entire cycle, but more recently, it was New Line's unexpected success with a dubbed, re-edited *Rumble in the Bronx* (Stanley Tong, HK 1995) which created a space once more for Chinese action stars in the US. Tony Rayns has likened the film to *Way of the Dragon* (Bruce Lee, HK 1972) – 'naive Hong Kong boy travels abroad to visit relatives and tangles with local gang' – while noting that Jackie Chan's 'stance is far more populist and far less Chinese-chauvinist than Lee's'.[26] Chan, as both Rayns and Fore note, has for some time been an transnational figure – his characters and films favour international locales – and yet his blend of comedy and action took longer to catch on in the West than Lee's superheroic persona. Chan's low-key 'patriotism' implicitly authenticates him for Rayns as a modern Hong Kong star – someone who represents a more complex sense of belonging than simply being 'Chinese'. Yet *Enter's* lack of Chinese-patriotism is often taken as a sign of its inauthenticity, an 'emasculation' which represents 'the West's antipathy towards Lee's nationalism'.[27]

Two things happen to Lee's ethnic populism in the film. On the one hand, it is pushed down in the mix – he defends the Chinese workers against a gwailo bully on the junk to Han's island, but significantly without landing a punch ('the art of fighting without fighting'). But ethnic pride is displaced most visibly onto Williams – Hollywood had a generic model for representing black (male) pride, and Warners were shrewd in gauging the demographics of kung fu's Western audience. But as Lee's patronising reference to 'Won Ton Kung Fu flicks' suggests, his sense of belonging, too, was contradictory. Even his fighting was 'neither wholly foreign nor wholly Chinese . . . very international'.[28] Lee bit, scratched and grappled, combined graceful traditional moves with Western boxing and street fighting. His image as Super-Patriot rests largely on *Fist of Fury's* Japan-bashing, although Abbas suggests that the film's anticolonialism was already slightly quaint, 'as if Bruce Lee were fighting again in a new Boxer Rebellion through the medium of cinema, in much the same way that Hollywood refought the Vietnam War'.[29] *Way of the Dragon* – Lee's most popular film in Hong Kong, but the last to reach the West (comedy again?) – softens this xenophobia Lee beats the Western heavies with 'Chinese boxing', but cautions his friends against dismissing 'foreign fighting'. It isn't Chinese boxing which defeats Chuck Norris in the Coliseum; rather, Lee's transnational Jeet Kune Do, a fighting style designed to transcend both 'style' and national-cultural tradition. Tang Lung (Lee) is 'part bumpkin, part martial arts master-philosopher',[30] and never quite coheres into a unified character. Teo is as troubled by this inconsistency as he is by *Enter*'s alleged co-opting. When he suggests that the bumpkin 'is emphasised at the expense of Lee's nationalism',[31] he seems to be longing for a fusion of the latter with the fighter-philosopher. Instead, Tang's move from parochial bumpkin to master fighter is channeled through the international language of his fighting style.

Enter the Dragon doesn't exactly back off from Lee's 'philosophy', even if it finds it equally difficult to consistently square it with generic imperatives. The 'restored' version of the film – in fact, the version originally released in Hong Kong – makes this more apparent. The additional material is a pre-credits conversation between Lee and the head monk about martial arts technique. Even Teo acknowledges that the sequence provides '(Lee's) only chance to expound on the spiritual principles of kung fu'.[32] In other words, there are issues around authorship here. Lee's fighting scenes are acknowledged prominently in the film's credits, and Rayns suggests grudgingly that they 'come as near as anything could to save the day'.[33] Lee's 'philosophical' input is a more complex commodity. In many ways, the Western 'kung fu craze' was bound up with commodifying two Others – violence and the 'Orient', fused together as mystical bodily harm. Hong Kong kung fu was much less 'philosophical' in the early '70s – it took directors like Lau Kar Leung and Samo Hung to later explore the principles of the art – much more unapologetically violent and revenge-driven. By contrast, Warners' *Kung Fu* was seen by more than one commentator as the '60s counterculture infiltrating the '70s mainstream, with its focus on 'peace, love, the natural way, ecology, a raising of consciousness'.[34]

Enter does seem to have been conceived as more of a 'straight' action film – the 'monk' scene was felt to slow down the action and cut from the Western print. Its restoration comes in the wake of a flood of books devoted to Lee's letters, essays, interviews and notebooks. The images of fluidity expounded by his character are familiar to anyone who's read such material: 'When the opponent expands, I contract; and when he contracts. I expand. And when the time comes, I do not hit – (holds up his fist) it hits by itself.'

I'm not trying to resurrect the auteur here, but authorship does complicate the idea of a Western co-opting as well as suggesting that a more international production does seem to have opened a limited space for such material (even if it took twenty five years for the scene to find a Western audience). The scene has other implications, because it gives Lee a dual narrative function, falling as it does in between his opening duel with Samo Hung and his recruitment by Braithwaite. Lee first hears of Han through the head monk, and his mission to 'restore the integrity of the Shaolin Temple' inscribes him into the Shaolin legends. But *Enter* is an odd Shaolin film – Western representations seem to have fallen for the prelapsarian exoticism of the locale before Hong Kong cinema established its more elaborate myths in the films of Chang Cheh and Lau Kar Leung. Where is this Shaolin Temple supposed to be? China? Hong Kong? And Lee both belongs and doesn't belong there – his black gloves and trunks and '70s hairstyle contrast with the robes and shaven heads of the other monks. The spectacle offered in the opening fight is a mixture of (kick)boxing and grappling, interspersed with Peking Opera-style tumbling. Once again, Lee is a 'mosaic', everywhere and nowhere, a mobile transnational signifier.

Lee's death made *Enter the Dragon* seem like a (flawed) culmination of the West's 1970s Eastern romance, rather than a transitional film, harbinger of a crossover which has only now arrived. *Rush Hour* makes for an interesting comparison – it refers explicitly to Hong Kong's post-colonialist status (even down to a villainous British governor), and embraces the Chinese-Afro-American bonding *Enter* didn't seem ready for. But make no mistake, its action scenes are Chan-lite, while *Enter* really did inject a new aesthetic into an American genre film. Watching the film with an audience recently was a revelation – the cavern fights were still impossibly thrilling, the audience gasped at the speed of the 'untelegraphed' punches meted out to Oharra and cheered the nunchaku scene usually missing from British prints. In addition, the new stereo soundtrack further amplified the sort of hyperbolic sound effects that could only emanate from a Hong Kong film. That this 'mosaic' doesn't always hold together adds to rather than detracts from its continuing fascination. That it still retains its following suggests that it addressed its diverse audience rather better than tends to be acknowledged.

Notes

1. John Little (ed.), *Bruce Lee Library Volume 5: Letters of the Dragon* (Boston, Rutland, Vermont and Tokyo: Charles E Tuttle Co., 1998), p. 181.
2. Tony Williams, '*Replacement Killers*', *Asian Cult Cinema*, Issue 19 (April 1998), pp. 29–31 (p. 30).
3. Stephen Teo, *Hong Kong Cinema: The Extra Dimension* (London: BFI 1997), p. 118.
4. Tony Rayns, '*Enter the Dragon* (Review)', *Monthly Film Bulletin*, Volume 41, Number 480 (January 1974), p. 6.
5. Tony Rayns, 'Bruce Lee: Narcissism and Nationalism' in *A Study of the Hong Kong Martial Arts Film*, 4th International Hong Kong Film Festival (Urban Council of Hong Kong, 1980), pp. 110–12 (p. 112).
6. Bey Logan, '*Enter the Dragon:* What Really Happened Behind the Scenes', *Martial Arts Legends Presents Bruce Lee* (August 1998), 19–32 (p. 19).
7. Bey Logan, *Hong Kong Action Cinema* (London: Titan, 1995), p. 43.
8. Ackbar Abbas, *Hong Kong: Culture and the Politics of Disappearance* (Minneapolis and London: University of Minnesota Press, 1997), p. 25.
9. Abbas, p. 23.
10. S. N. Ko, 'Under Western Eyes', in *Changes in Hong Kong Society Through Cinema*, 12th Hong Kong International Film Festival (Urban Council of Hong Kong, 1988), pp. 64–7 (p. 64).
11. Ko, p. 66.

12. Mike Roote, *Enter the Dragon* (London: Tandem, 1973), p. 57.
13. Abbas, p. 4.
14. Abbas, pp. 7–8.
15. Anne T. Ciecko, 'Transnational Action: John Woo, Hong Kong, Hollywood' in *Transnational Chinese Cinemas: identity, Nationhood, Gender*, ed. Sheldon Hsiao-peng Lu (Honolulu: University of Hawaii Press, 1997) pp. 221–37 (p. 223).
16. Robert Clouse, *The Making of Enter the Dragon* (Burbank, California: Unique Publications, 1987), p. 43.
17. Clouse. p. 44.
18. Sheldon Hsiao-peng Lu, Historical Introduction: Chinese Cinemas (1896–1996) and Transnational Film Studies' in Lu (ed.), pp. 1–31 (pp. 18–19).
19. Anne T. Ciecko, op cit and Steve Fore, 'Jackie Chan and the Cultural Dynamics of Global Entertainment' (pp. 239–62) in Lu (ed.).
20. Clouse, p. 18.
21. Rayns, 'Bruce Lee: Narcissism and Nationalism', p. 112.
22. *Marvel Special Edition: Master of Kung Fu*, number 15 (December 1973), p. 32.
23. Sax Rohmer, *The Mystery of Fu Manchu* (1913) in *The Fu Manchu Omnibus Volume 1* (London: Allison and Busby, 1995), p. 15.
24. Rayns, 'Bruce Lee: Narcissism and Nationalism', p. 110.
25. Lou Gaul, *The Fist That Shook the World: The Cinema of Bruce Lee* (Baltimore: Midnight Marquee Press, 1997), p. 131.
26. Tony Rayns, '*Rumble in the Bronx* (Review)', *Sight and Sound*, Volume 7, number 7 (July 1997), p. 51.
27. Teo, p. 117.
28. Liu Shi, 'Ng See Yuen: An Interview' in *A Study of the Hong Kong Martial Arts Film*, 1–31 (p. 145).
29. Abbas, p. 30.
30. Teo, p. 116.
31. Teo, p. 117.
32. Teo, p. 118.
33. Rayns, '*Enter the Dragon*', p. 6.
34. Richard Robinson, *Kung Fu: The Peaceful Way* (Manchester: Ensign, 1974), p. 28.

23

FISTS OF FURY: DISCOURSES OF RACE AND MASCULINITY IN THE MARTIAL ARTS CINEMA

Yvonne Tasker

It was undeniably the figure of Bruce Lee who popularized martial arts movies with Western audiences of the 1970s, even before his untimely death made him the stuff of legend. As well as being the first Chinese actor to become a major star in the West. Lee played a significant role in the redefinition of both the Hong Kong and the American action cinema. The martial arts cinema, itself part of the broader action traditions of a popular cinema that is defined by physicality and spectacle, encompasses a vast range of forms and subgenres. Chinese and American martial arts films, from both the 1970s and the present day, offer a fertile ground for an investigation of the play of sexualized racial discourses within the popular cinema.[1] In the pages that follow the operation of these discourses are discussed primarily in relation to the dominating figure of Bruce Lee, but also with reference to the work of recent Western martial arts stars, and the kung fu comedy associated with Jackie Chan. If these traditions have received little sustained critical attention, perhaps this is because critics tend to dismiss the products of the popular cinema as mindless, objecting to the visceral pleasures of physicality that are on offer. This lack of attention, however, will come as no surprise when we consider the marginal audiences with which the films are popular in the West, as well as the relative invisibility of Asian film culture.[2]

The typical action narrative operates around an axis of power and powerlessness, which is complexly articulated through the discourses of race, class,

From Harry Stecopoulos and Michael Vebel (eds) (1977), *Race and the Subject of Masculinities*, Durham: Duke University Press, pp. 315–35.

and sexuality that constitute the body of the hero. Themes of activity and passivity are central to all these discourses, as well as to the construction of the action hero. While the hero is, by definition, an active figure, he is also frequently rendered passive, subject to a range of restraints and oppressive forces. The hero is also defined in part by his suffering, which both lends him a certain tragic status, and demonstrates his remarkable ability to endure. The trajectory of tragic suffering is at its most extreme when enacted through the figure of the white male hero of recent Western action movies. While the black protagonists of these films, who usually act as partners to the white hero, are often damaged in some way, this seems to render them symbolically safe. By way of contrast, these same Western movies seem to need obsessively to cut up and punish the body of the white male hero, a body that they, not coincidentally, also offer up as sexual spectacle. In *Cyborg* (1989) the hero, played by Jean-Claude Van Damme, is described as a 'walking wound.' This phrase comes close to encapsulating the role of the white male hero in the contemporary action movie. He is both massively damaged and yet still functioning. It also indicates the potential purchase of a psychoanalytic discourse in understanding the complex ways in which figures of power and powerlessness are written over the body of a hero who is represented as both invincible and castrated.

'Race,' Masculinity, and the Action Tradition

In the action cinemas of both Hong Kong and America, the body of the hero or heroine is their ultimate, and often their only, weapon. A point of distinction between the two traditions lies in the way the Chinese hero often fights for and as part of a community, while within the American tradition the hero has become an increasingly isolated figure.[3] Both, however, tend to find themselves confronting a political system that is almost entirely corrupt, a villain who is the complete personification of evil. In Hong Kong films the use of the colonial past as a setting provides a specific populist point of reference. While some films are set in an unspecified or mythological past, the invocation of Japanese, Russian, or British forces allows for a more historically and culturally located narrative threat.[4] While Western films often tend toward the articulation of narratives centered on class conflict within a context of supposed racial harmony – the interracial male buddies – Hong Kong films are more likely to enact conflict in terms of the figures of colonial oppression, in which the enemy represents a threat from outside. The context of the anticolonial narrative is crucial for thinking about the racial discourses of masculine identity that are worked through in the Hong Kong martial arts cinema. As is evidenced most clearly in Bruce Lee's internationally successful films, the martial arts film of the 1970s deployed a discourse of macho Chinese nationalism that proved popular with a range of audiences. While the assertion of a powerful Chinese hero has an obvious appeal for Asian audiences, both in Asia and America, martial arts films were also hugely popular with black and white working-class audiences in the United States and in Europe during the 1970s. Such popularity can obviously be understood in terms of the production of fantasies of physical empowerment. These fantasies respond to the *constitution of the body through limits*.[5]

The redefinition of the swordplay film into the martial arts format familiar from the 1970s involved the increasing centrality of the fight, and hence the body, as a set piece. The action shifted to settings such as the martial arts school or the tournament, providing a showcase for the skills of the various performers.[6] A typical scenario consists of the fighting schools, in which the hero or heroine, who may be single or plural, fights to defend the honor of their school and the particular style of fighting associated with it against the incursion of a corrupt school, often associated with the Japanese.[7] In *The Chinese Boxer* a rogue Chinese who has been thrown out of the town some years before returns, bringing with him three Japanese karate experts who defeat the good school and take over the town. Only Wang Yu's character survives to take on and defeat these corrupt forces. In the film's final sequence, Wang Yu triumphs over the karate experts despite the machinations of their treacherous Chinese go-between, who has hidden himself under the snow. Within the anticolonial narrative of revenge, the collaborator is an ambiguous enemy. The figure of the traitorous intermediary, who in *The Chinese Boxer* is also a rapist, is interestingly written through sexual imagery in Bruce Lee's *Way of the Dragon* (U.S.: *Return of the Dragon*). A gender dysfunction of some kind comes to define the threat represented by this figure.

Way of the Dragon is set in contemporary Rome, a re-location that does not significantly alter the basic formulation of a Chinese community, here the owners and workers of a restaurant, under threat from an archetypal white capitalist with an army of hired thugs. The European location does allow for an explicit address to issues of Westernization, largely expressed through discourses of sexuality. The treacherous Chinese go-between is styled as a camp gay man who, dressed in outrageously bright Western clothes, minces about the restaurant cooing over Bruce Lee's muscles. Interestingly, he is one of the first characters in the film to realize what Bruce Lee's body is *for*, commenting on its hardness. As in his other movies, Lee's character holds back from fighting for some time and the film teases the audience as to when Lee will 'reveal' himself, a double moment in which he both reveals his body, removing his jacket, and his 'hidden' strength. The go-between functions not only as a passive figure against which the tough masculinity of Lee's character can be defined, but is also figured here in terms of a specifically (homo)sexual threat associated with Europe. The sexual naivete of Lee's character, Tang Lung, is indicated through his encounter with a European prostitute who takes him back to her apartment. He happily works out in front of a mirror but is horrified when she appears before him naked, running away in panic. Lee's absorption in his own image here is played off against those characters who have sexual designs on his body.

Set in Shanghai's international settlement, *Fist of Fury* (U.S.: *The Chinese Connection*) portrays the struggles of a Chinese school who are powerless against the political power of the Japanese school. A famous image from the film has Bruce Lee as Chen destroying a park sign saying 'No Dogs and Chinese.' This moment specifically enacts a fantasy that involves the refusal of physical limits. The film militantly champions a muscular Chinese national identity, despite the strictures of the law and against the insults of the Japanese. The go-between in this film acts as a translator for the Japanese – mediating between both language and culture. Disrupting a memorial service for their teacher, the go-between brings the Chinese a challenge, contemptuously referring to them as the 'Sick Man of Asia.' A close-up shows Chen's fist tightening, with the accompanying soundtrack amplifying and intensifying this physical expression of anger. Finally eschewing his promised restraint, Chen goes to the Japanese, defeating them all and declaring 'we are not sick men.' This assertion of nationalism is very clearly inscribed through the revelation of Lee's body – as he ritualistically removes his jacket – so that discourses of masculinity and nationhood are complexly bound up together in his star image. It is Lee's body that marks the assertion of a masculine national identity.

The American action cinema is more visibly concerned than other Hollywood forms with discourses of racial difference and masculinity. In a genre defined so much by physicality, black and Asian performers have had more opportunities to take on major roles. The spaces offered by such roles inevitably reinscribe stereotypical definitions of the physical, often further positioning black and Asian characters within a fantasized marginal space of criminality or deviance. Yet the martial arts film is also a genre in which racially overdetermined bodies, spaces for the projection of a range of fantasies, come into intimate physical contact. To this extent, racial difference functions partly within the films as a term that can deflect anxieties around their implicit homoeroticism. A violent physical confrontation, usually between men, forms the climax of the martial arts movie, which can be seen in terms of the staging or the performance of competing masculinities. In the memorable final fight from *Way of the Dragon*, Bruce Lee takes on karate champion Chuck Norris against the setting of Rome's Coliseum, a location that indicates the grandeur or at least the proportions of the occasion. The film offers competing masculinities and male bodies as a way of speaking about colonial conflict. Ritual images of limbering up, or extended training sequences, as well as the fights themselves, offer the male body as a sexualized spectacle, a spectacle that is inevitably overlaid with the complex meanings of the racially defined body.

The language and images through which the figure of the hero is articulated pose questions of gendered identity in terms of visual and verbal metaphors of hardness and softness. The hero's masculine identity is constructed as hardness. Using a range of methods to fight their opponents, the hero must avoid letting any stray kick or punch through his/her defense, so that the body functions as a sort of armor.[8] In *The Chinese Boxer* Wang Yu must make his hands like *iron*. The film's training sequences detail his disciplined struggle to become invincible, with images of him hardening his hands by placing them in a vat of heated iron filings, running and jumping with iron rods attached to his legs. These images provide a clear, since amplified, instance of the process by which a gendered identity is constituted through the necessary act of imagining, as well as resisting, bodily boundaries. We identify with a masculine identity that is constituted before our eyes, enacted through these narrative images of physical hardening. Judith Butler takes up this point when she suggests that 'the body is not a "being," but a variable boundary, a surface whose permeability is politically regulated.' Butler sees the body as 'a signifying practice within a cultural field of gender hierarchy and compulsory heterosexuality,' but the purchase of her analysis can also be extended in order to think about the racial constitution of the body (*Gender Trouble* 139). The symbolic centrality of a rhetoric of hardness in the martial arts films finds its parallel in those visual metaphors that express a fear of penetration, or of the softness that would allow it. As we'll see in the case of Bruce Lee, these fears are in part routed through the history of representation in which Chinese men and women have been constituted by the West as 'soft.'

A metaphoric language of gender that is intimately entwined with issues of place and status, is in operation in the fight film generally. For Western movies of recent years, a fear of softness is more directly connected to the deployment of a sexual, usually homoerotic, imagery of bodily penetration. The terrain of the action cinema is haunted by questions of masculine identity, that are in turn bound up with complex configurations of power and authority. As I've already implied, these ideological figures must be considered not only as they operate textually, but in terms of the audiences' relationship of identification to the figure of the hero. At the most obvious level, the figure of the graceful and ultimately triumphant martial arts hero offers a more perfect figure of identification for both male and female audiences, and in this sense our relationship to the image is one of primary narcissism.[9] The hero performs astounding physical feats with which we can identify – a process in which identity is *constituted through an identification* with the performance of the body. The notorious soundtrack of grunts that accompanies martial arts films forms part of the sensuous assertion of a physicality that transgresses limits. Our relationship as an audience to the adventures portrayed is also mediated through an identification with the Oedipal figure of the hero who struggles, who rebels against, but is subject to, the strictures of the social world.

Martial arts films combine sets of images that define the body in terms of aggression and sensuousness. It is no accident though that, given a particular understanding of masculinity, Western censors have read the films as primarily having to do with aggression. The sensuousness of movement is effaced, leaving only the violence of the body, a violence that is then projected onto a pathologized marginal audience. Yet if we reinstate the eroticized aspects of the graceful movement played out in these films, it also becomes apparent that the martial arts film has evolved as a cinematic form that allows men to look at men. In this the films legitimate a taboo look. More than this, they allow an identification with a male figure who other men will look at and who will enjoy being the object of that admiring gaze. In understanding this, the juxtaposition of martial arts and dance is a useful one. In Western culture, dance is constructed in opposition to fighting. It is also linked to the feminine, and often explicitly to images of male homosexuality. It is important to note though that this does not mean the *feminization* of the male dancer, a formulation that operates within a simple gender binary. Rather, dance offers the possibility of occupying a feminine position that involves, as with the martial arts film, an explicit location of the male body on display.

While Freud's theorized relationship between primary narcissism and homosexual desire (love of the self and the same) has proved problematic. I want to invoke this relationship here as one possible way of talking about the 'regressive' pleasures of the fight films. To some extent psychoanalysis functions to provide a framework within which terms such as 'regressive' and 'childish' do not carry the pejorative connotations that they do in everyday speech. Clearly regressive or childish pleasures are in operation through our identification with the hero as a more complete figure who triumphs over adversity. This fantasy of empowerment emerges from and speaks to those who, like children, find themselves in a position of powerlessness. In particular, an identification with the physical aspects of the hero's triumph is crucial – offering a very different set of pleasures to an intellectual identification. The regression at stake in the films can be seen as a resistance to (becoming) the father, a resistance that is radically different but nonetheless present in both the Chinese comedy films and the more earnest, or anxious, products associated with Bruce Lee and with more recent white stars. This resistance relates to the hero's location within a fantasy of omnipotence that is to some extent 'outside' the institutions that represent power.

In the revenge narratives around which many martial arts films are structured, the fight has an immense importance. The 'shift of the narrative discourse to violence.' suggests Chiao Hsiung-Ping, 'allows such a particularly intense and coherent statement of conflicts that the fight scenes become the real force carrying the narrative flow' ('Bruce Lee' 35). This understanding is echoed by Stuart Kaminsky who finds a Western point of reference for the films in the Hollywood musical, which has dance as its physical center, expressed in the set-piece musical number (see Kaminsky). Chiao Hsiung-Ping also links the figure of dance to images of physicality and the success of the martial arts films rather more effectively through an image from another hit film of the 1970s, *Saturday Night Fever*. We see the near-naked hero, Tony Manero (John Travolta) alone in his bedroom. On the wall are images of Sylvester Stallone (as Rocky) and Bruce Lee. All three men are figures who have achieved or seek to achieve success through their physicality – dance, boxing, kung fu – escaping the marginal spaces in which they find themselves through their achievements. The bodies of these working-class, marginalized men, which are their only resource, are turned through these forms into a spectacular site of pleasure rather than labor. Such images offer a physical constitution of identity that attempts to escape the policing to which the body is subject. The emphasis on physicality, then, allows the audience to identify with the construction of an oppositional identity sited on the body. This is pleasurable partly because the body is constituted through oppressive physical limitations.

Whilst Chiao's analysis was written retrospectively, critics at the time were not slow to posit links between the Western success of the martial arts films and a 'ghetto myth' through which dispossessed groups might identify with the hero's struggle to overcome. B. P. Flanigan's speculation on the success of the films is representative, asserting how it is 'obvious' that 'people who represent the most oppressed segment of a society would obtain great satisfaction, indeed enjoyment, in watching an antagonist be literally destroyed by the kung fu hero' (10). These equations – between audience and hero – are often rather schematic. The reference to the success of martial arts films with a black urban audience in the United States seems to represent an end point. The lack of further critical work suggests perhaps that the *process of accounting* is all, a process not unlike those regulatory processes of classification familiar from other spheres. An 'obvious' explanation can ultimately operate to confirm the marginalized audience in their marginal place, since explaining the appeal of the films somehow exhausts them. Is this because the films, like their audiences, are assumed to be 'simple'? By contrast, Chiao's analysis begins to unravel the complex articulation of race, class, and sexuality that is elaborated in the differing Chinese and American reception of these films, as well as within the revenge narratives of the films themselves.

While I am wary of generalization in relation to an area so often characterized precisely as 'simple,' I wish to risk one at this stage. This is to suggest that while both Hong Kong and American martial arts films are staging fantasies, the primary focus in each tradition is different. Within the Hong Kong cinema the films can be seen as primarily working through fantasies of empowerment that emphasize social relations. By contrast, the Americanized version of the martial arts format has increasingly become used as a space within which to stage homoerotic fantasies, primarily working through issues and anxieties around white male sexuality. Now it is nonetheless the case that both traditions employ a gendered rhetoric through which they articulate their narratives of revenge and struggle.[10]

Bruce Lee and the Remasculinization of the Chinese Body

'Remasculinization' may be a problematic notion within discourses about race and sexuality, potentially implying a return to a mythical gender stability, yet it nonetheless provides a way of situating a discussion of the central figure of Bruce Lee.[11] The significance of Lee's Western success lies partly in his articulation of a tough masculinity within nationalistic films that can be read against a history of 'feminizing' Western representations of Chinese men. The significance of this shift becomes even more apparent when we consider the one Western vehicle in which Lee starred, *Enter the Drogon*, a film that gives him an asexual persona and that seeks to rewrite his image into that of a representative of colonial authority. Before moving on to a discussion of Lee's films in this context, I want to make a brief digression into literature. In her novel of Chinese-American womanhood. *The Woman Warrior*, Maxine Hong Kingston writes fantasies of omnipotence precisely in terms of shifting gendered identities. Thus her narrator tells us '[W]hen we Chinese girls listened to the adults talking-story, we learned that we failed if we grew up to be but wives or slaves. We could be heroines, swordswomen.' She speculates on whether women 'were once so dangerous that they had to have their feet bound' (*Woman Warrior* 25). The polarized terms, of bondage and of the swordswoman's raging freedom, are initially assigned a sex and a gender – female/feminine and male/masculine – from which the text seeks to break free. Kingston uses another opposition – that between China and America – in order to partly deconstruct this gendered binary. Her various narrators are, for much of the text, caught between the two. Kingston's writing invokes a variety of cross-cultural perspectives within an American context, in which China is read, through Orientalist discourses, as a mystical/feminine space.

Kingston's second book, *China Men*, opens with a short fragment. 'On discovery,' which describes Tang Ao's journey to America, the 'land of women.' He is captured by women who remove his armor and slowly, painfully 'feminize' him. He is made up, his ears are pierced and his feet bound until, when he is serving food at court, we are told that his 'hips swayed and his shoulders swivelled because of his shaped feet.' He has become a beautiful and painful spectacle: ' "She's pretty, don't you agree?" the diners said, smacking their lips at his dainty feet as he bent to put dishes before them' (*China Men* 10). In this fragment and in the different narratives that follow, King-Kok Cheung sees both the book and its hostile critical reception from Asian critics as revealing 'not only the similarities between Chinese men's and Chinese women's suffering but also the correlation between these men's umbrage at racism and their misogynist behaviour' (240). In this she points to the impossibility of tackling questions of gender 'in the Chinese American cultural terrain without delving into the historically enforced "feminization" of Chinese American men, without confronting the dialectics of racial stereotypes and nationalist reactions or, above all, without wrestling with die-hard notions of masculinity and femininity in both Asian and Western cultures'(234). This perception is crucial in enabling King-Kok Cheung to both critique and contextualize the attempts by male literary editors to reproduce and update a heroic masculine tradition of Asian literature. In a footnote Cheung also refers to Bruce Lee, pointing to his significance in representations of Chinese masculinity but also to his rather inhuman characterization in *Enter the Dragon*, the American film that is taken up below.

When Bruce Lee died in 1973 he was given two funerals. Chiao Hsiung-Ping writes of the 30,000 people who attended his Hong Kong funeral, suggesting though that the event '*was only symbolic*' since the real thing 'was held in Seattle, and Steve McQueen and James Coburn were among the pall-bearers'

('Bruce Lee' 31; emphasis added). What was this double ceremony symbolic of? Perhaps it indicates something of the way in which Lee was positioned, and positioned himself, as a star in both Asia and America. Bruce Lee was, and remains, the only Chinese star to achieve an international visibility that included the West. He was also a very *visible* star in that his films tended to emphasize his physicality in a way that some have characterized as narcissistic. Given that the role of the movie actor is defined by display, the designation 'narcissistic' tends to be invoked only when critics feel such display is inappropriate or unsettling. In this sense it is significant that Lee's assertion of a strong, muscular Chinese hero should be so often dubbed unsettling by contemporary Western critics. Within his films Lee's lithe muscularity is played off in spectacular film battles against huge, white, muscular opponents: Chuck Norris in *Way of the Dragon*, Robert Baker in *Fist of Fury*. I've already noted the way in which Lee's films build up to the moment when he will fight, keeping him clothed up to that point as a form of disguise. Assuming a variety of disguises in *Fist of Fury*, Lee/Chen uses his *invisibility* as a Chinese man to spy on the Japanese school. The play of disguise and revelation is also a play, once more, on an accumulated history of images of softness and hardness, passivity and masculinity.

The hardness of Lee's body and of his star image emerges from a history of softness, a history of images in which both Chinese men and women had been represented as passive and compliant. In an early film appearance as a heavy in *Marlowe* (1968), James Garner suggests that Lee's character is gay, thus leading him to lose his temper and leap to his death. Garner's jibe picks up on the extent to which the display of Lee's body and physical grace was to be emphasized in his persona. The display of the male body in action is felt to be unsettling here, making too explicit as it does the homoeroticism implicit in these man-to-man showdowns. Later on in his career, Lee was turned down in favor of David Carradine for the lead role in the television series *Kung Fu*. Of Carradine, Chuck Norris is reported to have said, with rather disarming honesty, that he 'is about as good a martial artist as I am an actor' Lee himself pondered whether perhaps 'they weren't ready for a Hopalong Wong' (qtd in Glaessner 91). The earnestness of the Lee persona, along with the comedic sections of his films, can be situated against this cinematic context. Lee's struggle within America, which can be contrasted sharply with his success in Hong Kong, has emerged as a key element in the star image that has developed since his death. Chuck Norris conveys something of this in the following description of Lee, which is taken from Norris's indicatively entitled autobiography, *The Secret of Inner Strength*: 'Bruce lived and breathed the martial arts. I still recall the night I dropped in on him at home and found him in the den watching television. He was lying on his back in front of the TV set with his young son, Brandon, sitting on his stomach. Bruce had leg weights wrapped around his ankles. He had barbells in his hands. While bouncing Brandon on his stomach, he was inhaling and exhaling, thus tightening the muscles of his abdomen. At the same time, he was doing leg-ups and arm exercises' (67). Such testimonies form part of the mythology surrounding Bruce Lee, a mythos that is constructed through images of an obsessive commitment to training and the struggle to succeed, to become a star.

Lee's image speaks of a struggle to become hard, to negate an imputed softness. Another aspect of this is Lee's reputed refusal to follow any one school of fighting, instead appropriating and adapting a range of styles. Lee is complexly positioned as a star in both, and 'in-between,' Asia and America. Chiao Hsiung-Ping explores this positioning 'in-between' in terms of what she calls Lee's 'cross-cultural savvy.' Having worked in both industries, she points out, Lee was in a good position to judge what would appeal across the two. He was responsible for moves toward the use of martial artists rather than actors in Hong Kong films, as well as the reduction of rapid editing, camera tricks, the use of trampolines, and so on. Lee 'knew the generic importance of the fighting scene, but . . . strove for a "believable" kung fu, . . . Oriental fantasies were reduced and Western realism was emphasized' ('Bruce Lee' 33). In cinematic terms the meaning of this opposition between fantasy and realism is clear, avoiding trick camera work and so on. At an ideological level this opposition echoes a history of racial stereotypes, a history that seeks to represent the kinds of fantasies at work in the Western imaginary as somehow 'real.'[12]

If a strong masculinity is central to Bruce Lee's image, then this is accompanied by anxieties that prefigure the uncertainties that surround the personae of many white male stars today. That this image of the Chinese man was perceived as problematic within Hollywood is evident in *Enter the Dragon*. The film centers on three men, heroes who are constructed through the use of racial stereotypes. Bruce Lee plays Lee, who is the center of a film that is to a large extent a showcase for his skills. Along with Lee are a white American character called Roper, played by John Saxon (a B movie actor who received equal billing with Lee), and an African American, Williams, played by Jim Kelly, who went on to play the part of 'Black Belt Jones.' *Enter the Dragon* does not, however, go in for the extensive interracial male bonding that typifies many action pictures of recent years. While the three heroes talk to each other at various points, they do not act together and their stories are kept discrete. There is one key moment of recognizable male bonding in the film, between Williams and Roper when they first meet. Significantly, this moment centers on their shared experiences in Vietnam. Indeed, within the narratives of many American martial arts movies, Vietnam functions as the space/time when the hero acquired his fighting skills. Perhaps because of the very centrality of a 'Vietnam' constituted against an Oriental Other in American films, *Enter the Dragon* is clearly uncomfortable with its racial mix, a mix that represents Warner Bros.'s very tentative attempts to promote a Chinese star. Anecdotally, while the film is often seen by Western audiences as Lee's greatest achievement – and it is the film for which he is best known in the West, Asian audiences were suspicious of the film (Chiao, 'Bruce Lee' 37; see also Glaessner 93–6).

We are introduced to Lee in the Shaolin Temple, where an English official, Braithwaite, enlists his help against the evil Han (Shek Kin) who is involved in both drugs and sexual slavery. Han holds a martial arts tournament every three years on his fortress island as a way for him to recruit talent to his organization. The struggles against colonial opponents found in *Fist of Fury* and *Way of the Dragon* are replaced by Han who, with his white cat, is very clearly derived from a James Bondian lineage. Such a tradition does not offer a particularly fruitful space for the articulation of a Chinese identity, so that Lee seems to be placed once more in the role of Kato, the sidekick he had played years before in the American television series *The Green Hornet*. After Lee has agreed to act on behalf of the British, he is given a further motivation in a flashback that tells of the death of his sister (Angela Mao Ying). Roper is a compulsive gambler whose debts have led him to fight in the upcoming tournament. Williams's motivation for attending is less clear since we see him saying his good-byes wordlessly in an all-black martial arts school. As he is traveling to the airport Williams is harassed by two white policemen. Williams knocks the men out and steals their police car, signaling an underdeveloped narrative of racial conflict within America – narrative that is displaced through images of the Orient.

In the complex relationship between the articulation of a Chinese and a masculine identity in Lee's image, the following comments from Robert Clouse, director of *Enter the Dragon*, are indicative:

> He [Lee] had this strut . . . they showed me his first three films at Warner Bros. and . . . I said the first thing we have to do is kick the strut out of Bruce Lee. We're going to Westernize him to some degree. They wanted an international star. I said we would put him in carefully tailored suits instead of just his Chinese suits. We'll show him both ways. He should look as though he'd be comfortable in New York or London . . . [In *Enter the Dragon*] he comes strutting down the field toward the end of the big battle . . . And I said . . . You're beyond that now. A Western audience doesn't like the obvious strut. Let's play it straight there.' ('interview with Robert Clouse' 43)

Caught up in fantasies of racial and sexual identity, Clouse speaks through oppositions of savagery and civilization. Western suits versus Chinese suits. Gail Ching-Liang Low heads her discussion of cultural cross-dressing with a pertinent statement from Frantz Fanon that the 'colonised is elevated above his jungle status in proportion to his adoption of the mother country's cultural standards. He becomes whiter as he renounces his blackness, his jungle' (qtd in Low 83). Such a logic structures Clouse's desire to put Lee in Western clothes in order that he be 'comfortable' in the West, which is really to say that the West would be comfortable with him. Clouse's reference to 'playing it straight' in this context unwittingly indicates the homoerotic imaginary that underpins the cinematic performance of Lee's body – a performance in which the body is offered as sexual spectacle, as a site of pleasure rather than subjection.

This same logic is also expressed through Clouse's (failed) intention to *kick the strut* out of Lee. This phrase signals something of the fear and mistrust that develops around Bruce Lee's star status in the West, fears bound up with the tough nationalistic male identity that is championed in his Hong Kong films. I don't want to suggest that Lee was completely controlled by this discourse, since the parts of *Enter the Dragon* that he directed, and his own performance in particular, do emerge (complete with strut) as to some extent separate from the messy compromise that is the film's attempt to cater to a range of audiences. The confusion of the film is expressly clear in its mobilization of sexualized discourses of race. The three fighters are, in appropriately Bondian-decadent style, offered the choice of a harem of women. Roper selects the white woman who seems to be in charge, while Williams selects four Asian women. Predictably enough, Lee's character absents himself, selecting a woman he knows to be a spy who has been placed on the island.

It is Kelly as Williams who must bear the burden of the film's discourse about race. It is no surprise then that the stereotype of the black stud is invoked or that Williams does not survive to the end of the movie. It is he who also voices the film's social commentary, pointing regretfully to the ghettos of the city. Amidst the general success of Hong Kong action pictures in the America of the 1970s, producers were not slow to notice the appeal of these films to an urban black audience. Black martial arts films, which built on the success of films like *Shaft* (1971), invoked a hypersexualized image of the black man. By contrast, one of the most enduring Western stereotypes of the East is as a site of a mystical, asexual knowledge. Richard Fung captures this, setting out a representational dichotomy in which Asian men are either an 'egghead/wimp' or 'the kung fu master/ninja/samurai.' He is 'sometimes dangerous, sometimes friendly, but almost always characterized by a desexualized Zen asceticism.' Fung uses Fanon, who describes how 'the Negro is eclipsed. He is turned into a penis. He *is* a penis,' to draw a contrast with Western representations of the Asian man who 'is defined by a striking absence down there' (148). In *Enter the Dragon* Chinese sexuality is erased while blackness, in the figure of Jim Kelly, becomes the overdetermined space through which the film signifies both sexuality and racial difference.

Western Stars and the Martial Arts Cinema

A commentary on the workings of the Western action cinema is useful here in contextualizing the kinds of operation at work in a film like *Enter the Dragon* or more recent Orientalist fictions, such as *Showdown in Little Tokoyo*, which I discuss below. The American martial arts film, which is a subsidiary of the big-budget action picture, has very little cultural prestige attached to it. Indeed, Western martial arts stars frequently express the desire to move on from the so-called 'chop-socky' action film into more conventional action movies. Jean-Claude Van Damme is no exception, and his films have gradually moved away from showcasing martial arts into more traditional heroics. In any case, the overdeveloped muscular frames of the white Western stars are geared much more toward the sort of static, posed display involved in bodybuilding than the quick-fire action seen in the Hong Kong films. Given this tendency toward static display, it is perhaps not surprising to find that the films are centrally concerned with the sexual commodification of the (usually white) male body. The body is portrayed as sexual spectacle within a narrative that offers a critique of such commodification. Though there is not space here to develop the point fully, the different status of martial arts and other American action pictures can be understood partly through the sense that the martial arts form already carries the kinds of feminized associations that the Western imaginary has long ascribed to the East. The insistent homoeroticism of films featuring stars such as Van Damme, only makes it more important to distance him from such implicit feminization. Thus, it is black characters who once again take up the burden of a pathologized (homo) sexuality in the Western films.

A.W.O.L. (1990) casts Van Damme as Lyon, a soldier who has deserted the legion to visit his dying brother in America. He works his passage stoking the boilers of a ship, a typical plot device in that it both stresses the body as a site of manual labor and allows Van Damme to remove his clothes. Such moments of display are combined with set-piece fights. On his arrival Lyon meets Joshua, a crippled but street-smart black man, who initially seeks to exploit Lyon's fighting skill, though the two soon become buddies. The theme of the commodification of the working-class male body, typical of American fight movies, is also explicitly bound into the sexual implications of that commodification here, as Lyon finds himself working for 'The Lady,' who runs a high-class bare-knuckle fighting operation. The controlling figure of Cynthia, 'The Lady,' is a deeply fearful image of the powerful woman who at first seeks to control Lyon and then, when he spurns her sexually, matches him against a vicious white fighter known as Attila, who literally tears his opponents in two. The anxiety attendant on the commodification of the white male body is mediated here through the figure of the powerful (masculine) woman. The version of black masculinity articulated in these films is also crucial to securing the symbolic position of the hero. The recurrent figure of the 'damaged' black man is central, with the crippled Joshua fulfilling this role in *A.W.O.L.*, and Hawkins (who has a 'dead' eye) befriending Van Damme in *Death Warrant* (1991). The physical flaws of these initially hostile but ultimately dependable men make them symbolically safe in an anxious representational world. Blackness also functions then as a space within which to deal with fears around homosexual desire.

In *Death Warrant* Van Damme plays Burke, a cop who goes undercover in a maximum-security jail. The prison narrative is a favorite of the American action cinema, allowing as it does for the free play of homoerotic images and for the repressive mobilization of stock characters, such as the sadistic white warden and guards, dependable black old-timers, and hysterical, knife-wielding Latins. Here the hero is explicitly threatened with rape, an assault that the film's editing implies, though it cannot seem to explicitly state. While Western martial arts and other action movies thrive on interracial same-sex friendships, homosexuality or any notion of gay desire remains almost exclusively expressed in terms of threat and violence. The fight then provides the perfect space for male physical intimacy – since that intimacy is accompanied by a compensatory brutal violence. Serving to highlight the sexual significance of the 'castrated' black man in these fictions is another level of blackness conjured up by *Death Warrant* in the figure of Priest. He inhabits a mysterious realm beneath the prison: 'The lower you go the funkier it gets in this place,' Burke's cell mate tells him cheerfully, adding that he should 'cover his ass' and 'I mean that literally – it's not a figure of speech.' We are told that even the guards won't come here – it is a space then that is both sexual and totally other. Here we find Priest, surrounded by his 'ladies,' male/female inmates who function as profoundly unstable and hauntingly present figures in the film – images of the subterranean depths that lie beneath the sexual relations as relations of power that structure the prison world. The film both acknowledges and plays to the existence of gay desire, in its images and its narrative, while finally projecting this desire onto a space of pathologized black masculinity, in which sexuality is part of a more general excess.

An earlier Van Damme movie, *Kickboxer* (1989), not only teams the hero with a 'damaged' black man – Taylor, a cynical veteran scarred by his experiences in Vietnam – but also employs stereotypical images of the East. Thai kickboxing champion Tong Po embodies the Orient as sexual threat, alongside the figures of the mythic sage and the virginal maiden. The structure of this film is a familiar one in the West. A young white man persuades an ancient 'Oriental' man to teach him the skills of a secret martial art. At the same time, he typically meets an 'innocent' girl and falls in love. Although he seems to face impossible odds, he ultimately wins out in the final moments of the film. Now this is to some extent a familiar narrative of the Hong Kong cinema in the 1970s. The hero is initially beaten, learns a secret technique that makes him invincible, and, after extended torturous training, is ultimately triumphant – this is roughly the plot of *The Chinese Boxer*. But the version of this narrative that places the white hero at the center represents a significant rewriting.

To think about this further I'll refer briefly to an American cop movie. *Showdown in Little Tokoyo* (1991). Starring Dolph Lundgren and Brandon Lee, this is a rare film in its casting of a Chinese actor in a major heroic role. The film seeks to capitalize on an action-comedy tradition by casting Lee as a thoroughly Westernized Japanese-American, who to some extent undercuts the strong-silent performance of costar Dolph Lundgren.[13] In a perverse colonial logic, Aryan beefcake Lundgren plays a cop brought up in Japan who styles himself as a samurai warrior. His knowledge of Japanese tradition, language, and culture is played off against Lee's Westernized persona. The film's fantasy of cultural cross-dressing operates both to negate the homoeroticism implicit in the buddy relationship and to produce a complex fantasy of white mastery through the appropriation and penetration of the other's culture. Speaking of fantasies of cultural cross-dressing in nineteenth-century imperialist literature, Gail Ching-Liang Low points out that since 'the Orient becomes, through Western imagination, a site of excess sexuality and deviant behaviour that must be penetrated and controlled,' then the 'violation of a subject-culture may also be read as a sexualised text' (95).[14] In *Showdown in Little Tokoyo* this fantasy might be directly interpreted in terms of the racist articulation of American fears around Japanization. That these fears are bound up with masculine identity is perhaps most apparent in the 'comic' moment when Lee's character compliments Lundgren's on the size of his penis. Recalling Richard Fung's comments on Western myths of Asian sexuality as asexuality, it is clear that Lundgren's superwhite, muscular body functions as a fetish within the film. The body is clearly constituted by 'race,' and yet it also refuses the limits of that constitution. The freedom to shift, transgress, and adopt racial identities in this way is, of course, as Ching-Liang Low points out, available to different groups differently (98).[15]

Jackie Chan: Masculinity and Kung Fu Comedy

Jackie Chan's combination of action with slapstick comedy is quite distinct from the earnest and anxious suffering of the white stars, and from the dominating figure of Bruce Lee. His films are much more at ease with the hectic heroics of their male protagonists, heroics that are at once offered as spectacle and comically undercut. Comic interludes and punch lines punctuate even relatively tense narratives such as the *Police Story* films. I'd like to make some brief comments on Jackie Chan's films here as a way of talking about a very different kind of Hong Kong filmmaking to that associated with Bruce Lee. The films use a variety of physical set pieces – both comic and violent – drawing on a theatrical tradition that is committed to a different kind of spectacle than the more static bodily display at work in many American films. This is most apparent in the orchestration of group fights of amazing complexity, as in the bar room brawl and the final showdown of *Project A*. The more restrained playground battle in *Police Story 2* pitches Chan against a group of thugs, but even here, when the hero fights alone, the camera work is carefully choreographed around the scene, rather than the individual hero, as spectacle.

Of course, many of the films I've already discussed include comic moments, though I've not focused on this aspect of the action tradition. What distinguishes the quick-fire timing and slapstick comedy for which Chan has become famous is the infiltration of comedy into the fight scenes themselves, fights that as we've seen, form the center of the martial arts movie. In Chan's films, fights are played both seriously and for laughs, as when opponents come to blows and then back off shaking their fists or rubbing their heads in pain. Such moments admit both the possibility of pain and the vulnerability of the body. There is an indicative moment in *Wheels on Meals* when costars Chan and Yuen Biao are involved in a street fight. They look at each other, agree that their opponents are too tough and simply run away. Chan, while at times a very graceful fighter, also plays on the way in which both the body and technology lets its owner down. Thus he often seems to win his fights more by good luck and determination than skill. In the middle of a tense fight at the end of *Wheels on Meals*, Chan frees himself from a hold by tickling his opponent. Similarly, most of the people in a Jackie Chan film are *at some point* a fighter – characters are not written as professional fighters and they are not necessarily students or teachers in a martial arts school. Pauline Yeung, the romantic lead in *Dragons Forever*, who spends most of her time being rescued or wooed, suddenly, and quite inexplicably, produces a short set-piece display of fighting skill, knocking out a bad guy in the films final showdown.

In Chan's movies it is more often the case that women are either explicitly cast as, or ultimately revealed to be, girlish. They increasingly seem to represent a troublesome presence, both an annoying and a fascinating distraction from adventures and from the concerns of male friendship. Heterosexual romance is an important term for the definition of an adult masculine identity in the films, but is also the cause of myriad problems, as in the two *Police Story* films. The chorus of three women who keep getting in Chan's way in *Operation Condor: Armour of God 2* (1991) represents an extreme articulation of women-as-femininity-as-chaos. An inordinate amount of screen time is given over to the comic demonstration of female incompetence, by contrast to Western movies that are much more likely to exclude women altogether. The original *Armour of God* was reviewed and marketed in the West as Chan's attempt to cash in on the success of the *Indiana Jones* films. While these successful films do provide a reference point, there is more than a little naiveté in the assumption that Hong Kong always follows in the wake of Hollywood, especially given Hong Kong's long tradition of producing epic adventure films. So while some critics suggested the film was Westernized, they didn't in turn acknowledge the ways in which *The Armour of God* redefines and undercuts those Hollywood traditions that it does draw on. Indeed, Chan emerges from a changed industrial context in Hong Kong, and the figure of the adventurer is rewritten within its existing traditions. Chan plays Jackie, the 'Asian Hawk,' an ex–pop star turned adventurer who tracks down ancient artifacts for sale to the highest bidder. The film allows Chan to explore a Europe that is constructed as an alien and exotic territory. The hero is pitted against a fabulously bizarre sect of evil monks who are ensconced in a mountain retreat. A rather camp waiter tells them that the monks come down once a month to fetch supplies and women, establishing both the opponents and the terrain as sexually decadent. The terms of Orientalist fantasies are turned around on themselves, as Europe becomes the site of an exotic adventure for the Chinese heroes and heroine.

The film turns on the relationship between Jackie and his best friend Alan. Though Alan is to some extent a clownish character, this is set up differently to the physical comedy constructed around Chan. Though we see him early on performing in a spectacular stage show before a huge Hong Kong crowd, he lacks masculine competence within the film's terms. He is something of a fashion plate, modeling a series of stylish clothes throughout the film. Given this characterization it is not surprising that Alan is useless in a fight, pointing out hysterically that he doesn't believe in violence while holding onto Jackie for protection, getting them into trouble and needing to be rescued. If the fight bears the narrative discourse of the martial arts film, then a hero who cannot fight is an oddity. Within the film's discourse about masculinity Alan is clearly situated within a feminine position that is played for laughs. The comedy format allows for an articulation of masculinity that is to some extent fluid, not expressed exclusively in terms of a muscular hardness. Ultimately, though, *The Armour of God* falls back on blackness as a space of sexualized deviance. In one of the film's final sequences, when Jackie is attempting to steal the armor, four black furies are turned on him. These fighting women are kitted out in black corsets and stilettos. Both comic and fetishistic, these women represent the displacement of an exaggerated sexuality onto blackness. This image echoes the opening of the film, located in a fantasized Africa, in which Jackie fools a black tribe by talking gibberish. He escapes, stealing the sword that is part of the 'armour of god,' using a variety of gadgets and stunts. The structures at work here are replicated in the recent sequel, *Operation Condor* (1991), which again begins with Jackie fooling a black African tribe. This time he only narrowly escapes from the threat of marriage. The 'Asian Hawk' achieves his heroic identity at the expense of an Africa constructed as primitive and easily fooled.

Unlike Bruce Lee, the struggle for American success is not foregrounded in Jackie Chan's star image, though he also made a rather disastrous American movie with Robert Clouse at one point in his career.[16] 'Bruce had that hard tight look whenver he wanted it,' observes Clouse, the man who we recall wanted to 'kick the strut' out of Lee. Clouse goes on to remark that he 'thought Jackie Chan had it but he was soft' ('Interview with Robert Clouse' 9). Chan's 'softness' does not consist in a lack of muscularity or an inability to fight, but more in a refusal either to take the male body too seriously or to play the part of Oriental other. Chan's persona is built on the cheerful admission of vulnerability at work in his films – most obviously in the inclusion at the end of the movies of outtakes featuring stunts gone wrong. And while he frequently gets beaten up in his films, he is nonetheless in control. As Chan put it: 'In Hong-Kong, I can control everything. In Hollywood I'm just a Chinese actor who speaks bad English' (Rayns 84).

Discourses of race and masculinity are elaborated in vastly different ways in the various martial arts films discussed in this essay. I have sought to comment on some of the many contrasting traditions and subgenres, and to argue that the construction of racial and gendered identities in the genre is not as simple or as easily characterized as it may seem. Though many films work to reinscribe sexual and racial stereotypes, our readings also need to be situated within a historical and a cinematic context. The discussion of the very distinct star images and films of Bruce Lee, Jean-Claude Van Damme, and Jackie Chan emphasizes the radically different ways that the ideas, images, and themes associated with the martial arts genre can be inflected. Indeed, though I have used the term 'genre' here, it is probably evident from the range of films discussed that there is no clearly definable set of rules that can encapsulate the martial arts film across either the output of decades or the different industries of Hollywood and Hong Kong.

I have sought to argue, though, that there are certain themes recurring across different films – power and powerlessness, physical limitations and their transgression, narratives of revenge, and so on – that have a clear resonance for the discussion of the construction of masculine identities in the cinema. A central focus for this discussion has been the role of the body in the genre, with the suggestion that we can see the constitution of gendered identities in the cinema as operating through the act of imagining and resisting bodily boundaries. The discussion of various films and stars offered here can only further emphasize the extent to which ideas and images of masculine power – defined through such figures as the 'hard' male body, the ability to bear suffering, and ultimately to triumph – are intertwined with discourses of race, class, sexuality, and nationality.

NOTES

Thanks to Val Hill, Leon Hunt, and Gwion Jones for their ideas and comments.

1. While the primary focus of this essay is male martial arts stars, Hong Kong cinema has a long tradition of female fighters. Western martial artist Cynthia Rothrock went to Hong Kong to make films such as *Above the Law* (with Yuen Biao), while in Hollywood producers seem more likely to cast her as a 'girlfriend.'
2. Popular Asian cinema has an extensive circulation in the West through forms such as video. The point I'm making here is that these forms are marginal in comparison to the more widely available and more widely discussed Hollywood material. There are complex links between the popular cinemas of Hong Kong, Taiwan, Japan, and Bombay. These traditions are often ignored by Western criticism, though attention has been paid to more prestigious Asian films. For an excellent industrial survey see Lent.
3. This tendency is most evident in the frequent use of the figure of the Vietnam veteran, portrayed as a slightly unbalanced man who has lost his comrades in battle and been betrayed by his government.
4. I do not know of any Hong Kong action films that deal explicitly with the colonial present, though British figures are very visible, if marginal, in films – for example, the *Police Story* and *Project A* films. Chiao Hsiung-Ping describes *Project A: II* (1987) as 'given over to addressing the contradictory situation whereby Hong Kong now fears the 1997 return to the mainland and would rather remain colonised' ('Distinct Taiwanese' 160).
5. In *The Wretched of the Earth* Frantz Fanon writes that 'The native is a being hemmed in; apartheid is simply one form of the division into compartments of the colonial world. The first thing which the native learns is to stay in his place and not go beyond certain limits' (40). Fanon also emphasizes that the experience of the world through such oppressive limits generates fantasies of physical empowerment. See also Robins and Cohen, especially *Knuckle Sandwich: Growing Up in the Working-Class City* 94–103, in which they discuss the appeal of the martial arts; and see Walkerdine, for a discussion of class in relation to narratives of fighting. A key reference point for my argument here is Butler's *Gender Trouble*. Butler uses Foucault to discuss the constitution of the body through signs.

6. See Glaessner 54.
7. Glaessner outlines the function of the antagonist school in these films as 'a straightforward stand-in for the institutions involved in Japanese imperialism or for their less overt infiltration into Chinese life' (36).
8. The most useful reference point for a consideration of this play of qualities is in the work of anthropologist Mary Douglas, such as *Natural Symbols* and *Purity and Danger*. Theweleit takes up the image of the body as armor in relation to militarist culture in *Male Fantasies*. Theweleit, however, tends toward a pathologization of the ways in which identity is constructed through the establishment of bodily limits.
9. I'm referring here to Freud's essay 'On Narcissism' (1914), in which narcissism is situated as part of human development rather than a property of a perverse few.
10. Male buddy relationships are crucial to the Hong Kong action film and have become more explicitly eroticized in some recent films such as *The Killer* (1989). See Chiao, 'The Distinct Taiwanese' 163, for what she describes as a 'macho/gay feel' to some recent Hong Kong films. The distinction I'm seeking to draw here, though, is around the extent to which recent Western films quite obsessively center on relationships between men.
11. Jeffords interestingly uses the term 'remasculinization' in the context of recent representations around Vietnam. See her *The Remasculinization of America*.
12. Though he doesn't discuss China in an extensive way, Said's *Orientalism* is a crucial point of reference here. Bhabha's writings on colonial discourse develop these points within a psychoanalytic framework. See his 'Of Mimicry and Man: The Ambivalence of Colonial Discourse' and 'Sly Civility.'
13. Jackie Chan was also called on to play a Japanese character in the *Cannonball Run* films, part of an early attempt to break into Western markets.

    Brandon Lee seems aware that his father's name has given him an access to the American industry denied to other Chinese actors. The publicity machine seems determined to push this line, dubbing him 'Son of the Dragon.' See, for example, 'Interview with Brandon Lee.' Since this essay was originally written, Brandon Lee died in unusual circumstances and we have seen the much hyped release of his last film, finished with the help of computer technology. The turn to be taken by media mythology around his death remains to be seen.
14. Bhabha's writings (see note 12) are relevant here in terms of the processes of failed identification at work in the complex fantasies of mastery that structure colonial discourse.
15. Mercer offers an interesting discussion of Michael Jackson's changing image in this context in his 'The Boy Who Fell to Earth' 34–5.
16. The film was *The Big Brawl* (1980), which Clouse directed. This is not to suggest that Chan is somehow a more 'subversive' figure than Lee. Rather that the two emerged from very different historical moments.

Bibliographical References

Bhabha, Homi K (1984), 'Of mimicry and men: the ambivalence of colonial discourse', *October* 28, pp. 125–33.

Bhabha, Homi K (1985), 'Sly civility', *October* 34, pp. 71–80.

Butler, Judith (1990), *Gender Trouble: Feminism and the Subversion of Identity*, New York: Routledge.

Cheung, King-Kok (1990), 'The woman warrior versus the Chinaman Pacific: must a Chinese American critic choose between feminism and heroism', in Marianne Hirsch and Evelyn Fox Keller (eds), *Conflicts in Feminism*, New York: Routledge, pp. 234–51.

Chiao Hsiung-Ping (1981), 'Bruce Lee: his influence on the evolution of the Kung Fu genre', *Journal of Popular Film and Television*, 9.1.

Chiao Hsiung-Ping (1991), 'The distinct Taiwanese and Hong Kong cinemas' in Chris Berry (ed.), *Perspectives on Chinese Cinema*, London: BFI, pp. 155–65.
Douglas, Mary (1973), *Natural Symbols*, Harmondsworth: Penguin.
Douglas, Mary (1969), *Purity and Danger*, London: Routledge and Kegan Paul.
Fanon, Frantz (1967), *The Wretched of the Earth*, Harmondsworth: Penguin.
Flanigan, B. P. (1974), 'Kung Fu crazy, or the invasion of the "chop suey Easterners" ', *Cineaste*, 15.3.
Freud, Sigmund (1953–74), 'On narcissism', *The Standard Edition of the Complete Psychological Works of Sigmund Freud*, London: Hogarth, vol. 14, pp. 243–58.
Fung, Richard (1991), 'Looking for my penis: the eroticised Asian in gay video porn' in Bad Object-Choices (ed.), *How Do I Look?: Queer Film and Video*, Seattle: Bay, pp. 145–60.
Glaessner, Verina (1974), *Kung Fu: Cinema of Vengeance*, London: Lorrimar.
'Interview with Brandon Lee' (1991), *The Face* 37.
'Interview with Robert Clouse' (1988), *Inside Kung Fu*, August.
Jeffords, Susan (1994), *Hard Bodies: Hollywood Masculinity in the Reagan Era*, New Brunswick, NJ: Rutgers University Press.
Kaminsky, Stuart M. (1974), 'Kung fu film as ghetto myth', *Journal of Popular Film* 3, pp. 129–38.
Kingston, Maxine Hong (1981), *China Men*, London: Picador.
Kingston, Maxine Hong (1977), *The Woman Warrior*, London: Picador.
Low, Gail Ching-Liang (1989), 'White skin/black masks: the pleasures and politics of imperialism', *New Formations* 9, pp. 83–103.
Norris, Chuck, with Joe Hyams (1990), *The Secret of Inner Strength*, London: Arrow.
Rayns, Tony (1984), 'Entretien avec Jacky Chan', *Cahiers du cinéma*, September.

BIBLIOGRAPHY

Note on the Bibliography

The first section of the bibliography is organised around general topics, theories and methodologies; the second around the themes and cinemas examined in each section of *Asian Cinemas*. The rationale behind the bibliography's ordering of references by topic is to allow readers to target specific areas more closely and to make connections between different frameworks and topics, for example crosscultural analysis and Japanese cinema, that are not made explicit in this *Reader and Guide*. The bibliography invites readers to make these connections by thinking across topics and methodologies. Post-colonial theories, for example, can be found in the general section of the bibliography rather than under the headings of Hong Kong cinema. A wealth of material on Hong Kong cinema and Taiwanese cinema can be found in references contained under Chinese cinema, despite the fact that the *Reader and Guide's* focus in that section tends to be on Chinese film produced in the mainland.

While not exhaustive, we hope that the Bibliography provides a comprehensive mapping of literature on particular areas.

General Bibliography

Altman, Rick (1999), *Film/Genre*, London: British Film Institute.

Anderson, Benedict (1983), *Imagined Communities*, London: Verso.

Ang, Ien (2001), *On Not Speaking Chinese: Living Between Asia and the West*, London: Routledge.

Armes, Roy (1987), *Third World Filmmaking and the West*, Berkeley: University of California Press.

Bernstein, Mathew and Gaylyn Studlar (eds) (1997), *Visions of the East: Orientalism and Film*, London and New York: I. B. Taurus.

Bhabha, Homi (1992), *Nation and Narration*, London: Routledge.

Birch, David, Tony Schirato, and Sanjay Srivastava (2001), *Asia: Cultural Politics in the Global Age*, New York: Palgrave.

Blum-Reid, Sylvie (2003), *East-West Encounters: Franco-Asian Cinema and Literature*, London: Wallflower.

Bordwell, David (1979), 'The art film as a mode of film practice', *Film Criticism*, vol. 4, no. 1.
Burton, Julian (1985), 'Marginal cinemas and mainstream critical theory', *Screen*, vol. 24, no. 2.
Caughie, John (ed.) (1981), *Theories of Authorship*, London: British Film Institute.
Chen, Kuan-Hsing (ed.) (1998), *Trajectories: Inter-Asia Cultural Studies*, London: Routledge.
Curran, James and Myung-jin Park (eds) (2000), *De-Westernizing Media Studies*, London: Routledge.
Desser, David and Linda C. Erlich (eds) (1994), *Cinematic Landscapes: Observations on the Visual Arts and Cinema of China and Japan*, Austin: University of Texas Press.
Dissanayake, Wimal (ed.) (1994), *Colonialism and Nationalism in Asian Cinema*, Bloomington: Indiana University Press.
Dissanayake, Wimal (ed.) (2005), *Melodrama and Asian Cinema*, Cambridge: Cambridge University Press.
Dissanayake, Wimal, Kowk-Kan Tam and Terey Siou-Han Yip (eds) (2002), *Sites of Contestation: Localism, Globalism and Cultural Production in Asian and the Pacific*, Hong Kong: The Chinese University of Hong Kong Press.
Dyer, Richard (2003), *Heavenly Bodies: Film Stars and Society*, London: British Film Institute.
Dyer, Richard (1997), *Stars*, London: Routledge.
Erni, John Nguyet and Siew Keng Chua (eds) (2005), *Asian Media Studies*, London: Blackwell Publishing.
Feng, Peter X. (ed.) (2002), *Screening Asian Americans*, New Brunswick: Rutgers University Press.
Guneratne, Anthony and Wimal Dissanayake (eds) (2003), *Rethinking Third Cinema*, London: Routledge.
Hamamoto, Darrell Y. and Sandra Liu (eds) (2000), *Countervisions: Asian American Film Criticism*, Philadelphia: Temple University Press.
Hill, John and Pamela Church-Gibson (eds) (2000), *World Cinema: Critical Approaches*, Oxford: Oxford University Press.
Iwabuchi, Koichi (2002), *Recentering Globalization: Popular Culture and Japanese Transnationalism*, Durham: Duke University Press.
Iwabuchi, Koichi, Stephen Muecke, and Mandy Thomas (eds) (2004), *Rogue Flows: Trans-Asian Cultural Traffic*, Hong Kong: Hong Kong University Press.
Kaplan, E. Ann (1997), *Looking for the other: Feminism, Film, and the Imperial Gaze*, London: Routledge.
Lau, Jenny Kwok Wah (ed.) (2003), *Multiple Modernities: Cinemas and Popular Media in Transcultural East Asia*, Philadelphia: Temple University Press.
Leifer, Michael (ed.) (2000), *Asian Nationalism*, London: Routledge.
Lent, John A. (1990), *The Asian Film Industry*, Austin: University of Texas Press.
Mackenzie, Scott and Mette Hjort (eds) (2000), *Cinema and Nation*, London: Routledge.
Moore-Gilbert, Bart (1997), *Postcolonial Theory: Contexts, Practices, Politics*, London: Verso.
Naficy, Hamid and Teshome H. Gabriel (eds) (1993), *Otherness and the Media: The Ethnography of the Imagined and the Imaged*, Chur: Harwood Academic Publishers.
Neale, Steve (1980), *Genre*, London: British Film Institute.
Neale, Steve (1981), 'Art cinema as institution', *Screen*, vol. 22, no. 1.
Nygren, Scott (1991), 'Doubleness and idiosyncrasy in cross-cultural analysis', *Quarterly Review of Film and Video*, vol. 13, nos. 1–3.
Rosen, Philip (1996), 'Nation and anti-nation: concepts of national cinema in the "new" media era', *Diaspora*, 5: 3.
Said, Edward (1979), *Orientalism*, London: Penguin.

Stam, Robert and Ella Shohat, *Unthinking Eurocentrism: Multiculturalism and the Media*, London: Routledge.
Stam, Robert and Ella Shohat (eds) (2003), *Multiculturalism, Postcoloniality, and Transnational Media*, New Brunswick: Rutgers University Press.
Staiger, Janet and David Gerstner (eds) (2002), *Authorship and Film*, New York: Routledge.
Van der Heide, William (2002), *Malaysian Cinema, Asian Film*, Amsterdam: Amsterdam University Press.
Wexman, Virginia Wright (ed.) (2002), *Film and Authorship*, New Brunswick: Rutgers University Press.
Werbner, Pnina and Tariq Modood (eds) (1997), *Debating Cultural Hybridity*, London: Zed Books.
Williams, Alan (ed.) (2002), *Film and Nationalism*, New Brunswick: Rutgers University Press.
Williams, Patrick and Laura Chrisman (eds) (1993), *Colonial Discourse and Post-Colonial Theory*, Hemel Hempstead: Harvester Wheatsheaf.
Williams, Patrick and Peter Childs (1997), *An Introduction to Post-Colonial Theory*, Hemel Hempstead: Harvester Wheatsheaf.
Wilson, Rob and Wimal Dissanayake (eds) (1996), *Global/Local: Cultural Production and the Transnational Imaginary*, Durham: Duke University Press.

Japanese Cinema

Anderson, Joseph and Donald Richie (1982), *The Japanese Film: Art and Industry*, Princeton: Princeton University Press.
Anisfield, Nancy (1995), 'Godzilla/Gojira: evolution of a nuclear metaphor', *Journal of Popular Culture*, vol. 28, no. 3.
Bingham, Adam (2004), 'The spaces in-between: the cinema of Yasujiro Ozu', *Cineaction*, no. 63.
Bock, Audie (1985), *Japanese Film Directors*, New York: Kodansha International.
Bordwell, David (1979), 'Our dream cinema: western historiography and the Japanese film', *Film Reader 4*.
Bordwell, David (1979), *Ozu and the Poetics of Cinema*, Princeton: Princeton University Press.
Bordwell, David and Kristin Thompson, 'Space and narrative in the films of Ozu', *Screen*, vol. 17, no. 2.
Broderick Mick (ed.) (1996), *Hibakusha Cinema*, Kegan Paul International.
Burch, Noel (1979), *To the Distant Observer*, Berkeley: University of California Press.
Cazdyn, Eric (2002), *The Flash of Capital: Film and Geopolitics in Japan*, Durham: Duke University Press.
Davis, Darrel William (1996), *Picturing Japaneseness*, New York: Columbia University Press.
Desser, David (ed.) (1997), *Ozu's Tokyo Story*, Cambridge: Cambridge University Press.
Desser, David and Arthur J. Nolletti (eds) (1992), *Reframing Japanese Cinema*, Bloomington: Indiana University Press.
Iwabuchi, Koichi (1994), 'Complicit exoticism: Japan and its other', *Continuum*, vol. 8, no. 2.
Lehman, Peter (1987), 'The mysterious orient, the crystal clear orient, the non-existent orient: dilemmas of western scholars on Japanese films', *Journal of Popular Film and Video*, no. 30.
Martinez, Dolores P. (ed.) (1998), *The Worlds of Japanese Popular Culture: Gender, Shifting Boundaries and Global Cultures*, Cambridge: Cambridge University Press.
McDonald, Keiko Iwai (1983), *Cinema East: A Critical Study of Major Japanese Movies*, Rutherford: Farleigh Dickson University Press.

McDonald, Keiko Iwai (1989), 'Popular film', in Richard G. Powers (ed.), *Handbook of Japanese Popular Culture*, New York: Greenwood Press.

Miyoshi, Masao and H. D. Harootunian (eds) (1993), *Japan in the World*, Durham: Duke University Press.

Napier, Susan J. (1996), 'Panic sites: the Japanese imagination for disaster from Godzilla to Akira', in John Withier Treat (ed.), *Contemporary Japan and Popular Culture*, London: Curzon.

Nornes, Abe Mark and Fukushima Yukio (eds) (1994), *The Japan/America Film Wars: World War II Propaganda and its Cultural Context*, Chur: Harwood Academic Publishers.

Nygren, Scott (1993), 'Boundary crossings: Japanese and Western representations of the other', *Quarterly Review of Film and Video*, vol. 14, no. 3.

Philips, Alastair and Julian Stringer (eds) (2006), *Japanese Cinema*, London: Routledge.

Richie, Donald (1977), *Ozu: His Life and Films*, Berkeley: University of California Press.

Richie, Donald (2001), *A Hundred Years of Japanese Cinema*, Tokyo: Kodansha.

Sato, Tadao (1982), *Currents in Japanese Cinema*, New York: Kodanasha International.

Standish, Isolde (2005), *A New History of Japanese Cinema: A Century of Narrative Film*, London: Continuum.

Tsutsui, William M. (2004), *Godzilla on My Mind: Fifty Years of the King of Monsters*, New York: Palgrave Macmillan.

Washburn, Denis and Carol Cavanaugh (eds) (2000), *Word and Image in Japanese Cinema*, Cambridge: Cambridge University Press.

Yoshimoto, Mitsuhiro (2000), *Kurosawa: Film Studies and Japanese Cinema*, Durham: Duke University Press.

Hong Kong Cinema

Abbas, Ackbar (1997), *Hong Kong: Culture and the Politics of Disappearance*, Minneapolis: University of Minnesota Press.

Bordwell, David (2000), *Planet Hong Kong*, Cambridge: Harvard University Press.

Cheung, Esther M. K. and Yiu-Wai Chu (eds) (2005), *Between Home and World: A Reader in Hong Kong Cinema*, Hong Kong: Hong Kong University Press.

Chu, Yingchi (1993), *Hong Kong Cinema: Coloniser, Motherland and Self*, London: Routledge.

Cui, Shuqin (2000), 'Stanley Kwan's *Centre Stage*: the (im)possible engagement between feminism and postmodernism', *Cinema Journal*, vol. 39, no. 4, Summer.

Desser, David and Poshek Fu (eds) (2000), *The Cinema of Hong Kong*, Cambridge: Cambridge University Press.

Dissanayake, Wimal (2003), *Wong Kar-Wai's Ashes of Time*, Hong Kong: Hong Kong University Press.

Eng, David L. (1993), 'Love at last site: waiting for Oedipus in Stanley Kwan's *Rouge*', *Camera Obscura*, vol. 32, no. 1.

Erni, John Nguyet (ed.) (2001), 'Postcolonial Hong Kong', *Cultural Studies*, vol. 15, nos. 3–4.

Fang, Karen (2004), *John Woo's A Better Tomorrow*, Hong Kong: Hong Kong University Press.

Fu, Poshek (2003), *Between Shanghai and Hong Kong: The Politics of Chinese Cinemas*, California: Stanford University Press.

Ho, Sam (ed.) (2002), *The Swordsman and his Jianghu: Tsui Hark and Hong Kong Film*, Hong Kong: Hong Kong Film Archive.

Kar, Law (2004), *Hong Kong Cinema: A Cross-Cultural View*, New York: Scarecrow Press.

Lim, Bliss Cua (2001), 'Spectral times: the ghost film as historical allegory', *Positions: East West Culture Critique*, vol. 9, no. 2.

Pang, Laikwan (2002) 'Masculinity in crisis: films of Milkyway Image and post-1997 Hong Kong Cinema', *Feminist Media Studies*, vol. 2, no. 3.

Rodriguez, Hector (1997), 'Hong Kong popular culture as an interpretive arena: the Huang Feihong film series', *Screen*, vol. 38, no. 1.

Schroeder, Andrew (2004), *Tsui Hark's Zu Warriors From the Magic Mountain*, Hong Kong: Hong Kong University Press.

Stokes, Lisa Oldham and Michael Hoover (1999), *City on Fire: Hong Kong Cinema*, London: Verso.

Teo, Stephen (1997), *Hong Kong Cinema*, London: British Film Institute.

Wong, Ai-Ling (ed.) (2003), *The Shaw Screen: A Preliminary Study*, Hong Kong: Hong Kong Film Archive.

Chinese Cinema

Berry, Chris (ed.) (1991), *Perspectives on Chinese Cinema*, London: British Film Institute.

Berry, Chris (1992), ' "Race": Chinese film and the politics of nationalism', *Cinema Journal*. No. 2, Winter.

Berry, Chris (ed.) (2003), *Chinese Films in Focus: 25 New Takes*, London: British Film Institute.

Berry, Chris (2004), *Towards a Post-Socialist Cinema: The Cultural Revolution in the Films from the PRC*, London: Routledge.

Browne, Nick, Vivian Sobchack, Esther Yau, and Paul G. Pickowicz (eds) (1994), *New Chinese Cinemas: Forms, Identitites, Politics*, Cambridge: Cambridge University Press.

Chang, Hsu-Tung and Xudong Zhang (1997), *Chinese Modernism in the Era of Reforms: Cultural Fever, Avant-Garde Fiction, and the New Chinese Cinema*, Durham: Duke University Press.

Chow, Rey (1995), *Primitive Passions: Visuality, Sexuality, Ethnography, and Contemporary Chinese Cinema*, New York: Columbia University Press.

Cornelius, Sheila (2002), *New Chinese Cinema*, London: Wallflower.

Cui, Shuqin (2003), *Women Through the Lens: Gender and Nation in a Century of Chinese Cinema*, Honolulu: University of Hawaii Press.

Donald, Stephanie (1995), 'Women reading Chinese films: between orientalism and silence', *Screen*, vol. 36, no. 4.

Donald, Stephanie Hemelryk (2000), *Public Secrets, Public Spaces: Cinema and Civility in China*, Lanham: Rowman and Littlefield Publishers.

Kaplan, E. Ann (2005), 'Melodrama/subjectivity/ideology: western melodrama theories and their relevance to recent Chinese cinema', in Wimal Dissanayake (ed.), *Melodrama and Asian Cinema*, Cambridge: Cambridge University Press.

Lau, Jenny Kwok Wah (1991), '*Judou* – a hermeneutical reading of cross-cultural cinema', *Film Quarterly*, vol. 45, no. 2.

Lau, Jenny Kwok Wah (1995), '*Farewell My Concubine*: history, melodrama, and ideology in contemporary pan-Chinese cinema', *Film Quarterly*, vol. 49, no. 1.

Lu, Sheldon H. (ed.) (1997), *Transnational Chinese Cinemas*: Identity, Nationhood, Genre, Honolulu: University of Hawaii Press.

Lu, Sheldon H. (2002), *China: Transnational Visuality, Global Postmodernity*, New York: Stanford University Press.

Lu, Sheldon and Emilie Yueh-yu Yeh (eds) (2005), *Chinese-Language Film: Historiography, Poetics, Politics*, Honolulu: University of Hawaii Press.

Silbergeld, Jerome (2000), *China in to Film: Frames of Reference in Contemporary Chinese Cinema*, London: Reaktion Books.

Tam, Kwok-kan and Wimal Dissanayake (1998), *New Chinese Cinema*, Hong Kong: Oxford University Press.

Zhang, Yingjin (1997), 'From "minority film" to "minority discourse": questions of nationhood and ethnicity in Chinese cinema', *Cinema Journal*, 36, no. 3, Spring.

Zhang, Yingjin (1999), *Cinema and Urban Culture in Shanghai, 1922–1943*, California: Stanford University Press.

Zhang, Yingjin (2002), *Screening China: Critical Interventions, Cinematic Reconfigurations, and the Transnational Imaginary in Chinese Cinema*, Ann Arbor: University of Michigan Press.

Zhang, Yingjin (2004), *Chinese National Cinema*, London: Routledge.

Zhang, Yingjin and Zhiwei Xiao (eds) (1999), *Encyclopaedia of Chinese Film*, London: Routledge.

Turkish Cinema

Abisel, Nilgün (1994), *Türk Sinemasi Üzerine Yazilar*, Ankara: İmge Kitabevi.

Ahmad, Feroz, *The Making of Modern Turkey*, London and New York: Routledge.

Benedict, Peter, Erol Tümertekin and Fatma Mansur (eds) (1974), *Turkey: Geographic and Social Perspectives*, Leiden: Brill.

Bozdoğan, Sibel and Reşat Kasaba (eds) (1997), *Rethinking Modernity and National Identity in Turkey*, Seattle and London: University of Washington Press.

Büker, Seçil and Canan Uluyağci (1993), *Yeşilçam'da Bir Sultan*, Istanbul: Afa.

Erdoğan, Nezih and Dilek Kaya (2002), 'Institutional intervention in the distribution and exhibition of Hollywood films in Turkey', *Historical Journal of Film, Radio and Television*, 22 (1).

Ilal, Ersan (1987), 'On Turkish cinema', in John Downing (ed.), *Film and Politics in the Third World*, New York: Autonomedia.

Kafadar, Cemal (1995), *Between Two Worlds: The Construction of the Ottoman State*, California: University of California Press.

Kaplan Yusef (1996), 'Turkish cinema', in Geoffrey Nowell-Smith (ed.), *The Oxford History of World Cinema*, Oxford and New York: Oxford University Press.

Keyder, Çağlar (1987), *State and Class in Turkey: A Study in Capitalist Development*, London: Verso.

Scognamillo, Giovanni and Metin Demirhan (1999), *Fantastik Türk Sinemasi*, Istanbul: Kabalci.

Shafik, Viola (1998), *Arab Cinema: History and Cultural Identity*, Cairo: The American University in Cairo Press.

Shayegan, Daryush (1992), *Cultural Schizophrenia: Islamic Societies Confronting the West*, London: Saqi Books.

Suner, Asuman (2004), 'Horror of a different kind: dissonant voices of the new Turkish cinema', *Screen*, vol. 45, no. 4.

Tekeli, Şirin (ed.) (1995), *Women in Modern Turkish Society: A Reader*, London: Zed Books.

Woodhead, Christine (ed.) (1989), *Turkish Cinema: An Introduction*, London: SOAS, Occasional Paper 5.

Zürcher, Erik J. (1993), *Turkey: A Modern History*, London: I. B. Tauris & Co.

Indian Cinema and Bollywood

Arnold, Alison (1988), 'Popular film song in India: a case of mass market musical eclecticism', *Popular Music*, vol. 7, no. 2.

Chakravarty, Sumita S. (1993), *National Identity in Indian Popular Cinema 1947–1987*, Austin: University of Texas Press.

Desai, Jigna (2004), *Beyond Bollywood: The Cultural Politics of South Asian Diasporic Film*, London: Routledge.

Dhillon-Kashyap, Perminder (1998), 'Locating the Asian experience', *Screen*, vol. 29, no. 4.

Dwyer, Rachel (2005), *100 Bollywood Films*, London: British Film Institute.

Dwyer, Rachel and Divia Patel (2002), *Cinema India: The Visual Culture of Hindi Film*, London: Reaktion Books.

Ganti, Tejaswini (2004), *Bollywood: A Guidebook To Popular Indian Cinema*, London: Routledge.

Gokulsing, K. Moti and Wimal Dissanayake (1988), *Indian Popular Cinema: A Narrative of Cultural Change*, Stoke on Trent: Trentham Books.

Gopalan, Lalitha (2002), *Cinema of Interruptions: Action Genres in Contemporary Indian Cinema*, London: British Film Institute.

Kaur, Raminder and Ajay J. Sinha (eds) (2005), *Bollywood: Popular Indian Cinema Through a Transactional Lens*, London: Sage.

Manuel, P. (1993), *Cassette Culture: Popular Music and Technology in North India*, Chicago: Chicago University Press.

Mishra, Vijay (1985), 'Towards a theoretical critique of Indian Cinema', *Screen*, vol. 26, nos 3–4.

Mishra, Vijay (2002), *Bollywood Cinema: Temples of Desire*, London: Routledge.

Pendakur, Manjunath (2003), *Indian Popular Cinema: Industry, Ideology and Consciousness*, Creshill: NJ, Hampton Press.

Rajadhyaksha, Ashish and Paul Willimen (eds) (1999), *The Encyclopaedia of Indian Cinema*, London: British Film Institute.

Vasudevan, Ravi S., *Making Meaning in Indian Cinema*, Delhi: Oxford University Press.

Virdi, Jyotika (2003), *The Cinematic Imagination: Indian Popular Films as Social History*, New Brunswick: Rutgers University Press.

Taiwanese Cinema

Berry, Chris and Feii Lu (eds) (2005), *Island on the Edge: Taiwan New Cinema and After*, Hong Kong: Hong Kong University Press.

Brown, M. J. (2003), *Is Taiwan Chinese? The Impact of Culture, Power and Migration on Changing Identities*, Berkeley: University of California Press.

Corcuff, Stephane (ed.) (2002), *Memories of the Future: National Identity Issues and the Search for a New Taiwan*, London: M. E. Sharpe.

Edmonds, Richard Louis and Steven M. Goldstein (eds) (2001), *Taiwan in the Twentieth Century: A Reflective View*, Cambridge: Cambridge University Press.

Lu, Feii (1998), *Taiwan Cinema: Politics, Economics, Aesthetics*, Taipei: Yuanliu.

Lu, Tonglin (2001), *Confronting Modernity in the Cinemas of Taiwan and Mainland China*, Cambridge: Cambridge University Press.

Martin, Fran (2003), *Situating Sexualities: Queer Representation in Taiwanese Fiction, Film and Public Culture*, Hong Kong: Hong Kong University Press.

Ou, Alice (1993), *Taiwan Films*, Taipei: Variety Publishing.

Reynaud, Bérénice (2002), *City of Sadness*, London: British Film Institute.

Wu, I-Fen (2003), 'Looking for nostalgia: memory and national identity in Hou Hsiao-Hsien's *A Time to Live, A Time to Die*', *Cineaction*, no. 60.

Yip, June (2004), *Envisioning Taiwan: Fiction, Cinema, and the Nation in the Cultural Imaginary*, Durham: Duke University Press.

Yueh-Yu, Yu (2001), 'Politics and poetics of Hou Hsiao Hsien's films', *Post Script*, vol. 20, nos 2–3.

Bruce Lee

Chan, Jachinson (2001), *Chinese American Masculinities from Fu Manchu to Bruce Lee*, New York: Routledge.

Hoang, Nguyen Tan (2004), 'The resurrection of Brandon Lee: the making of a gay American porn star', in Linda Williams (ed.), *Porn Studies*, Durham: Duke University Press.

Hodge, Bob and Kam Louie (1998), 'The cult of the hero: masculinity and popular culture', in *The Politics of Chinese Language and Culture*, London: Routledge.

Hong Kong Film Archive, *The Making of Martial Arts Films – as Told by Filmmakers and Stars*, Hong Kong: Urban Council.

Hunt, Leon (2003), *Kung Fu Cult Masters: From Bruce Lee to Crouching Tiger*, London: Wallflower Press.

Lo, Kwai-Cheung (1996), 'Muscles and subjectivity: a short history of the masculine body in Hong Kong popular culture', *Camera Obscura*, vol. 39.

Shu, Yuan (2003), 'From Bruce Lee to Jackie Chan: reading the kung fu film in an American context', *Journal of Popular Film and Television*, 31: 2.

Wong, Day and Laikwan Pang (eds) (2005), *Masculinities and Hong Kong Cinema*, Hong Kong: Hong Kong University Press.

INDEX OF FILMS/TV PROGRAMMES

INDEX OF KEY TERMS